THE VISUAL CULTURE OF AMERICAN RELIGIONS

THE VISUAL CULTURE OF
AMERICAN RELIGIONS

EDITED BY

David Morgan & Sally M. Promey

UNIVERSITY OF CALIFORNIA PRESS
Berkeley   Los Angeles   London

Figure i.12, The Hanged Man tarot card from the Rider-Waite Tarot
Deck,™ is reproduced by permission of U.S. Games Systems, Inc., Stamford,
Connecticut, 06902. © 1971 by U.S. Games Systems, Inc. Further
reproduction prohibited. The Rider-Waite Tarot Deck™ is a registered
trademark of U.S. Games Systems, Inc.

University of California Press
Berkeley and Los Angeles, California

University of California Press, Ltd.
London, England

© 2001 by the Regents of the University of California

Library of Congress Cataloging-in-Publication Data

The visual culture of American religions / edited by David Morgan
    and Sally M. Promey.
        p. cm.
    Includes bibliographical references and index.
    ISBN 0-520-22520-1 (alk. paper)— ISBN 0-520-22522-8 (pbk. :
alk. paper)
        1. Art and religion—United States. I. Morgan, David, 1957-. II. Promey,
    Sally M., 1953-.
    N72.R4 V57 2001
    291.3'7—dc21   00-034378

Manufactured in the United States of America

10   09   08   07   06   05   04   03   02   01
10   9   8   7   6   5   4   3   2   1

The paper used in this publication meets the minimum requirements
of ANSI/NISO Z39.48-1992 (R 1997) (*Permanence of Paper*). ♾

To our students

CONTENTS

Color plates follow page 178.

PREFACE AND ACKNOWLEDGMENTS

Religion and the visual come together frequently in American life.[1] The academic study of their relations has a less consistent history. In the nineteenth-century United States, the first historians to write about the nation's visual arts noted the presence of religious content and concerns in their subject. For most of the twentieth century, however, various constraints have hindered the study of the visual culture of American religions. Despite a wealth of evidence to show how much art and religion have shaped one another, historians of American art, with a few notable exceptions, have been inattentive to the relationship between the two, often characterizing religion as captive to sectarian or ideological preoccupations, restrictive of creative individuality, and widely responsible for an inferior aesthetic.[2] Similarly, historians of American religion have viewed art—and, even more broadly, the domain of the visual—as merely illustrative of ideas and experiences that are properly and principally expressed in texts.[3] This manner of scholarly resistance on the part of both disciplines has resulted in a strong tendency to overlook the historical record and the rich opportunities that interdisciplinary study offers. In sharp contrast to these exclusionary biases, census data, polls, and historical analyses point again and again to the agency of both religion and the visual, suggesting that interpreters of American culture who neglect either one do so at the risk of missing critical evidence.[4]

The inclination to minimize the significance of religious visual culture has led to a kind of historical myopia in both art history and religious history. It would still, for example, come as a surprise to most art historians that a "religious" painting, *The Flagellants* (1889), by Milwaukee artist Carl Marr, was one of two most frequently visited and energetically celebrated pictures in the Fine Arts Palace at the 1893 World's Columbian Exhibition; that the only portrait for which agnostic Thomas Eakins received an official award from the Pennsylvania Academy of Fine Arts depicted a Catholic priest (Eakins painted seventeen priests among his "heroes of modern life"); and that a group of well known American painters competed in 1905 to provide the superior representation of a "modern" Jesus, with the resulting paintings widely toured and published in the following year. Perhaps most startling, when registered against late-twentieth-century art historical expectations, Alfred H. Barr Jr., founding director of the Museum of Modern Art, was also an observant Presbyterian who headed a Commission on Art for the National Council of Churches of Christ. This commission included among its leaders other prominent arts professionals like Perry T. Rathbone, Charles Rufus Morey, and George Heard Hamilton.[5]

By the same token, it would still be news to many historians of religion that American Protestants practice a visual piety as well as a textual one; that pictures are worthy of consideration as constituent, rather than subsidiary, elements of religious practice and experience; and that religious institutions in the United States have long maintained substantial connections to images and objects, to producers of art and artifacts, and to various arts organizations. Religious institutions and categories of experience, in fact, participated in defining the very terms that would describe and make possible American aesthetics. These examples indicate a conspicuous gap between lived history and the rhetorical and conceptual structures that support widely accepted scholarly attitudes toward art and religion in American culture. Suspicions of an inherently American Protestant iconoclasm, for instance, have long informed considerations of the relation between American art and American religion. To the extent that there is (or has been) an "American" iconoclasm, however, it is (and has been) a highly diverse, variable, and selective phenomenon, representing not the blanket destruction or even discouragement of art but the privileging of some visual forms concurrent with the rejection or reconfiguration of others.

Over the last few decades, historians in the fields of art and religion have paid increasing attention to the contexts of practice and reception. In art history (the primary disciplinary affiliation for this book's coeditors), scholars have enthusiastically acknowledged the interdisciplinary benefits extended by political, economic, and social histories, including the study of political and social sectarianisms. Nonetheless, most historians of American art continue to assign religion a negligible or inconsequential part in the formulation, production, reception, and theorization of art in the United States. Although this oversight might be taken to suggest otherwise, the emergence of modernity has not rendered religion defunct or anachronistic. To the contrary, recent sociological and historical studies suggest that religion flourishes in American culture.[6] Late-twentieth-century debates about public art funding have demonstrated repeatedly that religion not only has been but also remains an influential cultural and social force.

Twentieth-century attitudes toward art and religion have been informed by biases many and deep, with historical antecedents reaching as far back as the first European settlements on this side of the Atlantic ocean. In addition to other factors, for example, academic perceptions of the interrelation of art and religion have been shaped by assumptions about class. The fact that the upper classes have generally controlled what counts as art but not what counts as religion may go a long way toward explaining one important aspect of the seeming disjunction between religion and the visual in the United States.[7] Allowing only the intersections of artistic high culture and religious high culture to constitute the field of inquiry severely limits the scope of investigation. A first step toward greater understanding would thus be historical analysis that purposely stands at some critical remove from the usual intellectual and cultural hierarchies to consider how all sorts of people live with all sorts of pictures in the public and private spaces of their lives.

This is neither to propose that scholars cease to make appropriate distinctions, nor to suggest that they ignore cultural politics. It is rather to advocate an initial approach willing to be instructed by a wide spectrum of visual materials and human experiences. In this collaborative study, the designation "visual culture" includes, in principle, all visual forms. The selection of this term signals a commitment to rethink such usual categories as "folk" and official art, high and low, fine art and applied, architecture, illustration, craft, handmade and mass-produced images, objects of museum quality and objects of domestic display and everyday use. The scholarship represented here engages also the interstices between categories, the seams joining them; and it acknowledges the constructed character of cultural hierarchies and their historical enforcement. While this book is a modest step in the direction of this recommended mode of historical analysis, the selection of scholars and essays in these pages has been guided by these intellectual convictions.

The scarcity of scholarship in religious art and material culture attends a related lack of educational resources for the college classroom and the museum infrastructure in this country. In response to this situation, we approached the Henry Luce Foundation, an institution whose unparalleled commitment to art and religion in the United States has been exemplary, with a proposal. The foundation's generous support of our project funded a three-year collaborative program of consultation, research, and publication. Titled "The Visual Culture of American Religions," this program had a threefold aim: first, to significantly reverse the neglect of historical material and to explore new ways of understanding; second, to secure for the study of the visual culture of American religions a visible, multidisciplinary profile and a historical self-consciousness; and third, to pursue effective means of applying the new studies in the classroom and museum settings. To these ends, we convened a working group of scholars of American art, culture, and religion, who came together for three annual seminars to explore the historiographical, methodological, and museological aspects of our subject and to visit archives, historical monuments, and collections of objects.

Major support from Lilly Endowment allowed us to undertake the expanded dissemination of our findings. Lilly provided generous funding for the Winterthur Conference in 1999 and a traveling exhibition as well as additional support for production of this book. Lilly's long-standing interest in greater public understanding of American religions has helped us bring our research to audiences within and beyond the academy.

The project called "The Visual Culture of American Religions" has produced several tangible products: this book; a number of scholarly symposia; conference panels at the annual sessions of the College Art Association, the American Academy of Religion, the American Studies Association, and the American Historical Association; and a traveling exhibition of images and objects with an exhibition catalogue. Our intention, supported enthusiastically by the Luce and Lilly organizations, has been to attend to the public understanding of religion by seeking to foster critically and historically informed discussion and study of religious visual culture in the public spaces of the classroom, scholarly discourse, and the museum at a moment in American public life when a renewed interest in religion has encouraged scholars to engage with a broad public on the history of belief.

We are happy to thank our many fine colleagues in this project. An energetic spirit of interdisciplinary collaboration shaped our work together from the beginning. Negotiating the sometimes intimidating differences in critical theory, scholarly literature, and methodology, the group has convinced us that disciplinary boundaries are both constructive in the strengths they nurture and capable of weathering the creative transgression that scholarly imagination demands in order to advance the understanding of something as complex as the visual culture of religion. Our collaborators rose to every intellectual challenge with intelligence, resourcefulness, and great good will. It has been a pleasure and an honor to work with them. We extend a heartfelt and public "thank you" to each contributor. Personal thanks as well from members of our group to John Wesley Cook for his inspiration and support.

In addition, we wish to acknowledge our home departments and institutions—the Department of Art History and Archaeology at the University of Maryland (in Sally Promey's case) and the Department of Art at Valparaiso University (in David Morgan's)—for multiple kind acts of assistance large and small, including hosting group gatherings in 1996 (University of Maryland) and 1998 (Valparaiso University). In this regard, we also owe a debt of gratitude to the able staff of the Winterthur Museum, Garden, and Library (and to Gretchen Buggeln in particular) for hosting our 1997 seminar as well as allowing us to present our research at the Winterthur Conference in 1999. And finally, though by no means least, we thank Michelle Kloss and Jennifer Krzyminski Younger, graduate assistants to the planning and research phases of "The Visual Culture of American Religions," for their substantial contributions to the content, logistics, and mechanics of our project.

This book has occupied a significant place in our collaborative efforts. We have been fortunate indeed to work with Reed Malcolm, Lynn Meinhardt, and Nicole Hayward of the University of California Press. We are grateful for their enthusiasm, energy, and expertise.

INTRODUCTION

Toni Morrison opens her novel *The Bluest Eye* with the gift of a "blue-eyed Baby Doll." The doll is image as well as object, someone's fanciful representation of ideal babyhood. It is a gift promptly despised by its recipient, Claudia, a young African American girl, because it embodies the cultural archetype of everything that white America tells Claudia she lacks. But the doll is the idol of another black girl, the tragic and abused child named Pecola. In a grim recasting of the creation story in Genesis, the doll is the image in which Pecola would choose to be recreated since she is ignored by a world that sees only white skin and blond hair. Pecola is overlooked and unloved because in the blue eyes of Caucasian society, she is ugly. According to Platonic philosophy, the beautiful is good and true. Whatever is ugly doesn't really exist or exists only at a second or third remove from the beautiful. Claudia, who chooses rebellion and anger rather than Pecola's submission and assimilation, destroys the yellow-haired gift, gouging out its eyes, dismembering the pink-skinned body, and pulling off the head in fitful acts of iconoclasm. Other forms of visual culture also confront Claudia with the alban face of sweetness and light. She despises Shirley Temple and the aesthetic that the cherubic film star embodies and enforces with each cute smile and toss of her bouncy hair. Pecola, on the other hand, idolizes her. Pecola covetously devours Mary Janes, the peanut-butter candy wrapped in the icon of a "smiling white face." To her, the candy is a sacramental ingestion of the Beautiful. "To eat the candy is somehow to eat the eyes, eat Mary Jane. Love Mary Jane. Be Mary Jane."[1]

Morrison's novel is a jarring account of the power of images, of their insidious circulation in the moral economy of everyday life, of their unrelenting enforcement of social hierarchy in the visual terms of a racist aesthetic of beauty and ugliness. In search of whiteness, which is the search for visibility and love, Pecola is lured into the house of a light-skinned black boy whose living room displays a picture of Jesus. The boy's mother, returning home to find the dark, poor girl, a painful reminder of everything the woman does not wish to be, curses Pecola and orders her to leave. As Pecola walks out the door of the middle-class home, she passes beneath the picture of Jesus, who "look[ed] down at her with sad and unsurprised eyes, his long brown hair parted in the middle."[2] Dwelling in the white heaven of Mary Jane, Jean Harlow, Shirley Temple, and the blue-eyed baby doll, Jesus is a visual Platonic Form, an eternal ideal that orders the physical universe into a series of copies of itself. To see a picture of Jesus or Mary Jane is here to gaze upon a reproduction of the original beauty of Truth. White truth. This is the power of images that Morrison confronts and anatomizes in her novel. It is the power of images that ultimately plunges Pecola into insanity, but conducts Claudia through the gauntlet of self-awareness and, finally, brings her to adulthood and deliverance from the merciless aesthetic of whiteness.

THE POWER OF IMAGES

Claudia's destruction of the blue-eyed baby doll, as an affirmation of her own identity and will, is an action both individual and representative. As long as people have made images, they have also done violence to them. Iconoclasm is often a fundamentally religious behavior. In Morrison's story, Claudia's deed is explicitly about race and identity—but in its assertion of a seemingly transcendent visual ideal, its biblical referents, and its relation to the picture of the white Jesus, the narrative approaches the domain of religion. On Good Friday 1993, in the Freedom Plaza in Washington, D.C., the Reverend George Stallings performed a similar iconoclastic ritual of an emphatically religious quality (fig. i.1). Vested for Good Friday observances of the historical violence done to the body of the crucified Jesus, Stallings shredded and burned pictures of a white "mythological" Jesus, calling all the while for the iconoclastic and ritual "purification" of the image of the Caucasian Christ from African American experience.[3] Far from representing Stallings's conviction that these religious pictures are meaningless, useless scraps of paper and ink, the cleric's performance suggests the power he acknowledged in them and to which he responded. Efforts to destroy images, to protect their honor, or to conquer in their name presuppose that images matter, that they are invested with meaning, that they exert influence, that their welfare extends some hold over those who would break or revere them. This psychological fact and its social consequences suggest that images are relevant in the understanding of religion in several ways.

We count here at least four operations (and there are certainly others) by which images participate significantly in religious practice. First, images are understood to com-

FIGURE i.1
Reverend George
Stallings, Good Friday
iconoclastic ritual,
Washington, D.C., April
1993. © 1993 The
Washington Post. Photo
by Bill O'Leary. Reprinted
with permission.

municate between human and divine realms in an economy of ritualized exchange. Second, they help establish the social basis of communion by consolidating and reinforcing a range of allegiances, large and small. Third, images help create and organize memory. And fourth, they fuel constructive, synthetic acts of imagination in the kind of meaning-making practices that form a basic aspect of religious experience. As the reader will discern from the examples that follow, in specific occurrences the four operations are mutually compatible, and they frequently exist in simultaneity. A brief consideration of each one will clarify what we mean by the "power of images" in American religious life and map some of the ways the authors of this book have addressed visual practice and its significance in their essays.

Among adherents to a range of past and contemporary American religious traditions, images are widely used to achieve various forms of the first operation we have singled out. Here images communicate petitions to a deity; they serve in rituals for determining divine will or making decisions (in practices sometimes called divination), and they function as a visual technology for invoking or otherwise affecting natural or supernatural

FIGURE i.2 (SEE ALSO PLATE 1)
Nina Barr Wheeler, *Give Us Help*, World War II portable altar triptych, 60 in. x 96 in.
Courtesy Virginia War Museum, WM 86.129.9. Photo by Photo Reflections, Inc.

forces. This operation of images, what we are calling "communication," refers principally to a vertical dimension of relation, to some transaction between humans and the divine.

In this book Claire Farago and Harvey Markowitz, for instance, discuss the power of images to affect fertility, the growth of crops, or the success of the hunt or battle. In times of national hardship or war these kinds of expressions often become more visible in the official or public arena. During World War II, for example, a Citizens Committee for the Army and Navy cooperated with the American Academy in Rome and the American Academy of Arts and Letters to contribute "spiritual armor" in the form of portable devotional triptychs (figs. i.2–4) to the United States military to be used by chaplains leading worship in fields and barracks and on shipboard. While one stated purpose was to "serve all sects," some altarpieces appealed to specific Protestant, Catholic, or Jewish (fig. i.3) audiences, and some, especially those by Ellis Wilson, were intended for segregated African American troops (fig. i.4).[4]

Images also inform and facilitate the expression of religious petitions in circumstances of somewhat less extremity than world war. In 1986, in a vacant lot near the intersection

HEAR, O ISRAEL ᴛʜᴇ LORD OUR GOD ᴛʜᴇ LORD IS ONE ᴀɴᴅ THOU SHALT LOVE ᴛʜᴇ LORD THY GOD ᴡɪᴛʜ ALL ᴛʜʏ HEART ᴀɴᴅ WITH ALL THY SOUL ᴀɴᴅ WITH ALL THY MIGHT....

THE LORD IS MY GOD

FIGURE i.3
Louis Ross, *The Lord Is My God*, World War II portable altar triptych. Courtesy Virginia War Museum, from postcard. Photo by Photo Reflections, Inc.

FIGURE i.4
Ellis Wilson, *The Holy Family*, World War II portable altar triptych, 60 in. x 90 in. Courtesy Virginia War Museum, ᴡᴍ 86.129.10. Photo by Photo Reflections, Inc.

of Germantown Avenue and Tenth Street, in an economically deprived neighborhood in inner-city Philadelphia, artist Lily Yeh began a public mural project. Her efforts eventually expanded into the communal creation of a decorated park and gardens called the Village of Arts and Humanities. Yeh maintained, from the beginning of this enterprise, the connections of her art with a spiritual dimension of experience. In 1991, in a large-scale seven-figure mosaic composition called *Angel Alley* (fig. i.5), she visually invoked divine protection for the neighborhood and the artistic garden landscape that she and its residents had created. Visually suggesting Ethiopian prototypes and recalling the biblical guardians of paradise, Yeh's angels take their post as guardians of the garden.[5]

FIGURE i.5 (SEE ALSO PLATE 2)
Lily Yeh, *Angel Alley*, 1991. From the Village of Arts and Humanities
(begun 1986), North Philadelphia. Photo by Louis Nelson.

In Orthodox and Roman Catholic Christianity, icons and holy cards depicting saints are a fundamental part of the process of intercessory prayer and devotional life. Prayers directed to the pictured saint seek his or her assistance in securing divine favor. Another example in contemporary religious practice is the shrine to earth gods in Chinese folk belief (fig. i.6). The shrine reproduced here was assembled in a grocery store in Chinatown, Chicago, where it serves to present ritual offerings to what the store's proprietor called a "ghost" (*gui*) that attracts customers into the establishment. By offering the spirit incense and fruit, the store owner hopes to improve business. In rural China, the shrine is dedicated to *tu di gong*, earth gods who protect farmers and their households and ensure a fertile earth by guarding it against evil spirits. Farmers regularly make offerings to increase the fruit of their labor. Transposed to the urban, commercial culture of Chicago, the earth gods become spiritual beings that benefit the sale of the earth's produce.[6]

We have identified the second visual operation as communion. Under this operation, images identify individuals as members of kinship networks, communities, or nations as well as religious denominations, traditions, or institutions. This kind of image helps establish a *communitas*, incorporating a set of horizontal relations among individuals as well as a vertical communion with a reality greater than the self. Here, images may thus be said to function totemically. Several writers in this volume explore how this occurs. Thomas

FIGURE i.6
Shrine to earth gods. Grocery
store, Chinatown, Chicago,
1999. Photo by David Morgan.

Tweed, for example, discusses the way in which the National Shrine of the Immaculate
Conception reflects and shapes a sense of Catholic institution and Catholic self in Washington, D.C., and in the United States. Gretchen Buggeln investigates how a particular
sort of church building, and the process of its design and execution, structured and affirmed
a Presbyterian congregation's orientation toward the common purpose of community service. Ellen Smith studies the importance of the exchange of Yiddish New Year's postcards
among American Jews, and David Morgan writes about nineteenth-century schoolbook
illustrations as Protestant symbols of American *national* identity. Sally Promey explores
late-twentieth-century public display of religion and its role in asserting the varieties of
religious presence and practice that participate in the construction of American culture.

As a trip to the National Mall in Washington, D.C., clearly suggests, it is difficult to
overestimate the importance of visual symbols in the civil religion of the United States.
Civil religion, a particular form of the operation we are calling communion, is the name
given to the ritualized and symbolic performance of nationhood that underlies conceptions of American purpose and destiny. Beginning with the New England Puritans, who
laid the groundwork of American civil religion, one of the principal features of this phenomenon has been the conflation of ordinary historical events with the extraordinary realm
of divine activity and intention. George Washington, by these lights—and even in his own
lifetime—was construed as a kind of saint, an American divine man.[7] Numerous images
widely reproduced in the years following his death represented the first president's apoth-

eosis, his deification and bodily assumption into heaven in a sort of iconography usually
reserved for the representation of saints and of the Virgin Mary (fig. i.7).

The experience of civil religion is closely linked to its visual expression.[8] One of the
oldest, most traditional ways in which Americans have told themselves who they are is

by sacralizing their public heroes and erecting monuments to them as a way of publicly remembering what these individuals accomplished and how the present is rooted in the achievements of the past. The head of George Washington is certainly among the most widely recognized images in American culture. From the earliest days of the republic, first General, and then President, Washington was the "father" of the American nation. It was his military leadership and republican wisdom that helped birth the nation and guide it through its first, perilous moments. In 1785, the French sculptor Jean-Antoine Houdon went to Mount Vernon, Virginia, to create a bust of Washington (fig. i.8) by taking a mold from life. Houdon then cast a clay model, which he retouched according the neoclassical fashion of his day. As a result, Washington looks more like an ancient Roman senator or Greek hero than he does an eighteenth-century American landowner. The solemn expression, smooth complexion, square features, and prominent forehead conform to the classical ideal of nobility. Washington's actual appearance was translated into the visual language of heroism, appropriate for the nation's patriarch and the cult figure of its civil religion.[9]

Houdon's sculpture became the prototype for thousands of public monuments placed in parks, museums, libraries, and schools. It even ended up on the twenty-five-cent coin, the quarter. The bronze bust reproduced here carries on its back a "certificate and oath" (fig. i.9) from the New York bronze founder who cast it in 1898, indicating that the work is a "perfect reproduction of the Life-Cast" by Houdon. This assurance of authenticity mattered to patriotic Americans because they wanted "the real thing," an icon of their country's father. This image, like no other, has been an official symbol of American identity for generations; it symbolizes an ideal of heroic self-denial historically fused with the origin of the nation. Washington avoids any expression of personal emotion because he represents the amalgamation of individual and type into the single figure of the archetypal national hero. He does not call attention to himself but to the nobility of virtuous, even sacred, deeds.

The operation of communion also includes visual encounters that participants qualify with words like "depth," "absorption," "ecstasy," and "transcendence." In this case the appropriate activity in the face of images is a contemplative one; the catalyst is often, though by no means exclusively, a fine-art object, and descriptors frequently include vocabulary usually reserved for characterizing the sacred. Viewers, for instance, report an episode of engagement with an image or object that invites them to stand outside themselves, that provides a kind of transport from the ordinary to the "extraordinary," a transcendence of the everyday, and a communion with something beyond. The content to be discerned is something some audiences have labeled "the spiritual in art." A vast literature of analysis, support, and critique describes and documents this role of the visual in modern culture.[10] The fact that this literature has sometimes obscured or suppressed acknowledgment of other visual operations does not diminish the import of this use of art. It is a phenomenon and an experience in search of which many visits are made to art museums and galleries as well as to cathedrals and other conventional spaces of worship.

Beyond effecting communication and communion, religious images and visual practices are a powerful means of shaping memory and acts of commemoration. Images have long been used as a way of seeding the memory with information vital to maintaining a religious group's identity. Many believers have used images to teach children, to ritually observe sacred times and events, to commemorate heroes and deaths, and to study and preserve special knowledge. In each instance, the image bears cultural information

FIGURE i.10
Grave of Edith B. Hochberg, Sinai Temple Cemetery, Michigan City, Indiana, 1999. Courtesy Martin Hochberg.

FIGURE i.11
Jeffry C. Vornhagen, "Jesse,"
1997, cibachrome print.
Courtesy Jeffry C. Vornhagen.

and shapes memories considered essential for the well-being and identity of the group. David Morgan and Paul Gutjahr both explore the importance, among American Protestants, of illustrated texts as pedagogical devices. David Bjelajac scrutinizes the hermetic significance of painter William Sidney Mount's visualized arcana. The interior of the National Shrine, studied by Thomas Tweed, and many of the displays discussed by Sally Promey bear inscriptions, insignia, symbols, and signage that delineate the content of public remembering in and among individuals and groups. The point is not only to communicate but also to plant in memory the events and names that give a belief its history and character. Images are especially powerful forms of commemoration that contribute to both the communicative and communal needs of a religious group.

Commemorative images or visual symbols frequently take the form of shrines and memorials—war memorials and historical monuments that inscribe a landscape with the public meanings of an official narrative about past events and people (as in the civil religious images already considered)—but they can also be more private devices such as tombstones (fig. i.10) or memorials like a roadside cross (fig. i.11). In the instance of a Jewish grave (fig. i.10), stones are placed as a memorial act on the grave or the top of the tombstone by visitors who wish to leave a mark of their visit, a material form of the thought and feeling of remembrance. In the ancient world, Jewish graves were marked by a pile of rocks, a tradition alluded to today by the practice of placing stones at the grave. No less important, however, is the need to remember the deceased with something that is permanent. Flowers, wreathes, pictures, clothing, and such mementos are transient. Only stones will endure and make each act of remembrance a contribution to the gravemarker itself in a manner that recalls ancient burial practice. The material practice of depositing stones both remembers the person and the religious tradition in which the person and the mourner are joined. "In remembrance," as the Baal Shem-Tov, the founder of Hasidism, put it, "resides the secret of redemption."[11]

In the case of the roadside cross, photographed by Jeffry Vornhagen in a large series of pictures recording such memorials (fig. i.11), the assembled objects demarcate the places where violence happened and a loved one was lost. Vornhagen has documented the roadside memorial in ditches and along roadways and interstate highways as a material practice of mourning. These markers often begin as very simple devices, mere crosses or Stars of David, but then become the sites of pilgrimage and ritualized remembrance among survivors. As this process takes place, the memorials become more encrusted with iconography, artifacts, and decorations that distinguish the spot and name it with the particular identity of the deceased. Eventually, what began as a marker can become a highly personalized shrine exhibiting items that belonged to the person and therefore offer visitors a material trace of the loved one. For instance, at the top of the cross inscribed with Jesse's name (see fig. i.11) is attached a fragment of clothing, which may act as a relic. Personalized offerings left at the Vietnam Veterans Memorial on the National Mall or on the fence surrounding the Alfred P. Murrah Building in Oklahoma City, for example, represent, in more immediately accessible and official spaces, a similar—often religious—articulation of place.

Finally, our fourth operation, the power of images to generate meaning, to stimulate associations or suggest interpretive strategies for making sense of one's individual existence and communal life, is evident in many kinds of religious visual practice. From hieroglyphic bibles and religious parlor games to perceptions of sacred figures in trees, rocks, or the patterns of smears and smudges to even more esoteric and occult practices, images often possess a keen power to suggest associations or connections to the viewer's personal life.[12] Stewart Hoover has examined the facility with which visual media like television and the Internet are incorporated into the personal construction of meaning in the home. John Davis explores the sometimes lurid fascination with which many antebellum American Protestants gazed at Roman Catholic rites, cathedrals, and images. Davis finds evidence in this attraction for Protestant xenophobia, but also for a fantasized transcendence of the imaginal restrictions of Protestantism. David Bjelajac provides a detailed reading of layers of hermetic meaning embedded in William Sydney Mount's paintings in which things are more than they may seem on the surface.

As a popular form of visual meaning-making, tarot cards offer an emphatically personalized example of the use of images to divine hidden meanings or offer insights into a particular problem or question. Operating somewhere between spiritual counsel and psychotherapy, as a visual system of references to human fears, desires, pleasures, and pains, tarot cards are allusive, syncretistic emblems that invite an associative response. The reader, who is skilled at prompting associations with the rich iconography of the cards, ritually configures them before the client, who is motivated by a genuine desire to attain guidance. The images on the cards offer numerous possibilities of interpretation and therefore facilitate an interpersonal exchange between the two participants. For instance, instruction manuals on the interpretation of the card shown here, The Hanged Man (fig. i.12), indicate that the card can mean life in suspension, transition, change, reversal of

FIGURE i.12

The Hanged Man, tarot card, from the Rider-Waite Tarot Deck,™ known also as the Rider Tarot and the Waite Tarot. Reproduced by permission of U.S. Games Systems, Inc.

mind, boredom, abandonment, renunciation, repentance, readjustment, improvement, rebirth, surrender, lack of progress, sacrifice.[13] This range of meanings virtually assures some possible link between the card and the client. The process of the reading commences with the statement of a question by the client as he or she shuffles the deck and continues with the display of successive cards in prescribed positions. Each position in a ten-card spread—the most common divinatory configuration—has a different significance, from the client's current state or circumstances to immediate influence, goal, distant past, recent past, future influence, environmental factors, inner emotions, and final result.[14] The intrinsic meaning of each card is inflected by the position in the spread that it occupies. So the appearance of The Hanged Man as the first card, the client's current state, may indicate a circumstance of current change, but in the past or future positions would locate change of some kind at another point in life.

The cards act as an autonomous source of knowledge whose reading tailors an ambivalent and inclusive scheme of visual prompts to the particularities of the life of a client. Reading the cards is a progressively determined path of narration from the past to the present and from the vague to the concrete. The magic of tarot consists of making the client mindful of his or her life through the suggestive prompts of the cards. A process of appropriation, visually mediated by the cards, which lend the reading a material basis, offers a mirror into which the client peers to discern his or her own image. As anthropologist Stewart Guthrie has argued, because human beings have an inherent interest in discerning meaning in their environment, they prefer certain kinds of patterns, such as anything that looks like them (anthropomorphisms).[15] Tarot cards are the material elements of a story that the client, by collaborating with the reader, tells about herself. But the authority of the cards is important as a way of transfiguring the search for patterns into a revelation. When the client wonders if what she has heard could really be true, the reader needs only to remind her that the cards themselves have said so. The supportive literature is fond of stating that tarot is "a universal language that crosses all barriers."[16] This only enhances the autonomy of the cards. With the authority of a universal system, the reading is more compelling.

So far we have examined the power of images in terms of four, often overlapping, visual activities or accomplishments: communication, communion, commemoration, and imagination. Because images operate as vehicles of communication between the human and the divine, because they visualize the parameters of individual and communal identity, because they embody recollection, because they construct and posit worlds of meaning, they elicit a range of responses. In fact, images may be said to have power precisely because they elicit our response.

As Toni Morrison's novel makes clear, the power of images is perhaps most dramatically and insistently evident in the destruction of images, a phenomenon we might see as a fifth visual operation, but an operation occurring at a different conceptual level than the first four. Reaction to the content or configuration of any one of the first four operations, for example, may be the catalyst for the fifth. Far from signaling the insignificance of images, iconoclasm is a measure of the intensity of feeling and conviction associated with certain kinds of images. Iconoclasm is thus part of a larger visual-symbolic strategy. The process is a selective one: when one kind of image is proscribed, another generally takes its place. Some visual forms are vilified; others are invested with incommensurate authority. The destruction of specific images can thus generate powerful new alternatives, representing new paradigms of thought to replace the old.[17]

As a strategy, iconoclasm transforms icons into idols and seeks to break the spell the idol has over consciousness. In the concrete act of violating the image, iconoclasts denature an icon, seeking to show that it is not transparent, but that it actually obscures the mental vision of those who venerate it. Always a political act, iconoclasm can be a powerful form of liberation. In this book Erika Doss considers the double meaning of artist Robert Gober's violation of a statue of Mary, and Leigh Schmidt reflects on the Enlightenment's demythologizing of ancient oracles in pursuit of freedom from superstition and manipulation by priestcraft.

But iconoclasm can also descend into an orgy of violence in the service of absolutism and its insistence on controlling human beings. To introduce here another visual medium, the film *Blade Runner* (1982) portrays a futuristic world in which the Platonic fear of the image leads legal assassins or "blade runners" to hunt down genetically manufactured copies of human beings called "replicants." As offworld slave labor, the replicants are considered a threat to human purity and power. After several of them rebel against their state of servitude and short-term life spans, they return to earth like Frankenstein's monster to confront their "maker," the founder of a vast corporation that designs and manufactures replicants.

In an account of iconoclastic "blinding" or "defacing" similar in some respects to that perpetrated in Morrison's *The Bluest Eye*, the replicant leader, upon learning that there is no redemption from death for replicants, gouges out the eyes of the man who created them. The death of god at the hands of his creation unleashes a new round of violence. Deckard, the blade runner played by Harrison Ford, tracks the last replicants to terminate them. Yet the film is not the same kind of cautionary tale as Mary Shelley's *Frankenstein*. Unlike Victor Frankenstein, who chases his monstrous creation to the end of the earth, Deckard relents when he is saved from death by the leader of the replicants, who snatches him from a precipice with a hand pierced christologically by a nail. Deckard turns from his legally sanctioned slaughter when he in turn decides to save a replicant with whom he has fallen in love. As a result, the director's cut of the film ends with a blurring of the formerly enforced distinction between human and replicant, master and slave, truth and image. What began as a Platonic tale of grisly iconoclasm ends as a postmodern deconstruction of authenticity—but not as a nihilistic gesture.[18]

The power of images has been a subject of recurrent interest and concern at least since Plato decided to lock artists out of his ideal world, the mythical polis he dreamed up as Athens slipped into decline and out of the control of Plato's aristocratic pedigree. From Plato to modern advertising, belief in and fear of the image have located in it a power to be banned, controlled, or unleashed for its influence over what people feel and how they think and behave. Because of the deep entanglement of images in human hopes and fears, in desire, and in acts of violence, scholars over the past decade or so have come to use "visual culture" as a helpful rubric of scholarly analysis. As one species of the genus "material culture," visual culture invites the study of images that explores not only the aesthetic value or history of meaning ascribed to images, but also their social effects and patterns of popular reception, and the commercial, religious, domestic, and political uses of imagery, artistic or not. If material culture has made us aware of the function of stuff in everyday life—the semantics of office furniture, the spatial politics of suburban yards, the ideology of automobile design, the significance of how adolescents decorate their bedrooms—then visual culture denotes the rich and semantically dense range of meaning making that images of all kinds offer the student of human culture.

THE MATERIAL CULTURE OF RELIGION

The study of the material aspects of religion, which include images as well as buildings, furniture, food, clothing, and anything that contributes to religion's practice, affords scholars the opportunity to expand the range of evidence available for understanding religion as well as visual and material experience. In order to study the material history of belief to greatest effect, scholars do well to reorient their work in response to a principal question: How does religion happen materially? Not, How do material objects *illustrate* religious history? Not, What are the material *equivalents* of theological doctrines? Not, How did religion *influence* the way buildings or uniforms or chalices were made? But rather: In what manner are material things constitutive of religion? How do material objects participate in the practices that make up religious lives? How do such practices rely on material objects? How do these objects and their uses articulate social experience? How do objects help generate and maintain the narratives, institutions, and rituals that make sense of a lifeworld? How do objects interact with texts, theology, narrative, and ceremony, and serve thereby to naturalize ideology?

In other words, scholars studying the material culture of religion do not pose questions that make material culture ancillary to some Platonic reality called "religion," implying that the world of matter is a lower form of representation, a corporeal copy of a higher, spiritual Idea. The material culture approach to religion makes distinctive contributions to historical understanding only when scholars wrestle with the resistance of matter, with its ability to *make* religion, with its obdurate presence as something humans do as religious people that is not merely reducible to a prior theological text that can definitively tell us what the object means. Material culture is not a reflection of something else, but interacts with intellectual, ritualistic, performative, and aural cultures to constitute religion. This means that no particular form of culture defines religion, but participates with all others to do so. We can say, therefore, that such things as images, clothing, liturgical objects, and buildings are part of a social discourse of material forms, sensations, texts, and human behaviors that make up religion. This discourse is not in essence verbal, but is a system of exchange and representation that enfolds material, spoken, thought, and enacted human artifacts into the practices known as a particular religion.

Caution against privileging the study of religion with a linguistic model is important and has been sounded in various ways by other scholars.[19] We often talk about "reading" buildings and pictures and objects as texts. The metaphor is useful insofar as we realize its limits as a metaphor. It is important to bear in mind that material culture scholars read *texts* as objects. Book are things that clergy proudly display in their studies or families display on parlor tables; a love letter is something one carefully preserves, pressed between the leaves of a favorite book of verse. The danger of the metaphor is that scholars will be tempted to "read" objects and then discard them, having decoded their immaterial contents and thereby reducing the object to another archival text.

But objects don't work that way. There is no reason to reduce material culture to a linguistic model. As the scholar of visual culture W. J. T. Mitchell has pointed to the "pictorial turn" in the study of images, those engaged in the study of the material history of religion may speak of a "material turn," by which they mean the related attempt to understand objects not as substitutes for words, but as the nonverbal articulation of space, property, the past, present, and future, kinship, status, value, power, authority, friendship, alliance, loyalty, affection, sentiment, order, ethnicity, class, race, gender, sexuality, eating, dying, birthing, aging, memory, and nationhood—among other things.[20] All of these and their countless permutations happen to human beings in the shape of material things and would not happen the way they do or structure lifeworlds in the manner that they do without those material things. Human experiences and practices are not just words, stories, and ideas, but the concrete enterprises that give words and stories and ideas a place and a time to happen. In this regard, material culture can be said to be co-constitutive of religion.

If we understand a culture as a dynamic, ever-changing set of textual, spoken, performed, and material symbols that articulates a worldview, we can begin to understand images as the cultural devices that inspire people, deceive them, fuel their desires, chart out their migrations, and direct them along life's winding pathways. From television to church façades, images are powerful forms of communication, communion, commemoration, and imagination that both contribute to the making of culture and are made by it. Deeply inflected by and productive of the social relations and institutional arrangements that do much to shape everyday life, images are a body of evidence that historians should struggle to understand. The purpose of this book is to demonstrate in a variety of contexts and in manifold ways how visual culture can be fruitfully treated as evidential and not merely illustrational in the historical study of American religions. Written by specialists from a wide variety of disciplines, the book argues for an interdisciplinary approach that takes artifact, practice, and belief with equal seriousness.

HISTORICAL STUDY OF RELIGIOUS VISUAL CULTURE

Philosophers, cultural theorists, and aestheticians tend to ask what images are. For the historian, folklorist, and ethnographer, however, it is generally more fruitful to inquire what images *do*. The visual practices that authors study in this volume are organized in three sections. These sections reflect the particular areas of investigation that emerged, as our project coalesced, in relation to participants' common goals, the state of the discipline(s), and the methodological and institutional concerns laid out in this book's preface. Each of the three divisions underscores our commitments to explore in various ways the operation of religious visual culture in modern American society. First, religious images, monuments, and artifacts manifest a public visible presence and a public function in the United States and thus play a fundamental role in the formation of American public culture and national identity. Second, religion is a thoroughgoing participant in the social construction of reality, which consists of the meaning-making that believers undertake in the visual practices of daily life as well as in the corporate rituals of worship and civic cult. Finally, religious visual culture in the United States has had a significant share in the movements, innovations, and transformation of beliefs that characterize American modernity. In every case, the essays in this book pursue a critical analysis and interpretation of religious images, objects, and buildings embedded in the social practices of public and private life.

PART I: RELIGIOUS VISUAL CULTURE
AND PUBLIC IDENTITY

Of enormous importance throughout the history of the United States has been the creation of a notion and practice of public space in which specific rights are secured by pro-
scribing certain forms of speech and behavior. American society was founded on deep
political anxieties over the preservation of liberty. The Revolutionary maxim "The price
of liberty is eternal vigilance" registers these fears, suggesting that the work is never done,
that the loss of liberty is always a possibility. The Bill of Rights is concerned with threats
domestic as much as threats foreign in origin. The separation of church and state, which
has been argued, litigated, praised, and deplored in American history, acknowledges the
importance of religious freedom, but seeks to preempt the domestic menace of state ad-
vocacy of belief. American legal and cultural debates have repeatedly asked how to practice belief without state intervention and how to be governed by a state that does not advocate any sect. The rub, which has not been resolved, is this: Does religion belong in
public, as many believers insist? Or is faith a private matter, as Jefferson and many since
have contended?

For Sally Promey, the central questions are: What constitutes the public display of religion and how does it contribute to American public life? In pursuing answers to these
questions, Promey's essay expands and clarifies conventional definitions of her subject,
analyzes key parameters of visible religion in contemporary life, and reflects on the legacy
of the First Amendment, church/state relations, the limitations of the secularization
model, and the privatization of religion. Arguing the important activity of visible religion
in increasing public engagement with American pluriformity, she illuminates the participation of religion's public visual culture in the formation of national identity.[21]

David Morgan investigates the role of religion in the visual construction of the nation
as a public culture of symbols, rites, and institutions. He does so by studying early Protestant attempts to define the American republic as essentially Protestant but as part of a
civil religion. Protestants wished to avoid sectarianism by promoting a visual piety they
recommended to every American. Illustrated schoolbooks were part of a national dissemination of images and practices that patriotic individuals were supposed to honor. A
ubiquitous iconography of benevolence and heroes such as George Washington formed
the visual components of antebellum civil religion that sought to represent the nation as
a homogeneous monolith in the face of rising tensions and imminent threats to national
unity. Images participated in a social discourse of defining America and appealed to religion as the essential element of that definition.[22]

American Catholicism's quest for a monumental presence in the public culture of the
United States is the subject of Thomas Tweed's ethnographic study of the National Shrine
of the Immaculate Conception. Tweed's examination of the site and interviews with visitors and staff demonstrate that sacred space is politically motivated and historically and
socially constructed. Situated in the archetypal real estate of the American capital in Wash-

ington, D.C., the National Shrine inserts itself into the space of American civil religion and public symbolism. By 1920, when construction of the National Shrine began, many American Catholic leaders had determined that the best way to thrive in a dominant Protestant culture was not to adopt the antimodern stance of Pius IX, who had championed the doctrine of the Immaculate Conception, but to beat Protestants at their own game. Tweed argues that the location of the shrine has helped legitimate American Catholicism in a nation that has often seen in Catholicism the religion of the outsider.

There is no doubt that the shrine helps expand the definition of American civil religion, which has historically been dominated by Protestantism. A comparison of two images makes this very clear. Depicting a gathering of world inhabitants assembled to hear the millennial message of American Evangelicalism, the image reproduced in figure 2.9 decorated a certificate of membership in the arch-Protestant organization, the American Tract Society, which, according to Morgan, sought among other things to limit the influence of Catholic immigrants in the United States by assimilating (converting) them to a national ethos that was unmistakably Protestant. Figure 3.6, by contrast, a picture produced by a supporter of the National Shrine, gathers world inhabitants to celebrate the national prominence of Mary. Created less than a century after the Protestant image, figure 3.6 is no less zealous in its assignment of religious identity to the nation; it confirms the importance of shared, public symbols in establishing and maintaining a claim on national purpose and identity.

The visual culture of the public-minded religious community is the subject of Gretchen Buggeln's study of the reconstruction of a church building in Wilmington, Delaware. Faced with the task of replacing a Victorian structure destroyed by fire, a modern-day Presbyterian congregation searched its sense of identity in an urban setting that was no longer the neighborhood in which parishioners lived. Buggeln inquires how a congregation with a mission of community service sought to visualize its purpose. Her study raises important questions for the humanistic study of religion: How do religious communities build themselves? In what ways is architecture a kind of public signage? How does form accommodate function? How does a congregation make decisions about visual style and its public presence? Buggeln also very helpfully moves beyond architectural history's traditional preoccupation with façade, type, and style. Most interested in the disposition of interior spaces and their function in serving mission and defining the group's religious practice of service, Buggeln directs her analysis toward the process of a community's decision making, its collaboration with the architect, and the building's situation in a particular urban context.

PART II: RELIGIOUS VISUAL CULTURE AND THE CONSTRUCTION OF MEANING

While Promey, Morgan, Tweed, and Buggeln examine the public side of religion in the visual fabrication of meanings, John Davis, Erika Doss, and Stewart Hoover focus on how individuals use images and visual media in the private construction of religious world-view and belief. Images have performed powerful roles in articulating ethnic and creedal difference in the American cultural landscape. Davis's essay articulates antebellum Protestant attraction to portrayals of Roman Catholic ritual and ceremonial display. As Catholic immigrants arrived and the demographics of American identity changed, and as American Protestants traveled to Europe and turned increasingly to the arts as a means of national refinement, Catholic visual culture and artistic achievements impressed Protestants as both alien and irresistible. Protestant bigotry and hostility notwithstanding, envy of the exotic Catholic other in the nineteenth century, Davis suggests, was the beginning of "a breach in sectarian borders" that were irrevocably toppled a century or so later when the nation elected its first Roman Catholic president.

Doss frames her essay as a case study of Robert Gober, a sculptor whose installation of a highly autobiographical work in a public art gallery in California joins the public and private in a challenging, sometimes bewildering clash. Gober invests in the very common and shared symbols of Roman Catholicism the minutiae and particularities of his own life. The result moves us to ask whether it is the self clothed in public culture or the public clothed in the idiosyncracies of one man. Meaning is a negotiation between the two, neither strictly generic nor entirely idiomatic. Catholicism and its rich repository of visual forms constitute both the costume in which Gober's personal identity happens and the conditions against which personality takes shape as a pastiche that borrows at will from a common source of religious tradition. Impaled on a length of conduit, Mary presents herself to the viewer as a kind of telescope aimed at the cascade of water descending from on high. This melange of symbols marks a site in the secular and public space of the art gallery where grace flows and abounds, couched in memories and shared fragments, an assemblage that blurs the distinction between sacred and secular, public and private.

Stewart Hoover's essay suggests the uses of modern media that surpass or even subvert the intentions of media producers. Hoover illuminates the constructive practices in media reception, observing the way individuals fabricate meaning out of constituent elements selected from the highly mediated environments of home and work life. This is especially, though not exclusively, the case where religious content may be discerned. While conventional mass media and communications theory advocates an instrumentalist view of media, in which television or radio operate as channels directing message bullets aimed by producers at passive receivers, Hoover argues from ethnographic evidence for the meanings that ordinary people make, often irrespective of the intended messages that communicators are transmitting.

The visual culture of American religions has often been a place where social conflict and cultural contradiction have been manifest and in many cases where conflict has been negotiated. For instance, images have marked the historical collision of discrete understandings of the natural order and the power and knowledge that it divulges to those initiated into the mysteries of its operation. Images, in other words, have often mediated two very different realms of meaning: the physical world of nature and the invisible domain beyond it. This negotiation is the focus of chapters by Harvey Markowitz and David Bjelajac and, to a somewhat lesser extent, Claire Farago. Markowitz describes the workings of the Sioux worldview, in particular, the investiture of power in the material culture of images, body decoration, and the ritual practice of the Sun Dance. Markowitz explains how the symbols and color used by the Lakota Sioux were not understood simply as abstract devices that represented *wakan*, or wonder and power, but were themselves the sites where *wakan* resided in Lakota culture. But, with the restriction of the Sioux to reservations and the accompanying transformation from a nomadic to a stationary society, these Lakota presentations of spiritual and material power were redefined by both the market pressures of the Anglo-American capitalist economy and the desire of reservation artists to document a rapidly receding past. In the process, presentations of power become representations of history and event.

David Bjelajac examines how the paintings of William Sidney Mount are subtly encoded with the visual arcana of hermeticism, a body of secret knowledge that was rooted in an early scientific view of the unity of knowledge and the transparency of nature as a medium of metaphysical communication. The natural world was intelligible as a vast set of signatures, not mere arbitrary signifiers, but physical substances whose features manifested their invisible content and connection to the spiritual armature of all phenomena. These signatures were visual and Mount portrayed their harmony and universal manifestation in the color schemes and compositional structure of his paintings. To gaze upon his paintings was, for the hermetically minded, to see the connectedness of the universe as a revelation of an immanent deity. As capitalist entrepreneurs and industrialists converted natural resources into transatlantic capital, as fortune seekers dug for gold and sought out treasures thought to have been buried by pirates, and as pioneers and homesteaders transformed the wilderness and Indian territories into the inhabited property of private landowners, Mount persisted in discerning a spiritual content in nature.[23] In the spirit of American transcendentalism, Mount's painted hermeticism promoted a spiritual landscape that ultimately resolved the conflicts between nature and culture by regarding the natural as a revelation of what culture ought to recognize and celebrate.

American Catholicism is largely of two types: the northern European variety, which concerns Davis at the beginning of this section, and the Latino sort, a much older presence in North America, originating in the colonial enterprise of Spain in the New World. But Southwestern Catholicism can hardly be reduced to a simple notion of Spanish Catholic identity. Claire Farago looks carefully at the complex intermixture and hybridity of New Mexican santos, the devotional images created among Catholic Latinos, *mestizos*, and Indians in the nineteenth-century Southwest. Monolithic and final interpretations of meaning are not possible in a world undergoing constant change, in which one culture and religion were overlaid by successive strata of others, resulting neither in the complete erasure nor the total domination of any single cultural regime. Identity was never fixed and the influx of Anglo commerce did nothing to crystallize matters. In the second half of the century, mass-produced religious prints made in Europe and the northeastern United States entered the cultural marketplace of the Southwest, resulting in what Farago aptly calls the conflation and superimposition of different pictorial systems and different relations between natural and cultural orders. The enfolding of premodern colonized indigenous cultures with the industrial, mass culture of modern North America resulted in a cultural melange that also characterizes interaction and exchange in large parts of the world today.

PART III: RELIGIOUS VISUAL CULTURE
AND AMERICAN MODERNITY

As a modern nation-state, the United States has produced a society in which some of the most familiar hallmarks of modernity and modernization are evident: industrial production and the mechanization of labor; mass culture; and a secular ideology of Enlightenment that encourages an optimistic dependence on the instrumental power of science and technology to control nature. Leigh Schmidt explores the vicissitudes of modernity in the elegiac images of Elihu Vedder, an artist who agonized over his own experience and conviction of God's sensate remoteness and even absence. Why couldn't he hear God; why didn't God listen to Vedder's own desperate petitions? Secularization, hailed by the Enlightenment in the seventeenth and eighteenth centuries, argued for an increasing distinction between the natural and the supernatural that strained and ultimately broke the connection that Christianity posited between heaven and earth. Schmidt examines how proponents of the Enlightenment used pictures that purported to expose the oracles as the machinery of priestly deception. Although Vedder was nurtured by the Enlightenment's demythologizing of revelation, he longed to hear the oracles speak. But lacking the resources of a deeply rooted religious belief, he depicted desert mystics listening vainly at the stone lips of sphinxes, alone in the night of an empty, disenchanted cosmos. As Schmidt suggests, however, it is difficult not to sense a lingering anguish in Vedder's paintings. The artist was a casualty of Enlightenment as surely as those he painted were the victims of metaphysical superstitions.

One of the preeminent social and economic features of American modernity has been immigration, the massive mobilization of populations from Europe and Asia to North America. Images have played a role in this movement of peoples. Ellen Smith and John Giggie focus attention on migration to and within the United States. Smith investigates the way in which mass-mediated images—postcards—allowed Jewish immigrants to maintain vital links with the "Old World" as they entered a strange new one. Once here, Jews continued to celebrate Rosh Hashanah and made use of the commercial form of the postcard to convey greetings to family members back home as well as in the new world. As Smith suggests, the images on the cards helped Jewish immigrants in the United States see themselves as both Jewish and American.

When industrial mechanization reached the South in the wake of the Civil War, agricultural production was revolutionized and the reliance on manual labor was replaced by the new technologies of harvesting crops. As a result, an enormous labor pool of impoverished African Americans was free for the first time to leave the plantation and rural agrarian poverty and seek employment in the wealthier economies of the North. Major cities such as St. Louis, Chicago, and New York were the most frequent destinations. Giggie argues that understanding the religious lives of American Blacks after the Civil War depends in no small way on examining the material culture by which they practiced belief, in this case, the railroad cars in which they gathered to worship, the railroad stations at which they met the trains that took them north, and as evidenced in the trains themselves, where the material form of liberation was also a reminder of persistent racial oppression. Giggie scrutinizes the language used in sermons, letters, and autobiographies, the songs and music people performed, and the images they produced in order to reconstruct the experience of the railroad and its importance in the religious faith of African Americans.

Any account of modern American religions must give careful attention to the formative conditions of commerce, technology, and mass culture. Paul Gutjahr has discerned in the story of American Protestant Bible illustration from Isaiah Thomas to the present several recurrent visual features that would make readers of the Bible into viewers and attract viewers to be readers. Publishers deployed illustrations to commodify the Bible as well as to make strategic use of its popular commodification for theological purposes. In the late eighteenth and early nineteenth centuries, Isaiah Thomas and Mathew Carey used fine-art imagery and style to attract readership by associating their Bibles with the social virtue of aesthetic refinement. Antebellum Bible publishers inserted depictions of historical curiosities and archaeological miscellanea in order to rivet the viewer's attention and to apply illustrations to the task of evangelical apologetics. In the twentieth century, publishers believed that making the Bible relevant and accessible to popular readership would secure large markets, so they produced Bibles that were paraphrased in the vernacular and adorned by easily legible illustrations that clarify and accentuate biblical interpretation. Enterprising publishers brought technological innovations to bear on ventures that sometimes paid off handsomely. Gutjahr traces the evolution of biblical illustration as publishers explored ways of attracting readers in a very competitive marketplace. He contemplates two projects by the firm Harpers, one that succeeded and set the visual and technological standard in antebellum America, and one that failed utterly in the 1990s in spite of a wealth of technological and commercial resources.

This scheme of essays does not adequately represent either the variety of American religions or the range of genres and domains of visual practice. Whole traditions remain unmentioned or largely untreated. With regard to religion, virtually nothing on the visual cultures of American manifestations of Islam, Asian religions, Orthodox Christianity, Mormonism, indigenous religions such as Haitian vodou, or such noninstitutional religious forms as the occult, spiritualism, or New Age has been included. From the perspective of visual culture, significant visual media such as film and the Internet do not receive much attention. By contrast, several essays on Christian paintings and prints appear in the book. But comprehensive coverage was never our aim. Instead, we set out to assemble a group of rigorous case studies in the service of several goals: reflection on the mechanics and theoretics of academic inquiry with respect to religious visual culture; exploration of some of the subject's major issues and themes in the history of North American religious images; and demonstration by example of the significance of visual evidence for historians of American art, culture, and religion. This is surely a tall order by itself. For those who wish to examine traditions and innovations not discussed in these essays, the bibliography and the profiles of archives, museums, and collections at the end of the book will provide some useful assistance. Criticism for not including one topic or another is inevitable and not unjust. The book's subject, however, represents a field only now coming into view. *The Visual Culture of American Religions* will have served its purpose if it helps demonstrate the importance of further study and suggests some key directions for future investigation.

PART 1

RELIGIOUS VISUAL CULTURE
AND PUBLIC IDENTITY

1

THE PUBLIC DISPLAY OF RELIGION

Sally M. Promey

Congress shall make no law respecting an establishment
of religion, or prohibiting the free exercise thereof. . . .

AMENDMENT I, CONSTITUTION
OF THE UNITED STATES OF AMERICA

The public display of religion: the phrase itself generates a wide range of value-laden responses. In many quarters of the secular academy and among the mainstream liberal religious traditions, it seems to carry the implication of a breach in public decorum.[1] This sense of the violation of public good taste (and even democratic good citizenship) depends in turn on a number of factors. Prominent among these are, first, the recognition that religion rarely happens "in general," that it usually occurs in some particular or sectarian manifestation and, second, an understanding of "public" display that inclines attention toward images and objects "installed in public [facilities] by public agencies at public expense."[2] While few actually assume that all public display of religion is publicly funded, for many, consideration of the appropriate display of (largely sectarian) religion gets conceptually and categorically drawn into conversations about government endorsement or complicity—or some degree thereof—set off, philosophically and legally, against cultural pluralism and the establishment clause of the First Amendment.

The historical and practical interrelation of these two (cultural pluralism and disestablishment), furthermore, has produced a situation in which religion is counted not just as a matter of individual discernment and consent but also as something people do or ought to do in private. The privatization of American religion correlates historically, though perhaps not inevitably, with the separation of church and state. Religion, thus construed as ideally private, happens at the opposite end of the experiential spectrum from the other two terms of this chapter's title: "public" and "display." When the three terms come together in conversation, the initial assumption is often one of collision or conflict and, indeed, that is sometimes the case. Over the last two or three decades, for example, an increasing number of public display cases have come before the courts, with a few—the Ten Commandments posted in public school classrooms (*Stone v. Graham*, 1980) and nativity scenes on public property or supported by civic funds (*Lynch v. Donnelly*, 1984)—reaching the United States Supreme Court.[3] With respect to the character of the visual landscape of American religions as well as the separation of church and state glossed broadly, this chapter grants the critical importance of the establishment clause of the First Amendment. It more closely examines, however, the visible effects of disestablishment's constitutional sibling, the free exercise clause. For, as constitutional scholar Leonard W. Levy has pointed out, "religion saturates American public life," the establishment clause notwithstanding.[4] Here religion is not just something some people do, but something virtually all people see—daily—in public.

This chapter is an exercise in reframing consideration of the public display of religion. Most important, perhaps, it proposes expanding along several dimensions the common notion of religion's public representation. The result is a shift in emphasis toward "public" display that is plural, particular, and accessible. My subject does not exclude issues of government funding, property, and supervision but neither focuses nor stops there. While not minimizing the substantial importance of constitutionally bounded church-state relations in American religious expression, the accent here is on the nongovernmental operation of religious images and objects in the public arena.

My purpose is twofold. First, I want to define the public display of religion, as a category of visual experience, in a manner conducive to more inclusive academic inquiry. To date, the scant literature on the subject addresses particular forms (John Beardsley's work on yard art); particular functions (Edward T. Linenthal on public memory and sacred space); or particular aspects of public funding and legal history (Leonard Levy on the establishment clause and Wayne Swanson on *Lynch v. Donnelly*).[5] In addition, while there is a large body of scholarly writing on public art, acknowledgment of religion's presence in those conversations has been negligible, despite the frequency with which religious questions or phrasings have surfaced in recent contentions over art and public policy (witness Jesse Helms's labeling of Andres Serrano's work as "blasphemy").[6] My chapter represents an initial attempt to reorganize and reconfigure the subject of the public display of religion; to account, in the process, for all three terms and some of their relations; and to treat in a more comprehensive fashion the collection of materials usefully delineated within this visual field of information. Second, and perhaps of more immediate consequence, I wish to suggest that this conceptual arrangement of the public display of religion has significant implications in relation to the construction and consolidation of contemporary individual and group identity. Though it may have functioned differently in the past, in the early-twenty-first-century United States, the public display of religion plays a key role in manifesting the nation's plural character. Religion's public display thus makes visible pluralism's constitutive relation to American culture.[7]

The degree of ambiguity and complexity inherent in each term of the title ("public," "display," "religion") is greater than initial appearances might suggest. Each warrants its own discussion. The separate sections of my chapter take each term in turn, examining complications inherent in each as well as some of the intersections among the three.

PUBLIC

Though art may be a private act in its origins, this is not what we can
be expected to see as art becomes part of a system of public information. Art is a public system to which we, as spectators or consumers
[or participants], have random access.

LAWRENCE ALLOWAY, "NETWORK: THE ART WORLD DESCRIBED AS A SYSTEM"

Jesse Treviño's nine-story, hand-cut mosaic-tile mural, *Spirit of Healing* (fig. 1.1), is situated on the principal façade of the Santa Rosa Children's Hospital, a regional medical facility operated by the Sisters of the Incarnate Word, in San Antonio, Texas. A privately funded project, this ninety-by-forty-foot mural is, nonetheless, the largest work of "public art" in the city, easily visible to motorists on Interstate 10, a major San Antonio expressway. *Spirit of Healing* is "part of a system of public information" about the institution the mural adorns and about the people who inhabit the building, including the young patients and their parents as well as the medical personnel, the support staff, and the religious order that runs the hospital. Treviño indicates that publicness was a factor in the project's attraction for him: "It's not that I don't want my paintings in museums. I do. But the people are outside those museum walls. Public art, big pieces like this, brings the art out where everyone can see it."[8]

Despite the mural's public status, Treviño conceived aspects of its design in direct relation to his personal biography. Treviño, who was born in Mexico, became a United States citizen in 1970 and is now a resident of San Antonio. An artist by training and profession, he lost his right hand in military action during the Vietnam War. He subsequently retrained himself to paint left-handed. In the mural, the guardian angel's maimed left wing, while signifying life's general hardships, likely alludes to Treviño's own injury as well as directing attention, in its orientation, to the large cross in the background. In addition, and even more prominent than the angel's broken wing, Treviño's ten-year-old son, Jesse Jr., was the model for the child in *Spirit of Healing*. These rather intimate private associations, once known, become part of the mural's public meaning, aspects of the work with which particular audiences (parents, children, Latinos, veterans) identify.

Understandings of publicness occur in constant relation to and tension with notions of privacy.[9] In past and present practice, the public/private distinction has often been singled out as a way of approaching the problem of imagining religious action in a plural culture.[10] Though the word "public" has several possible meanings, from this historical perspective, public religion is oxymoronic; religion is a fundamentally private enterprise.

FIGURE 1.1 (SEE ALSO PLATE 3)

Jesse Treviño, *Spirit of Healing*. © San Antonio
Express-News. Photo by Robert McLeroy.

A Gallup poll conducted in 1988 reported that 80 percent of Americans agreed that religious beliefs belong to a voluntary and private domain, to be arrived at "independent of any church or synagogue."[11] (The percentages would undoubtedly have been even higher had government influence been considered along with that of religious institutions.) While the origins of "public" and "private" are traceable to ancient Greece and Rome, the early-twenty-first-century combination of privacy, individualism, and religious freedom has a specifically Euro-American lineage, including the early Puritan colonists and the Enlightenment thinkers whose works informed the founding of the republic. Assumptions of privacy reside at the very core of the historical construction of American religious liberty.[12] John Locke, for example, claimed in 1689 that the "true and saving Religion consists in the inward persuasion of the Mind."[13] Thomas Jefferson's famous 1802 letter to the Baptists of Danbury, Connecticut, the letter that introduced the phrase regarding the "wall of separation between Church and State," also asserted Jefferson's conviction that "religion is a matter which lies solely between man and his God."[14] By the late nineteenth century, there was widespread liberal agreement that the "inner spiritual life" was the "domain of sovereign individuality."[15]

The definition of religious privacy assumed in these quotations is more or less consistent with the one I follow here. What is private, for purposes of this chapter, is that which is relatively inaccessible to others. As political and social theorist Jeff Weintraub suggests, privacy includes the "things we are able or entitled [or required] to keep hidden, sheltered, or withdrawn from others."[16] Historically, such a definition of religious privacy has generally been constructed in supposed opposition to "public" established or state-supported institutional religion.[17] This chapter proposes augmenting the definition of "public" in three ways. The modifications I recommend have to do with matters of visual accessibility, of dynamic relation, and of the constitution of audience.

First, my use of the word "public" is linked to degree of accessibility rather than to issues of official or state or institutional administration. "Public" is thus, in the words of historian of religion John F. Wilson, a "means of signifying that which is generally available for common inspection."[18] Wilson's recourse to the phrase "common inspection" with respect to "public" and Weintraub's understanding of "private" as that which is "hidden" from view suggest that it does not necessarily take an artist or an art historian to cast *accessibility* (in relation to the public display of religion) as *visibility*. Who can see it and when? Where is it and what is the level of exposure? These are among the most relevant categorical questions. In addition to accessibility, the question of collectivity (most simply, the numbers of people to whom a public display is visually available) is not irrelevant.[19] But the sense in which collectivity intersects with this definition of public is a very specific one. The issue is not whether something is seen by an individual or by a group, whether it is viewed alone or in company. It is rather that the viewer knows that others can and will see too—and that they can and will do so with some facility. In other words, it is critical to this definition of public that many enjoy easy access to the object in question—but not necessarily that they do so at the same time. The viewing of a public display of religion can be a solitary experience without compromising its "publicness." Treviño's *Spirit of Healing* remains "public" whether there is one person or fifty people in the urban square in front of it.

Second, public is not rendered here as one term of a static, paired opposition (as in public versus private), but rather as one direction along a conceptual, practical, and experiential continuum of accessibility. It is upon the degree of visibility or invisibility that this definition hinges. Public and private are relative and dynamic terms. Rather than simple binary opposites, they are, as Robert A. White has argued for the similarly associated pairing of "sacred" and "secular," interdependent "dualities that are the enabling conditions for each other."[20] The shared boundaries that define the two are mutable; public and private are constantly in the process of formation and reformation with respect to each other. Along the spectrum that charts the two, the advance and retreat of one is always relative to the other.

Over the last century, in particular, technologies of mediation (e.g., half-tone print technologies, film, television, and electronic imaging systems, including the Internet) have complicated definitional categories, rendering "public" and "private" as increasingly elastic terms. Much that was formerly private has now been articulated into public expression by the mass mediation of culture, with its tendency to subject human experience and production to the "persistent gaze of publicity."[21] As media artifacts, W. J. T. Mitchell has argued, all art objects become public art. Because of publicity, the "'publicness' of public images goes well beyond their specific sites or sponsorship."[22] Even domestic religious objects and private devotional ones, when mediated by, for instance, the morning newspaper, take on a new "public" dimension for an expanded audience, though the objects simultaneously retain their "privacy" in the context of initial production and use.[23]

In the two modifications suggested above, the word "public" has its greatest applicability as an adjective, as in, for example, public space, public art, or public expression, where it now describes visual accessibility and where its relation to privacy is active and unstable. Third, and turning to the term's nominative usage, while I deem public spaces to be relatively more open and inclusive than private ones, no rhetorically all-inclusive "public" stands behind my argument. The public display of religion is observed not by a normative or representative public (singular) but by numerous *publics* (plural), multiple audiences, individuals and groups, who see religion around them as they conduct their daily lives and who approach the display of religion from many different perspectives. Though media exposure alters the equation, expanding the "geographical" referent and suggesting the advisability of attending to the macro- as well as the micropolitics of display, on the local level each example of display exists in its own "cultural space" and is not reducible to another.[24]

The publics for the display of religion are plural not only in any given place, but also in the sense that each public changes over time and new publics emerge. In addition, any number of relatively discrete audiences may aggregate to constitute a larger public or disintegrate into smaller units. To discuss a display's publics is thus to deal with entities both kinetic and partial. Whenever something is set out for others to see, what they see depends on both who they are and on what is displayed.[25] The plurality of publics for the display of religion increases the contingency of the display's significance. The public display of religion is thus fundamentally interactive, the full range of interpretive responses inherently unpredictable.[26]

DISPLAY

[Display] is not only endemic to human-being-in-the-world but fundamental to the process of constructing a human reality.

EDWARD L. SCHIEFFELIN, "PROBLEMATIZING PERFORMANCE"

In observance of Hanukkah 1993, five-year-old Isaac Schnitzer's parents placed a menorah in the front window of their home in Billings, Montana. Shortly after the arrangement of this domestic public display, someone launched a brick through the Schnitzers' window. In response to this blatantly antisemitic crime, non-Jewish residents of Billings (a town of eighty-five thousand with a Jewish population of approximately one hundred) put pictures of menorahs in their own front windows or on their doors to affirm their communal solidarity with the Schnitzers and with other local Jewish individuals and families. On 11 December 1993, in an editorial accompanied by a picture of a menorah to be clipped and used in this way, the *Billings Gazette* interpreted both the original family menorah and the town's visual and visible response to the crime as significant activities of public display. The editorial's author wrote:

> On December 2, 1993, someone twisted by hate threw a brick through the window of the home of one of our neighbors: a Jewish family who chose to celebrate the holiday season by displaying a symbol of faith—a menorah—for all to see. Today members of religious faiths throughout Billings are joining together to ask residents to display the menorah as a symbol of something else: our determination to live together in harmony, and our dedication to the principle of religious liberty embodied in the First Amendment to the Constitution of the United States of America. We urge all citizens to share in this message by displaying this menorah on a door or a window from now until Christmas. Let all the world know that the irrational hatred of a few cannot destroy what all of us in Billings, and in America, have worked together so long to build.[27]

The full shape of the display initiated by the Schnitzers' menorah did not stop with these newsprint images. One year after the act of antisemitic provocation, French photographer Frédéric Brenner assembled a deliberately diverse crowd of Billings residents ("cowboys, Indians, blacks, Latinos, ministers, priests, cops, you name it").[28] Directed by Brenner, this group staged a commemoration (fig. 1.2) designed to reaffirm respect for the many different religious and ethnic groups represented in the town's population. Wearing vestments and costumes that visually accentuated their differences, each participant raised aloft a Hanukkah menorah. Special crews provided electrical connections (note

FIGURE 1.2

Frédéric Brenner, *Citizens Protesting Anti-Semitic Acts, Billings, Montana, 1994.*
© Frédéric Brenner, and courtesy Howard Greenberg Gallery, New York.

the wires on the ground in the photograph) to light the bulbs representing candle flames.
Brenner signified the gathering's defiance of the initiating episode's specific violence by
shooting his photograph of the assembly through a sheet of glass penetrated, but not shat-
tered, by a projectile rock or stone. A two-story American flag draped (for the photo) from
a building in the right background asserted the perceived Americanness of this demonstration of plural and communal solidarity. The photograph that resulted from the performance staged by Brenner was subsequently exhibited as part of a traveling show that
began in September 1996 at the Howard Greenberg Gallery in SoHo. In the same month
the photograph was reproduced in *Life Magazine* with other images documenting American Jewish life and in a *New York Times* review of the SoHo exhibition. Brenner simultaneously published a book of his photographs titled *Jews/America/A Representation*. The
book included the shot he now called *Citizens Protesting Anti-Semitic Acts, Billings, Montana, 1994.* In this case, one display expanded, layer upon layer, to include other displays
that continued to bear a direct relation to the domestic ritual religious object in the
Schnitzers' front window. With each added "layer," new publics and new sorts of public-

ness accrued to the event and its iterations. Brenner's work first provided the rationale for, and then recorded, the commemorative performance. Both the collaboration between the photographer and the town and the image that documented the collaboration asserted for the Billings community an identity and a human reality actively alternative to that presented by the hate crime.

When used in conjunction with the modifier "public," "display" is a word that maintains a rich and resonant redundancy: the verbal form "to display" includes "to make public" (and, with just a bit of extrapolation, to make or create publics) among its synonyms. Display also sometimes carries with it connotations of ostentation, superficiality, or falseness.[29] But it is not in these evaluative senses that I employ the term here. Rather, I have deliberately selected display (over some of the possible, but categorically more limited, alternatives) in order to be inclusive of the widest possible array of experiences while still emphasizing the explicitly visual character of the specific phenomenon my chapter engages. "Art," for example, as one category of display, occupies an important and particular place in the public pictorial representation of religion. But, from the perspective of this chapter's subject, art is part

FIGURE 1.3
Billboard on the Pennsylvania Turnpike, "Consider This a Sign from God."
Courtesy Brad Perelman and Yitzak Francus. Photo by Sally M. Promey.

of a larger whole constituted by the numerous modes of visual communication represented in religious display. If the operative question is "Where do we see religion in the visual practice of daily life?" then the comprehensive response must be ventured, at least initially at any rate, without regard to the filtering mechanisms usually put into place by notions of aesthetic, intellectual, or economic hierarchy. We learn more about the way visual culture works when we look at a range of visual materials. The necessary second step, one that the prescribed length of this book's chapters precludes, is a return, with renewed understanding, to the various more tightly bounded categories of visual experience.

Display belongs to the realm of the visual; it is a visual device for the organization of space and experience.[30] The term "display" accommodates two significant aspects of the public visual culture of religion in the United States: exhibition and performance. Exhibition is conceived here as the public presentation of objects and images (including, for example, such things as pictures of various sorts, seasonal items like nativity scenes or menorahs, bumper stickers, postage stamps, and architectural façades). The category exhibition takes account of such specific displays of religion as Treviño's *Spirit of Healing* (fig. 1.1), a billboard on the Pennsylvania turnpike (fig. 1.3), and John G. Chapman's *Baptism of Pocahontas* (1840; fig. 1.4) in the Capitol Rotunda. The public exhibition of religion in the United States also includes the display of religious objects at one or more steps removed from original use, as, for example, in a recent showing at the Peninsula

FIGURE 1.4 (SEE ALSO PLATE 4)
John G. Chapman, *Baptism of Pocahontas at Jamestown, Virginia, 1613*, 1836–40, oil on canvas,
144 in. x 216 in., Capitol Rotunda, Washington, D.C. Courtesy Architect of the Capitol.

Fine Arts Center (Newport News, Virginia) of portable military altarpieces (figs. i.2–i.4)
used by World War II chaplains conducting religious services in the field.[31]

Performance, on the other hand, includes, in this context, the acting out in public of
explicitly and visually religious behavior. It comprises such displays as the seemingly ubiquitous rainbow-wigged figures at sports events holding up signs that read "John 3:16"; the
reportedly homeless man who dresses as Jesus and appears on the Capitol steps in Washington, D.C., each year around Easter; the Sikh Vaisakhi Day Parade in New York City;
and observances associated with the seasonal erection of Jewish, Muslim, and Christian
symbols on the National Mall (for example, the lighting of the "national" Hanukkah menorah and the ritual placement of the Islamic star and crescent). Display can thus be considered to include public ritual as "a kind of performative behavior" with a visual component.[32] The Rev. George Stallings's ritualized destruction of pictures of a white Jesus,
performed on Good Friday 1993 in Washington, D.C., is an especially apt example (fig.
i.1). Controversy and acts of iconoclasm themselves can be construed as cultural performances that serve to recall, foreground, and rework significant identity and boundary
issues within the American republic. Stallings intended his action, performed in clerical
garb outdoors along a major thoroughfare, to constitute a proclamation about the visual
appearance of Christianity's founder in relation to contemporary issues of race in the
United States.

The Stallings event also demonstrates how performance, by comparison with exhibition, much more assertively introduces the elements of time and motion into religious display. Once again, however, mass mediation complicates this picture by re-presenting performances in still images (as in, again, fig. i.i) and re-presenting the exhibition of pictures or objects in video formats that include both time and motion (for example, the appearance of a print version of Warner Sallman's 1940 *Head of Christ* in Spike Lee's 1991 film, *Jungle Fever*).

Even prior to media intervention, however, exhibition and performance are less clearly distinguished from one another than the forgoing might be taken to imply. The Billings, Montana, example (fig. 1.2) clearly includes elements of both exhibition and performance. So too does the spontaneous construction of public memorials, often including explicitly religious symbols or messages, that has occurred with increasing frequency in response to acts of violence and death like the shooting rampage at a public high school in Littleton, Colorado, in April 1999 or the 1995 bombing of the Alfred P. Murrah Building in Oklahoma City. One might choose to see many seasonal exhibitions of religion (attending such holidays as Christmas, Hanukkah, Sukkoth, and Kwanzaa) as a kind of performance on the basis of their temporary, periodic, and repetitive usage. The evangelical Christian preacher who constructs giant and elaborate sand sculptures of religious figures on the beach at Ocean City, Maryland, and then leaves them for the tides and tourists, only to return and start over again every ten days during the summer season, stands with one foot in each of our two categories.[33] And in cases involving many sorts of religious decoration of the human body (such as the head scarves worn by some Muslim women, yarmulkes, T-shirts imprinted with religious pictures, crosses, crucifixes, or Stars of David worn as jewelry, and religious tattoos), exhibition and performance merge in the practice of display.

As the religious ornamentation of human bodies plainly suggests, display organizes not just space and experience, but also identity and association within a given culture. More specifically, display generates a discursive space, a social and political arena, where cultural negotiations about identities both individual and collective take place.[34] Any given display is informed by the rules, conventions, and constraints deemed necessary to hold meaning in place in the specific discursive field the display occupies. Plural publics make prior discernment of "necessary" internal regulation an especially daunting task. Surely the fantastical architecture of the Mormon temple just off the outer loop of the Capital Beltway in suburban Maryland near Washington, D.C., (fig. 1.5) was intended by its designers to suggest a disjunction between sacred and profane, the disruption of ordinary activities and expectations. The desired disjunction from the ordinary, however, was not likely one that pursued the temple's conflation with secular fantasy lands. Nonetheless, over the years, the building's visual similarity (gleaming white and gold spires, strikingly surreal illumination, extreme verticality) to the built landscapes of Disneyland or the fictional Emerald City in the Land of Oz, combined with the temple's unavoidable visibility from the Capital Beltway, has elicited a form of editorial vandalism. From time to

FIGURE 1.5
Washington D.C. Temple,
Church of Jesus Christ of Latter-
day Saints (Mormon), viewed
from Capital Beltway, December
1999. Photo by Sally M. Promey.

time someone enacts a kind of textual counter-display, inscribing the words "Surrender Dorothy!" on the exterior barrier of the overhead train crossing that Beltway traffic passes under on immediate approach to the Mormon structure.

Different groups and individuals activate a particular display's meanings in different ways—or, as in the preceding paragraph, they activate different meanings altogether. Attempts to deal with the inherent instability of meaning in public display contribute to the display's visual character. Religious displays often seek to exercise control of interpretive possibilities by the inclusion of easily legible and widely recognizable symbols and images pared down to their most basic elements. Display may thus purposefully distance itself, in order to retain a high degree of control over meaning, from the sorts of complexities often required of "art." This phenomenon can be easily overstated, however. Even highly simplified images, symbols, and iconographies, achieving a substantial degree of cultural uniformity, may simultaneously retain a surprising variety. Think, for example, of the visual and narrative dynamics of different Christmas displays of nativity scenes. A very brief survey would need to take into account the handmade and the mass-produced; a wide range of media including wood, plastic, paint, and fabric; both two-dimensional and three-dimensional forms; and displays in which the crèche stands alone as well as ensembles of decorations that include a nativity scene.

Not infrequently the activity of viewing display elicits an alternative exhibition or performance that seeks to supplant the meaning that is initially asserted. During the December holiday season in 1998 and 1999, for example, one manufacturer marketed specially designed cardboard eyeglasses. Their lenses turned every bright light (Christmas lights, headlights, street lights, etc.) in the wearer's line of sight into a Star of David. The "magic glasses" thus reconfigured the Christian landscape of Christmas and opposed the cultural imposition of a particular seasonal identity.[35] Rather than merely neutralizing sectarian expression, the glasses wittingly and wittily transformed it. A billboard on the Pennsylvania Turnpike (fig. 1.3) incorporates the same sort of subtle and humorous rejoinder to Christianity's claims on the American religious economy. The large sign appears in the immediate line of sight for traffic traveling west on the turnpike. Against a startling background of celestial blue, a rainbow is arrayed: "Consider this a Sign from God!" the gold and white text announces, and then, "America's Jewish Bookstore."

RELIGION

There are, indeed, distinct alternatives to a coherent religious tradition
as the common cultural core thought by many to be required at the
center of our modern society.

JOHN F. WILSON, "THE PUBLIC AS A PROBLEM"

Of the three terms in this chapter's title, about this one ("religion") it would seem that there might be a substantial degree of intuitive agreement with respect to when and where the term applies. The evidence suggests otherwise. Religion, it appears, resides most definitively in the eye of the beholder. What counts as religion in public display varies with the audience(s) for a particular performance or exhibition. In February 1997 a coalition of sixteen Muslim groups wrote a letter of request to the justices of the Supreme Court of the United States; the members of the coalition understood their request to concern the public display of their own religious tradition. Specifically, they petitioned the court to remove the face from the figure of Muhammad (fig. 1.6) in the courtroom's larger-than-life-scale frieze representing eighteen great historical lawgivers, including Hammurabi, Confucius, Moses, Charlemagne, Napoleon, and John Marshall. The lawgiver portions of the frieze occupy the north and south walls of the courtroom chamber; allegorical figures representing

FIGURE 1.6
Adolph Weinman, figure of
Muhammad, as depicted in the
North Courtroom frieze of the
Supreme Court, 1931–32. Collection
of the Supreme Court of the United
States. Photo by Franz Jantzen.

various aspects or qualities of law (Wisdom, Truth, Justice, Divine Inspiration, Defender of Virtue) appear on the east and west walls. The courtroom frieze in its entirety was produced in the early 1930s by Beaux-Arts sculptor Adolph A. Weinman.

In a letter dated 11 March 1997, Chief Justice William H. Rehnquist maintained that the representation of Muhammad would not be altered because it "was intended only to recognize him, among many other lawgivers, as an important figure in the history of law . . . [and not] as a form of idol worship" or sacrilege, as Nihad Awad, director of the Council on American-Islamic Relations and the coalition's spokesperson, had contended. For Rehnquist and the court, Muhammad's image on the frieze constituted a historical representation of legal development and innovation. For Awad and the coalition, it was an inappropriate depiction of a figure whose meaningful identity was undeniably religious. While Muhammad's depiction remained unaltered, the court did order changes in the educational brochures distributed to tourists and visitors. The brochures now identify Muhammad as the "Prophet of Islam" rather than its "Founder" and contain this qualification: "The figure above [depicting Muhammad] is a well-intentioned attempt by the sculptor, Adolph Weinman, to honor Muhammad and it bears no resemblance to Muhammad. Muslims generally have a strong aversion to sculptured or pictured representations of their Prophet."[36]

An incident, now become anecdote, involving Sherman Minton, Supreme Court justice from 1949 to 1956, suggests that the courtroom's aesthetics (fig. 1.7) can be seen to complicate even further the issue at hand (the public perception of religious content). The justice's grandson, visiting the august chamber with Minton, was undeniably awed by the room's high coffered ceilings, extravagant gilding, marble luminosity, and thirty-foot Ionic columns. Looking up at Weinman's friezes, the ten-year-old reportedly exclaimed, "Granddaddy! Where's God?"[37] The city-funded Pawtucket, Rhode Island, nativity that sparked the Supreme Court case *Lynch v. Donnelly* was likewise viewed by some as inherently religious and by others as completely secularized and devoid of religious significance.[38] The decision on the case, delivered by then (and until 1986) Chief Justice Warren E. Burger, indicates the degree of categorical slippage and blurring. Burger's lengthy written opinion included the observation that the display of artistic "masterpieces" with "explicit Christian themes and messages" in the government-supported National Gallery of Art, constituted a plausible justification for toleration of the city-funded Pawtucket crèche.[39]

The categorical imprecision encountered with respect to the public display of religion accrues, in part, from the "location" of belief. Each display manifests at least three possible agents or loci of belief: the artist, maker, or performer; the patron (institutional, group, or individual); and the various audiences or publics who may well disagree among themselves about the absence, presence, or degree of religion that is represented. In some instances, the most meaningful constituent unit of interpretation for a particular display is a single person, with public display thus becoming a medium of private meaning-making. This may be the case even when a display does not overtly picture religion. For example, passersby offered markedly different interpretations of a tree trunk carved into the shape of an upraised arm and hand near a residence in Silver Spring, Maryland. The educational executive and fund-raiser who created the wood carving maintained that he understood this labor as "relaxing" and "therapeutic" and that he did not set out to make "a religious symbol." Among his neighbors, however, an Orthodox Jew saw in the work the "Hand of Moses." And a Muslim woman identified the sculpture's subject as the "Hand of Fatima," daughter of Muhammad.[40]

In social and historical analysis, where describing other peoples' understandings and perceptions of religion is paramount, psychologist of religion Roger Fallot makes a compelling case for adopting an expansive definition of the term, one that allows for the ambiguities and multivalencies of use. Public displays of religion represent a subject that may manifest both experiential and institutional dimensions. Experientially, religion may include a sense of ultimate or existential meaning, values, order, or purpose; an awareness of the sacred or the holy; or a sense of relation to a transcendent being or higher power. Institutionally, religion generally involves an identifiable collective or community of adherents as well as a set of defined beliefs, ideas, practices, rituals, and symbols.[41]

In the late nineteenth century, intellectuals and liberal religious congregants on both sides of the Atlantic voiced the often anxious opinion that modernity might necessarily

FIGURE 1.7 (SEE ALSO PLATE 5)
Adolph Weinman, east end of North Courtroom frieze, 1931–32. Collection
of the Supreme Court of the United States. Photo by Franz Jantzen.

be accompanied by a decline in religion (institutional and experiential). By the 1950s and
1960s, sociologists of religion had assumed and documented this decline, a phenomenon they called "secularization." In the 1990s, however, the scholarly literatures of the
history and sociology of religion have overturned the presumption that modernity—and
especially modernity in the United States—automatically defeats religious experience and

expression. The "new paradigm" for the sociological study of religion in the United States, according to R. Stephen Warner's already classic article,

> begins with theoretical reflection on a fact of U.S. religious history highly inconvenient to secularization theory: the proportion of the population enrolled in churches grew hugely throughout the 19th century and the first half of the 20th century, which, by any measure, were times of rapid modernization. . . . One [even] naive glance at the numbers is bound to give the impression that, in the experience of the United States, societal modernization went hand in hand with religious mobilization.[42]

Polls charting levels of religious belief and observance in the United States have consistently yielded figures substantially higher than intellectuals, especially, might have imagined. I single out intellectuals here because, outside of departments of religious studies, the academy has long practiced a policy of containment, marginalization, and suspicion of the subject of religion. In terms of the statistics of belief, however, a recent Gallup poll, for example, indicated that, over the last five decades, the number of respondents who claimed "belief in God" held remarkably steady, tallying 96 percent in 1997, compared to 95 percent in 1947.[43] While some have suggested that respondents perhaps inflated their estimates of their own levels of commitment to religion, the fact that such a large percentage saw belief in God as a desirable trait, and one with which they wished to identify, is surely significant.[44]

The polls suggest and almost all agree that what modernity *has* produced, rather than irreligion, is *pluralism* in belief and culture, especially in the United States, due largely to substantial immigrant populations and to a political philosophy that rests on religious and social freedoms.[45] It is not just the plurality of audiences, of course, but also the pluralism of American religions that influences the interpretation of religious content and that affects the attachment of the adjective "religious" to display. Like "public," and in similar pursuit of greater accuracy and precision, "religion" becomes a plural term, "religions." It goes almost without saying that American religions are not organizationally or administratively monolithic. In discussions of the separation of church and state, the two variables are not parallel. While "state" is a property of the whole society, "church" is not.[46] Numerous sociologists, historians, and journalists have commented on the increasing particularity of American religions, suggesting that religion in the United States not only is but has been all along the "vital expression of groups," a "refuge for cultural particularity."[47]

The historical conviction that religious variety in the United States could be navigated only by turning inward, by making religion private, is easily documented.[48] One outcome of this assertion has indeed been a high level of privatization in modern American religious experience. Today, however, rather than living in a culture in which religion must become ever more private in order to tolerate pluralism, we occupy a place in time and space in which pluralism (including religious pluralism) is becoming ever more public.

The new visual accessibility of religious pluriformity can be attributed to several recent phenomena. Chief among these are the social transformations attending what sociologists call the "new immigration." Between 1966 and 1990 nearly as many people immigrated to the United States as did between 1890 and 1914. The situation in terms of numbers of newcomers, then, is very similar to that of the turn of the last century. The new immigration, however, is even more heterogeneous in terms of race, ethnicity, religion, and language than any of its historical precedents.[49]

When Nathan Hatch argues that the prior existence of religious diversity in the American colonies accounted for the foundation of American religious liberty, the eighteenth-century pluriformity he has in mind was largely (though not exclusively) sectarian Protestantism.[50] By the mid-twentieth century, perceptions of religious pluralism in the United States had expanded to include Protestants, Catholics, and Jews. Today, historian Diane Winston observes that

> We no longer live in a Christian nation, or even a Judeo-Christian one. As *The New York Times Magazine* reported in December, the United States is now home to 800,000 Hindus (compared with 70,000 in 1977) and to as many Muslims as Presbyterians. The numbers of Sikhs, Jains, Buddhists, Eastern Orthodox, and Baha'i in this country are also increasing.[51]

Not only are the numbers of belief systems to which people subscribe expanding, but the diversity of American religion is further augmented by new compound religious ensembles. More and more people have adopted what Winston calls "trans-religiosity," "blending . . . beliefs, mythologies, and practices from varying traditions . . . without feeling any contradictions."[52]

For historians and interpreters of American visual culture it is especially significant that pluralism has become more public in terms of its *visual* accessibility. One outcome of the increasing visual accessibility of pluriformity is its tendency to challenge the "taken-for-grantedness" of individual values and beliefs, influencing—according to Peter Berger—"not so much what people believe as how they believe."[53] In a context of free expression, the pluralism of religious display questions assumptions of dominance on the part of any one expressive entity and dilutes the impact of the sort of exclusivist language often characteristic of religious truth claims. When many options are visibly present and available, a single option is less likely to be accepted as normative. Because no one expression can be taken to stand for the whole (for one unifying or universal religion), religious expression itself undergoes a sort of emancipation. The public display of religions (plural) thus gains the potential to contribute to the sense of cultural diversity rather than reinforcing the hegemony of any one group. This possibility is unlikely to yield immediate acceptance—or even necessarily toleration—of differences (as the desecration of Muslim symbols on the National Mall in December 1997 suggests), but religious pluralism is no longer something we do, in large part, in private.

Granting as an essential feature of his position significant local/regional, rural/urban

FIGURE 1.8
Intersection of New Hampshire Avenue and Norwood Road,
Montgomery County, Maryland, August 1997. © The Washington
Post. Photo by Nancy Andrews. Reprinted with permission.

variation in the extent and particularity of religious multiplicity, Warner argues that in the United States religion itself is configured as a "social space for cultural pluralism."[54] The more and more frequent public expression of plural religions on television, in movies, in the newspapers (with many major papers recently hiring religion reporters and establishing religion pages), and on the Internet supports his claim.[55] Again, mediation here enhances exposure and accessibility. It is one thing, for example, when Buddhists gather in Canton, Ohio, for private worship; another when a reporter for the *Canton Repository* publishes photographs of the worshipers; and still another when the story appears on the paper's website, accompanied by a picture of an elaborate Buddhist religious sculpture as well as the photographer's pictures of the liturgical "performance."[56]

Recent religious architecture contributes perhaps most emphatically to the sense of multiformity and juxtaposition in the visual landscape of contemporary American religions.[57] In Montgomery County, Maryland, on a principal commuter artery into Washington, D.C., a stretch of road less than ten miles long is home to almost three dozen religious congregations, including, among others, houses of worship for Hindus, Muslims, Buddhists, Jews, Catholics, and Protestants and liturgies spoken in Spanish, Chinese, Korean, Vietnamese, and Ukrainian languages as well as English and Hebrew. A Cambodian Buddhist Temple, for example, painted in lemon yellow with bright green and red, is sited for visual prominence. Especially striking, in terms of visual accessibility, is the constellation of buildings at the busy intersection of New Hampshire Avenue and Norwood Road (fig. 1.8).[58] Here, in a location passed daily not only by commuters but also by hundreds of children and youth on their way to nearby elementary and high schools, adherents of three different religious groups have constructed buildings that express their different subcultures and beliefs. Appearing in immediate and obvious proximity to one another, the white, turquoise, and gold architecture of the Ukrainian Orthodox Cathedral is set off against the minaret and copper dome of the Muslim Community Center's mosque and both contrast with the understated modernism of the adjacent congregation of the Protestant Disciples of Christ. Not only is pluralism more insistently apparent in the visual stimuli of everyday life, but consciousness of the potential for overtly religious public works of art to have a diversity of audiences is amplified by such display. Like museums or shopping malls, in an increasingly plural culture and open market economy—and even within a single religious tradition—religious display offers the potential for improvisation and accommodation to personal interpretations, expanding and reconfiguring, in the process, the boundaries of expectation.[59]

VISIBLE RELIGION AND THE CULTURAL PRACTICE OF PLURALISM

The reader will by now have gathered that I am casting a broad net with respect to the categories "religion," "display," and "public." I do so in order to direct attention to the ways American religions in the early twenty-first century alter our visual and thus, ultimately, our mental landscapes. The visual character of our surroundings shapes, supports, and transforms our conceptions of and assumptions about human experience.[60] Display is thus truly "fundamental to the process of constructing a human reality."[61] If, as Stephen Warner suggests, we view pluralism as "constitutive" rather than "degenerative" of American religion and culture, we begin to see that understanding this chapter's subject is not a purely academic exercise. In a society that claims among its most basic values and legal rights both the free exercise of religion and freedom of expression more generally, the public display of religion is quite simply something that people do. The objects and performances comprised in this display claim a place in the visual field of daily experience.[62] What we see contributes to our sense of who we are, collectively and individually.

Although there is often something distinctly territorial about display, when "territory" is marked by a multiplicity of signs, a different mechanism is at work than when one sign dominates. As American culture more openly and publicly (visibly) expresses its plural constituencies, the visible display of religion allows individuals and groups to approach and to imagine perspectives different from their own. Visible religion takes on an active cultural role: rehearsing diversity, practicing pluralism.[63] To paraphrase and generalize the words of Jesús Martín-Barbero, public display marks off space for the formation and re-formation of identity; it also stipulates a social arena for the configuration and re-configuration of community. Given this relation of display to the composition of both identity and community, the increasing pluriformity of American religion's public face encourages us to imagine and to reimagine, in public and in private, the permeable social boundaries of what it means to be "American."[64]

2

FOR CHRIST AND THE REPUBLIC

Protestant Illustration and the History of Literacy
in Nineteenth-Century America

David Morgan

WORD AND IMAGE IN
PROTESTANT ILLUSTRATION

In five centuries of history, Protestant image-making has rarely strayed far from the authority of the spoken or written word. A central tenet in Protestant belief, the sectarian scatter of American Protestants notwithstanding, has always been that "faith comes from what is heard" (Romans 10:17). For a culture enamored of the power of the printing press as the supreme tool for evangelism, "what is heard" was easily changed during the Reformation to "what is read." Yet because images were generally linked to words of one sort or another, there is hardly a time in the history of Protestantism when images were not part of Protestant practices of belief.

The collaborative relationship of image and text is evident from Luther's illustrated Bible to the *New England Primer* (fig. 2.1). The primary means by which most American children in the eighteenth and nineteenth centuries learned to read, the primer grounded literacy on a close coupling of images with spoken and written words. Beginning with the alphabet method of associating sounds with individual letters, then building short syllables and monosyllabic words, primers used pictures as a kind of visual glue for adhering sounds to letters. Thus, the opening pages of the primer featured the alphabet in large, graphic form to enhance the memorization of letters. Like several German and Latin primers before it, the *New England Primer* placed the letters of the alphabet beside small,

FIGURE 2.1
Alphabet page, in *New England Primer*. Exeter, New Hampshire, 1782. Courtesy American Antiquarian Society.

roughly hewn images of an object or a figure, with a brief rhyme that included the figure's proper name, typically composed of one or two syllables such as "Adam" and "Bible."[1] Sound, image, and script were combined to fix the letters in memory, which was then applied to the decoding of sentences and to reciting the catechism, which was appended to most versions of the *New England Primer*.[2]

Since the process of reading is an intrinsically visual one, students learning to read have long been assisted by images. The effects of this aid are several and significant. First, as already pointed out, and as a glance at a page from the *New England Primer* such as figure 2.1 confirms, images were mnemonic devices for the letters. A less obvious, but no less useful benefit of the image was epistemological: the image in a primer conveyed the notion that language corresponds very closely to the things it represents. Language, in other words, is a reliable and accurate way of representing things. There is a close, even seamless relation between the words children pronounce, the words they read and write, and the things to which words refer. The value of this assumption was considerable because it invested the use of language with confidence in the intelligibility of the world and the ability of language to name objects of experience. The significance of this power should not be underestimated for its effect on children. Empowered by literacy, children came into possession of a stable, semantically lucid world within the structure of language. Words could be relied upon both to describe the world and to engage other people in the social discourse of position and power. As a young slave, Frederick Douglass discovered that this was no less the case among African Americans in bondage. Douglass proclaimed in his autobiography that literacy inspired him to reject the conceptual chains of his enslavement and to grasp equality with the slave master.[3] Finally, another purpose of the image in the primer and other school books such as spellers and readers derived from the power of images to accentuate or reinforce a particular significance of a text. This was especially important in the case of a book's religious purpose. For instance, the alphabet as presented in the *New England Primer* and many others produced with religious instruction in mind corresponded not only to the physical world, but also to the world as devout Protestants viewed it: "A" was for Adam, "B" was for Bible, "C" was for "Christ crucify'd, for sinners died." Learning to read was also learning to read the world as Protestant American culture understood the world to be legible.

These mnemonic, epistemological, and ideological purposes of integrating word and image in illustrated primers conformed to an empiricism shared by many American educators. Illustrations of the alphabet in primers tended to portray single objects. Acting as visual nouns to which verbs were attached, images facilitated the notion that words existed in a one-to-one correspondence to an objective world. According to Thomas Gallaudet, evangelical reformer, founder of the American Asylum for the Education of the Deaf and Dumb, and the author of a primer that he intended for mainstream American education, "Children almost immediately refer to some sensible object, or visible occurrence or transaction, in their first efforts to acquire the meaning of words." Gallaudet grounded his primer on this principle and another, namely, "That the language of pictures, being founded in Nature, and thus a Universal Language, may, like the signs and gestures and pantomime employed in the instruction of the deaf and dumb, be used, as a key or translation to illustrate and explain written or printed language."[4] Images possessed a unique power to teach the meaning of abstract symbols because they anchored symbols to the concrete world of preliterate sensation. David Tower, author of *The Progressive Pictorial Primer* (1857), stated that "Words may paint a scene, or an action, to the full conception of a matured mind; but a child needs the actual representation before his eyes to make a distinct, true, and vivid impression."[5] Having mapped out in their opening pictorial alphabets such a stable semantic field—rooted explicitly or not in the empiricism that Gallaudet and Tower championed—most primers proceeded to use images to underscore salient scenes in narratives that would assist young readers to apprehend the gist of a text, illustrating "the *subject* of each lesson," as one pictorial primer put it.[6] Gallaudet divided his primer into two portions: the first a pairing of "pictures of sensible objects" with nouns, adjectives, verbs, and short phrases; the second a selection of biblical reading lessons, each of which is illustrated with an engraving that occupies nearly half of the page.

Seeing, reading, and speaking developed best as integrated skills and did so in tandem with meditation on religious subjects, thereby embedding piety in the mounting strata of literacy and sensation. As children's author Jacob Abbott put it in the preface to a volume in his Rollo series, a "child of three or four can easily be taught to explain the pictures, or as he will call it, tell the stories, in his own way, from memory, to a younger child. In this way his intellect, his imagination, his memory will be cultivated, but more than this, he will be taught to be kind to his little brother or sister,— he will secure a practical lesson in the happiness of doing good."[7] The mortar between the empiricist building blocks of American literacy was a piety that pedagogues thought indispensable to the acquisition of true literacy.

"A PICTORIAL AGE"

In 1836 one educator recalled that "When I attended school it would have been considered a crime to have looked into a book which contained engravings."[8] In fact, of course, the New England Primer had been minimally illustrated throughout most of the eighteenth century, but the early nineteenth century was a watershed in the history of illustrated books. Primers produced during the first several decades of the nineteenth century added increasing numbers of wood engravings because illustrated books sold well, but also for reasons of pedagogy. Some authors and publishers made a point of stipulating that the images were not present merely for the sake of pleasing children, but as a tool to assist students in learning how to read. The author of one primer explained the method of learning: "Direct the child's attention to the cut, and explain its parts and its use. Exhibit, in the next place, the word representing the name of the object, and require the child to repeat the letters. . . . In the review of each section, let the learner recur to the cuts."[9] The authors of a well-known primer and series of school books referred to the early nineteenth century as "a pictorial age in education as well as literature."[10] Beginning in the 1820s, children's literature and school books were widely and often densely illustrated. Often building on the model of the New England Primer's illustrated alphabet, publishers of primers added illustrated sections on syllables and words, followed by a series of illustrated sentences or brief stories, for which illustrations provided a subtler range of references and cues to assist young readers in decoding short narratives.[11]

The burgeoning of illustrated primers and other school books in pre–Civil War America coincided with two far-reaching social developments: the revivalism of evangelical Protestantism during what is generally referred to as the Second Great Awakening and the growing movement to establish publicly funded common schools. Responding to evangelical revivals throughout the Union, but especially in the Northeast and the South, voluntary organizations such as the American Tract Society (ATS) and the American Sunday School Union (ASSU) undertook the massive production and distribution of tracts, pamphlets, and books, which were often extensively illustrated and aimed at children and adult converts and potential converts. These inexpensive publications were intended to fan the flame ignited by the evanescent experience of revival gathering and preaching as well as to prepare the kindling for revival.[12]

Books, tracts, almanacs, newspapers, and primers were illustrated in order to attract attention, to add to their appeal, to assist in the understanding and memorizing of contents, and to allow students to grasp more quickly and surely the semantic essence of a written text. Paradoxically, the more the ideology of a Protestant republic stressed the free will and personal liberties of citizens, the more it relied on the persuasive influence of such moral technologies as education, mass print, and images to capture and retain the attention of children and immigrants.[13] As part of liberty's arsenal of education, images were considered a tool for inculcating virtue and assimilating whoever was different (immigrants) or unformed (children). Salesmen for the ATS made a point of hawking their wares at public schools as well as parochial, and the Tract Society was careful to produce picture books, primers, and collections of stories that could readily be applied in the "common" or public school room. The literature and imagery of these publications deliberately avoided sectarian extremes in order to find wider acceptance.

TEXTUAL LITERACY AS CULTURAL LITERACY

American victory in the Revolutionary War left a new nation facing an uncertain future. Pedagogues and moralists responded by emphasizing the importance of literacy as the precondition for a virtuous national character.[14] Noah Webster's *Spelling Book*, the first popular school book after the Revolution, included extensive directions about orthography and pronunciation since Webster understood the importance of literacy to be explicitly republican:

> To diffuse an uniformity and purity of language in America—to destroy the provincial prejudices that originate in the trifling difference of dialect and produce reciprocal ridicule—to promote the interest of literature and the harmony of the United States—is the most ardent wish of the author; and it is his highest ambition to deserve the approbation and encouragement of his countrymen.[15]

Seeking to distinguish American from British English, Webster taught young Americans how to speak as well as spell, read, and write. Literacy was everything one did with words and the fate of the nation depended on it.

Although the early editions of Webster's speller were illustrated only by an image of George Washington, the choice could not have been more significant. Secular or evangelical, most primers shared an iconography of moral conduct and republican virtue that antebellum educators considered inseparable from teaching young people how to read.

Textual and cultural literacy went hand in hand and are unmistakable in two familiar iconographical themes among illustrations in primers and other school books. The first portrayed the piety of the nation's great cult hero, George Washington; the second encouraged benevolent conduct as the seal of the nation's republican virtue. Both were ingredients in the emerging national cult of civil religion.

Portraits of General Washington decorated many frontispieces in early national primers. If the success and divine favor of the new republic needed evidence of pious leadership, it found the evidence visually corroborated in depictions of Washington at prayer in primers (fig. 2.2). This image was accompanied by a long passage in *The Illuminated American Primer* of 1844, which is an excellent example of the national piety the image was intended to foster. The passage states that Washington was observed "on his knees, and engaged in prayer" during "the darkest period of the Revolution, when the liberties of our country were well nigh extinct." The passage and image promoted a cult of Washington and of civil religion by rooting in the soil of battlegrounds a sacred quality: "Who can ever tread the ground where the American army was then encamped, and not recall the period when the eyes of that great man were directed to heaven, and when his knee bowed, and when he breathed forth his fervent supplications for the salvation of his country?" This civil religion claimed Washington as the preeminent symbol of an explicitly Christian national cult: "The sceptic never can plead his name. The philosophic infidel can never refer to him for authority. The atheist can never enroll him among those who believe that the universe is without a Father and a God. . . . The father of his country approached the Throne of Mercy in the name of the Redeemer."[16]

A second large class of illustrations that linked republican virtue with an American self-understanding of divinely sanctioned national mission were those that depicted acts of public benevolence such as almsgiving or otherwise assisting the indigent or incapacitated. Children were urged to do good and feel pity for beggars, the poor, the old, the lame, and the blind in illustrated primers throughout the antebellum period, at the same time that Protestant tractarian enterprises and social reform initiatives were aimed at their parents. This republican ideal contended that Americans inherited from the Revolution a national mission that required their commitment to the collective good in order to attain a providentially intended republic. Those of lower station were to be regarded with pity and encountered with sympathy, which meant offering alms, physical assistance, or encouraging words.

Antebellum primers commonly included an illustrated reading lesson on the subject of benevolence such as figure 2.3, from the *Boston School Primer* (1831), in which a boy on the way to school gives his cake to a destitute woman and her children, whose father was killed in "the war." Mingling patriotism with Christian charity (the primer's lessons include one on God's sovereignty, which is followed by the Lord's Prayer), the image and text interweave self-denial and pity in the education of young Christians. The well-dressed boy, perhaps shown outside of his own home, contrasts with the impoverished and homeless family. The needy were consistently shown as a distinct social class observed by the

PRAYER.

PRAYER is the simplest form
    of speech
  That infant lips can try;
Prayer, the sublimest strains
    that reach
  The Majesty on high.

FIGURE 2.2
General Washington at
prayer, from *The Illuminated
American Primer.* New York:
Turner & Hayden, 1844, 34.
Courtesy American
Antiquarian Society.

middle-class narrative voice and the illustrated bourgeois children. Sympathy meant extending condolences over the barrier of social difference, but not eradicating the distinction
itself. Indeed, compassion for those beneath one's economic status helped construct a
bourgeois ideology of American society that favored the middle class. This is the recurrent aim of the four sisters of Louisa May Alcott's *Little Women* (1868). Having suffered
a loss of fortune and corresponding status, the family stabilizes itself by cultivating a middle-class life of domestic order and civic virtue in acts of benevolence for the poor. Praising "the sweetness of self-denial and self-control" as the proper means of drawing nearer
to their heavenly "Friend," Meg, Jo, Beth, and Amy attempt to confront their respective
vanities. Meg, the eldest and most fashionably inclined among the four, is humiliated by

THIS little boy is giving his cake to a poor old woman, who has two small children, and nothing for them to eat. Their father was killed in the war, and she is searching out a house to live in.

FIGURE 2.3
Benevolent boy, from *Boston School Primer*. Boston: Munroe and Francis, 1831, 24. Courtesy American Antiquarian Society.

a reversal of the benevolent moment when she attends a soiree and is underdressed. Clad in the sturdy but outmoded fashion of a humbler class, she "saw only pity for her poverty" in the condescending attentions of her wealthy hosts.[17] The irony of her humiliation betrays the class interests of benevolent sympathy: elsewhere in the novel, Meg and her sisters are taught by their mother to express Christian pity for an impoverished family of German immigrants. Almsgiving of whatever sort became the bourgeois answer to the aristocracy's noblesse oblige of former centuries. Throughout Alcott's novel, the girls mourn their loss of status and praise their mother and one another for displaying "aristocratic" manners. Seen in this light, images of the benevolent boy (and girl) helped situate the acquisition of literacy in a moral and social setting. Illustrations helped install literacy within a particular cultural rhetoric about the importance of certain kinds of behavior as characteristic of class and national identity.[18]

Illustrated lessons about acts of benevolence were shared among religious and secular school books. Primers and readers such as Peter Parley's and McGuffey's form an intermediate class, because they fostered religious sentiments but avoided sectarianism. By offering only passages from the Hebrew scriptures, the Lord's Prayer, or brief texts that venerated divine wisdom and providence, these school books espoused a public piety or civil religion that was characterized by monotheism, filial obedience, patriotism, and benevolence.[19] In the *Fourth Eclectic Reader*, for instance, McGuffey summarized this republican piety very succinctly in a lesson entitled "Religion the only Basis of Society," excerpted from an address by William Ellery Channing:

> Religion is a social concern; for it operates powerfully on society, contributing, in various ways, to its stability and prosperity. Religion is not merely a private affair; the community is deeply interested in its diffusion; for it is the best support of the virtues and principles, on which the social order rests. Pure and undefiled religion is, to do good; and it follows, very plainly, that, if God be the Author and Friend of society, then, the recognition of him must force all social duty, and enlightened piety must give its whole strength to public order.[20]

Although McGuffey was a devout Presbyterian, he could approve of what a Unitarian divine said of the national importance of religion since Channing avoided sectarian controversy in order—as with fellow Unitarian Horace Mann and the common school movement initiated in Massachusetts—to affirm the central role of religion in the formation of all American citizens. For the same reason, Louisa May Alcott, daughter of one of New England's great Unitarian transcendentalists, could also situate her account of four sisters in a generically Protestant world. Whether it was the publication of such outwardly evangelical concerns as the American Tract Society or the countless secular primers published by George Cooledge or Harper's, which aimed for the broad marketplace of the common school, the same iconography of benevolence for the destitute taught almsgiving and pity as the social obligation of middle-class Americans out of regard for the moral welfare of the nation.[21]

RACE, CREED, AND THE ICONOGRAPHY OF THE REPUBLIC

Yet the sense of national unity was severely challenged by a spate of fundamental changes at midcentury that centered on racial, ethnic, and religious difference. Two are of special interest here: slavery and Catholic immigration. The national division over slavery violently called the very idea of national unity into question. Many conservative and liberal Protestants regarded the arrival of thousands of Roman Catholic immigrants as a fearsome threat to Anglo-Protestant hegemony.

Long before the Civil War forced their hand, benevolent societies such as the ATS had tried to steer a middle course on the issue of slavery, neither opposing nor advocating the "peculiar institution," but promoting the evangelization of slaves. This resulted in the use of an iconography of what may be called "the benevolent moment," as presented in figure 2.4, from an early tract produced by the ATS (originally issued by the Religious Tract Society in London), and used during the 1820s and 1830s. As seen in figure 2.4, the benevolent moment was that face-to-face encounter in which the evangelical tract was configured

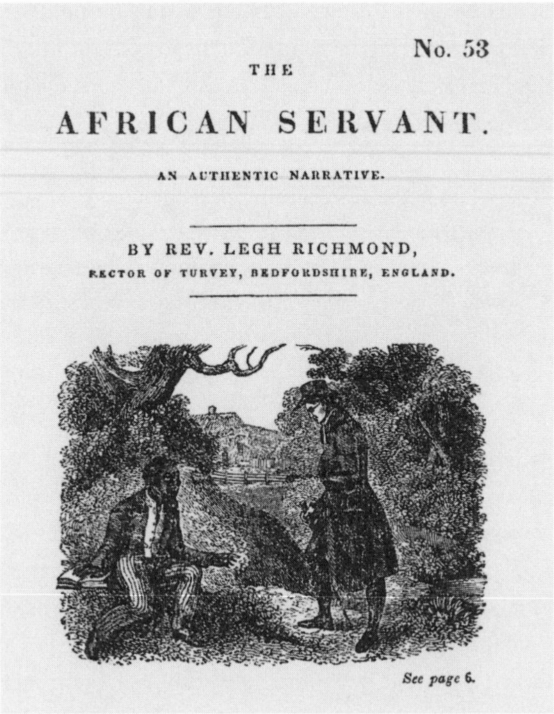

THE

AFRICAN SERVANT.

AN AUTHENTIC NARRATIVE.

BY REV. LEGH RICHMOND,
RECTOR OF TURVEY, BEDFORDSHIRE, ENGLAND.

No. 53

See page 6.

FIGURE 2.4
Alexander Anderson, engraver,
cover illustration to Reverend
Legh Richmond, *The African
Servant*. New York: American
Tract Society, ca. 1826.

as the means of a transformative exchange. The familiar iconography appears in an image of an encounter between the author of the tract, the Rev. Legh Richmond, and William, an African slave.[22] The genteel white man, with his hat, coat, and cane, condescends paternalistically to engage the slave in pious conversation—more a doctrinal interrogation—in which the slave demonstrates his preparation for conversion and baptism. The social differences are marked clearly in deportment, clothing, gesture, and height. Typically, the benevolent moment took place as an encounter between social unequals—White and Black, adult and child, teacher and student, bourgeois and indigent—and resulted in generating the sympathy, compassion, or pity that was the emotional experience of benevolence par excellence, which the tract reader vicariously imbibed.

The emotional intention of the image becomes transparent when we examine its contemporary inversion in abolitionist propaganda. Figure 2.5 illustrated an issue of *The Anti-Slavery Record* in 1835. The image portrays an unsympathetic slave owner from Virginia, set off as a haughty aristocrat by virtue of his staff, top hat, fine clothing, and unfeeling expression, who preys mercilessly on a slave and his imploring wife. The slave, named Peter Martin, was married to a free woman and was arrested, beaten, and imprisoned. He was freed, the story informs us, only when his wife raised six hundred dollars for his purchase.[23] In fact, the image does not appear to have been made for the story but may have been selected as a suitable illustration because it provoked indignation by inverting the

THE

ANTI-SLAVERY RECORD.

| VOL. I. | JULY, 1835. | NO. 7. |

[See page 63.]

SCENES IN THE CITY PRISON OF NEW YORK.

STEPHEN DOWNING.

This man was arrested as a fugitive, by a Virginia planter, and imprisoned in Bridewell, where he remained eighteen months. The inmates of the prison knew him well, and they were always ready to speak a good word for Downing. After the planter had got his *legal* right allowed, either because his lawyer's bill was so heavy, or because he hoped Downing's friends would *buy* him, he neglected to take him away for three months. By this delay he forfeited his right to do so, as was decided by Judge Edwards. But Downing's release was referred to the Supreme Court, which was to meet in two weeks. To the disappointment of every body, this was prevented by another *Judge*,* who, contrary to his promise, secretly wrote, for, and by a partial statement, obtained from the Supreme Court, at Albany, an order for the removal of poor Downing, and, before his friends were aware of the plot, he *was shipped for Virginia.*

* See Emancipator for November 4, 1834.

FIGURE 2.5
Cover illustration, *The Anti-Slavery Record* 1, no. 7, July 1835. Courtesy Billy Graham Center Museum.

benevolent moment that was calculated to ignite compassion. Both motifs, the benevolent moment and its inversion, were intended to mobilize the heart-struck viewer, though to different ends. The antibenevolent moment sought to elicit sympathy for the abolitionist cause; the benevolent moment for evangelical outreach. *The Anti-Slavery Record* applied the same strategy to the issue of education in figure 2.6, where the degree of pathos reaches melodramatic extremes. But the comparison of the well-dressed white teacher and black students in a classroom to a brutal, whip-bearing white master abusing black children in the fields fits the iconographic pattern of the benevolent moment and its inversion. Abolitionists could rely on the legibility of the antibenevolent moment precisely because it inverted a familiar motif.[24] As an intensification and politicization of evangelical rhetoric, this inversion followed a pattern among abolitionists such as William Lloyd Garrison and many others who applied the prophetic indignation and oratorical commonplaces of the evangelical preacher to the cause of abolition. Thus, the stark antithesis visualized in figure 2.6 parallels the contrast of salvation and damnation in evangelical oratory or sobriety and drunkenness in temperance propaganda.

The issue of literacy among slaves was, of course, of major significance. Since 1740,

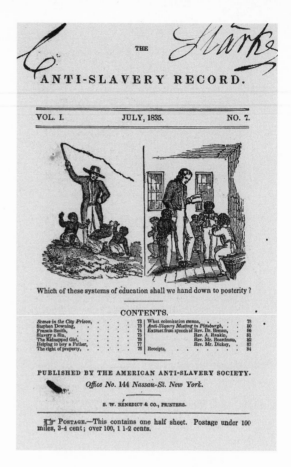

FIGURE 2.6
Two systems of education, wrapper
illustration, *The Anti-Slavery Record* 1,
no. 7, July 1835. Courtesy Billy
Graham Center Museum.

it had been a crime subject to a one-hundred-pound fine in South Carolina to teach a slave to write since it "may be attended with great inconveniences."[25] The life of Frederick Douglass made clear what these "inconveniences" could become: abandonment of submission to the "slave system" and escape to the North. In his autobiography, Douglass noted that "education and slavery were incompatible with each other." One of Douglass's sadistic masters reprimanded his wife for teaching Douglass the alphabet and claimed that learning spoiled a slave by making him unmanageable. Reading abolition literature, the young Douglass became aware of "the power of truth over the conscience of even a slaveholder."[26] The danger of literacy was the cancellation of difference, of social inequality.

The effort to educate African Americans did not enjoy federal organization until the final days of the Civil War with the establishment of the Freedmen's Bureau. Superintendents of schools were appointed by the bureau in July of 1865 and charged with the task of working with state officials and coordinating efforts with benevolent agencies that had come into being as early as 1861 when liberated slaves entered Union camps in the South in search of aid.[27] Important partners of the Freedmen's Bureau were the countless aid societies sponsored by church bodies throughout the North, but largely in New England.[28] Independent organizations also existed, the most important of which was the American Missionary Association, founded in 1846 in Syracuse as an outgrowth of the Amistad Committee whose treasurer was evangelical abolitionist Lewis Tappan. Following the Union army through the South in the spring of 1865, the AMA was the earliest organization to offer its services to former slaves.[29]

An examination of the many journals and annual reports of Freedmen's Aid Societies shows that a special place in the iconography of these groups was given to the portrait of the author of the Emancipation Proclamation. If George Washington had been the antebellum symbol of national unity, he was joined by Abraham Lincoln in educational efforts among former slaves as the icon of federal union. A former slave in Virginia reported that Lincoln's portrait hung in his house: "I love to look at it, and think how much I owe him." A teacher in a school for black children in Kingston, North Carolina, reported in 1866 that she created a banner with Lincoln's face for a school procession to celebrate the anniversary of the Emancipation Proclamation. "I think I may be excused if I say that this is the most beautiful thing of the kind I ever saw. All day long that noble face seemed to look down upon us, with a sweet and solemn gaze, that I am sure spoke eloquently to every heart."[30] Linda Warfel Slaughter, in her early study of former slaves in the South, reported that "Abraham Lincoln is to them [former slaves] a martyred saint, a buried Moses, who divided the turbid waters of slavery and led them through in safety." Freedmen's journals found African Americans corroborating this. When asked if Lincoln was her best friend, one black woman replied that he was, next to the Lord. When a Northern visitor asked black children in a Norfolk, Virginia, Freedmen's school whom they had to thank for their freedom, expecting "God" as the answer, she was surprised to hear a unanimous reply of "Abraham."[31]

The religious component of literacy efforts among former slaves quickly became an issue. When it came to educating former slaves, the ecumenical tolerances found in the civil religion of school books in the early republic broke down among evangelical and liberal Protestants. The evangelically inclined American Missionary Association promoted the combination of religious education with the acquisition of literacy skills while the American Freedmen's Union Commission, headed by Universalists and Unitarians, opposed any form of religious indoctrination.[32] The Freedmen's Aid Society of the Methodist Episcopal Church saw literacy campaigns among former slaves as a vital means of reversing gains among Roman Catholic missionaries, insisting that the "safety of the Nation demands" the intelligence and morality that Protestants could provide. "The African mind is susceptible to scenic attractions, and Popery knows how to skillfully use them. . . . If we aid this people with schools and churches we bind them with indissoluble bonds to Christ and the Republic."[33] Other societies sought to balance religious and secular instruction and to use only those creedal or doctrinal expressions "as all Christian can unite in."[34] And the Freedmen's Bureau itself sought to allay concerns of religious organizations that opposed religious instruction among Blacks.[35]

Having lost its white constituency in the South just before the outbreak of the Civil War over the issue of slavery, the American Tract Society produced several books for former slaves, including an illustrated primer in 1865.[36] In fact, the New York and the Boston wings of the ATS, split over the slavery issue since 1858, were the first groups to publish school books for African Americans, many of which included illustrations.[37] By the end of the war, the New York organization reversed its formerly sheepish position by creating and circulating its new primer. In 1867 the New York ATS donated five thousand copies of the primer to the Freedmen's Bureau for use in Southern "communities and families otherwise unsupplied with any educational facilities."[38] Another liberally illustrated publication of the New York ATS, *The Child's Paper*, was also used in Southern Freedmen schools in the instruction of reading.[39] The March 1865 issue reproduced figure 2.7 in an article by Helen Cross Knight (a regular contributor to the paper and former advocate of recolonization) that promoted the new primer. The benevolent moment of White-Black relations visualized before the war in figure 2.4 was recoded for use during and after the war as seen in the case of figure 2.7, which depicts the encounter between a Northern traveler and a tattered, newly emancipated black man. Instead of the aristocratic walking stick, the evangelical carries an umbrella beneath his arm. His Union military cap, traveling bags, and the artillery contingent in the background suggest that he represents the evangelical force from the North that followed the victorious army through the South. "What are you doing, uncle?" he asks. "I'se taking de fus step in de ladder of freedom," said the old man rising. "I don't know notin'. I warnt to know dreffully. I'se tank de heavenly Lord for dis book. It come fus; den de Bible." Knight constructs the former slave's reply to the Northerner's familiar mode of address in the patois of illiteracy no doubt to attempt to lend the exchange the appearance of authenticity. But the effect also dramatizes the presumed difference between the two speakers by rendering the Tract Society's appeal for aid condescending and the slave's attitude unambiguously submissive and gratefully dependent upon Northern compassion. The book the black man holds is the *United States Primer* which, Knight reminds the reader, promises to elevate whoever learns to read. Like so many other proponents of the republican ideal, the Tract Society had long insisted that by "an intelligent and moral people only, can a pure republic, and free institutions, be sustained and perpetuated."[40] Yet before the war this admonition had not been applied to slaves. With the sudden appearance of four million voting ex-slaves who resided largely in the dissident South, Northern evangelicals, who widely voted Republican, viewed the task of educating African Americans as paramount to the well-being of the nation.

Consistent with the New York–based American Tract Society's avoidance of controversy, the *United States Primer* itself includes no depictions of Blacks. It is, however, extensively illustrated. The use of images was no mistake. Reports from the field by teachers in Freedmen schools stressed the importance of visual teaching methods. "No people can be more easily taught through the medium of the eye than the freedmen; hence the rapidity with which they learn geography, and to read, write, and draw; and hence, too, the great utility of black-boards and maps, with which many of our schools are unsupplied."[41] Accord-

FIGURE 2.7
Freedman and friend, in
The Child's Paper 14, no. 3,
March 1865, 10. Photo by
David Morgan.

ingly, images were used as a counter strategy to check the advances of Catholic missionaries among African Americans. In 1877, the Methodist Freedman's Aid Society distributed fifty thousand "elevating and instructive pictures," presumably lithographs of religious or patriotic subjects, among Blacks in the South in order to "counteract the efforts of
the Romanists who are busily engaged in proselyting the freedmen by the distribution
of Romish pictures and images."[42] Rivalry over securing the allegiance (and socialization)
of former slaves is brutally clear in a cartoon by Thomas Nast, staunch Republican, Protestant, and bitter anti-Catholic, in which the visual rhetoric of the benevolent moment is
once again inverted (fig. 2.8). A priest, newly arrived from the corrupt Old World, seeks
to deceive a family of African Americans into accepting his seeming benevolence. Hidden behind the priest's back are the manacles of "priestly slavery" that would keep the

FIGURE 2.8
Thomas Nast, "A Roman Catholic Mission from England to the
'Heathens' of America," *Harper's Weekly Magazine*, 30 December 1871.
Courtesy American Antiquarian Society.

former slaves from the enlightenment that a republican education in the "U.S. Public School" would give them. Not content to leave any meaning implicit, Nast placed a Bible in one pocket of the family's father and a copy of the Emancipation Proclamation in the other.

Long concerned about the advances of Roman Catholic missionaries in the Mississippi Valley frontier, the ATS joined many other Protestant benevolent organizations to counter this threat to the uniformity of the Protestant character of the nation. These anxieties persisted throughout the nineteenth century, often achieving national attention in bitter debates over the use of public funds to support public and private schools in which religion was taught. The aims and self-interest of the Protestant campaign for a republican literacy were challenged by those who dissented from its hegemony. The religious interpretation of American republicanism advocated by many school book authors and publishers and school boards was ultimately millennialist. Images such as that on the certificate of membership in figure 2.9 visualized the ideal of millennial unity under the aegis of Protestant national identity. Members of many nations gather to listen to the prophetic announcements of one of the seven angels of the apocalypse witnessed by John and recorded by him in the Book of Revelation. Beneath the lithographic vignette appears the

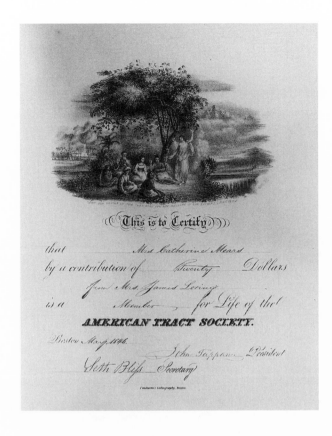

last portion of Revelation 22:2: "And the leaves of the tree were for the healing of the nations." By illustrating a certificate of membership in the American Tract Society, the image suggested that membership in the evangelical organization entailed affirmation of its millennial vision of harmony.

Mainline Protestants were widely unable to understand why Catholics, Adventists, and others could not subscribe to this vision of national Protestantism. The desire of Roman Catholics to maintain their religious and ethnic identity in educating their children was regarded as a fundamental threat. Catholics for their part felt menaced by the Protestant majority and resented the use of public funds to support education that involved Bible reading (especially from the authorized Protestant Bible, the King James version) as well as textbooks that endorsed nonsectarian Protestantism. Many Protestants refused to recognize the contradiction of privileging their notion of a Christian America in the common school while attacking Catholic attempts to apply tax revenues to private schools. From the 1830s through the remainder of the century, a series of court cases focused on the use of public funds in the common school that officially sanctioned religious instruction, even if that meant only public reading of the Bible with no commentary. Led by successive bishops in New York City, Catholics demanded public support for parochial

FIGURE 2.10

Thomas Nast, "Foreshadow-
ing of Coming Events in
Our Public Schools," *Harper's
Weekly Magazine*, 16 April
1870, 256. Courtesy American
Antiquarian Society.

schools since public schools widely justified Bible reading as a nonsectarian (Protestant)
practice of the moral formation of students. The controversy entered national politics as
Republicans (committed to the Protestant majority) opposed any funding for sectarian
schools while Democrats (enlisting immigrant and working-class Catholic votes) argued
that religious instruction of any kind did not belong in the public school.[43]

The conflict over the use of the Bible in the common school was compared by some
Protestants to the Civil War. In one of his notorious political cartoons Thomas Nast compared the assault of Catholics on the public school to the attack on Fort Sumter.[44] In another cartoon (fig. 2.10), published in *Harper's Weekly* in 1870, Nast also visualized the
threat as Protestant Republicans understood it. In this image, the public school classroom
has become the sanctuary of a Catholic church, with a priest presiding as another sweeps
away a pile of school books and the Bible. Students kneel at prie-dieux instead of sitting
at desks, and they gaze fixedly at a wall covered by Catholic imagery as yet another cleric
points to the portrait of a corpulent Pius IX. The portrait carries the text "He is Infalli-
ble," a reference to the doctrine of papal infallibility that was the major result of the Vatican Council of 1869–70 convened by Pius, the outspoken enemy of modern liberalism
and republicanism.[45]

It is evident that nineteenth-century visual culture developed an iconography about
literacy and education that helped delineate the shifting boundaries that separated public and private domains in American society. The nonsectarian civil religion disseminated
in school book imagery during the nineteenth century was a significant if inevitably ten-

dentious example of a public apparatus that struggled to interpret the First Amendment's establishment clause in terms of an accommodation of religious plurality (however narrowly defined). The opposition of Catholics, Seventh-Day Adventists, Unitarians, Universalists, and other religious groups outside of the Protestant mainstream (as well as many from within it) challenged the ideal of a Christian America—or at least the majoritarian Protestant right to define it. Illustrated school books were therefore part of a cultural politics created by American democracy, in which the rights of the majority collided with the constitutional principle prohibiting the governmental establishment of any religion, a debate that penetrates to the heart of the American experiment and shows little sign of subsiding today.

3

AMERICA'S CHURCH
Roman Catholicism and Civic Space in the Nation's Capital

Thomas A. Tweed

Eleven flags waved from the wooden speaker's platform, and more encircled the recently cleared ground as ten thousand Catholics gathered on 23 September 1920 to watch James Cardinal Gibbons lay the cornerstone for a national shrine in the nation's capital (fig. 3.1). The Byzantine-Romanesque building American Catholics would erect on that site during the decades ahead would be the largest Catholic church in the Western Hemisphere and the eighth largest in the world. Dedicated to Mary, since 1846 the official patroness of the United States, and built on the northeastern Washington campus of the Catholic University of America, by the 1990s it would attract 750,000 visitors annually. This chapter focuses on that building, the Basilica of the National Shrine of the Immaculate Conception (NSIC), which the promotional literature celebrates as "America's Church" (fig. 3.2).[1]

SHRINES AND THE NSIC

Although promotional literature sometimes uses the term "church" to describe the building, it is not a worship site for the Catholic faithful who live within a parish's geographical boundaries; it is a shrine, a sacred place that houses religious artifacts and attracts religious travelers.[2]

The variety of shrines is striking. They vary according to how they were founded; some commemorate a site where a saint performed an important deed, while others mark a spot

FIGURE 3.1

Cornerstone ceremony at
the National Shrine of the
Immaculate Conception,
23 September 1920.
Courtesy Basilica of the
National Shrine of the
Immaculate Conception.
Photo by S. I. Markel.
Used by permission.

FIGURE 3.2

Main entrance of the
National Shrine of the
Immaculate Concep-
tion. Courtesy Basilica
of the National Shrine
of the Immaculate
Conception.

where Mary appeared. Devotees also build shrines when a holy relic or image is brought from another place or when an object already on the site proves to have miraculous powers. Some shrines express gratitude for prayers answered. The NSIC and a small proportion of Christian shrines are devotional shrines, which devotees (usually clergy) deliberately mark off as sacred places, even though no miracles or apparitions occurred there.[3]

Shrines also vary according to their spatial placement and geographical range. Some shrines, like Lourdes and Muhammad's tomb, become international sites, drawing devotees from many nations. Others are national, as saints—like Our Lady of Guadalupe in Mexico—become intertwined with the nation's history and identity. Regional shrines attract pilgrims from a few provinces or a limited area, while local shrines draw devotees primarily from a single town or village. Narrowing the scope still more, some shrines decorate pathways, like roadside shrines, or mark the boundary between domestic and civic space, as with yard shrines. Homes become sacred, too, as devotees place images and artifacts associated with holy persons on bedroom walls or living room altars.

Recent technological innovations, especially the emergence of the Internet, have made some shrines even less spatially fixed. The NSIC and many other shrines now maintain web pages. The NSIC's Internet site allows cyberpilgrims to check schedules, learn doctrine, e-mail prayers, and even take a "virtual tour." Yet it is difficult to know *where* pilgrims are when they take a virtual tour: facing their computer, kneeling at the shrine, or hovering in cyberspace?[4]

Shrines were spatially complex, however, long before the introduction of cybertechnology since they are mediating spaces or transitional zones. They allow a vertical movement toward the sacred. Shrines elevate devotees and bring low the transcendent as pilgrims use artifacts and ritual to thank, promise, and petition the gods and saints. Shrines also allow horizontal movement outward into the social terrain and built environment. They move devotees between private and public sites, between civic and domestic spaces. So, for example, even though the NSIC is a national shrine by name and function, its geographical and social boundaries continually expand and contract. It is an international center since it attracts foreign visitors, and a local one since it draws Catholics from the metropolitan region. The gift shop, the mail, the Internet, and the media also extend the shrine's reach into the home. Devotees carry back a Marian statue to place on the dresser or a bumper sticker to affix to the Buick. At home they read a donation request from the shrine's rector or watch the shrine mass televised on Eternal Word Television Network (EWTN), a national Catholic cable station. Shrines propel devotees back and forth from kitchen to nave, erasing (or temporarily crossing) the boundaries between them.

To interpret these mediating architectural spaces is to position oneself in four domains: the building, the texts, the historical context, and the viewers. Decoding the building's meaning involves analyzing its form and function. As in the interpretation of architecture more generally, it means asking questions about the structure's design, materials, scale, site, and purpose. Texts are important, too. We should consider verbal and nonverbal representations of the building, including designer's drawings and writings. The "intentions"

FIGURE 3.3
Immaculate Conception
mosaic, 1930. Courtesy
Basilica of the National
Shrine of the Immaculate
Conception.

of architects, planners, or donors are not privileged sources, however, since those contend
with the meanings inscribed on the architectural space by other viewers and users. Pilgrims help produce the shrine's meanings by their responses to the space. In a similar
way, collective and individual ritual practice also shapes how users interpret the site. The
scheduled Eucharistic blessing of the sick and the spontaneous prayers of wheel-chaired
devotees at Lourdes, together with the retelling of miracle stories, make it a healing shrine.
And it is not only the NSIC's mosaic of the Immaculate Conception, America's patroness,
that marks it as national space for Catholics (fig. 3.3). The ceremonies and meetings of
national organizations, along with the visits of popes and presidents, also make it a national center, as when the National Conference of Catholic Bishops, the National Black
Catholic Congress, or the board of the National Council of Catholic Women gather at the
shrine—or when, as in 1966, a president's daughter is married there.[5]

To understand the meanings of the NSIC for designers, clergy, and visitors, I used historical and ethnographic approaches. I considered the usual historical sources, such as
the architectural plans, and asked the usual art historical questions about the building's
form and function. But I also have explored a wide range of archival sources, including
letters from pilgrims, records of donations, and photographs of ceremonies. For the earlier part of the twentieth century, those materials provide some clues about how ordinary
pilgrims understood the shrine. For the contemporary period, I also used participant observation as well as structured and unstructured interviews. If ritual shapes the build-

ing's meanings for users, it is important to observe it; if viewers inscribe meanings onto the space, then it is important to solicit their interpretations.

This approach has left me with a sense of the multiple, and sometimes competing, meanings of the shrine. In the remainder of this chapter, I consider some of those meanings as I focus on the clergy's suggestion that the NSIC is "America's Church."

NATIONAL CHURCHES
IN THE NATION'S CAPITAL

Even if its geographical reach expands and contracts, this devotional shrine is most fundamentally a *national* sacred space, as the clergy have emphasized and most pilgrims have acknowledged. But it is not immediately evident how Roman Catholics, or any U.S. denomination, can make claims on civic space in a nation without an official national religion. To call a religious site "America's Church," then, might seem presumptuous, even un-American. What are Catholic clergy doing when they call the National Shrine "America's Church"? Are they nostalgically longing for the medieval European past, when popes crowned emperors? Are they suggesting that Catholics have some special relationship with the American nation?

To make sense of Catholic views of the National Shrine, it is important to understand the cultural function of the capital in a nation with legally sanctioned separation of church and state. America's civil religion—that (always contested) piety connected with the political arena—has flourished since the 1790s at, for example, inaugural addresses, Memorial Day parades, and solemn political occasions. At the same time, the First Amendment's separation of church and state also has shaped religious life in the United States. Although some denominations (for example, Episcopalians and Congregationalists) have wielded disproportionate cultural power, federal and state statutes announce the government's commitment to religious toleration. In this political and cultural context, America's faiths have been forced to compete with one another to negotiate power, construct identity, and secure visibility. And the capital's urban landscape has been one site for these contests. In the United States, a nation with legally sanctioned religious diversity, the capital city has taken on special significance. Especially since the late nineteenth century, American religious groups have symbolically negotiated cultural power and denominational identity in Washington, D.C., by constructing national religious centers there.[6]

The idea to construct national churches in the U.S. capital arose more than two hundred years ago, and the clergy at one of D.C.'s most impressive sacred buildings have suggested that the venerable idea has been architecturally realized in the Episcopal Cathedral Church of Saints Peter and Paul, better known as the National Cathedral (fig. 3.4). As the National Cathedral's tourist guidebook proudly declares, the idea of an ecumenical national church in the capital originated with the federal city's chief designer, French-born artist, architect, and civil engineer Pierre Charles L'Enfant. His 1791 plans for Washington called for a church "for national purposes, such as public prayer, thanksgivings,

FIGURE 3.4
Washington National
Cathedral, Washington,
D.C. Courtesy Washington
National Cathedral.

funeral orations, etc. and assigned to the special use of no particular sect or denomination, but equally open to all." In part because some officials had difficulty reconciling the designer's proposal with the First Amendment's separating of church and state, it took another century before federal lawmakers acted on L'Enfant's suggestion. Yet in 1893, Congress granted a charter incorporating the Cathedral Foundation, and in 1907, President Theodore Roosevelt tapped in the cornerstone for that Gothic structure which, as the cathedral's guidebook and pamphlets proclaim, aims to serve as "a house of prayer for all people."[7]

And if an Episcopal house of worship—or any church affiliated with a single denomination—could have sated Americans' desire to symbolically stake out civic space in the nation's capital, that impressive structure might have. Given the American political context, however, it is not surprising that in the years ahead, other faiths would organize resources to take their place in the federal city's landscape. This symbolically negotiated competition for visibility and clout in the capital began in the 1890s, with the plan to build a national church, and it intensified during the first half of the twentieth century. So a century after Congress had sanctioned the National Cathedral, ten Washington, D.C., churches or shrines included "national" in their titles, and several others functioned (or aspired to function) as national denominational centers.[8]

Washington churches that function as national denominational centers but do not signal that in their title include First Baptist, Foundry Methodist, Church of the Holy City, St. Nicholas Orthodox Cathedral, and Metropolitan African Methodist Episcopal Church. Several of these do assert national status in their signs, cornerstones, or publications. The Church of the Holy City, which was dedicated in 1896, attracted funds from the denomination, and it calls itself the "National Swedenborgian Church." St. Nicholas's, the 1962 Russian sanctuary down the street from the Episcopal National Cathedral, functions as "the National Cathedral of the Orthodox Church in America." As its historical pamphlet notes, black Methodist clergy and laity imagined the "national character" of Metropolitan A.M.E. Church even before its cornerstone ceremony in 1881. In the 1870s, the Baltimore Conference instructed the congregation to build its new place of worship "in close proximity" to the Capitol and White House, and the red brick neo-Gothic structure, which was built near Fifteenth and M Streets, does stand in a central location. From there the church's cornerstone and congregational publications proudly announce that it is "the National Cathedral of African Methodism."[9]

Other Washington worship sites do not explicitly declare national denominational status, but, because of location, members, or influence, have been prominent in the capital's religious landscape. Three congregations that were among the first to build along Sixteenth Street, which by the early twentieth century became known as "the Street of Churches," fit this pattern: St. John's, First Baptist of the City of Washington, D.C., and Foundry United Methodist. Benjamin Henry Latrobe, one of the White House's architects, also designed the original St. John's, a neoclassical church just across Lafayette Square from the presidential residence. Latrobe imagined the 1815 Episcopal building as "the church of presidents," and every chief executive since James Madison has attended services there on occasion. Even though the National Cathedral functions as the capital's Episcopalian center, St. John's congregation preserves its original aspirations: by tradition, pew fifty-four is set aside for the current president. First Baptist's congregation built their first Sixteenth Street church in 1890, just as the street was becoming a prestigious ecclesiastical corridor, and in 1955, they dedicated a new Gothic revival building on the same prominent site. The pastor at the time recalled that members had vigorous discussions about moving, but they "decided to remain here at the geographical center of metropolitan Washington." The church's visibility derived in part from the political prominence of some of its members, who have included Presidents Truman and Carter. The same has been true of Foundry Methodist, an example of the auditorium church style that was in fashion when it was dedicated in 1904. This congregation, which has had a long and distinguished history that stretches back to 1815, moved to the center of attention in the 1990s because President Bill Clinton, a Baptist, and his wife Hillary, a Methodist, attended.[10]

Some churches whose titles include the term "national" are much less influential and visible, and they make national claims that few U.S. citizens or D.C. residents would accept. For example, the National Spiritual Science Center of Washington, D.C., which stands on Fern Street in the northwest section of the city, attracts few followers and little attention. Another of the ten bodies whose titles explicitly declare national status, the National Community Church, does not even have a building to call its own. This interdenominational congregation is associated with the Assemblies of God. Founded by the Reverend Mark Batterson in 1996, the group meets for worship in the AMC movie theater in Washington's Union Station. That site is four blocks from the Capitol, but the pastor's aim— "to impact the nation's capital"—seems out of step with the congregation's present worship site and social location.[11]

Other religious communities that signal national status in their titles make more plausible claims on the public arena. Some of those buildings are centrally located, as with two Sixteenth Street churches dedicated in 1930: the neo-Romanesque Universalist National Memorial Church and the neoclassical National City Christian Church, which stands several blocks over on Thomas Circle. The idea behind National City Christian Church originated with Alexander Campbell, who suggested in 1851 that the Disciples of Christ "ought to have the largest meeting house in Washington City." But the idea gained momentum only in the early twentieth century. The International Convention of the Disciples of Christ sanctioned the proposal for a national church in Washington, D.C., in 1919, and in 1930, followers dedicated National City. The Indiana-limestone building, which John Russell Pope designed and President Lyndon Johnson attended, has the same monumental character as Pope's other Washington, D.C., projects, such as the Jefferson Memorial. Situated high on a terrace overlooking Thomas Circle, a prominent location in the city, the church's façade—with its Ionic columns and broad steps—demands the attention of motorists and pedestrians.[12]

Other national churches, for example, the National Presbyterian Church on Nebraska Avenue and Van Ness Street, have somewhat less central locations in the city, but still manage to make notable claims on civic space. Presbyterians long debated the idea of a national church in Washington. That notion first came before the denomination's General Assembly in 1803, and regularly after that, but it was not until 1923 that denominational leaders appointed a commission to seriously consider a national church in the district. Rather than construct a new building, however, the denomination first designated an existing congregation, Covenant First Presbyterian in Washington, as "the national Presbyterian church." That church, its pastor Dr. Edward Elon stated in 1947, would serve several functions: It would represent the denomination in the capital, symbolize "the inseparable relationship between true religion and noble patriotism," and promote "the influence of the Presbyterian Church in national life." President Eisenhower and his wife joined, and the congregation had some local and national influence. But more than a decade later, the movement to build a new national church gained momentum, and in the fall of 1969, followers celebrated the dedication of the modern sanctuary, with its adjacent Chapel of the Presidents and 173-foot Tower of Faith, which announces Presbyterians' presence in Washington.[13]

"AMERICA'S CHURCH":
THE NSIC AS NATIONAL CHURCH

In a similar way, the NSIC announces a Roman Catholic presence. Catholicism has had a place in the District of Columbia since the city's founding, and many of its early leaders were Catholic. Further, the large number of Catholic institutions in Washington's contemporary landscape—including thirty-four seminaries, forty-four churches, three colleges, two cemeteries, and two hospitals—might attract notice. Yet the NSIC most vividly expresses American Catholic hopes to declare national status and claim civic space. During the past decade official communications from the shrine repeatedly have portrayed it as "America's Church." The first page of the forty-page illustrated guidebook published by the shrine uses the phrase. It also appears on the free introductory pamphlet, the official web page, and the fifteen-minute video, *A Hymn in Stone*, which traces the shrine's history.[14]

The phrase "America's Church" might be recent—shrine staff have used it regularly only since 1990—but the idea is not. From the start, the planners imagined the space as a national center, and that was how the Reverend Thomas Shahan, rector of the Catholic University of America in Washington, successfully pitched the idea to Pope Pius X in a private audience in 1913 (five years after Roosevelt presided at the Episcopal National Cathedral's cornerstone ceremony). After the pope granted his apostolic benediction, the shrine's planning and construction began. Four years after Cardinal Gibbons laid the shrine's cornerstone, clergy celebrated the first mass in the building—although the main altar would not be installed until 1927, and the lower church would remain incomplete until 1931. In 1946, the U.S. bishops voted to renew efforts to finish the original plans for an upper church. When the upper church was dedicated in 1959, the shrine measured 459 feet long, and it covered 77,500 square feet. The campanile, or Knights of Columbus bell tower, which the shrine director named for the primary donors, rose 359 feet from ground level (more than twice the height of the Presbyterian's Tower of Faith). If we consider scale alone, then, the clergy's suggestions that the building is "America's Church" would make some sense.

Yet it is more than scale the clergy have had in mind. The shrine makes (always contested) assertions to be "America's Church"—or in the more modest alternative they sometimes use, "America's *Catholic* Church"—in several ways. First, it is dedicated to the national patroness of the United States, Mary as the Immaculate Conception, and for Catholics who know the reference, that dedication links religious and national identity. Second, Protestants had long condemned Marian devotion as a spiritually dangerous medieval innovation, and the design and iconography of the 1920s lower church, which was dedicated to Our Lady of the Catacombs, offered a self-conscious visual rejoinder to Protestant charges: the lower church not only identified Mary with the nation but also established the antiquity and authenticity of Marian devotion. Third, the building proclaims Catholic unity, as its thirteen ethnic chapels also enshrine the U.S. church's diversity and

FIGURE 3.5
Asian Indian oratory to
Our Lady of Good
Health, chapel, National
Shrine of the Immacu-
late Conception. Courtesy
Basilica of the National
Shrine of the Immacu-
late Conception.

allow ethnic communities to symbolically take their place in the American ecclesiastical community (fig. 3.5). Finally, and this is my focus in this chapter, it functions as a national center in another way. For most clergy and many pilgrims, I argue, the shrine is "America's Church" because, like the National Cathedral and many other Washington sacred buildings, it claims civic space in the nation's capital.[15]

THE "SPIRITUAL CAPITOL": CLAIMING CIVIC SPACE

Shahan, the shrine's founder, and Monsignor Bernard A. McKenna, its director from 1915 to 1933, imagined the site as a national center, and one image they published in the shrine's magazine in 1922 vividly illustrated their hopes for the building (fig. 3.6). Drawn by the Reverend P. Raphael, O.S.B., the image depicts Mary as the Immaculate Conception; she hovers in the air with the Capitol on the viewer's left and the architect's design of the

FIGURE 3.6
The Reverend P. Raphael, o.s.b.,
untitled image of Mary as the
Immaculate Conception, from
Salve Regina 9, March 1922, 20.

NSIC on the right. Beneath the Virgin is an American flag, which two girls hold aloft. On the left, just beneath the Capitol, a bishop points to Mary; on the right, just beneath the shrine, a mother looks up reverently. At the bottom of the scene, two American Indian women hold a map of the United States, as they petition for the nation's protection. This image positions the Virgin, and the shrine, at the nation's center. And, as in this image, the architects and clergy hoped the shrine would claim a place for Catholicism in the civic landscape.[16]

And Catholics appeared ready to do that. Anti-Catholicism had not vanished by the second and third decades of the twentieth century, but some Catholics had edged toward the middle class and had begun to feel more comfortable in the nation. "Most of the nineteenth century was spent trying to dispel popular notions of the 'Whore of Babylon' seducing the American Adam . . . ," one Catholic historian has argued. "It was not until the period of World War I, when enough people were sufficiently convinced of one another's harmless intentions, that Catholics felt secure enough to claim America." Catholics did that in many ways. For example, *The United States: A History for the Upper Grades of Catholic*

Schools, a 1926 textbook, opened with a list of eighteen reasons that "I am proud of my faith and what it did for America" and closed with an inventory of sixty-five "notable Catholics in our history."[17]

Catholics also claimed America in the placement and design of the NSIC. When Shahan explained the shrine's purpose to potential donors in the first issue of its newsletter, *Salve Regina*, he suggested that readers' donations "would go far toward the creation of a most lovely church, whose noble proportions and interior beauty would appeal forever to the thousands of visitors to our National Capital!" And Shahan, McKenna, and the prestigious Catholic architectural firm of Maginnis and Walsh designed a shrine that would complement the government buildings and civic monuments in the District of Columbia's cityscape. The first designs had called for a Gothic structure; but the architect, Charles D. Maginnis, and the founder, Shahan, rejected that in favor of a composite Byzantine-Romanesque plan. They did this for several reasons. Gothic structures are expensive to build and slow to complete; and the Episcopalian National Cathedral, already being constructed across town, was Gothic. As important, however, the Byzantine-Romanesque plan blended best with Washington's built environment. As one 1922 article put it, "The architects . . . concluded that a domical style of architecture would best convey the *national character* of the project." In particular, the clergy and architects imagined the site would complement the Capitol: "The Shrine is by no means to be considered as intended to rival the Capitol; architecturally it complements it, rather; its grandly proportioned mass will be as manifestly ecclesiastical in motive as that of the Capitol is secular." In print and in sermons, the clergy have made the same point again and again. For example, a year before the upper church was dedicated, a Jesuit from nearby Georgetown University put it this way: "In Washington, District of Columbia, two sovereignties have built two capitols. Our continent-conquering forefathers have built our glorious capitol there; and our Catholic ecclesiastical fathers have erected our spiritual capitol there, on the campus of the Catholic University of America, in the glorious National Shrine of the Immaculate Conception." Contemporary readers, who are more sensitive to the social consequences of gendered language and westward expansion, might squirm at this priest's celebration of "our continent-conquering forefathers," but his main message is clear: the NSIC stands as the spiritual capitol of the nation.[18]

Catholic "ecclesiastical fathers" planned that spiritual capitol, and most of the surviving public record offers their view of the site. But how have the laity imagined the building? Have they shared the clergy's vision of the shrine as a symbol of Catholic presence in America's political center? We will never know what most donors and pilgrims have thought since they left no record, but the published and unpublished letters from early devotees and donors offer hints. Consider a few donation letters printed in one issue of *Salve Regina* in 1920, the year Gibbons laid the cornerstone. A New Yorker sent one dollar "to burn a Vigil Light in honor of the Blessed Virgin and for my intention that I may be cured of a sore eye." She added, "My son 7 years old also sends $1 that he may get along well in school and that his father will get strong." An elderly man from Pennsylvania mailed in ten dollars "to help you in this great work in erecting the Shrine in honor of Our Blessed Mother." And he added a petition: "Dear Father, please say a little prayer for me to our Dear Mother for the grace of a happy death." Unpublished letters sent to the shrine clergy during those early years are similar. The writers, many of them women, often identify themselves as "a child of Mary," and it is their personal devotion to her, and not the shrine's claims on public space, they mention. And, of course, the letters ask Mary for favors— about a wide range of personal worries, including health, family, and money. One un-published letter, written six months before the stock market crash of 1929, expressed wor-ries about money. (More letters like this flooded the shrine's office after the Depression set in.) The unemployed Irish-American letter writer appealed to Mary, and to the Rev-erend McKenna, for aid in getting his job back. And he ended with a vow: "If I am suc-cessful I will write you and when able I promise a donation to the National Shrine of Mary."[19]

Contemporary pilgrims and donors bring similar personal concerns—about family, money, and health—to the Virgin at her national shrine. Consider two examples. One spring day in 1997, I met Jane, whom I spoke with for more than an hour in the shrine's cafete-ria. This forty-one-year-old Marian devotee, who prays the Rosary regularly and visits the shrine often, revealed that she suffers from mental illness. And Jane attributes her present stability, and the absence of the delusions that haunt her, as much to the Virgin's inter-cession as to the prescription drugs: "She keeps me out of the hospitals," Jane explained.[20]

Cheryl, a forty-eight-year-old African American Charismatic Catholic, first told me a story about how the Virgin "healed" her relationship with her mother in 1990. And then she recounted how Mary cured her brother's addiction:

> The very beginning of my devotion to Our Lady was a result of a miracle she worked for me. My brother was an alcoholic and drug addict. His addiction had grown to a point where I knew he would die. I am an intercessor. So I decided to offer intercessory prayer for him. I was praying in tongues. All of a sudden a hand grabbed my throat from behind. In a nasty snarling voice I heard, "Leave him to dwell with the demons for he has blasphemed against God." I was really scared. I was on my knees in my bedroom and I was alone. Never had I been prevented from praying. I immediately thought Our Lady can handle this. I didn't know [how] to ask Our Lady for prayer. I went to my prayer group that week and one of the members said he was going to Knock. I didn't know what that meant. He explained that it was a shrine to Our Lady in Knock, Ireland, and people left petitions for Our Lady's help. I got a piece of paper and wrote, "Please save my brother." Within one month, after eigh-teen years of addiction, my brother was in Narcotics Anonymous. He has been clean and sober for eight years by the grace of Our Lady.[21]

As they told these personal stories about healing, Cheryl and Jane did not mention the civic significance of the shrine, but both did at other times during our conversation. The shrine's placement in the District of Columbia is important, Jane told me, because "This shrine is for all America, and Washington is the capital." Even if they visited to offer personal prayers about health, money, or family, almost all the pilgrims I have interviewed made the same point: it mattered that planners had positioned the shrine in the capital, at the center of American political life. One female devotee who regularly visits the shrine offered a common lay interpretation: "It places Mary's shrine in the heart of American government."[22]

If many lay devotees notice that the shrine claims space for Catholicism (and Mary) among Washington's civic monuments, some Catholics challenge those claims. Eleanor, a conservative Marian devotee, forcefully rejected the shrine's nationalist aspirations. "It's a church under *Rome*, not America," she explained. This sixty-one-year-old Californian stressed Catholicism's links with its international center and relativized the authority of the nation. Roberta, a more liberal Alaska-born pilgrim, reported that she does not think of the building as America's church, although she does see it "as very American and very Catholic." Its location in the national capital was important, she suggested, but only for the pragmatic reason that it attracts tourists to the shrine. For her, it is "very American," not because its location signals Catholic presence or its architectural style recalls Washington's civic monuments but because the shrine, with its sixty-two chapels and many statues and mosaics, "includes a bit of everything."[23]

Most lay Catholic visitors told me that they find the massive building "impressive" and "awesome," and some even said that the title "America's Church" was appropriate because "it is the most beautiful church in America." Yet some Catholic priests, seminarians, and lay elites acknowledge the shrine's scale (and its position in the capital) but bemoan its Byzantine-Romanesque design. A Catholic University graduate student, who visits the shrine regularly, mockingly described it as "neo-ugly." One priest who teaches at a northeastern Catholic university seemed surprised that anyone would spend time studying this building, and he gleefully confided that his friends, local seminarians and priests, crudely describe the domed structure as a feature of Mary's anatomy (fig. 3.7). In his award-winning memoir, James Carroll, the Catholic novelist and former Paulist priest, also derides the shrine's design. He dismisses the building, which he had visited regularly as a child, as a "towering Byzantine beach ball," and he contrasts it with the "elegance" and "purity" of the Gothic National Cathedral. In another passage, Carroll recounts a 1963 visit to the shrine:

> We climbed the broad stairs to the entrance of the great basilica, with its brilliant blue mosaic beach ball of a dome. At the door, we glanced back toward the city spread out behind us, and now I imagine what we saw on that pristine early autumn day: the Capitol dome, the Washington monument, the spires of my own Georgetown, and to the west, on the hill opposite this one, the towers of the National Cathedral (Episcopal), a pure Gothic masterpiece and a Protestant rebuke to the garishness of our church here.

Carroll ends this passage expressing spire envy—that widely shared aesthetic longing for Gothic's elegant verticality—by recalling a seminarian's joke from those days (1963 to

FIGURE 3.7 (SEE ALSO PLATE 6)
Dome of the National Shrine of the Immaculate Conception.
Courtesy Basilica of the National Shrine of the Immaculate
Conception. Photo by James Pipkin.

1969) when he attended the nearby Paulist Father's seminary: The Virgin appeared on the top step of the shrine, and then, clarifying her wishes for devotees, Mary offered a new command: "Build me a *beautiful* church on this spot."[24]

If some Catholic clergy and lay elites joke about the building's design, most non-Catholic tourists, and even some Catholics, do not even know about the shrine. One Lutheran tourist who managed to find her way to the building told me that "many Christians, I'm sure, have never heard of this shrine. Before today I was one of them." Part of the problem is that although Catholic Tourists of America, and other Catholic agencies, have been co-ordinating visits to shrine since 1924, the site still does not appear on most Washington sightseeing tours.[25]

Nonetheless, several hundreds of thousands of Catholic and non-Catholic tourists visit the shrine each year. For example, one day while I was there twenty-three (mostly Protestant) eighth graders from a rural public school in Ohio and three busloads of (mostly Protestant) sixth graders from a suburban public school in New York arrived to see the shrine. The sixth graders toured the building, then cruised the gift shop for religious trinkets: holy cards, key chains, Marian statues, coffee mugs, postcards, and T-shirts. One of the students, a twelve-year-old Evangelical from Long Island, reported, "I don't like the gift shop." When I asked why, he told me, "It's too religious." But, he added quickly, as his friends gathered to listen, "The building is cool." Most of the eighth graders from Ohio, who toured several days later, agreed. Their visit to the shrine, however, was unplanned. The principal's wife explained: "We went to another Washington memorial [this morning], but it was closed. So we decided to come here. We take the eighth graders each year, but usually we do not go to the Basilica, only the National Cathedral, which is on their tour." "The kids liked the National Cathedral yesterday," she continued, "but some are saying they like this even better. To my surprise, they end up liking the two churches best. Some kids have taken two rolls of film in here. We can't get them out of here." One student who was reluctant to leave, a fourteen-year-old Methodist, explained the shrine's attraction: "We went to the National Cathedral yesterday, and I thought 'How could anything be better?' . . . This place is great. It makes you feel welcome. It's everybody's church." Not all non-Catholic tourists feel that welcomed by the shrine—or take that many photographs—but many do manage to find their way to the national Catholic center.[26]

Yet many tourists who never visit the shrine still notice it, as the architect and clergy had hoped. Even though it is not on the tours or on the mall or among the usual D.C. tourist spots, visitors and locals can spot the dome and the campanile, second in height only to the Washington Monument, throughout the metropolitan area. The Rev. Thomas J. Grady, the shrine's director when the upper church was dedicated, made this point. "Draw a circle around the shrine . . . eight or nine miles," Grady told readers of a 1959 article. "On the perimeter would be Chillum in Maryland, Silver Spring in Maryland, Arlington across the Potomac in Virginia—also the Pentagon and the National Airport in Virginia, the Washington-Baltimore Parkway. From all these places one can see the shrine. Within the district and from many, many places, even across town, one can see the shrine. The dome and bell tower are definitely on the Washington skyline."[27]

Although the shrine staff still worry that the building does not get the attention it deserves, by the end of the 1990s it was more visible than ever. After years of being ignored, it now appears in the American Institute of Architects' architectural guidebook to the city. And the local media have noticed, too. In 1997, the front page of the *Washington Times*'s weekend section praised the shrine as a "dazzling jewel" and encouraged tourists and locals to visit. A story in the *Washington Post* gushed even more. That story trumpeted the new lights on the dome. "Washington night owls may have noticed recently a spectacular new adornment to the city's skyline—the brilliant multicolored dome of the National Shrine of the Immaculate Conception, high on its northeast hill." The reporter continued by noting that the "fabulous dome" has been there for years, but the site often has been overlooked. "Though it is every bit as monumental as the Washington National Cathedral—the great Gothic edifice on Wisconsin Avenue—the shrine has always suffered unfairly by comparison." After noting some of the reasons for that—it

FIGURE 3.8
"Washington, D.C.," postcard, 1993. © 1999 by
Werner J. Bertsch. All Rights Reserved.

isn't Gothic, the site's less prominent, and Washington "isn't a Catholic city"—the reporter
praised the shrine, arguing that "the lack of recognition is patently undeserved."[28]

Washington postcards—another sign of visibility—also now include the shrine. One
reproduces an aerial photograph of the shrine's exterior, and beneath that in large orange
letters, "Washington, D.C." Another postcard displays sixteen Washington, D.C., buildings
and monuments, including the NSIC (fig. 3.8). The Georgetown Jesuit who in 1958 had
compared the shrine and the Capitol would be happy to discover that the "spiritual capitol" appears on this postcard immediately beside the "secular capitol." The postcard suggests that the shrine, and American Catholicism, has found its place in the civic landscape—
even if the shrine still cannot get on the tours and even if the National Cathedral and other
religious sites continue to challenge its claim to be "America's Church."[29]

CONCLUSION

When clergy dedicated the shrine's upper church in 1959, decades before they trumpeted
the site as "America's Church," American Catholicism stood poised to secure its place in
the capital. By 1965, U.S. Catholics had gained proportional representation in national

government: twelve Catholic senators and ninety-one Catholic representatives served in Congress. A symbol of national Catholic presence, John F. Kennedy, had entered the White House four years earlier.[30]

But even that did not propel the NSIC, or any Washington, D.C., Catholic church, to national attention. The Washington congregation with presidential membership usually draws the media spotlight, which happened with Eisenhower and First Presbyterian, Johnson and National City, Carter and First Baptist, and the Clintons and Foundry Methodist. But the shrine was unable to claim the only Catholic president, Kennedy, as a regular. In fact, the president's appointment books, and all available written and oral sources, indicate that Kennedy never even visited the shrine while he was in the White House. Nor could any Washington, D.C., parish boast of the president's exclusive allegiance: he alternated among several churches, including St. Matthew's, St. Stephen's, and Holy Trinity. Further, because of his well-grounded worries about anti-Catholicism, Kennedy withdrew his piety to the private sphere, forced by some anti-Catholic opponents to continually reaffirm his commitment to fortify the boundary between church and state. In this cultural context—and given his minimal interest in the traditional Marian devotionalism that predominated at the shrine—it is not surprising that Kennedy stayed away. But because he did, the NSIC missed its chance—or its first chance?—to be illumined by the presidency's reflected light.[31]

The result was that even after the political rise of American Catholics, and the post-1960s decline of the national Protestant establishment, centrally located Presbyterian, Methodist, Baptist, Disciples, and Episcopal churches continued to enjoy substantial visibility and influence in the capital. As the twentieth century closed, two Washington houses of worship seemed especially prominent: the current presidential church, which was Foundry Methodist while the Clintons occupied the White House, and the Episcopalian National Cathedral, the site of many religious ceremonies with civic significance. By almost any standard, the National Cathedral stands as the most venerated and visible religious structure in Washington, and it seems to have won the struggle to serve as a national spiritual center. As one Catholic pilgrim at the NSIC acknowledged, and shrine clergy reluctantly admit, "Most in D.C. think of the National Cathedral as America's Church."[32]

Even if few non-Catholics accept the National Shrine's self-designation, and if the building's claims on national space are always contested, the Catholic sanctuary dedicated to America's patroness still has enjoyed some success. For example, it attracts more annual visitors than any other religious building in the capital except the National Cathedral. And, as the planners had hoped, the NSIC dominates the skyline as motorists approach northeastern Washington from the Maryland border; its soaring tower and monumental dome come in view from many sites in the district. It is as prominent in Washington's religious landscape as any of the churches that declare denominational centrality or assert national status.

And by prominently positioning the denomination in Washington's cityscape, I have suggested, Catholics have followed (and helped create) an important but unrecognized component of America's public religious practice. In the United States, with its legally sanctioned diversity, faiths have negotiated political power, constructed denominational identity, and secured public visibility by positioning national churches in the nation's capital. A century after Congress consecrated the plan for a National Cathedral, the practice of building denominational centers in the District of Columbia had been firmly established. It had become part of the American way of being religious. The Catholic shrine, then, stands as one of many sacred buildings that, more or less successfully, symbolically claim their place near America's political center.[33]

4

ARCHITECTURE AS COMMUNITY SERVICE
West Presbyterian Church in Wilmington, Delaware

Gretchen T. Buggeln

In the early morning hours of Friday, 17 September 1993, members of West Presbyterian Church watched in disbelief as a fire that began in the attic tore through their 1871 building, sending the roof crashing through the sanctuary floor. When the smoke finally cleared, most of the façade and the side walls, as well as the greater part of the rear addition, were still standing. Smoke, water, and falling debris, however, had severely damaged what was left of the building. Within hours, the inner-city congregation had been thrown into a precarious position. Without its building, not just West Church's programs but also its very identity had to be rethought.

Protestant theology is clear on the point that the church is people, not buildings. Yet buildings play a crucial role in congregational self-definition, community recognition and action, and even individual spirituality. Without a building, West Church lost its mooring. One longtime member of the church said her first thought when she heard about the devastation was "Where will we ever go to church now?" In the grief of the moment, she did not see how the struggling church could exist without its place in the West Center City neighborhood.[1]

The study of church architecture usually begins and ends with the construction of a new church and an assessment of its architectural significance. But church buildings have an ongoing, dynamic relationship with a congregation.[2] As objects of material culture, church buildings tell us about the spiritual and social dimensions of religious community.[3] These structures also, for better or worse, *shape and limit* the possibilities open to that community. As an active participant in community life, a church building may be a blessing or a burden, a missionary, or a lumbering coworker desperately in need of ministration itself. Congregations constantly reevaluate the purpose and suitability of their architectural capital.

Church buildings have another important yet less obvious audience. As public buildings, churches invite a sense of general proprietorship from a community. They tend to be large, architecturally distinctive structures that work their way into the cognitive maps of those who are in and around them. Historic buildings often become important markers—in Wilmington, for instance, there are the neighborhoods known as "Trinity Vicinity" (for Trinity Episcopal Church) and "Quaker Hill." The history of the West Presbyterian congregation and its buildings illuminates both the evolving character of urban Protestantism and the special role church buildings play in a community.

When the original members of West Church drew together in the late 1860s, Wilmington was a rapidly growing city with an economy based on large industry—shipbuilding, railroad cars, carriages, and ironwork. By the turn of the century, Wilmington was becoming a corporate city with a growing class of managers and researchers. More recently, financial corporations have been drawn to Wilmington by Delaware's liberal tax laws.[4] Residents of West Center City have felt these forceful changes. As is the case in many American cities, a neighborhood immediately surrounding the commercial downtown has been plagued with a disproportionate amount of crime and neglect. What was once the new home of skilled workers in heavy industry became the home of the economically disadvantaged. Although blessed by a rich history and architectural character, attempts to revive the West Center City neighborhood have met with only moderate success. Hopeful rejuvenation in the late 1970s could not be sustained, and Wilmington's primary efforts to gentrify migrated to Trolley Square, a neighborhood northwest of downtown. Today West Church's neighborhood is relatively stable yet continues to struggle with vacant and decaying buildings that are magnets for illegal activity. West Church is in the middle of one of the most crime-ridden sections of the neighborhood. Throughout these changes, it has survived by its adaptability and its commitment to place.

The congregation facing the 1993 disaster was a small remnant of what had once been the largest Protestant church in the state of Delaware. In its heyday, the second quarter of the twentieth century, West Presbyterian Church had a regularly scheduled radio program, the largest Sunday school in the city, a lengthy roster of social programs, and a membership that grew to more than eighteen hundred. After World War II, the West Center City neighborhood, which had been largely blue-collar Italian, went through dramatic changes. Whites left for the growing suburbs north and west of the city, and African Americans moved in. A 1957 special session report revealed that 50 percent of the all-white congregation lived in the suburbs and that membership was dropping precipitously.[5] Although tempted at that juncture to leave the city, the majority of the congregation voted to remain committed to its urban mission—a decision that split the church. In the 1960s,

FIGURE 4.1
Samuel Sloane, "West
Presbyterian Church," 1871,
from A. J. Clement,
*Wilmington, Delaware: Its
Productive Industries and
Commercial and Maritime
Advantages*, 1888. Courtesy
Winterthur Museum,
Garden, and Library, Printed
Book and Periodical
Collection.

a young pastor and a team of interns led the congregation to open West Church to the
neighborhood with the hopes of combating crime and neglect and integrating the membership. Over time, summer camps, tutoring programs, day-care centers, and eventually
breakfasts for the hungry and the meetings of Narcotics Anonymous replaced the Camp
Fire Girls, Boy Scouts, and the Ladies Aid Society who had previously used the West Church
facilities.[6] Even during the 1968 riots, the church hung on, a model of Civil Rights–era
liberal Protestant activism. By the time of the fire in 1993, a congregation of about 150,
now firmly committed to urban ministry, had achieved a modicum of stability. Under
similar circumstances, many urban congregations have either relocated or shut down entirely. The fact that the West congregation stayed reflected its original and continued emphasis on service to the community, which the church calls "mission."[7]

The 108 men and women who began the congregation in 1868 were members in
good standing of the three major Presbyterian churches in Wilmington—First, Hanover
Street, and Central—who felt called to begin a new church in a growing area. The 1871
building (fig. 4.1) was evidence of this call and the optimism behind it; a congregation of
barely two hundred built, and carried the debt for, an edifice that could seat five times its
number.[8] The rectangular brick church with Gothic details was a fashionable giant that

muscled its way into new urban territory and commanded attention. A local newspaper described the church at its dedication:

> The building is of the Gothic style, and quite handsome. It is just what the builders intended it to be, a substantial edifice, and neat in appearance. It is built with pressed brick, trimmed with a handsome stone. On the top are four pinnacles front and 2 back; adding greatly to the appearance of the building. . . . The edifice is 108 feet by 65 feet, outside, and the auditorium is a large room 86 feet by 61 with a vestibule 10 feet wide, and a small entrance 4 feet wide.
>
> There are 156 pews in the auditorium which will seat 800 persons down stairs, and 150 in the gallery; about 1,000 can be comfortably seated. The ceiling is arched and beautifully frescoed, while 13 tasty gas brackets are up around the room, and there will be a chandelier in the centre. The auditorium is 35 feet high. The seats are all made in a semi-circular form, and nicely cushioned. The pulpit is an arched niche in the west end of the building . . .[9]

Downstairs, a hallway separated the Ladies Parlor and Infant Room from the Lecture Room, and opened into a large Sunday school room.[10] Beyond the Sunday school room were restrooms and a library. The cellar was "fitted up" with a pantry and kitchen. All aspects of the building were assumed to be of public interest. The newspaper noted the architect, Samuel Sloan, as well as the names of contractors and other firms supplying masonry, decoration, and furnishings, even plumbing.[11] A week later, another article detailed the finances of construction: of the $66,120 spent on the church, $40,120 was still owed to creditors.[12]

During the period following the Civil War, many Wilmington congregations built new, costly structures, similarly accepting enormous debt as the price of moral progress. It was assumed that church construction, architectural style, and the advance of Christianity all bore an important relationship to the public good and enhanced Wilmington's ability to attract industry and respectable new citizens.[13] Grace Methodist, built in 1865, was a remarkable, serpentine stone, Gothic church, which, according to contemporary assessment "gave a better ideal for public buildings."[14] Union Methodist (1866), First Unitarian (1868), St. Paul's Roman Catholic (1869), Delaware Avenue Baptist (1870), and then West Church (1871) followed in succession.[15] With rhetoric typical for the period, a local newspaper reported that West Church was "a credit to the congregation and an honor to the city."[16]

The West Church building committee was made up of successful men who considered the work both religious and civic duty and ran the project like a business.[17] After the completion of the 1871 church, the session minutes expressed relief that the project was over, for the "necessary secularizing tendencies of the work" had interfered with their forward motion.[18] There is no indication that there was a significant, shared, *spiritual* dimension to the process of design or construction of West Church.

The West Church plan was a familiar auditorium with functional secondary spaces.

Rather than the term "sanctuary," period accounts of Protestant churches refer to an "auditorium," a room designed for orderly, passive reception of the word of God and its interpretation by the minister. The Washington Street entrance, reached by granite steps, was authoritarian and imposing. The interior—forward-facing pews in a fixed arrangement, stained-glass windows, pastel colors—was what a Protestant of the day would expect. Placement of secondary rooms was also Protestant *status quo*. The use of the Gothic style—however pedestrian—was timely and fashionable, yet it also revealed the desire to create something "substantial" with vague historical and romantic associations. Everything about the church suggests a forward-looking congregation comfortable with the integral role of Protestant institutions in society.[19] The Calvinist refrain "Let all things be done decently and in order" was the tag line for church worship and programs.[20]

While West Church was a model achievement, it was never a "society church" in the elite sense. It served an economically diverse membership and constantly maintained its emphasis on service, operating a city mission (1894–1969), a mission to the Italian community (1905–25), a huge Sunday school, and social programs that were progressive in their day. People went to West because they lived in the neighborhood, because the ministry was vital, and because the building was inviting and comfortable. By 1894, the congregation, and notably the Sunday school, had grown to the point that a large addition on a lot off Wollaston Street, to the back of the sanctuary, was a necessity.[21] In 1906 and 1912, more rooms were added to the Wollaston Street addition. Approximately once every decade through World War II, major or minor renovations updated the facilities for the sake of fashion and comfort.[22] The building served the congregation's evangelistic mission of "extending the kingdom of Christ" in Wilmington and its social purpose of keeping together the many parts of an institutional machine.[23]

By midcentury there appeared a gap between both the worship and outreach needs of the congregation and the capabilities of the building. In 1960, West Church addressed the changing racial and economic configuration of West Center City by deliberately setting out to study the neighborhood and establish a "practical and realistic ministry to it."[24] As a result, the building was opened to the neighborhood for its needs: week-day kindergarten, Friday-night teen center, study center three nights a week, meetings of the West Center City Neighborhood Association, and a popular summer program.[25] The congregation, desiring that the community feel comfortable in the church, sold the original furniture and attempted to make the church rooms more inviting. As a tool for community outreach, the church building was in many ways inadequate. One member recalls another fire that started in the basement in the sixties. That time, the fire department had been able to put it out before any significant damage was done. Rev. Thomas Luce, the charismatic minister who shepherded the congregation through the turbulent sixties, reportedly leaned over to his associate and whispered, "Too bad the fire department got here at the right time."[26]

The church survived both rioting and the fallout of urban renewal, but the membership rolls continued to shrink, and it was difficult simply to maintain the structure, despite growing awareness of its historical importance. Donations of money and time barely allowed the congregation to keep up with maintenance. In the early eighties, for instance, the congregation responded to the suggestions of the Delaware Energy Commission by suspending the ceilings in the meeting rooms, insulating walls and windows, and installing fluorescent lights and sanctuary ceiling fans to circulate heat. Painstaking volunteer work restored the sanctuary's stained-glass windows.[27] At this point, one might say that caring for the building itself had become part of the congregation's mission, for, although approached with a certain fondness, it consumed the congregation's resources and energy. The church was both an asset and a liability, far from a perfect fit with the congregation's size and urban ministry. The enormous, dark sanctuary was particularly unsuitable for a small congregation trying to add warmth and familiarity to Sunday worship. Renovations made to the sanctuary in 1986 included moving pews together in the front of the sanctuary in an attempt to create a more intimate worship space for the sixty or so worshippers expected each Sunday. "It was awful," current Pastor Jeffrey Krehbiel, who arrived in 1992, recalled. "We got lost in there . . . you did *not* have a very distinct sense of community." This was the state of affairs in September of 1993.[28]

Pastor Krehbiel can say in retrospect that "one of the best things that ever happened" to his church was the devastating fire.[29] That was not, however, immediately apparent. The stunned congregation was faced with a major decision: restore the church to the old design, rebuild according to a new design, move to a new location, or disband. Estimates for restoration came in at close to 5 million dollars; the church's insurance settlement was $2.2 million. With a small endowment and limited fund-raising capability, rebuilding was an intimidating concept. Yet it was clear within a matter of days that the congregation, strongly encouraged by Pastor Krehbiel, would remain committed to its urban ministry and its place on the corner of Eighth and Washington.

In many ways, this second building project was distinguished from the one of the previous century. First, building was a collaborative, inclusive process with an important spiritual dimension. Second, because the issue was not building but *re*building, the congregation was thrown into the contested arena of history and memory, not just its own, but that of the Wilmington community. The result was a building far different from the imposing and confident structure of 1871, and its very form illuminates, with its tensions and compromises, the complicated position of the late-twentieth-century urban church.

On 19 September, Pastor Krehbiel delivered his first sermon after the fire to his congregation gathered in the Boy Scout building across Eighth Street. He used the disaster to direct the church to its mission and to fill the events of the previous few days with spiritual significance. His text was Jeremiah 29:4–8, "Seek the welfare of the city where I have sent you into exile, and pray to the Lord on its behalf, for in its welfare you will find your welfare." "God has called us to this place," he reminded his congregation, "and God is not finished with us yet." For this congregation with a significant cohort of middle-class suburbanites, he discovered, the loss even had a didactic purpose. "It may be just at this moment," preached Pastor Krehbiel, "that we have more in common with the suffering people of this city than at any time before in our history. As a congregation we have such a long history of reaching out to those in need, and now we find ourselves with the shoe on the other foot. Who better to be a friend of the homeless than a church with no home?"[30]

A combination of "friends and supporters in the neighborhood, the presbytery, and the religious community" offered appreciation and encouragement to the members of West Church.[31] Four other Presbyterian churches from the city sent "goodwill ambassa-dors" to that first worship in the Boy Scout building and provided flowers and commun-ion vessels. After considering many offers of temporary housing, the congregation chose the YMCA building at Eleventh and Washington. West Church worshipped there "in ex-ile" for more than two years, rallied, and even took in new members at this time. Tem-porary homes were found for the congregation's mission programs. "We had a great time!" said one member about worship at the Y.[32] Pastor Krehbiel is also nostalgic about those days when the congregation went from a "big, formal sanctuary . . ." to a "room where we had to create the worship space."[33] He sees it as a turning point in the worship life of his congregation.

On 31 October, members of the church met at a suburban Presbyterian church for a retreat led by Bob Bolt, associate executive presbyter of the New Castle Presbytery. The goal of the meeting was an open discussion regarding "the mission priorities for the use of our space at Eighth and Washington." According to Pastor Krehbiel, by the time of that meeting, the majority of members were convinced that the proper course was to build a new church "that would meet our needs more faithfully."[34] Although financially impos-sible and practically undesirable to rebuild according to the 1871 plan, some members desired to save portions of the old building and incorporate them into the new. One mem-ber who had been involved in the recent restoration of the Grand Opera House (also 1871) wrote an eloquent letter to the session hoping to convince them to save at least the façade of the old church. His impression was that Wilmington had not been a responsible care-taker of its architectural heritage and the decision West Church was facing involved a key element of stewardship. He claimed the old church was "historically noble," its ruins all that was "left to remind us of the architectural and aesthetic value" of the old building. "It was large and ornate. It was rich and warm. But all of that is gone. Only the hand-some brick exterior walls and buttresses, with their window and door arches of alternat-ing shades of sandstone remind us of what was there."

Many people had been drawn to those ruins; others had seen the image in newspa-pers. This façade, if incorporated "imaginatively" into a new building, "will be the best advertisement imaginable of the continuing presence of our ministry at Eighth and Wash-ington Streets."[35]

Those ruins, unfortunately, were also a public health hazard, and at this time the city notified the congregation that if it did not proceed immediately with either stabilization or demolition, it would be in violation of the law. The church consulted structural engi-neers, architects, and builders, who estimated that stabilization would cost more than

$100,000 and that there would be many other expenses to update the foundation and restore disintegrating brick work.[36] Given this estimate, and under the pressure of the violation notice, the church decided to go ahead with demolition and applied to the city for a permit. The Department of Licenses and Inspections denied this request with the surprising justification that the West Church property was in the Quaker Hill Historic District, hence all such action would have to be cleared through the Design Review and Preservation Commission (DRPC).[37]

Suddenly, a whole new constituency had a stake in the project. The Historic District, established in 1986, was the effort of concerned residents attempting to save the architectural heritage of one of Wilmington's most historically important neighborhoods.[38] Besides nineteenth-century row and semidetached houses, the neighborhood was notable for its historic churches, including its anchor, the 1816 Friends Meeting House. Attorney Bayard Marin, then president of the Quaker Hill Neighborhood Association and the Quaker Hill Historic Preservation Foundation, had seen the district as an antidote to all the negative pressure in the neighborhood: "everything was anti, anti-drugs, anti-whore, anti-everything." Architectural preservation claimed something positive for the neighborhood, boosted morale, and, residents hoped, wouldn't hurt property values either. Marin insists that these efforts have not been "intended to dislocate people," but simply to improve and stabilize a neighborhood with rich potential and monumental problems. The old 1871 church had been a neighborhood asset; it looked imposing, even from I-95, and "made a statement identifying the entrance to Quaker Hill."[39]

From the church's perspective, news of its inclusion in preservation efforts was unwelcome, even unfair.[40] The congregation looked at its place at the far end of the district, noted that the buildings on every other corner of their intersection were not included in the boundaries, and took offense.[41] It seemed that the district had sneaked its way up and grabbed its property without so much as a "by your leave." To the congregation, the district represented the moneyed efforts of gentrification, a bourgeois purpose at odds with its mission. While not averse to architectural preservation, members resisted anything that would inhibit the success of their programs and the well-being of the people they served. West considered itself a "neighborhood church" yet the vast majority of its members did not live in the neighborhood. West Center City was for them a surrogate or second neighborhood where they felt profoundly invested, despite their nonresidency. Although most members were committed to making a difference there, their feelings about the place are clearly different from those of residents.

The meeting of the DRPC the following January was predictably frustrating for parties on both sides. The church was anxious about its violation notice (but was told, in essence, that it was negotiable) and eager to proceed with its plans. From the perspective of the DRPC, those plans were vague at best, and the significance of the old church, and potentially the new building as well, necessitated a more cautious pace. One church member accused the DRPC of letting "bricks and mortar" issues take precedence over pressing "social issues" and the conversation reportedly became quite heated at points. The church was "proposing to retain what is symbolic and important, while building a struc-ture that would suit [its] current goals and mission in this neighborhood." The DRPC, however, heard other voices at the meeting as well. One West Center City resident came forward and described the "emotional and spiritual links" she had with the church. Another stated that "the physical structure means a lot to many residents and is a vital part of the community, beyond just the services that the congregation provides." In response, the DRPC requested that demolition be delayed until the church could understand and "be responsive to the community," select an architect, and present it with more detailed plans.[42]

Over the next few months, West Church more aggressively pursued a discussion with neighborhood residents to see what they had to say about the old building, the congre-gation, the neighborhood, and the future. Several surprising facts came to light. First, many people in the neighborhood considered West Church their "home church" even though they didn't know its name. Because of a long-ago baptism, attendance at a wed-ding or funeral, participation in a social service program, or perhaps simply because of proximity, some persons recognized "that church at Eighth and Washington," or "that brick church up there" as an institution in which they shared some ownership. Second, it was important to people to have a church in their neighborhood. For them it provided, Pastor Krehbiel explained, some "stability." And that was not simply for the social ser-vices the church offered. "It meant something to them," he emphasized, "that there was a group that *worshipped* here."[43] Third, it *did* matter to these people what the building looked like. One interviewee, who had lived in Quaker Hill for nine years and was active in its neighborhood association, asked specifically that the church be beautiful, not sim-ply another social service center like the YMCA or the Scout buildings. She urged the congregation to "remember that it was still a church," the interviewer recorded, "and should have the appearance of a church."[44]

By May 1994, the architectural search committee had chosen George Yu of Philadel-phia as the architect for their new design. Yu had completed more than twenty-five church-related projects, including a recent addition and renovation of Wilmington's Westmin-ster Presbyterian on Delaware Avenue. In Yu's initial presentations to the building committee, rather than appear with a complete design, he prepared several rough mod-els of how the church might progress. One design, for instance, recommended that the old façade be retained as an entry to a courtyard garden, leading to an entirely new build-ing. The search committee was drawn by his "collegial manner and the aesthetic beauty in his designs, especially in his use of natural light."[45] He also made a much-appreciated effort to understand *them*, stressing that the design process would be a collaborative one. At the outset of the project, Yu met with more than thirty members to discover their hopes for the new building. He encouraged them to think in terms of function and feeling. Work-ing in small groups, members described qualities associated with places of worship, places of learning, places of gathering, and used descriptive phrases such as "sunny and warm," "inviting," and "an inspiring place of simple beauty." The sanctuary and the fellowship hall, it was decided, should be about the same size, seating two hundred. Practical concerns were addressed: bathrooms should be convenient; the nursery should be near the sanctuary.[46]

In October another congregation meeting was held to discuss specifically the new sanctuary. At this meeting, the pastor and architect talked about "the history, theology, and aesthetics of worship space, including the symbols, furnishing, and arrangement of the room." The pastor encouraged members to read an article by John W. Cook, "To a Parish on the Verge of Construction or Renovation." Cook's advice, published by and for the United Church of Christ (UCC), came to Pastor Krehbiel's attention through his sister, a Chicago-area architect attending a UCC church. He had searched in vain for any parallel documents circulated by the Presbyterian Church. The document is a text completely without plans; in it, Cook focuses on ideas and patterns, not on models. But those ideas are very pointed, and many resonated with West Church's aims. They range from the general ("Beauty is a moral choice") to the specific ("Discourage wall-to-wall carpets"). Church architecture should be integrated into its neighborhood; spaces should be accessible to all. In his missive, Cook stresses that worship should be inviting, flexible, and meaningful, and the architectural setting should be just that, a "setting" that supports the action. In many ways what Cook describes—a multifunctional room, natural light, acoustical clarity, simple and bold symbols—is closer to a Puritan meeting house than a twentieth-century mainline church.[47]

Yu's designs for West Church (fig. 4.2) stressed multiple use and suitability for mission and incorporated some of the design elements, if not the actual materials, of the 1871 building. One tower was to be retained on the corner of Eighth and Washington, the three-gable entrance was to be rebuilt at street level, the façade along Eighth Street was to be reused. Significant markers—portions of old stained glass, the 1871 date stone, a marble baptismal font that remarkably survived the fire—would remain as "symbols of memory."[48] His proposed sanctuary, whether by design or coincidence, was in line with the space suggested by John Cook—a simple, flexible, peaceful space that would be comfortable for a small group of worshippers.

In late July 1994, the Division of Licenses and Inspections issued the permit to demolish the old structure.[49] In January 1995, George Yu and the congregation presented their construction plans to the DRPC in a meeting that was informative and mostly nonconfrontational. Members of the Neighborhood Association and the preservation community had long since resigned themselves to the fact that this new building would retain very little of the original structure, and most seemed relatively satisfied with Yu's designs. Bayard Marin, who was probably not alone, remained perplexed about what Yu called the "dynamic symmetry" of the new building and found the one-tower façade aesthetically disturbing. Yu called this tower a "pivot point, tying the L shape of the building together," and argued for the "balance" of asymmetrical elements. But such discussion was minimal; most of the meeting centered on the use of materials and security concerns.[50] The DRPC voted unanimously to approve the plans and construction began soon after the meeting.[51]

FELLOWSHIP HALL

KITCHEN

NARTHEX

8TH STREET

SANCTUARY

SCALE

FIGURE 4.2
West Presbyterian Church,
1997. Plan: George Yu
Architects. Scale: one tick
equals one foot.

WASHINGTON STREET

Despite concerted efforts at economy, the projected budget still came in well over the amount of the insurance settlement. A successful fund-raising campaign, "Ashes to Action," raised the needed $450,000 to make up the difference in construction costs.[52] Contributions came from members, former members, and nonmembers, other Wilmington churches, other Presbyterian churches, and foundations. The achievement of the fundraising campaign demonstrates that the community valued the church and its programs and wanted to see the congregation back in business. Donors, by and large, were those much more concerned with the services the church provided than the look of its building.

Between the 1993 fire and the 1997 dedication of the new building (fig. 4.3), the project played a considerable role in the spiritual life of the congregation. In part this was due to changes in both the practice of architecture and the shape of worship. George Yu refers to building design in general as "a soul searching thing." "Architecture," he says, "is very spiritual."[53] Yu led the congregation on retreats in which he directed, as Pastor Krehbiel put it, a lot of "right brain stuff" among the attendees.[54] The spiritual dimension of the project was also a sign of changes within mainline Protestant churches, where younger clergy in particular, trained to think creatively about liturgy, actively teach their parishioners to find meaning in ritual.[55] West Church is far to the left of center in its denomination (Presbyterian Church USA). Its drive for inclusivity has led the church to welcome gays and lesbians, strive to accommodate persons with disabilities, celebrate with a wide range of music, and use gender-neutral language and "feminine images of God alongside more traditional masculine images."[56] Even before the fire, the worship committee

FIGURE 4.3 (SEE ALSO PLATE 7)
West Presbyterian Church, Wilmington, Delaware, 1998,
George Yu Architects. Photo by Gretchen T. Buggeln.

was seeking to make worship more "joyful, raucous, participatory," and "focused." "Worship at West Church is not a 'spectator sport,'" Pastor Krehbiel has written.[57] The disaster became an unexpected opportunity to think deliberately about how architecture and worship might work together, and that was a spiritual as well as a practical problem.

Although George Yu claims emphatically that his designs emerge from the congregations he serves, not his personal beliefs, clearly a combination of both is involved. Currently, he attends a Presbyterian Church in Swarthmore where he has been an elder. Yu grew up in Shanghai, Hong Kong, and Brazil and was educated in Catholic schools. He attended college at North Carolina State and architecture school at the University of Pennsylvania where he studied under Louis Kahn. Before opening a private practice, he worked for Romaldo Giurgola, assisting on such major projects as the Australian Parliament House. He is well traveled and sophisticated; once he pointed to the round window on the front façade of the new West Church and offhandedly remarked, "I don't know what

FIGURE 4.4
West Presbyterian Church, sanctuary, 1998. Photo by Jeff Hamilton.

that is—that was the year I went to Tuscany." Yu uses this metaphor to describe his work: "I design the piano, the music is [the congregation's] own liturgy."[58] This metaphor is apt, for the designer of the piano determines, if not the expression itself, at least its range.

Yu likes to listen to congregations, to find their "real essence." But he also likes to challenge their expectations about their buildings, suggesting, for example, that the sanctuary be an octagon, as it is in the new West Church. Although people "like stained glass because they think stained glass is church," Yu steers his clients in the direction of clear light—"I like to use light the way it is," he says. He also encourages them whenever possible to use the talents of independent craftsmen rather than purchasing mass-produced artifacts. The woodworkers who made the cherry cross, table, pulpit, and music stand for West Church, for example, are a husband and wife team trained at the Rhode Island School of Design. They have worked with Yu on a number of other projects and their style, while fresh and simple, is nonetheless in the vanguard of modern design, not the popular vernacular. Yu enjoyed working with the West congregation because they were sure of their mission, yet flexible and adventurous. He points out that the exterior rectilinearity of the church building does not match the articulation of space inside, resulting in surprising arrangements of windows and walls, particularly in the clerestory of the sanctuary (fig. 4.4). The West congregation understands this disjunction as something that not only gives the building interest, as the light plays off the interior surfaces in unlikely ways, but is also as symbolic of the order within (the congregation) and the order without (the neighborhood) existing in constructive tension.[59]

FIGURE 4.5
West Presbyterian Church, Wollaston Street
entrance, 1998. Photo by Jeff Hamilton.

The new West Church is inconspicuous and nonthreatening. The front entrance off Washington Street is rarely used. On Sundays, the congregation enters through the Eighth Street entrance (the entrance used the rest of the week is on Wollaston Street), where nothing readily distinguishes the building from any other social service institution (fig. 4.5). Historical elements are consciously placed reminders of the congregation's specific history. The worship space is intimate, comfortable, largely unadorned. Muted earth colors blend with natural light. The exterior of the building in particular is, to unfamiliar eyes, a strange hodgepodge of parts and styles. Yet the form and details of the building are to an unusual extent invested with meaning by the congregation. Their reaction to the new sanctuary is uniformly positive, even though for some of them it challenges their long-held ideas of worship space. There is "something very informal about the whole thing," says one older member.[60] One woman, a member of the building committee, enjoys the fact that "the light comes in different all the time. It changes. It moves." And she finds that the congregation is "much more together."[61] A younger man, who joined the church since the rebuilding and never set foot in the old building, appreciates the "centeredness of the sanctuary," which "comes at you" when you walk in. This member, a young professor at the University of Delaware, lives four blocks away. He appreciates the quality of the light inside, the fact that there are "no bad seats," and the feminist, nonhierarchical aspects of the new sanctuary.[62]

The religious theorist Jonathan Z. Smith has written that "ritual relies for its power on the fact that it is concerned with quite ordinary activities placed within an extraordinary setting."[63] The current West Church is an extraordinary setting for the present congregation. Although the building's exterior and most of the interior is far from awe-inspiring, the new sanctuary arguably has the same numinous quality of the plain-style, Protestant meeting houses that have charmed and even transported generations of admirers. But this new building is very different from its predecessor, particularly in its posture in the neighborhood, which is almost monastic in its emphasis on service and presence, rather than evangelism and growth.[64] The community at large values it primarily for the social—not the spiritual—services it provides. Whereas the church in its first generations relied primarily on its Sunday school to raise membership, it is unlikely that many of the people served by the current West Church's programs will become church members. The architecture seems to presume this from the start, given the locked doors and the segregation of the sanctuary from the rest of the building. The building is not triumphantly optimistic, in the sense of its predecessor—even by removing partitions between the main space and the meeting rooms, the sanctuary could hold scarcely more than two hundred people. But it is practical. And Protestants worshipping in urban congregations today have to be realistic as they face a larger community that for the most part welcomes their social ministry while not privileging their theology.

The new West Presbyterian Church does fit the needs of its congregation, but it remains to be seen if the new building's effect on the community will match that of the 1871 structure. It would be difficult to understand the present building without a keen knowledge of the congregation's relationship to it. With that knowledge, however, the building reveals both deliberate and unintended messages about the congregation and its relationship to the community it serves. Its three constituencies—the congregation, the neighborhood at large, and those that are served by its social programs—all put conflicting claims on the building. It is no surprise that the resulting structure, in its eccentricities, has none of the bold coherence of the earlier building. Instead, it embodies the tensions of the church within its neighborhood. The blending of old and new reveals both the compromises made with historic preservation interests and the congregation's own relationship to its notable past. The segregation between its parts balances the spiritual needs of the congregation against its service to the community. And the fact that the building exists at all demonstrates the integral role of place in the formation of religious identity.

PART 2

RELIGIOUS VISUAL CULTURE AND THE CONSTRUCTION OF MEANING

5

CATHOLIC ENVY

The Visual Culture of Protestant Desire

John Davis

Gilbert Stuart's life-sized portrait of the first Catholic bishop of Boston, Jean Lefebvre de Cheverus, presents a man whose expressive animation virtually demands an active, participatory response from his audience (fig. 5.1). Stuart successfully merges the energized, shallow space of his canvas with the space of the observer, fostering an interactive visual environment in which an exchange takes place, in which viewers ultimately turn away and leave this picture having received something from the sitter beyond a generalized impression of the physiognomy of an historic personage. To a degree, this is a hallmark of Stuart's portraits, and in *Jean de Cheverus*, the artist's fluid, sensuous brushwork creates the familiar sense of the momentary and suggestive that often moves his depictions out of the flat, cartographic realm of direct likeness into the slower, more rounded world of character and expression. Light breaks and flickers across the Bishop's crimson-edged cape. Silvery razor stubble highlights the set of his mouth, lips pressed together as though about to form words. Cheverus sits forward, his silk-enveloped forearm seemingly testing the tension of the picture plane while his finger marks a page in a book—a pause in a larger temporal span of activity in which the acknowledgment of the viewer is only one of a series of connected actions.

There are other elements of the composition, however, which speak more specifically to the identity of the sitter. The prim, downward-pointing V of the bishop's chin nestles within the wide chevron of the collar, leading the eye to his heavy metal cross below. This

FIGURE 5.1
Gilbert Stuart, *Bishop Jean-Louis Anne Magdelaine Lefebvre de Cheverus*,
1823, oil on canvas, 36¼ in. x 28½ in. Bequest of Mrs. Charlotte
Gore Greenough Hervoches du Quilliou, 21.9. Courtesy Museum of
Fine Arts, Boston. Reproduced with permission. © 1999 Museum
of Fine Arts, Boston. All Rights Reserved.

centrally placed marker of faith would have stamped the image for an early-nineteenth-
century audience as Roman Catholic, as would the physical act of benediction so important to the implied "narrative" of the portrait.[1] Cheverus's right hand, its index finger tipped
in light, extends forward, displaying the episcopal ring of office. It seems to enter and activate the space of the viewer, and by virtue of its blessing, it effects a shift from a com-

mon secular environment—with the usual grand-manner portrait trappings—to one that might be thought of as approaching an ecclesiastical or ritual space. Above, for example, the ubiquitous baroque swag of drapery advances to form a sheltering canopy, much like a baldachin or an enclosed pulpit. Directly beneath it, the light slows and the air thickens, a shadowy suggestion, perhaps, of an intoxicating cloud of incense surrounding the bishop.[2]

Experiencing this evocative, direct connection to a Gilbert Stuart sitter is not surprising, but when the visual communion takes place with a Roman Catholic prelate, the encounter becomes much more notable. In the realm of Catholic imagery disseminated to the public at large during the antebellum era, the sympathetic image of Jean de Cheverus holding our gaze as he bestows his benediction is unusually active and forthright.[3] The bishop's renown as a preacher and his beloved status within the Boston community no doubt go a long way in explaining the portrait's singularity. Still, it must be remembered that during his lifetime, any public assertiveness on the part of a Catholic cleric in the overwhelmingly Protestant United States was likely to be met with considerable hostility. Indeed, it was Cheverus who established one of the earliest Ursuline convents in the United States in 1820, presiding over the taking of vows of the first novices; this was the same community that was attacked fourteen years later by a Charlestown mob, burned, and left in ruins in one of the most infamous acts of anti-Catholic violence in the United States.[4]

Within this climate of general hostility, it is intriguing to learn that the portrait of Cheverus was commissioned by a Protestant patron, displayed in Protestant homes, and exhibited repeatedly in that bastion of Protestant culture, the Boston Atheneum. Engravings after the Stuart likeness were also distributed throughout the city.[5] The Cheverus portrait, in fact, is only one example of the wide-ranging antebellum phenomenon of Protestant audiences consuming images of Catholics—often engaged in the ritual and ceremonial performance of their faith. Believers at prayer, priests and monks prosecuting their offices, large-scale sacramental spectacles in grandiose church interiors: these are just some of the windows onto the Catholic experience that fascinated the American Protestant majority.

But these visual spectacles were not merely windows, but also doors—doors through which non-Catholics could pass, leaving their "Protestant shoes" behind, in the words of poet and Harvard professor James Russell Lowell. In his European travels, Lowell actually did much more than metaphorically bare his feet. Instead, while visiting St. Peter's in Rome, he allowed his romanticized conception of Catholicism to wash over his entire body and ignite his senses, imagining the Church as

feeding the soul not with the essential religious sentiment, not with a drop or two of the tincture of worship, but making us feel one by one all those original elements of which worship is composed; not bringing the end to us, but making us pass over and feel beneath our feet all the golden rounds of the ladder by which the climbing generations have reached that end; not handing us drily a dead and extinguished Q.E.D., but letting it rather declare itself by the glory with which it interfuses the incense-clouds of wonder and aspiration and beauty in which it is veiled.

In a lengthy, rhapsodic passage, Lowell goes on to celebrate the Catholic church as historically universal, part of a shared cultural legacy of all that is unfettered, pleasurable, and imaginative—this, in contrast to the more attenuated, mensurational bent of his own Protestantism, constantly "unrolling [its] pocket surveyor's-plan."[6]

Even the most extreme of Protestant skeptics found themselves subject to the suggestive powers of the Roman Catholic liturgical experience. Grace Greenwood, writing about the same time as Lowell, fills her travel account with caustic criticisms of Catholic doctrine and practice, yet bombarded by the aural, visual, and olfactory stimuli of Christmas mass in St. Peter's, she surprises herself by dropping to her knees:

> I then felt to a wonderful degree the magnetism of worship, emanating from the kneeling crowd around me, and for a few moments no devoutest Catholic could have responded more unresistingly and reverently to all those solemn appeals to the senses. To my eyes, the beauty and gorgeousness of the scene grew most fitting and holy; with the incense floating to me from the altar, I seemed to breathe in a subtile, subduing spirit; and to that music my heart hushed itself in my breast, my very pulses grew still, and my brain swam in a new, half-sensuous, half-spiritual emotion. For a moment I believe I understood the faith of the Roman Catholic.

The moment did not last long, however. Following a standard script for such Catholic transferences, Greenwood ultimately breaks out of her reverie, almost blinking, as she suddenly recalls a simple image of the "meek and lowly" Christ. She has refound what she later refers to as her "Protestant eyes," and their focus on a humble Judean scene effectively banishes the Roman pomp and ceremonial from view.[7]

Together, the accounts of Lowell and Greenwood—sometimes melding, sometimes oscillating between the visual and the corporeal—illustrate the phenomenon that literary historian Jenny Franchot has called "the bodily gaze of Protestantism." In her comprehensive study of the dual attraction and repulsion experienced by American Protestants before the institutional and symbolic edifice of Catholicism, Franchot describes this positioned viewing as "a gaze that acknowledged its spiritual desire, celebrated Catholicism as spectacle, and fantasied the consumption of this foreign substance rather than conversion to it."[8] It was thus a gaze that allowed viewers to self-project into the visceral experience of externalized worship, to sample and to taste of the surroundings—but only within certain limits. This imagining and performing of Catholicism permitted an entrance into ritual space, a kind of voyeuristic identification with "exotic" spiritual exercises; it offered a release to Protestants, transporting them out of their normal, quotidian existence.[9] Yet no matter how absorbing the vicarious journey might be, the experience was almost always undertaken with the expectation that there would be a retreat back to the familiar world of Protestant boundaries, a world embraced for its rationality and decorum. These were religious tourists, not pilgrims; their displacement, whether it involved actual visits to the cathedrals of Europe or simply a trip around the corner to the latest traveling picture exhibition, was temporary, liminal, and controlled.

At the root of this fascination with religious difference are some broad and important distinctions between Catholic and Protestant manifestations of the sacred. In general terms, it would be difficult to make too much of the central tenet of Catholic worship that looks for all redemptive experience in the actualized body of Christ—and this extends beyond the pivotal eucharistic celebration. Most important Catholic rituals are linked in some way to Christ's historical and corporeal being. They are "external rite[s] ordained by Christ,— the visible sign of an invisible grace or spiritual benefit," in the words of one antebellum scholar attempting to explain the essence of the Church to the American populace.[10] To be effective, these rites must usually be performed publicly in the presence of a participating laity attuned to their sights, sounds, smells, and kinesthetics; they are a *physical* form of belief. In contrast to this focus on body language as a primary means of access to God, most mainstream Protestants took pride in the incorporeal nature of their faith. Belief was lodged in the *logos*, and this emphasis on the word depended on the cultivation of rational faculties, to the exclusion of sensory experience. The inability of some Protestants to navigate the religious borderlands of mind and body was at times comical, as Margaret Fuller Ossoli discovered while attending vespers at the Gesù, in Rome: "A number of Americans there, new arrivals, kept requesting in the midst of the music to know when *it* would begin. 'Why, this is *it*,' some one at last had the patience to answer; 'you are hearing vespers now.' 'What,' they replied, 'is there no oration, no speech!' "[11]

But this is by no means the complete picture. During the first half of the nineteenth century, the Protestant encounter with Catholic ritual was grounded as much in the political and social realm as it was in competing theologies. Bodies are at issue here as well, notably the millions of immigrants who poured into the United States during the decades preceding the Civil War.[12] The threat to Protestant dominance within the public sphere that such a drastic population shift represented had profound ramifications. Intolerance of ethnic difference grew rapidly; the Irish in particular were vilified as ignorant, rowdy troublemakers whose sheer numbers would result in a destabilization of the labor market and the established political order. For a time, religious riots occurred with some regularity—in Charlestown in 1834, New York City in 1832 and 1835, and Philadelphia in 1844. An explosion of anti-Catholic literature—books, pamphlets, and newspapers such as the *American Protestant Vindicator* and the *Christian Watchman*—fueled this nativist movement, and some of the most important figures in the visual arts in the United States, such as Samuel F. B. Morse and James Jackson Jarves, became leading figures in the "No-Popery" campaign. Their movement culminated in the secretive "Know-Nothing" political party, a short-lived populist group that enjoyed astonishing success at the polls in 1854 before slavery eclipsed anti-Catholicism as the issue of the day.[13]

FIGURE 5.2
James Jackson Jarves,
"A Roman Preacher," *Harper's
New Monthly Magazine* 9,
July 1854, 167.

These political developments are crucial for understanding the Protestant interest in Catholic imagery, because the majority of nativist attacks focused not on the immigrants themselves, but on the priestly hierarchy of the church, as well as the manner of worship it ordained and presided over with uncontested authority. As Jarves wrote, "The sin lies not with those who *believe*, but upon them who *deceive*." The vilification of the office of the pope, for example, knew no bounds, and his clerical subordinates—ranging, in the nativist view, from conniving, princely cardinals to dirty, drunken Franciscans—were seen as carefully organized troops marshaled by the Vatican to squeeze every last cent from the Catholic laity. Their means of compelling such obeisance was the mysterious and hypnotic rite of the mass, and here, it was the precise calibration and display of the ritually clothed celebrant that most baffled, and most intrigued Protestant viewers. "Will the Roman Catholic ask his priest, whom he now sees crossing himself, what is the use or meaning of all this crossing, capering, and twirling of his limbs and body?" wondered a rebellious former Catholic priest named William Hogan. Or, as Nicholas Murray, another Protestant convert from Catholicism, put it, "Why does the priest dress so? What book does he read from, when carried now to his right, and now to his left? . . . Why bow down, and strike my breast, when the little bell rings? What does it all mean?"[14]

More often than not, it fell to unsympathetic outsiders to explain what it all meant. Few were as assiduous in the task as Jarves, whose Italian travel accounts go well beyond most of his contemporaries in their obsessive documentation of the details of Catholic worship and "priestcraft." His articles for *Harper's* and his lengthy *Italian Sights and Papal Principles, Seen through American Spectacles* provide a compendium of favorite topics

FIGURE 5.3
James Jackson Jarves,
"Vows to the Virgin," *Harper's
New Monthly Magazine* 9,
August 1854, 323.

for anti-Catholic writers: indulgences, image worship, Vatican greed, the veneration of relics, the pagan origins of church ritual, and the low morals of monks.[15] More interesting, perhaps, than his text are the dozens of engraved illustrations which, together, limn a varied and savvy portrait of clerical manipulation and fanatical excess. This is an unusually large corpus of images, each one embedded with subtle and not-so-subtle messages that can effectively stand independent of the text. Florid processions surrounded by kneeling peasants are a favorite, as are abject physical expressions of deference, such as the kissing of the toe of the bronze statue of St. Peter or the slipper of the pope. Gestures are exaggerated, and hands and arms are often lifted above heads in rapturous supplication. Images of saints abound in the crowded interiors, and there is often an impression of decorative surfeit—an almost oppressive busyness of line—which encourages in Jarves's reader a kind of jumpy, nervous viewing of the plates.

Some of these visual cues are seen at work in two typical illustrations, "A Roman Preacher" and "Vows to the Virgin" (figs. 5.2 and 5.3). In the former, the most feared of Catholic functionaries, a black-robed Jesuit, is elevated above a throng of presumably simple *contadini*, the women all wearing traditional headdresses.[16] Separating him from the people he would instruct is a row of forbidding attendants, each one hooded and brandishing a flaming torch; these penitential figures were particularly reviled by American visitors, who recoiled at their secretive costuming. Placed on either side of the preacher are objects designed, in different ways, to illicit equally disgusted reactions from Protestants. The crucified Christ, especially if life size, as is the case here, was generally perceived as unnecessarily morbid and graphic by Americans; the preference was always for the unembodied symbol of the cross over the crucifix. Yet in the engraving, Christ appears rather forlorn and neglected by the Catholic preacher. Teetering on the edge of the platform, the Savior cedes center space to a framed and draped icon, which here seems to be the favored object of veneration. The swaying priest's efforts to direct attention to the painting are clear enough, as is the doubly mediated experience of the sacred that results.

The purported fervor with which images, particularly those of the Virgin, were embraced by Catholics is even more evident in the second engraving. The charge of idolatry, and more specifically, "Mariolatry," was one of the most sensitive and omnipresent issues of debate between Catholics and Protestants. "On almost every corner, over almost every church door, and in many other places, you are forced to behold a carved and painted image. . . . Some of these, particularly some representations of the Virgin with the infant Savior in her arms, are hardly *decent* to be seen," wrote one Maltese missionary to the *New York Observer* in 1830. In a subsequent article in the same paper, the potential dangers of weak personal morals in the viewer were linked to a taste for icons: "The necessary effect of any attempt to exhibit the Deity to the human senses, by pictures or images, must be to degrade to an incalculable degree, our conceptions of him; partly as it is adapted to mingle the passions and affections of the human nature with our conception of the Divine."[17] In the engraving, the tremulous, rocking entreaty of the woman before the painting labeled "Maria" hints at the intellectual and physical abandon warned of by Protestants. Like the crowd in "A Roman Preacher," she is separated from the object of her attentions, in this case by a wall at half height. Lamps, draperies, and other framed images crowd the principal painting, but the simple symbol of the cross is nowhere to be found. Other objects, however, are quite carefully and pointedly included: the Roman relief at left reminds viewers of the pagan origins of the practice of idolatry, and the alms box at right, the ever-present sentinel at such shrines, cuts through the festive trappings to reveal the "true" motivation for creating the spectacle.

Perhaps the most impressive effort at illustration is a group of engravings accompanying Jarves's account, which exhaustively catalogues twenty representative clerical "types" occupying places at the Papal court (fig. 5.4). Introducing this ethnographic collection, he writes, "Throughout the whole edifice of the Roman hierarchy, costume forms a very important and conspicuous part. It is nicely graduated with decreasing splendor and diversified cut from the pope, cardinals, archbishops, and the inferior clergy, who are almost lost amid richly-laced petticoats and purple skirts, to the laughable attire of the sacristans, choristers, and the dirty and dolorous robes of the monastic orders." Although Jarves maintains that "the nomenclature of papal costume is intelligible only to those who pass their lives in wearing it," the whole point of his delineative exercise is to enable his Protestant audience to gain access to this inside information, to crack the Catholic sartorial code.[18] This desire for knowledge of the internal workings of Catholic ritual is played out diagrammatically as well, in a full-page plan detailing the placement of more than fifty categories of officials in the Easter Sunday procession in St. Peter's. These officials (archbishops, mace bearers, etc.) are keyed in the plan to their corresponding engravings on subsequent

FIGURE 5.4
James Jackson Jarves,
engravings of clerical types
demonstrating sartorial
hierarchy, *Harper's New
Monthly Magazine* 9, June
1854, 25.

pages, so that the personages depicted might be imagined in their proper relationship to the other members of the entourage, and to the spectators. The entire essay appears organized for an audience with a seemingly indefatigable appetite for such ceremonial minutiae, an interest that obviously extends beyond simple curiosity and moves, through the vivid prose and spatially indexed imagery, into a more experiential realm.

Jarves's vituperative tone does not in any way disallow a certain degree of pleasure that the reader might take in the vicarious experience of these festive occasions. Indeed, the male figure included at right in "Vows to the Virgin" offers a hint of the detached, touristic viewing (focusing both on the aesthetic, ritual environment and the worshippers who perform within it) which was the preferred Protestant means of witnessing the theatrical components of the rite. This figure is clearly differentiated from the praying woman in dress and in posture; he is more refined, measured, relaxed, and contained. Jarves ends his lengthy description of the Holy City by leaving a possible clue as to his identity: "Two classes alone of strangers can enjoy Rome. Artists who live only in their ideal world, or visitors who turn Rome into a watering-place."[19] Both the artist and the tourist, he implies, seek out a kind of fantasy environment of pleasure and leisure. Both travel, as well, in a state of openness to new varieties of sensory experience. This expectation of aesthetic sustenance was instrumental in moving painted depictions of Catholic ritual and prayer into an ambiguous middle ground, one situated between the competing realms of enticement and revulsion.

In an essay examining the modern art museum as a ritual space, Carol Duncan traces an important shift in Western aesthetic thought that bears directly on this Protestant experience of the alternative spirituality of Catholicism. Beginning in the late eighteenth century, philosophers accorded increased importance to aesthetic phenomena as productive of a specialized state of perception and judgment. "In this sense," writes Duncan, "the invention of aesthetics can be understood as a transference of spiritual values from the sacred realm into secular time and space. Put in other terms, aestheticians gave philosophical formulations to the condition of liminality, recognizing it as a state of withdrawal from the day-to-day world, a passage into a time or space in which the normal business of life is suspended."[20] The second point is perhaps the more pertinent here, establishing the world of art as a place of refuge from the daily restrictions of life in regulated, polite society. For within the realm of Catholic imagery, the Protestant experience of the sacred was not so much supplanted by the *secular*, as it was fused to the *aesthetic* in a way that raised previously temporal definitions of beauty to a new level of spirituality. Art and Catholicism, for many, became linked, and the latter took on both the positive and negative attributes of the domain of the senses.

Artists were, perhaps, best situated to perceive and explore this connection. James De Veaux, one of the most enraptured of American painters traveling in Italy, made a direct analogy in his diary in 1843: "These Catholic priests are all painters in feeling, and get up these sights in [such] wondrous and impressive style." Recognizing the inherent artifice of this pageantry, he nonetheless counted himself an admirer: "How rapidly the imposing and solemn splendor of this religion grows on one! I must leave Italy, or some day find myself a deserter from my own family, and bowing to the forms of this fascinating worship." Orville Dewey, a Unitarian minister unusual in his embrace of much of the "art" of Catholicism, also joked about his enthusiasm: "You will think I am becoming a Catholic outright. But seriously, I do not wonder that some number of those who visit Rome do become so—especially artists, enthusiastic persons, Etc."[21]

Such reactions must be understood against the background of the "Oxford" or "Tractarian" movements, the campaign within high church circles of the Church of England, and subsequently, American Episcopalians, to reestablish and value the more theatrical and performative aspects of the liturgy.[22] Aesthetically, it manifested itself in a romantic longing for the mystery and beauty of medieval worship, particularly the taste for the Gothic, which, while certainly fueling the Episcopal high-church campaign, spread as well into American Protestant circles at large. ("I wish we had more of these things with us Protestants," confessed the Unitarian Dewey.) Alarmed, the editor of the *Christian Examiner*, James Walker, warned of "a class of Protestants, more inclined to mysticism than to rationalism, with whom it is growing into a fashion to speak unguardedly of religion as founded on sentiment rather than on knowledge and argument, and who appear to think that symbols, and scenic exhibitions, and the fine arts, provided they act powerfully on the imagination and the feelings, have quite as much to do in regenerating and sanctifying the soul, as truth."[23]

The implication in Walker's description is that these Protestants were culpable—weak and even libertine in their surrender to "the imagination and the feelings." For others, such as Rev. George E. Ellis, blame lay with the Catholic church, which was perceived as sending out aesthetic tentacles in the hopes of converting Protestants, making them victims of their own sentimental nature: "The Church has most powerful influences to address to the eye, the imagination, and the feelings. It is most richly furnished with means to engage the sentiments, the affections, the love of beautiful and imposing forms, and the admiration of abstract qualities embodied in pleasing or gorgeous symbols. These are susceptibilities which are akin to the religious sentiment in very many breasts." Nicholas Murray went even further with the analogy, likening Catholic churches to secular theatres: "People resort to them, not to worship God, but in accordance to custom, or as they would resort to an opera or to an exhibition of the arts."[24]

Research examining the issue from a Catholic perspective appears, in some respects, to confirm the importance of visually impressive ritual in the lives of laypersons and converts. Ann Taves, for example, documents a considerable increase in lay devotional activities during the antebellum period; she describes a concerted campaign among American Catholic clerics to cultivate a ritualistic attachment to the mass, the images of Mary and the Sacred Heart, and the patriarchal institution of the church. And Stephanie Wilkinson, in her study of Catholic popular fiction, finds that nineteenth-century conversion accounts, an important self-affirming genre for the American Catholic community, inevitably locate a "rising interest in the aesthetics and rituals of the Church" as a turning point in the convert's embrace of Catholicism.[25]

There is, perhaps, no better example of the widespread enthusiasm for the poetic and sentimental aspects of Catholic ritual than Robert W. Weir's painting of a young novice making her convent vows, *Taking the Veil* (fig. 5.5). Although this work was not completed until the early 1860s, Weir had begun it thirty years earlier and had been interested in the theme ever since he witnessed such a ceremony in Rome in 1826. Tapping into the Protestant fascination with nuns and the secret life of the cloister, as well as the general antebellum celebration of virginal feminine beauty, *Taking the Veil* was probably the most successful work of the artist's career, exhibited to wide acclaim and more than a thousand paying visitors at Goupil's Gallery, in New York.[26] While ostensibly depicting the specific

FIGURE 5.5 (SEE ALSO PLATE 8)
Robert W. Weir, *Taking the Veil*, 1863, oil on canvas,
49½ in. x 39¾ in. Courtesy Yale University Art
Gallery, 1900.49.

consecration of one Carlotta Lorenzano in the church of San Guiseppe, the archaic dress and generalized Gothic interior give the image a more universal, international tone. Weir, a high-church convert to the Episcopal church, was a passionate devotee of the Gothic (he designed and built a revival-style church in Highland Falls, New York), and in 1846, he wrote a firm defense of religious art within a Protestant context. Like his colleague, Daniel Huntington, who also made an adult conversion to Episcopalianism, Weir sought to downplay the more sectarian aspects of Catholic art, rendering it discreetly "safe" for Protestant consumption. It is in this context that we can understand his decision to mask most of the potentially offensive body of the crucified Christ, displayed on the altar at right, by the baldachin curtain and the rising tendrils of incense. To a degree, Weir appears to have been successful at dulling the Catholic edge of this affecting ritual experience. One press account referred to it as "a gentle thought from what is universal in Catholicism," and another dubbed it "a beautiful poem that overrides all prejudice."[27]

Yet it is not so easy to dismiss the specific Catholic content of this scene or to assume that Weir's finely wrought image successfully transcends Protestant perceptions of otherness in the pageantry of the Church of Rome. The ceremony of a novice taking the veil was, perhaps, the most notorious of public Catholic rituals, sought out by Protestants and described in great detail in a number of European travel accounts—often in negative terms.[28] It was also something occasionally witnessed by Americans in their own country. "A great number of Protestants" reportedly attended Boston's first ceremony of novices taking the veil, presided over by Cheverus in 1820. In fact, even the most vehement nativist writers made it a point to encourage their readers to look in on American Catholic services. Hogan suggested this practice no fewer than five times in his *High and Low Mass:* "I would recommend to my Protestant fellow-citizens to avail themselves of the first opportunity to visit some Catholic church, when high Mass is performed. It will prove a sorrowful source of amusement to as many of them as may be true Christians."[29]

One such Christian published an account in *Harper's* of attending a "Veil" ceremony at the Convent of the Sacred Heart, in New York, only five years before Weir's canvas was exhibited in that city. As was the case with viewers of the painting, the author was momentarily overcome with the impressive beauty of the scene: "I . . . lost my reason in my sympathy. I did not feel so much that a home was losing its member, and God's field its laborer, as that heaven was gaining a saint." This daydreaming, however, was only a brief interlude. The remaining paragraphs function as a scathing indictment of all that the ceremony represented—especially in the author's perception of the Church's "casuistry" in luring untried, innocent maidens to a life of imprisonment. Completing this tale with a rather predictable comparison, the writer left behind the "dim, religious light of the chapel" and exited to the "sunlit street," whereupon he retired to the home of a friend, surrounded by his relatives and children. Watching the women of this idyllic domestic refuge, he made a final devastating juxtaposition: the "life of gloom and sterility" he has just witnessed at the convent versus the "cheerful, loving, filial service" rendered by the "Protestant lay Sister" embraced by her family.[30]

Clearly, part of the interest in viewing such a ritual lay in the temporary escape it afforded into a shadowed Catholic interior. Weir's viewers were provided a brief and poignant glimpse of a life very much at odds with public expectations of feminine duty and destiny, a spatialized spectacle made all the more fearsome and thrilling by the finality of the initiate's eventual journey deep into the cloister. And it is this experience, it is worth stressing, that was recreated in the plush interior of Goupil's. Henry Tuckerman, for example, employed the same contrasts as those of the visitor to the Sacred Heart, finding the "hushed and darkened room" in Goupil's a soothing retreat from busy Broadway. The manipulated light, the *"draperies formant chapelle*," in the words of one French publication: all combined to reproduce the sensation of attending the theatrical ceremony in person. "The method of its arrangement for exhibition heightens its impressiveness," explained one critic. "It is as if the actual spectacle were witnessed from the window of a darkened cloister." Tuckerman also indulged in this sort of sensual projection: "The spectator has but to exclude surrounding objects from his vision, and gaze earnestly and exclusively at the picture, to imagine that he hears the low music of a chant and inhales the odor of incense." Here was a sensory experience available even to the timid or squeamish Protestant, one who might otherwise blanch at the thought of entering an actual Catholic church and subjecting fellow Christians to the kind of ethnographic scrutiny advocated by nativist writers.[31]

The success of *Taking the Veil* is due, in large part, to the way in which Weir invokes the senses of his viewer. The organ and choir in the background and the striking play of colored light cascading diagonally down the wall stimulate the eye and ear. Closer to the picture plane, the swinging censer wafts plumes of incense in several directions, and on the pavement in the immediate foreground, the juxtaposition of soft rose petals against the cold, hard marble activates the sense of touch. It is a powerful effect, and the language of at least one visitor to Goupil's betrays a struggle with the artistic and religious allure inherent in the composition: "I did not admire or understand at first blush. . . . I criticised, complained of this and that, relented now and then, was drawn back and again, until, beginning to learn my own deficiencies of vision, *I was at last completely conquered and converted;* and of this tumult, which he had innocently created, the artist quietly at home was entirely unconscious."[32]

This remarkably confessional prose, written by an "Amateur" who clearly reveled in his experience, hints at the power of the dramatic environment in which Weir's painting was enfolded. But what was created was not so much the ability to participate in the rite as to count oneself among its privileged spectators. The critic's fantasy of watching from within a "darkened cloister" was no doubt prompted by the spatial construction of the painting itself, with viewers positioned to one side of the main altar, mirrored by the devout crowd in the distance occupying a corresponding transept of the church. "Antebellum Americans," as Franchot has observed, "both watched Catholicism and watched one another doing so."[33] Still, there is no question as to the main event of the canvas. Every gaze, in the end, centers on the maiden and the bishop. Bending toward each other, the parenthetical curves of their backs rising to culminate in the gold miter, they share an exchange to which all others, including the ecclesiastical attendants, are merely witnesses.

For viewers of such images, then, there are different degrees of connection to the Catholic subjects depicted. A comparison of *Taking the Veil* with the portrait of Cheverus nicely demonstrates the distinction between a direct interaction with the subject played out across shared, contiguous spaces (Stuart) and the indirect, spectatorial link, a more one-sided relationship with viewers somewhat disengaged from the active, narrative space (Weir). In a well-known analysis, Meyer Schapiro discussed these two modes (the frontal and the profile) in terms of personal address and spiritual content. Frontality, he argued, is the equivalent of first-person speech, creating an "I-you" relationship that he characterized as "a vehicle of the sacred or transcendent." The profile representation, in contrast, simulates third-person speech, the impersonal "he" and "she," which, in narrative terms, is "detached from the viewer and belongs with the body in action."[34]

Poststructuralist critics such as Margaret Iversen have questioned the rigidity of Schapiro's binary polarities, arguing for a more subtle analytical model of viewer engagement. Others interested in visual modes of address have turned to Emile Benveniste's similarly oppositional dyad of discursive and historical enunciative systems—the former a "here and now" situation requiring the presence of both speaker and listener, the latter a more distanced utterance that uses time, as much as space, to disconnect the listener from the narrative, as well as the actively embodied narrator.[35] Indeed, each model is illuminating here, and whether we term it "profile," "third-person," or "historical," the mode chosen by Weir does, in fact, create a "safe" proscenium space for the actors—a construct in keeping with the view that Catholic art needed to be visually buffered, rendered less threatening and immediate. Among all the enthusiastic reviews of the painting, only one seemed alert to this issue, registering its disappointment at Weir's timidity. The critic of the *Commercial Advertiser* looked in vain for "the spiritual meaning" and "mystery" of the ceremony. "These figures are little more than automatons," he concluded. "They make no impression on us."[36]

These dynamics of viewer address can also be played out in a landscape mode. Thomas Cole and Samuel Morse were both early travelers to Italy who responded to the beauty of the *campagna* and took up the subject of Catholic worship within that setting. At first glance, Cole's *Il Penseroso* and Morse's *Chapel of the Virgin at Subiaco* are remarkably similar (figs. 5.6 and 5.7). Each features a prominent roadside shrine dedicated to the Virgin and a kneeling peasant before it. In the distance, sunny hilltop villages provide the paintings with a discernibly Italian context, as well as a compositional foil to the principal narrative elements. Yet the degree to which the artists allow their viewers an opening, a means of access to the spiritual experience of prayer, could not be more different. Cole, who had been baptized in the Episcopalian Church only a year before painting *Il Penseroso*, practiced a faith, somewhat alone among American Protestant sects, that was just then working out a place for devotional imagery—often melodramatic and elegiac in tone—in its ritual and worship.

FIGURE 5.6

Thomas Cole, *Il Penseroso*, 1845, oil on canvas, 32⅜ in. x 48¹⁄₁₆ in.
Courtesy Los Angeles County Museum of Art, Trustees Fund, Corporate
Donors, and General Acquisition Fund.

Morse, in contrast, was perhaps the most conflicted American artist ever to take up
the subject of Catholicism, one who would go on to be a principal public mouthpiece for
the nativist political movement in the United States. His journals and letters include page
after page filled with obsessive, numbing descriptions of the elaborate pageantry and public worship he encountered in Catholic Europe, and his profession predisposed him toward an artistic interest in the rich displays he witnessed. Yet his rigorous and conservative Protestant beliefs prevented him from truly immersing himself in the experience.
Though he might devote day after day to chasing after still one more mass or festival, he
never pretended to give way to what he termed "the charms of mere sense." Morse was
torn, in Paul Staiti's words, between "ritual and faith, image and actuality, mind and
body."[37] In his life and in his art, limits had to be found that would prevent a complete
descent into the allure of the externalized and despised Catholic religion.

We see those limits imposed in his *Chapel of the Virgin*, a depiction of a shrine near a
famous Benedictine monastery east of Rome. Performing in profile, Morse's kneeling
worshipper is tiny and distanced from the viewer. She and her companions occupy an

FIGURE 5.7
Samuel F. B. Morse, *Chapel of the Virgin at Subiaco*, 1830, oil on canvas,
29¹⁵⁄₁₆ in. x 37 in. Bequest of Stephen Salisbury, 1907.35. Courtesy
Worcester Art Museum, Worcester, Massachusetts.

artificial platform that is separated from the natural surroundings (and from the viewer) by a near-vertical cliff, a plunging gulch that effectively functions as a kind of religious *cordon sanitaire*, ensuring little possibility of empathy with the figures. The most significant barrier to viewer participation, however, is the absence of the object of veneration from the pictorial field. The icon of the virgin remains frustratingly invisible, and the chapel itself appears to block out the sun. The effect of Morse's decision to deny his viewers the experience of the image is to render it even more mysterious, to leave the impression that it possesses special attributes designed for Catholic eyes only. The viewer feels cheated, excluded. Encoded in Morse's angular and overdetermined composition is a hint of the secrecy that prompted so many Protestants to demand access, for example, to the cloistered confines of the convent or the private spaces of the confessional.[38]

Cole's canvas offers much more to the viewer. The painting of the virgin, even if not fully frontal, is visible enough to dominate the foreground and invite contemplation. It addresses itself to its audience in much the same way as Stuart's portrait of Cheverus. The abject posture of the woman, seemingly lost in spiritual reflection before the consoling image, encourages in the viewer a similarly ardent and direct connection to the icon. Lacking Morse's misty ravine, Cole's shrine is completely accessible, with the steps leading up to it serving as a visual guide to its approach. With no other distracting figures present, the focus is on the personal experience of the worshipper, rather than the spectacle of her worship. The ability to share in her relationship with the Madonna and Child allows for a more private communion with Cole's peasant protagonist. As an artist, he is comfortable with such acts of pure devotion. His composition—picturesque, gentle, and flowing where Morse's is cool, clinical, and static—serves as a window to the spiritual power of images, as well as the inward, emotional quality of worship they can prompt. It graphically conveys this power, without descending into the derogatory visual syntax of the Jarves engraving. Cole appears to be expressing in paint the thoughts of the minister, Dewey, whose liberalism even allowed him to flirt with the practice of praying to saints for intercession: "Why should it be thought a thing so monstrous, that I should ask some sainted friend that has gone to heaven . . . to help me, or to intercede for me?"[39]

Orville Dewey, clearly, was willing to go further than most in his quest for an authentic, vicarious Catholicism. The trigger for Dewey, as for the majority of American Protestants, was the complete sensory experience of the Roman Catholic interior. "I have become a perfect church worshipper," he wrote. "I pass some hours of every day in these places—places more sacred in everything that belongs to the appearance, arrangement, and keeping of them, than any other that I ever saw." Aware of the heretical nature of his yearnings, he nevertheless admitted, "I seldom enter these churches without an impulse to go and kneel at some of the altars."[40] Dewey's frank words may be taken as a public acknowledgment of the more private (and pervasive) Protestant desires that ensured the success of a rich variety of commercial presentations of Catholic interior spaces during the early nineteenth century. Yet his definition of the sacred is rather carefully formulated. Catholic churches are not, in his mind, *inherently* sacred—recognized as holy through some kind of essentialized, local power—but rather, are *rendered* so through "the appearance, arrangement, and keeping of them." Their sacrality, then, is socially constituted; it is culturally and aesthetically produced. By inference, and assuming the right environmental conditions, this special character was therefore capable of being *reproduced*, recreated along with the attendant ritual performances that governed such spaces.[41]

This, in any event, is one explanation for the remarkable number of church views by European and American artists exhibited in the United States during the antebellum era. Although most are no longer extant, a scan of the advertising pages of almost any urban newspaper turns up a succession of panoramas and dioramas of European church interiors, often quite large in scale, which traveled the theatrical circuit of the eastern states. Some were true multimedia events, such as Louis Daguerre's double-effect diorama entitled *Midnight Mass in the Church of St. Etienne du Mont, at Paris*, shown in New York, Boston, and Philadelphia in 1840–41.[42] The better-known St. Peter's Basilica was an even more popular subject for public displays of this type. Although a Catholic structure, St. Peter's consoled Tuckerman by being almost unconditionally available, "open to all and at all times," and this sense of being embraced, absorbed in its vast spaces, he felt, was better delineated on canvas than in words. Following the lead of such published touristic accounts, American reviewers began appropriating St. Peter's as a universal site of Christianity, "the temple alike of Catholic and Protestant," as one New York critic put it in 1842.[43] By far the most successful rendition of this interior by an American artist was the painting by George Cooke, exhibited throughout the South for more than fifteen years beginning in 1829. Reviews repeatedly spoke of "its effect upon the senses as exceeding in sublimity all that the artificial world can produce."[44]

Throughout the antebellum era, however, Catholic interior scenes were consistently judged against one benchmark, one almost unaccountably successful image from the early decades of the century. When Cooke's *Interior of St. Peter's* was shown in Washington, for example, a newspaper critic was enthusiastic, but had to acknowledge that despite its virtues, it was "almost, if not quite, equal to the Capuchin Chapel, exhibited here some years ago," and even twenty-five years later, Weir's *Taking the Veil* was held up to the same yardstick: "Many of our readers will remember that famous interior, 'The Capuchin Chapel.' . . . We think that this painting of our countryman will be said by the best judges to bear a favorable comparison with that." François-Marius Granet's composition, *The Choir of the Capuchin Chapel*, was indeed world famous, the best-known image of its type in Europe and America. The reception and exhibition history of this work help shed light on the actual visual experiences of Protestant viewers of Catholic ritual, and its astounding popular success provides an intriguing case study with which to conclude.[45]

The original painting, executed sometime around 1814 by Granet, was exhibited at the Parisian Salon in 1819, where it caused a sensation. But the image had already become widely known by that time, copied repeatedly by Granet and sold to a variety of important patrons. He is known to have made well over a dozen versions, and in April 1818, one such copy was ordered by an unidentified American merchant, who brought it to the United States, apparently on speculation.[46] Purchased shortly thereafter by Bostonian Benjamin Wiggin, the canvas was made available to a number of interested visitors to the Wiggin home and was lent on many occasions during the next forty years to charitable exhibitions in Boston, Providence, and other cities. This was likely the same version that traveled to Philadelphia in 1820, taking that town by storm and prompting the important local artist, Thomas Sully, to make a trip to Boston the following year to execute an exact copy of the Wiggin painting (fig. 5.8). It was this copy, more than any other version, that established the popular fame of the subject, for Sully actively promoted the picture for years, making it a constant attraction at Earle's Gallery in Philadelphia (which he partly owned) and sending it out on lengthy tours to Charleston, Norfolk, Baltimore, Newburyport, Boston, Saratoga Springs, and New York City. Further copies of the Sully version were then made by Philadelphia artists J. Borthwick and John Clarendon Darley, the latter of which was sold on Sully's behalf in Mexico four years later for $500. Over time, the original copy earned Sully thousands of dollars, and many of his fellow artists—such as Charles Bird King, John S. Cogdell, and Rembrandt Peale—were quite eager to rent it from him or

FIGURE 5.8 (SEE ALSO PLATE 9)

Thomas Sully, *Interior of the Capuchin Chapel in the Piazza Barberini*, 1821, oil on canvas, 68½ in. x 50½ in. Copy of François-Marius Granet's *Choir of the Capuchin Chapel*, ca. 1814. Collection of Mr. and Mrs. Lawrence Goichman. Courtesy Sotheby's.

copy it yet again. It was one of the most influential compositions of its era, and later historians have traced its imprint in the work of Charles Fraser, Henry Inman, John Krimmel, Morse, Henry Sargent, and Edward Troye, among others.[47]

What can account for the sustained and enthusiastic reception of the *Capuchin Chapel*? The subject, certainly, would have fascinated any American curious about the mysterious rites practiced behind monastery walls. The Capuchin order, a severe and ascetic branch of the Franciscans, provided an especially picturesque spectacle with their tonsured heads, long beards and hoods, and heavy robes. Much was made of this eerie, cloistered lifestyle—in 1820 the picture was linked in the advertising pages of American newspapers to Sir Walter Scott's romantic (and largely anti-Catholic) novel *The Monastery*, and a poem exploring the unnatural exclusion of women in the lives of these men (entitled "Love at the Capuchin Chapel") appeared in a Charleston newspaper when the picture came to town.[48]

But closely allied with this esoteric subject was the dramatic presentation of the tenebrous chapel. Light is restricted, with the sole source of illumination forcefully located just above the crux of the one-point perspectival system. The architectural planes of the room thus divide it into disjunctive pockets of light and dark, yet the most important figures, the priest and his attendants, are etched with a fiery glow, their long, ponderous shadows claiming the central ritual space. Around this central group, the rustle and murmur of the somber monks shuffling to their places almost seems audible. One enters slowly from the wings, while another, in the foreground, has fallen to his knees and lowered his head to his clasped hands, a physical and religious act of complete submission similar to that in Cole's later *Il Penseroso*. The grave character of such body language, as well as the overwhelming scale of the space when compared to the tiny humans, seems all the more ominous given the chapel's suggestive illumination. With the shutters thrown open in the rear, the strong sun streams through the panes of glass, setting both the cruciform mullions and the cross atop the lectern in relief. Placed just under the arcing brow of a truncated barrel vault, this brilliant opening seems almost personified—the eye of God fixed on his believers, generating, defining, and animating the space. When the nearly six-foot canvas is hung on the wall at a normal height, this powerful nodal point appears at the adult viewer's eye level. The highly frontal composition, in effect, stares back at its audience.

This visual "lock" with the viewer was a crucial component of the three-dimensional illusion of the *Capuchin Chapel*, its most commented-upon feature. "The beholder immediately looses [sic] the impression that he is gazing upon a surface of canvass. The perspective is so perfect that one is obliged to recollect himself continually, to realize that a plain [sic] surface is actually before him," wrote the *Providence Patriot and Columbian Phenix*. Much like awestruck Protestant visitors to the Catholic cathedrals of Europe, viewers essentially forgot themselves before the painting (or at least forgot their American surroundings). Indeed, the language of the reviews sometimes adopted the suspicious vocabulary of anti-Catholic writers who worried about the aesthetic lure of the church's imagery. Thus, the *Carolina Gazette* spoke of "the power of this seductive and almost magical arrangement of harmonies and contrasts. We are, for a season, spell-bound, and imagine we are actually in the midst of those silent and abstracted figures."[49]

"Being there" was obviously of great importance to some antebellum audiences, but the degree to which this taste for trompe l'oeil was socially differentiated, was perceived to be class based, is revealed in a series of comments by artist Charles Willson Peale. The elderly Peale was astonished at the initial success of the *Capuchin Chapel* in Philadelphia: "A picture now Exhibiting in Philada. attracts an abundance of Visitants," he announced to Thomas Jefferson. To his son Raphaelle, he described it as "the inside of a Chapel of the Roman Catholick," and to another son, Rembrandt, he relayed the information that it "excited so much admiration here as being the *finest picture ever seen.*" Rembrandt, in Baltimore, had already heard about the picture from Thomas Sully, to whom he wrote in reply, "Your account of the Picture which excites so much attention was interesting to me, and encreased my desire to see what kind of painting does so completely satisfy such numbers." His father thought he knew the reason. Untutored viewers, he felt, were blindly following the lead of a few influential spokespersons: "And of course others must join in the praise of it! and when people have not much to talk about this will fill up the chasm. Perhaps it is well for [the] professors of the fine Arts, that connoisseurs should talk, and the lads & Lasses catch the clue; and thus display their taste for the sublime & Beautifull." Still, the enthusiasm of such lads and lasses was not necessarily a good thing for the fine arts. "Mr. Thackara," he reported, "says the taste of the Citizens is a burlesk on the Arts. A Gentleman who had seen [the *Capuchin Chapel*] & was praising it in high strains, Thackara asked him in what its merit consisted, he replyed, that it was a perfect deception, as being every thing in a painting."[50]

Why might Peale, who had repeatedly demonstrated a love of trompe l'oeil throughout his long career, adopt such a censorious tone? It may be that in this context, he was actually associating such trickery not so much with low-brow appetites for the simulation of the real, as with Roman Catholicism, a faith with which he was decidedly uncomfortable. Peale is known to have opposed the marriages of two of his sons to "low bred Roman Catholicks," as he described one family of potential in-laws, but more revealing is his comment upon seeing the new Catholic church of St. Patrick's in New York in 1817. Installed on the wall behind the altar as an intended "extension" of the space of the sanctuary was a large-scale trompe l'oeil mural of Jerusalem, and this he tellingly found "as usial, rich & Massy to attract admiration of weak minds." Peale's deprecatory description of St. Patrick's places his naive viewer inside a kind of painted shadowbox, or camera obscura, and this is exactly the way in which the *Capuchin Chapel* was presented in Philadelphia. In a darkened room with no other pictures present, he relates, a controlled environment was carefully produced by the unnamed entrepreneurs: "It is placed in the most advantageous light, with Green Baise, table height, in front keeping the Spectators about 6 or 7 feet from the Picture. And also a curtain of the same materials on the side to keep the Company from viewing it in a bad light and 6 [Tin] tubes are laid in the front on the baise for the Visitors to view the Picture through them."[51]

This is a remarkably explicit description of what we might term, following Jonathan Crary, the technological "production of the observer" through exhibition practices. Crary's examination of the shift toward a subjective, "modern" construction of vision in the early nineteenth century provides something of a framework for understanding the visual and corporeal experience of a visitor to the *Capuchin Chapel*. While the conservative Albertian space of Granet's composition is different from the more complex, binocular phenomena he discusses, Crary's larger thesis is relevant here: "As observation is increasingly tied to the body in the early nineteenth century, temporality and vision become inseparable. The shifting processes of one's own subjectivity experienced in time became synonymous with the art of seeing, dissolving the Cartesian ideal of an observer completely focused on an object."[52] Essentially, the placement of the viewer's body in the dim, draped exhibition space at a certain distance from the canvas, as well as the yoking of that body to the tin tube described by Peale—a "tool" for seeing that forges an artificial connection to the ritual space of the painting—creates an absorptive viewing experience that is no longer separate from the objectified image. Vision becomes a temporal and phenomenal event generated by the viewer, and it encompasses—is inseparable from—the action taking place in the choir of the Capuchin church. Here, perhaps, is a clue to the visual power of images like the Granet and Weir, where, oddly enough, access to Catholic spirituality is provided in an environment in which that very notion is contested. Despite the circulation of these pictures in an anti-Catholic discourse, the rituals they describe nevertheless encourage responses that are clearly empathetic.

There is, in fact, a direct connection between Crary's discussion of early-nineteenth-century optical experience—its "arrangements of bodies in space, regulations of activity," and so on—and the language and concerns of ritual studies. Most recent writing on ritual seeks to demystify it somewhat, to cease to think of it solely as a doorway to some dematerialized realm of the numinous, and instead, to recognize it, like sacred space, as socially produced and socially productive. Like most spatial practices, it is generated by the body, revolves around it like an axis, and ends by leaving its imprint on it. Following Pierre Bourdieu, theorists have concentrated attention on this "ritualized social body" and its interaction with, in Catherine Bell's words, "a symbolically constituted spatial and temporal environment." The exhibition chamber of the *Capuchin Chapel* is surely one of these environments, with its set-apart, restricted space, its expectations of a certain decorum and formalized viewing practices, its focusing of the mind and senses through enframement, and its invitation to witness a performance—even, through its trompe l'oeil cultivation of the senses, to take part in that performance. That this is an entrepreneurial, commodified space (with an admission fee) and a culturally charged, contested space (where Protestants are, to a degree, engaging in an act of trespass and appropriation) is immaterial to the process of ritualization, for these characteristics, according to David Chidester and Edward Linenthal, are fundamental to the production of American sacred space.[53]

Of course, this cultural and religious intersection of Protestant and Catholic is at the heart of all the works considered in this chapter. While the antebellum climate of antipathy encourages a reading of such imagery in oppositional terms, ritual theory may provide us with a way of understanding this material as more of a potential bridge, a means for Protestants to explore and experience difference while still reserving the option of resisting or "misreading" it. There is no longer an agreement among scholars that ritualization requires absolute belief or submission. Clifford Geertz finds ritual ceremonies to be "the point at which the dispositional and conceptual aspects of religious life converge for the believer, but also the point at which the interaction between them can be most readily examined by the detached observer."[54] Thus, for both the participant and the outsider (the "detached observer"), ritual forms a site of cultural transmission and negotiation, but not necessarily one of spiritual commitment. Moreover, in the texts and images considered here, the categories of participant and outsider are often blended, with Protestant viewers, to varying degrees, giving themselves up to the imaginative and corporeal experience of Catholic worship, whether that experience takes place in St. Peter's Basilica or Earle's Gallery in Philadelphia.

Protestants clearly reacted to Catholic images in many ways and used them as tools for a bewildering variety of purposes. The same visual representation might serve as a one-dimensional piece of evidence used to support a xenophobic polemic, while also providing an imaginative opportunity for more open viewers to temporarily "inhabit" Catholic bodies as part of a critique of their own religious community. But between these two extremes lies a vast interpretive space that shifted constantly during the antebellum decades. Within that space, pictures such as Granet's *Capuchin Chapel*, Weir's *Taking the Veil*, and even Stuart's *Jean de Cheverus* performed important cultural work in that they facilitated a kind of exchange or transfer. At a time when conventional language often failed the cause of interreligious understanding—or even became its principal impediment—the phenomenon of the Protestant consumption of images of Catholic ritual can be seen as an alternative means of establishing communication through the empathetic experience of the body and the senses. Ritualization often encapsulates and displays the core units of social identity that define an individual's worldview and map his or her place in the larger culture. It is difficult to conceive of a better transmission point, a better location for opening a breach in sectarian borders, than this locus of thought, action, and social connectivity—for it is here that each potential viewer is given an opportunity to chart his or her own course through the colliding worlds of the sacred and the secular.

6

ROBERT GOBER'S "VIRGIN" INSTALLATION
Issues of Spirituality in Contemporary American Art

Erika Doss

In September 1997, American artist Robert Gober (b. 1954) unveiled an untitled installation piece in the Geffen Contemporary, a gallery of the Los Angeles Museum of Contemporary Art (fig. 6.1).[1] The installation's central element was a larger-than-life-scale and rough-surfaced concrete sculpture of the Virgin Mary, dimly but dramatically lit and surrounded by gray walls and floors. The figure perched on a storm drain and was pierced through the midsection with a six-foot length of standard, screw-ribbed, steel culvert pipe, cast in bronze. Set in the wall behind her was a steep wooden staircase, a cascade of water flowing down its cedar risers and into an open drain. On either side of the Virgin were placed two old-fashioned and vastly oversized silk-lined suitcases, opened and inviting, their bottoms also resting on grated drains. Peering down into these drains, viewers gazed upon colorful tidal pools filled with plastic-cast plants and painted fiberglass stones and shells. Looking through the drain directly below the body of the Virgin, they saw scattered oversized coins (mostly Lincoln-head pennies) dating to 1954; looking through the two suitcase grates, they glimpsed the hairy legs of an adult male and the smoother legs and feet of a diapered infant, dangling between the man's calves (fig. 6.2).

In keeping with the nature of much contemporary installation art, Gober's piece was extravagant and interactive, a consciously complex mix of objects, subjects, and viewers engaged in a demanding interplay of spaces, materials, and senses. Indeed, first encountering the multilayered installation from above, from the vantage of a low balcony

FIGURE 6.1

Robert Gober, view of untitled installation, 1995–97, including cast-concrete
sculpture of the Virgin Mary pierced by six-foot length of bronze-cast steel culvert
pipe; staircase waterfall; two oversized custom-made suitcases; four cast-bronze
drains; and subfloor pools of water. Geffen Contemporary Gallery, Museum of
Contemporary Art, Los Angeles. Courtesy Paula Cooper Gallery, New York.
Photo by Russell Kaye.

in the museum reception area, visitors descended into the deliberately theatrical space
and became active participants in the entire tableau. Looking and hearing, then being
caught up in momentary insights and flashes of understanding were all key to this installation: Gober guided viewers to look through the shaft planted in the Virgin's belly to
see—and listen to—the staircase waterfall behind her; to look down into the grated drains
to discover the subterranean sources of the sounds that filled the gallery; to look over the
project's entire grand-scale narrative; to reflect on Gober's and their own ideas and assumptions about seeing and belief, about the intersections between art, icons, religion,
and spirituality in contemporary America (fig. 6.3).

Gober's revelatory installation may be contextualized within the increased importance
of issues of faith and the sacred in contemporary America, albeit often on conflicted and
alternative terms. "Americans' fascination with spirituality has been escalating dramatically," writes sociologist Robert Wuthnow, and even a cursory glance at recent cultural
currents substantiates his claim. Nearly half (47 percent) of those interviewed in a 1998

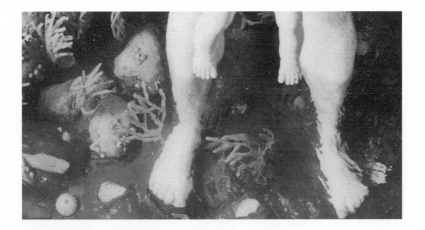

USA Weekend poll cited spirituality and religious faith as the single most important factor in their lives after good health and personal happiness. Among the most popular television programs in the late 1990s were *Touched by an Angel* and *7th Heaven*, both of which offered ecumenical moral tales about faith and the power of prayer. Inspirational books such as *The Celestine Prophecies* and *Chicken Soup for the Woman's Soul* topped certain bestseller lists. Untold numbers flocked to the labyrinth movement, making pilgrimages to walk along designated "sacred paths" for "physical healing, personal transformation and religious transcendence." "What Would Jesus Do?" bracelets ("witnessing tools to help you spread the word of Jesus Christ") and reworked corporate logos (T-shirts on which the words "Tommy" and "Hilfiger," for example, have been changed to "Today" and "He Forgives") are popular among teen audiences. So-called megachurches ("religion's answer to Home Depot," offering one-stop salvation shopping with everything from sermons and Twelve-Step groups to sports clubs) have mushroomed in popularity across America, as have spiritually flavored musical tunes and bands (from Joan Osborne's hit single "What If God Was [One of Us]" to contemporary Christian rock groups like Jars of Clay and Striper).[2]

A recent wave of exhibitions, from "The Spiritual in Art: Abstract Painting, 1890–1985" (Los Angeles County Museum of Art, 1986) to "Winged Evocations: A Kinetic Sculptural Installation & A Meditation on Flight and Its Association with Divinity" (Allen Memorial Art Museum, Oberlin College, 1998), suggests that contemporary American art museums and galleries have also turned to the subjects of faith and spirituality.[3] Contemporary American artists ranging in diversity from Gober, Albert Chong, Keith Haring, Amalia Mesa-Bains, Ed Paschke, and Betye Saar to Andres Serrano, Cindy Sherman, Jaune Quick-to-See Smith, Kiki Smith, Mike and Doug Starn, Renée Stout, Bill Viola, and Yolanda Lopez, among others, have explored the intersections between iconography, religious orthodoxy, and issues of faith in various bodies of work. And recent books such as *An Art of Their Own: The Spiritual in Twentieth-Century Art* (1989), *Icons of American Protestantism: The Art of Warner Sallman* (1996), and *Visual Piety: A History and Theory of Popular Religious Images* (1998) further suggest burgeoning attention to the study and meaning of the visual cultures of religion and spirituality.[4]

Given the much vaunted "return to religion" among the baby-boom generation, it may seem unsurprising that the contemporary American art world has also turned its attention to spirituality and sacredness.[5] Yet what do works such as Gober's "Virgin" installation really tell us about his understanding of religion and faith and, by extension, that of his baby-boomer peers? Further, what does it mean when avant-garde artists such as Gober participate in larger mainstream cultural conversations about religion and spirituality and do so on reflective and introspective (rather than wholly dismissive) terms? Indeed, with the apparent abandonment of the Enlightenment project among many postmodern Western intellectuals, what has happened to an aesthetic avant-garde originally formed as a force of modernist reaction against, among other things, institutional religion (compare to the Catholic church in France)? Given the secular spiritual status that many modern art objects and images acquired in the twentieth century, and the similarly consecrated "aesthetic chapel" reputation of the typical art museum, what does it mean when artists such as Gober, and museums such as MOCA, now choose to link with a broader cultural search for the sacred?[6]

At first take, it might seem that this religious revival in contemporary American art is based mainly on "difference." That is, many recent art museum exhibitions have focused on the religiosity of African American, Chicano, Native American, queer, and/or women artists, suggesting, by way of repeated attention to artists already marginalized in the mainstream art world, that issues of art and religiosity are mainly the concern of multicultural artistic "others," who are also perceived as nonmodern (either antimodern or postmodern) artists. Such views bear further scrutiny. They rest, for example, on still current as-

FIGURE 6.4
Albert Chong, *Winged Evocations*, 1998, kinetic installation, Allen
Memorial Art Museum, Oberlin, Ohio. Photo courtesy of the artist.

sumptions that art that is attentive to issues of faith, spirituality, and the sacred is essentially
a form of mainstream religious proselytization, and that as such, it is nonmodern and
has no place within the historical and critical framework of the avant-garde.

Many in the art world harbor suspicions that a contemporary art of spiritual expression is fundamentally "religious art": art that professes a certain faith tradition, that aims
to place believers within the vicinity of the holy (and to persuade nonbelievers of divine
authority), and is thus less critically engaged with what is assumed as modernism's primary focus on formalist evolution and artistic self-expression. By extension, many critics
insist that the categories of modern and contemporary art, and religion, are quite separate and distinct. John Berger, for example, remarks, "The spiritual value of an object, as
distinct from a message or an example, can only be explained in terms of magic or religion. And since in modern society neither of these is a living force, the art object, the 'work
of art,' is enveloped in an atmosphere of entirely bogus religiosity." Insisting that faith is
part of a lost (and unrecoverable) historical past and religion is "the Other to modernism,"
such critics link religious art with premodern and hence primitive times and peoples.[7]
Following this train of thought, Albert Chong's 1998 *Winged Evocations* installation (fig.
6.4), Renée Stout's *Fetish #4* (1989), Amalia Mesa-Bains's *Altar for Dolores Del Rio* (1988),

and Jaune Quick-to-See Smith's *Genesis* (1993) are thus understood as the products of marginalized cultures and peoples (Afro-Caribbean, African American, Chicana, and Native American, respectively) who have somehow managed to sustain their belief systems in these modern times and are, thus, less artists than spiritualists.

Obviously, these sorts of assumptions are completely misguided, historically uninformed, insulting, and more than a little ironic, especially when artworks such as Gober's "Virgin" installation, Bill Viola's video installation *Saint John of the Cross* (1983), the Starn brothers' *Triple Christ* (1985–86), Andres Serrano's *Piss Christ* (1990), Keith Haring's *Altar* (1990), and Kiki Smith's *Virgin Mary* (1993) (fig. 6.5) are also recognized for their explorations of spirituality and faith. That their makers are also among the most critically considered and, in some cases, commercially successful contemporary artists, and thus hardly constitute art world "others," belies the blatant contradictions inherent in assumptions that American art attentive to issues of religiosity and spirituality is primarily an ethnic, racial, or multicultural phenomenon, or that modern and contemporary art and religion are separate and distinct entities.

It is interesting, then, that much of the art world's attention to the spiritual and religious underpinnings of contemporary visual culture remains grounded in assumptions of its "outsider" status, its cryptic eccentricity, its mystical and romantic strangeness, and its inherent "difference" from mainstream art. Even well-intended exhibitions such as "Dreams and Shields: Spiritual Dimensions in Contemporary Art" (Salt Lake Art Center, 1992), which surveyed the work of some forty artists from seven Western states, tend to distinguish "shamanistic" artists with "spiritual vision" from those painters and sculptors more evidently understood to occupy a critical and cultural mainstream. As art historian Joanne Cubbs writes (in a discussion of religious visionary art), "What is often missing from the art world view of this work is a real consideration of its most fundamental meaning, its spiritual origins and religious function, both within the individual lives of its makers and its relationship to a broader cultural context." To do so, of course, would force the art world to reckon with its own position within that context, to admit to its own primary market and institutional interests, and to adopt both an interdisciplinary approach and a consciously self-critical consideration of who and what ranks as an "outsider" or an "insider" in official art-world culture. But this sort of interrogation might seriously challenge and even undermine the art world's own belief systems; as Cubbs adds, "Beyond all of its eulogies to creative vision, the art world reveals a final distrust of other, possibly more miraculous worlds and their products."[8]

However uncomfortable the art world is with the proposition, religiosity is very much part of the modern-art project. Indeed, twentieth-century American art is riddled with modernists of diverse styles and inclinations who have closely examined their own religious beliefs and practices, and those of others, from early abstractionists such as Arthur Dove, Marsden Hartley, and Georgia O'Keeffe to postwar artists ranging from Ad Reinhardt, Barnett Newman, Robert Motherwell, and Mark Rothko to John Cage, Robert Irwin, Andy Warhol, Brice Marden, Ana Mendieta, Betye Saar, and others. Their work clearly

FIGURE 6.5
Kiki Smith, *Virgin Mary*, 1994, wax, pigment, papier
maché. Courtesy Pace Gallery, New York.

challenges misunderstandings of the assumed separation of a modernist avant-garde from religious inquiry. It also complicates easily made assumptions of the supposed links between religious proselytizing and the spiritual in art: while the Rothko Chapel constitutes more traditional understandings of religious space (although on ecumenical terms), Mendieta's ritualized "earth-as-body" performances and sculptural "siluetas" of the late 1970s and early 1980s followed both feminist and avant-garde threads in an exploration of the religious cultures of her Cuban and Catholic childhood.[9]

Such art further thwarts assumptions of what critic Suzi Gablik views as the "desacralized mentality" of modern times. In such books as *Has Modernism Failed?* (1984) and *The Reenchantment of Art* (1991), Gablik insists on the separation and independence of modern art and spirituality. Other critics similarly argue that "today there is little or no patronage of traditional religious art," that "contemporary art audiences are often uncomfortable viewing overtly religious or spiritual imagery," and that it is only the "artists' own sense of spirituality that initiates and informs the spiritual and religious art of our time." If the artwork and museum and gallery patronage of the above artists contradicts such statements, so too does the growing national presence of organizations such as CIVA (Christians in the Visual Arts), which sponsors well-attended conferences on spirituality and Christian themes in contemporary art, and the popular and critical reception of galleries such as MOCRA (Museum of Contemporary Religious Art) at Saint Louis University, which features a rotating permanent collection of "interfaith" modern art. "The artists whose work we're showing here," remarks MOCRA founder and art historian Father Terrence E. Dempsey, "may not be artists who are professing a particular faith tradition, although many are. But all are inquirers."[10]

It is this position of spiritual and religious inquiry that most clearly envelopes Robert Gober's "Virgin" installation. Implicit in his inquiry is his self-critical examination, and personal reconstitution, of Catholicism, including one of its primary symbolic attributes: the body of the Virgin Mary. Born in Wallingford, Connecticut, Gober was raised a Catholic: attending catechism classes, becoming confirmed, serving as an altar boy. If, from an early age, he was drawn to the church's rich and dramatic visual culture of "body-bound imagery, from the ecstasy to the suffering," he was also, as critic Dave Hickey remarks, "the homosexual son of Catholic working people, the infant blessed and damned in the earliest memory with an awareness that his 'nature' is at odds with the 'nature' of the culture in which he lives."[11] As Gober relates, the Catholic church was the "ultimate moral authority from which a lot of social mores emanated: it was part of a broader configuration of institutions that included the law, newspapers, criminality, family and even folklore."[12] Within the religious dogma of Catholic moral authority is its contemporary censure of homosexuality, around which many of Gober's personal artistic explorations have been rooted since he began his art career in the late 1970s. His "Virgin" installation resonates with references to his Catholic upbringing, reckoning with his spiritual roots and his conflicted relationships with a mainstream religious institution that has declared his being morally corrupt and profoundly anti-Catholic.

Gober is joined by a number of other contemporary artists who have likewise been inspired by the tensions within their Catholic backgrounds and, in particular, an emphasis within Catholicism on the human body and the links between the corporeal and the divine. Karen Finley, Mike Kelley, Robert Mapplethorpe, Andres Serrano, Kiki Smith, Joel-Peter Witkin, and David Wojnarowicz are among recent American artists whose work is permeated with references to Catholic culture symbols and themes, from Serrano's obsession with the icons of religious devotion (including *Piss Christ* and *Madonna and Child II*, 1987) to Witkin's "radical challenge to the Christian belief in resurrection and an afterlife," as reflected in his photographs of crucified nudes (*Penitente, New Mexico*, 1982) and severed heads (*Head of a Dead Man, Mexico*, 1990). Kiki Smith's fascination with religious statuary and the abject female body is evident in such works as *Lilith* (1994) and *Virgin Mary*, the latter representing Mary in the traditional pose of outstretched and comforting arms but whose nudity, shaved head, flayed skin, and exposed musculature reveal Smith's central interest in imaging the vulnerable body and physical trauma. Raised Catholic in a family of artists (her father, Tony Smith, was a leading minimalist sculptor, and her mother is an actress and opera singer), Smith remarks that Catholicism, "as a visual tradition, is a tradition of manifesting things physically that aren't necessarily physical," and that it is "also a history of martyrdom—a religion of physical suffering."[13] Indeed, while Gober's installation posits Mary as a divine conduit of grace, Smith's sculpture focuses on the temporal and spatial reality of her human and fleshly body.

"The Catholic perspective," argues critic Eleanor Heartney, "pushes certain artists toward the corporeal and the transgressive." Catholicism's doctrinal emphasis on the human body as a vessel of divine spirit (as embodied in the Immaculate Conception, the Crucifixion, the Resurrection, the Transubstantiation of the Host into the body and blood of Christ, and the Ascension and Assumption of the Virgin), has produced centuries of fleshly and carnal works of religious art. Given this history, Heartney remarks, "It's no wonder that such physicality has served as a source of inspiration for many contemporary artists."[14] This is especially the case at a time when the body commands center stage among the issues over which many Americans fiercely disagree: abortion, AIDS, artificial intelligence, euthanasia, genetic engineering, overpopulation, pollution, reproductive rights, sexual difference, and sexual practice (or sex in general). Obviously under siege, the body has become a site of extraordinary cultural, physical, political, psychological, and social stress.

Throughout his career, Gober's attentiveness to the body has focused on its vulnerability and repression. Sculptures made in the 1980s of sinks, urinals, chairs, and cribs, all handmade of plaster, wire lath, wood, and steel, absent the spigots, drains, and cushions that make them useful and displayed in museum and gallery spaces where their utility is forbidden anyway, quietly allude to the invisible human bodies for whom they ostensibly exist. These sculptures are "unabashedly anthropomorphic," writes one critic, noting that some of their titles allude to human emotions and states of being—such as *The Silly Sink* and *The Subconscious Sink*, both dating to 1985. Gober's pitched and tilting cribs, writes another critic, "express the artificial restraint, the physical and emotional confinement experienced during childhood"; his "pristine" sinks and urinals "implicate the body that stands before them to cleanse and relieve itself." Gober's first sink sculpture was, in fact, made when a close friend of his was dying of AIDS, and "in retrospect," writes Gary Garrels, "he recognized in it a procedure of cleansing."[15]

In recent works, Gober has more directly referenced the physical destruction of AIDS in a series of wax cast body fragments, each again made by hand with consummate craftsmanship, some from casts of his own body, some clothed, and others accompanied by props such as sheet music (or tattooed musical notation), candles, and drains. *Untitled* (1991) (fig. 6.6), for example, featured the disembodied legs of a man lying face down on the floor, clad in a funereal black suit, three white candles planted on his body; *Untitled* (1991–93), similarly featured a recumbent man clad only in white underpants, tube socks, and sneakers, his buttocks, thighs, and calves hideously cratered with plastic "drains" that mimicked the Kaposi's sarcoma that often ravages those with full-blown AIDS. Prostrate and diseased, these sculpted body parts reference human vulnerability in an age of AIDS; as Gober remarked in 1997, "How could I not be affected by it? I'm a gay man, and I was living in the middle of the epidemic." Yet as troubling as these severed sculptural limbs are, they also resonate with Gober's faith that the body, even ravaged and destroyed, may also be a source of redemption. Discussing these specific works in 1993, Gober observed: "There was the butt with music, the butt with drains, and the butt with candles, and they seemed to present a trinity of possibilities from pleasure to disaster to resuscitation."[16] As mordant as these body fragments are, in other words, they also retain a sensibility as holy relics and ex-votos or corporeal conduits of faith.

This allegorical "trinity of possibilities" is echoed in Gober's "Virgin" installation, which resonates with bodies (that of Mary, the standing men and diapered infants, even Lincoln on all those pennies) that similarly speak to euphoria, violation, and salvation. Indeed, the entire multilayered installation stands as a metaphor for the body: as a charged physical space, as a container for the self, for memories and desires, and, significantly, as an analog to the house or home. Freud wrote of the correlations between the house and the human body in his 1919 essay "The Uncanny," suggesting that "dream images of the house and its attributes—specific rooms, staircases, windows, and doors— represent, in highly veiled form, libidinal desires and individual body parts."[17] Centuries earlier, of course, the pioneering architects of Christian churches recognized those correlations as well, designing consecrated spaces for worship and ceremony in a cruciform configuration that replicated the body of Christ on the cross, and thus urged believers to an understanding of the continuities between the corporeal and the divine, the secular and the spiritual, the body and faith.

Gober, who once made dollhouses for a living, has long been attentive to the forms and meanings inherent in Christian architecture. One of his earliest works, titled *Prayers Are Answered* (1980–81), was a three-foot-tall plaster and wire lath model of a dilapidated Romanesque church, its interior gutted and one of its exterior walls painted in the awkward

FIGURE 6.6
Robert Gober, *Untitled*, 1991–93,
detail from installation at the
Galerie Nationale du Jeu de
Paume, Paris, wood, wax, leather,
cloth, human hair, silkscreened
background. Courtesy Paula
Cooper Gallery, New York. Photo
by Russell Kaye.

funky style of the community mural movement of the 1970s. Much of his other early work consisted of similarly scaled toy houses, painstakingly outfitted in precise architectural details and miniature furnishings. While most were simply dollhouses, others more obviously critiqued the abiding myths surrounding idealized American understandings of house, home, and domesticity, backed by homilies such as "There's no place like home," "Home sweet home," and "A man's home is his castle." Gober's work *Untitled (House)* (1978–80), for example, featured a rather grand Tara-like mansion severed through its midsection.[18] In *Prayers Are Answered*, Gober similarly critiqued another primary institution within Western and American culture: the Christian church. Still standing but greatly diminished, Gober's decomposed church is utterly devoid of human and spiritual significance, implying that without humanity, the house of God is only an empty shell. Interestingly, Gober's title for this piece presaged the last published work of another American artist, also gay: Truman Capote's *Answered Prayers: The Unfinished Novel* (1987).

Originally planning to construct a large-scale, three-level house with a basement, and then a church, for the MOCA commission, Gober reconstituted the links between body, house, and the general cross-plan of Christian cathedrals in the 1997 installation: the

FIGURE 6.7
Robert Gober, view of
untitled installation,
1995–97, detail of Virgin
Mary. Courtesy Paula
Cooper Gallery, New York.
Photo by Russell Kaye.

transept established by the two suitcases, the nave by the directions of the culvert pipe, the apse by the staircase fountain. And while the pierced Virgin could be read as a violation of the female body, or as Gober's attack on Catholicism, it is, writes critic Libby Lumpkin, "perfectly articulate within the tradition of medieval Christianity as a personification of the church." As she remarks: "Just as Jan van Eyck's oversized Mary in his *Madonna in a Church*, with columnated robe, personifies the basilica in which she stands, the ribs of Gober's culvert pipe reprise the vaults of late medieval cathedrals, which themselves were meant to symbolically transform the interior of the church into Mary's womb (or the body of Christ, depending on the particular exegetic source)." While Gober's Virgin Mary (fig. 6.7) may personify the traditional Holy Church, her impoverished appearance, her pierced state—and, thus, her sterility—also allude to Gober's description of the "sick and hypocritical" nature of a mainstream religious institution that denies the diversity and differences within its faith community.[19]

Importantly, however, Gober's installation does not close on this metaphorical point of despair and pessimism about the vagaries of Christian dogma. Rather, toying with existing Catholic imagery, Gober restaged and remade the multilayered iconography that embodies the "Virgin" installation into a personal religious narrative emphasizing inclusiveness and enlightenment. There are several different levels, for example, to Gober's installation, each corresponding to earthly or heavenly realms, and each linked with the other. The surface of the installation, the level occupied by the barefoot Virgin, the suitcases, the sewer grates, and the gray concrete floor that museum visitors walk upon, represents the secular world, the world of the body and of various manmade structures and institutions—the house, the church, the city. The entire installation, in fact, references Los Angeles's vast, urban spaces: a city built on top of a desert, now with an insatiable thirst for water imported from the Owens Valley and pumped through a life-giving aqueduct whose building was one of the major feats of twentieth-century American engineering. If Gober's watery staircase points to the "city of angels'" dire environmental state—most eloquently dissected by Los Angeles critic and historian Mike Davis in such books as *City of Quartz* (1990) and, most recently, *Ecology of Fear: Los Angeles and the Imagination of Disaster* (1998)—the giant sculpture of the Virgin further recalls the ongoing furor over the design and construction of Our Lady of the Angels Catholic Cathedral, being built just a few blocks from MOCA.[20]

Gober's statue of the Virgin is pockmarked and worn, modeled by the artist and his assistants out of wet clay, cast in concrete, and then sandblasted to create a softened or eroded appearance. If her visage is that of a generic Madonna, her body is based on that of a female model hired by Gober "to give the figure the attributes of a real woman." Draped in heavy plaster robes, Gober's sculpted Virgin also recalls Bernini's *The Ecstasy of Saint Teresa* (1645–52), a similarly clad figure of a "real woman" who is also, as MOCA curator Paul Schimmel remarks, represented as being pierced or penetrated. Bodily and psychic suffering were central features of the mystic spirituality of the Spanish Carmelite nun Teresa of Avila (1515–82). In *Interior Castle*, written in 1577 as a spiritual manual for the nuns of her order as they prepared to marry Christ, the bridegroom of the soul, Teresa described Christ's presence in the body as a penetrating form of desirable pain:

> So powerful is the effect of this upon the soul that it becomes consumed with desire, yet cannot think what to ask, so clearly conscious is it of the presence of its God. Now, if this is so, you will ask me what it desires or what causes it distress. What greater blessing can it wish for?
> I cannot say; I know that this distress seems to penetrate to its very bowels; and that, when He that has wounded it draws out the arrow, the bowels seem to come with it, so deeply does it feel this love.[21]

The Virgin represented within Gober's installation is thus part of a much longer and larger tradition within Catholicism itself that has emphasized, particularly in the visual representation of women, the links between the physically tormented human body and the divine.

The "Virgin" installation's two enormous suitcases, carefully handcrafted of pigskin and forged hardware over a wooden frame, are symbols of travel. Whether used for business or pleasure, they are the stereotypical containers in which we pack the things we own and need. They are hugely oversized, indicative of modern materialism or, on even more prosaic terms, our contemporary cultural baggage. And their lids are open, inviting viewers to look inside, to rummage through their contents, and to form their own ideas about what they mean, about Gober's intentions, and about the entire installation. At first glance, the suitcases are empty—one must stand over them to notice the grates at their bottoms and then to peer through the grates to see the entire panorama of Gober's multilayered installation. "For me," Gober remarks, "the suitcases are about being an adult, where you go and what you take with you."[22] On one level, they reference Gober's solid critical reputation as a mature artist whose art-world status is rewarded with a prestigious solo exhibition at the Geffen Contemporary. On another, the suitcases seem pointedly autobiographical, symbolic devices that hint at Gober's own deliberate "packaging" of his art career, his image, and his personal memories—in much the same vein as Gustave Courbet's monumental (and equally enigmatic) painting *The Painter's Studio: A Real Allegory Summing Up Seven Years of My Life As an Artist* (1854–55). Especially, the suitcases are visual passageways through which viewers are led into Gober's underground, into the sewers.

Essential but odious, sewers exist to wash away the grit and garbage of daily life, cleansing our lives and our bodies of impurities, flushing our detritus down the drain, out of sight, out of mind. Yet through the sewers of Gober's "Virgin" installation, inside the drains modeled on generic urban grates, is another world, a watery Edenic realm charged with light and color (fig. 6.8). This is Gober's heaven: a natural paradise bursting with luminous colors and teeming with life, a place of rejuvenation, a lowly wishing well of gleaming coins, a spiritual counterpoint to the cold, gray, sterile, and impoverished world of earth above. The watery staircase on the installation's floor level is the primary link between these two worlds. Using water as a metaphor for cleansing and renewed life (one thinks of baptism, for example), Gober also draws on the stairway to reference the biblical notion of the heavenly ladder, the stairway to heaven that Jacob dreams and that in medieval art was often associated with images of the Virgin Mary, who represented a conduit between earth and heaven. That the risers are extraordinarily steep suggests the hardships involved in heavenly pursuits; that they lead up and down and yet only the downward path embodies promise and potential, hints of Gober's primary aim of upsetting prescribed Catholic paths. Indeed, inverting the spatial conventions of "heaven above" and "earth below," Gober's source of salvation is underground, under the earth, under the floor, under the overbearing structure of the museum cum church, in a tidal pool that suggests genesis, fortune, and new beginnings. "In Gober's antipodean world," remarks Schimmel, "up is down, down is up, light is dark, and dark is light; good and evil, father and son, mother and father, are all remixed. It is an alternative world."[23]

Indeed, the sense of genesis that pervades this "alternative world" is very much about Gober: it is no accident that the male legs in these pools are modeled on his own, and that most of the coins date to 1954, the year of Gober's birth—and that most of them are Lincoln-head pennies, and thus reference an icon of American emancipation. As Gober remarks, his art is pointedly autobiographical: "Most of my sculptures have been memories remade, recombined and filtered through my current experiences." Recollecting his Catholic memories, Gober's "Virgin" installation asserted his difference within a sacred world of his own making. Positing both his personal liberation from and his recovery of Catholicism, Gober's work hinged on his vision of spiritual reformation. As he remarks, "I have no problems with Catholicism in terms of faith, I just object to the way it's taught. I wanted to ventilate that and complicate that, in terms of life."[24] While clearly following the modernist paradigms of self and formalist exploration, Gober joined other contem-

Robert Gober, view of untitled installation, 1995–97, detail
of subterranean tidal pool. Courtesy Paula Cooper Gallery,
New York. Photo by Russell Kaye.

porary American artists in assessing the symbols and metaphors of spirituality and probing the human need for faith in these modern times.

"Imbued with a charged spirituality," one critic remarked, Gober's piece was also "free
from all traces of irony and similar distancing mechanisms."[25] Perhaps because of his re-
fusal to engage the modernist binary opposition of art versus religion—as has been suggested was the primary intent behind Andres Serrano's *Piss Christ* and other photographs—
many critics found Gober's "Virgin" installation surreal and ambiguous. Most were most
attentive to Gober's reformation not of spirituality, but of material culture: his "method
of artisanal fabrication," his apparent fascination with creating art that looks ready-made
but isn't. Few completely ignored the issues of spirituality inherent in the installation, yet
most were hesitant to explain or critique them or to delve into their significance for the
artist, for audiences, and for contemporary American art in general. In 1993, when asked
why few art critics had been attentive to the spiritualist dimensions in her own work, Kiki
Smith remarked, "Well, it's not a very popular subject matter. It's not popular for people
to think about the psychic or the spiritual life." Smith alludes to lingering art-world dis-
comfort regarding the spiritual in contemporary art; as one critic rather nastily remarked
about her work in 1997: "Kiki Smith's recent show, 'Reconstructing the Moon,' finds her
continuing her quasi-spiritual mystico-sentimental journey into the pathetic." Yet, as

Smith's former gallery dealer Joe Fawbush comments, "We sold quite a few pieces from her first show [in 1988]. And this was at the time when Peter Halley and Neo-Geo were all the rage. But people relate to her work. They respond to it on a spiritual level."[26]

Indeed, public response to Gober's "Virgin" installation reveals just how much audiences long for a contemporary art that is engaged with issues of spiritual faith and practice. To be sure, the exhibit did arouse some controversy and the *Los Angeles Times* printed a handful of letters from writers who said they were "insulted" and "offended" by Gober's "image of a defiled Virgin Mary." The director of media relations for Los Angeles's Roman Catholic Archdiocese called Gober's work a "nightmare" and decried his desecration of "sacred images." And the Catholic League for Religious and Civil Rights, based in New York, announced that any museum that chose to exhibit the work was, "like Gober, a bigot."[27] But others saw within Gober's installation the visual and material manifestation of the vitality of religious faith in their lives. One woman, a self-described "devout Roman Catholic," wrote that she "found the imagery breathtakingly beautiful and inspirational," and added: "I do admit that being confronted with the need for faith is disquieting. But then good art is never comfortable." Another woman, calling herself "an artist, a practicing Roman Catholic, and a feminist who is very much involved in the church and maintains a devotion to Mary," and who also, "as a woman," has "felt disenfranchised from the very church in which I am an active participant," found the MOCA installation "one of the most profoundly sacred spaces I have encountered in an art venue."[28]

The author of this letter, Linda Ekstrom, an artist and art teacher at Santa Barbara Community College, wrote a much longer defense of Gober's piece for the *National Catholic Reporter* in late 1997, in which she pointed out that the debate over the piece "says more about the ambiguous relationship between art and religion today than about the merits of the work." "Perhaps the controversy will be useful," she remarked, "if it reminds believers that art is most useful to religion when it is free to reconsider and rethink symbols, rather [than] being condemned for performing this vital service." No church or faith "can claim exclusive ownership of Mary as a symbol," Ekstrom cautioned, encouraging readers to understand that Gober's manipulation of Mary was perfectly within his rights and, more importantly, essential to Catholicism's own evolution. "Where once art imitated theology," she added, "it is now quite possible that contemporary art might influence theological notions by challenging the status quo with new forms. The church has always been enriched by the tension that comes with diversity."[29]

Evoking tension, and thereby questioning mainstream religious tenets and teachings, was precisely Gober's goal. Like much of contemporary American art, the "Virgin" installation was configured around issues of his personal identity. Yet it was also very much a sociopolitical piece that encouraged the reformation of a more inclusive Catholic church, and encouraged its audience to continue to wish for change—tossing pennies into alternative wells, hoping for spiritual rebirth and rejuvenation.

Finally, Gober's "Virgin" installation may suggest change within the art museum, or at least more of an art-world openness to a contemporary art that consciously focuses on issues of spiritual practice and belief. MOCA has long done this, mounting exhibitions, for example, of Betye Saar's installations and her Vodun and Swahili inspired altarpieces in the mid-1980s and the 1990s, and inviting museum visitors to contribute their own offerings to the artworks (flowers, coins, photos, letters, and the like).[30] The museum's most recent acceptance of Robert Gober's similarly spiritually attuned artwork suggests that the art world may be rethinking its frequently biased assumptions about both the makers of such art and its supposed status as religious propaganda, and recognizing, instead, its deep significance and vitality in the lives of contemporary Americans.

7

VISUAL RELIGION IN MEDIA CULTURE

Stewart M. Hoover

In any given week, Americans spend more time with the mass media of television, radio, popular music, film, videos, magazines, books, the Internet, and the web, than with any other activity. To a great extent, the popular media have become our cultural environment, mediating our experiences with current events, providing us with information and entertainment, and helping define what we value and what we consider worth our attention. This is not to say that the media are all-powerful, but that they play a prominent role in the lives and identity of the American people.

Most social and cultural institutions have been slow to recognize the growing importance of the media. For most of this century, mass communication was largely thought of as ancillary to more fundamental centers of social and cultural influence such as family, schools, church, and state. With the advent of television and the rapid growth in television penetration into the American household after the 1960s, attention has begun to shift. Educators now recognize the influence that the media have on education. Our political discourse is now seen to be integrally linked to the media that cover it. Parents un-

The author and editors regret that requests for permission to reproduce stills from *Northern Exposure* and *The Ten Commandments* were denied by Universal Studios and Paramount "due to a variety of legal concerns and business considerations."

derstand that television, music, video games, and other media are playing an important role in the socialization and development of children.

While many have begun to take media seriously, the world of religious believers has been slower to catch on. Even though important changes in religion have been historically connected to changes in media (the impact of the development of printing on the Protestant Reformation, for instance), it has been difficult for religious authorities to grasp the nature and extent of the challenge posed by the modern mass media of communication. There are some obvious ways that religion and the media interact and interrelate. There are religious programs such as those of the televangelists and publications such as religious magazines, books, websites, and pamphlets. The news media also cover religion, and there are vibrant debates about the nature and quality of this coverage.

While these obvious examples draw a good bit of attention, they are only the tip of the iceberg. For if the media in general (not just the small marginal audiences that exist for religious media and the specialized audiences that exist for religion journalism) are coming to play an important role and to claim more of the time and attention of American audiences, we need to ask a larger, more fundamental question. If religion operates in the integration of experience, identity, and meaning (as most authorities on religion assume it does), then the media in general must be playing a more profound role in contemporary religious experience than we might realize. Media, after all, are nothing if not primary sources for the identities and meanings that people shape for themselves in everyday life.[1]

As a way of investigating this more profound contribution of media to contemporary religion, we can look at two specific examples from television. One is a representation of religion within a specific program, the other an instance of the presence of religious ideas and meanings in the practice of viewing itself. These two examples constitute two facets of the interaction between media objects (programs) and their audiences and offer a concrete basis for interpretation and discussion. Why are both of them present in a consideration of the visual nature of mediated religious discourse? One of them is fundamentally a discussion of a visual representation; the other one is less directly so. In the end, I hope to show that the visual character of much of mass communication is only part— but a very important part—of the explanation for the significance and meaning of media for contemporary religion.

A PRIEST IN *NORTHERN EXPOSURE*

Northern Exposure was one of the most significant television programs of the early 1990s. During its network run, it laid the groundwork for a new thematic turn in American television, focusing on generational and cultural meanings in a format that often played fast and loose with the notion of cinematic realism. It was also a highly *visual* program. The opening credits turned on a series of visual cues to roles, relationships, and characters in the program. In the particular episode we'll think about here, the major transition (a trip from Alaska to Detroit) is charged with powerful and referential images of travel and of the locations departed from and traveled to.

Religion was a fairly common theme in many episodes. Most often, this religion was of the diffuse sort, probably most appropriately described by the term "spirituality." Eastern mysticism was part of the regular output of the local radio station. Native American spirituality appeared frequently. And, in a surrealist turn, spirits and spirit beings were sometimes visualized.

Much less common than spirituality and mysticism was what we might call "conventional religion," the kind we associate with traditional faith groups. There were exceptions to this, however, and it is to one of those that we will now refer. The plot of this episode revolved around two of the main characters, Maggie O'Connell and Joel Fleischman (whose on-and-off relationship was a continuing story arc in the series) traveling to Detroit for Maggie's grandmother's birthday.

As they arrive at Maggie's home in a Detroit suburb, the two main characters enter a world of middle-class anomie, family dysfunction, and religious uncertainty expressed through the angst of repressed sexuality and unrequited longing for escape. Simple, straightforward stuff. Grandma has locked herself in the bathroom because she cannot stand her daughter (Maggie's mother). Maggie and "Gran" bond across the generations. Maggie's brother Jeffie and sister-in-law Stephie are clearly on the rocks, a fact that Stephie announces both to Fleischman and to the family pastor who is there for the birthday celebration.

It is to this clergyman, Pastor Harding, that we turn. He is young, callow, and clearly inexperienced. He is described early on by a parishioner as a "fine young man" who followed in his father's footsteps. The father had been ". . . our pastor for over forty years." The young pastor is involved in three key interchanges during the party. In the first, he corners Fleischman at the buffet table to ask him about Jewish views of death. "Judaism is a system of ethical behavior," the pastor begins. "There is no thought of an eternal reward."

FLEISCHMAN: Eternal reward? You mean, like heaven?
PASTOR: Right, and don't get me wrong here—I like the idea of goodness for its own sake. But on the other hand, doesn't it, well, *gnaw* at you. . . . There's no afterlife, that this is *it*, that afterward, there's *nothing*. I mean, even if that were *true*, how can you *live* with that? How can you *stand* it?
FLEISCHMAN: . . . I just don't think about it.

Pastor Harding's views are, to say the least, traditionalist, in this regard. His traditionalism and inflexibility are further demonstrated when he encounters Stephie in the kitchen, as she makes a tearful and abrupt announcement to him:

STEPHIE: I'm leaving Jeffie . . . our marriage is over. . . . I've tried to be a good wife, I've really tried. . . . Six years . . . what have I got to show for it.

We don't even have a child together. Jeffie said it would ruin my figure . . . my waist would go, my breasts would fall, as though he would even *notice*. You know, I have a body you could break bricks on, my waist is flat as a skillet, my breasts *float*. . . . And what do I do? I take courses. . . . It would really be funny if it weren't so *pathetic*.

And the pastor? He simply turns pale and begins to fumble nervously with his glass. Stephie turns to him, and says, ". . . Reverend, you don't look so good." A humorous ending to a very emotional scene, at the expense of Pastor Harding. The reality of his ineffectualness is finally confirmed in a third vignette where, alone with Fleischman, he confesses to the doctor all of his regrets, misgivings, and insecurities about the responsibilities of the pastorate. Fleischman counsels him with a combination of common sense and self-help. The scene is constructed by Pastor Harding's movement through a doorway, into an enclosed space, signaling a confessional moment between the two men, physician/Jew/confessor sequestered with the pastor/Christian/confider. The camera then moves in for a close-up of the two, as Fleischman listens to and counsels the troubled clergyman, who appears in profile, as if sitting in the confessional booth, speaking through a screen that separates the two. The disparaged pastor slumps, hands hanging uselessly between his legs, in a gesture of childlike discouragement.

What is most significant to our discussion here is what Pastor Harding is wearing. He appears in the classic black suit and clerical collar most closely identified with the Roman Catholic priesthood. This visual sign of his vocation is actually rather jarring. It is a lovely spring day, and everyone else is dressed in light colors appropriate to the season and to the occasion of a birthday party. In the midst of this tableau, like a lead weight, looms the figure in black. His dress is, furthermore, quite confusing as a visual representation. Combined with the fact that the family name is O'Connell and Maggie is frequently addressed as "Mary Margaret," the clerical dress might convey Catholicism. And yet, the pastor has followed "his father" into this particular pulpit. These seeming contradictions are not addressed or resolved.

WATCHING A SOAP OPERA
WITH GRANDMA

We don't often talk in depth about our experiences of television and the other media. When we do, or when we have the opportunity to listen in on extended discussions, we can learn a great deal about how the actual practice of viewing television (or consuming other media) relates to the rest of daily life and experience. Here is an excerpt from an interview with a woman talking about her experience with a particular kind of programming—soap operas—and how viewing these programs relates to other aspects of her life. She describes herself as a religious woman and comes from a deeply religious background. She is thus always conscious of religion as she and the interviewer talk about her experiences.

Barbara watched *Days of Our Lives* every day with her strict Methodist grandmother during summer vacation when she was growing up. Barbara's aunt objected, but Barbara continued to watch soap operas, even scheduling her classes around them in college. Her favorite was *General Hospital*. Eventually, after the grandmother died, the aunt had a change of heart, and herself became devoted to *The Young and Restless*.

BARBARA: Yeah, but you know I hate to admit it, but I love soap operas, and I probably, sometimes though when they're being really vicious and mean, I think, "Oh, this is probably not a good thing to be watching."

INTERVIEWER: Do you apply to soap operas what you . . . were telling me before, that you like the way the characters mesh together? [She had said this about *Seinfeld* and *thirtysomething*.] That's certainly what soap operas do.

BARBARA: I think it's probably just entertainment. [Laughs.] You kind of get caught up in the characters' lives, I guess, probably. I don't watch them on a regular basis, just when I'm home I'll kind of flip one on. [Laughs.] . . . [*General Hospital*] was one I watched all through college. I would schedule my classes around it.

INTERVIEWER: Oh, so you were a serious watcher then.

BARBARA: I was back then. My mother just hated it, too. But my grandmother who I used to spend summers with, that was her big thing, was she had her soap operas, and she would catch me up every summer when I'd go down.

INTERVIEWER: So you had a real family link with it.

BARBARA: Well, my mother just thought it was horrible, my grandmother would do that. [Laughing.] . . .

INTERVIEWER: [Continuing discussion about watching with her grandmother.] And did you have discussions about who was doing what?

BARBARA: Yeah. My aunt thought it was just horrible. She would say, "Oh, Mother don't do that!" [Laughs.]

INTERVIEWER: Oh, so your aunt and your mom had . . . it's so interesting.

BARBARA: It was almost, my grandmother—My aunt worked all day, so what was I gonna do?

INTERVIEWER: Plus it must have been fun for you in some way.

BARBARA: Yeah. It was kind of like it was naughty. [Laughs.] It was like I was doing something naughty. So!

INTERVIEWER: Did your grandmother have anything to say about your aunt and your mother's disapproval?

BARBARA: No, my grandmother was pretty feisty, so she didn't have anything to say about anybody telling her what to do. [Laughs.] I think they get to that age where she thought she could say and do anything that she wanted because she was old.

INTERVIEWER: Well, no wonder you still like it. I mean that's a pretty big experience.

BARBARA: And then my friends when I was in high school, we liked to do that.

INTERVIEWER: Oh, you talked about it with your friends?

BARBARA: Tim [her husband] thinks it's horrible. [He says] "I can't believe you still watch that junk!" I would just turn it on every once in a while when I'm home for lunch.

INTERVIEWER: Did he know that you scheduled your classes around it?

BARBARA: Oh, yeah. Do you remember Luke and Laura? Did you ever watch it? That was a big story line a lot of people were caught up with.

INTERVIEWER: You know, I never did. I wish I had.

BARBARA: We would be in the college commons area, and there would be all these people around the TV! [Laughs.]

INTERVIEWER: Oh, that's where you would watch it, you wouldn't watch it in your room?

BARBARA: No. It's so funny. You have to watch it with a group of people, because it's so much fun.

INTERVIEWER: Oh, so you'd talk and make fun of it?

BARBARA: Oh, yeah. Yeah.

INTERVIEWER: Did they tend to be girls?

BARBARA: Oh, yeah, girls. The guys kind of rolled their eyes. So that's questionable. I think I probably shouldn't watch that kind of stuff, because it's not real wholesome or uplifting. Most of the characters are a big mess!

CONSIDERING TELEVISION AND RELIGION

These examples focus on television, and so will the remainder of my discussion. This is not to say that television is the most important of the media for our considerations here. It is, however, the dominant medium, and much that we can learn from talking about it can be applied to other visual media. There are clues in both the representation of the pastor in *Northern Exposure* and in the experiences recounted by Barbara that television plays a role, in both subtle and profound ways, in the religious lives of its viewers through means that are not yet clearly understood.

The vignettes from *Northern Exposure* and their representation of the clergy tell something about contemporary religion, about what it is possible to say and do in the way of depicting the values, symbols, and ideas of "the traditionally religious." The program is also significant for our understanding of the specifically visual capacities of such media representations. Barbara's experience tells us something as well. Whereas she and her grandmother might have been expected, based on their rather strict religious backgrounds, to have eschewed such popular entertainments as soap operas, they instead found pleasure in the viewing.

In order to understand these practices better, we need to consider the nature of contemporary religion and media. We can then return to an investigation of our specific examples. The story here is that the evolution of religion and the evolution of television co-

incide in such a way that we can begin to consider the extent to which the media are becoming an important context of religious practice, though it is practice of a particular kind.

RELIGIOUS CHANGE

Religion in America is today undergoing great change. This change has two dimensions:
1) change in the intrinsic nature of religious identity and religious practice, and 2) change
rooted in generational shifts in these things. The most basic thing we can say about contemporary religion is that it has become increasingly disconnected from religious institutions, doctrines, and histories. Stephen Warner, a sociologist of religion, has called this
a "new paradigm" in religion, where the achievement of meaningful religious ends is more
important than how one gets there.[2] And what is this end? Today, a primary religious motivation seems to be identity. Wade Clark Roof, another sociologist, has called this
"seeker" or "quester" religiosity, where individuals see themselves to be on a spiritual journey devoted to creating an ideal "self."[3] This means that religious consciousness is consistent with the overall nature of contemporary life, which Anthony Giddens has suggested is oriented toward the self and self-identity.[4] Religion is thus less about belief (in
the sense of adhering to a particular creed) than it is about behavior and how specific behaviors are directed toward acquiring ideas, symbols, and resources from which one can
craft a consciousness unique to oneself.

It is also important to say that this kind of religion is made possible by the notion that
one's religious life is in one's own hands. This idea, called "religious autonomy" by scholars, marks a fundamental shift. Autonomy takes responsibility for religious life out of the
hands of clerical and other institutional authorities and places it in the lap of the individual. The fact that the point of religion is increasingly perfection of the self means that
the importance of history and doctrine also declines. Today, people tend to think of religious ideas as situated on the shelf of a religious marketplace from which the seeker is
free to take them in acts of imaginative consumption. Rather than occupying a vertical
relationship with a sacred tradition that descends over the ages to the present, the religious marketplace offers a supply of possibilities from which the consumer selects ideas
and symbols for the construction of his or her own identity.

No one suggests that these trends are universal or absolute. They are, instead, trends
exerting different influences in a variety of religious settings. There is much evidence,
however, that these are the ways that many Americans are thinking about religion. And
there are clearly profound implications for the context of contemporary religion. Today
we can think of religion as increasingly independent of churches, temples, synagogues,
and mosques as well as their histories and authorities. Religion today floats more freely
and can begin to find its way in the wider context of American culture, a culture that is
largely defined by the institutions and practices of the mass media.

There are many examples of this new religious practice. The most obvious is the so-
called new age religiosity, which consists of the appropriation of religious symbols, ideas,

and values from many sources and shaping these borrowings into a religious identity. But the more traditional religions of today increasingly appropriate new elements as well. Some groups, for example, are incorporating newly crafted "rites of passage" into their practice. Others are borrowing Eastern or Native American values.[5]

One of the most important features of this new religiosity is the horizontal nature of its understanding of symbols and values. Because the traditional authorities no longer hold sway, their symbols no longer are seen in a hierarchical relationship to other symbols. They are all part of the symbolic marketplace. More importantly, certain of the "traditional" symbols and values are actually now less important and valuable. This is particularly true of the notion of religion itself. The term "religion" has lost a good deal of its value in contemporary discussions. People are much more likely to talk about spirituality than religion, for example, and other ideas such as belief and faith are today less valuable than in the past.[6]

It may be that this new religiosity is in part a reaction to a perceived repression of modes of practice and identity that today seem attractive: the body, experience, objects, rituals, and the visual. The argument goes something like this. For most religious authorities in the nineteenth and twentieth centuries, it has been necessary to stress certain ways of knowing and understanding religion. Historian Peter Williams has noted that this has meant that "popular" religion, and its practices, have been repressed in favor of scholarly, intellectual, and—most importantly—text-based ways of doing and knowing religion.[7] Against this authoritative tradition (and its "sacred" texts and traditions) stands a popular tradition that is rooted in individual and small-group meaning quests and that finds its resources by appropriating values, ideas, and symbols from sources such as media commodities (often thought to be "profane") and rites of viewing and consumption.

Our purpose here is to consider "the visual," but we should recognize that the visual culture of religion is embedded in a larger discourse about the sources and bases of religion.[8] It is important that we understand that in some ways none of this is very new. As Williams and other historians have shown us, American religion has always been appropriative and has always found some of its resources in the sphere of media culture and its commodities.[9] The nineteenth-century revival movement was a kind of entertainment medium of its own. A wide variety of religious objects, rituals, and commodities have always been available and used, at least by some sectors of religious culture. Another historian, David Nord, has shown that, in fact, the secular American publishing industry owes much of its origins to sectarian and religious publishing.[10]

While it is thus not an entirely new phenomenon, we can see that the media have also been changing in ways that encourage a connection with religion. Most importantly, the media have been diversifying in recent years. The array of channels, publications, and sources widens all the time. This has accelerated with the emergence of the Internet and World Wide Web, but this diversification is also evident in the "older" media of television and radio and the publishing industry.

The range of sources now available has led to more particularity and specificity in individual sources and channels. Twenty years ago, there were only three major television networks in the United States, and the diversity of their offerings was more limited. Today, a plethora of channels is available, and some of these channels are searching out more particular and specific audiences. This has meant that for religion in particular, there has been an increase in its presence in these contexts.

Northern Exposure is only one example. In the same decade a number of other network programs with religious themes also appeared. Some, like the critically acclaimed *Nothing Sacred* (a drama program about an iconoclastic young priest serving an urban parish), failed, while others, such as the highly rated *Touched by an Angel*, succeeded. On public broadcasting there was an explosion in the number of programs dealing with explicit and implicit religion, including pledge-period headliners like the New-Age guru Deepak Chopra. And when we talk to viewers like Barbara, we find a wide range of programs providing religious images and ideas to them, from *The Simpsons* to the *X-Files*.

The simplest way to describe the situation is to say that the media marketplace has begun to act like a marketplace. As consumer demand in the form of seeker religiosity began to move out of the context of the formal religious institutions, a range of suppliers has emerged to serve that demand.

MEDIA PRACTICES

We can see this new religion and the media coming together in a way that would be invisible if we looked only at explicitly religious media or explicitly mediated religion. In the way that an American anthropologist might look at cultural practices in a non-Western society, we can look at the cultural practice of religion in the media age and ask questions about how things might be working.

When we take such an anthropological view, research shows us some of the outlines of these processes. We might consider first the question of what people get out of their media consumption. There seem to be three basic kinds of motivations for media use. First is pleasure. There are many times and many contexts in which all people say is "I like it," and there is not much more to be said. There are tactile, visual, auditory, and cultural satisfactions to most media, and people mostly are drawn to them to satisfy such tastes.

The second motivation for media use is what we might call "social currency." For example, people do watch news programs to find out what is going on in the world, but there is a deeper sense in which this is important. It is important both to know what is going on and to know that one knows what is going on. Social currency also plays a role when people watch specific entertainment programs with other people in order to talk about the programs afterward. People become "fans" of certain shows, and identify with other fans of the same. Friends and family members watch certain programs together and talk about them with each other. In all of these ways, media practices are integrated into the structure of social relations in families, peer networks, and other settings.

A third result of media consumption is that it provides concrete values, symbols, tastes, and other touch points by which people are grounded in space and time. This is what we might call an ontological motivation for media use, and it is related most directly to what we think of as one of the most fundamentally religious of meaning quests. But it is also a motivation that is rooted in the "seeking" I discussed earlier. If the purpose of the quest is the development of an evolved sense of identity and selfhood, media provide a major resource that grounds the individual rather concretely and directly in contemporary lived culture.

We further find that as people construct meanings in media culture they do so by means of three interrelated frameworks we might call "discourses." The first of these is "discourses *in* the media." These are the discourses that articulate and bind audience readings with media objects (programs, symbols, experiences, etc.). The basic question here is "Do they (the audience) get it?" That is, does the audience understand a given program on its own terms, and have an understanding of its intentions, meanings, and pleasures? This discourse is related to questions of competence as well as pleasure and is bounded by the terms of reference of the media objects and rituals of media consumption.

The second of the discourses is "discourses *about* the media." These discourses take place outside the ritual or reception context per se but are rooted in media experience. They are the concrete mechanism whereby media become involved in social currency in social and family settings, but they also can have more instrumental functions, as when people talk about news or current events.

The third category of discourse is "discourses *of* the media." These occur when informants engage in discussions about the place and position of the media within the larger contexts of their beliefs, values, and behaviors. Self-consciousness plays an important role. The most common example of these discourses is the frameworks within which people talk about the "shoulds" of their media lives. Most people know they should watch less television. Most of them know they should watch more educational or public television. Most of them know that it is bad for children to watch violence. But this is also a discourse that positions the audience (individual, household, or family) with regard to the media. This positioning has much to say about values of class, ethnicity, identity, and meaning. Audience claims about the media become important markers of taste that can then contribute to grounding in space, time, and history.[11]

ANALYZING THE EXAMPLES

By looking at religion and media through the lens of what I have said about religious and media evolution and how media are used in meaning construction in media, we can begin to see where the themes and influence of traditional sources of meaning such as religion enter into the practices of audiences.

I'll look first at the example of *Northern Exposure*'s Pastor Harding. Such a program provides concrete representations of religion, but it is important to note the kind of religion that is represented. In the scenes from *Northern Exposure*, we see a confrontation between "traditional" religion and the new "seeker" religiosity of the self. And the latter is the kind of religion that clearly prevails. One way of describing the program's argument about the nature of the pastorate is to say that, today, the doctors are the priests and the priests are irrelevant. In the midst of so much unhappiness and dysfunction, all religion can do is ponder the nature of the afterlife.

But the most important element for my discussion is the way the pastor is visually represented. His dress signals the fact that he is superfluous to the goings-on in the household. He stands out, like a billboard announcement, in the midst of living and breathing beings.

What is even more interesting to ponder is the extent to which the clerical dress is one of the few visual clues available in the iconography of the media for the representation of "the religious." This may, in fact, be part of the explanation for the confusion over this pastor's exact denomination. Television critic Walter Goodman has suggested that Catholicism, in the form of such classics as *Going My Way* and the *Bells of St. Mary's*, is the generic religion of American media. This is a controversial claim, but in one important sense seems supportable: that Catholicism provides, in a way that Protestantism does not, a visual nomenclature of religiosity. Priests and nuns in traditional dress are easy to represent. The visuality of the Mass is also a highly salient aspect of religious practice that is less distinctive in most Protestant services.

The intriguing implication of this is that television finds itself increasingly in difficult straits when it wishes to represent religion. The salient images of traditional religion do not hold sway in an era when the authorities that support those images are in decline. A new kind of religion—and a new iconography—must emerge.[12] To rising generations that are increasingly ignorant of traditional religion and its sacred and popular iconographies, these images will become more and more determinative of their understanding of faith and spirituality.

The visual gesture of Pastor Harding in black in *Northern Exposure* at one moment binds a number of claims, beliefs, and discourses. As an image, it floats (in a leaden way) in the midst of a network of lived relationships that raise the essential crises of the self in modern, suburban life. Its singularity is a powerful argument about its isolation from the reality around it. It represents visually what the dialog describes verbally—that religion as we know it is old news. As a visual object, it also makes claims about history and about the future. For the viewers of *Northern Exposure* (an audience dominated by the generation of the baby boom), it connects in a single moment their self-understanding with an implicit expression of their tastes and desires in religion and spirituality.

What about Barbara and her soap opera viewing? One of the clearest ways that our three discourses come into play is in the common situation where informants watch something on television that they know they should not. We see many examples of this, cases where parents, in particular, describe themselves as presiding over a household that would never watch *Baywatch*, for example, and yet who know a great deal about the program, more than they would know if they did not actually watch it.

But there are examples of much more complex and nuanced tensions between the discourses. Barbara provides an example of discourse *of* and discourse *about* in negotiation and in tension. First of all, the interpretive framework or discourse received from her religious faith (a discourse *of*) has receded almost entirely into the background. It is still there, conditioning her discussions with the interviewer, but also mixed with a second discourse *of*, the broader social opprobrium attached to soap opera viewing.

There is, for Barbara, simple pleasure, both in the text itself and in the naughtiness of viewing it in resistance to received proscription. There is a level of ritual social connectedness or social currency. Her experience of viewing partly defined her relationship with her grandmother. And, the grandmother's own situation is interesting, too. She was a regular viewer of a type of television frowned upon by two different sources of authority—her religion and society in general.

There was also connectedness for Barbara, a discourse *about*, that integrated her with classmates in college, and there is a continuing discourse *of* with her husband, who criticizes her guilty pleasure.

Examples such as this illustrate the complex and nuanced nature of the relationship between religious and social values and audience practices in the media sphere. It is not really possible to see a clear line separating "religion" and "the media" here. It is also not only a question of how people find religious meaning in television. Distinctions do exist in the form of received scripts (from secular as well as religious sources) about the soap opera genre and the viewing of television in general. But Barbara is integrated into the audience for *General Hospital* in a rather transparent way. She exhibits two of the levels of motivation we discussed earlier. There is pleasure in the text/object itself and a further pleasure in the resistance represented by viewing it. There is also social currency in her co-viewing, first with her grandmother (there is pleasure in that, of course) and then with her cohorts at the university.

There is ontological salience (grounding in space and time) but of a complicated sort. On the one hand, her awareness of discourses *of*, which look down on the soap opera from various perspectives, is meaningful, and she must negotiate a place for herself with regard to them. She does this by describing her involvement as "in the past" and only incidental today. She is, in effect, saying, ". . . who am I? I am *not* a soap opera viewer," an important definitional task. But, she is also aware that, at one point in her life, she was positioned in a more naturalized way within the ritual of soap opera viewing, and specifically within a broad ritual of a particular story arc within the program, the famous "Luke and Laura" cycle.

Barbara's experience with *General Hospital* illustrates the extent to which meaning construction in the media sphere is a negotiation and a struggle. It is not a straightforward process, but one that derives from interrelated discourses, behaviors, saliencies, and practices.

So, what can we say about the role of visual representation in mass-mediated religion? While there has been a great deal of attention paid recently to the visual culture of American religion, our understanding of what happens in the case of mass-mediated visual images is more limited and more speculative.[13]

Among these speculations are the following. First, the visual mode is a means of communication in contemporary life whose centrality in contemporary life is supported by the essentially visual nature of much of mass media. Second, the fact that the media are visual is thought to have led to a situation (part of what is known as the "postmodern condition")[14] where generations of Americans are becoming increasingly "visually literate." Third, the visual mode is claimed by some to pose a threat to traditional religious authority because it is nonlinear and because it disconnects signs from their traditional referents. Fourth, media images often are kinetic—that is, they move—and thus are thought to have a particular kind of power over thought and emotion. Their movement, critics fear, can lead to the manipulation of viewers.

The examples can tell us something about these ideas in two ways. We can say some things about certain of these notions directly, but more importantly, they tell us something new about how we should think about these questions. In other words, are the questions appropriate, or should they, themselves, be rethought?

We do know that the first proposition makes sense; the media of communication, and their visual nature, have come to a more important place in cultural discourse. Much of what we know today is visual or visually coded information, and it does seem to make sense that we are increasingly visually oriented in our ways of learning and talking about contemporary cultural experience. Further, our example from *Northern Exposure* works because it places a traditional, authoritative marker in opposition to emerging meaning and spiritual sensibilities. It redefines the priesthood and does so through a not-so-subtle visual language.

But when we begin to think about the question of the impact or effect of visual imagery on viewers in their own reception of these images, a caution begins to form. As the interview with Barbara demonstrates, the viewing of television is integrated into a whole pattern of social relations in such a way that the effect cannot be clearly claimed to flow in any one direction. Barbara gets a range of things from her television viewing. Some of what she gets is in the programs themselves, in their imagery and in their claims. But a great deal of what she gets comes from her use of these programs and the act of viewing, as meaningful markers of her own sense of self-identity.

The media provide an important visual cultural context for American religion. The film *The Ten Commandments* socialized and enculturated a whole generation into a certain visual nomenclature of the Abrahamic faiths. Its own visual legacy has come to determine a great deal of what has come after in both "mediated" and "religious" representations of religion. Talking with viewers indicates that a wide range of entertainment programs today provide resources to religious seeking and questing that are less clearly linked to and grounded in the old ways of representing religion.

Our major learning emerges from this realization. To understand the nature of religion as visually mediated, we need to come at it from two directions. First the imagery itself, as we have seen in the example of the portrayal of Pastor Harding. Second is what people are doing with imagery. Here, we find religion and media interacting and cross-fertilizing each other through their shared discourses about representation and meaning practice. Part of our problem is that we have tended to think of religion and media as separate spheres. By looking at cases where media are actually used, we understand that this is no longer adequate. As Barbara demonstrates, religion and media both contribute to her understanding of who she is. In a way, religion helps define her media diet for her. Pastor Harding demonstrates the extent to which the obverse also occurs. The media are also involved in the definition of contemporary religion.

8

FROM PRESENTATION TO REPRESENTATION IN SIOUX SUN DANCE PAINTING

Harvey Markowitz

INTRODUCTION

During the final third of the nineteenth century, the United States confined, through treaty and force, the seven tribes of Lakotas or Teton Sioux to reservations located within the present-day Dakotas.[1] In accord with the policy of Indian "civilization and Christianization" of that era, these reservations served as controlled environments where agents and missionaries labored to undermine the cultural and religious foundations of Lakota identity while simultaneously inculcating members of the *tiyospayes*, or the kin-based bands constituting each tribe, with the institutions and mores of Western society. Although the Indian Bureau placed top priority on transforming the Sioux from nomadic buffalo hunters into yeoman farmers, it aimed at nothing less than a total Westernization of Lakota thinking, believing, and acting.

In view of the Indian Bureau's ethnocidal agenda, there is little surprise that the Lakota Sun Dance should top its list of targets for eradication. For not only was this ceremony the most important of all Lakota religious observances, but it also provided an annual occasion for the normally far-flung *tiyospayes* to assemble and reinforce their shared life-world of language, values, and customs.[2] Drawing primarily upon the testimony of holy men from the Oglala, Hunkpapa, and Sicangu Lakota tribes, this chapter explores the nature and role of pre- and postreservation Sun Dance painting. Part 1 summarizes some of the fundamental precepts of Lakota spirituality, focusing particular attention on the concept of sacred power. Building upon this foundation, part 2 begins with a summary of the purposes and structure of the Lakota Sun Dance. It then describes the character and function of sacred painting as part of the ritualized production of selected elements of Lakota Sun Dance visual culture. The chapter concludes with a discussion of postreservation Sun Dance painting, illustrated with works by three noted Sioux artists.

LAKOTA SPIRITUALITY AND *WAKAN*

The Lakotas conceived, organized, and celebrated their spirituality according to a set of categories that was, at once, logically coherent and fluid. The existential core of this system was their wonderment at a profoundly mysterious universe. Any object, being, or process capable of generating this experience they referred to as *wakan*, reserving the term *Wakan Tanka*—literally "Great Wonder"—for the most unfathomable and awesome of these marvels.

According to the Oglala holy man Good Seat, "anything might be *wakan*."[3] The following list, by Good Seat's contemporary Little Wound, provides the merest sample of the highly diverse phenomena that Lakota considered inherently or potentially *wakan*. "Animals," Little Wound stated, "may be *wakan* . . . Things that do not live may be *wakan*. When anything is food, it is *wakan* because it makes life in the body. When anything is hard to understand, it is *wakan* because mankind does not know what it is . . . Little children are *wakan* because they do not speak . . . Anything that is very old is *wakan* because no one knows when it was made . . . Anything that is poison or anything that intoxicates is *wakan* . . ."[4]

In addition to perceptible aspects of their environment, Lakotas attributed spiritual existence and power to cultural categories that post-Enlightenment, Western thought has come to regard as abstractions, lacking external reality. They thus believed that certain shapes, quantities, and colors were endowed with the *wakan* attributes of their invisible archetypes that could be activated through the proper rituals and prayers. Two noteworthy examples were the circle (*cangleska wakan*) and the number four (*topa*).

Expounding on the *wakan* character of the circle, Oglala holy man Thomas Tyon noted:

> . . . the circle [is] sacred because the Great Spirit caused everything to be round except stone. Stone is the implement of destruction. The sun and the sky, the earth and the moon are round like a shield, though the sky is deep like a bowl. Everything that breathes is round like the body of a man. Everything that grows from the ground is round like the stem of a tree. Since the Great Spirit has caused everything to be round mankind should look upon the circle as sacred for it is the symbol of all things in nature except stone . . . For these reasons the Oglala make their tipis circular, their camp circle circular and sit in a circle in all ceremonies.[5]

Concerning the spiritual significance of the number four, Tyon declared:

> . . . the Lakota grouped all their activities by fours. This was because they recognized four directions: the west, the north, the east, and the south; four divisions of time: the day, the night, the moon, and the year; four parts to everything that grows from the ground: the roots, the stem, the leaves, and the fruit; four kinds of things that breathe: those that crawl, those that fly, those that walk on four legs, and those that walk on two legs; four things above the world: the sun, the moon, the sky, and the stars; four kinds of gods: the great, the associates of the great, the gods below them, and the spirit kind; four periods of human life: babyhood, childhood, adulthood, and old age; and finally, mankind had four fingers on each hand, four toes on each foot, and the thumbs and the great toes of each taken together are four. Since the Great Spirit caused everything to be in fours, mankind should do everything possible in fours.[6]

Lakotas traced the *wakan* character and powers of various phenomena to the potency (*tonwan* or *towan*) of their spiritual essences (*sicun*). According to Oglala holy man Sword, "Every object in the world has a spirit and this spirit is *wakan*. Thus the spirit of the tree or things of that kind, while not the spirit of man, are also *wakan*."[7]

Lakotas believed that certain beings, objects, and processes were endowed with *tonwan* of extraordinary force and mystery. They thus, for example, consider the talents of exceptional hunters, warriors, and artists as products of their spiritual potencies. Exceeding all other humans in spiritual prowess were the *wicasa wakan* (holy men or shamans) to whom the spirits had entrusted the tribe's sacred language and *wicohan wakan*, sacred traditions. Among the greatest of these customs were socially beneficial ceremonies, such as those for treating illnesses and finding lost objects, that were revealed to shamans in *wowihanble*, visions. These visions generally included prayers and songs that gave shamans the power to *yuwakan*, or consecrate objects or beings, either by activating the *tonwan* of the latter or infusing them with *tonwan* from the shamans' own *sicun*. Speaking of his own abilities to *yuwakan*, Oglala shaman Feather on Head thus stated, "I am a great medicine man. I have mysterious powers . . . I can give magic power to things. I can make the mysterious things."[8] As is discussed in part 2, the ability of shamans to "make" mysterious things played an essential role in Sun Dance painting.

For Lakotas the most wondrous of all beings were those spiritual powers—the *Wakanpi*—whom they considered as the source of all *tonwan*. According to Sword, the *Wakanpi* were all things that were above humankind and "greater than mankind in the same way that humankind is greater than animals."[9]

The majority of Lakotas referred to the most powerful and benevolent of these *Wakanpi* as *Taku Wakan*, spirit relatives, or simply *Wakan Tanka*, Great Wonder. However holy men addressed them in their sacred language as *Tobtob kin*—the "Four times Four." This squaring of the holy number four indicates not only their great reverence for these beings, but also their belief that they were sixteen in number, comprising four hierarchical divisions of four gods each. In order of rank these divisions were: *Wakan Akantu* (the Superior *Wakan*), to which belonged *Wi* (Sun), *Skan* (Energy), *Maka* (Earth), and *Inyan* (Rock); the *Wakan Kolaya* (the associates or kindred of the superior *Wakan*), made up of *Han Wi* (Moon), *Tate* (Wind), *Wohpe* (the Beautiful One/White Buffalo Calf Maiden), and *Wakinyan* (Thunder Beings); the *Wakan Kuya* (the lower or subordinate gods), comprising *Tatanka* (Buffalo Bull), *Hunumpa* (Two Leggeds), *Tate Tob* (Four Winds), and *Yumni* (Whirlwind); and the *Wakanlapi* (spirit kind or *Wakan*-like), among whom were *Nagi* (Spirit), *Niya* (Ghost, Life), *Nagila* (Spirit-like), and *Sicun* (the potency of a *Wakan* being).[10]

In addition to the good *Wakanpi*, Lakotas posited the existence of many evil deities who delighted in causing them misery and anguish. From available testimony, it is not entirely clear how the evil *Wakanpi* fit into the Lakota pantheon. They had a leader named *Iya*, an ogre of tremendous size and maliciousness. However, neither he nor his wicked minions were members of the *Tobtob kin*. "*Tobtob*," Lone Bear stated, "is all kinds of good spirits. It is," he continued, "Four-times-four . . . The bad spirits are not of the *Tobtob*."[11] With specific reference to *Iya*, Short Feather asserted, "*Iya* is a Great Spirit [*Wakan Tanka*]. He is a bad spirit. He does not take part in the council of the Great Spirits. He is jealous of the Sioux and tries to do them harm all the time."[12]

The exclusion of the evil *Wakanpi* from the company of the *Tobtob kin* makes sense when one realizes that the Lakotas thought the Four times Four constituted a *tiyospaye* that operated according to the same social and ethical principles as their own extended families. They therefore considered it perfectly reasonable that the good gods had banished the evil *Wakanpi* from the sacred family. Exile, after all, was precisely the punishment that they meted out to *tiyospaye* members who refused to conform to the moral principles of the group. Bereft of kinship ties—the ultimate horror for a Lakota—the evil *Wakanpi* degenerated into a state of chaos, reflected in their "unclassed" status.[13]

Owing to the debased and predatory nature of the evil *Wakanpi*, Little Wound cautioned his fellow Lakotas that these were "to be feared" and that they "should think of [them] as an enemy." Regarding the good *Wakanpi* he conversely advised, "Mankind should please [them] in all things . . . They should be pleased by songs and ceremonies. Gifts should be made to them . . . They should think of them as they think of their mothers and fathers."[14] For their part, as was befitting good relatives, the *Taku Wakan* were obligated to attend to the needs of Lakotas by honoring properly offered petitions for prosperity and health. As Sioux anthropologist Ella Deloria once pointed out, it is significant that the Lakota verb *cekiye* signified both to recognize a kinship relationship and to offer prayer.[15]

The Lakotas' well-populated pantheon has led some students of religion to classify them "polytheists." Aside from the general problems plaguing this term, it is a particularly unsuitable characterization of Lakota spirituality. Although the Lakotas believed that there were many *Wakanpi*, they nevertheless considered all of them embodiments of a greater, intangible unity. As Little Wound lucidly observed, "*Wanka Tanka* are many. But they are all the same as one."[16] Lakotas associated the *sicun* of each *Wakanpi*, whether good or bad, with a color. According to Sword, "Red is the color of the sun; blue, the color of the moving spirit; green, the color of the spirit of the earth; and yellow, the color of the spirit of the rock. These colors," he continued, "are for other spirits. Blue is the color of the wind; red is the color of all spirits. The colors are the same for the friends [*Wakan Kolayapi*] of the Great Spirits. Black is the color of the bad spirits."[17]

As will be discussed in relation to Sun Dance painting, these colors were in fact more than mere emblems. Rather, they functioned as *owa wakan*, sacred hues, endowed with *tonwan* of their *Wakanpi*'s *sicun*. In a real sense they *were* this *tonwan*, made present and active through a shaman's ritual and prayer.

THE LAKOTA SUN DANCE
AND SUN DANCE PAINTING

Among the sixteen *Wakan Tanka*, the Lakotas most revered and loved *Wi*, the Sun, ranking him first among the Superior Gods, and chief of the *Tobtob kin*. They believed that because of his high station and his special love for the Lakota people, *Skan* (the god of energy) had granted him the holiest of colors, red, as his emblem.[18] According to Tyon and other Lakota holy men: "Red is the color that belongs to the Sun . . . This color is evoked by shamans, and represents the coming and the going of the Sun. When one wears red the Sun is pleased and will listen to such a one. The Indians are red, so they are the favorite people of the Sun. The Sun provides everything for them."[19]

In appreciation for the sun's special affection for the Lakotas, they celebrated their greatest ceremony, *Wiwayang wacipi*, or Sun Dance, in his honor.[20] Describing the complex nature of the ritual, several Lakota holy men concurred that the "ceremony of the Sun Dance may embrace all the ceremonies of any kind that are relative to the Gods . . ."[21]

However, aside from the many supplementary rituals, the Lakotas performed the Sun Dance to accomplish three important ends. It was first a means for individuals to thank the sun, and the other *Wakanpi*, for favors granted the preceding year. A warrior thus might take part in the Sun Dance to acknowledge the spiritual aid he had received in killing enemies, stealing horses, or surviving a battle. Second, participation in the ceremony was a way of petitioning spiritual intercession, perhaps for the recovery of a loved one, a successful buffalo hunt, or a year free of pestilence. Finally, undertaking the Sun Dance was an important means for securing spiritual power from *Wi* or the *Wakanpi*.[22]

Lakotas divided their Sun Dance ceremony into four parts, as was fitting its sacred nature: first, a period when candidates chose their mentors and readied themselves for their future sacrifice; second, the time set aside for people to assemble at the dance site; third, the interval allotted for establishing the camp and performing required predance ceremonies; and fourth, the day given over to the dance itself.[23]

While no rule dictated when candidates should begin their instruction, the complex nature of the Sun Dance ceremony necessitated that they select and begin working with their mentors well in advance of the celebration. The celebration, itself, always took place at the same time: when the buffalo were fat, new sprouts of sage were a span long, when chokecherries were ripening, and the moon was rising as the sun was going down; in mid-June or early July, according to the Western calendar.[24] By contrast, the site where the Sun Dance was held changed from year to year.

The arrival of Sun Dance participants and spectators at the ceremonial site marked the beginning of an eight-day period of predance activities. This period was divided into two four-day phases. The first four days, known as the "preliminary camp," provided the opportunity for socializing and conviviality.[25] However, it was also a time for assigning key ceremonial roles, including that of the Sun Dance leader, the individual who would scout for the Sun Dance tree, and the men and women who would ritually fell it.[26]

The second four-day phase, referred to as the "the ceremonial camp," began with the performance of several preparatory rituals and climaxed four days later with the Sun Dance.[27] On the first day, the Sun Dance leader selected the area for the campsite and, with the help of the mentors and candidates, cleansed it of malevolent spirits. Once the area had been expunged of evil powers, the people pitched their tipis in a great, sacred circle—*cangleska wakan*—with the sacred spot where the Sun Dance pole would stand at its center. Ceremonies for procuring and consecrating the cottonwood tree that would serve as this pole occupied most of the second day. The raising of the pole and the construction of the pine-covered dance lodge took place on the following day. At dawn on the fourth day, the mentors painted the candidates, provided them with their final instructions, and conducted them to the arena for the beginning of the dance.

Lakotas could perform the Sun Dance in a variety of forms and at various levels of intensity.[28] Some individuals confined their sacrifice to dancing in addition to observing the fast stipulated for all participants. Others added lacerations or offerings of flesh to their ordeal. Finally, some Lakotas chose to break loose from ropes that had been implanted in their skin and attached to buffalo skulls or the sacred pole. This last type of sacrifice, which recapitulated a sacred drama of capture, torture, captivity, and escape, itself took various forms. According to anthropologist Frances Densmore, the "two most common forms of this treatment consisted in the piercing of the flesh over the chest with skewers attached by cords to the crossbar of the sacred pole, and the fastening of buffalo skulls to the flesh of the back and arms. The two more severe and less common forms were the suspending of the entire body by the flesh of the back and the fastening of the flesh of both back and chest to four poles at some distance from the body, the poles being placed at the corners of a square."[29]

No matter what mode of sacrifice he chose, a dancer was required to lock his gaze on the sacred pole, while keeping in step with the drums and praying to Wi. Many of these prayers took the form of songs. As Tyon observed, "If they wish for many buffalo, they will sing of them; if victory, sing of it; and if they wish to bring good weather, they will sing of it."[30]

By themselves, however, the prayers and sacrifices of the Sun Dancers were insufficient to elicit the blessings of Wi. It was, instead, absolutely essential that they be performed within a space and with ceremonial objects that had been consecrated through elaborate rituals of *yuwakan*. As suggested above, most of these rituals took place during the three days of the "ceremonial camp" that preceded the Sun Dance itself.

LAKOTA PAINTING
AND THE SUN DANCE

For Lakotas, the process of painting was part of a broader cultural domain, *owapi*, under which they assigned all manners of marking or coloring a surface. Within this category they distinguished between representational and sacred painting. It was the primary function of representational painting to illustrate important events in the lives of individual Lakotas and the histories of *tiyospayes*. The vast majority of such works were by warriors who wished to depict their glories on the warpath and during horse-raiding forays. In addition, however, representational painting included chronologies known as *waniyetu iyawapi*, or winter counts, which provided pictographic accounts of those events that *tiyospayes* considered the most important occurrences in their collective past and after which they named their years.

In contrast to representational painting, it was the chief objective of ceremonial painting to *present* or manifest the *wakan*. Such painting was always performed as part of the process of *yuwakan* that included sacred songs and prayers that served to activate the *tonwan* of the specified colors or designs.

The painting performed as part of the Sun Dance was almost exclusively of a sacred nature. Among the most important of these rites of *wakan owapi* were the paintings of sacred tree or pole and its effigies and the bodies of the Sun Dance candidates.

PAINTING THE SACRED POLE
AND ITS EFFIGIES

The ceremonial painting of the Sun Dance tree was part of a complex series of rituals by means of which the tree was transformed from an ordinary cottonwood to a sacred pole. These rites began on the third day of the preliminary camp with the selection of a scout who was responsible for locating a cottonwood tree of suitable height, mass, and configuration to withstand the struggle of dancers attempting to break free of its "hold." His designation as "scout" was fitting, for the Lakotas considered the tree an enemy to be captured and brought back to camp.[31]

The actual capture of this "enemy" occurred on the second day of the ceremonial camp. One by one, four men who had been chosen to fell the tree took their positions. Each first told the onlookers of the great deeds that entitled him to this honor and then, wielding an ax, feigned three blows before actually striking the cottonwood with the fourth.[32] This rite was believed to subordinate the tree's spirit to the will of its captors.[33] A chaste woman was then handed an ax to deliver the final blows and, as the tree dropped earthward, its fall was broken before touching the ground.

From this moment forward, the tree was considered a "captive" that would serve the Lakotas as the sacred pole in their Sun Dance. Placing the prisoner on a litter, four teams took turns hauling it back to the ceremonial camp. The return journey was punctuated by four stops, made in order to change crews. During each of these stops all of the carriers howled like wolves, "for this is the cry of returning warriors who come bringing a captive."[34]

When the team bearing the sacred tree finally returned, its members moved slowly through the camp circle until reaching the center. They then carefully placed the sacred hostage on the ground so that its head faced east and its stump touched the lip of a hole in which it would stand.

While a crowd that had gathered to greet the captors looked on, the Sun Dance leader and mentors performed the ritual of painting the tree. This ritual began with the leader removing the tree's outer bark. Once the tree had been suitably stripped and smoothed, he painted it from the bottom branches to base with red perpendicular lines. The use of red as the first and primary paint was replete with significance. As has been previously stated, this color was the emblem of the sun and pleasing to all the good *Wakanpi*. Thomas Tyon thus observed, "Red is the color spirits like best."[35]

As the leader painted the sacred pole he would chant ceremonial songs whose majesty and power are suggested by the following verse: "With voice sounding forth, I appear; With voice sounding forth, I appear; With face showing, I appear; I cause the buffalo bull to roam over your land. With voice sounding forth, I appear; I cause the buffalo bull to roam over your land, Those I give to you."[36] The chanting of this and other songs served to activate the *tonwan* of the paints, thereby rendering them, and the tree they covered, mysterious, powerful *wakan*.

When the Sun Dance leader finished painting the tree, he attached offerings to a crossbar that had previously been placed in a crotch of branches located near the pole's crest. These gifts included two rawhide images, one that had been cut into the shape of a man (fig. 8.1) and the other resembling a bison (fig. 8.2). A review of the literature discloses varying interpretations concerning the precise beings whom these effigies were intended to represent. However, one of the more detailed accounts is provided by the Sicangu religious leader Short Bull, whose Sun Dance paintings are discussed in part 3. According to Short Bull, the two effigies, which were "made with ceremony," symbolized enemy warriors and *Tatanka Gnaskiyan*, the Demon Buffalo, respectively.[37]

Before attaching these effigies to the crossbar, the Sun Dance leader painted them black, the color of the evil spirits, again amidst sacred songs. Short Bull stated that this ceremonial painting was performed to give to them "the receptivity of an enemy and of the Demon Buffalo so that whatever is done to these images occurs to the enemy and to the demon."[38]

What was "done" to the rawhide effigies generally occurred immediately after the sacred pole was planted in the center of the Sun Dance lodge. Men clad in their warrior dress and carrying bows and arrows and guns entered the shelter and rushed toward the

FIGURE 8.1 (LEFT)
Human effigy, collected
ca. 1911–12, rawhide. State
Historical Society of North
Dakota, SHSND 948.

FIGURE 8.2 (BELOW)
Bison effigy, collected
ca. 1911–12, rawhide. State
Historical Society of North
Dakota, SHSND 949.

pole, shooting repeatedly at the enemy figures. These acts, according to Densmore, indicate that the "enemy and buffalo had been conquered by supernatural help."[39]

With the conclusion of this attack on the effigies, a team of men hoisted the pole to an upright position, pausing four times in accord with sacred tradition. Mysterious, *wakan*, the pole now dominated the arena, waiting for the dance to begin.

PAINTING THE SUN DANCERS

Upon arriving at the Sun Dance site, the candidates were expected to consider themselves *wakan*, sacred, by living apart from nondancers and foregoing all the pleasures of the encampment. They also commenced an elaborate series of rites intended to strengthen and purify their bodies and spirits for their upcoming sacrifice. In one of these rites, known as *inikage,* or sweatbath, water was poured over heated rocks as prayers were offered to the *Wi* and the other *Wakanpi.* Lakotas believed that the steam released during this ceremony was the rocks' *ni,* or breath, that both cleansed and empowered the candidates.[40] In addition to *inikage,* the candidates repeatedly fumigated themselves (*azilic'iayapi*) with sage, believing that the smoke from this plant repulsed evil spirits.[41]

Lakotas believed that these practices transformed the candidates' bodies into suitably pure canvasses to be painted with the sacred designs and colors required for the dance. This ceremony, referred to as *wakan owicawapi,* was performed by the candidates' mentors just before they were escorted into the dance arena.[42] The mentor began by applying a primer of paint directly to his candidate's flesh. While firsthand accounts of this ceremony differ on what parts of the body received this undercoat, most agree that they were colored with red. According to Deloria, "The traditional painting was like this: The entire face was given a vermilion base . . . [and] the whole body is given a red base."[43]

As with the tree, the painting of the candidates with red both signified and made them holy. In this regard, it is significant that some reports note that the dancers' hands and feet were left unpainted. Short Bull, for example, stated that all the dancers were prepared alike, "each with body painted red except his hands."[44] In his extended treatment of the Sun Dance, James Dorsey provided an explanation for this practice that underscores the spiritual significance and power of red. He wrote, "Meanwhile, the men who have been selected for the purpose [of painting the candidates] redden their entire hands, and it devolves on them [the Sun Dancers] to dance without touching anything, such as the withes connected to the Sun Dance pole or buffalo skulls; all that they are required to do is to extend their hands towards the sun, with the palms turned from them."[45]

After the mentors had completed painting the candidates with red undercoat, they decorated them with additional colors and designs. These decorations varied from one dancer to another. Some signified the form of dance he would perform. Others portrayed the dancer's or his mentor's spirit friends, or animals with whose *tonwan* the dancer wished to be blessed. Regarding this last type of design, the Hunkpapa Lakota Siyaka reported that his mentor had painted the image of a black deer's head over his mouth, explaining that ". . . the deer could endure thirst for a long time without losing his strength."[46] This power would have certainly been considered of inestimable value to someone who would soon be dancing under a hot sun for an entire day.

By the time the mentors had finished their painting, each of the candidates was covered with an abundance of sacred colors and designs, some of which he shared with his fellow Sun Dancers and others unique to his own spiritual experiences and desires. However, whatever their particular character, as Oglala High Bear noted, "all [were] *wakan.*"[47] Bedecked with sacred paintings, the candidates were paraded single file into the arena. The time had finally arrived for them to fulfill their pledges to *Wi.*

FROM PRESENTATION TO REPRESENTATION
IN SUN DANCE PAINTING

Immediately after the federal government relocated the Lakotas to their respective reservations, agents and Christian missionaries launched an all-out assault on Lakota religious beliefs and practices, including the Sun Dance. The efforts to eliminate the Sun Dance culminated in 1883, when Congress outlawed the ceremony.

However, despite these pressures to eliminate the Sun Dance, documentary and oral sources provide abundant evidence that members of many Lakota communities continued to practice the ceremony in secret. Because of their clandestine nature and the government's clampdown on travel by Lakotas outside their agencies, these observances were smaller and less elaborate than those of their prereservation predecessors. Nevertheless, they served to preserve many of the beliefs and practices associated with the ceremony, including its traditions of sacred painting.

In the midst of this ceremonial continuity, a new form of Sun Dance painting rapidly emerged as a result of market forces brought about by the Lakotas' increasing contacts with Whites. In a radical departure from customary Sun Dance painting, whose primary function was to present the *wakan*, Lakota artists began representing the ceremony in drawings and paintings for sale to non-Indian customers. For the first time, native-produced paintings of the Sun Dance appeared.[48]

Among the original painted depictions of the Sun Dance were the ones made by Sicangu holy man Short Bull (c. 1845–1915). As part of his research on the Sun Dance, in 1912, physician-ethnologist James R. Walker paid Short Bull twenty-five dollars to portray the ceremony in watercolors accompanied by "descriptive notes" on their content. In fulfillment of this commission, Short Bull produced two paintings on ducking canvas, one representing the third and another the fourth day of the Dance, the latter of which is reproduced here (fig. 8.3). However, as he was literate neither in English nor in Lakota, Short Bull hired his nephew to record his explanations of the pictures. In 1918, Walker transmitted the paintings to the American Museum of Natural History, where they remain.[49]

In keeping with his patron's ethnographic interests, Short Bull packed his paintings with ceremonial and cultural details that only a Lakota who had participated in many such observations could have known. However, these paintings stubbornly resist being pigeonholed as ethnographic illustrations. Rather, they burst with an energy emanating from the artist's lived experience of ceremony. Like many of his fellow holy men, Short Bull feared that the federal government's assimilationist policy would soon obliterate all traces of the Lakota gods and their ceremonies. In addition to illustrating the Sun Dance, he desired that his paintings demonstrate to future generations the passion with which Lakotas dedicated themselves to the *Wakan Tanka* and their greatest religious observance.

Beyond providing experientially grounded depictions of Sun Dance customs, Short Bull's paintings are of crucial importance for tracing the evolution of early reservation

FIGURE 8.3
Short Bull, *The Fourth Day of the Sun Dance*, 1912, water-based paint on
canvas, 29¼ in. x 66¾ in. Courtesy Department of Library Services,
American Museum of Natural History.

Lakota art. As has been mentioned, they belong to the first generation of Lakota representations of the Sun Dance. However, aside from their innovative content, they also display fascinating continuities and changes with customary methods of Lakota representational art. Thus, for example, in keeping with these methods, Short Bull portrayed his subjects in flat, unmodeled tones without any attempt at foreshortening to give them dimension or depth.[50]

And yet, a careful examination of the artist's painting of the fourth day of the Sun Dance displays several significant differences with customary Lakota representationalism. Thus, while Short Bull adhered to the prereservation tradition of portraying human faces in profile with their bodies turned sideways or at three-quarters' stance, he drew three of his subjects—one of the Sun Dancers, a drummer, and a woman on horseback at the right of the dance arena—facing forward. Even more unusual are the drummers portrayed with their backs to the viewers. Finally, because of the ethnographic nature of his commission, Short Bull was required to depict his human figures in relationship to inanimate objects, that is, the Sun Dance arena and tipis. This concern for context was not a characteristic of prereservation Sioux art.

Evidence is lacking to determine whether these divergences resulted from Short Bull's exposure to works by European or American artists or to drawings by contemporary Sioux "ledger book" artists who drew scenes of traditional Indian social life for sale to non-Indians. What is certain is that during the generation following Short Bull's, increasing numbers of Sioux artists adopted and adapted the formal and stylistic techniques of Western "easel painting" to depict customary tribal practices, including the Sun Dance.

FIGURE 8.4
Oscar Howe, *The Sun
Dance*, 1942, oil on plaster,
16 ft. x 20 ft. Collection of
University of South Dakota.
© 1983 Adelheid Howe.

The best known of these artists is, undoubtedly, Oscar Howe (1915–83), a Yanktonai Sioux or Nakota, who is often referred to as the "father" of new Indian art. In 1938, the United States Indian Bureau sent Howe to the Santa Fe Indian school, where he associated himself with Dorothy Dunn's "Studio" program. The goal of the Studio was to foster the development of Indian art. However, as art historians John A. Day and Margaret Quintal have pointed out, while "Howe and his peers were exhorted to be true to their tribal traditions, they were ultimately indoctrinated with the tenets of conventionalized Southwestern Indian art and its romantic subjects, unmodeled pastel colors, formal compositions, concern for descriptive detail and limited spatial depth."[51]

After graduating from Santa Fe in 1938, Howe enrolled in the Indian Art Center at Fort Sill, Oklahoma, where he received training as a muralist. His first major project after leaving Fort Sill was to decorate the interior walls of the newly constructed civic center in Mobridge, South Dakota, a predominantly non-Indian community close to the Standing Rock Sioux Reservation.

Howe chose as the subject for his murals episodes depicting Sioux history, culture, and religion. This was a bold gesture given the perennially tense relations between the Indian and white residents of Mobridge. However, it was also entirely consistent with Howe's goal of bridging the gap between Indians and Whites through art. "A person," Howe once wrote, "is better for knowing and experiencing (not just understanding) two cultures."[52]

The ten murals Howe created for this project represent a perfect blend of his institutional training and his desire to communicate the beauty and nobility of Sioux history and life in paint. One of his subjects is the Sun Dance (fig. 8.4). However, the pastelled

romanticism of this mural communicates an experience of the ceremony entirely different from that conveyed by the vibrant colors and stark composition of Short Bull's canvas. A feeling of serenity fills Howe's work, quite at odds with the raw energy that pul-
sates through Short Bull's drawing. Howe depicts his four dancers in a state of rapture,
absorbed by the power of their prayers and sacrifice.

Shortly after completing the Mobridge murals, Howe was inducted into the military
and spent the next four years fighting in World War II. Following his return from the war,
he progressively abandoned the muted romanticism of the Santa Fe Studio until, by the
early 1960s, he had developed a painting style far removed from the aesthetic principles
and techniques of his early works. The abstract, angular quality of Howe's postwar paintings prompted many critics to conclude that he had been inspired by Cubism. However,
Howe spurned this assessment, countering, "It has always been my version of Indian
traditions to make it my own way, but every part comes from Indian and not white culture. I have wrongly been labeled a Cubist . . . From an all-Indian background I developed my own style."[53]

The Sun Dancers (fig. 8.5) was painted by Howe at the peak of his artistic powers. Its
bold colors and sharp lines dramatically evoke the carnal force and spiritual ecstasy of
the moment when the dancer breaks free from the ropes that have tethered him to the
sacred pole. It is a supreme example of the "dynamic energy, poetic presence and sense
of reverence" that characterize Howe's mature style.[54]

The works of few contemporary Sioux artists are as filled with a reverence for Lakota
spiritual traditions as those by Arthur Amiotte. Born in 1942 on the Pine Ridge Sioux
Reservation, Amiotte apprenticed with several Lakota practitioners of the Sun Dance. He

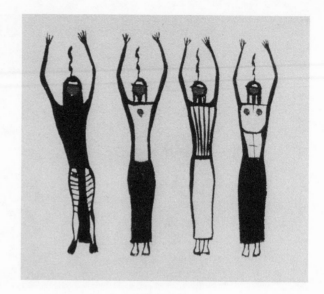

FIGURE 8.6
Arthur Amiotte, *The Sun
Dance*, 1982, acrylic on canvas,
48 in. x 72 in. Courtesy
Arthur Amiotte.

has stated that his understanding of the ceremony is based primarily in these relationships. "[F]or the one who understands it [the Sun Dance]," Amiotte has written, "there is a profound realization in the dance, a sacred ecstacy, a transformation whereby he realizes the wholeness and unity of all things. The spiritual, the temporal, the gross, the profane, the common all come together at one time. Through this the individual transcends all that we know of this life and finally arrives at the real world, the real place."[55]

The Sun Dance painting by Amiotte included with this essay (fig. 8.6) is part of his series *Work from the Shamanic Tradition*, which he completed in the early 1980s. It depicts four dancers (again the sacred number) at a moment of transcendence, lifting their arms in thanks and praise to *Wi*. Amiotte's use of stark, bold lines and few details serves to keep the viewer focused on his central theme: the timeless merging of sacred, profane, community, and self achieved through the path of *Wiwayang Wacipi*, Sun Dance.

CONCLUSION: PRESENTATION, REPRESENTATION, AND *WAKAN*

Responding to complaints by fellow Lakotas that contemporary Sun Dance celebrations had strayed from sacred traditions by incorporating elements of Western, material culture, Arthur Amiotte wrote in 1982, "Today we may hear criticisms of the use of tin buckets, kettles, loudspeakers at the Sun Dance. I think we should realize however," he cautioned, "that Lakota culture has never been static; it has never been monolithic. It always has been undergoing a process of change. In fact, the process of life itself is one of transformation. As cultural beings, what is important to us it that, despite our having taken on many aspects of modern technology, the sacred intent continues to remain the same. That is," he concluded, "the very core of the meaning of sacred Lakota traditions."[56]

Amiotte's recognition of the dynamic, multivalent character of Lakota cultural and spiritual traditions is crucial to understanding the history and character of Sioux Sun Dance painting. In its original form, Sun Dance painting played an essential role of endowing ceremonial equipment and participants with the sacred power, *tonwan*, required for the celebration's performance. As has been described, this consecration was accomplished through the rituals of *yuwakan* that enlivened or transmitted spiritual potency to the painted colors and designs. In prereservation times, Sun Dance painting was exclusively a ceremonial art, serving to present, make manifest, *wakan*.

During the early reservation era, Sioux artists began painting Sun Dance scenes for sale to non-Indian customers. While the first such artists generally utilized customary techniques and aesthetic standards of Lakota representationalism, they also selectively adopted those elements and methods of Western art that they needed to depict their new subject matter and to please their clients. As years passed however, increasing numbers of Sioux artists trained in or were influenced by Euro-American easel painting and adapted the techniques of this foreign tradition to portray scenes of Sioux life, including portrayals of the Sun Dance.

From the beginning, however, Sioux artists intended their depictions of the Sun Dance to be more than mere illustrations. The most successful among these artists, including Short Bull, Oscar Howe, and Arthur Amiotte, have created works that communicate the spiritual power of the ceremony. Though not *wakan owapi*, ceremonial painting, they nevertheless represent the sacred in ways that reveal the depth of feeling and self-sacrifice that lies at the heart of the Sun Dance ceremony. In so doing, these paintings are abiding tributes to the Sioux people and their spirituality.

9

WILLIAM SIDNEY MOUNT AND THE HERMETIC TRADITION IN AMERICAN ART

David Bjelajac

Two years after he painted *Eel Spearing at Setauket* (fig. 9.1) in 1845, the New York genre painter William Sidney Mount (1807–68) wrote a brief note in his diary that implicitly invites a religious interpretation of his humble Long Island scenes: "Man comprehends but one thing at a time. God all things, and is every where."[1] Early in his career, the largely self-taught Mount had imitated the biblical paintings of Benjamin West (1738–1820), the Pennsylvania-born artist, who had served as president of London's Royal Academy of Art from 1792 to 1820.[2] However, Mount, a native Long Islander, never left the United States to study old-master European history paintings, and he soon abandoned dramatic scriptural subjects. As he later wrote in another diary entry from the mid-1840s: "There has been enough written on ideality—and the grand style of Art etc—to divert the artist from the true study of natural objects. For ever after, let me read the volume of nature—a lecture always ready and bound by the Almighty."[3] Since God is everywhere, Mount insisted that "a painter's studio should be everywhere."[4] Furthermore, in order to represent both "high life and low life" truthfully, the artist persistently searched for and experimented with indigenous Long Island pigments. Apparently he believed that these native materials would better enable him to capture the local color, light, and atmosphere of his home environment. Mount's *Eel Spearing at Setauket* represents a young Long Island boy's initiation into nature's dark secrets. In this sublimely silent, translucent picture, the social

FIGURE 9.1 (SEE ALSO PLATE 11)
William Sidney Mount, *Eel Spearing at Setauket*, 1845, oil on canvas,
28½ in. x 36 in. © New York State Historical Association, Cooperstown,
New York, N-395.55. Photo by Richard Walker.

polarities of race, class, and gender seem subsumed by the orderly architecture and cyclical processes of God's creation.

Foreshadowing Mount's intense interest in Spiritualist séances and mediums during the 1850s, *Eel Spearing at Setauket* expressed a hermetic philosophy, which presumed that every object down to the smallest granule of Long Island sand was a divine microcosm corresponding to or mirroring the spirit world.[5] However, as we shall see, the artist's humor and hermetic, democratic tendency to find the divine within the humble unintentionally subverted the traditional orthodoxy supporting a providentially sanctioned racial inequality, thereby guaranteeing that his painting would receive a relatively cool public reception.

Originally entitled *Recollection of Early Days—"Fishing along Shore,"* Mount's *Eel Spearing at Setauket* was painted for George Washington Strong (1783–1855), a wealthy and learned New York lawyer, who desired a picture that nostalgically recalled his boyhood on the north shore of eastern Long Island. The boy in the boat has been identified as Strong's nephew Thomas, who represents his uncle in his youth. The African American woman is Rachel Holland Hart, who had worked as a slave for Strong's father, Judge Selah Strong (1737–1815).[6] St. George's Manor, the Strong's family home, appears on the horizon. Surrounded by a wooden fence and golden fields of farmland, the large white mansion partially emerges from behind a protective stand of trees.

Mount also intended the picture as a warm evocation of his own Setauket youth and as an expression of artistic purpose in learning how to read God's book of nature. In 1847, Mount responded to a letter from the landscape painter and explorer Charles Lanman (1819–95), who was planning to write a book on American fishing. Mount, an expert fisherman, wrote an account of how he learned to fish.

An old Negro by the name of Hector gave me the first lesson in spearing flatfish and eels. Early one morning we were along shore according to appointment, it was calm, and the water was as clear as a mirror, every object perfectly distinct to the depth from one to twelve feet, now and then could be seen an eel darting the sea weed or a flatfish shifting his place and throwing sand over his body for safty [sic]. "Steady there at the stern," said Hector, as he stood on the bow (with his spear held ready) looking into the element with all the philosophy of a Crane, while I would watch his motions, and move the boat according to the direction of his spear. "Slow now, we are coming on the ground," on sandy and gravelly bottoms are found the best fish. "Look out for his eyes," observes Hector, as he hauls in a flatfish, out of his bed of gravel. . . . "Stop the boat," shouts Hector, "shove a little back, more to the left, the sun bothers me, that will do, now young *Master* step this way. I will learn you to see and catch flatfish. There," pointing with his spear, "don't you see those eyes, how they shine like diamonds." I looked for some time and finally assented that I did—"Well, now, don't you see the form of the whole fish (a noble one) as he lies covered lightly in the sand. Very good now," says he, "I will strike it in the head," and away went his iron and the clear bottom was nothing but a cloud of moving sand, caused by the death struggle.[7]

For the future painter, the family servant's fishing instructions constituted an important lesson in perceiving and interpreting nature's changeable and hidden colors. As Mount concluded, "When flatfish are out of their beds it often takes an experienced eye to see them, the body being covered over with brownish or rusty spots resembling the ground or bottom."[8] The color camouflaging challenged human vision, particularly when the fish attempted to "keep out of sight" by moving "along with the shadow of the boat." Mount recalls this boyhood expedition as an almost magical treasure hunt. Hector served as a powerful seer, who instructed his young master to focus upon the fish's eyes, which "shine like diamonds."[9]

Mount's fishing expedition may be interpreted in relation to a more professional type of treasure hunt. As much as possible, Mount attempted to paint his pictures with local Long Island pigments. In 1843, he and his brother Shepard Alonzo Mount (1804–68), a

PLATE 2

Lily Yeh, *Angel Alley*, 1991. From the Village of Arts and
Humanities (begun 1986), North Philadelphia. Photo by
Louis Nelson.

PLATE 3

Jesse Treviño, *Spirit of Healing.* © San Antonio
Express-News. Photo by Robert McLeroy.

John G. Chapman, *Baptism of Pocahontas at Jamestown, Virginia, 1613*, 1836–40, oil on canvas, 144 in. x 216 in., Capitol Rotunda, Washington, D.C. Courtesy Architect of the Capitol.

PLATE 5
Adolph Weinman, east end of North Courtroom frieze,
1931–32. Collection of the Supreme Court of the United
States. Photo by Franz Jantzen.

PLATE 6

Dome of the National Shrine of the Immaculate Conception.
Courtesy Basilica of the National Shrine of the Immaculate
Conception. Photo by James Pipkin.

PLATE 7
West Presbyterian Church, Wilmington, Delaware, 1998,
George Yu Architects. Photo by Gretchen T. Buggeln.

Robert W. Weir, *Taking the Veil*, 1863, oil on canvas, 49½ in. x
39¾ in. Courtesy Yale University Art Gallery, 1900.49.

PLATE 9

Thomas Sully, *Interior of the Capuchin Chapel in the Piazza Barberini*,
1821, oil on canvas, 68½ in. x 50½ in. Copy of François-Marius
Granet's *Choir of the Capuchin Chapel*, ca. 1814. Collection of Mr. and
Mrs. Lawrence Goichman. Courtesy Sotheby's.

PLATE 10

Oscar Howe, *The Sun Dancers*, casein on paper. Collection of
University of South Dakota. © 1983 Adelheid Howe.

PLATE 11

William Sidney Mount, *Eel Spearing at Setauket*, 1845, oil on
canvas, 28½ in. x 36 in. © New York State Historical Association,
Cooperstown, New York, N-395.55. Photo by Richard Walker.

PLATE 13

Jacob K., Girl playing piano, Jewish New Year postcard, postmarked 17
September 1910, 3⅜ in. x 5⅜ in. Hebrew Publishing Company, New York
City. No. 85. Courtesy American Jewish Historical Society, New York, New
York, and Waltham, Massachusetts. AJHS 3333.033. Photo by Edward Dougherty.

לאור   מחושך

Happy New Year   לשנה טובה תכתבו'

PLATE 14

Immigrant steamship, Jewish New Year postcard, 3⅜ in. x 5⅜ in.
Hebrew Publishing Company, New York City. Series 6, no. 36. Courtesy
American Jewish Historical Society, New York, New York, and Waltham,
Massachusetts. AJHS 3333.375. Photo by Edward Dougherty.

PLATE 15
Romare Bearden, *Tidings*, 1973, mixed media collage, 16 in. x 24 in.
Courtesy of Bank of America Corporation.

PLATE 16

"Crossing the Red Sea," from *The Bible Alive*, 1993, facing
page 52, by John D. Clare. © HarperCollins Publishers Ltd.
Reprinted by permission of HarperCollins Publishers, Inc.

fellow painter, searched for native pigments along the high sandy banks bordering Long Island Sound. He later wrote a friend:

> As we strolled along the bank we picked up pieces of *brown, yellow,* and *red.* . . . Shepard struck his hoe a few feet up the bank and we were astonished to see a lot of bright *red* running down the bank and mingling with the sand. It was a rich day for us—we worked with the spirit of gold diggers, and were well paid. The red found in balls, was in tint like India red, and venetian red—some of these sandstone balls contained purple, some yellow, and some red, like orange vermillion. While digging in another part of the bank, about seventy feet above tide water, we dug out a white powder. . . . I have used it in painting. I think *Titian* must have used something like it, in toning the flesh of his pictures.[10]

Without ever leaving the United States, Mount apparently believed that he could learn the secrets of European old-master painting simply by excavating the sandy shores of his native home. Titian (c. 1487/90–1576), the Venetian Renaissance painter, was especially admired by English and American painters for reportedly possessing a secret oil glazing formula that could capture nature's true colors.[11] Like an alchemist who appeared to transmute base metals into gold, Titian had a coveted reputation for refining earthly pigments into glassy, translucent glazes that glowed with the internal light of God's Word.

During the late eighteenth century, members of London's Royal Academy of Art, led by Benjamin West, were duped by a pair of confidence artists who claimed to possess an Italian manuscript revealing the Venetian secret of color.[12] The British caricaturist James Gillray (1756–1815) lampooned West and the other academicians who fell for the fraudulent document (fig. 9.2). Above a crowd of academicians and their apelike protégés, Mary Ann Provis, one of the hoaxers, paints a demonic portrait of Titian, using her secret glazing formula as the concoction boils in a cauldron heated by a vast alchemical furnace. Rising from behind the portrait, a phoenixlike eagle triumphantly clutches the Venetian manuscript amidst a cloud of smoke and flames.

The fraudulent Venetian manuscript was a reminder to subsequent generations of American artists that God's book of nature was an infinitely superior text for learning the craft secrets of color. Providing a parallel model for Mount's early, primitive education in the secrets of color, West's official biography, published in 1817, reported that a "party of Indians" gave the young Pennsylvanian his first lessons in how "to prepare the red and yellow pigments with which they painted their ornaments."[13] John Galt, the biographer, adds that "a Painter who would embody the metaphor of an Artist instructed by Nature, could scarcely imagine any thing more picturesque than the real incident of the Indians instructing West to prepare the prismatic colours."

American Indians did not simply personify the mysteries of nature, they also seemed to communicate a secret wisdom descended from ancient Egypt. As a young painter studying in Rome, West saw an Egyptian obelisk decorated with hieroglyphics and immediately equated this mysterious language of the ancient East with the enigmatic figural drawing of contemporary American Indians.[14]

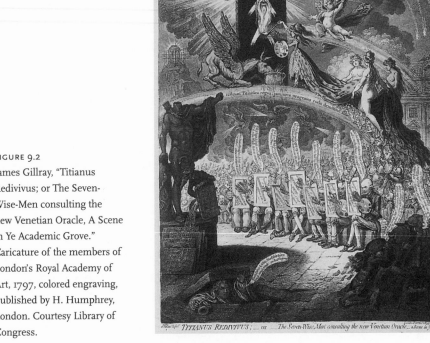

FIGURE 9.2
James Gillray, "Titianus
Redivivus; or The Seven-
Wise-Men consulting the
new Venetian Oracle, A Scene
in Ye Academic Grove."
Caricature of the members of
London's Royal Academy of
Art, 1797, colored engraving,
published by H. Humphrey,
London. Courtesy Library of
Congress.

Even after the French Egyptologist Jean-Francois Champollion (1790–1832) translated
the Rosetta Stone hieroglyphs to prove that they represented arbitrary phonetic signs, antebellum American artists and writers continued to believe that at least some of the signs
were figurative or symbolic representations of Egyptian wisdom, encoding the secrets of
God's creation.[15] Indeed, the American landscape painter Thomas Cole (1801–48), a close
colleague of Mount's, argued that all human languages were essentially visual in origin,
being derived from the mimetic, universal languages of painting and sculpture:

> Sculpture and painting if not the first Arts which man ever exercised are undoubtedly those
> by which the others were seized in their swift flight and bound in enduring symbols to be
> transmitted through the long centuries to man. The primal rudiment of all literature, the
> Alphabet owes its origin to one of the Arts as may be seen in the Hebrew letters, each of
> which was the representation of some object, or animal, whose spoken name commenced
> with it. Indeed, it is impossible that any significant sound could originally have been rep-
> resented without a form significant of some natural object. And thus it may be said that
> all literature originated in the Arts of Design.[16]

Cole therefore concluded that the visual arts imitate "the great Creative power" and through their perfection "the world blooms again in something of its pristine glory."[17]

American artists' elevation of their craft practices to a universal means of religious knowledge drew on the hermetic tradition of ancient wisdom or divine knowledge (*gnosis*), which proposed a vitalistic alternative to mechanistic interpretations of the universe.[18] Closely identified with the occult art of alchemy, the ancient predecessor of modern chemistry, hermetic philosophy encouraged the empirical investigation of nature in the arts and sciences.

During the Renaissance, the Florentine scholar Marsilio Ficino (1433–99) translated into Latin an ancient collection of Hellenistic Egyptian manuscripts attributed to the mythic Egyptian magus Hermes Trismegistus, who supposedly had lived prior to Moses and Plato.[19] Even after a seventeenth-century French skeptic proved that this *Corpus Hermeticum* actually dated from late antiquity, the English natural philosophers Sir Robert Boyle (1627–91), Sir Isaac Newton (1642–1727), and many other men of science continued to believe that the hermetic texts contained a profound understanding of nature's vitalistic processes and of God's original act of creation.[20] Contrary to the Mosaic book of Genesis, which taught that God had created matter out of nothing, the hermetic creation myth proclaimed that the cosmos flowed directly from God's divine substance and endowed humans with the godlike power to perfect nature through the progressive acquisition and use of its hidden wisdom.[21] Founders of London's scientific Royal Society were inspired by the seventeenth-century hermetic myth of a secret Rosicrucian brotherhood dedicated to investigating the book of nature and perfecting all arts and learning.[22] Influenced by hermetic thought, the empirical, natural philosophy of Sir Francis Bacon (1561–1626) encouraged Royal Society founders and later men of science to enlist the expertise of artists and artisans, whose experiments with different raw materials and craft techniques promised to reveal many of nature's secrets.

Blending science and religion, Baconian empiricism captured the imagination of antebellum American Protestants, who sought visible, material proofs for God's presence in the universe.[23] Thus, Benjamin West's failure to discover the Venetian secret of color was lamented in an encyclopedic *Brief Retrospect of the Eighteenth Century* (1803) by the Presbyterian clergyman and Baconian natural philosopher, the Rev. Samuel Miller.[24] Preferring a vitalistic optics that founded the "whole doctrine of colours on chemical principles," Miller rejected Newton's quantification of optics as too mechanistic, too independent of an ever-present, divine creative force.[25]

Membership in Freemasonry shaped Miller's hermetic, Baconian interpretation of nature.[26] Perhaps more than any other social institution, the fraternal order of Freemasonry popularized the image of artists and artisans as hermetic philosophers, chemists, and seekers of nature's hidden wisdom. Originally a guild of professional stonemasons, modern Freemasonry, beginning in eighteenth-century Britain, became a philosophically "speculative" fraternity of middle- and upper-class men, who drew analogies between Masonry's building secrets and the Divine Architect's Masonic principles for shaping the

WASHINGTON'S APRON
PRESENTED BY BROTHER LAFAYETTE
PROPERTY OF THE GRAND LODGE OF PENNSYLVANIA
SESQUI-CENTENNIAL OF
BROTHER GEORGE WASHINGTON'S
INITIATION AS A FREEMASON

FIGURE 9.3
Madame Lafayette, George
Washington's Masonic apron, ca.
1784, embroidered silk. Courtesy
The Masonic Library and Museum
of Pennsylvania, M.1908.13. The
Grand Lodge of Pennsylvania,
Philadelphia.

geometric and luminous order of the universe. Freemasons traced their lineage not only to the construction of Solomon's temple in Jerusalem but also to Hermes Trismegistus, the legendary inventor of all the arts, and even earlier to Adam's prelapsarian knowledge of God's creation.

Following the Revolutionary War, Freemasonry in America became a powerful expression of nation building.[27] George Washington, the nation's leading Freemason, wore a Masonic apron decorated with hieroglyphic emblems symbolizing the three craft degrees of Apprentice, Fellow Craft, and Master Mason (fig. 9.3). The apron itself was a Masonic emblem of innocence and identified its elite owner with the artisanal mysteries of stonemasonry and the divine architecture of nature.

After Washington had toured Long Island in 1790, many towns there soon established Masonic lodges, attracting socially aspiring and affluent men from the area's leading farming and business families.[28] Mount's maternal grandfather, Jonas Hawkins (1752–1817), who had served as a major in the Continental Army, probably had been a Freemason. A farmer and storekeeper, Major Hawkins owned a tavern in Stony Brook, which became the regular meeting place for the Suffolk County Lodge of Freemasons.[29] After the death of his father, who owned a similar establishment at nearby Setauket, Mount and his family moved to live with Grandfather Hawkins. The old Revolutionary War officer's tavern was an especially appropriate site for Masonic lodge meetings because, according to legend, Washington himself had stopped for a visit on his grand tour.

FIGURE 9.4

Thomas Cole, *The Voyage of Life: Youth*, 1842, oil on canvas, 52⅞ in. x 76¾ in.
© Board of Trustees, National Gallery of Art, Washington, D.C., Ailsa Mellon
Bruce Fund, 1971.16.2. (2551) (PA).

Although Mount did not join the Freemasons, he did apprentice in the New York City
workshop of his older brother Henry Smith Mount (1802–41), which specialized in signs
and ornamental paintings. Sign painters and portraitists were frequently commissioned
by Freemasons to decorate Masonic aprons and other objects with the fraternity's mysterious emblems.[30] Thomas Cole, who became a Freemason in 1822, incorporated Masonic-
inspired imagery in many of his landscapes.[31] His allegorical series *The Voyage of Life* appealed to Freemasons, who associated the three craft degrees with the three principal
stages of adult life: youth, manhood, and old age.[32] Apprentice, or first-degree, Freemasons were commonly urged to pursue "useful knowledge" and were warned against fanciful "castle building," a message that Cole visually expressed in *Voyage of Life: Youth*
(fig. 9.4).[33]

In contrast to Cole's foolish youth, who dismisses his guardian angel to pursue a mi-
rage, Mount's young apprentice in *Eel Spearing at Setauket* wisely focuses his gaze on the
colors and elements of earthly life. He carefully listens to his black guide, who possesses
a wisdom traceable to ancient Egypt. According to contemporary Masonic journals, which
were intended for artisans and mechanics as well as fraternity brothers, the descendants

of Noah's son Ham, traditionally identified as black Africans, had been experts in the "hermetical art" of chemistry:

It appears that, soon after the Deluge, the family of *Ham* made great progress in the Art. For the Egyptians, whose family is called Ham in Scripture, and who are said to be the descendants of *Ham*, applied themselves very much to this branch of study, and made many discoveries; such as embalming bodies of the *dead*, making Vases, fabricating a kind of nitre, making common salt, and even *wine;* and it is said, they knew the art of distillation.

It was in Egypt that the famous Hermes Trismegistus lived, who has been regarded by many heathen nations as the inventor of *all* the arts. He is said to be the author of all the learning of the Egyptians, and believed by many to have been Chanaan, son of Ham, or Abraham, or Joseph.[34]

Mount's diaries strongly suggest a similar interest in the hermetic, Egyptian origins of chemistry and painting. In them, he advocates using Egyptian "mummy" as a transparent brown pigment to glaze paintings.[35] Benjamin West, who equated Egyptian and American Indian hieroglyphs, regarded the tarlike pigment mined from communal Egyptian tombs as equivalent or superior to asphaltum as a shading color for flesh tones.[36] But surely Anglo-American artists had a less pragmatic attraction to the dusky pigment. Its painterly transmutation into a transparent glaze was a magical, alchemical act of resurrection from the darkness of the grave. Mingled with Long Island pigments to illuminate humble Long Island subjects, Egyptian mummy could implicitly suggest that the hermetic arts of the East had traveled westward to the New World.

Mount's *Eel Spearing at Setauket* describes a scene of "natural magic," in contrast to the "black magic" depicted in *The Money Diggers* (fig. 9.5) by New York artist John Quidor (1801–81). This earlier painting of Long Island's hermetic lore features a caricatured African American ("Black Fisherman Sam") among a trio of treasure hunters.[37] Like Quidor's satirical painting, Mount's diaries poked fun at the popular mania in antebellum America for seeking buried pirates' treasure with divining rods and other occult devices.[38] More closely allied with the tradition of Baconian science, Mount's hermeticism, as expressed in his painting of youthful apprenticeship, celebrates the ceaseless pursuit of nature's hidden secrets as a means for knowing God's wisdom. Though the artist financially depended upon the New York City art market, he still shared the treasure hunters' fundamental assumption that true material and spiritual values were to be discovered in the fertile soil of the American landscape rather than the unpredictable cycles of an urban capitalist economy.

Perhaps deferring to his patron's particular memories, Mount does not represent Hector, his own boyhood fishing mentor, in *Eel Spearing at Setauket.* Instead, he chose an African American woman, whose racial identity led one New York critic to call her "the amphibious negro-woman," identifying her with the fishing prey or nature's reptilian creatures.[39] While Mount probably would not have disputed this analogy, he conceived the

John Quidor, *The Money Diggers*, 1832, oil on canvas,
16⅝ in. x 21½ in. Courtesy The Brooklyn Museum of Art.
Gift of Mr. and Mrs. Alastair Bradley Martin, 48.171.

black guide as an adept of the air as well as of land and sea. Like Hector, the old woman
was also a "crane," a traditional, emblematic hieroglyph for the virtue of Vigilance, since,
according to iconological texts, fish-eating cranes seem to "stand like centinels," keeping
watch with one clawed leg poised in concentration.[40]

The woman's golden spear rises high into a sunlit sky to mark the apex of a pyramid
formed by the base of the boat and an imaginary diagonal line that extends upward from
the young boy's tensely poised body and golden brown oar. However, the black and white
human figures are also framed by a visually cropped, inverted triangle of water reflections leading from both the oar and the spear and downward into the sand home of eels
and flatfish. Not sharing the vantage point or keen vision of the fisherwoman, we can't
see the hidden prey. But Mount suggests a serpentine presence by painting the watery
reflection of a rope that circles around the bow of the boat like an eel or snake. The prongs
of the forked spear virtually touch this curved form reflected in the water. The reflected
image of the spear creates an additional illusion of a serpentlike creature coiled around
a staff. Indeed, immediately behind the boat, the rippled mirror reflection of the golden

FIGURE 9.6
William Hogarth,
The Painter and His Pug,
1745, oil on canvas, 35 in. x
27½ in. Courtesy Tate
Gallery, London.

land in the background gently curves in a serpentine line across the entire length of the painting.

In his *Analysis of Beauty* (1753), the English painter William Hogarth (1697–1764) argued that the human eye enjoys "winding walks, and serpentine rivers, and all sorts of objects, whose forms . . . are composed principally of what, I call, the *waving* and *serpentine* lines."[41] Hogarth compared the aesthetic pleasure derived from intricate serpentine lines to "the joys of hunting, shooting, fishing, and many other favourite diversions."[42] He argues that just as dogs like the chase more than the actual capture of their prey, so does the human mind love the pursuit of mysteries, riddles, and difficult allegories or symbolic forms. In 1745, Hogarth painted a half-length portrait of himself with his pug or pet dog seated next to a palette on which is drawn the serpentine line of beauty (fig. 9.6). Similarly, in *Eel Spearing at Setauket*, a pet dog alertly replicates the intense gaze of his young master, who rows the boat in pursuit of the serpentine prey. Hogarth, a Freemason, traced the hermetic origins of the serpentine line to ancient Egypt, equating it with the form of an Egyptian pyramid. Both signified a creative, animating "flame of fire."[43]

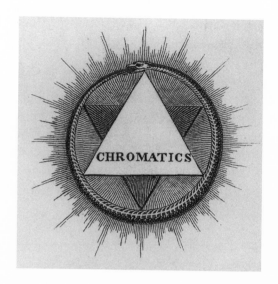

FIGURE 9.7
Title page from George Field,
*Chromatics; Or An Essay on the Analogy
and Harmony of Colors*. London: A. J.
Valpy, 1817. Courtesy Library of the
National Museum of American Art and
National Portrait Gallery, Smithsonian
Institution, Washington, D.C.

Like the serpentine line, the pyramid suggested the endless variety of nature: "There is no object composed of straight lines, that has so much variety, with so few parts, as the pyramid: and it is constantly varying from its base gradually upwards in every situation of the eye, (without giving the idea of sameness, as the eye moves round it). . . ."[44]

Mount's painting seems to expand on Hogarth's observation "that there is scarce an Egyptian, Greek, or Roman deity, but hath a twisted serpent . . . or some symbol winding in this manner to accompany it."[45] The presence of St. George's Manor in the background evokes associations with St. George, a medieval Christian dragon slayer, who personified chivalrous virtue and was the patron saint for England's honorific knights of the Royal Order of the Garter.[46] While the African American woman assumes the pose of St. George, she merely foreshadows the bright future of her young master, George Washington Strong, a "veray parfit gentil knight," as declared by his classmates at Yale College.[47]

St. George's rescue of a virginal woman from the subterranean lair of a serpentine creature was appropriated by hermetic philosophers. They defined alchemy as a spiritual descent into the blackness of death and dissolution followed by an ascent toward resurrected, perfected being. Gold or the luminous "reddening" of refined matter symbolized this consummate state.[48] The reptilian imagery, overlapping, light-dark triangles, and reddish, heated color key of Mount's painting may be interpreted in relation to the alchemical, hermetic color theory of the English pigment manufacturer George Field (1777–1854), whose writings were repeatedly referred to by Mount and other leading antebellum American painters.[49] The title page of an 1817 color treatise by Field features a mysterious hexagram formed by overlapping triangles surrounded by an uroboros, or circular serpent biting its own tail (fig. 9.7).[50] As in *Eel Spearing at Setauket*, the inverted dark triangle, representing the chthonic, earthly realm, is only partially visible. In both the schematic emblem and Mount's naturalistic painting, the dominant, upright triangle symbolizes the supremacy of God's solar light, an analogue for the animating, spiritual light of his divine presence within nature.

Viewed in relation to the hexagram, or six-pointed star, *Eel Spearing at Setauket* also possesses a circular motion that unites upper and lower realms of light and dark. Near the center of the painting, a basket handle in the boat is reflected in the water to suggest in miniature the circular motion of the open composition cropped by the frame below.

The image of a snake biting its tail traditionally signified infinity and the eternal cycles of nature. Alchemical texts associated the circular serpent with liquid mercury, a changeable metal that supposedly facilitated the transmutation of base materials such as lead into more precious substances such as gold. Without a fixed shape, fluid mercury signified the flux of nature. Amphibious like a reptile, quicksilver easily adapted to the elements of earth, water, and air and reached perfection through fire, the fourth element.[51] Vermilion, or red mercuric sulphide, a favorite artists' pigment, resembled gold and signified alchemy's ambition to perfect nature by marrying opposites, liquid mercury and fiery sulfur.[52] Field's hexagram of light and dark triangles also expressed his belief that God ordered the universe through a dialectical balance of opposites and a series of harmonic, triadic relationships. Field arranged pigments by threes: primary (red—yellow—blue); secondary (orange—purple—green); and tertiary (russet—olive—citrine). Each color represented a different tonal synthesis of light and dark principles. Drawing on alchemical tradition, Field regarded red as the most perfect color because it balanced the tension between light and dark, thereby expressing the original harmony of God's creation.[53]

In *Eel Spearing at Setauket*, Mount's palette of mostly reddish or warm russet colors, presumably derived from local, native pigments, more than *represented* the prosperous, idyllic Long Island environment.[54] Critics frequently thought Mount's colors either too hot or too cold. Nevertheless, they virtually all agreed that his compositions were so "characteristic" and "closely painted to nature" that he literally seemed to *present* a particular slice of Long Island's rustic life and landscape.[55] Furthermore, Mount's defenders argued that his choice of humble subjects rather than noble and heroic themes better demonstrated his artistic, magical powers. An artist who could sublime low life into high art, as did the Dutch masters of the seventeenth century, performed a true sorcery or alchemy worthy of the "finger of God."[56]

Frequently called on by bereaved families to paint the portraits of corpses or recently deceased loved ones, Mount had a reputation for resurrecting the dead with the warm "fresh colors of life."[57] Similarly in *Eel Spearing at Setauket*, he bestowed new life on Long Island's past before economic modernization entirely erased the pastoral balance between nature and rural inhabitants. In New York City, critics lamented that the "noisy world" of "modern travel" or "the gigantic engine" of the railroad train was now invading Long Island, destroying its solitude and tranquility. Meanwhile, Mount's silent painting of frozen figures and crystalline light appears to arrest the cyclical flux of nature and human life in a quintessential, perfect moment of time.[58] The russet-brown farmland and its reflection in the water suggest the alchemical relationship between traditional Long Island agriculture and fishing. For farmers, decaying fish fertilized golden crops of apples, corn, and grain.[59]

In 1845, the same year that Mount painted *Eel Spearing at Setauket*, a fellow Democrat, the New York newspaperman John L. O'Sullivan, argued for the annexation of Texas and Oregon. He claimed that the United States possessed a "manifest destiny to overspread and to possess the whole of the continent which Providence has given for us for the development of the great experiment of liberty and federated self-government entrusted to us."[60] The dispute with Great Britain over the territory of Oregon stimulated a consensus among nationalists with opposing political views. They generally agreed that the American and English peoples had a common root in the Anglo-Saxon race, which was chosen by God to civilize the world with the light of divine wisdom.

As a topographical portrait of the Strong family home on St. George's Manor, located in Brookhaven township near the village of Setauket, Mount's painting expressed the racial underpinnings of manifest destiny, the Anglo-Saxon roots of his patron's and his own seventeenth-century ancestors.[61] Having emigrated from the Puritan colony of Massachusetts, the original English residents of Brookhaven had placed themselves under the jurisdiction of Connecticut and its colonial governor John Winthrop Sr. (1606–76).[62] In 1836, the state of Connecticut celebrated the two hundredth anniversary of its founding. That same year, George Washington Strong purchased a new edition of Cotton Mather's celebrated history of New England, *Magnalia Christi Americana* (1702).[63] The Rev. Mather identified Connecticut's first governor as "Hermes Christianus," or the Christian Mercury, a devout Puritan and hermetic philosopher.[64] John Winthrop Jr. attained legendary stature by alchemically roasting ores to produce gold. He also employed his knowledge of alchemy to seek an elixir to cure all diseases.

At Yale College, George Washington Strong was a classmate of Francis Bayard Winthrop (1787–1841). Winthrop's father, Francis Bayard Winthrop Sr. (1754–1817), donated much of John Winthrop Jr.'s vast library of alchemical books to Yale in 1800, during Strong's residence at New Haven.[65] The Strongs and Winthrops developed close family ties through education and marriage and Long Island property interests. They also shared the common religious assumption of the New England and New York elite that hermetic, natural philosophy, or an empirical, Baconian knowledge of God's creation, could prove the truths of Holy Scripture.[66]

George Templeton Strong (1820–75), the son of Mount's patron, disliked *Eel Spearing at Setauket*, although he failed to specify why in his otherwise informative diary.[67] The culturally urbane and socially conservative son belonged to a generation more distant from the family's agrarian roots. He probably was embarrassed by the image of his lawyer-father's youthful apprenticeship to an "amphibious negro-woman." Neither Mount nor the Strongs favored abolishing slavery. Slavery seemed to represent the natural hierarchy of God's creation. Abolitionism, conversely, represented political factionalism that threatened to throw "the whole system" of government into "a state of discord and dissension."[68]

Mount did portray the humanity of African Americans in his art. Nevertheless, his hermetic language of color and light-dark relationships relegated blackness to the bottom or primitive origins of nature's cyclical processes. Darkness represented the chaotic stage of death and dissolution that precedes the stages of renewal or material and spiritual refinement.[69] Viewed in relation to the narrative of Mount's career, the African American woman assumes her proper role, like Hector, as a philosophical crane or a mercurial serpent who instructs the artist in the colorful secrets of nature. When interpreted alternatively as a model for George Washington Strong, future lord of St. George's Manor, the aging African American woman more humorously steps outside her natural role to assume the pose and identity of St. George, a refined Christian knight revered by American Anglo-Saxons and the English monarchy. Mount's comic violation of the divinely ordained social hierarchy implicitly calls attention to the rosy-cheeked young boy as a true American manifestation of St. George. Yet, the painting's crystalline surface and classical geometry seems to freeze this unnatural momentary pose into a permanent state. Influential New York critics and Strong's son apparently were more disturbed than amused by Mount's work. They likely felt uncomfortable with the painting's unintended but implicit message that the book of nature's universal, hieroglyphic language may be arbitrary and open to alternative social and cultural constructions. In the racially charged atmosphere of the mid-1840s, even an old woman wielding a fishing spear could generate a discordant note, casting doubts upon America's providential fulfillment of Eastern, hermetic wisdom.

10

TRANSFORMING IMAGES
New Mexican Santos between Theory and History

Claire Farago

An international market in mass-media religious images precipitated complex local effects in nineteenth-century New Mexico. After midcentury, stylish and affordable prints imported from the eastern United States, Europe, and Mexico were increasingly favored over locally manufactured paintings and sculptures. The technology of lithography itself has been viewed as the primary agent of this vast cultural change.[1] Nineteenth-century New Mexico's visual culture was facilitated by a combination of new print technology, political restructuring of the region (New Mexico became a U.S. territory in 1848), and a better transportation system that in a few decades brought more people and goods to Santa Fe, Albuquerque, and the surrounding region than it had ever known in its long human history. The human dynamics of the situation are, of course, multifaceted. Once the transcontinental railroad system and its local infrastructure were in place around 1880–85, even inhospitable areas like the Hopi mesas received schoolmasters, missionaries, archaeologists, photographers, and tourists, including one adventurous German art historian, as early as 1896.[2]

The following study focuses not on the impersonal power of institutions and vast technologies, however, as important as these are in any social history, but on the recovery of individual human agency from the material record. How did the local populations deal with the sudden infusion of new economic resources? Specifically, did imported, inexpensive lithographs and chromolithographs meet existing needs for domestic religious images? Did the cheap and novel prints instill new consumer desires? Viewed as evidence of the dynamic social function of religious images in local communities, the mass-media images introduced to New Mexico in the nineteenth century take on new significance. It will be argued here that the "organic" process by which these anonymous images acquired local identities, far from erasing the cultural distinctiveness of the region, repeated long-standing patterns of active reception, appropriation, and inflection.

Like several other studies in this volume, this chapter deals with mass-media illustrations in mainstream America, but the region it studies is not predominantly Protestant, like the eastern United States.[3] This is a case study of a region colonized by Spanish Catholics at the turn of the seventeenth century, a large, geographically and culturally heterogeneous area which Pueblo, Athapaskan, and other Native American peoples had settled at least since the thirteenth century. What we now call the American Southwest was invaded by the Spanish in the sixteenth century and settled by (statistically significant numbers of) people of northern European descent only since the second half of the nineteenth century.[4] New Mexico's religious orientation is predominantly Catholic, and its Spanish Catholicism is built over a cultural base that is not part of the Judeo-Christian-Islamic tradition. Moreover, New Mexico's institutional affiliation is different from that of most regions that appear in this collection of essays: New Mexico was part of New Spain until 1821, taken over by U.S. military forces in 1846, and was not yet a state at the turn of the century. In other words, New Mexico was a distinct, heterogeneous cultural entity involved in a lengthy process of being incorporated into the United States during the time that the visual culture discussed in this essay initially circulated among its population.

What difference does this configuration of Catholicism, strong Native American presence, and territorial status make as far as New Mexico's visual culture is concerned? In the United States, mass-mediated visual culture emerged over the course of the nineteenth century, made possible by a combination of mail-order entrepreneurship, a reliable postal system, uniform currency, widespread literacy, and dependable long-distance transportation. Mass-produced publishing enterprises flourished in the United States, thanks to a predictable supply of raw materials and the requisite technology, competitive producers, and capital, writes David Morgan in *Protestants and Pictures*.[5] This so-called market revolution reached New Mexico almost as early as it did the eastern seaboard; that is, the new technology of lithography was already being imported in the 1820s and 1830s, and the most active period of demand, from the 1860s to the early twentieth century, coincides with trends elsewhere.[6] In the territory of New Mexico, however, mass-media visual culture was entirely imported and, therefore, a relatively scarce (though desired and affordable) presence compared to the continent east of the Mississippi River Valley. Firsthand accounts vividly capture the remoteness of New Mexico from the East Coast—in 1860 and later, the trip necessitated months of uncomfortable travel.[7]

In the regional economy of central and northeastern New Mexico, mass culture did not replace local artistic production: their interrelationship is the subject of this chapter.[8] Native American imagery was common to everyone's daily environment and is, therefore, central to any discussion of New Mexico's artistic culture. A similar case can be made for the international circulation of manufactured and handmade goods shipped from central Mexico to the northern frontier of New Spain since the beginning of the seventeenth century.[9] One important effect of considering the role of mass media in the reception of religious images in New Mexico is that it dispels any assumption about the intrinsically "American" emergence of mass culture. Indeed, it dispels any lingering notion that a necessarily direct relationship exists between ethnic identity and artistic expression whatsoever. Some of the same publishing houses that supplied the Protestant market elsewhere supplied New Mexicans with Catholic images of the Virgin, Christ, saints, and other holy figures. Currier, later Currier and Ives of New York, and Kurz, later Kurz and Allison of Chicago, were two of the largest U.S. firms that competed in the New Mexico market, along with the French firm of Turgis, the Swiss firm of Benziger (see for example, fig. 10.1), and many others less well known.[10] Although relatively few of the thousands of paper images that circulated in the Spanish Colonial period and later survive—due to the ephemeral nature of the medium—their existence is documented in wills and inventories. Their appearance can thereby often be reconstructed indirectly through surviving painted and sculpted images that are based on the same compositions and pictorial formulas in widely scattered geographical locations.[11] How else than through the intermediary of prints disseminated internationally do we account for common features, despite disparities in terms of historical, socio-economic, and religious factors, in different geographical areas as widely separated from one another as India, the Philippines, Mexico, and South America, asks Yvonne Lange, one of the only scholars to study the circulation of prints in New Mexico.[12]

From the earliest period, prints in the Spanish colonial world were complex, multinational productions. Several New Mexican subjects have been traced to their Mexican and European print sources.[13] This research demonstrates that New Mexican artists—who worked outside any formal institutional setting as far as we know—exercised considerable independence in adapting compositions and combining motifs from different visual sources.

International patterns of print distribution involving New Mexico were established in the early modern period to serve the Catholic community. This situation is substantially different from the conditions observed elsewhere in this volume by David Morgan and Paul Gutjahr, and by other scholars writing about Protestant print culture in the eastern United States during the same period.[14] Many surviving nineteenth-century religious prints collected in New Mexico are simultaneously labeled in several languages, suggesting that European publishing houses distributed the same image to different ethnic groups. A survey of seventy-two prints in the collection of the Museum of International Folk Art in Santa Fe produced the following statistics indicative of these international distribution practices: of sixty-four prints with printed texts, fifteen were multilingual, usually in Spanish and English, often with a third language, including French, German, Italian, Portuguese, or Latin. Of the images with text in a single language, three were in French, nine

FIGURE 10.1

El Sagrado Corazon de Jesus, Isleta tinsmith, frame, tinwork with painting on glass.
Benzinger Brothers, oleograph of Jesus Christ, ca. 1905, Santa Fe, private collection.
Reproduced from Lane Coulter and Maurice Dixon Jr., *New Mexican Tinwork,*
1840–1940, Albuquerque: University of New Mexico Press, 1990, color plate 13.

FIGURE 10.2

José Maria Apodaca, page advertising chromolithographs of St. Joseph with the
Christ Child and Virgin and Child, Benzinger Brothers trade catalogue, ca. 1890,
frame, tinwork with wallpaper inset panels. International Folk Art Foundation
Collections in the Museum of International Folk Art, a unit of the Museum of
New Mexico, Santa Fe. Photo by Blair Clark.

in German, one in Italian, thirteen in Spanish, nineteen in English, and two in Latin.[15]
Nineteenth- and twentieth-century trade catalogues provide additional evidence of the mediated process between ethnicity and cultural production. Trade catalogues illustrate images in different styles side by side, making it clear that the choice—whether Italo-Byzan-
tine, High Renaissance, Murillo, or some other artistic or cultural identity—was up to
purchasers, whether individual buyers, peddlers, or suppliers to stationers, religious shops,
or popular shrines (fig. 10.2). The clients' links with the parent cultures of these styles
ranged from direct to nonexistent—and the differences are most often indistinguishable
from our historical vantage point.

Despite this anonymity of reception, in its colonial and postcolonial setting, mass-
media prints still acquired distinctive local characteristics. In New Mexico, where woodcuts, engravings, lithographs, and chromolithographs competed with locally produced paintings and sculptures (whose compositions ultimately derived from print sources in many

FIGURE 10.3
Mora Octagonal Workshop.
Nicho on wooden stand, ca.
1850, tin, glass, polychromed
wood. Santa Fe. Private
collection.

cases), local characteristics took the form of elaborately shaped and painted tin frames made of salvaged materials, in which prints were carefully placed in wallpaper surrounds or arranged in recessed boxes with decorations of flowers, corn, and objects reminiscent of offerings conventionally placed at domestic shrines (fig. 10.3).[16] By the 1840s, manufactured goods made in the eastern United States were made available by Yankee traders to upscale Hispanic households in the Santa Fe region.[17] By the 1850s, European and American lithographs were sold locally and a number of tinworking workshops, each with its own distinctive style, were operating in competition with one another.[18]

FIGURE 10.4
Christ with a youth, first communion card, French
chromolithograph, dated 10 June 1909.

Few studies have been published to date on consumerism in Catholic settings.[19] The
following observations, gleaned from regional studies of New Mexican culture focused
on other subjects, is intended to suggest useful avenues for further research. The rapid
emergence of mass-mediated visual culture in New Mexico in the mid–nineteenth century coincided with the efforts of the new American bishop, French-born Jean Lamy, and
his staff of French priests, who began arriving in 1851, shortly after the Mexican-Ameri-
can War of 1846 made New Mexico a U.S. possession. The French Catholic clergy tried
to eliminate the use of locally made religious images, which they considered unworthy
of veneration.[20]

In keeping with these dynamic economic conditions and new institutional pressures,
local adaptations of mass-mediated images show a complex process of reinterpretation at
work. French, Swiss, and German chromolithographs and their American-made imitations
introduced many devotions unfamiliar to the Spanish Catholic audience of New Mexico.[21]
Some of these images may have been aimed at recent immigrant Catholics, but it is likely
that locals associated the new subjects with devotions already familiar to Spanish Catholics
in the region. One case that can be documented, thanks to a handwritten Spanish inscription
on the border of the print, misidentifies an image of Jesus Christ with a youth, as this motif appears in French announcements of First Communion from the second half of the
nineteenth century (fig. 10.4). Its Spanish-speaking New Mexican owner reidentified the
image as a "Señor San José y el Niño Dios" (St. Joseph with Christ Child), even though

FIGURE 10.5
Christ with a youth, chromolithograph, ca. 1895, frame
by Isleta tinsmith, c. 1885–
1920; print inscribed in ink:
"Señor San José y el Niño Dios,"
tinplate, glass, paper illustrated
with floral motifs in ink and
watercolor. Collections of the
Spanish Colonial Arts Society
Inc., on loan to the Museum
of International Folk Art, a unit
of the Museum of New Mexico,
Santa Fe. Photo by Blair Clark.

the "Christ Child" is lacking a halo (fig. 10.5).[22] It is easy to imagine that many other new variants on familiar figures, like the blond and blue-eyed Christ illustration (see fig. 10.1), were also interpreted by New Mexican audiences on the basis of long-standing local expectations and traditions rooted in Spanish Catholicism.[23]

It is difficult to estimate the level of consternation that these new introductions generated, but the existence of linguistic and other cultural barriers must have been considerable. This can be inferred from many examples, such as the framed page of a Benziger Brothers trade catalogue, c. 1890 (already cited; see fig. 10.2), which consists of three images in different styles with inscriptions below listing the prices of the images offered. The inclusion of the price list in English by the frame maker who cut out the page from a trade catalogue and treated the images as objects of religious devotion is more understandable in light of the fact that many imported lithographs and chromolithographs of the period do include real inscriptions, most frequently lines of scripture, in languages other than Spanish.[24] While mass-media technology took artistically sophisticated images to New Mexican worshippers at modest prices, the new paper images also introduced linguistic slippages and other dislocations of meaning.

What can we make of the active reception of mass-media religious images in New Mexico? Mass culture is generally defined as a socio-cultural system that produces and consumes manufactured commodities. Media studies may disagree over the exact moment that mass culture emerged in a given place, but they uniformly insist on its difference from precedents. The present study, while it draws upon the methods and modes of inquiry in media studies, emphasizes continuities that these explanations do not address. Recent studies of mass culture stress how the circulation of supply and demand is driven by resources of time and money to create, satisfy, and renew consumer desire. But what exactly is "consumer desire"? The following discussion of New Mexican material and visual culture is mainly concerned with the ways in which people create symbolically meaningful worlds out of objects in their daily environments. It considers a broader framework for recovering the agency of consumers than most studies of mass-media culture by suggesting that technically innovative forms of religious imagery such as lithography, chromolithography, tinwork, printed wallpaper, and even such industrialized forms of ornamentation as imitation cut lace, blind embossing, and shot silk threads incorporated into the paper, can be viewed successfully as part of a longer cultural continuum. This diachronic perspective, drawn at the intersection of entrepreneurship and religious practice, proceeds from the argument that personalizing a mass-produced religious image is the mid-nineteenth-century equivalent of commissioning a local artist to make a unique version of a conventional religious subject. Both kinds of images are forms of symbolic ordering—"aesthetic construction" in that communication with the supernatural takes place through the selection and placement of material objects. While the materials involved may be commercial givens, or not, they are all manipulated for personal pious use.

From anthropology to media studies to cognitive psychology to linguistic semiotics, groundbreaking research is mapping the ways in which meaning is constructed and the openness of signification maintained through our relationships with the material world of objects. This case study, in foregrounding the basic human activity of making symbolically meaningful worlds out of objects in one's environment, recasts the cycle in which consumer desire operates in a Catholic setting. The aim of the following analysis is to understand the mechanisms of meaning formation. Since recovering the *process* of signification is the goal of interpretation, it matters less that a certain meaning was intended by an individual than it does to understand a certain range of meanings that intended viewers located in that image.

THE EPISTEMOLOGY OF ORNAMENT

From the surviving evidence, at this preliminary stage of research, it is possible to reconstruct an international circulation of prints in competition with locally manufactured paintings and sculptures. What holds true for chromolithographs available in the region since the mid–nineteenth century can be transferred to a consideration of religious art in the era before this advanced print technology was introduced. Prints in tinwork frames, like the painted and sculpted religious images locally manufactured since the late eighteenth century, feature elaborate framing devices, including geometric patterns and other motifs derived from both indigenous artistic traditions and imported materials (such as

Puebla blue-and-white majolica imitations of Chinese Export ceramics) (figs. 10.1, 10.2, 10.3, and 10.5).

What can we make of these formal visual qualities, distinctive of the region for 250 years or more, that span this range of representational technologies? First, it must be acknowledged that the material evidence raises difficult interpretative questions of how a profit-driven private industry and the official attitudes of the institutionalized Catholic Church toward religious images intersected. Most of the scholarly effort to date has been spent on classifying the surviving New Mexican paintings and sculptures by artist, style, and approximate date.[25] These efforts tell us little about the ways in which these images functioned for their audiences. The imagery of the religious art undoubtedly derives from European models, but as studies of colonial art elsewhere have begun to demonstrate, dispossessed cultural traditions often survive by assuming the pictorial language of the dominant culture. Is it possible to recuperate such complex aspects of colonial art in the absence of textual documentation? New Mexico offers a formidable challenge to interpretation because textual sources that have made it possible to document Nahua-Christian relations farther south, for example, are completely lacking.[26] The visual evidence tells us only that the paintings and sculptures produced in the region were technically simplified, made primarily from locally produced materials, by anonymous artists who were relatively untrained in European representational practices.

Recent attempts to understand Latin American colonial art as a dialogue between European and indigenous cultures stress the ability of native artists and audiences to participate actively in the process of cultural assimilation. The most challenging and disputed issue is not what survived nor where, but how and why.[27] To get to these issues in colonial New Mexico, we must acknowledge that its cultural diversity was far more complex than present-day terminology suggests.[28] Although Native Americans resisted outside intrusion since first contact, the groups we recognize today are partly a *product* of colonialism.[29] In the Resettlement period (after 1696, following the Pueblo Revolt of 1680), Pueblo towns coexisted with Hispanic settlements of farmers and artisans in the valley served by the Rio Grande, intimately connected by their physical setting, common enemies (mostly raiding nomadic Amerindians with whom they sometimes traded goods and slaves), and economic codependency.[30] Although segregated by lifestyle and language throughout the eighteenth and during a large part of the nineteenth century, some Native Americans intermarried with the colonial population, and the pueblos supplied Hispanic households with textiles, pottery, baskets, food, and tribute labor.[31] Native American imagery was familiar everywhere, and internationally manufactured luxury goods shipped from central Mexico to the northern frontier of New Spain were not uncommon sights, especially if less expensive Mexican and New Mexican colonial imitations are taken into account.[32] After Mexico's independence from Spain in 1821, trade increased dramatically, ushering in the era of mass consumerism.

It is in these cultural circumstances, two to three centuries after first contact, that the social processes associated with New Mexican Catholic images can be located. Certainly most New Mexican santeros (makers of santos), no matter what their background, never had access to European art at its richest site of activity, that is, in European urban centers and courtly environments. Instead, European and Mexican colonial images, especially religious prints, provided New Mexican artists with models.[33] It would be a drastic oversimplification to assume that the colonists' religious attitudes were identical with those of the institutionalized Church, which did not present a unilateral front in New Mexico or elsewhere in any event.[34] New Mexican artisans and farmers practiced lay forms of Catholicism. Recent ethnographic studies of contemporary practices at community shrines managed by local parishes help us imagine how social groups negotiated with each other in New Mexico's past.[35] The historical record documents a wide range of responses to eighteenth- and nineteenth-century New Mexican santos, from the ecclesiastics who found them so defective that they ordered them destroyed, to early-twentieth-century art collectors whose aesthetic pleasure, though genuine, nonetheless lacks historical and religious understanding.[36]

THE SEMIOTIC OPENNESS OF NEW MEXICAN SACRED ART

Catholic theories of images maintained that the exemplary representation of the saint or other holy figure appeals to the human imagination through the sense of sight.[37] Ornamental borders and settings help set off the sacred image from its surroundings and engage the senses in the service of worship, while the portrait of the saint acts as an intermediary between the human and the divine realms: the likeness of the image, whatever the artist's personal style, is an aid to the beholder in recognizing another order of likeness in the process of coming to knowledge of God. The extent to which secondary embellishment served the clarity and purpose of the depiction was, of course, a continuing matter of great importance since the Catholic Reformation. Not surprisingly, eighteenth- and nineteenth-century descriptions of New Mexican santos, written mostly by ecclesiastics, military personnel, and traders and their spouses, conflate issues of religious decorum and artistic quality judged in terms of European norms. The presence of signifying elements in framing and background areas of the image, peripheral to the figure, could be easily overlooked by these audiences.

University of Chicago social psychologists Mihalyi Csikszentmihalyi and Eugene Rochberg-Halton argue that artifacts in our daily environment secure the continuity of the self over time by maintaining traces of the past in the present and indicating future expectations.[38] The claim, based on empirical research, is remarkable in that it reverses the common assumption that material objects reflect our preexisting identities. Viewed in this context, the geometric patterning and plant motifs unique to New Mexican devotional art— ignored in the historical record and modern scholarship alike—take on new significance. The migration of motifs across cultural traditions provides only a starting point for discussion, however: viewed in isolation, the communicative function of individual motifs is

FIGURE 10.6
Pedro Antonio Fresquís, *St. Damascus*, late eighteenth–early nineteenth century, wood with gesso and water-based paint. Collections of the Spanish Colonial Arts Society Inc., on loan to the Museum of International Folk Art, a unit of the Museum of New Mexico, Santa Fe. Photo by Blair Clark.

difficult to assess. New motifs may be no more than novel representations of familiar subject matter. A St. Damascus (fig. 10.6) attributed to the earliest known New Mexican–born santero, Pédro Antonio Fresquís (1749–1831), offers a more complex case of artistic hybridity.[39] As the only known treatment of the subject in New Mexican art, this saint's image may have been ordered by a patron for specific reasons we cannot reconstruct. There are, however, other, internal clues about the intended audience of this image. This *retablo* incorporates motifs that have multiple cultural origins. It depicts landscape according to a medieval European convention for drawing mountains, which is also a widely used Pueblo

FIGURE 10.7
Vase, eighteenth century, earthenware
with tin glaze, Puebla, Mexico. Museum
of New Mexico Collections in the
Museum of International Folk Art, a
unit of the Museum of New Mexico,
Santa Fe. Photo by Blair Clark.

pictorial device that predates European contact. This "scallop" motif is relevant to the present discussion because it suggests that what we might call "visual homologies" encouraged artists to appropriate and reinterpret the pictorial vocabulary of foreign artistic traditions. The entire image is in fact an assemblage of motifs borrowed from different sources, several of which have multiple identities. The stylized tree on the left is derived from a Puebla majolica imitation of Chinese export ware (fig. 10.7) that was available in New Mexico.[40] The slender plant on the right is probably a young corn stalk, a subject that is depicted in several pre-Hispanic kiva murals, though the naturalistic style of representation here betrays knowledge of European sources.

There are more features to consider at the level of syntax, or the formal organization of the image. The awkward way in which the artist inserted the figure of St. Damascus into a landscape setting poses a quandary for the contemporary viewer. It is probable that Fresquís depended for the figure on a Mexican "statue portrait" engraving such as the commemorative prints in Francisco de Florencia's *Origen de los dos célebres santuarios de la Nueva Galicia*, 1757.[41] In its transformed setting in the Fresquís *retablo*, however, the saint is no longer associated with a specific shrine. Did the artist intend to depict a shrine statue or the real saint in a landscape? From our perspective, it is not possible to decide which reading is "correct." If the former, which particular shrine does the image commemorate? If the latter, why did the artist not disguise the sculptural source of his borrowing when he placed the figure into a landscape setting? Building a composition from available parts in this manner compromises the illusionism of the image, while at the same time introducing new principles of organization and a different (nonspecific, private?) identification.

The semiotic or discursive openness of the Fresquís santo, and of many other New Mexican examples, raises the question of who the intended audience for such obviously and multiply hybrid objects could have been. The following discussion suggests that the unprecedented visual effect of these images, due to the ways in which motifs and stylistic conventions from different pictorial traditions are combined, signals the formation of a new category of spectators within a complex social fabric.

PUEBLO SOURCES: "MANAGING THE INTERSTICES WITH A MEASURE OF CREATIVITY"

The transformative power of the work of art on the beholder is one of the most basic issues with which students of visual culture grapple. It is not enough to imagine that the work of art elicits individually different aesthetic responses.[42] How do we account for the *culturally* determined dispositions of spectators without falling back on discredited assumptions of cultural coherence? Let us suppose, for the sake of argument, that the primary cultural conditioning of some New Mexican santeros and their audiences was Pueblo.[43] Certainly their individual perception would have been very different from viewers familiar primarily with European representational practices. Homi Bhabha's concept of hybridity offers a starting point for discussion. He maintains that the colonial subject introduced slippages, (mis)translations, and excesses of meaning while mimicking the forms of another, unfamiliar culture.[44] A conceptually hybrid work by this definition is one that both imitates and destabilizes authorized forms of representation. In these circumstances, individual understanding varies widely at the collective level.

Néstor García Canclini's analysis of the socio-economic role of artistic production in hybrid cultures enlarges upon this issue of collective identity in a heterogeneous society.[45] His study of contemporary Latin America is concerned with the various ways in which different parts of the social sector seek autonomous goals. The interactions of those who, in Canclini's words, have "no possibility of changing the course [of history]," who manage the "interstices with a measure of creativity and to their own benefit," are the audiences that interest us the most.[46]

For beholders with some knowledge of both European and indigenous cultures, certain homologous motifs, framing devices, and landscape settings such as the plant forms frequently introduced in secondary areas of New Mexican santos, might have functioned as supplements to their orthodox Christian significance. Contemporary ethnographic evidence reinforces this hypothesis. Some contemporary *curanderas*, or lay healers, employ images of saints along with herbal remedies to effect their cures. Since herbal healing practices are established in both European and Native American culture—conjoined in New Mexico by their shared geographical setting—ethnobotanical evidence can help us understand the santo-using populace as a bicultural one that may have used plant imagery in santos to denote the traditional notion of the icon's healing power.[47]

Healing, moreover, has broad connotations in Pueblo culture. The powerful aesthetic presence of the actual New Mexican landscape in which these Christian images originally circulated makes it especially difficult to dismiss prominent references to land as anything but a signifying element. To consider the possible healing significance of the plant forms and landscape references in santos from a Pueblo point of view, we can turn to a much wider range of artistic production because the motifs and organizational principles of indigenous painting in the region of New Mexico and Arizona occupied by the Pueblo and their ancestors transcend media, technology, and function.[48]

FIGURE 10.8

San Buenaventura Church, exterior view, Second Cochiti Mission,
ca. 1910. Courtesy Museum of New Mexico. Photo Carter H.
Harrison, neg. no. 2302.

Images were produced in a Pueblo setting in a variety of media. Pueblo-style decoration even appears on the interior and exterior walls of some mission churches. For example, a late-nineteenth-century photograph of the now destroyed mission church of St. Bonaventure at Cochiti Pueblo documents a painted handprint and snake symbol on the front posts (fig. 10.8). Throughout the Pueblo world, handprints are widely understood as petitions or signatures, and similar images are found at ancient rock-art sites near the church. Snakes are important messengers to the underworld, where all life emerges and all life returns.[49] The choice and placement of such symbols on Catholic churches therefore suggests an attempt to incorporate Pueblo beliefs into a Christian context.[50] The undeniable coexistence of Pueblo and Christian sacred symbols here and elsewhere increases the possibility that visual elements I have been calling "secondary" and "ornamental" in the devotional panels used in homes and community chapels are not just meaningless formal survivals and decorative motifs.

The once-popular notion that santos are Pueblo supernaturals in disguise has been discredited for good reason (and I do not wish to revive the argument here).[51] The material and historical record of cultural exchange points to far more complex acts of assimilation and appropriation. Pueblo acceptance of Christianity is almost universally dismissed by anthropologists as merely a superficial veneer on native beliefs, but judging from the extensive visual record of shared pictorial motifs and stylistic conventions, this may not be accurate. Missionaries in Latin America, even when they acquired linguistic skills, unavoidably transformed Christian concepts into indigenous ideas in the process of translation—because words are inseparable from worldviews. The visual evidence suggests that a similar process of cultural (mis)translation took place through images in New Mexico.

Rather than pursue an argument about religious syncretism that the available records cannot sustain, I accept the artistic hybridity of New Mexican santos as an aspect of their Catholicism, defined in local terms. Pre-Hispanic images of katsinas recall many santos in their formal presentation and function as guiding spirits. Formal similarities include the frontal presentation of costumed figures with attributes, often plants, and spare indications of landscape suggesting planting and harvest. The visual similarities between santos and katsinas are only general, but striking nonetheless. An examination of the changing representations of katsinas over the course of the nineteenth century leaves no doubt that they incorporated European stylistic elements, above all an increasingly naturalistic figure style. The Pueblo peoples themselves, as Frederick Dockstader has argued, may not have been aware of their stylistic appropriations.[52] The question before us now is whether stylistic appropriations also occurred in the opposite direction. It is worth asking what form of Christianity the Pueblo Indians could have initially practiced. As noted earlier, the missionaries failed to learn the native languages. Under these circumstances, the teaching of Christian doctrine must have been exceptionally reductive. The initial language barrier suggests why the New Mexican repertory of religious imagery is almost completely lacking in narrative painting, the requirements of which would have defeated the linguistic skills of most missionaries. After the sobering experience of the Pueblo Revolt in 1680, Franciscans and secular priests who returned to the region encouraged a certain amount of freedom to adapt Catholic ceremonies to local circumstances.[53] For example, sacred Pueblo performances keyed to the agricultural cycle were, in the seventeenth century as they are today, celebrated in many Pueblos in conjunction with saints' days and other events of the Catholic liturgical calendar.[54]

The historical framework of interpretation established thus far needs to be refined in one important respect to avoid perpetuating simplistic ethnic and cultural distinctions: we actually know very little about Christianity within the Pueblos, which remain relatively antagonistic to intrusion. It is doubtful that many santos in museum collections today originated in the context of a Pueblo lifestyle. The genealogical records indicate that by c. 1790, a large segment of the New Mexican population was *mestizo*—at least one-third of its thirty-thousand inhabitants.[55] Beginning in the mid–eighteenth century, shortly before the earliest surviving santos were manufactured in New Mexico, land grants were issued to *genízaros* living in the barrios of Albuquerque and elsewhere and other peoples, mostly of mixed ethnic origins at the bottom of the socio-economic scale, to found villages that could serve the urban centers of Santa Fe, Santa Cruz, and Albuquerque as buffers against nomadic Indian attacks. In the narrow sense, *genízaros* designate Plains Indians sold into slavery in childhood who earned their freedom when they reached adulthood.[56] In actual practice, the term often encompassed many other former Indian slaves and outcasts, including those who left their traditional lifestyles as adults and therefore carried extensive cultural knowledge with them. These settlers soon established themselves as farmers and artisans capable of ascending the socio-economic ladder. In the border zones of predominantly *genízaro* villages like Abiquiu and Tomé, where cultural interaction was intensive and sometimes fatal, people with limited knowledge of any given cultural tradition—but with a demonstrated capacity for negotiating between cultures— united against common danger. Although Catholic devotional images had been produced in what is now New Mexico since the 1630s, and possibly earlier, surviving local artistic production postdates 1696 and was most concentrated during roughly the same period that *genízaro* communities thrived, from about 1780 until about 1860.[57]

There is extensive visual evidence to support the view that artists with some direct knowledge of Amerindian culture were involved in the production of santos. It would be a drastic oversimplification of a complex social network to suggest that all santos originated in marginal communities. Yet it is significant that New Mexican Catholic devotional images typically go beyond the habitual dispositions of their separate cultural precedents by conflating and superimposing different motifs and systems of pictorial organization. The unresolved, ruptured, openly hybrid visual character of many New Mexican santos is strong enough to suggest, independently of other forms of documentation, that authorized meanings derived from institutionally sanctioned Catholicism were altered by bicultural artists to meet local needs.

LOCATING CONSUMER DESIRE

Mass culture, in the form of religious prints and recycled metal and paper decorations, began to replace locally produced santos in the mid–nineteenth century. By the end of the century, local manufacture of paintings had all but ceased.[58] The rapidly emerging fashion for imported, brightly colored prints of religious subjects, depicted by academically trained artists, elaborately framed in regionally crafted materials, were within reach of the most modest households and appealed to upwardly mobile socio-economic aspirations as well. Moreover, these lithographs were encouraged by the institutionalized Catholic Church under Lamy and his successors, who strongly disapproved of regionally manufactured paintings and sculptures and believed them unfit for veneration.[59]

The range of styles evident in the tinwork frames that once held these nineteenth-century prints, although awaiting further study, is analogous to the diversity of painting and sculpture styles by New Mexican santeros. Throughout, the innovativeness of artists in combining visual sources and improvising available materials is a distinctive feature. In this short chapter, there is not the opportunity to present the extensive visual evidence necessary to support the demographic data and historical record. I have tried only to suggest, in a broad-ranging and fundamentally speculative way, that the same conditions that once helped people endure hard lives now encourage us to ponder multiple viewing perspectives. Images of the Virgin, Christ, and saints helped people withstand natural disasters, raiding Indians, land speculators, and illness. Beyond the current challenge to better understand the complex, mediated relationship between ethnic identity and cultural expression, the enduring transformative power of santos lies in the convergence and palimpsesting of distinct artistic traditions. How meaning is formed—how it remains an open-ended process in the mind of the receiver—has been the driving force of the foregoing analysis. With that discussion in mind, let us return to the question posed toward the beginning of this chapter: What is consumer desire?

Catholic images circulating in a predominantly Catholic society appear to present an exception to standing accounts of consumer desire that associate it with disenchantment. Briefly stated, disenchantment is the collapse of the general assumption that independent agents and "spirits" were operative in nature.[60] Consumerism defined in the context of lay Catholicism is not a form of disenchantment, above all, because the worshipper participates in a world where agents or "spirits" *are* considered operative in nature. The religious image, and the prayers and material offerings associated with it, are the visible symbols of human pleas for divine assistance and part of what one expert has called "a complete motivational system."[61] In this context, it matters not whether an image is painted or printed: what matters is its ability to intercede on behalf of the petitioner.

This is not to say that the introduction of mass-produced religious prints did not add to the social fragmentation of New Mexico's population, or that aspects such as imitation, emulation, innovation, manipulation, and status seeking that have been identified with consumerism were not operative forces.[62] Mass consumerism did not control the regional economy of images as it did elsewhere in the United States. The evidence presented here shows that "national" and "regional" systems of cultural production were not separate spheres of activity, but linked by a network of trade that requires further study to be well understood. The fruits of such study will have significant implications for mass consumer theory in general, which has not dealt with this economic "hybridity" as far as I am aware. Moreover, local inflections of mass-media prints were grounded in an understanding of saints and other holy figures as personal patrons, efficacious mediators, as they were elsewhere. The New Mexican reception of Catholic religious prints since the early colonial period suggests the metaphor of "resonance" to convey what happens in-between the poles of completely decontextualized expropriaton and fully informed understanding.[63]

PART 3

RELIGIOUS VISUAL CULTURE AND AMERICAN MODERNITY

11

VISUALIZING GOD'S SILENCE
Oracles, the Enlightenment, and Elihu Vedder's
Questioner of the Sphinx

Leigh E. Schmidt

New Englander William Frederick Pinchbeck, who described himself as "a mechanic and a philosopher," liked a good show. In 1798, he had made decent money displaying a Pig of Knowledge that he had trained to appear to tell time, do arithmetic, and identify concealed cards; he even boasted (in his advertising, it should be noted with a wink) of touring "every principal city in the Union" and exhibiting his Learned Pig "before the President of the United States with unbounded applause." So it was with a mix of professional jealousy and scientific curiosity that Pinchbeck set out in late 1804 to see one of the latest attractions to come to the American circuit of entertainments, "a certain Philosophical Machine lately arrived from France, which engrosses universal attention," the Acoustic Temple (fig. 11.1). The exhibition, its "INEXPLICABLE AURICULAR AND OPTICAL ILLUSION," its principles of construction, its disembodied female voice, its mechanical sophistication with hidden tubes and large trumpets for the transmission of sound, captivated Pinchbeck, so much so that he studied the temple long and hard in preparation for building his own for display in the Washington Museum in Boston.[1]

The "wonderful and incomprehensible exhibition" was sold in part as an occult mystery, with all the forbidden allure of Hermetic magic: "In a temple, representing those where the Egyptians delivered their oracles, is a small altar, and a crystal (as described by Dr. Dee, &c.) for consulting spirits." Pinchbeck was a knowledgeable magician, some of his neighbors thought too knowledgeable for his soul's good (of course, some of these

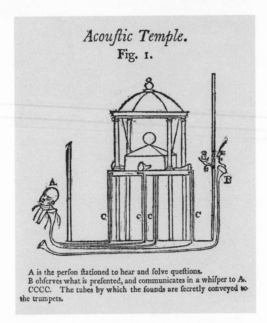

Acouſtic Temple.

Fig. 1.

A is the perſon ſtationed to hear and ſolve queſtions.
B obſerves what is preſented, and communicates in a whiſper to A.
CCCC. The tubes by which the ſounds are ſecretly conveyed to the trumpets.

FIGURE 11.1

"Acoustic Temple," from
William Frederick Pinchbeck,
*The Expositor; Or Many
Mysteries Unravelled.* Boston:
1805, 81. Courtesy American
Antiquarian Society.

same people, Pinchbeck noted rue-
fully, had feared that the Learned
Pig was bewitched and should be
put to death; many had seen a ghost
that haunted the local churchyard;
and still more believed in the devil
and the pacts that magicians struck
with evil spirits). For these folks,
the specter of John Dee, the Elizabethan magus, might give the Acoustic Temple and the
Astonishing Invisible Lady who spoke out of it a magical and even dangerous aura, but
Pinchbeck only scoffed at such gullibility. If anything, it was Dee the mathematician, not
Dee the necromancer, who appealed to him. "Where superstition waves her bloody banners," this would-be Voltaire exhorted, "Philosophy and the arts must hide their heads."[2]

And that is how the Acoustic Temple was really sold—as a performance that evoked
the magical in order to dispel that very enchantment. Certainly Pinchbeck, who wrote
two tracts on this and similar amusements, wanted people to garner that sort of lesson
from the Acoustic Temple, the original as well as his facsimile. Anyone who witnessed
this reproduced Egyptian oracle, he confidently asserted, would "easily conceive how the
Pagan priests by making use of tubes deceived the people, and by thus imposing on their
credulity, induced them to believe that these idols or oracles returned answers to their
questions." The Acoustic Temple beckoned natural philosophers and "amateurs of Science," all those dedicated to the advance of learning and invention, to a performance of
the Enlightenment, a vanquishing of superstition and priestcraft, a spectacle of disenchantment. As one 1805 broadside explaining "this wonderful deception" proclaimed, "Attend, and never after give credit to the improbable tales of Witchcraft and Supernatural
Agency." The amused questioner of this Egyptian oracle would come away satisfied that
oracular voices were illusions and that the ingenious mechanisms of the Enlightenment
exposed them as such.[3]

The Acoustic Temple stood at an important crossroads. It looked back to the early Enlightenment repositioning of the oracles from a Christian narrative of demonic presences,
miraculous silencing, and apocalyptic anticipation into a natural history of superstition

FIGURE 11.2

Elihu Vedder, *Prayer for Death in the Desert*, ca. 1867, oil on canvas, 14 in. x 49½ in. Courtesy Brooklyn Museum of Art. Gift of The American Academy of Arts and Letters, 55.40.

FIGURE 11.3 (SEE ALSO PLATE 12)

Elihu Vedder, *The Questioner of the Sphinx*, 1863, oil on canvas, 36¼ in. x 42¼ in. Courtesy Museum of Fine Arts, Boston. Bequest of Mrs. Martin Brimmer, 06.2430. Reproduced with permission. © 1999 Museum of Fine Arts, Boston. All Rights Reserved.

FIGURE 11.4

Elihu Vedder, *The Questioner of the Sphinx*, 1875, oil on canvas, 11 in. x 12⅘ in. Gift of Mr. and Mrs. Stuart Riley Jr., 1974.330. Courtesy Worcester Art Museum, Worcester, Massachusetts.

and priestly fraud. It also pointed ahead to a quintessentially modern predicament: for a growing number of despairing souls, the world seemed increasingly shorn of all revelatory presences, and the demystified oracles came to stand as mute testimony to the stony silence of the heavens. The American visionary artist Elihu Vedder painted, especially in his early work of the 1860s, that loss of religious vision—or, more precisely, the absence of God's voice (figs. 11.2–4). All too aware of what he could no longer hear, Vedder rendered for the eye the silences of an uncommunicative deity. In this chapter, Vedder's images and musings are set against the larger reimagining of the oracles during the Enlightenment, of which Pinchbeck's museum display was one performative embodiment.

In dwelling on the fate of oracular voices, this chapter also calls attention to the interfaces of visual and auditory cultures—namely, the visualization of demonic utterances, slippery voices, mechanized sounds, and divine silences. The Acoustic Temple, the promotions claimed, was designed "to open the eyes of those who still foster an absurd belief in *ghosts, witches, conjurations, demoniacs,* &c." and to "enable the attentive observer to form a just idea of the artifices" that charlatans have long used to impose on "the *credulous* and *superstitious.*" The eye was expressly used to train the ear, to discipline it against the hearsay of the revelatory. With Vedder's *Questioner of the Sphinx,* too, the visual pictured a lesson about hearing, one that showed how forlorn listening had become once the ear had been formed in these auditory habits of suspicion. These images, spectacles, and performances worked not only on people's eyes then, but on their ears as well. Seeing things needs to be part of a larger history of the senses in which different modes of perception are understood not only to blur into synesthesia, but also to work on one another.[4]

ORACULAR PRESENCES

Dreams, omens, sacrifices, speaking statues, whispering trees, visions, miraculous water, cures, trances, and prophecies—was it any wonder that the pagan oracles demanded notice, whether the offerings of devotees, the fearful denigrations of early Christian apologists, or, subsequently, the scandalized outrage of the *philosophes?* As the bearers of such extraordinary powers, the oracles entered the Christian imagination ambivalently: they were signs of demonic danger, but they were also tests of the power of Christian redemption. For the early church fathers—Origen, Eusebius, Athanasius, Jerome, Augustine, and on down the line—the silencing of the oracles was a hallmark of the signal turning point in the new sacred history, the advent of Christ, the reversal of the devil's thralldom over humanity since the Fall. So, despite their dismissal as idolatrous shams, the oracles proved useful, even compelling, for Christian apologists. They were emblematic of history's fundamental hinge; their swinging closed was the sign of the new opening in God's time; the pagan oracles ironically became part of the very axis of redemption. This mapping of Christian history was long dear to Protestants and Catholics alike. As Jonathan Edwards observed in his *History of the Work of Redemption,* "The famous heathen oracles in their temples where princes and others for many past ages had been wont to inquire and to receive answers with an audible voice from their gods, which were indeed answers from the devil, I say, those oracles were now silenced and struck dumb, and gave no more answers. . . . Thus did the kingdom of Christ prevail against the kingdom of Satan." Well into the eighteenth century, the demonized oracles were revered for the shape they gave to Christian history, for the mapping of a universal narrative of redemptive time.[5]

The Christian history of the oracles was given visual form in the frontispiece to one

FIGURE 11.5
Frontispiece to Jean Baltus,
*Réponse à l'histoire des
oracles, de Mr. de Fontenelle,
de l'Academie Françoise,* 2d
ed. Strasbourg: Doulssecker,
1709. Courtesy Firestone
Library, Princeton
University Library.

defense of that traditional narrative in the early eighteenth century by the French Jesuit
Jean Baltus. The oracles were pictured as alive with demonic presences, dark spirits
seething out of the mouths of statues and seers and also out of the pagan temple in the
background (fig. 11.5). The mouth, marked visually as the orifice of demonic ingress and
exit, strongly suggested the vocality of possession, that the very words these soothsayers
uttered were inspired not by God, but the devil. In turn, it is the light of the cross, held
aloft by a female figure representing the church, that exorcises the evil spirits and silences
(even tramples) their material forms. Given this paradigmatic scene of crushing violence
and religious displacement at the foundations of the Christian narrative, it is no wonder
that the ancient silencing of the oracles often proved in the early modern world a reiter-
able script for colonial and Christian mastery. As one eighteenth-century Jesuit mission-

ary in the East Indies attested, the ancient wonder of divine suppression was still being performed in his confrontations with indigenous oracles; the demons in the heathen idols were falling silent in the face of the same ancient signs—the proclamation of the gospel, the invocation of Christ's name, and the presence of the cross.[6]

Pagan divination proved useful too because some early Christian writers, following prior Jewish appropriations, managed to make a few of the oracles augurs of their own eclipse. The Sibyls were creatively Christianized as gentile prophets of the Messiah, earlier texts interpolated and new ones concocted in order to strengthen the Christian cause against paganism. These reinterpreted and recast Sibylline prophecies, with their hymns to Christ and revelations of Judgment, became widely enough accepted that Augustine numbered the Sibyls among those who belonged to the City of God, and eventually Michelangelo even enshrined them with the Hebrew prophets on the ceiling of the Sistine Chapel. These inspired prophetesses also proved an enduringly rich source for Christian apocalypticism, nurturing centuries of eschatological commentary from Lactantius to Joachim of Fiore. "I will speak the following with my whole person in ecstasy / For I do not know what I say, but God bids me utter each thing." So was the heady opening to one Sibylline book. The "wondrous words" of these urgent prophecies still inspired some eighteenth-century exegetes, who continued to lay them alongside John's book of Revelation to help calculate the events of the millennium, the full circle of God's drama. One English Protestant commentary from 1713, for example, insisted that the Sibyls had actually predicted the Reformation and had offered detailed clues for discerning the millennial import of current political events.[7]

The ancient oracles not only had a living presence in the Christian imagination, but also in occultist traditions. In one of the most alluring passages in the writings ascribed to the Egyptian magus Hermes Trismegistus, a corpus that was crucial to the Renaissance revival of magic, the teacher heralds the gnostic power of the initiated to realize a genuinely oracular statue, "statues living and conscious, filled with the breath of life, and doing many mighty works; statues which have foreknowledge, and predict future events by the drawing of lots, and by prophetic inspiration, and by dreams, and in many other ways."[8] Henry Cornelius Agrippa's *Three Books of Occult Philosophy*, published in translation in London in 1651, offered this gloss on that Hermetic expectation:

No man is ignorant that supercelestiall Angels or spirits may be gained by us through good works, a pure minde, secret prayers, devout humiliation, and the like. . . . Let no man therefore doubt that in like manner . . . the Gods of the world may be raised by us, or at least the minist[e]ring spirits, . . . So we read that the antient Priests made statues, and images, foretelling things to come, and infused into them the spirits of the stars, which were not kept there by constraint in some certain matters, but rejoycing in them, *viz.* as acknowledging such kinds of matter to be suitable to them, they do alwaies, and willingly abide in them, and speak, and do wonderful things by them; no otherwise th[a]n evill spirits are wont to do, when they possess mens bodies.

In Hermetic magic, this was one of the most compelling and controversial aspirations—to bring down the spirits into material form and allow them to speak. Ancient oracles thus lived on in early modern occultism where they were commonly revered as part of the mystic discovery of "the highest secrets of the Divine Essence." On the eve of the Enlightenment, the ancient oracles still throbbed with various presences.[9]

ORACULAR FRAUDS

With their commanding history in antiquity and with their second life in the Christian tradition and Renaissance occultism, the oracles presented a very tempting target for seventeenth- and eighteenth-century philosophers. The assault on the oracles proved, indeed, one of the most prominent opening wedges of learned historicism and skepticism in the early Enlightenment. With all the tales of supernatural signs and voices, these divinatory practices stood as the very embodiment of enthusiasm, superstition, and priestly artifice, a primeval fount of all that was still wrong with religion. Also, because of the hallowed place the oracles had come to hold in Christian renderings of sacred history, they were—as a number of historians of the Enlightenment have shown—a prime location for testing new critical, historical methods, for trying the chronicles of demon possession, miraculous expulsion, and prophetic prediction by the standards of natural history. To explain the oracles through mechanistic means and to rework the way they were remembered would assist the unfolding of the Enlightenment: at minimum, it would perform the necessary work of exposing popular superstition and magical beliefs; for the more radical, it would do even more—it would unhinge the givenness of the Christian narrative of redemptive time.[10]

The modern brief against the oracles was in part a pastiche of repositioned classical, patristic, and Protestant materials, but the argument began to take on its own original form with historical reevaluations of the Sibylline prophecies. Just as seventeenth-century scholarship redated the writings of Hermes Trismegistus and announced their primeval Egyptian pretenses a fraud, so too did the learned go after the primordial attributions of the Sibylline revelations, their supposed anticipations of Jesus and their millennialist prophecies. It was the "common Opinion of the Modern Criticks," one defender lamented in 1715, that "the *Sibylline* Oracles, quoted by the most primitive Christians, were spurious, and forged by some among themselves, a little before the middle of the Second Century; and from such a forged Copy were alledg'd by those Primitive Writers for their Religion." That argument quickly became common intellectual property among learned debunkers. Modern critics, like the Protestant scholar David Blondel, thought that they were doing Christianity a service by cleansing it of these Sibylline counterfeits: that such fraudulent texts had for too long encouraged "the extravagant Imagination of the *Millenaries*," that acceptance of their inspiration validated the enthusiasm of disorderly women, and that, at bottom, truth could not be served by forgery. Disposing of the Sibyls was seen as a judicious historical correction, but this knowledge also served as another

FIGURE 11.6

"Priestly Shams," from Antonius van Dale, *De oraculis veterum ethnicorum dissertationes duæ.* Amsterdam: Boom, 1700. Courtesy Firestone Library, Princeton University Library.

way of delegitimating Christian sectaries. The historical critique proved astonishingly thorough and effective. By the end of the eighteenth century, attempts to vindicate the Sibylline prophecies had collapsed into silence. Few bothered to read these prophecies devotionally after the new scholarship removed them from the realm of religious vision and firmly consigned them to the category of political imposture.[11]

The attack soon widened well beyond the Sibyls to take on all the oracles. The most popular and enduring work in this bombardment was Bernard le Bovier de Fontenelle's *History of the Oracles, and the Cheats of the Pagan Priests,* first published in French in 1686, then translated into English in 1688, and appearing frequently thereafter over the next century and a half. Fontenelle's work was based on the sprawling scholarship of a Dutch Anabaptist physician of Socinian sympathies, Antonius van Dale, whose *De oraculis veterum ethnicorum* (1683) provided the bedrock upon which Fontenelle played. Together van Dale and Fontenelle showed their allegiance to the republic of letters, to the overarching philosophical community committed to the new learning and to the vanquishing of superstition. For those who would defend Christian claims about sacred history and demonic presences, Fontenelle's fashionable book, more than van Dale's expansive tome, stood as one of the wickedest in "this wicked age of free-thinkers, and free-writers," the embodiment of a new demon, "the evil Spirit of *Criticism*." The influence of the revised history on the *philosophes* was decisive, so much so that Voltaire could remark in his entry on the oracles in the *Philosophical Dictionary* that "there is no man of education and respectability who now calls it in question." Its influence was regularly evident in the rhetoric of subsequent deists, several of whom had a presence in the early American republic, including Ethan Allen, Tom Paine, Elihu Palmer, and the cosmopolitan wayfarer John Stewart.[12]

The works of Fontenelle and van Dale provided a new history of the oracles shorn of demons and centered on the frauds of priests, especially the mechanisms by which they deceived the people for their own ends of wealth and power. In imagining all this priestly treachery, engravings served an important role of visualizing and thus exposing these stratagems, a way of making manifest the subterranean passages, the hidden acoustic devices, and the concealed confederates that the *philosophes* imagined littered the ancient temples. Van Dale's treatise contained numerous plates that made apparent the technological sources of all the smoke and mirrors, the secrets of priestly powers, and the tactics of disorientation that led people to think they were seeing or hearing the gods (fig. 11.6). Likewise, in an illustration of Fontenelle's text (fig. 11.7), the focus was placed on the fabrication of revelation, the use of an acoustic tube to make a statue speak in what amounted to the complete naturalization of Hermetic magic. Indeed, in this Enlightenment image, the base of the statue was cut away to let the distanced viewer see the priestly treacheries practiced upon the ear. Though the technological fantasies of Fontenelle and van Dale had precedents in exponents of natural magic like John Baptista della Porta and Athanasius Kircher, their joined history of impostures crucially spurred the imagination of the literati.[13]

Soon this vision of imposture was driving showmen as well. That "Philosophical Machine lately arrived from France," the Acoustic Temple, served, in effect, as a performative materialization of the new history. By the early nineteenth century, the Enlightenment's brief against the oracles had been crystallized in various rational recreations: oracular heads, speaking busts, acoustic temples, invisible ladies, and Delphic figures, all of which built on earlier reimaginings of the oracles, even as they turned the oracles into ever more commonplace amusements. In his celebrated *Letters on Natural Magic* (1832), the eminent natural philosopher David Brewster further popularized such oracular entertainments, imagining in great detail the optic and acoustic deceptions of pagan priests and allowing various stage entertainments to serve as exposés of such deceptively mediated voices. In an image that Brewster borrowed from *Nicholson's Journal of Natural Philosophy*, a woman is hidden in another room, enabled to speak out of an elaborate contrivance through the favored technologies of speaking tubes and speaking trumpets (fig. 11.8). Again the viewer is let in on how the ear is deceived, helping the eye to discipline the ear against such acoustic illusions.[14]

FIGURE 11.7

"Feigned Oracle," from Bernard de Fontenelle, *Oeuvres diverses*. Amsterdam: no publisher, 1742, 1:345. Courtesy Northwestern University Library.

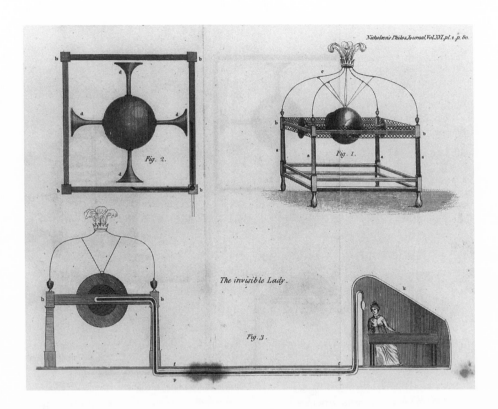

Nicholson's Philos.Journal.Vol.XVI.pl.1.p.80.

Fig. 2.

Fig. 1.

The invisible Lady.

Fig. 3.

FIGURE 11.8

"The Invisible Lady," from *Nicholson's Journal of Natural Philosophy, Chemistry, and the Arts*, 1807, 16, facing page 80. Courtesy Library Company of Philadelphia.

The turning of the supposed fraud of the oracles into an amusing spectacle is worth dwelling on. The learned account of Englishman Edward Daniel Clarke, whose extensive travel narratives (published from 1811 to 1819) proved popular on both sides of the Atlantic, is especially suggestive. Clarke's travels, at once Protestant, genteel, and enlightened, stand as a consummation of the new history of the oracles—its culmination in a leisured touring of antiquities.[15] Where Fontenelle and van Dale had to rely on reinterpreting classical authorities, Clarke was able to appeal to the archaeological record as the spread of colonial empires multiplied the possibilities for both scholarly digging and amateur plunder (Clarke himself was an avid collector of marble statuary). At Telmessus, Clarke visited an "Oracular Cave" where he thought he uncovered a concealed recess in which a soothsayer hid, "so that when persons entered the vault to consult the oracle, a voice, apparently supernatural, might answer where no person was visible." At Argos, he found "one of the most curious *tell-tale* remains yet discovered among the vestiges of Pagan priestcraft: it was nothing less than one of the *Oracular* Shrines of *Argos* alluded to by *Pausanias*, laid open to inspection, like the toy a child has broken in order that he may see the contrivance whereby it was made to speak." From this enlightened angle of vision, the oracles had become little more than mechanical toys, a source of childlike amusement.[16]

The scene that followed, indeed, remade the learned travelers into children at play. Having sighted "a secret subterraneous passage" underneath "the *fictile* superstructure" of the altar, Clarke imagined a priest creeping along this tunnel, and then hiding behind "some colossal statue" and impersonating the voice of the gods before prostrate votaries. Then the fantasies of Enlightenment knowledge turned into performance, into playacting: "We amused ourselves for a few minutes by endeavouring to mimic the sort of solemn farce acted upon these occasions: and as we delivered a mock oracle, *ore rotundo*, from the cavernous throne of the altar, a reverberation, caused by the sides of the rock, afforded a tolerable specimen of the '*will of the Gods,*' as it was formerly made known to the credulous votaries of this now-forgotten shrine." The Enlightenment's script predetermined the lesson that Clarke drew from this scene of archaeological "discovery" and mimetic play. "Surely it will never again become a question among learned men," he (fore)closed the interpretation of this shrine, "whether the answers in them were given by the inspiration of evil spirits, or whether they proceeded from the imposture of priests." Clarke's "modern curiosity" amid these Grecian ruins is revealing mostly for what it could not imagine or hear. His was a performance that enacted absence, a recreation that made emptiness apparent. For Clarke, Enlightenment knowledge of the oracles was experienced as a form of learned play, a fantastic delight in the hollowness of the signs, a personal amusement grounded in a politics of demystified enthusiasm.[17]

ORACULAR SILENCES

Not all took such delight in the reigning modern story about the oracles that the Enlightenment crafted. Imposture, deceit, and credulity, if effective critical weapons against "superstition," were not consoling religious visions. Enlightenment *philosophes* sought a silent and predictable heaven—no ethereal, prophetic, inspired, angelic, demonic, or oracular voices—and for those who inherited these "modern" assumptions, the universe often became a coldly unresponsive place. One Romantic answer was to seek muselike inspiration in art, in poetry, and in painting. The artist might be prophet and seer, might through the imagination recapture the oracular or through creative self-expression become the conduit of the transcendent. Some counter-Enlightenment critics, such as the Platonist Thomas Taylor and the essayist Thomas De Quincey, came to the explicit defense of the ancient oracles against "the spirit of triumphant ridicule" embodied in the work of van Dale and Fontenelle.[18] Still, these highbrow efforts at oracular recovery often proved faint and nostalgic. Romantic visions, whether those of Wordsworth or Carlyle or Emerson, issued frequently in corroborating laments over the disenchantment of the world (a phrase that sociologist Max Weber, after all, borrowed from Romantic sources). Often the result was a sentimentalized picture of irreclaimable faith rather than the successful birth of Emerson's new bards of the Holy Ghost. In lamenting the lost resonance of Michelangelo's Sybils, for example, the nineteenth-century American artist John La Farge suggested that the oracles survived only decoratively—"the poetry, the charm, the intense importance has faded." For centuries the Sibylline verses "ran up and down the discussions of the Church, . . . now we do not even know what is meant by a Sibyl."[19]

The American painter Elihu Vedder offered a dreamscape of that loss. When combined with his autobiographical musings and his verse, a vivid canvas emerges of those oracular silences and longings. As Vedder observed late in life, "It is not for me to pass judgment on Doubt or Doubters, that concerns Philosophers and Theologians; but as a painter I can at least give its portrait with some hope of success, after an intimacy of many years standing." Vedder's religious wandering is one index of the disenchanting powers of the Enlightenment, and the demystified oracles of the Egyptian desert became a powerful way for him to visualize his own hearing loss.[20]

Growing up in Schenectady, New York, in the 1830s and 1840s, Vedder found himself in a world charged with the oracular, the marvelous, and the evangelistic. Raised in a Universalist home, he was spared the "nightmare" of hell, but its "endless torture" still crowded in around him through those who "daily dinned [it] into my companions" and through those who railed against the Universalists for denying those very torments. Damnation and salvation encircled him in portentous combat: revival preachers, evoking macabre scenes of drunken desolation, pleaded with the young boys to sign temperance pledges, and old-time Dutch Calvinists, like one of his grandfathers, held out for the starkness of double predestination and for resignation to that divine decree. Sunday school seemed purgatorial—a place where he propounded questions about God "that have remained unanswered to this day" and where he felt "treated as if I were an imbecile." Relief came (at least once anyway) when another boy found a particularly indelicate Bible verse and pointed it out to the teacher for elucidation.[21]

Greater mysteries than Sunday school and hellfire lurked around him. At one point his father was away on business for a considerable time, and, as the letters home grew ever more despondent, the family's straits seemed severe. So his mother "in her trouble" sought out a fortune-teller, and "now," Vedder wrote, "comes this strange thing":

> The Fortune-Teller told my mother that she had a husband over the water; that she had a letter saying he was coming home; but that a letter would arrive from him in a few days that would change all her plans; this letter would tell her that all was going well with him and that she and her children must go to him. All this came true,—every word of it.
>
> But this was not all. The Fortune-Teller told her that there seemed to be no reason why she should not live to a good old age, except that in a certain year all was very dark; could she get through that year alive, she would live a long time. She gave the year, and in that year my mother died.[22]

Even in his seventies, as he was putting together his digressive memoirs, Vedder remained burdened by this grim diviner, this dead-on voice of fortune.

Other childhood seers haunted him, one especially, his Aunt Eve. "I was growing up and filled with all the modern theories as to our relations with the Infinite, so my aunt seemed to me a being of another age. She never read the Bible, knowing it by heart." But it was not so much her intimacy with the Bible or even her deep conviction of her own sinfulness that lingered. "I have never lost the impression made on me when she related with deep emotion her last Vision," Vedder acknowledged. "She no more doubted the truth of these visions than I doubted the fact of my existence":

> She told me—they always came to her just before dawn. "I was standing in a barn with wonderful beams, and up in the beams it was full of beautiful little angels all singing softly and playing on curious instruments, and they made the sweetest music I ever heard, though I often hear sweet music. And a beautiful angel stood before me and said: 'Eve, I am told to ask you what is the dearest wish of your heart. You may tell me and it will be given to you.' And I answered: 'I want to look on the face of my Saviour.' Slowly a great light grew about me and I knew some one stood before me, and I knew it was the Lord, and I covered my face and did not look. I felt I was unworthy to look on Him, or to speak to Him; and then the light went away and has never come back again."[23]

Eve's evangelical "vision" is as much auditory as visual: It is what she hears that is so striking: the singing, the heavenly instruments, the sweet music, and the angel's voice. She could not bring herself to look upon the face of her Savior or to speak to him. It is no wonder that Vedder remembered this story vividly or that his own spiritual life should feel so flat in comparison.

For Vedder, religion became art, and art a religion. In school he had been exposed for the first time to William Blake, "the mad painter," and Blake's visionary poetry absorbed him throughout his life, though Vedder baldly refused to fashion himself a mystic or a prophet. His remaking of one childhood story from a tale about Christianity to one about the aesthetic is suggestive of this creative translation. Relocated because of his father's business to Cuba, Vedder, with his own thinned-out Protestantism, was there "struck with the gorgeous ceremonials of the Church" and with the legends of the Catholic saints. As a schoolboy, he wanted to build his own shrine:

> Collecting all the tinsel and most gaudy materials I could, and little highly coloured prints of Saints and gods and goddesses, and fashionable beauties, I erected an altar in a large unused room, and fitted it up beautifully with flowers and little candles, and then was ready for business. I formed my congregation by getting together all the little darkies of the neighbourhood, who came willingly enough to see the splendid sight.

Vedder, both artist and colonialist in training, thinks he will teach the "little darkies" how "to worship on bended knee" the gods of his own imagination, but finds resistance instead from one of the boys who refuses to kneel at his altar (perhaps appalled by this presumptuous manipulation of his own sacred materials). With candles aflame, the altar, "a dream of beauty and magnificence," turns into "a general blaze" as a result of this "beast of a boy-Luther" (Vedder, with his own slipping religious identity, tellingly transformed the boy into a defiant Protestant). The aged Vedder mused that with better luck he "might have founded a cult of the beautiful, a religion of Art for Art's sake." "Who knows? I never tried it again," he concluded disingenuously, for much of his life was an effort to make art stand in for a visionary faith that had turned into an empty vacillation—a hollowness that was never satisfyingly filled by his ceaseless appropriations of the other, whether Catholic saints, Egyptian monuments, or Buddhist images.[24]

By the early 1860s, in his midtwenties, Vedder was living meagerly in New York City and painting some of his most enduring works. Several entailed religious themes, and many of them were characterized by fruitless searching and arid silence. In *The Lost Mind* (1864), a distracted woman wanders in the desert, the vacancy of soul mirrored in the barrenness of the landscape. The same wasteland was evoked in *Prayer for Death in the Desert* (1867; fig. 11.2), in which the wanderer makes futile supplication to the parched heavens. The hermit or saint in the desert captivated the young Vedder, but it was not the visions found there but the silences, the lost seekers, the recluses without demonic or angelic visitors:

> We're never told of all those others
> Who fled the world their souls to save,
> Those poor wandering half-crazed brothers
> Who found in the desert but a grave.[25]

If Vedder was an artist of the fantastic and the visionary, he regularly painted against the grain of the mystical and the prophetic. As in *The Dead Alchemist* (1868), Vedder's seekers perished in the midst of seeking before any secrets could be communicated. For Vedder, there was always the foreboding of mystery, as in the fortune-teller's dark prognostications, but there was never the epiphany of Aunt Eve and her evangelical piety.

Vedder's most revealing painting of unrevealing oracles is *The Questioner of the Sphinx* (1863; fig. 11.3), a work that drew on the popular fascination with Egyptian monuments and archaeology—an enchantment embodied in the Egyptian revival, which left its architectural mark across the United States in the first half of the nineteenth century. In the early 1860s, Vedder had to rely on books, prints, and museums for his Orientalist images of Egyptian exoticism (including a major exhibition at the New York Historical Society in 1861). He would later travel to Egypt and become all the more absorbed, like other American and European tourists, by the "grandeur" of the architecture and the "silence" of the desert, "always the Desert—perhaps the best of all."[26]

In the painting, the solitary wayfarer puts his ear to the stony lips of the Sphinx awaiting an oracular answer that does not come. Vedder underlined this unrequited listening by painting a second version of the same scene twelve years later in which the wizened pilgrim has aged considerably—as if he has grown old in God-forsaken waiting (fig. 11.4). As critic James Jackson Jarves interpreted the first version of the painting in 1864, the twilight inquirer confronts "the inscrutable statue, and asks to know the Great Secret of life, but receives no answer except the devouring silence, solitude, and death that encompass him."[27] The Sphinx, like the stilled statue of Memnon, is mute and blank; no "ancient song" is heard from the carved lips, morning or evening. Such silence recalls the treatments of Egyptian monuments in learned commentaries, like that of David Brewster, who relished showing how the Egyptian priests had achieved their jugglery, especially how they had made the colossus of Memnon seem animated. Having solved to his satisfaction the puzzle of Memnon's sounds, Brewster patted himself on the back: "It is curious to observe how the study of nature gradually dispels the consecrated delusions of ages, and reduces to the level of ordinary facts what time had invested with all the characters of the supernatural." Vedder's art reflects that stony demystification; the saints, the prophets, the oracles all seemed dead quiet; such "pious tales" had been torn "to bits," Vedder said, and nature itself offered no pantheistic or Emersonian solace, only scorched wastes. The votary might still kneel at the statue's lips, desirous for a moment of Hermetic magic, but that waiting was no longer freighted with possibility or even the dubious effects of priestly illusion.[28]

His Orientalist imaginings of desolation—half-naked Egyptians kneeling before deanimated stones—allowed Vedder to (melo)dramatize his own prison house interiors of lost Christian faith. At about the time Vedder painted his first version of *The Questioner of the Sphinx*, he was getting by in shabby lodgings in New York City, often living hand-to-mouth between sales of his paintings: "It was in this bare room, kneeling at the window one night, that I made my great prayer—the last. I only asked for guidance, not for anything else, and it was an honest prayer. The only answer was—the brick walls and iron shutters." With self-contradiction he did note praying one more time later in life, but the result was the same. He prayed for "an innocent life; but it was found that the great laws could not be disturbed for such a small matter,—in fact were not disturbed in the least." In the one other passage in his autobiography where he takes up prayer directly the conclusion is equally dark. This time, writing of his brother's anxious devotions, Vedder noted bluntly: "He wanted a direct answer from the Lord—and no answer came." The silent oracles of antiquity were a stark monument for Vedder, a dreamscape not of revelation but of fatalistic silence. *The Questioner of the Sphinx* was not necessarily nostalgia on Vedder's part then—a picture of where the gods once spoke but sadly spoke no more. As in *Prayer for Death in the Desert*, it was not evident to Vedder that God had ever spoken.[29]

Vedder was left with "the Voice of Doubt which is never still" and at least a pair of divided interior voices—his own Dr. Jekyl and Mr. Hyde, he called them. "Truth changes from day to day—and so do I," Vedder wrote in what could stand as an epitaph for the joined modern displacements of God and personal identity. He saw, indeed, in the initial letter of his last name a pictorialization of this very splintering:

> Thus I diverge on either hand.
> An I—divided, cannot stand,
> Falling apart it forms a V—
> Which I much fear resembles me.

Outside this fragmented interior he found only a faint echo of his own whispered longings—an Egyptian desert that he first imagined and then came to know rather wanly as a tourist where "ruined temples" and ancient monuments still sat in forlorn if "poetic" silence, just as he had already dreamed them in his younger days. Other voices he heard turned "the harmonious music of the Spheres" into an unsettling cacophony of shrieks:

> Even while gazing at the starry sky,
> Comes to his ears the agonizing cry
> Of thousands of victims as they die.[30]

Vedder managed to transfigure the loss of the revelatory voice into a Melvillean art, but that aesthetic transformation provided an empty comfort.

In 1896, the Pabst Brewing Company found another oracular use for Vedder's *Questioner of the Sphinx*—as an advertising image in which Vedder's spiritual thirsts became something easily quenched by a commodity of the American marketplace. The appropriation angered the artist not because of the commercial use—he had already lent his talents to manufacturers of comic valentines and Christmas cards—but because the company had not paid him for it (he eventually accepted $250 from Pabst as repayment). That the *Questioner of the Sphinx* became an advertisement was peculiarly fitting: in a world pictured as devoid of the oracular, advertising took on the aura of the vanished gods and made all kinds of new commodities the answering voice to these modern longings. Given Vedder's own grim faith, the consumer culture may actually have arrived on an errand of mercy, providing at least a satisfying diversion. His desert pilgrim might not hear God, but at least he could have a beer.[31]

The visionary piety of Vedder's Aunt Eve or the oracular power of his mother's fortune-teller had lost place to the Baconian inquisition of nature in which the prophetic had been mechanized. The scientific and technological absorption of the oracular had left Vedder's world hushed, but hardly tranquil. Where natural philosophers from Fontenelle to Brewster took the new history of the oracles as a triumph of rationality, Vedder painted it as an absence but discerned few resources for reanimating the world. In the face of the obvious flourishing of religion in American culture, it is sometimes easy to forget the casualties of the Enlightenment. Vedder was among them. He used one of the learned's fondest images of disenchantment—the demystified oracle—as an image not of advancing reason or enlightened amusement but as a picture of a disquieting silence. Vedder may have wanted to imagine (in Orientalist fashion) an alternative dreamscape of sibyls and sphinxes, but his images, memoirs, and poems all testify to an interior life shaped far more by the skeptical strands of the Enlightenment than any counter mythologies, whether evangelical, Romantic, or occultist. For Vedder, all these counter-Enlightenment strategies ultimately proved powerless to breathe presence back into absence.

12

GREETINGS FROM FAITH
Early-Twentieth-Century American Jewish New Year Postcards

Ellen Smith

I have been expending a few of my rare leisure moments in surveying . . .
the latest thing in New Year greeting cards. . . . Certainly, these multi-colored
pasteboard creations, frosted and be-ribboned, run the gamut of emotions.
Some are grave and some are gay, and all seem infected in varying degree with
the emotions that assail one when standing on the threshold of another year.
But happily the merrier cards preponderate.

GABRIEL COSTA, "SOME QUAINT NEW YEAR CARDS"

At the turn of the twentieth century, the traditional form of exchanging Rosh Hashanah [Jewish New Year] greetings underwent a visual, spatial, and social revolution.[1] From simple written greetings and neighborly face-to-face exchanges of good wishes, the form of Rosh Hashanah greetings changed format, and in doing so, partially redrew the social and religious geography of the early-twentieth-century Jewish experience. Jewish New Year postcards, eagerly adopted at the height of the international postcard craze (c. 1895–1920) by Jewish people on both sides of the Atlantic Ocean, gave visual expression to the confusion, disruption, complexity, and promise of Jewish life during the height of emigration within and from Europe (fig. 12.1). Newly emerging groups of people charged with creating, marketing, and dispensing the postcards staged and codified images of the rapidly changing Jewish experience across three continents and two generations of Jewish life. Incorporation of the postcards into the social and religious behavior of early-twentieth-century Jewry changed the roles and voices of women. Postcards made visible the crucial role of consumer culture in defining immigrant American Jewish culture. And for the late-twentieth-century historian, Rosh Hashanah postcards provide a unique insight into the way Jews envisioned themselves.[2]

Unlike postcards produced by commercial firms to sell to mass audiences, Jewish New Year cards were produced internally to the Jewish community. Jewish studio artists and on-site photographers captured Jewish images that were produced by Jewish firms and

FIGURE 12.1 (SEE ALSO PLATE 13)
Jacob K., Girl playing piano, Jewish New Year postcard, postmarked
17 September 1910, 3⅜ in. x 5⅜ in. Hebrew Publishing Company,
New York City. No. 85. Courtesy American Jewish Historical Society,
New York, New York, and Waltham, Massachusetts. AJHS 3333.033.
Photo by Edward Dougherty.

sold through Jewish merchandisers and peddlers to Jewish consumers who exercised careful choices among a vast array of merchandise. Once purchased, choices regarding visual images, messages, and recipients became conscious constructions of Jewish senders, particularly women. These same women often also collected New Year postcards, both ones received and as series of images purchased and sent straight to the album book.

Jewish New Year postcards thus give a unique opportunity to examine images of Jews as they were created, acquired, and distributed by and for the Jewish community itself. No outsiders aimed to capture the "exotic" or the "other" in these images. Rather, the postcards help us gain insight into how the Jewish community saw itself: how it chose to depict its members and its behaviors and further encode itself through the printed labels and written messages integral to the meaning of the cards. The postcards allow us to examine, in visual form, the complex interaction between Jewish religious culture and a broader national American and international culture as it was experienced by Jewish immigrants at the turn of the twentieth century.

The custom of exchanging New Year greetings dates back at least to medieval Germany.[3] Jews believe that during the ten days between the beginning of Rosh Hashanah and Yom Kippur, three books in heaven are opened. "Thoroughly righteous" Jews are inscribed in the Book of Life, the clearly wicked in the Book of Death. The majority of Jews are judged during the intervening ten days, and at the end, are either entered for life or for death in the coming year. Several medieval rabbis urged that Jews should greet fellow Jews during this dangerous time, both in person and in writing, with the phrase, "*L'Shanah Tovah Tikatevu*" ["May you be inscribed for a good year"], a phrase that appears in Rosh Hashanah correspondence and cards to this day.

From Germany the custom of including New Year greetings in correspondence spread throughout western and eastern Europe. By the nineteenth century, greetings were sent personally in letters and in long lists printed in small font in newspapers and periodicals. Families would issue broad New Year greetings to family and friends and sign their names.[4] By the late nineteenth century, the tradition of exchanging New Year greetings was poised to exploit the growing international postcard market.

Modern postcards first developed in Austria at the end of the 1860s and were elaborated in the 1870s, especially in Germany. Originally, addresses appeared on one side of the card, written messages on the other. At the end of the nineteenth century, small images began appearing on the cards, but it was not until 1902 that England first permitted the back of the card to be divided so that both message and address could appear on the same side of the card. With the front now free, the "picture" aspect of the postcards expanded. The earliest American-produced postcards appeared for the 1893 World's Columbian Exposition in Chicago. By 1907, the United States permitted divided backs, and the golden age of postcards entered its maturity.[5]

Postcards could be manufactured relatively quickly. For locally photographed or staged images, production could be completed in two to three weeks. For images captured abroad, production might take four to five weeks, including time to ship the image to the publishing house, print the postcard, and reship the image to distributors and sellers.[6]

Postcard production was highly competitive and quite secretive. Postcard sales, based on sales figures of one-cent stamps, reached 668 million in the United States in 1908, 833 million in Great Britain in 1909, and 398 million in Austria in the same year, just to cite a few examples.[7] With such lucrative markets at stake, producers raced to manufacture the newest and most innovative postcards. Details of images, of production techniques, even formulas for colors, were closely guarded by the manufacturers. One of the difficulties of researching the technical aspects of postcard production is that postcard companies, eager to protect their trade secrets, often did not commit such details to paper lest they fall into competitors' hands. Records of printing and production companies are notoriously thin in many areas of intense interest to historians.

The records of the Jewish production houses share a doubly difficult fate. Of the inventories, records, and archives that may have been kept among the European Jewish production houses, many were destroyed during World War I. What the Great War did not eradicate, World War II did, as Jewish businesses throughout eastern and western Europe were systematically destroyed during the Holocaust. Comprehensive information on types and sales of images, wholesale purchasers, and trends and tastes in the market simply did not survive.

But during the heyday of Jewish postcard production, photographers, producers, and distributors blanketed the world with the product. Before World War I, the major production houses for the international postcard market were in Europe. In Poland, key houses included Verlag Jehudia, Verlag Synaj, Verlag Central, Verlag Lebanon, Alt-naj-land, Omanut, and the production house of S. Resnik. These names often appear on the verso (back, non-image) side of the cards. German production houses are less commonly named, but the phrase "Printed in Germany" (and occasionally "Printed in Saxony") appears on the backs of many cards. That these European-produced cards are stamped on the fronts and backs with English writing indicates both the relatively recent adoption of a universal trademark language and the fact that Europe and North America numbered among the markets for these cards. Cards printed in Poland often contain printing in Polish, German, Russian, and French, suggesting the international breadth of the greeting card market.[8]

With the passage of restrictive trade acts against Germany in 1915 and the entry of the United States into World War I in 1917, already disrupted lines of trade between Germany and America were severed. American publishing houses, active since the 1880s, increased their production to fill North American demand. Among the most important were three New York City publishing firms: Hebrew Publishing Company, founded in 1883; the Williamsburg Art Company; and the Bloch Publishing Company, founded in Cincinnati in 1854 and in New York City in 1901. Most of the surviving postcards in American institutional and private collections today come from one of these three houses.[9]

The taste for exchanging these Jewish New Year cards was enormous. Reflecting on the new custom's explosive popularity, the *American Hebrew* of 18 August 1905 speculated that distance stoked the engines. When European communities were small, the article's author observed, and families and friends lived in proximity to one another, there was little call for greeting cards. "It was then both practical and possible to convey all the personal greetings of the festivals, as well as the social news of the home circle, by word of mouth."[10] But with the breakup of European Jewish communities from the middle of the nineteenth century onward—due primarily to migrations to larger European cities and to Palestine, Canada, and the United States—new forms of communication needed to be found. The colorful, inexpensive New Year postcards filled the vacuum perfectly. Gabriel Costa, writing from London in 1913, observed, "There have been years when the post offices of the Ghetto have exhausted their stocks of halfpenny stamps, so keen has been the demand for postal facilities on New Year's eve."[11]

Postcards were sold in a variety of ways, and the postcards themselves often illustrated the possibilities. Peddlers and pushcart vendors sold postcards from the streets. Storefronts transformed windows into showcases for the colorful and sparkling stock.[12] Jewish retail outlets featured the postcards each fall, as did non-Jewish retailers, including, for example, John Wannamaker's on Tenth Street and Broadway in New York City.[13] Vendors of all types vied to capture the growing market for Jewish New Year greetings.

Jewish New Year postcards were also advertised heavily in Jewish newspapers and periodicals. The ads seem aimed both at individual purchasers and at wholesale buyers. Yiddish and English-language advertisements peppered newspapers, journals, and inventory listings each year in late summer and early fall. A September 1909 "Catalogue of Jewish Books mainly published, imported or controlled by Bloch Publishing Company" (printed with a "Hebrew Almanac for the Year 5670") advertises "New and Novel Jewish Post Cards" on the inside back cover.[14] A September 1910 listing of Bloch Publishing Company inventory, probably from their fall book catalogue, proclaims, "We have prepared a fine selection of Fancy Post Cards, with the New Year Greeting. All orders made up of various designs." The advertisement then goes on to list postcards for purchase in a range of increasingly expensive and fancy options:

Lot

A.	Fancy Post Cards, embossed in colors.	Per doz.	.15
B.	Fancy Post Cards, embossed in gold and colors.	Per doz.	.25
C.	High-grade Post Cards, embossed in colors.	Per doz.	.50
D.	High-grade Post Cards, embossed in plush, gold and colors.	Per doz.	.75

DIRECTIONS FOR ORDERING: When ordering please state HOW MANY Cards are wanted, and we will make a careful selection. DO NOT ASK FOR SAMPLES.[15]

Postcards were also produced and marketed as collectors' series, with new issues being released every year.

Not all postcards created by Jewish people, or for a Jewish market, were New Year postcards. Postcards produced with Jewish content covered the full range of images found throughout the international postcard market. These specifically Jewish cards included scenes of cities in Europe, Palestine, and America, with special focus on their Jewish quarters, cemeteries, and buildings. Postcards depicted Jewish holidays, ceremonies, and scenes from daily lives. The cards offered images of traditional and modern Jewish men, women, and children; of rabbis and Jewish celebrities. Holy sites occupied an important niche, along with new Jewish settlements emerging around the world. Jewish people in non-Western communities, looking very similar to the series of "exotic" people postcards popular throughout the entire international postcard market, were offered by most publishing companies.[16] Postcards reproduced paintings and graphic works by Jewish artists. Others celebrated modern inventions, contemporary costumes and customs, and the technological promises of the modern world.

All of these wonders of the world were for sale in a three-by-five-inch format, singly or in series. The same images appeared in several versions. Depending on one's budget, a postcard could be purchased in sepia, in black, blue, or white, or in full color. Each type came in a matte or glossy finish. Postcards could be embellished further with embossing, ribbons, glitter, or moving parts.[17] And among this tantalizing array of postcard images and styles, Jewish New Year postcards decisively dominated the market.[18]

Though not all postcards were Jewish New Year postcards, any image could be and often was made into one. Jewish New Year postcards often incorporated symbols of other holidays, both Jewish and American. Recognizing the rising market for *L'Shanah Tovah* cards at the turn of the twentieth century, non-Jewish publishing houses recycled surplus cards toward a Jewish audience, probably selling their overstock to the Jewish production companies in late summer. One card in the collection of the American Jewish Historical Society (AJHS) shows a dove carrying an envelope: a plausible image of Jewish New Year cards emphasizing the literal delivery of a message.[19] But the sealing wax on the card displays a four-leaf clover, likely left over from St. Patrick's Day. The same card appears with "*Shanah Tovah*" stamped on it, but with the sealing wax showing a heart for Valentine's Day, another with a lily for Easter.[20] Even more obviously, a valentine-style postcard, printed in Germany and aimed for a European market, becomes a Jewish New Year card with a few choice phrases printed onto it. The Fourth of July and Easter number among other secular and Christian holidays whose postcards were recycled into Jewish New Year cards.[21]

By overstamping a card with "*L'Shanah Tovah Tikatevu*," and mistranslating the greeting as "New Year Greetings" or some other phrase redolent of secular rather than Jewish New Year sentiments, any card became suitable for the Jewish market. But more to the point, the Jewish market could accommodate such reinterpreted messages and delighted in doing so. No subject or image was too foreign, too threatening, too competitive. Images were coopted, visually retranslated with the addition of a holy tongue, and embraced into the social and religious behaviors of Jewish people.

Father Time, a symbol of the secular New Year, is also appropriated into Jewish New Year cards. A studio-posed New Year card from the late teens or early 1920s (fig. 12.2) ties traditional Jewish themes of multigenerational gathering and the old blessing the young with non–Jewish American imagery.[22] But the translation of Father Time into Jewish Time favors the Jewish. Despite the common American props of hourglass and sickle, this Father Time looks more like a *rebbe* [rabbi or teacher] or an *abba* [family father] with his long beard, white robe traditional to Rosh Hashanah, and headcovering that most Jewish viewers would recognize as a yarmulke. The Yiddish poem on the left-hand side of the card refers to luck and good fortune, capturing more the flavor of Eastern European Jewish greetings than a Christian grim reaper softened for commercial Western audiences of the twentieth century.[23]

So paramount was Rosh Hashanah—the pinnacle of all Jewish holidays—that card producers felt comfortable appropriating any and all holiday images and overstamping them in Hebrew with "*L'Shanah Tovah*" (fig. 12.3). The system allowed publishers to use up their overstock and to issue series of cards on Jewish life that were marketed as Rosh Hashanah postcards. The system also suggests that at least until the end of World War I, for Jewish-American consumers, Rosh Hashanah overstamped all other celebrations. The

FIGURE 12.2

Father Time, Jewish New Year postcard, Verlag Central. Printed
in Germany. 3½ in. x 5⅜ in. Courtesy American Jewish Historical
Society, New York, New York, and Waltham, Massachusetts.
AJHS 3333.105. Photo by Edward Dougherty.

cards speak simultaneously of the persistence of traditional religious modes of worship
and emphasis, and of the immigrants' increasing ability to adapt the new world of America to their own.

But as Jewish New Year cards could include everything, they were also about nothing.
With the exception of photographic scenes of Jewish sites, most Jewish New Year postcards were studio staged: imagined, fictive, and fantasy scenarios of Jewish life in Europe
and the United States. The staging was highly manipulated and culturally self-conscious
(fig. 12.4).[24] Scenes were staged to appeal to a variety of perspectives and tastes. A series
of postcards depicting a young girl dressed as an angel, for example, portrays her holding up scales. In one version, a thoroughly modern, post–World War I woman looks up
as the scales tip toward a heart and away from a pile of gold. Love, the card assures, is
worth more than money. Another card shows the same scene with a modern man looking on. But a third card in the series features an "orthodox" man and woman looking on.
Not love, but a baby, weighs in at greater value. A message of children, fertility, and family are targeted for more traditional tastes. The worth of modern, romantic love's value
can also be purchased for the same penny.[25]

The "nothingness" of these postcards goes to the core of their meaning. The scenes

and memories they may evoke are tied to nonplaces: fictive, created, manipulated stage sets with moveable characters and changeable messages. The holidays, families, and religious behaviors depicted are decisively separated from physical places where they actually may have been taking place. Memory is tapping into something physically nonexistent. Memory in these cards thus becomes less about nostalgia—which locates the present in the past—than about using the familiar as an element in the building of new lives. As overt visual manipulations, the cards recognize that the viewer, likely a recent immigrant or part of a family that has been disrupted by immigration, is, like the producers of the cards, in the process of structuring new places and spaces of meaning. The cards in this sense are not visual tricks, but reinforce the ability—even, perhaps, the right—of the viewers to construct new realities, new places of meaning, of their own.

If the postcard images encompassed both everything and nothing, they also encompassed the viewer. Unlike many postcards on the market, the Jewish New Year postcards were almost invariably staged to include the viewer in the scene. The great panoramic postcard shots taken from a distance were often photographed from above or below eye level to exaggerate size and scale and often did not include people at all.[26] Jewish New Year postcards staged more human-scaled scenes and almost always at the eye level of the viewer. Virtually every studio-produced card is posed so that the viewer seems to be on the same platform as the actors in the cards. Images were organized so there was usually an opening in the front of the scene: a place at the table for the viewer or room to stand beside those gathered. Unlike other posed shots of people where the subject stares the viewer back directly in the face and blocks access to the space, the characters in the New Year cards most commonly are looking at one another or the activity in which they are participating. The viewer thus slides into the scene as just another participant and as one who belongs (see, for example, fig. 12.3). The viewer is the additional visitor at the table, the additional member of the crowd. An individual holding the card is not merely looking, but participating and belonging. The cards thus universalize access into a single Jewish world, uniting human and fictive characters, senders and recipients. Everyone is part of the scene; everyone belongs. The cards, by staging an eye-level, open-front setup and welcoming the viewer in directly, conveyed a clear message of belonging and intimacy to the users, uniting the hundreds or thousands of people who may have sent or received them. In their visual structure, the cards reinforced the human, communal aspects of the holiday and the need to reassert—and to create through this new form of greeting—the lines of community that now needed to include the far-flung places of disrupted and re-forming Jewish life.

Beyond the personal intimacy and expanded communal bounds the cards created, the cards delivered another important message about the contemporary Jewish community: the look of the people themselves. Between the 1880s and the 1930s—the period of the development and highest popularity of these Jewish New Year cards—political anti-semitism in Europe was elaborated and codified. Visual typologies and taxonomies of difference were set down in the nineteenth century and informed modern antisemitism, which defined for the first time the Jewish people as a racial type. Such characterization of Jews as a people with distinct physical attributes influenced politics, science, and social policies of the decades.[27] How to allow Jews to move from restricted residential areas, schools, and occupations into the mainstream of European civic and political life occupied national European debates on the meaning of "nation" and the role Jews could play in it for three generations. Could a minority population with distinct language, costume, and religious behaviors meld into the main body of the new nation-states? And if Jews were no longer immediately distinguished by their clothing, their speech, their places of work, or homes, how would they be recognized by the society at large?

Sander Gilman, among others, argues that the creation of a visual antisemitism—the invention of a set of physical traits ascribed specifically to Jews—was a conscious and deliberate act of political and social invention to relabel Jews once their traditional defining physical attributes had been removed through political and legal emancipation.[28] The characteristics of physical antisemitism were quite specific. Jews were portrayed either as too fat or too skinny: in either case, people who as a generalized racial type inhabited visually abnormal bodies. The scale of their frames also hinted either at extreme poverty or overindulgent wealth: in either case reflecting a reputed lack of civilized moderation or ability to maintain even a modicum of stable, middle-class life. Men were additionally often characterized with bulging, hooded eyes; large, hooked noses; fleshy oversized lips; large jutting ears; knobby and knocked knees; and flat, pigeon-toed feet. Their bodies rendered them grotesque and unfit for the valued callings of the modern nation-state, including work on the land and service in the military. In an era when social, scientific, and political theory converged to indicate that the highest civilization was a series of progressive improvements, the physical type ascribed to male Jews indicated that their fitness and genetic tendencies were on a downward slide, opposite the rising and "higher" racial types. To drive the point home further, syphilis was often ascribed to Jewish men: one of the era's most dreaded and destructive illnesses was deemed endemic to a people. Ugly and degenerating body types, riddled with a wasting, degenerative disease easily passed on through dangerous and illicit sex into the healthy population: Jews as a type, so the antisemitic argument went, were naturally devolving toward extinction, and the general population's dealing with them could lead to their own death.[29]

Jewish women fared no better. They were typed in the same terms as men: overweight or underfed, with overlarge ears, eyes, noses, and mouths.[30] But Jewish women were alternately characterized as beautiful and exotic; as buxom and seductive; as creamy-skinned or dark beauties.[31] Here, too, they were dangerous. Non-Jewish men, drawn by seductive powers too difficult to refuse, broke up their own families and by consorting with Jewish women, so the polemic went, would likely catch syphilis or other venereal diseases, infecting themselves and their entire community. Beautiful or ugly, Jewish men and women were dangerous visual dynamite and physical dealings with them could destroy the outside culture.

Visual representation of Jews by the non-Jewish community often followed these physical assumptions. Outside of Jewish production, postcards of Jews from "exotic" regions paralleled displays of other "exotic" peoples, stressing the primitive and "dirty" qualities of the men and the dangerous erotic and seductive qualities of the women. In these postcards, viewers, rather than being welcomed into the scene as participants, occupied a different position. They stared at or stared down: the interaction between subject and viewer was confrontational, with the balance of power contested.[32] Photographic postcards of Jews produced for a general audience also often stressed the primitive qualities under which Jews of the time lived: from hovels in North Africa and Palestine, to the daylight madness of pushcarts and impoverished crowds on Hester Street in New York City. Such cards kept the viewer at a safe distance and visually contrasted sharply with the world in which the presumed viewer lived. Such cards were rarely overstamped as Jewish New Year postcards.

New Year postcards created by Jews and for a Jewish audience "image" Jews in radically different terms. The faces on the cards, whether staged, drawn, or photographed, rarely conveyed any of the physical stereotypes ascribed to Jews by the antisemitic tracts. If there is a racial "type" conveyed in these postcards, the type in no way bears the traits described above. Very few postcards in the AJHS collection present Jews with prominently hooked noses. Most other postcards present men and women and children with faces that would be indistinguishable in a crowd in any part of Europe or America.[33] This absence of the most overt of ascribed Jewish physical traits in the cards is striking. Even when the costumes, the social and religious activities, and the languages portrayed in the cards are foreign to the larger society, the physical look of the people themselves is not. Jewish people, these cards visually reinforce, look like everyone else, and so visually belong to, and fit into, their new environments.[34]

This message of "normalcy" was likely quite reassuring to the cards' consumers. Buyers, senders, and recipients of Jewish New Year postcards, based on the locations of the sellers and the addresses and postmarks on the surviving cards that were actually written on and sent, seem to have been immigrants and their children still living in the first and second neighborhoods of immigrant settlement. These locations include New York City, but also small towns where "Jewish streets" might mean merely one or two blocks.[35] In a strange new country, where the language, customs, and people were confusing and difficult to decode, the first message immigrants received from the cards was that they belonged.

The subject of many of the cards further attempted to reinforce the sense of belonging. Several of the cards deal with the immigration experience itself and leave no room for ambiguity. In some cards, immigration to America or Palestine was the right move. One card of the genre shows a steamship heading to Palestine, and the extensive Yiddish message stamped across it relates the need and advantages for the move.[36] Cards of the second decade of the 1900s present Zionist messages in a variety of forms.[37] Even more explicit is the rare postcard illustrated in figure 12.5. A steamship moves from the right of the card to the left, from Europe to America, as the background moves from brown-

לאור   מחושך

Happy New Year   שנה טובה תכתבו

FIGURE 12.5 (SEE ALSO PLATE 14)
Immigrant steamship, Jewish New Year postcard, 3⅛ in. x 5⅜ in.
Hebrew Publishing Company, New York City. Series 6, no. 36. Courtesy
American Jewish Historical Society, New York, New York, and Waltham,
Massachusetts. AJHS 3333.375. Photo by Edward Dougherty.

ish gray and cloudy to the clear bright sky on the American side. Lest the viewer missed
the point, the double-headed eagle emblem of czarist Russia hovers above the dark side
of the card, while a strong, beckoning American eagle faces the ship and hovers above
the light. Four doves of peace fly above the steamer toward the eagle. The few printed
words tie the visual to the textual, and deepen and sacralize the message. Where the image is political, the text is biblical. Carefully chosen Hebrew words from Leviticus proclaim: "The Lord has taken us *from darkness to great light.*"[38]

Other cards celebrate the right choice of America through celebration of its wonders.
A large portion of the surviving cards feature the material and technological advantages
America offers, particularly its varied and accessible modes of transportation and communication: cars, planes, trains, bicycles, boats, telephones, and radios. These modern
inventions were celebrated as desirable advantages of the contemporary world and also
for their ability to keep loved ones close (fig. 12.6).[39] But immigrants can also fit into their
new nation without necessarily adopting all of its new ways. A postcard (fig. 12.7) portrays the *Tashlikh* ceremony, a prayer service performed on the first day of Rosh Hashanah,
when Jews gather beside fresh running water and symbolically cast their sins into the

FIGURE 12.6 (ABOVE)
People in automobile, Jewish New Year postcard, Williamsburg Post Card Company, New York City. Printed in Germany. 3⅝ in. x 5½ in. Courtesy American Jewish Historical Society, New York, New York, and Waltham, Massachusetts. AJHS 3333.339b. Photo by Edward Dougherty.

FIGURE 12.7 (RIGHT)
Tashlikh service near Brooklyn Bridge, Jewish New Year postcard, Williamsburg Post Card Company, New York City. Printed in Germany. 5½ in. x 3⅝ in. Courtesy American Jewish Historical Society, New York, New York, and Waltham, Massachusetts. AJHS 3333.302a. Photo by Edward Dougherty.

water. Here, the ceremony is conducted beside the East River with the Brooklyn Bridge behind it. Three immigrant generations, cleanly dressed and well fed, worship in harmony and at seeming peace. The setting by the East River is significant religiously, but also important socially and experientially. Many of New York City's Jewish immigrants would have sailed past the East River upon their arrival in America, and the Brooklyn Bridge itself connected two areas near intensive Jewish settlement in New York: Brooklyn and the Lower East Side of Manhattan. Once again, the card conveys, Jews had landed on the correct side of the water, in a place they belong socially, religiously, and physically. Freedom, home, and faith merged in the context of the most sacred holiday within the Jewish year.[40]

The cards registered many other aspects of the immigrants' religious and daily activities. Street scenes, travels to and from synagogues, worship within synagogues, religious celebrations in the home, family meals, families socializing around dining room tables, and many other images, blur lines between the sacred and secular. The cards portrayed virtually every aspect of the immigrants' lived experiences and by portraying those experiences as Rosh Hashanah cards, located them in a sacred, religious context. The cards smoothed over the difficulties of immigrant life, and envisioned a sense of calm and belonging. This visual imposition of order and balance onto scenes that may have been anything but, not only served to reassure, but also provided a promising glimpse of the future: a topic very much on the minds of Jewish people during the ten days of the Jewish New Year. The cards thus reinforced hope in the future in a visual language appropriate to the users' daily lives and in a sacred language appropriate to the awesome days of the Jewish New Year. In these cards, faith, future, and daily life were tightly bound.

Collectors with whom I spoke often debated whether these cards also created pleasant scenes of religious life to reassure family in Europe that traditional life continued well in America.[41] My own reading is that these cards are less about reassurance to family in Europe than they are about choices one could make in America. The range of images is so vast, that depending on the intended receiver, one could send romantic cards, humorous cards, scenes of religious life, or scenes of secular life. Taken as a whole, the series of images produced each year embraced the full gamut of experiences, homogenizing them and placing all those experiences on the same level. Each was valid; each could be rationalized and made calm and beautiful; and each card might depict one of the many overlapping aspects of an individual's life. If there was confusion and conflict and tension in the daily lives of the immigrants, the cards suggested that all might coexist in a neatly ordered numbered series of images for that year. As a consumer of the cards, one could choose images reassuring to the recipient, but also reassuring to oneself. The cards are thus less about tradition or the past than about ordering a disordered universe. Such order could be created by both the cards' producers and the cards' consumers.

Much has been written in recent years of the relationship between the Jewish immigrant experience and consumerism. Andrew Heinze and Jenna Weissman Joselit in particular argue that American Jews' role as consumers was decisive to their adjustment to

America and the creation of their identity as Americans: that their self-styled entrance into American culture was often facilitated through material goods as much as through hard work, self-help, and education.[42] A studio-posed postcard of a young girl playing the piano for her grandparents (fig. 12.1) declares that such consumerism and religious life could coexist and strengthen one another. The girl is a well-dressed Edwardian young lady; her grandparents, clearly of an older world, are nonetheless well clad. Their costumes, combined with the finely appointed parlor furniture and the piano, capture the three areas of consumer goods most often adopted by immigrant Jewish families (often on credit) as the first and visible signs not so much of their success, as of their belonging. Among all the immigrant groups, Jews came to America with the firm intention to stay, not to earn money and return after several years to a prior homeland. The intention of Jews to stay was key to their investment in consumer and durable goods as it was a symbol of their desire to fit in and to show their successes. But the card goes further. This was not just any parlor in America, for the piece the child plays for her grandparents is *Kol Nidre*, the opening prayer of the Yom Kippur service, chanted by the *hazan* [cantor] three times. It is among the most solemn prayers uttered in the course of the Jewish year. The curtain lets us know that we are viewing a staged scene, but the "sound" of the card would have resonated to the most real depths of its recipients, and the stamped New Year greeting would trump the staginess of the image with the higher reality of the holiday and the Kol Nidre service. There is no dissembling about the fiction of the scene, but neither is there any dissembling about its highest meaning or its truth. The parlor constructed by consumer sensibilities nurtures human activity and interaction revolving around faith. In America, each can strengthen the other.

The choosing of consumer goods, including the New Year postcards, was most often done by women. Even in the absence of companies' sales and marketing records, most of the cards that portray the selling of Jewish New Year cards, and most of the advertisements in the newspapers of the day, depict the sales being made to women. Displays of cards in windows catered to wives, mothers, and daughters doing the marketing. Of the cards in the AJHS collection that were actually sent, at least 70 percent appear to have been written and sent by women.[43] Such behavior parallels established trends in the larger secular market.

This entry of women into the consumer market of Rosh Hashanah cards helped fashion a new role for Jewish women in America, part of a larger series of role changes women experienced throughout immigration.[44] With the Jewish New Year cards, this expanding role for women took a unique shape and even sound. Traditionally, Jewish women had important, but prescribed voices in religious celebrations. In the traditional synagogue, they were physically segregated and trained in Hebrew and Yiddish prayers differently than were boys and men. At home, their role was often determinative, orchestrating weekly, yearly, and life-cycle celebrations and conducting important portions of home-based worship. But the tradition of a communal or public religious visibility and voice for women was generally limited.

Jewish New Year postcards partially changed the situation. Women of all ages were depicted liberally throughout the genres of the New Year cards. In the history of imaging Jews, these postcards are among the first formats that broadly envision and disseminate visual categories of Jewish females. Women appear in virtually every scene, except those depicting activities inside the synagogues.[45] Jewish New Year postcards helped bring women into the visual universe of Jewish experience.

Through the postcards, women also acquired new activities around Rosh Hashanah. They chose the cards, chose the recipients, and sent the cards to friends and family, potentially around the entire globe. In so doing, they created new maps of their community. With a stack of cards and stamps on the kitchen table, distances could be narrowed, families could be reunited, and the boundaries of neighborhood, family, and friends could be redrawn. So important was this responsibility of creating new maps of community through the mailing of Rosh Hashanah cards that the *American Hebrew* worried in 1905 that "New Year presents the same difficulty as the issue of wedding invitations. We have to debate where one can safely draw the line."[46] That this responsibility for grouping and defining community was in the context of a religious holiday gave women a public voice and power few had formerly possessed.

This new positioning of women in relation to a key religious holiday parallels the changing role of women in American Judaism and Jewish life during these years in several important ways. With rabbis late in arriving to America, American Judaism evolved from its earliest days with relatively more power residing in lay communities than was the case in Europe. As the nineteenth century turned into the twentieth, and as male immigrants found it increasingly difficult to observe the Saturday Jewish Sabbath and earn a living in predominantly Christian America, synagogue attendance began to tip toward a female majority, another change from Europe. As in Europe, Jewish women also often worked in the family (usually small retail) business, but in America, the availability of consumer goods and opportunities gave them many more options and potentially more power with their purse. Women's behavior expressed through the Jewish New Year cards typifies the elaboration of women's roles through alternative paths in America that contributed to their increased responsibility, visibility, and voice.[47]

The cards themselves sound this "new voice" of American Jewish women. Figures 12.8, 12.9, and 12.10, all published by Williamsburg Postcard Company, probably around 1915, capture the range of roles open to Jewish women in America. Figure 12.8 portrays two modern, but demure and traditionally pious young Jewish women. The text reinforces their traditional roles and voice. Not the women, but a narrator, describes "The tear of a Jewish girl / Her prayer, her pleading glance / They will not be lost in the abyss / They will not go unanswered."[48] Figure 12.9 offers a modern woman engaged in a less pious and more self-directed romantic activity. The apparently happy object of her suitor's affections, she nevertheless allows him the initiative, and the voice in the card is his. "My pretty little girl, my pure and gentle one / My darling flower / Give me your pure, lovely heart / Take me in your arms."[49] But in figure 12.10, the woman is not only modern and romantic, the aggressive

A happy New Year

לשנה טובה תכתבי.

אַ מײדעל פֿן אַ אידישע מאַכטער,
אַ תפלה, אַ בעטענדיקער בליק –
זײ װײסען אין תהום נישט פֿערפֿאַלען
און קימען נישט לעדינג צורק...

FIGURE 12.8

Pious women, Jewish New Year postcard, Williamsburg Post Card Company, New York City. Printed in Germany. 5½ in. x 3½ in. Courtesy American Jewish Historical Society, New York, New York, and Waltham, Massachusetts. AJHS 3333.314b. Photo by Edward Dougherty.

romantic voice is hers. Speaking in that most modern of all ways, by telephone, she urges her lover, "I wish you strength and vigor / To love me with truth and ardor / May not a single dark cloud / Darken your sky."[50] In the context of religious New Year cards, the new possibilities for women are expressed in a combination of physical representation and the narrative power of text/voice.

Women added their text/voice in one more important way to the New Year cards: through the messages they wrote on them. Historians would prefer that more cards had survived with text actually written on them. Those that survive in the American Jewish Historical Society collection are primarily written in English, by women, and convey broad and general greetings. But the signatures are often affectionate and convey how much the recipients are missed. The final layer of interpretation is thus imposed on the cards.

שענענקט מייזעלע, – רייְנענקה,עדוֹי־ע
ליעפּענקט פֿלום !
גיב מיד דיין שענענקע,העַרצעַלע רייַנע,
נעהם מיד ארום !

לשנה טובה

A happy
New Year!

FIGURE 12.9
Romantic couple, Jewish
New Year postcard, Williams-
burg Post Card Company, New
York City. Printed in Germany.
5½ in. x 3⅝ in. Courtesy
American Jewish Historical
Society, New York, New York,
and Waltham, Massachusetts.
AJHS 3333.335a. Photo by
Edward Dougherty.

From the initial creation and manipulation of the image to its overstamping with
"*L'Shanah Tovah*"/"Happy New Year" that encloses nearly all of lived experience in the
religious and holiday message; to the addition of printed text by the production company;
to the human addition of hand-written greetings and messages, the final voice and layer
of added interpretation is that of the sender. The final mediation of staged image, printed
message, and actual experience in the cards is usually managed by women.

Yet as the cards may indicate increased voice and visibility for women, in their time
they simultaneously conveyed the context of nonempowerment through the very form
of the postcards themselves. Naomi Schor argues, as does Colleen McDannell, that every
behavior associated with picture postcards at the turn of the twentieth century—buying,
writing, sending, and collecting them—was seen by the male world as "feminine," and

FIGURE 12.10

Telephone conversation, Jewish New Year postcard, Williamsburg Post Card Company, New York City. Printed in Germany. 5½ in. x 3⅝ in. Courtesy American Jewish Historical Society, New York, New York, and Waltham, Massachusetts. AJHS 3333.336. Photo by Edward Dougherty.

therefore associated with "the trivial, the picturesque, and the ephemeral."[51] Handling miniature objects; collecting photographs, postcards, and other imaged forms in albums and notebooks; and writing letters and postcards themselves, were thus marginalized, as were those who conducted such tasks. The alternative worlds of access and participation marketed to women and embraced by them may simultaneously have drawn new lines of perceived segregation and marginality around them. That women did not necessarily accept that judgment argues once again for the fluidity of the joined powers of word, image, and human perception.

Marketplace, message, the modern world and faith—all came together in neat series of 3-by-5-inch Jewish New Year postcards that imaged Jews for themselves and circumscribed every aspect of American life, tension, experience, and promise with the language of Jewish religion and daily life. The cards embraced the chaos, took possession of it, and, in the context of the Jewish New Year, made it holy. As visual images, they created a reality both reflective of experience and promising for it. As consumer items, they created and made visible new arenas of choice and new structures of power, gender, voice, and influence through them. The cards bridged physical distances and redrew defining boundaries around community and family. From far-flung production centers, they moved through distributors to neighborhood sellers to the intimacy of the household, and back out again to reencompass the world. Perhaps no other turn-of-the-twentieth-century visual form captures the tensions and the creativity of Jewish life in America better than these modest, much-overlooked, penny cards. Jewish New Year postcards brought the experience of America into the visual culture of an emerging modern American Judaism. In so doing, the postcards may have helped define and shape that culture by offering a particular cultural model of integration, choice, and control.

13

"WHEN JESUS HANDED ME A TICKET"

Images of Railroad Travel and Spiritual Transformations
among African Americans, 1865–1917

John M. Giggie

In the early 1930s, when asked by a researcher with the Works Project Administration to reflect on the trials of his spiritual life, an elderly ex-slave pointed to a moment shortly after his eighteenth birthday when he "began to think seriously about the salvation of my soul." The onetime bondsman, never named in the surviving interview, vividly recalled an image from a special dream that forever changed him. The image was of a railroad station, where he stood nervously next to Jesus. Suddenly, remembered this black Southerner, "My knees got weak, and I knelt to pray. As I knelt Jesus handed me a ticket. It was all signed with my name. I arose to my feet and handed it in at the window and was told to take my place with the three men standing on the platform and wait."[1] The symbolic meaning of receiving a ticket from Jesus and waiting at the railroad station was immediately plain to this African American Christian: he was saved.

As this former slave's memory made clear, the railroad was a rich setting for the unfolding of religious drama among southern African Americans after the Civil War. Ex-slaves commonly symbolized spiritual and political journeys as railroad journeys and experienced episodes of conversion as times when "Jesus handed me a ticket." Indeed, they often underwent moments of religious transformation when taking the train or envisioning doing so, revealing the railroad to be a modern locus where African American dreams of deliverance intersected with technology.[2]

To examine the relationship between images of rail travel and the sacred lives of ex-slaves is to show how the study of material culture can shed new light on the field of African American religious history. In the case of ex-slaves living in the late-nineteenth-century South, it illuminates subtle ways that politics and culture merged with religion in the practice of daily life. First, in visions, prayers, and songs that included railroad imagery, Blacks blurred the racial boundaries of legal segregation that defined train travel, suggesting how problems of racial hierarchy entered spiritual life. Second, black men and woman symbolized the railroad differently, reflecting the importance of gender in the experience of religious struggle and change. Finally, by the turn of the twentieth century, African Americans widely viewed the train as a contemporary means to escape northward toward liberty and the Promised Land, intimating that they incorporated the railroad as part of their identity as a chosen people journeying from slavery to freedom as did the Jews in the Hebrew Scriptures.

. . .

At first glance, it is rather curious that the railroad developed as an important symbol in African American religious life after freedom. After all, the railroad was a place where Blacks were lynched and suffered the indignities of segregation. But it was also the region's most important symbol of change and continuity with its slave past.[3] And for black Southerners, the train was critical to their material progress as a people. They saw it as a shiny new technology that offered them an unprecedented freedom to move and get ahead.[4] Like many politicians of the day, Blacks firmly believed that the financial rebirth of the South depended on an expanded railroad infrastructure and they loudly applauded the thousands of miles of new track laid after 1865.[5] The construction of a new line or station in a county always fired hopes of financial opportunity for black residents, signaling prosperity to come, new jobs, and better markets for cotton and farm supplies. The growth of the railroad, moreover, was critical to the expansion of black institutions sworn to uplift the race. African American religious leaders relied on the train to help them travel widely and win converts for their churches, recruit students for their schools, and solicit subscribers for their newspapers and facilitate delivery of them. Illustrations of a locomotive speeding across a stretch

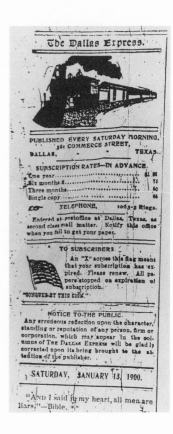

FIGURE 13.1

Train masthead, from the *Dallas Express*, 13 January 1900, Dallas, Texas.

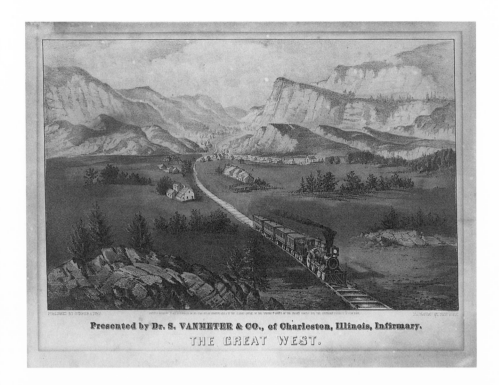

Presented by Dr. S. VANMETER & CO., of Charleston, Illinois, Infirmary.

THE GREAT WEST.

FIGURE 13.2
Currier & Ives, *The Great West*, 1870, lithograph.
Courtesy Chicago Historical Society.

of track appeared regularly on the mastheads and banners of African American publications dedicated to racial progress, such as the *Dallas Express* (fig. 13.1).[6]

Significantly, African Americans depicted the train as a symbol of progress differently than most white Americans of the day. For many Whites living in the late nineteenth century, Currier & Ives, the popular lithographers from New York City, captured the main meaning of the railroad. As seen in their 1870 print *The Great West* (fig. 13.2), the train represented the taming of a wilderness, particularly of virgin land lying west of the Mississippi River, and the relentless advance of modern civilization and technology.[7] It was a vehicle that helped Anglo-America implement the notion of manifest destiny or the basic belief that white men were destined to rule from coast to coast.[8] To African Americans, however, such railroad scenes and the popular interpretation of them lacked any sense of the train's importance to the project of directly improving black life or—more negatively—its role in demonstrating the practice of racial hierarchy.

For the railroad was, of course, a form of segregated transportation, especially in the South. In 1896, in the landmark case of *Plessy v. Ferguson*, the Supreme Court affirmed that separation by race was a natural and legal practice so long as Blacks were provided with cars "separate but equal" to those of Whites.[9] Separate coach laws and practices lay at the heart of a dilemma faced by African Americans in the late-nineteenth-century South. Strive as they might to prosper, and as prosperous as they might become, the color of their skin limited their mobility in white society. The problem of railroad segregation painfully demonstrated that middle-class aspiration or even status was no "ticket" to better accommodations or fairer treatment.[10]

The contrasting meaning of the railroad to Blacks—it promised freedom and coercion—made it a powerful site to probe the limits of racial difference. That act of probing was made easier by the very nature of train travel in which, surprisingly, racial contact was nearly as common as racial segregation. On the railroad, the races mixed to a degree unrealized in other segregated public spaces, such as parks, pools, schools, libraries, and restrooms; on the railroad, people came face-to-face with the maddening inconsistencies of division by color. For even as segregation on trains became the law of the land, Southerners of all types—Black and White, male and female, poor and affluent—never fully avoided the sight, sound, or smell of each other when traveling by rail. The structural design of platforms, waiting areas, and train cars ensured a large degree of racial mixing as did both the habit of integrating cars to fill every available seat and the practice of racial passing, when light-skinned Blacks slipped undetected into white-only sections. Once the train departed the depot and the immediate reach of local authorities, it was temporarily a type of self-contained society, where Blacks and Whites examined the meaning of segregation.

When African Americans represented the railroad in their lives, then, it was not strictly as a vehicle to be damned or avoided. Of course, many black writers viewed the train as a symbol of freedom lost: as one discontented black journalist put it in 1890, segregation aboard the railroad proved that "[o]ne by one all the results of the war, secured at such tremendous cost in life and property, are being frittered away. . . ."[11] More commonly, though, Blacks appropriated images of train travel to frame expressions of deliverance. It was a practice begun during slavery, particularly in the upper-South region, when bondsmen dreamed of riding the underground railroad north toward freedom. Similarly, northern white and black abolitionists sometimes delivered their antislavery message by representing the political drive toward emancipation as a train ride.[12] For example, the 1844 cover illustration of the sheet music to the song "Get off the Track!" prominently featured a locomotive whose wheel cover was titled the "Liberator," the name of the newspaper founded in 1831 by William Lloyd Garrison, an architect of abolitionism; a train car emblazoned with the movement's war cry, "Immediate Emancipation"; and a conductor ringing a "Lib[ert]y Bell" (fig. 13.3). The song's lyrics reinforced the notion of the railroad as an emblem of social change. As verse seven read:

All True friends of Emancipation
Haste to Freedom's Rail Road Station
Quick into the Cars get seated

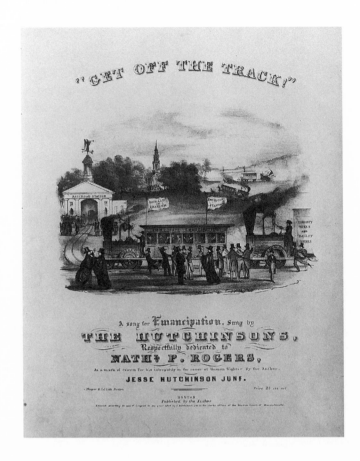

All is ready, and completed
Put on the Steam! All are crying
And the Liberty Flag flying.[13]

The African American idea of the train as a vehicle of deliverance gained wide prominence only after 1865, however, when railroad companies emerged as a powerful economic
force in the South and frequently provided the physical structures in which Blacks worshipped. Indeed, their sheer size and wealth often made them more important than local banks or creditors to black congregations in need of land and money to build a church.
Their discarded train cars and deserted depots were quickly put to use as churches by
cash-starved congregants. The location of their stations typically influenced patterns of
church growth because the Blacks who moved close to the depots in search of opportunity eventually founded new congregations or relocated older ones. And, finally, their waiting areas and open-air platforms often were the settings for revivals, prayer meetings,
and church fund-raisers.

As their places of worship and work increasingly depended on the railroad, Blacks slowly began to incorporate visual elements of it into their speech and imagination. Most basically, they began to rely on the locations of depots to describe the locations of houses of worship and important gatherings. When C. H. Andrews Jr. told of his hometown of Leverett, Mississippi, in a letter to a newspaper, he began by declaring that "[o]ur town is on the edge of the Delta near no railroad. . . ."[14] The invitations to the 1888 Annual Meeting of Baptist leaders from Phillips, Lee, and Monroe counties in eastern Arkansas included the date, time, place—and nearest train stop. "Our Association meets Friday before the third Lord's day in August, at St. Matthew's. Your presence with us is greatly desired. Your nearest point to the church is at Palmer Station."[15] Concurrently, presiding elders started to identify their pastors and congregations in public by stating how far they lived from the nearest whistle stop. In a published report on where his ministers labored and churches lay, for example, Presiding Elder J. W. Hudson of Baton Rouge ticked off line after line in a common form, as in: "Bro. P. W. Clark, pastor of Wesley Chapel, [is] thirty-five miles from the city of Baton Rouge, and three from the town of Wilson, on the Mississippi Valley Railroad."[16]

Simple convenience, of course, lay behind publicly identifying the location of churches, meetings, and ministers according to their distance from a railroad stop; the announcement provided future visitors with an easy landmark to navigate their way. Yet part of the meaning of such identifications also lay in closely aligning the key institutions of spiritual life with the railroad. The act of connecting missions and people to points on an imagined railroad map encouraged Blacks to envision religious stories as railroad stories.

These religious stories usually shared the conceit of a spiritual journey as a railroad journey. They took two basic forms, institutional narratives of church and denominational growth and personal narratives of individual spiritual transformation. As an example of the first type, Christian Methodist Episcopal minister J. W. Spearman penned a letter in 1904 to his denominational weekly, *The Christian Index*, that evoked the idea of conductors piloting a train to heaven to describe the work of earlier church fathers. He prompted readers to recall that their history was a product of the labors of men that took "passengers who have purchased their tickets at the Calvary's union station stamped with the blood of Christ and the insignia of God to meet Christ the Lord."[17]

Like Spearman, Rev. Pierre Landry, pastor of St. Paul's Methodist Episcopal Church in Shreveport, Louisiana, borrowed the idea of a railroad trip to develop a fund-raiser for a new church roof in 1890. He also gave the image more concrete form, selling tickets to a fictitious "railroad excursion." These were no ordinary tickets, however, as purchasers found out upon examining them closely, but were actually small printed cards that deftly combined references to the church's financial need, the story of Exodus, and experience of train travel. "We are now passing through the tunnel of Mount Indebtedness with one more river to cross. With your help we will soon bridge the same and extend this line over into the promised land of Free Deliverance. Fare for the round-trip. Pullman palace coaches, $20; vestibule palace coaches, $15; parlor reclining chair, $10; first-class passengers coaches, $5; second class passenger coaches, $1."[18] By structuring his appeal as a train ride, the reverend achieved two goals at once. He crafted a modern fund-raiser that deftly combined modern technology and biblical verse. He also offered the idea of a train as a vehicle to take Blacks where they had long wanted to go—on a journey toward "the promised land of freedom."

Significantly, Rev. Landry minimized the problem of segregation in his "railroad excursion." This is not to say that he ignored or accepted it. Rather, by "selling" fares to elite sections of the train typically denied Blacks because of their race the minister implicitly poked fun of the laws of separate accommodation. But directly protesting separate coach laws was not of paramount concern to Landry in the fund-raiser; he simply explored the problem of segregation in a creative way that generated donations. Similarly, other preachers began to imagine segregated travel not strictly as an abhorrent fact of life but additionally as a test of the ability of denominational leaders to withstand hardship with poise and dignity. In 1904, Arkansas clerics with the Christian Methodist Church labeled segregated travel a challenge to the discipline and desire of any man hoping to serve God. After their annual state meeting, one minister remarked that "accommodations for colored people on railroads is [sic] poor at best, and they are often made to go for many days with a hungry stomach." But riders "should learn a lesson of enduring hardships. If any undergraduate enters the Methodist itinerary to have his path-way bedecked with blooming roses and fragrant flowers, he has simply mistaken the profession."[19]

In episodes of individual conversion, Blacks experienced salvation as literally "going on a train" and blurred the lines between what was simply railroad imagery and what was a genuine moment of transcendence.[20] This was the case for former Alabama slave Joe Hutchings, who described his 1903 conversion as a time when he "began to shout saying halalujah [sic]. . . . Oh, it is a good thing to serve the Lord. I am going to heaven. . . . I am going on the train. . . . The [rail]road is tedious, you will have troubles of many, but god will be with you."[21] Similarly, in a 1904 letter published in a black Tennessee newspaper, an unnamed writer described his participation in a recent heart-pounding revival by referring to himself as a passenger on a fast-moving train. The evangelist leading the revival was both conductor and engineer, the one who "booked the gospel train" and "thundered [it] along the rail of time." He "didn't carry us very far," said the author, "before seemingly all the 'blood bought' souls began dashing fuel at the place that makes the steam rise. Then the old train traveled at a rapid rate and soon we were standing at the 'Judgement' seat."[22]

The practice of constructing spiritual journeys from the physical components of rail travel developed as a new part of the oral tradition of African American worship, particularly in chanted sermons. By the early 1900s, ministers widely incorporated the sounds of bells, whistles, hissing steam, and conductors' voices into their preaching as devices to enliven the sermon, order its tempo, and pace its lyrics. In "Black Diamond Express to Hell," for example, a sermon delivered first in the 1910s, Reverend A. Nix, an Alabama preacher, opened by speaking a biblical passage: "I take my text this morning in Matthew seventh chapter and thirteenth verse. 'Hear ye in at the straight gate for wide is the gate and broad is the way that leadeth to destruction and many be here that go in there.'" He then began the sermon in a slow and clear voice.

> This train is known as the Black Diamond Express Train to hell. Sin is the engineer.
> Pleasure is the headlight
> and the Devil is the conductor.
> I see the Black Diamond as she start off for hell.
> The bell is ringin'. Hell-bound! Hell-bound!
> The devil cries out, "All aboard for hell!"

Nix performed the second verse in a pattern that he would repeat in every subsequent verse. Echoing a conductor as his train came into a station, Nix first bellowed the name of the railroad stop, which was actually the title of a specific sin. He then started to describe the unfortunate lives of the men and women who lived there, speaking faster and louder with every word while women from his church joined in, humming, singing, and yelling "amens" and "hallelujahs." Eventually he cadenced his voice to resemble the chugging rhythm of a train as it built up steam and pulled away from the station.

> First Station! Is Drunkards-ville.
> Stop there and all the drunkards get aboard.
> Have a big crowd down there drinking.
> Some city! Some drinkin' shimmy, some drinkin' moonshine, some drinkin' white mule
>   and red horse.
> All you drunkards you gotta go to hell on the Black Diamond Train!
>
> That Diamond starts off for hell now.
> Next station! Is Liar's Avenue.
> Wait there! And let all the liars get on board.
> Have a good crowd of liars down there.
> Have some smooth liars, some unreasonable liars, some professional liars, some
>   barefaced liars, some ungodly liars, some big liars, some little liars, some go to
>   bed lying, get up lying.
> Lie all day! Lie on you and on me!
> A big crowd of liars!
> You got to go to hell on a Black Diamond Train.

The song climaxed when the Devil hopped aboard and took the train straight to hell.[23]

In "Black Diamond Express," Nix created a modern story of spiritual decline by describing a train making a run to hell and stopping along the way at stations named for

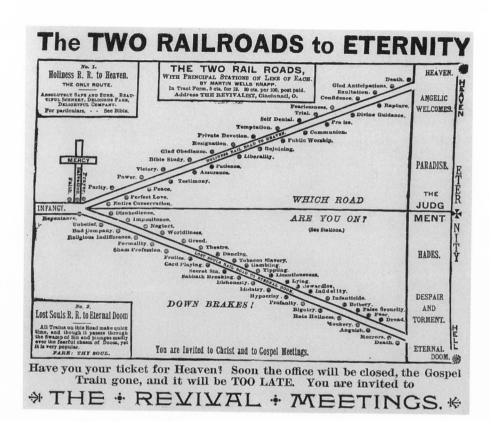

FIGURE 13.4
"The Two Railroads to Eternity," "The Revivalist,"
Cincinnati, Ohio, c. 1900.

different types of transgressions. To help visualize the message in these types of chanted sermons, ministers sometimes passed out illustrations, such as "The Two Railroads to Eternity" (fig. 13.4).[24] In these printed diagrams, the lyrics gained a degree of urgency and clarity as the two tracks to the two different resting places were plainly drawn and sins clearly labeled as train stops.

Rev. J. M. Gates, a Baptist preacher from Atlanta, Georgia, also incorporated the sights and sounds of the railroad in his sermons. In "Death's Black Train Is Coming," a chanted sermon given first in the early 1910s, Gates and his congregants from Mt. Calvary Church sang of a train coming to take the faithful to heaven. Like Nix, Gates began the sermon by issuing a spoken invitation to his audience. He explained that the purpose of the song was simple: convert sinners and excite a popular need to repent and turn to God. "Ahh, I want to sing us a song tonight, and while I sing I want every sinner in the house to come to the anxious seat and bow, and accept prayer. You need prayer. Subject of this song,

'Death's Black Train is Coming.' It's coming too." He then started to sing, slowly and by himself, in a plaintive tone. He began with the refrain and the first verse.

> O, The Little Black Train is coming.
> Get all you business right.
> You'd better set you house in order
> For that train may be here tonight.

> There some men and there some women.
> That care nothing for the Gospel life.
> 'Till they hear the bell ringing and hear the whistle blow.
> O, the little black train in sight. (refrain)

Gates then picked up the pace and increased his volume, and the women joined in during the singing of the refrain.

> O, that little black train and its engine
> With one little baggage car
> Has all your deeds and your wicked thoughts.
> Meet you at the Judgement board. (refrain)

> If you want to get on the mornin' train
> If you want to go home and live in peace
> You'd better have your ticket in you hand.
> Be standing at the station
> With you ticket in your hand
> For the little black train is coming
> And you goin' to join that band. (refrain)[25]

In chanted sermons, Gates, Nix, and scores of other unrecorded black preachers offered the best example of how African Americans appropriated visual and aural images of railroad travel as modern means to experience episodes of grace such as conversion.

. . .

In examples of spiritual stories and prayers uttered by black women, however, the railroad emerged as a place of power and transformation in distinctive ways. Black men often symbolized the train as a vehicle taking them to heaven or hell. So did African American women, but they also experienced it as a setting for overcoming threats of bodily harm. The difference between the genders probably reflected the greater degree of physical danger faced by black women than men when riding a train, a frequent topic in their letters and diaries. Female passengers often described the perils they faced, especially when traveling alone. In her autobiography, Mary Church Terrell, a well-to-do black woman from Memphis, Tennessee, vividly recalled her encounter with an aggressive white man who "made some ugly remarks." It was nighttime, and she was by herself. "I was terror stricken and started to the door when the train slowed to a stop. He seized me and threw me into a seat and then left the car."[26]

The threat of physical and sexual abuse that haunted black women on the railroad made it a potent site for instances of female spiritual empowerment. Mrs. V. K. Glenn was a well-traveled Christian Methodist Church missionary who told a story of how God helped her to diffuse a tense stand-off at a depot. It was the end of an unsuccessful visit to a rural church, and she was unsure if she ought to continue her evangelizing. She stood at the local whistle-stop, without money and as the object of attention for a group of approaching men whose intentions were suspicious. "I was out among strangers. My heart was heavy and tears came into my eyes." As the train neared, she likely expected to be denied passage because she had no money; as the men advanced, she probably anticipated a confrontation of some sort. Yet neither happened. Instead, she wrote, "I saw Jesus as he stood watching the birds of the air and the foxes going to their home, and said 'Foxes have holes, birds of the air have nests, but the Son of Man hath nowhere to lay his head.'" Identifying with Jesus as he spread an unpopular gospel among an unthankful people, Glenn stiffened her resolve to continue her work. She also received a more pedestrian sign of God's approval: "Just about train time I looked up and . . . [the men] came up and gave me some money."[27]

For church women like Glenn who depended on traveling by train to spread the word of God, the act of conquering hardships posed by riding the rails confirmed their sense of a calling to act as evangelists. This type of affirmation was important to women because many denominational bishops and male leaders doubted the ability of women to travel and proselytize alone and questioned the propriety of such activity. Take the case of Peggy Lesure, also a missionary with the Christian Methodist Church, who described how God frequently weighed in on her behalf at railroad stations and bolstered her sense of calling as a missionary. In one story, Lesure lost her money en route to Oscilla, Georgia. Standing in a railroad yard, tired and frightened, she cried out, "O God tell me something." A reply came quickly. "I heard that same voice that pilgrims heard in olden times. It said, 'Go right in and tell the Agent to give you a ticket to Oscilla, I will see that he gets his money.'" At this point, Lesure probably hesitated. Blacks rarely received tickets on credit or approached the ticket counter unless all white passengers had been serviced, which usually was the time when the train had arrived. Yet Lesure she did as she was told, broke social custom, and was rewarded for her faith by receiving a ticket from the conductor without paying for it. She continued her work.

In another incident, Lesure boarded a train but left her purse with the ticket in it at the station. As the train departed and as she braced for a battle with the conductor, a ticket agent "caught the train before it got a good start and threw my purse in the window." In her mind, the ticket agent helped her because "God's hand" compelled him to do so.[28] Similarly, Lesure detailed another episode in which her train "struck a weak place on the river bridge." "The train was shaking, the passengers began to scream." She jumped into

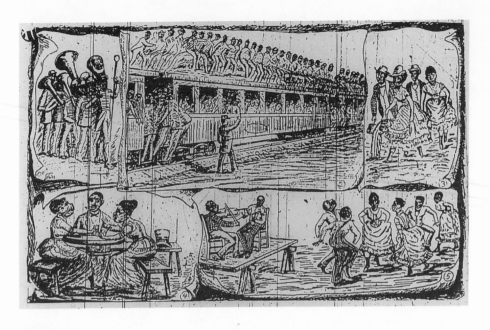

FIGURE 13.5

"The Excursion Craze," from the *Indianapolis Freeman*, 17 August 1889.
Original caption reads: (1) The Drum Major. (2) The Excursion Ready to
Pull Out. (3) On the Way to the Train. (4) The Minister and two of his
Flock "Rushing the Growler." (5) A Virginia Reel.

action. "I ran and helped the porter shut down the windows. I sat down and began singing:
'Life's Railway to Heaven.'" The train quickly stabilized. When asked by the conductor
how she stayed so calm, Lesure replied, "Sir, when I boarded your train, I had two tickets, and if your train can't make it, thank God, I have a ticket that hasn't been punched."[29]
Lesure expressed confidence in her own salvation in railroad terms: she invoked the image of two tickets, one punched by the conductor and the other held by God. God's intervention on the railroad legitimated her belief in the justness of her labor.

At times, the railroad served as an explicit symbol of social tensions developing within
black communities. Many railroad companies sponsored popular Sunday "excursions,"
which were local train rides to county seats or nearby cities for a day of sight-seeing and
recreation. Yet for some ministers and laymen, these excursions excited the worst in
African American Christians. Critics sometimes made their points visually, through images such as the one titled "The Excursion Craze" (fig. 13.5). In a quick series of illustrations, the author depicts the sinful behavior attending Sunday train rides. Instead of observing the Sabbath, passengers listened and watched the marching bands that frequently
sent off the train, jostled for seats, donned their best clothes to enter the train and not a
church, gambled, and danced in public.

. . .

As black Southerners increasingly imagined spiritual journeys as train rides and experienced moments of spiritual transformation at depots and aboard railroad cars, they gradually married their hopes for geographic deliverance from the land of segregation to the
train. Among a people who spiritually identified with the children of Israel, the train
emerged as the form of transportation to take them out of the wilderness and into the
Promised Land. The image of the train as a vehicle of literal deliverance was widely popularized through a new style of music that began in Delta train stations, churches, and
gin houses in the late 1800s. It was a form of music that Americans of a later generation
would call the early blues.

In the early blues, one man with a guitar, often accompanied by a bass player, string
man, and harmonica player, sang in a three-line, twelve-bar, a-a-b pattern. He frequently
"bent" his guitar, making it buzz by holding a piece of metal to its throat and scraping a
pick along its strings. His lyrics flowed freely, connecting to a general theme in a loose,
associational manner.[30] It was a protean and improvisational form of music that adapted
to the mood and need of the artist and audience. The flexible structure allowed the performer to seize quickly on one person's sorrow or trouble and turn it into a shared emotion through song and sound, affording the individual a sense of relief and comfort. Like
a minister chanting a sermon and repeating a favorite verse to the supportive cries of his
congregation, the early blues artist often repeated a phrase known to all, and he and the
audience sang it back and forth in a call-and-response pattern. Many of the new musicians played at churches and some were even preachers. Throughout the 1890s and early
1900s, they traveled the Delta on trains and played at depots and churches alike.[31] Up
and down the rails running parallel to the Mississippi River, African Americans sang,
performed, and heard this new music and made it a fresh way to deny, push away, and
even transform the toils of the day into cries of redemption and escape.[32]

The new blues musicians often sang of riding a train to freedom. Sometimes the ride
was simply a way to escape a general sense of despair that accompanied agricultural life
in the Delta. Tommy Johnson, the son of a part-time preacher born in 1896 in Crystal
Springs, Mississippi, played what he called a repertory of "church songs" in the Delta.[33]
In "Slidin' Delta," a title that was also the name of a local express, Johnson cried to the
"Lord" that he might grab the train and leave the "world."

Delta Slide done been here and gone.
Well, the Delta Slide, just done been here and gone.
When you hear the Delta, baby, it's fore dey want to ride.
Hear the Slidin' Delta, fore dey want to ride.
Says if I don't get to join it, baby, gonna sure, lord, lose my mind.
Cryin', lord, lord, lord, lord, lord.
Lord, I wonder, what in this world I'm gonna do.
Lord, I can't do nothin' but hang my head and cry.

Baby, when I leave, I ain't comin' here no more.
When I leave here, ain't comin' here no more.
Lord, I'm goin' away to worry you off my mind.[34]

Like Johnson, Henry "Rag Time Texas" Thomas, an itinerant musician and preacher, identified the train with a sense of spiritual deliverance. He explicitly sang of a voyage in religious terms. In "When the Train Comes Along," he waited at a depot for Jesus to come and take him away on a train. Thomas sang:

I may be blind, I cannot see.
I'll meet you at the station when the train come along.
The train come along, the train come along.
I'll meet you at the station when the train come along.

I'm prayin' in my heart, I'm cryin' out of my eyes.
That Jesus has died for my sins.
I will meet you at the station, I'll meet you in the smoke.
I will meet you at the station when the train come a[long].
When the train come along, the train come along.
I'll meet you at the station when the train come along.[35]

Similarly, Blind Lemon Jefferson, a frequent visitor to the Delta, invoked the train as a vehicle of religious passage. He specifically sang about the journey of the children of Israel as a journey taken on a train. In "All I Want Is That Pure Religion," he described traveling across the Jordan River without fear because "Jesus gonna be my engineer."

When you're journeyin' over Jordan don't have no fear, Hallelu.
When you're journeyin' over Jordan don't have no fear, Hallelu, Hallelu.
Journeyin' over Jordan don't have no fear,
Jesus gonna be my engineer.
Sayin' you gonna need that pure religion, Hallelu, Hallelu.

Well, your train is comin' round past the curve, Hallelu.
Train is comin' round and it's passin' the curve, Hallelu, Hallelu.
Train is comin' round and it's passin' the curve.
Think I'm leavin' this distressful world.
Sayin' you're gonna need that pure religion, Hallelu, Hallelu.[36]

Musicians like Blind Lemon Jefferson popularized and set to music the notion of the train as a vehicle of passage to Canaan Land. They connected disparate parts of a modern religious identity for African Americans, synthesizing their long-standing affiliation with the ancient Hebrews, their contemporary quest for a fuller experience of freedom, and their confrontation with the rapid growth of the railroad as the New South's dominant expression of economic change and racial status quo.

FIGURE 13.6
"The Great Southern Exodus," from the *Indianapolis Freeman*, 5 November 1892.

. . .

Starting slowly in the 1880s but accelerating during World War I, southern Blacks moved north. Driven from their homelands by decades of violence and poverty and pulled by the lure of well-paying industrial jobs and racial detente in cities such as Chicago and St. Louis, thousands of African American migrants believed that they were finally arriving in a promised land of freedom. In "The Great Southern Exodus," an illustration typical of the type run in black newspapers, Blacks crowded the railroad station and queued up to take trains heading northward (fig. 13.6).[37] It was an image that captured many of the popular meanings of the railroad to Blacks. The eight white men lining the column of black wayfarers and glaring at them recall the station as a place of racial tension. In the left foreground, the small black boy selling copies of the [Indianapolis] *Freeman*, an African American newspaper popular in the Mid-west and South, reminds the viewer of the importance of the railroad to the viability of African American institutions such as the press. The entrance of the long line of black travelers into the depot evokes the train as a means of deliverance from slavery and hardship. Specifically, the notion of geographic deliverance is clearly affirmed by the title of the picture, "The Great Southern Exodus," and the underlying caption, which gives as a reason for the movement a need to flee "Democratic hate." The five small frames that crown the image further emphasize the link between exodus and liberty. In the first (moving left to right), the quest for new opportunity is summed up in a sketch of a black man standing in a land office. The sketch is labeled "The Negro in Kansas," a reference to the 1879 migration of hundreds of Blacks from

Mississippi, Louisiana, and Arkansas to Kansas in search of the promise of cheap and available land.[38] Blacks also leave the South, as the next four scenes make clear, to escape violence—the whipping of black women, lynchings, the memory of the hunting of runaway slaves with dogs. They also depart to avoid living as an ornament of pleasure for wealthy Whites, as suggested by the banjo player strumming for white dancers.

In "The Great Southern Exodus," the theme of religious deliverance is evoked by the architecture of the railroad station, which loosely resembles more a black country church than a country whistle-stop. The effect suggests that the railroad station was a physical setting for revivals and prayer meetings. The notion of a biblical exodus, of a people wandering toward the Promised Land, can be appreciated by comparing the image to an earlier famous painting by George Caleb Bingham, *Boone Escorting Settlers through the Cumberland Gap* (1851–52; fig. 13.7). The visual parallels are striking: a people cutting through the middle of a threatening landscape and directly into the viewers' space; a central male figure acting as a leader; a dog in the left corner; and a man in the right corner carrying a gun (in Bingham's work) or a banjo (in the "Exodus") cocked at the same angle. The two images make a similar thematic statement, too. Daniel Boone, like a Moses figure, leads a stream of pioneers into a promised land of virgin territory to capture the promise of manifest destiny.[39] In the "Exodus," the foremost man leads a winding line of wanderers to the train station and on their own mission of manifest destiny—on a journey toward a Canaan Land of freedom.

The historical importance of the train with both geographic and spiritual deliverance was not lost on a group of 147 black Mississippians who each purchased a one-way ticket for Chicago in 1916. When their train passed the Ohio River, a border that they believed divided the North from the South, the migrants stopped their watches, knelt in the car, and sang of deliverance as tears streamed down their faces. They sang:

I done come of [th]e land of Egypt
aint that good news.
O Canaan, Sweet Canaan
I am bound for the land of Canaan.[40]

The tears shed by those Blacks dramatized their belief that the South's cursed history held power over them no more. A vehicle of segregation had become, at last, one of liberation.

Tragically, the Blacks who moved north discovered shortly after their arrival that geographic relocation did not secure racial harmony. Deadly race riots in the summer of 1917 made that clear. In the end, the African American journey toward unfettered freedom begun in 1865 continued for nearly a century, until a black minister from Birmingham, Alabama, drew on the motifs of his forefathers and told the nation about taking a journey to the mountaintop and reaching, finally, the Promised Land.

Significantly, the railroad persisted as a powerful visual symbol of African American religious life throughout the twentieth century, perhaps most notably in the abstract art

FIGURE 13.7

George Caleb Bingham, *Daniel Boone Escorting Settlers through the Cumber-land Gap*, 1851–52, oil on canvas, 36½ in. x 50¼ in. Courtesy Washington University Gallery of Art, St. Louis. Gift of Nathaniel Phillips, 1890.

of Romare Bearden. Bearden was born in 1911 in Charlotte, North Carolina, and spent much of his youth in the segregated South. As a child, he remembered visiting railroad stations with his grandfather, a preacher, and watching the trains come and go. For him, the train "was an exciting symbol of a different world. . . . [It] was always something that could take you away and could also bring you to where you were."[41]

Bearden eventually migrated by train to Pittsburgh, Pennsylvania, and finally to New York City, where he trained as an artist and lived most of his professional life. But he never forgot those childhood Sundays spent at the depot in North Carolina. The train was special to him, and he called it "a journeying thing."[42] He regularly incorporated it into his collages and paintings as a symbol of passage. In *Tidings* (1973; fig. 13.8), for exam-

FIGURE 13.8 (SEE ALSO PLATE 15)
Romare Bearden, *Tidings*, 1973, mixed
media collage, 16 in. x 24 in. Courtesy of
Bank of America Corporation.

ple, a woman is visited by an angel, whose winged figure stands in front of a locomotive
and steepled chapel. By including the train in the moment when Mary learns of her role
as the mother of the son of God, Bearden re-creates the biblical drama of the Annunci-
ation. The figures are black and the train helps to form the setting for the experience of
prophecy and deliverance.[43] It is a visual recalling of the historic role of the railroad in
African American spiritual life after slavery, evoking it as a place where God's will that
his chosen people be free was made known and tested.

14

AMERICAN PROTESTANT BIBLE ILLUSTRATION FROM COPPER PLATES TO COMPUTERS

Paul Gutjahr

INTRODUCTION

Although some four hundred and fifty new English Bible translations have been introduced into the United States since Robert Aitken printed the first American edition of the Bible in 1777, only a handful have gained much ground against the persistent popularity of the King James Version.[1] Not until the relatively recent appearance of the New International Version in 1978 did another translation of the scriptures seriously threaten the preeminence of the King James's popularity among Bible-reading Americans.[2] This is not to say that no other version has enjoyed popularity among American readers.[3] One of the most striking American translation success stories was Today's English Version (TEV).

The American Bible Society introduced the TEV in 1966 as *Good News for Modern Man*. A version bent on giving people the Bible in a "language common to both the professor and the janitor, the business executive and the gardener, the socialite and the waiter," the American Bible Society initially printed 150,000 copies of *Good News*.[4] Almost immediately, the printing sold out. Within one year, five million copies had been distributed; in the next twenty years, seventy-five million copies of TEV were in circulation.[5]

There were many reasons for the success of TEV, but there is little doubt that readers flocked to this new Bible edition because of its illustrations.[6] In fact, it was the first American translation of the scriptures to reach beyond the study of words to use pictures to

Let him down on his bed into the middle of the group. (Lk 5.19)

FIGURE 14.1
Annie Vallotton, illustration for Luke 5, *Today's English Version New Testament*, 162–63. © 1966, American Bible Society. Reprinted by permission.

help interpret the original biblical languages (fig. 14.1). The artist for the TEV's illustrations was the Swiss illustrator Annie Vallotton.[7] Thinking that most Bibles had the same "old dull appearance," being printed entirely on gray "tedious" pages, Vallotton wanted to give the traditional scriptures a new, more engaging look.[8] She approached the American Bible Society with a plan of "holy daring," namely that their new translation might "flourish" with drawings to capture the attention of readers.[9] The American Bible Society agreed to take a chance on the idea, and a novel illustrated translation project was born.

In an interview after the initial success of *Good News for Modern Man*, Vallotton succinctly explained her views on Bible illustration by stating: "An illustration automatically suggests an interpretation, and this is a danger where the Bible is concerned. That is why I have tried hard to make my illustrations a kind of 'bait' to arouse and develop interest on the part of the reader."[10] Vallotton captured two of the defining characteristics in American biblical illustration. First, that American editors and publishers had a long history of using pictures as "bait" to attract readers to their versions of the scriptures. Second, that illustrations always "automatically suggest an interpretation."

The following chapter is an exploration of the most pronounced trends found in American Protestant Bible illustration during the last two hundred years, a study that bears witness to the fact that while biblical illustrations might be used as bait to attract readers, they can also constantly switch that text's meaning through their content and placement.

Bible illustrations subvert the Protestant belief that the Word alone matters (*Sola Scriptura*) when that Word arrives in the company of dozens, if not hundreds, of interpretation-shaping illustrations.

FINE ART

One can paint the history of American Bible illustration in broad strokes by surveying five recurrent strategies used by publishers to interest readers in their biblical editions. While all five of these strategies may be found in the same Bible edition, they never appear in the same edition with equal weight. An illustrated edition almost always foregrounds one of these five strategies to engage its reader.

The first of these trends can be characterized as a desire to associate the Bible with great art and high cultural refinement. The first illustrated Bible published in America was Isaiah Thomas's folio edition of 1791, an edition clearly in the tradition of associating God's word with the conventions of fine art.[11] With the desire to make his folio Bible edition as elegant as any book published in Europe, Thomas commissioned fifty copperplate illustrations favoring a rococo style, one of the fine art styles popular in the late eighteenth century.[12] Thomas probably chose the rococo style because of its close associations with enlightened rationality and "the very limit of upper-class refinement."[13] The rococo style was bent on portraying beauty in a sensuous way as seen in its frequently erotic representations of classical figures in the pleasure parks and villas of European aristocracy.

Thomas attempted to recode the rococo for his Bible readers by fusing beauty with certain key virtues such as honesty, courage, and wisdom in the context of biblical scenes. For example, the folio's illustration of Susanna is filled with the rococo conventions of frequent use of S and C curves, cherubs and children, clamshells and nature motifs, and a pronounced emphasis on the feminine, but at the same time it emphasizes Susanna's chastity and courage in resisting the lascivious advances of two elders (fig. 14.2). By linking beauty and virtue, Thomas strove to refine his viewer's sensibilities and encourage them to think of virtuous action as a beautiful thing.[14]

Thomas's portrayal of women in the rococo style brought with it certain problems. Dominant among these was the fact that the rococo style favored women with bare breasts. This convention is seen throughout the folio's illustrations. Pictures of Eve show her bare breasted, while illustrations of Queen Esther and Mary Magdalene show them with their nipples exposed. Such depictions resonate with the deeply patriotic leanings of Thomas, who may have been eager to adopt the highly politicized nature of the breast in the revolutionary France of his day. In France, artists and writers had come to use women's breasts as a key symbol in depicting a carefully nurtured and vibrantly healthy body politic.[15] While Thomas's illustrations may have evoked the political and refined artistic sensibilities of Europe, they upset the more religiously conservative sensibilities of many of Thomas's Bible readers. Upon being allowed an early glimpse of the folio's illustrations, the famous writer and Congregational minister Jeremy Belknap thought "The position of the figures

FIGURE 14.2
"Susanna Surprised by the
Elders in the Garden," Holy
Bible, Worcester: Isaiah
Thomas, 1791, plate 31.
Courtesy The Lilly Library,
Indiana University,
Bloomington, Indiana.

in the first plate very bad, especially Eve, whose [*sic*] is in a very indecent posture."[16] Thomas may have been attempting to cultivate a refined and patriotic sensibility through his illustrations, but Belknap saw them stimulating less virtuous, inappropriate appetites.

Thomas's aspirations and Belknap's response reveal the brutal truth that pictures do not contain a single, readily apparent, message. Although illustrations had long been used to accent, or further explicate, the Bible's written text, the visual commentary they provided was not always easily interpreted.[17] Pictures are frequently not straightforward interpretive devices. While illustrations may emphasize some aspect of a written narrative, they can also distract from, even subvert, the narrative they illustrate.[18] Words may say one thing, pictures another. As seen in Belknap's response to Thomas's intentions for fine art, the Bible's sacred message was subverted by the "indecent" illustrations that accompanied it. What was spiritual and refined to one reader could be virtually pornographic to another.

CURIOUS THINGS

The second strategy is not so much concerned with fine art as it is with placing illustrations within Bibles to attract the reader. This strategy dates back in American Bible publishing to the earliest years of the nineteenth century, and it is well exemplified in the first markedly successful American publisher of Bibles, Mathew Carey of Philadelphia. Publishing a vast array of books for more than three decades (including more than sixty editions of the King James Bible between 1801 and 1824), Carey was one of the few financially successful publishers in the early United States.[19] Much of this success was due to Carey's keen ability to judge the book market. He had a good sense of what the public wanted, and when he began publishing Bibles, he was careful to remain informed about his purchasers' preferences. Perhaps no one was more helpful in feeding him information about book buyers and Bibles than Carey's itinerant bookseller, Mason Locke Weems.

Weems worked for Carey for more than twenty years and was instrumental in getting Carey to publish his first Bible editions.[20] Being on the front lines of bookselling, Weems saw a large market for cheap Bible editions; he begged Carey to send him such volumes. As the demand for Carey Bibles grew in the early 1800s, Weems began to see a trend toward buying ever more elaborate editions of the Bibles: editions filled with more illustrations, tables, and notes. He told Carey to fill his editions with such extras because a volume containing "more Curious things than were ever seen in any other bible, wou'd be a great Matter."[21]

Weems's encouragement to include "Curious things" is reflected in another aspect of early-nineteenth-century American culture, namely the immensely popular practice among many Americans to collect, arrange, and display various objects in what came to be known as curiosity cabinets.[22] As a means of education and entertainment, countless Americans in the late eighteenth and early nineteenth century spent time collecting and arranging their own little museums in small cabinets or on shelves, sometimes occupying whole rooms. These collections foregrounded a mixture of edification and entertainment, whereby the viewer could learn new things about the natural and humanmade worlds. Museums such as Peale's in Philadelphia and later Barnum's in New York capitalized on this interest in collected and displayed pieces of material culture. Peale and Barnum used elaborately orchestrated displays and exhibitions as a means of first arresting a viewer's attention and then educating that viewer.[23] The curious things Carey included in his Bibles were bent on employing much the same strategy.

Among the extra material Weems sought to have included in Bible editions was an ever increasing array of illustrations. By 1816, Carey was obliging him with editions filled

FIGURE 14.3
"The Prodigal Son," from Holy Bible, Philadelphia: published
by Mathew Carey, 1813, plate 23. Courtesy Beinecke Rare Book
and Manuscript Library, Yale University Library.

with as many as seventy maps and illustrations.[24] Instead of using representations of established religious art to illustrate his Bibles, Carey hired his own illustrators. These illustrators provided Carey with pictures that one was not tempted to associate primarily
with the more refined tastes and techniques of the Italian renaissance or French rococo
traditions. Instead, although his pictures contained vestiges of the rococo style, they were
heavily weighted toward the neoclassical style.

The neoclassical style, characterized by sharp, robust perpendicular lines, followed upon
the heels of the rococo in both Europe and the United States, and became a prevalent architectural and artistic style in the early American republic.[25] It was founded upon the
classical architecture of Greece and Rome, full of columns, square steps, domes, and
squat-based buildings. The neoclassical became popular in the United States largely because of its association with the best attributes of ancient Greek and Roman society, where
honesty, sacrificial service, and devotion to country were held to be the supreme virtues.
A young American democracy admired these attributes and counted them as essential to
the survival of a country that stood as the first great modern experiment in democracy.[26]

Carey underlined his pictures' stylistic resonance with republican virtue by centering
many of his pictures on scenes full of didactic content in an attempt to teach his readers

moral lessons. One of his favorite illustrations featured the return of the prodigal son (fig. 14.3). Here, Carey used neoclassical devices such as pillars and squat, solid architecture to serve as framing devices for a scene centering on filial devotion. As scholars have shown, the story of the prodigal son was a central cultural trope in the early American republic, capturing the tension between a wayward son and a forgiving father. The son was frequently depicted as the citizens of the United States, while the father stood for England and later as various forms of centralized authority.[27] A neoclassical illustration of such familiar biblical and political content could quite possibly have underlined themes of republican responsibility amid republican freedom to readers who were familiar with tracts, sermons, political speeches, and works of art that used the story of the prodigal son to comment on various features of a young republic attempting to find its way.

There were other interpretive possibilities, however, for Carey's placement of the prodigal son illustration in his Bible editions. These possibilities did not so much center on republican virtue, but underlined different interests readers might bring to the text. A close look at Carey's prodigal son illustration demonstrates Carey's willingness to take Weems's advice about "Curious things." Carey's pictures may have been drawn using the favored style of the neoclassical, but they were frequently pictures that took a certain degree of license with the biblical narrative. For example, Carey's prodigal son illustration included a bare-breasted woman being molested in the top right-hand corner of the picture; no trace of such a woman can be found anywhere in the biblical text. Carey may have given his readers republican virtue on one level, but he was also stocking his Bibles with a range of exciting extras to attract readers as well. If one looks carefully, many of Carey's illustrations take on a gamelike quality that rewards the attentive viewer with amusing, salacious, and sometimes violent additions to the biblical text they purportedly portray.

The lesson to be remembered in this second strategy of American religious publishing is that economics can play a large part in which illustrations are chosen for a particular Bible edition. The curious quality of Carey's images quite possibly boosted sales because of the various ways in which readers could interpret and enjoy the many extras included in Carey's Bible editions. These pictures clearly demonstrate that while illustrations could comment on the biblical text, they could also connect to contemporary cultural tropes and engage readers who found amusement in what they saw. Pictures could sell Bibles for a number of reasons, and these reasons did not always involve illustrations that added theological insight or cultural refinement to the biblical text.

APOLOGETICS

The third trend found throughout American Bible illustration is theologically calculated. It focuses on the issue of biblical apologetics. American publishers have long used pictures in their Bible editions to underline the biblical text's trustworthiness. Most often, this strategy has taken the form of linking the Holy Land to the Bible.

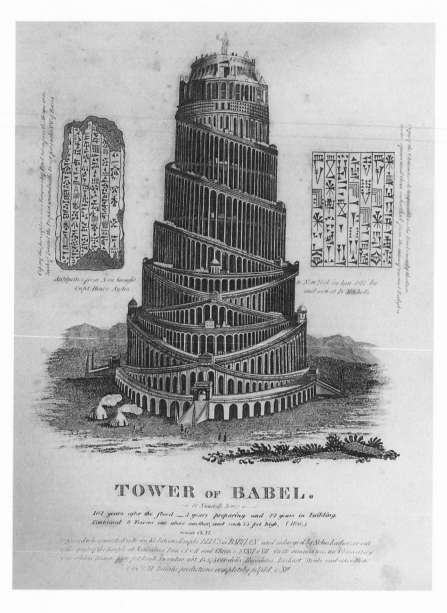

TOWER of BABEL.
— or Nimrods Tower —
102 years after the flood — 3 years preparing and 22 years in building.
Contained 8 Towers one above another, and each 75 feet high. (Hist.)
Genesis Ch. XI.

FIGURE 14.4
"Tower of Babel," from Holbrook Bible, 1818.
Photo by Paul Gutjahr.

The first hint of this trend appears in early-nineteenth-century Bibles, where pictures of artifacts from the Middle East are used to testify to the authenticity of God's word. John Holbrook's 1818 Bible edition provides a clear example of this strategy (fig. 14.4). Here, a picture of the Tower of Babel is shown flanked by two cuneiform tablets. The captions under these two tablets read: "Antiquities from Asia brought to New York in Jan. 1817 by Capt. Henry Austin and now at D. Mitchell's." The left side of the picture further reveals that one of the tablets is a "Copy of the Inscription in a fragment of Brick . . . at the Tomb of Daniel the Prophet. . . ." In adding these two tablets, Holbrook helped inaugurate a trend in American biblical illustration that concentrated on linking the Bible's text with contemporary travels and archaeological excavations in Egypt and Palestine.[28]

Although a wide range of Americans would show interest in the Middle East in the early nineteenth century, the region held a special allure for American Protestants.[29] By the 1820s, American theological scholarship began to feel the first shock waves of new trends in European biblical criticism. This criticism involved historical, chronological, and philological attacks on the accuracy of various portions of the scriptures, placing a heavy emphasis on the need to understand the context of the scripture writers in order to understand their message. Through this lens, the historicity of the Bible became all important. American biblical scholarship began to reflect this concern with the Bible's trustworthiness by producing a body of work that concentrated on the accuracy of biblical manuscripts and traditions of interpretation.[30] As textual critics increasingly argued over the accuracy of the actual biblical text, certain biblical scholars moved from strict textual analysis to another biblical text—the Holy Land.

This turn toward shoring up the Bible with its land of origin found two powerful, early-nineteenth-century advocates in William A. Thomson and Edward Robinson. Thomson, a missionary in the Middle East, wrote an immensely popular, multivolume work entitled *The Land and the Book*.[31] In it, he set forth a belief that gained vast popularity among antebellum Protestants by calling the Holy Land one "vast tablet whereupon God's messages to men have been drawn, and graven deep in living characters by the Great Publisher of glad tidings, to be seen and read [by] all to the end of time. The Land and the Book—with reverence be it said—constitute the ENTIRE and ALL-PERFECT TEXT, and should be studied together."[32]

While Thomson wrote for the masses, the Congregational theologian Edward Robinson made an international reputation for himself by journeying to Judea and writing on the Holy Land's geographical affirmation of biblical truths.[33] Through his extensive scholarly publications that mapped Judea physically, socially, and historically, Robinson founded a school of Protestant biblical apologetics that attempted to strip bare false impressions of the Bible's meaning by linking the study of the Bible to the Holy Land.[34] As other scholars argued over issues of biblical chronology, philology, and historicity, Robinson chose to emphasize the actual existence of the Holy Land.[35] The very existence of such sites as the town of Bethlehem, the River Jordan, and Calvary stood as tangible proof that the events reported in the Bible actually took place. How could one doubt the trustworthiness of the biblical narrative when the places where Jesus was born, baptized, and died still existed for all to see?[36]

While travelers had ventured into the Middle East from America since the opening decade of the nineteenth century, Thomson and Robinson would motivate countless

Protestants to explore the Holy Land personally.[37] Many Protestants returned from such pilgrimages with their faith reaffirmed, yet not every American Protestant could take advantage of these faith-building excursions.[38] Many could, however, find Bibles that brought the Holy Land to them through lavish illustrations and detailed maps. In the midst of the growing apologetic importance of the Holy Land in American Protestant thought, biblical illustrations of the Holy Land became visual texts that allowed the Bible reader to travel vicariously to various biblical sites and authenticate and illuminate the biblical narrative through these mental transmigrations.

Illustrations emphasizing the trustworthiness of the biblical text by linking it to archaeology persisted into the twentieth century. Although the technology used to represent the archaeological links changed from wood block to steel engraving and lithography, and then to photography, the basic belief that the Holy Land provided vibrant testimony to the trustworthiness of the Holy Book remained. Perhaps the most widely distributed twentieth-century Bible edition built around highlighting the apologetic connections between the Bible and Middle Eastern locations and archaeological finds was the American Bible Society's *The Good News, The New Testament with Over 500 Illustrations and Maps*. Released in 1955, this version of the New Testament was a radical departure for the American Bible Society. Since its inception in 1816, the society had prided itself with providing people with the Bible's core text "without note or comment."[39] Now, the American Bible Society was offering a heavily illustrated version purporting to underline the trustworthiness of the biblical message and promising interpretive insights into the biblical narrative. Millions of copies of this New Testament edition (which was printed in six languages) flowed from the American Bible Society in the 1950s.[40]

The Rev. Gilbert Darlington, long-time treasurer of the American Bible Society and director of its publication department, selected the edition's photographs.[41] Although the format of the edition was intended to imitate the photo-magazines of the day, such as *Time* and *Life*, one is struck by the way in which the photographs concentrate on showing off the archaeological and topographic integrity of the Holy Land and various other ancient sites in a way that supports the integrity and authenticity of the New Testament.

Darlington pursued the project with single-minded devotion, committed to the vision that the version's photographs should picture only items and "scenes familiar to Our Lord and to the apostles" because there was "no surer way to get people to know the world of Jesus of Nazareth."[42] His attention to detail is evident in the three years he spent in negotiations to obtain an aerial photograph of the Island of Patmos.[43] Another clue to Darlington's attention to authentic detail is seen in the way a team of scholars headed by Dr. F. W. Albright checked the accuracy of each historical introduction to the New Testament books, the archaeological inscriptions reproduced to clarify scripture passages, and the caption of every one of the 581 photographs.[44]

The technology may have changed, but the goal had not. Biblical characters, artifacts, and places—this time represented with all the vibrancy and immediacy of the photographic art—still bore vivid witness to the authenticity of scripture.[45] Darlington's commitment to authentic detail and accuracy falls in line with a tradition of American biblical illustration where the pictures were carefully chosen and placed, so that they might visually underline the trustworthiness of the biblical text.

RELEVANCE

The fourth strategy in American Bible illustration appears far less frequently than the three mentioned above. It revolves around making the Bible's text relevant to its readers through pictures. Possibly due to a confluence of conditions in the mid–twentieth century, including the geometric growth of Bible edition production, the expansion and diversification of the United States' general population, and the increasingly fractured market of Bible readers, this fourth strategy seems to have begun in the 1940s and continues on a limited scale today. Beginning in the 1940s, publishers offered Bible readers editions with notes and pictures that were specifically bent on making connections between contemporary society and the biblical narrative.

Perhaps the most striking Bible edition to employ this strategy is John Stirling's *The Bible for To-day*, first published in 1941. Stirling, who had a long interest in presenting the Bible to laypeople, had already worked on Bible atlases, children's Bibles, and study Bibles before the appearance of *The Bible for To-day*, a volume he spent twenty years preparing.[46] Declaring his edition to be "the divine revelation for our own times," Stirling made it clear that this edition was the "news of God for the men and the women of this generation."[47] In one of the volume's largest and most centrally located pictures, Stirling's edition encourages its readers to look "by all means" at the world and "know what is going on in every part of it" (fig. 14.5).

Stirling's vision involved getting his readers to appreciate the relevance of scripture to every aspect of their modern lives. He pushed the accessibility of his Bible by formatting his edition like other books of the day, minimizing chapter and verse markings, and replacing such markers with short section titles such as "The Remorse of Judas" and "The Burial of Jesus."[48] He also wanted to connect biblical events with contemporary equivalents by linking pictures of the contemporary world, drawn mostly by the artist Rowland Hilder, to specific biblical texts. Thus, the skilled workmen of Proverbs are portrayed as contemporary draftsmen, a father is shown teaching his son wisdom as they both survey their city from a high-rise building's balcony, and the mighty powers that are mentioned in First Corinthians are echoed by an illustration of a contemporary power plant. In contrast to editors who wanted to associate the Bible with its Middle Eastern past through illustrations, Stirling wanted to make it clear that "viewed without its local colour, the Bible is neither oriental nor ancient. Its backgrounds are the common, ordinary backgrounds of human experience in every age, everywhere, and are thus the setting for divine revelation."[49]

Stirling's vision for a relevant Bible edition would find one of its most popular manifestations in *The Way*, a paraphrase of the Bible released in 1971 and targeted for high

BY ALL MEANS LET US LOOK AT THE WORLD AND

But let our eyes be clear and penetrating that we may grasp the full significance of the living scene. It is not enough to behold the glories of the present world, or gaze in wonder at the latest inventions of the mind of man. We must look with prophets' eyes beneath the surface of things, and beyond the events of the moment to the things that are to come.

708

KNOW WHAT IS GOING ON IN EVERY PART OF IT

We must give a thought to the things that are not seen, to the forces that are at work in the hearts of men, and the end to which they are working. Above all we must ask: Is all well with the world, in the eyes of the Living God? Even in the eyes of men, is life to-day what it should be?

709

FIGURE 14.5

"By All Means," from *The Bible for To-Day*, ed. John Stirling, New York: Oxford University Press, 1941, 708–9. Courtesy Oxford University Press.

school and college students.[50] Within five years, *The Way* had sold almost five million copies as young readers were drawn to its contemporary illustrations and a format that sought to address their world.[51] *The Way* is filled with dozens of photographs of young people placed next to scripture passages in such a way as to link the contemporary setting to the biblical message. For example, the Uruguay spokesperson, Fanny Schnur, is shown speaking at a roundtable discussion with one hundred teens from fifty states on the topic "Protest: A Right and a Responsibility."[52] This photo, with a short essay entitled "Be a Rebel with a Cause," introduced the Gospel of Mark by telling readers that Christ was "the greatest spiritual Activist who ever lived." By positioning Christ as the greatest example of activism ever known, *The Way* sought to appeal to the cause-oriented American youth of the late 1960s and early 1970s.[53]

Other illustrated Bibles in this tradition include editions focused on addressing the history and concerns of different ethnic groups. One of the earliest examples of such an edition appeared in 1940, when the large Philadelphia Bible publishing firm of A. J. Hol-

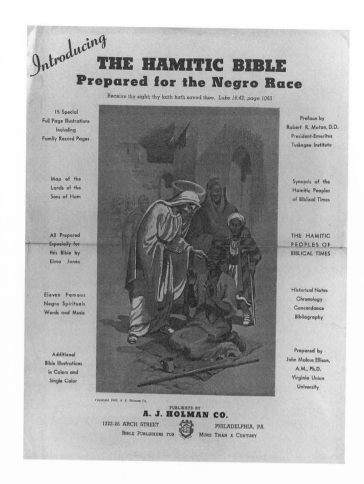

man released *The Story of the Hamitic Peoples of the Old and New Testaments with Original Subject Illustrations* (fig. 14.6). This edition had been specially "prepared for the Negro Race."[54] In a way that would foreshadow the specialized study and devotional Bible editions that would begin to proliferate in the 1980s, this volume strove to make the Bible relevant for its readers by explaining the significance of "The Land of Ham," or Africa, and its people to the Judeo-Christian tradition.[55]

The Story of the Hamitic Peoples used the term "Hamitic" to signify both a place and a racial grouping, and the edition was bent on increasing "Bible reading among American Negroes."[56] The edition wished to show that the "the Sons of Ham" (Noah's descendants characterized by darker skin) had a critically important history that comes "back again from the ages into the present time."[57] By including a "Synopsis of the Hamitic Peoples of Biblical Times" with a bibliography for further study, a "Chronology of Events Bearing upon the Origin and History of the Hamitic Peoples," the words and music to eleven spirituals, a bibliography of sources on Africa and religion, and fifteen original illustrations featuring "Negro" characters, the edition attempted to provide a means for African Americans to trace their lineage to biblical characters, as well as connect the biblical narrative to their contemporary lives.

Through these editions' illustrations, Bible publishers and editors underline the fact that the biblical text is not trapped in ancient history but has a voice for the modern age. As the literary scholar Perry Nodelman has argued, there is a collaborative effect between words and pictures once they are juxtaposed to one another. Joining visual and verbal texts creates a kind of collaborative third text. Nodelman states: "On their own, pictures and words each first allow a number of different narrative possibilities; together they make each more specific."[58] Joining words and pictures can channel a narrative in more specific directions, and for the aforementioned editions, those involved in Bible production use these more specific narrative avenues to collapse the ancient biblical narrative with the contemporary world. As a consequence, they are able to fuse ancient and modern worlds.

PUSHING THE TECHNOLOGICAL ENVELOPE

The final strategy focuses more on process than it does on a specific genre. It concerns the interaction between product and means of production. Changes in printing technology have allowed an ever wider range of possibilities in Bible formatting and illustration. Sometimes the technology has driven content in ways that have had radical repercussions for the biblical text. Throughout the history of American Bible publishing, various new technologies have played a prominent role in changing not only how Bibles were produced and distributed, but also how they were advertised as revivifying the sacred word through modernity. One of the best ways of understanding the complex relationship between product and means of production is to look at two Bible editions set apart because of the way in which they were produced with groundbreaking print technologies. In the early 1840s and then again in the early 1990s, the firm of Harper and Brothers produced strikingly different Bible editions; the first was a spectacular success, the second was a spectacular failure.

In 1843, the firm of Harper and Brothers began to print the first installments of their *Illuminated Bible*, a Bible edition they advertised as "the most splendidly elegant edition of the Sacred Record ever issued."[59] Others readily agreed. The volume quickly became known as the most spectacular book ever printed in the United States, and it changed forever the need American religious publishers felt to illustrate their works. After the *Illuminated Bible*, illustrations became not only an expected but also an integral part of American religious publishing in the nineteenth century.[60]

In looking at the tremendously successful *Illuminated Bible*, it is important to note that although their firm was fast becoming the largest publisher in the United States, the Harpers had not printed a Bible for almost twenty years when Joseph Alexander Adams, a local printer and engraver, went to them with a proposal to produce the grandest Bible the United States had ever seen.[61] What promised to make Adams's edition so special

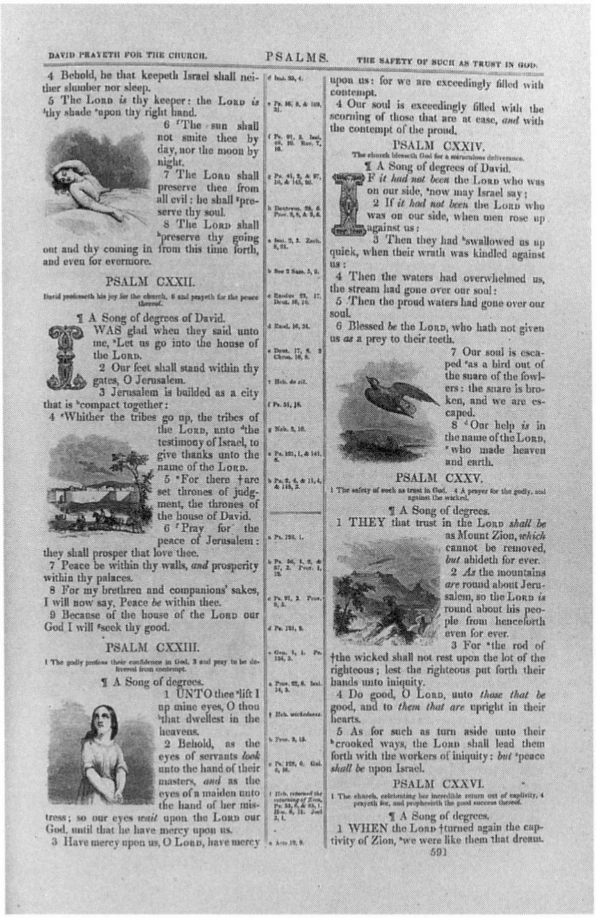

DAVID PRAYETH FOR THE CHURCH. PSALMS. THE SAFETY OF SUCH AS TRUST IN GOD.

4 Behold, he that keepeth Israel shall neither slumber nor sleep.
5 The LORD *is* thy keeper: the LORD *is* thy shade upon thy right hand.
6 The sun shall not smite thee by day, nor the moon by night.
7 The LORD shall preserve thee from all evil: he shall preserve thy soul.
8 The LORD shall preserve thy going out and thy coming in from this time forth, and even for evermore.

PSALM CXXII.

David professeth his joy for the church, 6 and prayeth for the peace thereof.

¶ A Song of degrees of David.
I WAS glad when they said unto me, Let us go into the house of the LORD.
2 Our feet shall stand within thy gates, O Jerusalem.
3 Jerusalem is builded as a city that is compact together:
4 Whither the tribes go up, the tribes of the LORD, unto the testimony of Israel, to give thanks unto the name of the LORD.
5 For there †are set thrones of judgment, the thrones of the house of David.
6 Pray for the peace of Jerusalem: they shall prosper that love thee.
7 Peace be within thy walls, *and* prosperity within thy palaces.
8 For my brethren and companions' sakes, I will now say, Peace *be* within thee.
9 Because of the house of the LORD our God I will seek thy good.

PSALM CXXIII.

1 The godly profess their confidence in God, 3 and pray to be delivered from contempt.

¶ A Song of degrees.
1 UNTO thee lift I up mine eyes, O thou that dwellest in the heavens.
2 Behold, as the eyes of servants *look* unto the hand of their masters, *and* as the eyes of a maiden unto the hand of her mistress; so our eyes *wait* upon the LORD our God, until that he have mercy upon us.
3 Have mercy upon us, O LORD, have mercy upon us: for we are exceedingly filled with contempt.
4 Our soul is exceedingly filled with the scorning of those that are at ease, *and* with the contempt of the proud.

PSALM CXXIV.

The church blesseth God for a miraculous deliverance.

¶ A Song of degrees of David.
IF *it had not been* the LORD who was on our side, now may Israel say;
2 If *it had not been* the LORD who was on our side, when men rose up against us:
3 Then they had swallowed us up quick, when their wrath was kindled against us:
4 Then the waters had overwhelmed us, the stream had gone over our soul:
5 Then the proud waters had gone over our soul.
6 Blessed *be* the LORD, who hath not given us *as* a prey to their teeth.
7 Our soul is escaped as a bird out of the snare of the fowlers: the snare is broken, and we are escaped.
8 Our help *is* in the name of the LORD, who made heaven and earth.

PSALM CXXV.

1 The safety of such as trust in God. 4 A prayer for the godly, and against the wicked.

¶ A Song of degrees.
1 THEY that trust in the LORD *shall be* as Mount Zion, *which* cannot be removed, *but* abideth for ever.
2 *As* the mountains *are* round about Jerusalem, so the LORD *is* round about his people from henceforth even for ever.
3 For the rod of †the wicked shall not rest upon the lot of the righteous; lest the righteous put forth their hands unto iniquity.
4 Do good, O LORD, unto *those that be* good, and to *them that are* upright in their hearts.
5 As for such as turn aside unto their crooked ways, the LORD shall lead them forth with the workers of iniquity: *but* peace *shall be* upon Israel.

PSALM CXXVI.

1 The church, celebrating her incredible return out of captivity, 4 prayeth for, and prophesieth the good success thereof.

¶ A Song of degrees.
1 WHEN the LORD †turned again the captivity of Zion, we were like them that dream.

591

FIGURE 14.7
Page from book of Psalms, Harper's *Illuminated Bible*. New York: Harper Brothers, 1846, 591. By permission of the University of Iowa Libraries (Iowa City).

was its more than sixteen hundred illustrations. No previous American-made Bible had ever had more than one hundred illustrations.

Aside from the enormous number of engravings, Adams wanted to distinguish his volume by placing his pictures on the same pages as the text, rather than the far more common publishing practice of printing illustrations on separate sheets and then binding them with the text (fig. 14.7). Adams promised to accomplish this wonder through a new printing process called electrotyping; a procedure that involved coating stereotyped, wood block or intaglio plates with a thin layer of copper, thereby strengthening them for use in high-speed, high-pressure presses. Electrotyping allowed for large print runs of extremely fine quality text and pictures, and the Harper's *Illuminated Bible* was the first volume printed with the technology.[62]

The *Illuminated Bible* was an immediate success. The initial press run of fifty thousand quickly sold out, and the Harpers decided to run another twenty-five thousand copies in 1846. During the next two decades, sales would remain strong enough for the firm to issue two more printings, in 1859 and 1866.[63] The Harpers made so much money on this Bible edition that they were able to build a new building for their publishing business, and Adams became so wealthy that he was able to retire early. Factors contributing to the success of the *Illuminated Bible* are complex, but it was known in the 1840s as a Bible edition that bypassed all common conventions for illustrating Bibles by offering its readers so many pictures to help them interpret the scriptural text. On one level, the Harpers were able to lure purchasers to their Bible because it was different, innovative, potentially edifying, *and* entertaining.[64] If one jumps 150 years to the early 1990s, it is amazing to see the same drama played out for the Harper publishing firm, but this time with strikingly different results.

In 1993, HarperCollins released *The Bible Alive*. Still a publisher who rarely put out a Bible edition (and then, mostly study Bibles), HarperCollins invested heavily in *The Bible Alive* project, believing that it would be a publishing coup similar to the *Illuminated Bible*. *The Bible Alive* was to be distinctive for two reasons. First, it did not include the whole biblical text, but only a stripped down narrative that was simplified both in vocabulary and narrative complexity. Second, *The Bible Alive* used "a cutting-edge process of photo manipulation to portray scenes from the Bible in their actual settings" to make it a "Bible like no other" by giving the reader a "you-are-there" experience of reading the scriptures (fig. 14.8).[65] The edition's subtitle underlined the distinctive abilities of the volume with the words: "Witness the Great Events of the Bible." What antebellum Bible publishers had started for readers in linking the Holy Land with the biblical text in order to create vicarious travel experiences to Judea found a more contemporary permutation in *The Bible Alive*. This edition promised readers a visual, virtual-reality experience, that would allow them to become actors in the biblical drama.

HarperCollins put a great deal of money into this volume; above all, they keyed their investment dollars on the visual aspects of the edition. Computer specialists were hired, photographic locations were scouted, equipment was transported and dozens of actors were engaged to play parts ranging from Adam to Rahab to Jesus to Saint Paul. Harper-Collins also put a great deal of advertising muscle behind the edition, aggressively putting out ads in a wide range of both secular and religious periodicals.[66] The glory days of the *Illuminated Bible* (and its printing innovations that rocked the publishing world) were seemingly within reach once again. Unlike the *Illuminated Bible*, however, *The Bible Alive* was a dismal failure. The edition sold poorly from its first release, and by 1996, all remaining volumes had been pulped. Just four years after its release, *The Bible Alive* had all but disappeared.

There are many possible reasons for the failure of *The Bible Alive*. A close look at figure 14.8 quickly reveals some of the problems with the edition's illustrations. The computer graphics, which are supposed to give the reader a "you-are-there" feel, appear artificial, understated, and poorly produced. The Egyptian soldiers pursuing the Israelites across the Red Sea look superimposed against a fake background, as does the blurry horse in

FIGURE 14.8 (SEE ALSO PLATE 16)
"Crossing the Red Sea," from *The Bible Alive*, ed. John D. Clare,
1993, facing page 52. © HarperCollins Publishers Ltd. Reprinted
by permission of HarperCollins Publishers, Inc.

the foreground. The Egyptian soldiers also seem to be smirking to themselves, as if they
can anticipate just how ridiculously this picture will turn out. Finally, the waves that supposedly threaten to destroy them (and all of Pharaoh's army) seem more like a mild com-
puter-generated tide on a beach rather than a menacing wall of water full of death and
destruction.

Whatever the reasons for the failure of *The Bible Alive*—which might reach beyond the edition's poor production values to include misjudging a target audience and a failure to realize that the book medium has certain limitations that will forever keep it from being a movie or a video game—of concern here is how becoming enthralled by a new production technology was integral in the creation of a new illustrated Bible edition. HarperCollins sought to capitalize on the rapid changes in computer-manipulated graphics and the popularity of such graphics by offering readers a version of the Bible that might be able to compete with other media that used the same graphic technologies. *The Bible Alive* is a vibrant example of how methods of production exercise a profound influence on the final product.

Of particular interest here is the interaction of these computer-manipulated images with the biblical words they were meant to illustrate. In an attempt to grab the reader through a you-are-there graphic feel, the editors of *The Bible Alive* radically simplified the actual biblical text. They included only short snippets of Bible passages and then surrounded these passages with all sorts of images. What needs to be understood is that when verbal and visual texts are juxtaposed, there arises a competition between the texts for the reader's attention and interpretive energy.[67] This competition is most often decided in favor of the picture. Both the *Illuminated Bible* and *The Bible Alive*, by including so many pictures and having these pictures produced by a technology that was novel, and thus even more intriguing to the reader, strengthened an already extant proclivity to favor pictures over written text in the reading enterprise.

Thus, any insight a picture offers into the interpretation of a text is foregrounded, often to the exclusion of what the written text might actually say. In so heavily illustrating their Bible, it is possible that Harpers and Brothers and HarperCollins created innovative Bible editions that made their readers concentrate more on the Bible's illustrations than on the Bible's words. This pictorial focus could encourage a radical simplification in the reader's interpretive process by highlighting one or two elements of an often extremely complex narrative at the cost of the narrative as a whole. This radical simplification is accented in *The Bible Alive*, where the text itself was abridged and simplified. Consequently, using pictures so centrally in Bible editions such as the *Illuminated Bible* and *The Bible Alive* contributed importantly to eroding a reader's ability to critically engage with a complicated text. Certain segments of American Protestantism that continue to hold the Bible's words as the central tenet of their religious tradition bemoan this erosion, seeing it as a key element in a shift from complicated, theological reasoning to a more simple, and often emotional, discourse in American Protestant communities.[68]

CONCLUSION

While the intellectual design of a book is often the only thing that interests scholars, it is important to note that books are far more than the words they contain. Those words take a corporeal form, which inextricably intertwines intellectual and material designs. Not only are a book's words important, but a book's type, binding, illustrations, format design, dust jacket, paper, price, and methods of distribution can all work to influence the way a reader ultimately interprets a book's words. Illustrations compose just one aspect of a book's design, which may exercise a significant interpretive influence on the words they accompany. The reality that the words found in books are never disembodied from the material form in which they reach their readers is a lesson worthy of note. The long and diverse history of American biblical illustration is important not only as an exercise in the development of a certain genre of art, but as a way to investigate how American Bible producers have long exercised a profound influence on crafting the mutable medium, and thus the mutable meaning, of a supposedly immutable book.

NOTES

PREFACE AND ACKNOWLEDGMENTS

1. The authors and editors use the terms "America" and "American" to refer to the United States of America, understanding of course that the terms might equally apply to Latin America and all of North America.

2. Early exceptions include the works of Charles C. Eldredge, Neil Harris, David C. Huntington, Barbara Novak, Roger Stein, and Joshua Taylor cited in this book's bibliography.

3. Among those scholars whose primary affiliations are with the field of religion or with theological education, John Cook, Jane Dillenberger, John Dillenberger, and John Dixon early acknowledged the significance of the visual; see the selected citations of their work in this book's bibliography.

4. For statistics on religion and religious belief in the United States, see, e.g., George Gallup Jr. and J. Castelli, *The People's Religion: American Faith in the 90s* (New York: Macmillan, 1998); E. H. Hastings and P. K. Hastings, eds., *Index to International Public Opinion, 1994–95* (Westport, Conn.: Greenwood Press, 1996); and Roger Finke and Rodney Stark, *The Churching of America: 1776–1990* (New Brunswick, N.J.: Rutgers University Press, 1992). On the significance of the visual in contemporary American culture, see, e.g., Ian Heywood and Barry Sandywell, eds., *Interpreting Visual Culture: Explorations in the Hermeneutics of the Visual* (London: Routledge, 1999); Nicholas Mirzoeff, *The Visual Culture Reader* (London: Routledge, 1998); David Morgan, *Visual Piety: A History and Theory of Popular Religious Images* (Berkeley and Los Angeles: University of California Press, 1998); James Elkins, *The Object Stares Back: On the Nature of Seeing* (New York: Harcourt, Brace, 1996);

and Constance Classen, *The Color of Angels: Cosmology, Gender, and the Aesthetic Imagination* (London: Routledge, 1998).

5. On Carl Marr's painting, see Carolyn Kinder Carr, "Prejudice and Pride: Presenting American Art at the 1893 Chicago World's Columbian Exposition," in *Revisiting the White City*, exh. cat. (Washington, D.C.: Smithsonian Institution, 1993), 83, 105. The second of the two paintings was a narrative image of domestic sentiment, Thomas Hovenden's *Breaking Home Ties*, 1890, an image that could also fairly be construed to represent religious content. On Eakins's clergy portraits, see Kristin Schwain, "Figuring Belief: Thomas Eakins's Clergy Portraits," Fellows Talk, National Museum of American Art, 9 April 1999, unpublished manuscript; see also Elizabeth Johns, *Thomas Eakins, The Heroism of Modern Life* (Princeton: Princeton University Press, 1983); and Evan H. Turner, "Thomas Eakins at Overbrook," *Records of the Catholic Historical Society of Philadelphia* 81, no. 4 (Dec. 1970): 195–98. On the 1905–6 competition and touring exhibition, see R. N. C., "New Conceptions of Christ," *Brush and Pencil* 17, no. 4 (April 1906): 148–57; and William Griffith, "Christ as American Artists See Him," *The Craftsman* 10, no. 3 (June 1906): 286–99. On Alfred Barr Jr. and his colleagues on the Commission on Art, see Sally M. Promey, "Interchangeable Art: Warner Sallman and the Critics of Mass Culture," in *Icons of American Protestantism,* ed. David Morgan (New Haven: Yale University Press, 1996), esp. 172–74.

6. Finke and Stark, *Churching of America;* R. Laurence Moore, *Selling God: American Religion in the Marketplace of Culture* (New York: Oxford University Press, 1994); and R. Stephen Warner, "Work in Progress toward a New Paradigm for the Sociological Study of Religion in the United States," *American Journal of Sociology* 98, no. 5 (March 1993): 1044–93.

7. Nathan O. Hatch, "The Whirlwind of Religious Liberty in Early America," in Richard Helmstadter, *Freedom and Religion in the Nineteenth Century* (Stanford: Stanford University Press, 1997), 29, 32; Paul DiMaggio, "Cultural Boundaries and Structural Change: The Extension of the High Culture Model to Theater, Opera, and the Dance, 1900–1940," in *Cultivating Differences: Symbolic Boundaries and the Making of Inequality,* ed. Michèle Lamont and Marcel Fournier (Chicago: University of Chicago Press, 1992), 21–57; and Lawrence W. Levine, *Highbrow/Lowbrow: The Emergence of Cultural Hierarchy in America* (Cambridge, Mass.: Harvard University Press, 1988).

INTRODUCTION

1. Toni Morrison, *The Bluest Eye* (New York: Penguin, 1994), 50.

2. Ibid., 92–93.

3. See, for example, "Religion's Changing Face: More Churches Depicting Christ as Black," *Washington Post,* 28 March 1994, A1.

4. Marion Aigner, "Religion and Art Follow Our Fighting Men," *American Art* (Nov. 1942): 20–21, 38. See also William C. Barker, "American Triptych Art: Spiritual Armor," *The Correspondent* (spring 1997): 2; Barker, who is curator at the Virginia War Museum, is preparing a longer manuscript on these altarpieces.

5. We thank Ellen Menefee and Louis Nelson for sharing materials on Lily Yeh.

6. The authors would like to thank Professor Wai-Tung Cho for assistance in translation.

7. Catherine L. Albanese, *America: Religions and Religion* (Belmont, Cal.: Wadsworth, 1981), 283–309.

8. Four murals, painted in the mid–nineteenth century for the Capitol Rotunda, represented not just moments of consequence in the nation's past, but also the construction of a coherent historical narrative in relation to divine providence and agency. Perhaps not coincidentally, John Chapman, whose rotunda mural, *The Baptism of Pocahontas* (fig. 1.5), was the first one completed (1836–40), also produced many of the illustrations for the immensely popular Harper's *Illuminated Bible*. In *Baptism of Pocahontas*, Chapman asserted his conviction that American "civilization" depended upon the conversion of the land and its native populations to the Christianity of the early European colonists. See Vivien Green Fryd, *Art and Empire: The Politics of Ethnicity in the U.S. Capitol, 1815–1860* (New Haven: Yale University Press, 1992), 45–59, esp. 47. Similarly, the other three rotunda murals (John Vanderlyn's *Landing of Columbus*, 1836–47; Robert W. Weir's *Embarkation of the Pilgrims*, 1836–43; and William H. Powell's *Discovery of the Mississippi*, 1847–55) all include emblems of religious (here Christian) conviction or conversion.

9. For a detailed discussion of Washington's importance in American public culture, see Karal Ann Marling, *George Washington Slept Here: Colonial Revivals and American Culture, 1876–1986* (Cambridge, Mass.: Harvard University Press, 1988). On American civil religion and Washington, Catherine L. Albanese, *Sons of the Fathers: The Civil Religion of the American Revolution* (Philadelphia: Temple University Press, 1976), 143–81.

10. See catalogues for two exhibitions on this subject: *The Spiritual in Art: Abstract Painting, 1890–1985*, exh. cat., Los Angeles County Museum of Art, 1986; and *Negotiating Rapture: The Power of Art to Transform Lives*, ed. Richard Francis, exh. cat., Museum of Contemporary Art, Chicago, 1996.

11. On the mourning ritual, see Maurice Lamm, *The Jewish Way in Death and Mourning*, rev. ed. (New York: J. David, 1977), 76, 195.

12. For examples of discerning images in visual marks, see Stewart Elliot Guthrie, *Faces in the Clouds: A New Theory of Religion* (New York: Oxford University Press, 1993), 142–46; and David Morgan, *Visual Piety: A History and Theory of Popular Religious Images* (Berkeley and Los Angeles: University of California Press, 1998), 124–51.

13. Stuart R. Kaplan, *The Encyclopedia of Tarot*, 2 vols. (New York: U.S. Games Systems, 1978), 1: 330. Meanings vary widely from one tarot to the next, though certain themes are apparent. Oswald Wirth, a nineteenth-century occultist who drew on a wide variety of sources such as rosicrucianism, alchemy, freemasonry, and ancient magic when he created designs for a set of tarot cards in 1889, stated that The Hanged Man meant "The soul freed from the enclosing body. Mysticism. Priest . . . Redeeming sacrifice. Activity of the soul. Remote intervention. Telepathy"; Oswald Wirth, *The Tarot of the Magicians* (York Beach, Maine: Samuel Weiser, 1985), 112. A third source also lists sacrifice, but adds "unjust calumny, death through violence, early death, the discovery of scientific and metaphysical truths hidden in the earth"; Basil Ivan Rákóczi, *The Painted Caravan: A Penetration into the Secrets of the Tarot Cards* (The Hague: J. C. Boucher, 1954), 49. For an excellent study of the association of tarot and the occult, see Ronald Decker, Thierry

Depaulis, and Michael Dummett, *A Wicked Pack of Cards: The Origin of the Occult Tarot* (New York: St. Martin's Press, 1996).

14. Kaplan, *Encyclopedia of Tarot*, 1: 343–44.

15. Guthrie, *Faces in the Clouds*, 91–121; on the autonomy of images, see David Freedberg, *The Power of Images: Studies in the History and Theory of Response* (Chicago: University of Chicago Press, 1989); Elkins, *The Object Stares Back*; and W. J. T. Mitchell, "What Do Pictures *Really* Want?" *OCTOBER* 77 (summer 1996): 71–82.

16. Kaplan, *Encyclopedia of Tarot*, 1: 327. See also Angeles Arrien, *The Tarot Handbook: Practical Applications of Ancient Visual Symbols* (New York: Jeremy P. Tarcher/Putnam, 1997), 12.

17. For further discussion of this dynamic, see Sally M. Promey, *Spiritual Spectacles: Vision and Image in Mid-Nineteenth-Century Shakerism* (Bloomington: Indiana University Press, 1993).

18. There is a considerable literature on *Blade Runner*. For a broad range of essays, see *Retrofitting Blade Runner: Issues in Ridley Scott's* Blade Runner *and Philip K. Dick's* Do Androids Dream of Electric Sheep?, ed. Judith B. Kerman (Bowling Green, Ohio: Popular Culture Press, 1991); and W. M. Kolb, "*Blade Runner*: An Annotated Bibliography," *Literature Film Quarterly* 18, no. 1 (1990): 19–64.

19. See, for instance, Colleen McDannell, *Material Christianity: Religion and Popular Culture in America* (New Haven: Yale University Press, 1995), 1–16.

20. W. J. T. Mitchell, *Picture Theory* (Chicago: University of Chicago Press, 1994), 11–34.

21. See also Sally M. Promey, *Painting Religion in Public: John Singer Sargent's* Triumph of Religion *at the Boston Public Library* (Princeton: Princeton University Press, 1999).

22. See also David Morgan, *Protestants and Pictures: Religion, Visual Culture, and the Age of American Mass Production* (New York: Oxford University Press, 1999).

23. Alan Taylor, "The Early Republic's Supernatural Economy: Treasure-Seeking in the American Northeast, 1780–1830," *American Quarterly* 38 (spring 1986): 6–33.

CHAPTER 1

1. I selected the title of my chapter for its accurate description of my subject—but also for its mildly provocative character. Historian of American church history Martin E. Marty had a similar sense of impropriety in mind when he titled his 1988 presidential address to the American Academy of Religion "Committing the Study of Religion in Public"; Martin E. Marty, "Committing the Study of Religion in Public," *Journal of the American Academy of Religion* 57, no. 1 (spring 1989). Like the "public display of affection" (a behavior proscribed in the United States military—where it earns the acronym PDA—and discouraged or regulated in public high schools), the subject of my chapter carries a trace of the illicit, the outcome of yoking the modifiers "public" and "display" with the topic "religion."

Modest portions of the text of this chapter first appeared in the introduction and epilogue to Sally M. Promey, *Painting Religion in Public: John Singer Sargent's "Triumph of Religion" at the Boston Public Library* (Princeton: Princeton University Press, 1999). My manuscript-in-progress, titled *Religion in Plain View: The Public Aesthetics of American*

Belief, explores the history of the public display of religion in the United States from the eighteenth century to the present.

2. Here the "sectarian" is not a less formalized, less developed alternative to the "established church" but refers to any particularist expression of religious affiliation. For contemporary religion, especially, it is difficult to imagine the religious expression of a group or individual that would qualify as genuinely "nonsectarian." Furthermore, recent world events have brought to wider public attention the recognition that there is no more one Judaism or one Islam than there is one Christianity or even one Protestantism.

    W. J. T. Mitchell, "The Violence of Public Art: Do the Right Thing," in *Art and the Public Sphere,* ed. W. J. T. Mitchell (Chicago: University of Chicago Press, 1990), 38.

3. In 1868, the Fourteenth Amendment brought the states into conformity with national civil liberties standards; in 1940 *Cantrell v. Connecticut* asserted that the Free Exercise Clause imposed the same restraints on the states as on the nation; in 1947 *Everson v. Board of Education* ruled that the Establishment Clause extended in the same way. Since the 1940s, in part because of these decisions, establishment cases, most often concerned in some way with public school education, have appeared with increasing regularity on court dockets. Only a few cases have explicitly concerned the public display of religion as it is defined in this chapter. See Wayne R. Swanson, *The Christ Child Goes to Court* (Philadelphia: Temple University Press, 1990), especially 7, 12.

4. See Leonard W. Levy, *The Establishment Clause: Religion and the First Amendment* (Chapel Hill: University of North Carolina Press, 1994).

5. See, for example, John Beardsley, *Gardens of Revelation: Environments by Visionary Artists* (New York: Abbeville Press, 1995); Edward T. Linenthal, "Locating Holocaust Memory: The United States Holocaust Memorial Museum," in *American Sacred Space,* ed. David Chidester and Edward T. Linenthal (Bloomington: Indiana University Press, 1995), 220–61; Levy, *Establishment Clause;* and Swanson, *Christ Child Goes to Court.*

6. See, for example, Mitchell, ed., *Art and the Public Sphere;* Erika Doss, *Spirit Poles and Flying Pigs: Public Art and Cultural Democracy in American Communities* (Washington, D.C.: Smithsonian Institution Press, 1995); and Harriet F. Senie and Sally Webster, eds., *Critical Issues in Public Art: Content, Context, and Controversy* (New York: HarperCollins, 1992).

7. See R. Stephen Warner, "Work in Progress toward a New Paradigm for the Sociological Study of Religion in the United States," *American Journal of Sociology* 98, no. 5 (March 1993): esp. 1052. In my chapter, following Peter Berger, pluralism describes "the coexistence and social interaction of people with very different beliefs, values, and lifestyles"; Peter L. Berger, "Protestantism and the Quest for Certainty," *Christian Century* 115, no. 23 (26 Aug.–2 Sept. 1998): 782. "Pluralism" is thus a state of affairs roughly synonymous with social pluriformity, where such pluriformity assumes some degree of engagement with difference. Here pluralism is an American reality as well as an American ideal, historically grounded, though not explicitly articulated, in the First Amendment.

    Historian of religion Diana Eck asserts the relationship of both pluralism and religious display to identity formation when she describes the "culture wars" of the early 1990s as a "national identity crisis"; Diana L. Eck, "Challenge of Pluralism," *Nieman Reports* 47, no. 2 (summer 1993): 7, as mounted on the Diana L. Eck, "Pluralism Project" website, http://www.fas.harvard.edu/~pluralism/html/article-cop.html.

8. Quotation is taken from an unidentified newspaper clipping, "Mural to Provide Residents with Healing Image," 28 Sept. 1997, Treviño archives, courtesy of Carolee Youngblood. Treviño describes himself as a "realist" painter; in 1994 he had a one-artist show at the National Museum of American Art, Smithsonian Institution; see http://www.jesse trevino.com. The artist based his guardian angel on a local cemetery statue; the cross in the painting reiterates the large-scale cross on the adjacent hospital wing. The hospital itself is sited next to an urban park across from Market Square.

9. See, for example, Jeff Weintraub, "The Theory and Politics of the Public/Private Distinction," in *Public and Private in Thought and Practice*, ed. Jeff Weintraub and Krishan Kumar (Chicago: University of Chicago Press, 1997), 1–3.

10. John F. Wilson, "The Public as a Problem," in *Caring for the Commonweal: Education for Religious and Public Life*, ed. Parker J. Palmer, Barbara G. Wheeler, and James W. Fowler (Macon, Ga.: Mercer University Press, 1990), 13. Nathan Hatch has recently suggested that the fact of colonial religious diversity (rather than the fulfillment of heroic aspirations for religious liberty) provided the basis for religious freedom in the United States; Nathan O. Hatch, "The Whirlwind of Religious Liberty in Early America," in *Freedom and Religion in the Nineteenth Century*, ed. Richard Helmstadter (Stanford: Stanford University Press, 1997), 29–53.

11. Cited in Warner, "Work in Progress," 1075.

12. Richard Helmstadter, "Introduction," in *Freedom and Religion*, ed. Helmstadter, especially 5–8.

13. Quoted in Robin Lovin, "Beyond the Pursuit of Happiness: Religion and Public Discourse in Liberalism's Fourth Century," in *Caring for the Commonweal*, ed. Parker, Wheeler, and Fowler, 47.

14. Quoted in Robert T. Handy, "Changing Contexts of Church-State Relations in America, 1880–1920," in *Caring for the Commonweal*, ed. Parker, Wheeler, and Fowler, 30, 34.

15. Ibid., 37.

16. Weintraub, "Theory and Politics," 6; and Allan Silver, "'Two Different Sorts of Commerce'—Friendship and Strangership in Civil Society," in *Public and Private in Thought and Practice*, ed. Weintraub and Kumar, 45.

17. See Helmstadter, "Introduction."

18. Wilson, "Public as a Problem," 15; see also Stanley I. Benn and Gerald F. Gaus, "The Public and the Private: Concepts and Action," in *Public and Private in Social Life*, ed. Stanley I. Benn and Gerald F. Gaus (New York: St. Martin's Press, 1983), 20–21.

19. Weintraub, "Theory and Politics," 4–5.

20. Robert A. White, "Religion and Media in the Construction of Cultures," in *Rethinking Media, Religion, and Culture*, ed. Stewart M. Hoover and Knut Lundby (Thousand Oaks, Cal.: Sage Publications, 1997), 40, 45.

21. The quoted phrase belongs to Jean Bethke Elshtain, "The Displacement of Politics," in *Public and Private in Thought and Practice*, 167; see also Stewart M. Hoover, "Media and the Construction of the Religious Public Sphere," in *Rethinking Media, Religion, and Culture*, 283–97.

22. Mitchell, "Violence of Public Art," 30.
23. The Internet represents a particular challenge to conventional notions of privacy. See, for example, artist John Snogren's website, "Heavenly Visions Byzantine Icon Studio," where he markets icons for contemplative use; http://www.heavenlyvisions.com; see also Mark A. Kellner, *God on the Internet: Your Complete Guide to Enhancing Your Spiritual Life via the Internet and Online Services* (Foster City, Cal.: IDG Books, 1996).
24. W. J. T. Mitchell, "Introduction: Utopia and Critique," in *Art and the Public Sphere*, 2.
25. In its adjectival usage, and in relation to our purposes here, "public" describes the picture, object, monument, place, or performance seen. In its nominative usage, the emphasis shifts from the object to the spectator, from the thing that is visible to the person who sees it, from production and placement to reception. The most fruitful understandings of the public display of religion will involve the consideration neither simply of things nor of people but of the relations between things and people.
26. On the contingency of performance, see Edward L. Schieffelin, "Problematizing Performance," in *Ritual, Performance, Media,* ed. Felicia Hughes-Freeland (London: Routledge, 1998), 197–98.
27. Editorial from the *Billings Gazette,* 11 December 1993, as quoted in *Jews/America/A Representation,* essay by Simon Schama, photographs by Frédéric Brenner (New York: Harry N. Abrams, 1996), 58.
28. As quoted in Vicky Greenberg, "The American Chapter of the Jewish Saga," *New York Times,* 22 September 1996, H33.
29. Often associated with these suspicions of ostentation, connections to commerce also make an appearance here. In a consumer culture like that of the early-twenty-first-century United States, the staging and the interpretation of display assume a commercial set of relations. It is not just the role of display in "making [its subject] public" that seems ill-suited to apparent preferences for religion "in private." The "taint" of commerce, too, sometimes preconditions initial negative reactions to religion's public display. Ironically (in this regard), the public display of American religion has enjoyed a long and even venerable acquaintance with commerce. As historian R. Laurence Moore points out, American religion played a critical and formative role in shaping modern consumerism; R. Laurence Moore, *Selling God: American Religion in the Marketplace of Culture* (New York: Oxford University Press, 1994), 35, 43. American religious culture is thus an entity complicit and conversant in the mechanisms of commercial display. Public display is an important aspect of the "open market" of religion in the United States; Warner, "Work in Progress," 1050–51. As the face of global commerce has become more uniform in the course of the late twentieth and early twenty-first centuries, the face of American religious display (both within a single religious tradition and among different religions) has also become more various.
30. Karen-Edis Barzman's unpublished research on spectacle has informed my own thinking in this regard; see Karen-Edis Barzman, "Ritual and Vision: Renaissance Spectacle and the Performance of Images," lecture delivered on 11 March 1999, University of Maryland.
31. The Virginia War Museum owns the ten triptychs included in the 1997 summer exhibition.

32. Felicia Hughes-Freeland, "Introduction," in *Ritual, Performance, Media*, ed. Hughes-Freeland, 3.

33. Minister and sand sculptor Randy Hofman sprays his creations with diluted Elmer's Glue to protect them from the wind; he illuminates them with colored lights at night. The groups of figures, about twelve feet high and as many wide, take about seven hours to complete and generally include one or more representations of Jesus. Hofman has been making them each summer since 1974. When a reporter asked about motivation for his figures, Hofman replied: "I'm just trying to remind people who may be away from home for the first time as young adults that God is still watching"; Lyndsey Layton, "Ocean City Sighs as Tide of Tourists Ebbs," *Washington Post*, 30 August 1998, B1 and B4.

34. Warner, "Work in Progress," 1059.

35. See, for example, Ivan Karp, "Introduction: Museums and Communities: The Politics of Public Culture," in *Museums and Communities: The Politics of Public Culture*, ed. Ivan Karp, Christine Mullen-Kreamer, and Steven D. Lavine (Washington, D.C.: Smithsonian Institution Press, 1992), 1–6, 14. I am grateful to Ellen Smith for bringing these eyeglasses to my attention. The manufacturer of these "Gemini Hol✿day Specs©" is Gemini Kaleidoscopes of Zelienople, Pennsylvania.

36. For the quotation from Rehnquist's letter, see Tamara Jones, "Supreme Court Won't Alter Frieze Depicting Muhammad," *Washington Post*, 13 March 1997, B1 and B8; for quotation from tourist brochure, see "Courtroom Friezes: North and South Walls," Fact Sheet, Office of the Curator, Supreme Court of the United States, 25 January 1999.

37. Quoted in Joan Biskupic, "Lawgivers: From Two Friezes, Great Figures of Legal History Gaze upon the Supreme Court Bench," *Washington Post*, 11 March 1998, H1 and H4.

38. Swanson, *Christ Child Goes to Court*.

39. Ibid., 141.

40. Meredith Narcum, "A Hand That Grabs Attention: Different Meanings Evoked by Tree-Carving," *Silver Spring Gazette*, 14 January 1998, A1 and A11.

41. Roger D. Fallot, "The Place of Spirituality and Religion in Mental Health Services," in *Spirituality and Religion in Recovery from Mental Illness*, ed. Roger D. Fallot (San Francisco: Jossey-Bass, 1998), 4–5; see also Robert Wuthnow, *Producing the Sacred: An Essay on Public Religion* (Urbana: University of Illinois Press, 1994), 3.

42. Warner, "Work in Progress," 1049. Roger Finke and Rodney Stark assign this phenomenon to disestablishment and to the rise of an open market in religion in the United States; Roger Finke and Rodney Stark, *The Churching of America, 1776–1990* (New Brunswick, N.J.: Rutgers University Press, 1992).

43. See, for example, Bill Broadway, "Poll Finds Americans 'As Churched as Ever': Beliefs in God Have Changed Little Since 1947, But Faithful Sample More Forms of Spirituality," *Washington Post*, 31 May 1997, B7.

44. See, for example, Adam Walsh, "Church, Lies, and Polling Data," *Religion in the News* 1, no. 2 (fall 1998), 9–11.

45. Berger, "Protestantism and the Quest for Certainty," 782. See also Hatch, "Whirlwind of Religious Liberty in Early America," on religious pluralism and the foundation of American religious liberty.

46. Warner, "Work in Progress," 1046–47.

47. Ibid., 1047, 1060. See also Diane Winston, "Campuses Are a Bellwether for Society's Religious Revival," *Chronicle of Higher Education*, 16 January 1998, A60; Richard Cimino and Don Lattin, *Shopping for Faith: American Religion in the New Millennium* (San Francisco: Jossey-Bass, 1998); and Mark Silk, "A New Establishment?" *Religion in the News* 1, no. 2 (fall 1998): 3.

48. For a discussion of one prominent artist's expression of this conviction, see Sally M. Promey, *Painting Religion in Public*.

49. Warner, "Work in Progress," 1061.

50. Hatch, "Whirlwind of Religious Liberty in Early America," 29–53.

51. Winston, "Campuses Are a Bellwether," A60.

52. Ibid.

53. Berger, "Protestantism and the Quest for Certainty," 782.

54. Warner, "Work in Progress," 1058. In many parts of the United States, Christianity retains precedence in the visual landscape. The prevalence of Christian display in large areas of the country is nonetheless modulated by the *varieties* of Christian expression and by the display of wider (non-Christian) religious pluralism in the mass media, on television and in the newspapers, for example.

55. See, for example, Mark Silk, "Why *Religion in the News*?" *Religion in the News* 1, no. 1 (June 1998): 3. This increasing publicness of religion is not the result of religion in the United States entering the marketplace; it may be, rather, one result of its always having been there. See Moore, *Selling God*.

56. See Charita M. Goshay, "Buddhist Truth: Buddhist Monk Leads Local Group in Search," *Canton Repository*, 13 February 1999, and http://www.cantonrep.com.

57. See Diana Eck, "Challenge of Pluralism," 2, 4–6, on religious architecture and the visibility of a "new multireligious reality."

58. Susan Levine, "A Place for Those Who Pray: Along Montgomery's 'Highway to Heaven,' Diverse Acts of Faith," *Washington Post*, 3 August 1997, B1 and B4–B5.

59. Simon Coleman and John Elsner, "Performing Pilgrimage: Walsingham and the Ritual Construction of Irony," in *Ritual, Performance, Media*, 46–47.

60. W. J. T. Mitchell, "Introduction," in *Landscape and Power*, ed. W. J. T. Mitchell (Chicago: University of Chicago Press, 1994), 1.

61. See Schieffelin, "Problematizing Performance," 205, where Schieffelin discusses the performance aspects of what I have called "display." Ian Heywood and Barry Sandywell, too, understand visual culture as part of a "socio-historical realm of interpretive practices"; Ian Heywood and Barry Sandywell, "Introduction: Explorations in the Hermeneutics of Vision," in *Interpreting Visual Culture: Explorations in the Hermeneutics of Vision*, ed. Ian Heywood and Barry Sandywell (London: Routledge, 1999), xi.

62. Warner, "Work in Progress," 1052; and Lawrence Alloway, *Network: Art and the Complex Present* (Ann Arbor, Mich.: UMI Research Press, 1984), 3, 8.

63. Pluralism can be understood as a cultural practice because it assumes some degree of social interaction. The visual expression of plural religion organizes varying degrees of engagement between individuals and the diversity of American culture. In the case of the United States, religion can be construed as a principal conceptual location for encountering difference, for the cultural practice of pluralism.

64. Jesús Martín-Barbero, "Mass Media as a Site of Resacralization of Contemporary Cultures," in *Rethinking Media, Religion, and Culture*, 102. Martín-Barbero speaks of mass-mediated expression in particular.

CHAPTER 2

1. George Emery Littlefield, *Early Schools and School-Books of New England* (Boston: The Club of Odd Volumes, 1904), 152. The Latin grammar by Johann Comenius, *Orbis Pictus*, 1657, which was frequently translated and reprinted, organized vertical columns of images beside sentences and the letters of the alphabet, anticipating the configuration seen much later in the *New England Primer*—see Clifton Johnson, *Old-Time Schools and School-Books* (New York: Dover Publications, 1963), 15–19. On the revival of Comenius's book in the late nineteenth century, see Mitford M. Mathews, *Teaching to Read Historically Considered* (Chicago: University of Chicago Press, 1966), 141–43.

2. On the *New England Primer*, see Paul Leicester Ford, ed., *The New England Primer: A History of Its Origins and Development* (New York: Dodd, Mead, 1897) and Patricia U. Bonomi, *Education and Religion in Early America: Gleanings from The New England Primer*, 13th Annual Phi Alpha Theta Distinguished Lecture on History, 1993 (Albany: Department of History, State University of New York, 1993); on the primer and other school books in use during the colonial period, see Littlefield, *Early Schools and School-Books of New England;* and Johnson, *Old-Time Schools and School-Books*, 69–99. The *New England Primer* was first published by a Boston and London printer named Benjamin Harris around 1690. For primers other than the *New England Primer*, see Charles F. Heartman, *American Primers, Indian Primers, Royal Primers, and Thirty-seven Other Types of Non-New England Primers Issued Prior to 1830* (Highland Park, N.J.: Printed for Harry B. Weiss, 1935).

3. Frederick Douglass, *Narrative of the Life of Frederick Douglass, An American Slave*, ed. Houston A. Baker Jr. (New York: Penguin Books, 1985), 78.

4. T[homas] H[opkins] Gallaudet, *The Child's Picture Defining and Reading Book* (Hartford, Conn.: H. & F. J. Huntington; Boston: Richardson, Lord & Holbrook; New York: Jonathan Leavitt, 1830), iv. For biographical material on Gallaudet (1787–1851), see Henry Barnard, "Educational Biography. Thomas Hopkins Gallaudet," *The American Journal of Education* 1, no. 4 (May 1856): 417–32; abridged from Henry Barnard, "Tribute to Gallaudet. A Discourse on the Life, Character, and Services of Thomas Hopkins Gallaudet, LL.D., delivered before the Citizens of Hartford, 7th January 1852, with an Appendix, containing History of Deaf-mute Instruction and Institutions."

5. [David B. Tower], *The Progressive Pictorial Primer* (Boston: Bazin & Ellsworth; Portland: Francis Blake, 1857), Preface, n.p. The empiricist understanding of the human mind stressed that the mind of the young child was a blank slate waiting to be inscribed. As one author of an illustrated primer published in 1842 put it:

> There is perhaps no period of life having a more important influence upon the future improvement of the child, than that through which he passes during his rudimental studies. The mind then, unencumbered, and like "the pure unsullied sheet," is ready to receive any impression that may be made upon it. In order to give the juvenile mind a proper impulse, such as will produce a favourable result in after life, the rudiments of literature should be

presented, if possible, in a form at once interesting and attractive. And this can only be done, by putting such books into the hands of children, as will engage their attention, and render study pleasant and agreeable: such only, as will arouse their dormant energies, and call into action those noble faculties with which they are endowed by their Creator.

Rensselaer Bentley, *The Pictorial Primer* (New York: Saxton & Miles; Boston: Saxton, Pierce; Philadelphia: A. S. Barnes, 1842), Preface, n.p. Bentley intended his illustrated primer for just this purpose.

6. The quotation is from Charles W. Sanders and J. C. Sanders, *Sanders' Pictorial Primer* (New York: Mark H. Newman, 1846), 4, emphasis in original. For illustrated readers, see John Pierpont, *The Young Reader* (Boston: Richardson, Lord, and Holbrook, 1831), containing eighteen wood engravings by Abel Bowen among others. McGuffey's spellers and readers were illustrated on an even greater scale—see Stanley W. Lindberg, *The Annotated McGuffey: Selections from the McGuffey Eclectic Readers, 1836–1920* (New York: Van Nostrand Reinhold, 1976) and Harvey C. Minnich, *William Holmes McGuffey and His Readers* (New York: American Book Company, 1936), 113–41—as were the Peter Parley books by Samuel G. Goodrich. See for example, *A Present from Peter Parley to All His Little Friends* (Philadelphia: Thomas Holden, 1831), with 220 engravings. Pierpont, McGuffey, and Goodrich each included explicitly religious material in their school books.

7. Jacob Abbott, *The Little Learner. Learning to Talk* (New York: Harper & Brothers, 1856), viii.

8. Quoted in Rudolph R. Reeder, "The Historical Development of School Readers and Method in Teaching Reading" (Ph.D. thesis, Columbia University, 1900), 68; *American Annals of Education and Instruction* 6 (1836), 226. For helpful bibliographies of early school books, see Joe Park, ed., *The Rise of American Education: An Annotated Bibliography* (Evanston: Northwestern University Press, 1965) and *Early American Textbooks, 1775–1900* (Washington, D.C.: United States Department of Education, 1985). For a discussion of school texts and illustrations, see Johnson, *Old-Time Schools and School-Books.*

9. J[onathan] Lamb, "Advertisement," *The Child's Primer; or First Book for Primary Schools* (Burlington, Vt.: Chauncey Goodrich, 1830), 3.

10. Charles and J. C. Sanders, *Sanders' Pictorial Primer*, 4.

11. Examples of these primers are Samuel Worcester, *A Primer of the English Language* (Boston: Benjamin B. Mussey and Hilliard, Gray, 1835); the countless republications of the *New England Primer*, such as those published in Boston by the Massachusetts Sabbath School Society in the 1830s and 1840s as well as other versions of the same by the American Tract Society such as the one produced by Frances Manwaring Caulkins, *The Tract Primer* (New York: American Tract Society, 1848); and *The American Pictorial Primer* (New York: George F. Cooledge & Brother, 1844).

12. The explosion of illustrated school books was part of the larger increase in illustrated publications in the antebellum period such as newspapers and magazines. This development was a component of the emergence of a mass culture in the first half of the nineteenth century that should be understood in terms of the market revolution and the increase of literacy in the United States. For a discussion of literacy in this cultural context, see William J. Gilmore, "Literacy, The Rise of an Age of Reading, and the Cultural Grammar of Print Communications in America, 1735–1850," *Communication* 11, no. 1 (1988), 23–46; Mary Kupiec Cayton, "Print and Publishing," in *Encyclopedia of Amer-*

ican Social History, ed. Mary Kupiec Cayton, Elliott J. Gorn, and Peter W. Williams, 3 vols. (New York: Scribner's, 1993) 1: 2427–45; and David Morgan, *Protestants and Pictures: Religion, Visual Culture, and the Age of American Mass Production* (New York: Oxford University Press, 1999), chaps. 1, 6.

13. For an insightful discussion of this paradox, see David B. Tyack, "Forming the National Character: Paradox in the Educational Thought of the Revolutionary Generation," *Harvard Educational Review* 36, no. 1 (winter 1966): 29–41.

14. Scholarly literature on the antebellum ideology of education as the basis of the civic virtue of a republican citizenry includes: Lawrence A. Cremin, *American Education: The National Experience, 1783–1876* (New York: Harper & Row, 1980); Ruth Miller Elson, *Guardians of Tradition: American Schoolbooks of the Nineteenth Century* (Lincoln: University of Nebraska Press, 1964); J. Merton England, "The Democratic Faith in American Schoolbooks, 1783–1860," *American Quarterly* 15, no. 2, pt. 1 (summer 1963): 191–99; Carl F. Kaestle, *Pillars of the Republic: Common Schools and American Society, 1780–1860* (New York: Hill and Wang, 1983); E. Jennifer Monaghan, *A Common Heritage: Noah Webster's Blue-Back Speller* (Hamden: Archon Books, 1983); Timothy C. Smith, "Protestant Schooling and American Nationality, 1800–1850," *The Journal of American History* 53, no. 4 (March 1967): 679–95; and Tyack, "Forming the National Character."

15. Noah Webster, *The American Spelling-Book* (New York: Samuel Campbell, 1792), ix. For a collection of important pedagogical treatises from this time, see Frederick Rudolph, ed., *Essays on Education in the Early Republic* (Cambridge, Mass: The Belknap Press of Harvard University Press, 1965).

16. "Washington at Prayer," *The Illuminated American Primer* (New York: Turner & Hayden, 1844), 35–36.

17. Louisa May Alcott, *Little Women* (New York: Penguin, 1989), 82, 86.

18. The theme of almsgiving as well as its iconography was inherited from British pious literature. For a brief history of British almsgiving, see W. K. Jordan, *Philanthropy in England, 1480–1660* (London: Allen & Unwin, 1959); Ian Williams, *The Alms Trade: Charities, Past, Present and Future* (London: Unwin Hyman, 1989), 5–53; and Clive Berridge, *The Almshouses of London* (Southampton: Ashford Press, 1987). On the history of charities and philanthropic organizations in eighteenth- and nineteenth-century Britain, see Ford K. Brown, *Fathers of the Victorians: The Age of Wilberforce* (Cambridge, Eng.: Cambridge University Press, 1961), 317–60; and Thomas Walter Laqueur, *Religion and Respectability: Sunday Schools and Working Class Culture, 1780–1850* (New Haven: Yale University Press, 1976). The benevolent portrayal of beggars and the indigent occurs in the work of Thomas Bewick, the British engraver who inspired the American Alexander Anderson to emulate his technique in countless American Bibles, school books, and American editions of Bewick's *History of Quadrupeds*. See, for example, the images reproduced and discussed in John Brewer, *The Pleasures of the Imagination: English Culture in the Eighteenth Century* (New York: Farrar, Straus and Giroux, 1997), 523–25.

19. William H. McGuffey, *McGuffey's Eclectic First Reader*, rev. ed. (Cincinnati, Ohio: Winthrop B. Smith, 1853), 36; Peter Parley [Samuel G. Goodrich], *What to Do, And, How to Do It; or, Morals and Manners Taught by Examples* (New York: Wiley & Putnam, 1844), 34. On religious belief in McGuffey's Readers, see John H. Westerhoff III, *McGuffey*

and His Readers: Piety, Morality, and Education in Nineteenth-Century America (Nashville, Tenn.: Abingdon, 1978), 40–46, 74–108. Other examples of primers that include benevolent imagery as well as such religious items as the Lord's Prayer or verses from the Old Testament, reference to the Ten Commandments, or to the importance of prayer, but avoid any reference to particular doctrines or to Jesus Christ are: *The Atlantic Primer* (Dover, N.H.: Samuel C. Stevens, 1829), 15; *Child's Instructor; or A Present for Sister* (New Haven: S. Babcock, 1830), 16; *The American Juvenile Primer* (Philadelphia: Turner & Fisher, 1838), 19; *The National Pictorial Primer* (New York: George F. Cooledge & Brother, 1844), 30; *The Illustrated Primer* (New York: George F. Cooledge & Brother [1857?]), 43; *The Mother's Primer* (St. Louis: South-Western Book and Publishing Company [1869?]), 19; and *The Home Primer* (New York: McLoughlin Brothers, 1875), n.p. (15, 24).

20. William H. McGuffey, *The Eclectic Fourth Reader*, 6th ed. (Cincinnati, Ohio: Truman and Smith, 1838), 143. The passage was also reproduced in (Unitarian) John Pierpont's *The National Reader* (Boston: Hilliard, Gray, Little, and Wilkins, and Richard and Lord, 1827), 142–43.

21. The following are examples of secular primers including benevolent imagery: Lindley Murray, *First Book for Children* (Philadelphia: Benjamin Warner, 1819), cover; *The American Pictorial Primer* (New York: George Cooledge, 1845), 47; Rensselaer Bentley, *The Pictorial Primer* (New York: Saxton & Miles, 1844), 19; *The Beautiful ABC Book* (Philadelphia, 1852), 2; *The New York School Primer* (New York: Philip J. Cozans [1855?]), 17; *Fisher's Holiday Primer* (Philadelphia: Fisher & Brother, 1857), n.p. (28); *The American Pictorial Primer* (New York: Richard Marsh, 1861), 10; Charles W. Sanders, *Sanders' Union Pictorial Primer* (New York: Ivison, Phinney, Blakeman, 1868), 32; *The Father's Pictorial Primer* (Cambridgeport, Mass: L. S. Learned, 1869), 10; see also Abbott, *The Little Learner*, 38, 168.

Instances of the imagery to be found among religious primers are: Jonathan Fisher, *The Youth's Primer* (Boston: Samuel T. Armstrong, 1817); *Boston School Primer* (Boston: Munroe and Francis, 1831), 24; *The Picture Reader* (New Haven: S. Babcock, 1833), 29; Theodore Dwight, *The New Picture Primer and Table Book* (New London: Bolles & Williams, 1841), 22; *The Child's Christian Primer* (New York: T. W. Strong [1843?]), 17; *Burke's Picture Primer* (Macon, Ga.: Burke, Boykin, 1864), 10; and *The United States Primer* (New York: American Tract Society, 1864), 62. The motif is also found throughout publications by the American Tract Society and the American Sunday School Union—see for instance *The Family Christian Almanac for 1873* (New York: American Tract Society, 1873), 44.

22. Rev. Legh Richmond, *The African Slave*, no. 53, in *The Publications of the American Tract Society*, 14 vols. (New York: American Tract Society, n.d. [1842]), 2: 218. The tract indicates that the scene took place on a rugged and lonely seashore.

23. "Peter Martin," *The Anti-Slavery Record* 1, no. 6 (June 1835), 63.

24. A similarly melodramatic depiction of the slave-owning mania appears in a woodcut in the *Anti-Slavery Almanac for 1839*, where a crowd of Whites attack a "School for Colored Girls" in the North, setting it on fire and pelting it with stones as two young black girls escape from a side door, *The American Anti-Slavery Almanac for 1839*, 1, no. 4 (New York: The American Anti-Slavery Society, 1839), 15.

25. Rena L. Vassar, ed., *Social History of American Education*, 2 vols. (Chicago: Rand Mc-Nally., 1965), 1: 269. In 1834 the law added six months imprisonment to a fine of one hundred dollars (271). Other Southern states followed suit during the years preceding the war. In 1854, for instance, a white woman was imprisoned by a judge in Virginia for teaching free black children to read (276).

26. Douglass, *Life*, 82, 78, 84.

27. By 1 January 1866, the Freedmen's Bureau reported 90,589 black students, 1,314 teachers, and 740 schools nationwide. Six months later the number of students, both children and adults, was estimated at 150,000. One-third of the teachers were black. Linda Warfel Slaughter, *The Freedmen of the South* (Cincinnati, Ohio: Elm Street, 1869), 99–100. State organizations for the education of Blacks were also formed. Although for a population of four million Blacks these numbers were very small, particularly in light of the fact that the 1860 census shows that 94 percent of free males were literate, only 31 percent of all school-aged children in the South were enrolled in schools in 1860; among Blacks, 3.5 to 4 percent were enrolled in the south-central and south-Atlantic regions. David B. Tyack and Elisabeth Hansot, *Managers of Virtue: Public School Leadership in America, 1820–1980* (New York: Basic Books, 1982), 29, 32; Gilmore, "Literacy," 2421. For a good, statistically based study of literacy rates, see Lee Soltow and Edward Stevens, *The Rise of Literacy and the Common School in the United States: A Socioeconomic Analysis to 1870* (Chicago: University of Chicago Press, 1981).

28. On Freedmen's Aid Societies, see Henry Lee Swint, *The Northern Teacher in the South, 1862–1870* (New York: Octagon Books, 1967), 3–22; James D. Anderson, *The Education of Blacks in the South, 1860–1935* (Chapel Hill: University of North Carolina, 1988), 4–32; Joe Martin Richardson, *Christian Reconstruction: The American Missionary Association and Southern Blacks, 1861–1890* (London: University of Georgia Press, 1986); and Robert C. Morris, *Reading, 'Riting, and Reconstruction: The Education of Freedmen in the South, 1861–1870* (Chicago: University of Chicago Press, 1982).

29. Swint, *The Northern Teacher*, 11–13.

30. "Extracts from Teachers' Letters," *The Freedmen's Record* 2, no. 2 (February 1866), 26, 28.

31. Slaughter, *The Freedmen of the South*, 178; "Extracts from Teachers' Letters," *The Freedmen's Record* 2, no. 1 (January 1866), 6; "Anecdotes and Incidents from a Visit to Freedmen," *The Freedmen's Record* 1, no. 9 (September 1865), 148.

32. Swint, *The Northern Teacher*, 38–39.

33. "Peril from Romanism," *Ninth Annual Report of the Freedmen's Aid Society for 1876*, in *Freedmen's Aid Society of the Methodist Episcopal Church* (Cincinnati, Ohio: Western Methodist Book Concern, n.d.), 12, 13.

34. "Education and Religion," *The National Freedman, A Monthly Journal of the New York National Freedman's Relief Association* 2, no. 8 (August 1866), 210.

35. After visiting schools organized by the Freedmen's Bureau in several cities in Virginia, Delaware, and North Carolina, the Rev. J. Brinton Smith, secretary of the Protestant Episcopal Freedmen's Commission, wrote: "While nothing of a secular character in their instruction had been neglected, the children had been taught, when age permitted, the Ten Commandments, the Lord's Prayer, and what is usually called the Apostle's Creed—

the symbol of faith of all orthodox evangelical Christians." Quoted in J. W. Alvord, *Fourth Semi-Annual Report on Schools for Freedmen, July 1, 1867* (Washington, D.C.: Government Printing Office, 1868), 14. Alvord was the general superintendent of schools in the Freedmen's Bureau. Lacking common school buildings, Freedmen schools were often held in churches and Sunday school facilities.

36. On the Tract Society's controversy over slavery, see Morgan, *Protestants and Pictures*, chap. 3.

37. The Boston ATS organization, which left the larger group in 1858 because of its reticence to oppose slavery, was the first to publish materials for Freedmen. Some of these publications are: *Picture Lesson Book* (ca. 1862); Isaac Brinckerhoff, *Advice to Freedmen* (1864); Israel P. Warren, ed., *The Freedmen's Primer, Or First Reader* (1864); *The Freedman's Second Reader* (1865), and *The Freedman's Third Reader* (1866). The New York ATS organization published the following: *United States Primer* (1864); and Rev. Jared Bell Waterbury, *Friendly Counsels for Freedmen* (ca. 1866). For a discussion of the ATS literature for Freedmen, see Morris, *Reading, 'Riting, and Reconstruction*, 188–202. The Rev. Brinckerhoff's *Advice to Freedmen* included a frontispiece that showed a black father returning home with shovel and corn over his shoulder, being greeted warmly by his children and wife, who stands beside the door of their cabin. The image follows the pattern of the Tract Society's antebellum illustrations of humble white laboring families at peace in rustic rural settings. Isaac W. Brinckerhoff, *Advice to Freedmen*, AMS Reprint Series, vol. 4, ed. Robert C. Morris (New York: AMS Press, 1980).

38. Reported in Alvord, *Fourth Semi-Annual Report on Schools for Freedmen*, 13.

39. As reported in *The Freedmen's Record* 1, no. 9 (September 1865), 148.

40. W. C. Brownlee, *An Appeal to the Patriot and Christian, on the Importance of the Gospel, its Ministry, its Sabbath, and its Ordinances, to the Well-being and Perpetuity of Our Free Institutions*, Tract no. 253 (New York: American Tract Society, n.d. [1831]), 3.

41. Report from the Arkansas department, in Alvord, *Fourth Semi-Annual Report on Schools for Freedmen*, 47.

42. "Pictures," *Tenth Annual Report of the Freedmen's Aid Society of the Methodist Episcopal Church . . . for 1877* (Cincinnati, Ohio: Western Methodist Book Concern, 1878), 10. The article stated that the pictures were "to adorn their humble homes, educate the inmates in the truths of the Bible, and stimulate them to holy lives."

43. David B. Tyack, "Onward Christian Soldiers: Religion in the American Common School," in *History and Education: The Educational Uses of the Past*, ed. Paul Nash (New York: Random House, 1970), 212–55; Diane Ravitch, *The Great School Wars: New York City, 1805–1973: A History of the Public Schools as Battlefield of Social Change* (New York: Basic Books, 1974), 3–76. For a thoughtful discussion of the arguments, see R. Laurence Moore, "Bible Reading and Nonsectarian Schooling: The Failure of Religious Instruction in Nineteenth-Century Public Education," *The Journal of American History* 86, no. 4 (March 2000): 1,581–99.

44. "Fort Sumter," Plate 107 in Morton Keller, *The Art and Politics of Thomas Nast* (New York: Oxford University Press, 1968).

45. For a brief discussion of Nast's views on politics, religion, and public education, see Keller, *Art and Politics of Thomas Nast*, 159–62.

CHAPTER 3

I want to thank David Morgan and Sally Promey, and the other members of the project, for their helpful comments on earlier drafts. I also am grateful to Notre Dame's Cushwa Center for the Study of American Catholicism, which offered research support.

1. On the cornerstone ceremony, see William P. Kennedy, *National Shrine of the Immaculate Conception* (Washington, D.C.: Salve Regina Press, 1927), 62–65. For a history of the campus where the shrine rests see C. Joseph Nuesse, *The Catholic University of America: A Centennial History* (Washington, D.C.: The Catholic University of America Press, 1990). The NSIC is the second largest church in the United States; the Cathedral Church of Saint John the Divine, the massive Episcopalian structure in New York City, is the largest. On that Episcopalian cathedral see Peter W. Williams, *Houses of God: Region, Religion, and Architecture in the United States* (Urbana: University of Illinois Press, 1997), 67–68. To put the scale in perspective, the NSIC's area in square feet (77,500) is less than St. John's in New York (121,000) and St. Peter's in Rome (227,069) but more than Chartres's (68,260) and Cologne's (65,800) cathedrals. The NSIC is also the second largest basilica church dedicated to Mary in the world; the largest is Our Lady of Peace in Yamousoukro, capital of the West African nation of Ivory Coast. The NSIC's director of Visitor Services, Sister Mary Josellen Dajer, S.N.D., offered the estimate of the shrine's annual visitors in an interview, NSIC, 6 June 1997. The dimensions of the NSIC are offered in the free eleven-page pamphlet distributed at the shrine: *Welcome to the Basilica of the National Shrine of the Immaculate Conception* (Washington, D.C.: NSIC, n.d.).

2. The original meaning of "shrine" in Old English *(scrin)* and Latin *(scrinium)* suggests that it is a box or repository. In this original sense, shrines are boxes that contain a dead body or venerated relic, and devotees often construct shrines over tombs or place remains in them. (For example, in 1932 the NSIC's clergy interred the Rev. Thomas J. Shahan, the shrine's founder, in its crypt church.) Pilgrims travel to shrines in many traditions. For example, the Prophet Muhammad's tomb in a Medina (Saudi Arabia) mosque attracts Muslims. Followers of Shinto, Japan's indigenous religion, clap their hands to call the *kami* (divine presences) at the mountain shrines on Mt. Koya. Among the most famous Christian shrines is Lourdes, where the Virgin Mary appeared to a fourteen-year-old peasant in 1858, and ever since, pilgrims have journeyed to southeastern France to petition Mary for personal favors and to bottle the spring's healing water. Some sites, for example civic monuments, do not claim to be religious but function like shrines. The name of one Civil War memorial in Virginia, the Stonewall Jackson Shrine, even explicitly claims religious parallels. Named by the United Daughters of the Confederacy and local Virginians who owned the site before the National Park Service assumed control, the small white house commemorates the place where one of the most celebrated Confederate generals died. As a Park Service employee who conducts tours at the Virginia shrine observed, for many white Southern visitors with Confederate roots "it is a genuine place of pilgrimage." Reinforcing the site's religious meaning, a plywood sign across the street at Guinea Station Souvenirs unself-consciously announces in large hand-painted letters that the store sells "RELICS," which turn out to be Confederate suspender buckles and uniform buttons unearthed at Southern battlefields. Personal Interview, Frank O'Reilly, Na-

tional Park Service, 14 June 1998, Stonewall Jackson Shrine, Guinea Station, Virginia. On tourist sites and civic monuments as sacred spaces, see Edward Tabor Linenthal, *Sacred Ground: Americans and Their Battlefields*, 2d ed. (Urbana: University of Illinois Press, 1993); John Sears, *Sacred Places: American Tourist Attractions in the Nineteenth Century* (New York: Oxford University Press, 1989). For a brief introduction to shrines, see "Shrines," in *Encyclopedia of Religion*, ed. Mircea Eliade (New York: Macmillan, 1987); "Shrine," in *The HarperCollins Dictionary of Religion*, ed. Jonathan Z. Smith (New York: HarperCollins, 1995); and Thomas A. Tweed, "Shrine," in *Contemporary American Religion*, ed. Wade Clark Roof (New York: Macmillan, 2000).

3. Two students of Christian pilgrimage have identified seven types of modern Catholic shrines: significant-site shrines, ex-voto shrines, devotional shrines, spontaneous-miracle shrines, acquired-object shrines, found-object shrines, and apparitional shrines. See Mary Lee Nolan and Sidney Nolan, *Christian Pilgrimage in Modern Western Europe* (Chapel Hill: University of North Carolina Press, 1989), 216–90. William A. Christian Jr.'s books on popular religion in Spain also offer helpful information about the nature and function of shrines. See especially *Local Religion in Sixteenth-Century Spain* (Princeton: Princeton University Press, 1981); and *Person and God in a Spanish Valley*. 1972. Rev. ed. (Princeton: Princeton University Press, 1989). For a list of Catholic shrines in the United States see J. Anthony Moran, *Pilgrim's Guide to America: U.S. Catholic Shrines and Centers of Devotion* (Huntington, Ind.: Our Sunday Visitor Publishing Division, 1992).

4. Shrines can be spatially complex, even mobile, in other ways. For example, consider the portable Buddhist shrine from Japan's Edo Period (1615–1867) displayed in Salem, Massachusetts's Peabody Essex Museum. It is a lightweight black lacquered wood box with engraved brass fixtures. It opens to reveal a polychrome image of the Bodhisattva Jizo, the patron of travelers, whom the proselytizing monk carries on his back as he spreads the Buddha's teachings across the countryside. For a reproduction and discussion of this artifact see Thomas A. Tweed and Stephen Prothero, eds., *Asian Religions in America: A Documentary History* (New York: Oxford University Press, 1999), 155. Basilica of the National Shrine of the Immaculate Conception, www.nationalshrine.com, 4 June 1998. For other Catholic websites see Thomas C. Fox, *Catholicism on the Web* (New York: MIS Press, 1997); and Jeff Zeleski, *The Soul of Cyberspace* (San Francisco: HarperSanFrancisco, 1997), 99–120.

5. The art historian Thomas A. Markus discusses "three domains"—he omits historical context—and advocates a similar approach to interpretation in *Buildings and Power* (London: Routledge, 1993), 3–28. For a useful collection of writings on architecture by twentieth-century philosophers and cultural theorists, see Neil Leach, ed., *Rethinking Architecture: A Reader in Cultural Theory* (London: Routledge, 1997). My approach to interpreting artifacts, including buildings, has been shaped by reception theory, and there is an enormous literature on that. For helpful applications see David Freedberg, *The Power of Images: Studies in the History and Theory of Response* (Chicago: University of Chicago Press, 1989); David Morgan, "Would Jesus Have Sat for a Portrait?": The Likeness of Christ in the Popular Reception of Sallman's Art," in *Icons of American Protestantism: The Art of Warner Sallman*, ed. David Morgan (New Haven: Yale University Press, 1996), 181–206; and James Elkins, *The Object Stares Back* (New York: Simon and Schuster, 1996). I used

a similar approach in *Our Lady of the Exile: Diasporic Religion at a Cuban Catholic Shrine in Miami* (New York: Oxford University Press, 1997), 99–115. I suggest there, too, that the meaning of architectural spaces is inscribed, in part, by the practices held within. On that see also James W. Fernandez, *Bwiti: An Ethnography of the Religious Imagination in Africa* (Princeton: Princeton University Press, 1982), 377, 408–12; and Lindsay Jones, *Twin City Tales: A Hermeneutical Reassessment of Tula and Chichén Itzá* (Niwot: University Press of Colorado, 1995), 186–210. The wedding between Luci Banes Johnson and Patrick Nugent was held at the NSIC on 6 August 1966. It was only the second wedding in that building because wedding ceremonies, as well as baptisms and funerals, usually are not allowed in a shrine and take place only in a parish. For one cover story on the wedding, complete with a photograph of the shrine's exterior, see "The Wedding in Washington," *Newsweek*, 15 August 1966, 17–21.

6. Civil religion is the set of religious beliefs, myths, symbols, saints, and rituals associated with the political realm. Usually that term is understood to mean the loosely framed faith that arises outside the churches, although in the variant I discuss in this essay, civil religion in the nation's capital can be denominationally coded. In the modern West, the idea of civil religion goes back to Jean-Jacques Rousseau, who proposed a widely shared civil religion that might encourage citizens' loyalty to the democratic state. Robert Bellah's 1967 essay ("Civil Religion in America," *Daedalus* 96 [winter 1967]) sparked the late-twentieth-century scholarly discussion of the topic. A great deal of debate followed. The widely cited works on civil religion include Catherine L. Albanese, *Sons of the Fathers: The Civil Religion of the American Revolution* (Philadelphia: Temple University Press, 1976); Robert N. Bellah, *The Broken Covenant: American Civil Religion in Time of Trial* (New York: Seabury Press, 1975); Conrad Cherry, ed., *God's New Israel: Religious Interpretations of American Destiny*, 1971. Rev. and updated ed. (Chapel Hill: University of North Carolina, 1998); and Russell E. Richey and Donald G. Jones, eds. *American Civil Religion* (New York: Harper and Row, 1974). Francis D. Lethbridge of the American Institute of Architects has divided the history of the federal city's architecture into four phases: 1) 1791–1850, Late Georgian and Classic Revival; 2) 1850–1900, Romantic Revival; 3) Classic Eclecticism, 1893–1940; 4) 1940–present. It was during the third period that the District of Columbia became an important site for the contest among faiths for public presence. Most of the important national churches, or their functional equivalents, were started or completed during this period, which began with influences from the 1893 Columbian Exposition and the 1901 McMillan Plan. The latter modified and enlarged the original design for the capital by Pierre Charles L'Enfant; it was named for the senator, James McMillan, who served as chairman of the Senate District Committee and appointed a commission to study the plan of the city. For Lethbridge's periodization, and discussion of the third period, see Francis D. Lethbridge, "The Architecture of Washington, D.C.," in *AIA Guide to the Architecture of Washington, D.C.*, ed. Christopher Weeks (for the Washington Chapter of the American Institute of Architects), 3d ed. (Baltimore: The Johns Hopkins University Press, 1994), 5–6, 12.

7. L'Enfant's description of his plan was hand printed on the manuscript he presented Congress in December 1791. That plan first appeared publicly in a Philadelphia newspaper: *Dunlop's American Daily Advertiser*, 26 December 1791. See also Papers of Charles L'En-

fant, Library of Congress, Manuscript Division, District of Columbia. Many books chronicle the planning and history of the District of Columbia; one of the best is Kenneth R. Bowling, *The Creation of Washington, D.C.: The Idea and Location of the American Capital* (Washington, D.C.: George Mason University Press, 1991). On the architecture of the capital, two volumes are especially helpful: Weeks, *AIA Guide;* and Pamela Scott and Antoinette J. Lee, *Buildings of the District of Columbia* (New York: Oxford University Press, 1993). On D.C. churches, see Williams, *Houses of God,* 72–76. The quotation from the National Cathedral's tourist guidebook is taken from *Washington National Cathedral* (Washington, D.C.: Washington National Cathedral, 1995), 17. For more on that building, see Richard T. Feller, *Completing Washington Cathedral for Thy Great Glory* (Washington, D.C.: Washington Cathedral, 1989).

8. The D.C. churches with "national" in their titles include the following ten: National Baptist Memorial Church, National Community Church on Capitol Hill (Assemblies of God), Basilica of the National Shrine of the Immaculate Conception, Ukrainian Catholic National Shrine of the Holy Family, National City Christian Church (Disciples of Christ), National Memorial Church of God, Washington National Cathedral (Episcopal), National Presbyterian Church, National Spiritual Science Center, and Universalist National Memorial Church. Three other D.C. churches explicitly call themselves national centers in their own literature or on their signs: Church of the Holy City ("the National Swedenborgian Church"), St. Nicholas Orthodox Cathedral ("the National Cathedral of the Orthodox Church in America"), and Metropolitan A.M.E. Church ("the National Cathedral of African Methodism"). Five others function as national denominational centers or at some time have claimed to: St. John's Church (Episcopal), First Baptist, Foundry Methodist, Saint Sophia Greek Orthodox Cathedral, and Founding Church of Scientology. Others hint at national aspirations by using "capital" in their titles, including Capital Memorial Seventh-Day Adventist Church and Unity Center of Truth in the Nation's Capital. Three churches outside the federal city's limits, but still within the larger metropolitan area, publicly claim national status: The National Church of God (Ft. Washington, Md.), National Apostolic Church (Silver Spring, Md.), and National Wesleyan Church (Hyattsville, Md.).

9. The quotation is from "Metropolitan A.M.E. Church: A Brief History," in *Metropolitan African Methodist Episcopal Church*, undated, four-page church pamphlet, Metropolitan A.M.E. Church, Washington, D.C. The other two churches highlighted here also mention their national status in church publications: *Church of the Holy City*, undated, four-page church pamphlet, Church of the Holy City, Washington, D.C.; and *St. Nicholas Orthodox Cathedral*, undated, folded 8.5"-x-11" church pamphlet, St. Nicholas Orthodox Cathedral, Washington, D.C. For historical information on the latter, see also *St. Nicholas Russian Orthodox Church: Fiftieth Anniversary*, commemorative brochure (Washington: St. Nicholas Russian Orthodox Cathedral, 1980).

10. The quotation is from former pastor Edward Hughes Pruden, *Building the House of God: Some Memories* (Washington, D.C.: First Baptist Church of the City of Washington, D.C., 1986). Foundry Methodist's history is chronicled in Homer Calkin, *Castings from the Foundry Mold: A History of Foundry Church, Washington, D.C., 1814–1964* (Nashville, Tenn.: Parthenon Press, 1968). By the early twentieth century it had become fash-

ionable for denominations to seek a site on Sixteenth Street. The churches on that street include: St. John's (1816; 1881–90; 1919); First Baptist Church (1890; 1955); The Church of the Holy City (1896); Foundry Methodist (1904); Church of the Sacred Heart (1923); All Souls Unitarian Church (1924); Universalist National Memorial Church (1930); National Baptist Memorial Church (1933); Unification Church [Washington Chapel, Church of Jesus Christ of Latter Day Saints] (1933); and Third Church of Christ, Scientist (1970). On the architecture of that corridor see Sue A. Kohler and Jeffrey R. Carson, *Sixteenth Street Architecture*. 2 vols. (Washington, D.C.: Commission of Fine Arts, 1978–85). Most of these churches are discussed in the two best guides to the city's architecture: *AIA Guide* and *Buildings of the District of Columbia*, and in Williams, *Houses of God*, 72–76.

11. The quotation is from Mark Batterson, "A Church for All Audiences," *American Horizon* (Sept./Oct. 1998): 16–17. For excerpts from a sermon by Batterson, see "Esther's Saving Her People Is the Potential of Everyone," *Washington Times*, 5 October 1998, A2. For a journalist's account of the congregation, see Peri Stone, "G-Rated Service: Church Calls Movie Theater Home," *Chicago Tribune*, 6 November 1997.

12. Campbell is quoted in a work that contains valuable historical information: Hilda E. Koontz, *A History of the National City Christian Church* (Washington, D.C.: Print and Mail, printed as a private edition, 1981), 1. Across Thomas Circle from National City Christian Church is the older Luther Place Memorial Church (1870), a red sandstone Gothic structure built to offer thanks for the ending of the Civil War. It is less self-consciously national in character (and less imposing) than the Disciples of Christ Church across Thomas Circle, although as a centrally located church in the capital it takes on some significance for the denomination's identity and visibility. On this Lutheran church see Scott and Lee, *Buildings of the District of Columbia*, 295.

13. The quotations are from *The National Presbyterian Church: The First Two Hundred Years, 1795–1995* (Washington, D.C.: The National Presbyterian Church, 1996), 19.

14. On the early influence of Roman Catholics in the district see William Warner, *At Peace with All Their Neighbors: Catholics and Catholicism in the National Capital, 1787–1860* (Washington, D.C.: Georgetown University Press, 1994). Michael P. Warsaw, *The National Shrine of the Immaculate Conception: America's Church* (Washington, D.C.: The National Shrine of the Immaculate Conception, 1990). (The shrine's gift shop manager reports that this guidebook is the best-selling item: Dennis Zeigler, letter to the author, 6 June 1998.) *Basilica of the National Shrine of the Immaculate Conception*, folded paper pamphlet (Washington, D.C.: National Shrine of the Immaculate Conception, n.d.). *A Hymn in Stone*, video, fifteen minutes (Washington, D.C.: National Shrine of the Immaculate Conception, n.d.).

15. The shrine centers on Mary—as many official proclamations have reminded devotees—because Mary, under the title of the Immaculate Conception, is the official patroness of the United States. At the meeting of the Sixth Provincial Council of Baltimore on 13 May 1846, Archbishop Samuel Eccleston of Baltimore and twenty-two American bishops officially placed the United States "under the special patronage of the holy Mother of God, whose immaculate conception is venerated by the piety of the faithful throughout the Catholic Church." For two examples of the clergy reminding devout readers of Mary's national role see the Rev. Donald Macleod, "Patroness of the United

States," *Salve Regina* 7 (1 Aug. 1920): 39; and "November Dedication," *Mary's Shrine* 20 (Aug. 1959): 2. On the second meaning of "America's Church," note that Protestants had dismissed Catholic veneration of Mary as idolatry. When the lower church was being built, some Catholics detected a softening among Protestants on this, as one unsigned article in a Catholic magazine suggested: "A Consoling Sign of the Times," *Ave Maria* 18, new series (7 July 1923): 21. But Protestant charges that Marian devotion was an inauthentic innovation persisted. The shrine's founder, Thomas J. Shahan, tried to answer those charges in a book he published two decades before he formally began his quest for a national shrine, and the design of the shrine's crypt church, with its recalling of the Catacombs, reflects his concern to defend Marian devotion. See Thomas J. Shahan, *The Blessed Virgin in the Catacombs* (Baltimore: John Murphy, 1892). The third meaning of the shrine as "America's Church"—as unifier of U.S. Catholicism—has been emphasized more recently. The shrine, and especially its thirteen ethnic chapels, symbolically holds together the enormous diversity of the U.S. Catholic Church, with its multiple national and ethnic heritages. This theme emerged early in the construction of the shrine. On this, see Shawn Perry, "The Perpetual Chorus of Peoples," *Mary's Shrine* 36 (Dec. 1975): n.p. However, the theme has been highlighted in the 1990s. See any of Monsignor Michael Bransfield's official explanations of the phrase America's Church," as with the one printed on a fund-raising pamphlet for the recently completed Filipino oratory. There he promises Filipino donors that by supporting the ethnic chapel they can find their place in the shrine, and so the U.S. church: *Share in the Joy and Privilege of Building a Chapel for Our Lady of Antipolo*, folded paper flier (Washington, D.C.: National Shrine of the Immaculate Conception, n.d.). Bransfield's comments there were taken from an earlier piece: Monsignor Michael Bransfield, "The National Shrine: America's Catholic Church," *Mary's Shrine* 54 (spring/summer 1994): 2–3. On ethnic representation at the shrine, and the Filipino oratory in particular, see Tweed, "Proclaiming Catholic Inclusiveness: Ethnic Diversity and Ecclesiastical Unity at the National Shrine of the Immaculate Conception," *U.S. Catholic Historian* 18 (winter 2000): 1–18.

16. This untitled image by the Rev. P. Raphael, O.S.B., was printed, and praised, in "Patroness of the United States," *Salve Regina* 9, no. 3 (March 1922): 21.

17. William M. Halsey, *The Survival of American Innocence: Catholicism in an Era of Disillusionment, 1920–1940* (Notre Dame: University of Notre Dame Press, 1980), 3. William H. J. Kennedy and Sister Mary Joseph, *The United States: A History for the Upper Grades of Catholic Schools* (New York: Benziger Brothers, 1926), v–vi, 665–67.

18. [Thomas J. Shahan], "The National Shrine: Idea, Means, Results," *Salve Regina* 1, no. 1 (Jan. 1914): 2. Sylvester Baxter, "The National Shrine of the Immaculate Conception, Washington, D.C.," *Architectural Record* 52 (July 1922): 3–15; italics mine. Eugene B. Gallagher, S.J., "The Land of the Immaculate Conception," *American Ecclesiastical Review* (Dec. 1958): 380. Monsignor Thomas J. Grady, the shrine's director when the upper church was dedicated, reported that the architectural firm listed these three reasons that Maginnis and Shahan chose Byzantine-Romanesque over Gothic, and he noted a fourth reason: the influence of John Glennon, later Cardinal Glennon of St. Louis, a close friend of the architect and founder. Glennon had a "strong preference for Romanesque."

Thomas J. Grady, "National Shrine of the Immaculate Conception," *American Ecclesiastical Review* (Jan.–June 1957): 148–49. The first history of the NSIC, which the shrine published in 1927, offered five reasons they had placed the building in Washington (Kennedy, *National Shrine*, 12–14.): 1) "Every nation has some great National Monument in honor of our Blessed Mother"; 2) "The City of Washington is our chief Catholic educational center"; 3) "The Catholic University of America was solemnly dedicated by our Bishops to Mary Immaculate as the patroness of Catholic learning"; 4) "To advance the religious education of our student body"; 5) "Washington is a city of monumental buildings, attracting thousands of visitors annually; the temporary home of our numerous government officials. . . ." In most ways, the first and last reasons were most important to Shahan, McKenna, and most clergy.

19. "Our Collector's Circle," *Salve Regina* 7 (15 March 1920): 14. Jere Brennan to the Rev. Bernard A. McKenna, 4 March 1929, Box D-2, Archives, NSIC. Shrine officials reported that they received an overwhelming number of letters from devotees in those early years. For example, in June 1922 they claimed that the "letters received in the *Salve Regina* office in the past two years, if placed end to end in a straight line, would form a path from Washington, D.C., to Quebec, Canada." Quoted in Kennedy, *National Shrine*, 87. The circulation of the free newsletter also was substantial, even in those early years. On the feast of the Immaculate Conception in 1917, the Rev. McKenna, the shrine's director, told those who gathered at the periodical's offices after the mass that "75,000 *Salve Reginas* were being sent out every six weeks to Catholics throughout the United States and Canada." Quoted in Kennedy, *National Shrine*, 56.

20. Here, and throughout, I use pseudonyms when quoting and citing interviews. For each interview I list, in order, the number, date, gender, age, birthplace, and residence. All interviews were at the NSIC, unless I indicate otherwise. Interview #7 (Jane), 6 June 1997, female, age 41, born California, resides Maryland.

21. Interview #35 (Cheryl), 13 June 1998, female, age 48, born New York, resides Virginia.

22. Interview #7 (Jane). Interview #36, 13 June 1998, female, age 54, born California, resides Maryland.

23. Interview #6 (Eleanor), 6 June 1997, female, age 61, born New Mexico, resides California. Interview #37 (Roberta), 13 June 1998, female, age 46, born Alaska, resides Washington, D.C.

24. On the shrine as "most beautiful": Interview #19, 27 June 1997, female, age 54, born Philippines, resides New Jersey. On the shrine as "neo-ugly": Interview #38, 13 June 1998, male, age 32, born Kentucky, resides Washington, D.C. James Carroll, *An American Requiem: God, My Father, and the War That Came between Us* (Boston: Houghton Mifflin, 1996), 93, 155, 141.

25. On 18 May 1924, Catholic Tourists of America began to arrange pilgrimages to the shrine. On this see Kennedy, *National Shrine*, 93. Several similar Catholic groups sponsor and coordinate tours today.

26. The Lutheran visitor: Interview #33, 13 June 1998, female, age 22, born Maryland, resides Virginia. The quotations from my encounters with the students were recorded in my fieldnotes: Fieldnotes, 4 June 1997, NSIC, sixth-grade students from a public middle school on Long Island, New York; Fieldnotes, NSIC, 7 June 1997, eighth-grade stu-

dents from a public junior high in Kingston, Ohio. The (Protestant) principal of the small Ohio junior high told me that only two of the twenty-three students on the Washington trip were Catholic.

27. Thomas J. Grady, "America's Great Tribute to Mary," *American Ecclesiastical Review* (July–Dec. 1959): 217.

28. The NSIC first appeared in the American Institute of Architects' guidebook to Washington in 1994: Weeks, *AIA Guide*, 288. Denise Barnes, "A Mosaic of Faith: Shrine to the History of Catholic People in America and Tribute to the Almighty," Washington Weekend, *Washington Times*, 9 January 1997, M4–M6. Benjamin Forgey, "Letting the Shrine Shine," Style Section, *The Washington Post*, 24 August 1996, B1, B7.

29. "The Basilica of the National Shrine of the Immaculate Conception," postcard (exterior of the basilica), Washington, D.C.: Silberne Sales, n.d. The text on the reverse side: "The National Shrine, the largest Catholic Church in the United States and the seventh largest in the world is contemporary in style, with strong Byzantine-Romanesque influence. Built as were medieval cathedrals without any steel skeleton, brick, tile, or concrete, the National Shrine stands as a great symbol of the faith and devotion of Catholics throughout the United States." "Washington, D.C." postcard (sixteen local buildings and monuments), photographs by Werner J. Bertsch (1993), made by Kina Italia, in Milan, Italy, distributed by L. B. Prince, Fairfax, Virginia. The postcard represents sixteen sites, and two are religious: the NSIC and the National Cathedral. Among the other sites included are the Jefferson Memorial, White House, Smithsonian Castle, Capitol, Pentagon, Lincoln Memorial, and Washington Monument.

30. Patrick W. Carey, *The Roman Catholics* (Westport, Conn.: Greenwood Press, 1993), 109.

31. "Index to the President's Appointment Books, 1961–63," John F. Kennedy Library, Boston, Mass. Kennedy's appointment books indicate that he attended three local Catholic churches—St. Matthew's, St. Stephen's, and Holy Trinity—but never visited the NSIC. I also have failed to find any mention of the NSIC in any autobiographical or biographical material, and oral history confirms the conclusion that he never attended. Sal Mazzuca was an altar server at the NSIC and for many years a tour guide there. He also served as part of President Kennedy's secret service detail for a time. In an interview, he confirmed the archival sources in the presidential library. Mazzuca recalls escorting Kennedy to several D.C. churches—"most often Holy Trinity"—and he maintains that "as far as I know, he never went to the National Shrine." Sal Mazzuca, interview with the author, 20 February 1999. The most frequently cited source on Kennedy's religious views remains Lawrence H. Fuchs, *John F. Kennedy and American Catholicism* (New York: Meredith Press, 1967). That book, and passages in other articles and books, offer important information about Kennedy's religious life, but a fuller study is needed. There are reasons to think that he was more shaped by Catholic faith than some interpreters have suggested.

32. Interview #37 (Roberta), 13 June 1998, female, age 46, born Alaska, resides Washington, D.C.

33. As the district's traditional religious corridors like Sixteenth Street have become crowded, new spaces have opened where faiths, increasingly more than just Christian denominations, continue (and revise) the tradition of marking Metropolitan Washington's landscape. New Hampshire Avenue, along a ten-mile stretch in Montgomery County, con-

tains nearly three dozen congregations. "Religion Row" or "Highway to Heaven," as Washington journalists have christened it, boasts not only twenty-nine Christian churches, but also a Jewish synagogue, Muslim mosque, Hindu temple, and Buddhist temple. Because these houses of worship are outside the district and few of these congregations claim national status, they have less significance for understanding the contest for civic space in Washington. Most local interpreters have taken Religion Row as a sign of the new ethnic and religious diversity of the city and the nation. Nonetheless, the congregations' relative proximity to the capital adds some symbolic power. See Susan Levine, "A Place for Those Who Pray: Along Montgomery's 'Highway to Heaven' Diverse Acts of Faith," *Washington Post*, 3 August 1997, B1–4. Muslims and Jews already had claimed space within the district's boundaries before the emergence of New Hampshire Avenue as a religious corridor in 1958. For example, Adas Israel Synagogue was built in 1876 at Sixth and G Streets NW, and moved in 1907 to Sixth and I. The Islamic Center of Washington, D.C., opened in 1957 on Massachusetts Avenue's Embassy Row. The organizers included mostly foreign Muslims from the Middle East, and it was planned to nurture Muslims who served in Washington's embassies. As the American Muslim population has expanded since 1965, however, the site has taken on more significance for the construction of religious identity and negotiation of political power. Although it hardly rivals the National Cathedral as a national religious site, leaders at the mosque have quietly made claims on the civic arena, as with one bumper sticker they sell in the gift shop: "In God We Trust" it reads in large white letters. Just below that, the artifact claims the traditional American motto for Islam by citing the Qur'an (67:29). On the origin and history of that mosque, see Muhammad Abdul-Rauf, *History of the Islamic Center: From Dream to Reality* (Washington, D.C.: Colortone Press, 1978).

CHAPTER 4

The author would like to thank the pastor and congregation of West Church, the architect, and members of the Wilmington preservation community who graciously contributed to this project.

1. Member Interview #1, 14 July 1998, member of building committee.
2. For a fresh, interesting discussion about the changing relationships between buildings and people, see Neil Harris, *Building Lives: Constructing Rites and Passages* (New Haven: Yale University Press, 1999).
3. For an excellent study that concentrates on the social relationship between architecture and community, see Dell Upton, *Holy Things and Profane: Anglican Parish Churches in Colonial Virginia* (New York: Architectural History Foundation and MIT Press, 1986).
4. The religious history of Wilmington is largely unstudied, except for scattered congregational histories. A 1981 church tour guidebook provides some summary history of existing buildings and congregations; see Carolyn Z. Roland, "Guidebook: First Annual Cityside Church and Synagogue Tour of Wilmington, Delaware (1981 typescript, Historical Society of Delaware). For general Wilmington history, including some religious

history, see Carol E. Hoffecker, *Wilmington, Delaware: Portrait of an Industrial City, 1830–1910* (Charlottesville: University Press of Virginia for the Eleutherian Mills-Hagley Foundation, 1974) and Hoffecker, *Corporate Capital: Wilmington in the Twentieth Century* (Philadelphia: Temple University Press, 1983).

5. See Michael Ryan Kirkpatrick, "West Presbyterian Church: Facing New Frontiers in Mission—the 1960s" (unpublished paper, 1992), typescript, Historical Society of Delaware.

6. Currently, most of the programs that use the West Church facility are not run specifically by the church, but by other Wilmington interfaith or even secular organizations. It is significant that the church opens its doors for community programs that are *not* under its direction; the building is consciously seen as a community resource.

7. For a concise history of the West Church neighborhood through the 1960s, see Kirkpatrick, "Facing New Frontiers." See also *Centennial Yearbook* (West Presbyterian Church, 1968); *Seventy-Fifth Anniversary, West Presbyterian Church, Washington and Eighth Streets, Wilmington, Delaware* (Wilmington, Del.: Hambleton Printing and Publishing, 1943).

8. The congregation was not out of debt until April of 1945. WPC Session Minutes, 11 April 1945.

9. *Every Evening*, 1, no. 98 (28 Dec. 1871).

10. This description is based on the account in *Every Evening*, 28 December 1871, as well as similarities to the United Methodist Church (now Tabernacle Baptist) at Fifth and Washington, built in 1866.

11. Samuel Sloan was a Philadelphia architect known primarily for his house pattern books published in the 1850s and 1860s.

12. *Every Evening*, 1, no. 99 (29 Dec. 1871).

13. See Hoffecker, *Portrait*, 71–83. For an excellent study of how religious institutions were charged with maintaining moral order in rapidly industrializing cities, see Paul Boyer, *Urban Masses and Moral Order in America, 1820–1920* (Cambridge, Mass.: Harvard University Press, 1978).

14. *History of Wilmington: The Commercial, Social and Religious Growth of the City during the Past Century: Embracing a Record of Its Churches, Public Schools, Public Buildings, Parks, Residences* . . . (Wilmington?: F. T. Smiley, 1894), 44–45.

15. The 1850s was also a decade of significant church building: John Notman's St. John's Episcopal (1857), St. Mary's (the second Roman Catholic church in Wilmington, at Sixth and Pine, 1858), Church of the Holy City (Swedenborgian, 1857), Central Presbyterian (1857), and Brandywine Methodist (1857).

16. *Wilmington Daily Commercial*, 4, no. 1621 (28 Dec. 1871).

17. Chairman of the Building Committee was James Morrow, a forty-nine-year-old Irish immigrant, one of the church's founding members and a successful businessman. Another committee member was the manufacturer Charles Baird, who also served many years as director of the Sunday school, president of Wilmington Board of Education, member of the Board of Directors and former president of the Wilmington YMCA. See Charles Baird obituary, WPC Session Minutes, 8 June 1898.

18. Session Minutes, 1 April 1872, as cited in "Did You Know?" history column of *Chronicle of West Presbyterian Church*, 1 December 1983, 10. I have been unable to locate the original of the first session minute book in the church's archives.

19. See Boyer, *Urban Masses*.

20. *West Presbyterian Church Manual* (comp. G. H. Smyth, 1872).

21. The 1894 addition, 27' x 8' x 58', contained a kindergarten room and secretary's quarters in the basement, primary and junior rooms on the first floor, and two large rooms on the second floor. The congregation operated two missions. The Front Street Mission, begun in 1894, located on Market Street, was renamed the Baird mission after Charles Baird's death in 1898 and after several moves settled at 400 W. Second Street. Services were held there until 1969. The Italian mission was begun in 1905 and a building built in 1911. That work continued until 1925.

22. In 1916, for example, about $13,000 was spent for carpets, upholstery, painting, rebuilding the organ, general repairs, and work on the support systems. *Annual Report of the Treasurer of West Presbyterian Church*, 1916.

23. See West Presbyterian Church, *Seventy-Fifth Anniversary*.

24. Session Minutes, 21 February 1960.

25. See *Centennial Yearbook* and Kirkpatrick, "Facing New Frontiers."

26. Member Interview #2, July 1998.

27. *Chronicle*, 1 June 1982, 5.

28. Interview, Rev. Jeffrey Krehbiel, 22 January 1998.

29. Ibid.

30. Rev. Jeffrey Krehbiel, sermon delivered 19 September 1993, printed in *Chronicle*, 25 October 1993, 6–7.

31. Ibid.

32. Member Interview #2.

33. Krehbiel Interview, 22 January 1998.

34. Ibid.; see also "Members Reflections after the Fire," *Chronicle*, 1 December 1994.

35. Bob Stoddard, "The Case for the Preservation of the West Presbyterian Church Facade," presented to the West Church Session, 31 October 1993.

36. Krehbiel interview.

37. Ibid.

38. See *Wilmington City Historic District* (City of Wilmington: Wilmington Public Library, 1998).

39. Interview, Bayard Marin, 17 November 1998.

40. For an interesting discussion of the politics of contemporary urban historic preservation, see Dolores Hayden, *The Power of Place: Urban Landscapes as Public History* (Cambridge, Mass.: MIT Press, 1995).

41. *Chronicle*, 5 March 1994; Krehbiel interview.

42. DRPC Minutes, Special Meeting, 21 January 1994.

43. Krehbiel interview.

44. Interview Report, 9 February 1994 (on file at church).

45. *Chronicle*, 1 May 1994.

46. *Chronicle*, 1 June 1994.

47. The first quotation in this paragraph is from *Chronicle*, 1 October 1994. The others can be found in John W. Cook, "To a Parish on the Verge of Construction or Renovation," pamphlet published by the United Church Board for Homeland Ministries, Division of Evangelism and Local Church Development, in Partnership with the Fellowship of UCC Architects, n.d.

48. The congregation first encountered this term when looking at Yu's designs for the re-construction of Jerusalem Evangelical Lutheran Church in Schuylkill Haven, Pennsyl-vania, where the congregation had survived a similar fire. See *Chronicle*, 1 May 1994.

49. See *Chronicle*, 1 September 1994. Minutes of the DRPC, 26 July 1994.

50. There remains, to this day, some tension regarding the restoration and replacement of the wrought iron fence surrounding the property. During the meeting, Yu assured one questioner that "they would salvage as much as possible, since the church wanted a fence around the entire building for security." Several nonmembers present at the meeting offered their services for this restoration and for landscaping. According to Rev. Kreh-biel, these services were never rendered. See DRPC Minutes, 19 July 1995.

51. DRPC Minutes, 4 January 1995.

52. *Chronicle*, 1 September 1994. See "Ashes to Action: Rebuilding Community in the 21st Century," campaign brochure. The church hoped to raise $600,000.

53. Interview, George Yu, 23 June 1998, Philadelphia.

54. Interview, Krehbiel.

55. Krehbiel is a 1984 graduate of McCormick Theological Seminary in Chicago, which tends to be somewhat to the left of center, focused on urban ministry and experimental liturgy and worship. See McCormick Theological Seminary, *152nd Academic Year Bulletin, 1981–82* (Chicago: McCormick Theological Seminary, 1991).

56. *Chronicle*, 5 March 1994.

57. See Krehbiel, "Pulpit, Font, Cross, and Table," winter 1997 sermon series. Reprinted by the church.

58. George Yu interview.

59. Ibid.

60. Member interview #2.

61. Member interview #1.

62. Member interview #3, 23 July 1998, Wilmington (telephone interview).

63. Jonathan Z. Smith, *To Take Place: Toward Theory in Ritual* (Chicago: University of Chicago Press, 1987), 109.

64. I am grateful to Mark Parker Miller for this insight.

CHAPTER 5

I am greatly indebted to David Steinberg, whose generous, careful reading opened some im-portant new avenues of thought—not all of which, unfortunately, I have been able to follow in this chapter. For their research assistance, I would also like to thank Amanda Glesmann, Amy Kurtz, Laura K. Mills, and Gena Schwam.

1. The large pectoral was standard for depictions of Roman Catholic religious. A similar weighty cross and yoke, for example, stabilize the composition and form the primary iconographic identifier in George Whiting Flagg's *A Nun* (c. 1836, New York Historical Society), exhibited at the National Academy of Design in 1836. The particular placement of the Catholic priest's thumb and fingers in the act of blessing was noted, described, and often ridiculed by many Protestant observers. See, for example, [James Jackson Jarves], "The Holy Week at Rome. First Article," *Harper's New Monthly Magazine* 9 (June 1854): 27; and Samuel F. B. Morse, *Samuel F. B. Morse: His Letters and Journals*, ed. Edward Lind Morse, 2 vols. (Boston: Houghton Mifflin, 1914), 1: 339, 347.

2. Stuart, who worked in his youth as a church organist in London and who spent some six years (1787–93) in Catholic Ireland, would certainly have been capable of such direct allusions to the experience of a mass. According to Richard McLanathan, Stuart was particularly sensitive and sympathetic to the situation of the Irish Catholic majority living under English domination (*Gilbert Stuart* [New York: Harry N. Abrams, 1986], 74).

3. The best comparison within Stuart's own oeuvre is his portrait of Cheverus's superior, Bishop (and ultimately, Archbishop) John Carroll (c. 1803–5, Georgetown University), which while employing some of the same compositional elements, presents a tentative, almost wincing portrayal of the highest official of the American Catholic Church. Unlike Cheverus, Carroll appears as a man loathe to offend, constitutionally unable to put himself forward.

4. The history of the Charlestown convent burning is extremely complex. Its notoriety stemmed in part from the remarkable success of the sensational publication, *Six Months in a Convent* (Boston: Russell, Odiorne, and Metcalf, 1835), by Rebecca Reed, a onetime convent student and Catholic convert. Recent attempts to shed light on this important incident include Daniel A. Cohen, "Miss Reed and the Superiors: The Contradictions of Convent Life in Antebellum America," *Journal of Social History* 30 (fall 1996): 149–84; Jeanne Hamilton, "The Nunnery as Menace: The Burning of the Charlestown Convent, 1834," *U.S. Catholic Historian* 14 (winter 1996): 35–65; and Maureen A. McCarthy, "The Rescue of True Womanhood: Convents and Anti-Catholicism in 1830s America" (Ph.D. diss., Rutgers University, 1996). Cheverus, a French-born priest from an aristocratic family, left revolutionary France in 1792 and arrived in Boston four years later. He was consecrated and installed as the first bishop of the large New England diocese in 1810, where he fostered an unusual degree of interfaith harmony until he was recalled to France in 1823. Early in his career, he discovered the extent of anti-Catholic sentiment when he traveled to Northampton, Massachusetts, to confess two Irish Catholic prisoners, where he met with a less than enthusiastic welcome from the town's innkeepers and citizens. For this episode, see Annabelle M. Melville, *Jean Lefebvre de Cheverus, 1768–1836* (Milwaukee: Bruce Publishing, 1958), 136; and P. H. Gallen, "Father Cheverus in Northampton," in *How Popes Are Chosen and Other Essays* (Boston: Stratford, 1927). The most comprehensive account of antebellum Protestant antipathy toward Catholics remains Ray Allen Billington, *The Protestant Crusade, 1800–1860: A Study of the Origins of American Nativism* (New York: Macmillan, 1938).

5. On the eve of Cheverus's departure from his episcopal seat in the United States, the portrait was commissioned by the prominent Bostonian, Mrs. John Gore, descending

through several generations of her family. It was exhibited at the Boston Atheneum in 1827, 1828, and 1854. On the engravings, see Melville, *Cheverus*, chap. 17 n. 19.

6. James Russell Lowell, *Fireside Travels*, 4th ed. (Boston: Houghton Mifflin, 1881), 288, 290. The first edition was published in 1864; it describes his European experiences of the 1850s.

    I am indebted to Jenny Franchot's discussion of Lowell in her indispensable *Roads to Rome: The Antebellum Protestant Encounter with Catholicism* (Berkeley and Los Angeles: University of California Press, 1994), 215, 270–72.

7. Grace Greenwood, *Haps and Mishaps of a Tour in Europe* (Boston: Ticknor, Reed, and Fields, 1853), 199–200, 273.

8. Franchot, *Roads to Rome*, 234. In her introduction, Franchot describes her book as arguing "that anti-Catholicism operated as an imaginative category of discourse through which antebellum American writers of popular and elite fictional and historical texts indirectly voiced the tensions and limitations of mainstream Protestant culture" (xvii). It is my hope to extend some of Franchot's excellent insights more squarely into the realm of visual production and reception.

9. I have examined a similar phenomenon, involving late-nineteenth-century Protestants and Jews, in John Davis, "Holy Land, Holy People? Photography, Semitic Wannabes, and Chautauqua's Palestine Park," *Prospects: An Annual of American Cultural Studies* 17 (1992): 241–71.

10. W. Joseph Walters, "Catholic, Roman," in *An Original History of the Religious Denominations at Present Existing in the United States*, comp. I. Daniel Rupp (Philadelphia: J. Y. Humphreys, 1844), 137. Walters appears to be aware of the great sensitivity surrounding the issue of Catholic ritual. Thus, his defense of these "ceremonies" is surprisingly weak and noncommittal: "The Catholic Church deems them useful. They give a peculiar dignity to the sacred mysteries of religion . . . but neither the ceremonies nor the vestments belong to the essence of religion. The Church established them in the first ages. She could, if she deemed it advisable, set them aside any day, and the sacrifice would be equally holy" (155). For a better summary of the importance of ritual in Catholicism, see Jay Dolan, *The American Catholic Experience: A History from Colonial Times to the Present* (Garden City, N.Y.: Doubleday, 1985), 229–31. In a very different context, Eleanor Heartney has compellingly explored the ways in which the Catholic focus on the physical body has informed the work of such transgressive artists as Robert Mapplethorpe, Andres Serrano, and Kiki Smith. See Heartney's "Postmodern Heretics," *Art in America* 85 (February 1997): 33–39.

11. Margaret Fuller Ossoli, *At Home and Abroad, or Things and Thoughts in America and Europe* (Boston: Crosby, Nichols, 1856), 276–77.

12. Estimates differ, but the Irish and the Germans together account for the vast majority of immigrants, most of them Catholic, during the period of c. 1820–50. By 1860, more than 3 million U.S. residents, a tenfold increase in thirty years (or roughly 10 percent of the general population), were Catholic. For some representative figures, see Billington, *Protestant Crusade*, 37, 239; Martin E. Marty, *Pilgrims in Their Own Land: 500 Years of Religion in America* (Boston: Little, Brown, 1984), 272; Ann Taves, *The Household of Faith: Roman Catholic Devotions in Mid-Nineteenth-Century America* (Notre Dame: Uni-

versity of Notre Dame Press, 1986), 7; and Mark A. Noll, *A History of Christianity in the United States and Canada* (Grand Rapids, Mich.: William B. Eerdmans, 1992), 205–6.

13. In general, see Billington, *Protestant Crusade,* for a comprehensive discussion of nativist literature and political strategies. The two most important anti-Catholic publications of Jarves and Morse were James Jackson Jarves, *Italian Sights and Papal Principles, Seen through American Spectacles* (New York: Harper & Bros., 1856), portions of which had previously appeared in *Harper's New Monthly Magazine;* and perhaps the most influential of all such essays, Brutus [Samuel F. B. Morse], *Foreign Conspiracy against the Liberties of the United States* (New York: Leavitt, Lord, 1835), which was first published as a series of letters in the *New York Observer* in 1834. Two of Morse's brothers had founded the *Observer,* a widely read anti-Catholic newspaper, in 1823.

14. Jarves, *Italian Sights,* 254; William Hogan, *High and Low Mass in the Roman Catholic Church; with Comments* (Boston: Jordan and Wiley, 1846), 54; and Kirwan [Nicholas Murray], *Letters to the Rt. Rev. John Hughes, Roman Catholic Bishop of New-York* (New York: Leavitt, Trow, 1848), 32–33. In a telling index of the capacity of Protestant audiences to consume even the most insignificant details of Catholic ceremony, Hogan's book translates every word of the Latin mass and obsessively parses each aspect of its ritual, always in unfailingly sarcastic terms. A similar tract, this time addressed to Catholics in an effort to convince them "that the Mass is opposed to God's own word" (177), is John Rogerson Cotter, *The Mass and Rubrics of the Roman Catholic Church, Translated into English, with Notes and Remarks* (N.Y.: D. Appleton, 1846), which launches into a critique of the experience of the mass from the very moment of entering the church and dipping one's finger in holy water.

15. The best treatment of Jarves's anti-Catholic prose is found in William L. Vance, *America's Rome: Volume Two. Catholic and Contemporary Rome* (New Haven: Yale University Press, 1989), chap. 1.

16. Greenwood describes Jesuits as "sinister-looking . . . in their sombre robes, moving about by twos, at a peculiar, stealthy, prowling gait—walking presentments of the very blackness of spiritual darkness" (*Haps and Mishaps,* 176). Morse's voice was perhaps the loudest in its warnings about Jesuit conspiracies to undermine American democracy. See, for example, Morse, *Letters and Journals,* 2: 330.

17. "A Month in Malta," *New York Observer,* 2 October 1830; Robert Hall, "The Roman Catholic Church," *New York Observer,* 20 April 1833. See also Thomas Hartwell Horne, *Mariolatry: or, Facts and Evidences Demonstrating the Worship of the Blessed Virgin Mary by the Church of Rome* (Hartford: Henry S. Parsons, 1844).

18. [Jarves], "Holy Week at Rome," 27.

19. Jarves, *Italian Sights,* 358–59.

20. Carol Duncan, *Civilizing Rituals: Inside Public Art Museums* (London: Routledge, 1995), 14.

21. Robert W. Gibbes, *A Memoir of James De Veaux, of Charleston, S.C.* (Columbia, S.C.: I. C. Morgan, 1846), 110, 109; Orville Dewey, *The Old World and the New; or, A Journal of Reflections and Observations Made on a Tour in Europe.* 2 vols. (N.Y.: Harper & Bros., 1836), 2: 110. See also Theodore E. Stebbins Jr., "American Painters and the Lure of Italy," in *The Lure of Italy: American Artists and the Italian Experience, 1760–1914* (Boston: Museum of Fine Arts, 1992), 49.

22. For an interesting, first-person account of these theological disputes in the 1840s, which resulted in a doctrinal crisis and purge of the student body of New York's General Theological Seminary, see Clarence Walworth, *The Oxford Movement in America* (1895; reprint, New York: United States Catholic Historical Society, 1974). One of the elements of this story that bears on the present subject is the delight with which General Theological students made touristic visits to Catholic churches in New York City to see the Latin mass being performed.

23. Dewey, *Old World*, 2: 126; James Walker, "Reaction in Favor of the Roman Catholics. A Discourse Delivered before the University in Cambridge, at the Dudleian Lecture, May 10, 1837," *Christian Examiner* 23 (September 1837): 13. Not surprisingly, art periodicals were some of the most vociferous in their support of increased pomp in Protestant worship. See, for example, "Paletta" [author], "Ritualism," *Watson's Art Journal* 7 (3 August 1867): 230.

24. G[eorge] E. E[llis], "The Artistic and Romantic View of the Church of the Middle Ages," *Christian Examiner and Religious Miscellany* 46 (May 1849): 346; Kirwan [Nicholas Murray], *Men and Things as I Saw Them in Europe* (New York: Harper & Bros., 1853), 79.

25. Taves, *Household of Faith*, vii-viii, chap. 2, passim; and Stephanie Wilkinson, "A Novel Defense: Fictional Defenses of American Catholicism, 1829–1869" (Ph.D. diss., University of Virginia, 1997), 149.

26. The most complete account of the facts surrounding the painting is Susan P. Casteras, "Robert W. Weir's *Taking the Veil* and 'The Value of Art as Handmaid of Religion,'" *Yale University Art Gallery Bulletin* 39 (winter 1986): 13–23. On Weir in general, see Irene Weir, *Robert W. Weir, Artist* (New York: Field-Doubleday, 1947); and *Robert Weir: Artist and Teacher of West Point* (West Point, N.Y.: Cadet Fine Arts Forum, 1976). Sketchy financial accounts for the Goupil's exhibition in February and March 1863 are found in the curatorial records, Yale University Art Gallery. For the elaborate preparations made by Weir to generate publicity for the exhibition of his work, see his letter to John F. Weir, 7 January 1863, Robert F. Weir Papers, Archives of American Art, microfilm roll 531, frs. 906–8.

27. "Mr. Weir's Picture of 'The Nun Taking the Veil in Rome,'" letter to the editor of the *New York Times*, 19 April 1863; and "Domestic Art Gossip," *Crayon* 7 (October 1860): 298. These articles appear to be the source for the view of the painting as rising above sectarian doctrine, which has largely governed most twentieth-century interpretations. Wendy Greenhouse makes the connection between Weir and Huntington in her comprehensive study, "Daniel Huntington and the Ideal of Christian Art," *Winterthur Portfolio* 31 (summer/autumn 1996): 124. She provides an excellent discussion of Huntington's sometimes tortured flirtation with Catholicism, as well as the Catholic-Episcopal divide within the realm of art. Weir's essay on religious art appeared as a letter to the editor in *The Churchman* 16 (5 Dec. 1846): 2. The masking of the crucified Christ in *Taking the Veil* can be explained by a comment made by Weir in a later interview: "A year or two ago I painted the two Marys at the tomb, but left the figure of Christ to be imagined. I have often so left it. One feels a delicacy in even attempting the delineation" (clipping, "An Artist at Home," *New York Evening Post* [c. 1877], Weir Papers, AAA 531: 1389). An unusual example of the crucifix treated as a prominent iconographic device in an

American painting is William James Hubard's portrait of Charles Carroll of Carrollton, the only Catholic signer of the Declaration of Independence (Metropolitan Museum of Art, c. 1830).

28. These accounts are discussed in Vance, *America's Rome*, 181–84, where Ossoli's frank opinion of the spectacle is quoted: "The effect on my mind was revolting and painful to the last degree" (183). One reason for the literary popularity of this subject was likely the confluence of Catholic ritual and a female protagonist. Dolan, for example, finds the nineteenth-century culture of ritual "identified with the feminine personality" and "riddled with emotionalism and sentimentalism" (231), and one antebellum writer found discussions of Catholic ceremony "addressed chiefly to female sensibilities" ("Artistic and Romantic View," [351]).

29. Hogan, *High and Low Mass*, 63. The Boston ceremony is described in Melville, *Cheverus*, 214; see also Hamilton, "Nunnery as Menace," 36.

30. "The Ladies of the Sacred Heart," *Harper's New Monthly Magazine* 17 (July 1858): 205–6.

31. [Henry T. Tuckerman], "Professor Weir's New Picture," *New York Evening Post* 19 February 1863; unidentified French clipping, Weir Papers, AAA 531: 1453; "Professor Weir's New Picture," unidentified clipping, Weir Papers, AAA 531: 1457. There was a minority of Protestant writers who were mortified by the indelicate, touristic objectification of Catholics in their own houses of worship. See James Fenimore Cooper, *Gleanings in Europe: Italy* (Albany: State University of New York Press, 1981), 255; Dewey, *Old World*, 2: 47–48; and Ossoli, *At Home and Abroad*, 262.

32. "Mr. Weir's Picture" (emphasis added).

33. Franchot, *Roads to Rome*, 238.

34. Meyer Schapiro, *Words and Pictures: On the Literal and the Symbolic in the Illustration of a Text* (The Hague: Mouton, 1973), 41, 38.

35. Margaret Iversen, "Saussure v. Peirce: Models for a Semiotics of Visual Art," in *The New Art History*, ed. A. L. Rees and Frances Borzello (Atlantic Highlands, N.J.: Humanities Press International, 1988), 87–89. Emile Benveniste, *Problems in General Linguistics*, trans. Mary Elizabeth Meek (Coral Gables: University of Miami Press, 1971), 205–11. Benveniste's applicability to modes of representation is discussed in Craig Owens, "Representation, Appropriation & Power," *Art in America* 70 (May 1982): 15.

36. "Art Intelligence," *Commercial Advertiser*, 24 February 1863.

37. Morse, *Letters and Journals*, 325; Paul J. Staiti, *Samuel F. B. Morse* (New York: Cambridge University Press, 1989), 178. Although Morse's religious views have been considered by a number of authors, Staiti's treatment (especially 2–8, 177–86) is the most thoughtful and complete. See also John Dillenberger, *The Visual Arts and Christianity in America: The Colonial Period through the Nineteenth Century* (Chico, Calif.: Scholars Press, 1984), 72–75. For an early comparison of the attitudes of Cole and Morse, see Oliver W. Larkin, "Two Yankee Painters in Italy: Thomas Cole and Samuel Morse," *American Quarterly* 5 (fall 1953): 195–200.

38. Staiti also finds the painting "unconvincing," and "rigidly ordered" (*Morse*, 181, 186). The most complete account of the commission and execution of the painting is Louisa Dresser, "*The Chapel of the Virgin at Subiaco* by Samuel F. B. Morse," *Worcester Art Museum Annual* 4 (1941): 65–71, where the subject is described by Morse in a letter to his

patron, Stephen Salisbury, as "a good example of those shrines before which the contadini bow the knee, and worship the Virgin" (68). Virgin worship is also mentioned in Morse's *Foreign Conspiracy*, 71.

39. Dewey, *Old World*, 2: 62. To avoid divorcing the Cole canvas from its original context, it should be stated that it is one half of a pair of paintings with a loose Miltonic theme, *L'Allegro* and *Il Penseroso*. See the catalogue essay in Ilene Susan Fort and Michael Quick, *American Art: A Catalogue of the Los Angeles County Museum of Art Collection* (Los Angeles: Los Angeles County Museum of Art, 1991), 113–17. For an interesting painting falling somewhat in the middle of the Cole-Morse spectrum outlined above, see John F. Kensett, *The Shrine—A Scene in Italy* (Mr. and Mrs. Maurice N. Katz Collection, Naples, Florida, 1847). Wayside shrines were frequent subjects of North American artists in Italy and in Latin America. A very different visual dynamic, however, is created in the series of paintings entitled *Ave Maria* by Louis Rémy Mignot, the only Catholic artist working among the East Coast cadre of antebellum landscape painters. Although lacking the human protagonists of Cole and Morse, these paintings, each one depicting a South American church bathed in a golden crepuscular glow, seem—through their titles—to intone an entreaty to the virgin; they function, more or less, as visual prosecutions of a prayer. See Katherine E. Manthorne's discussion in *Louis Rémy Mignot: A Southern Painter Abroad* (Washington, D.C.: Smithsonian Institution Press, 1996), 93–96.

40. Dewey, *Old World*, 2: 111, 150.

41. These divergent understandings of sacred space (the "substantial" versus the "situational") structure one of the major historiographic debates in the fields of religious history and ritual studies. The former view—associated with Mircea Eliade—finds certain numinous locations to be, more or less, independently productive of sacred space, while the latter theory—most often traced to Emile Durkheim and Claude Lévi-Strauss—sees the sacred as culturally determined, ritually enacted through social practices. See the discussion of David Chidester and Edward T. Linenthal in *American Sacred Space* (Bloomington: Indiana University Press, 1995), 5–10.

42. See "Daguerre's Dioramas," *New York Commercial Advertiser*, 23 September 1840; quoted in Keven J. Avery, "The Panorama and Its Manifestations in American Landscape Painting, 1795–1870" (Ph.D. diss., Columbia University, 1995), 49. Avery (39–51) gives a representative sampling of such dioramic presentations. For the success of the same composition in Paris, see Helmut Gernsheim and Alison Gernsheim, *L. J. M. Daguerre: The History of the Diorama and the Daguerreotype* (N.Y.: Dover, 1968), 34–36.

43. "Editor's Table," *Knickerbocker* 19 (June 1842): 592; and "An American" [Henry T. Tuckerman], *The Italian Sketchbook* (Philadelphia: Key & Biddle, 1835): 24.

44. "George Cooke," *Constitutional Whig* (Richmond), 20 January 1829. The best source on Cooke, who converted to Catholicism as a young man and then later repudiated the faith in a switch to Methodism, is Donald D. Keyes et al., *George Cooke, 1793–1849* (Athens: Georgia Museum of Art, 1991). See also *Descriptive Catalogue of Paintings in the Gallery of Daniel Pratt, Prattville, Alabama, Together with a Memoir of George Cooke, Artist* (Prattville: Howell & Luckett, 1853); Beth Abney, "George Cooke and the Chapel Painting," *Papers of the Athens Historical Society* 2 (December 1979): 63–75; and Laquita Thomson, "Daniel Pratt's Picture Gallery," *Alabama Review* 47 (July 1995): 163–76. A visit to the Vatican,

whether through painted images or an actual physical experience, regularly provided American Protestants with an opportunity to give way to elemental emotions, to shed outward respectability as they succumbed to the sublimity of the space and the thrilling promiscuity of the crushing crowds. Thus James Fenimore Cooper—speechless, trembling, and numb—found himself weeping unaccountably in St. Peter's, his confused young son clinging to him in fright. Grace Greenwood, buffeted by the surging Holy Week mob, seemingly lost her faculties, laughing out loud "in a wild, hysterical way." She took an almost giddy pleasure in this "strange world, in which I seemed lost," and others, such as N. P. Willis, also noted "a lost and unexamining, unparticularizing feeling which I cannot overcome in this place—a mind borne quite off its feet and confused and overwhelmed with the tide of astonishment." See Cooper, *Gleanings*, 192; Greenwood, *Haps and Mishaps*, 280, 395; N. Parker Willis, *Pencillings by the Way* (Auburn: Alden, Beardsley, 1853), 381—all of whom are discussed in Vance, *America's Rome*, 95–98.

45. "The Paintings on Four and a Half Street," *Daily National Intelligencer* (Washington, D.C.), 20 September 1837; and "Art Matters," *New York Evening Express*, c. March 1863, undated clipping, Weir Papers, AAA 531: 1383. See also "The Athenaeum Gallery and the Allston Collection," *Bulletin of the American Art Union* 3 (October 1850): 110. The bibliography on Granet has grown considerably in recent years. Most helpful for the Capuchin canvases are: Edgar Munhall, *François-Marius Granet: Watercolors from the Musée Granet at Aix-en-Provence* (New York: Frick Collection, 1988), which reprints Granet's memoirs; Isabelle Néto-Daguerre and Denis Coutagne, *Granet: Peintre de Rome* (Aix-en-Provence: Musée Granet, 1992); and Isabelle Néto, "Un tableau de Granet au Musée des Beaux-Arts de Lyon: Le Choeur des Capucins de la place Barberini," *Bulletin des Musées et Monuments lyonnais* 1–2 (1994): 4–17.

46. Néto ("Un tableau de Granet," 12) refers to him as "un amateur non-identifié," while a Boston newspaper of the time calls him simply "an American merchant" and states that the copy purchased was the sixth by Granet ("The Capuchin Chapel," *Boston Daily Advertiser*, 23 April 1827).

47. The history of this important phenomenon remains to be accurately pieced together. The following are the most important sources (other than period letters and reviews) that shed light on Granet's popular composition and its influence: William Dunlap, *History of the Rise and Progress of the Arts of Design in the United States*, 2 vols. (1834; reprint, New York: Dover, 1969), 1: 288, 2: 134–35; Edward Biddle and Mantle Fielding, *The Life and Works of Thomas Sully (1783–1872)* (Philadelphia: Wickersham Press, 1921), 339, 396–99; Frances Batty, "Famous Painting by Thomas Sully Discovered in London House by Art Dealer," *Philadelphia Sunday Ledger*, 16 January 1927; Paul Staiti, "The 1823 Exhibition of the South Carolina Academy of Fine Arts: A Paradigm of Charleston Taste?" in *Art in the Lives of South Carolinians: Nineteenth-Century Chapters*, ed. David Moltke-Hansen (Charleston: Carolina Art Association, 1979), PSb-2; Steven Eric Bronson, "Thomas Sully: Style and Development in the Masterworks of Portraiture, 1738–1839" (Ph.D. diss., University of Delaware, 1986), 179–80; Maurice Poggi, "The Travelling Exhibition in America in the 1820s and 1830s" (master's thesis, University of Delaware, 1989), 11, 21–26, 35, 40; Staiti, *Morse*, 75, 96; Anneliese Harding, *John Lewis Krimmel: Genre Artist of the Early Republic* (Winterthur, Del.: Winterthur Museum, 1994), 166–67; Ellen Hickey

Grayson, "Art, Audiences, and the Aesthetics of Social Order in Antebellum America: Rembrandt Peale's *Court of Death*" (Ph.D. diss., George Washington University, 1995), 253, 466, 494, 496–97, 501; and John Davis, *The Landscape of Belief: Encountering the Holy Land in Nineteenth-Century American Art and Culture* (Princeton: Princeton University Press, 1996), 135–36.

48.   *Charleston Courier*, 25 February 1822. Many American authors "played" at being monks or longed to experience the cloistered life when they visited Europe. See Willis, *Pencillings*, 340–41; and Gibbes, *Memoir*, 63. Some, inspired by the renown of the Granet image, went out of their way to visit the Capuchin church in Rome, with their reactions ranging from Nicholas Murray's revulsion and disgust to Rembrandt Peale's nonchalance. See Kirwan [Nicholas Murray], *Romanism at Home. Letters to the Hon. Roger B. Taney, Chief Justice of the United States* (New York: Harper & Bros., 1852), 75–77; and Rembrandt Peale, *Notes on Italy* (Philadelphia: Carey and Lea, 1831), 150.

49.   "Capuchin Chapel," *Providence Patriot and Columbian Phenix*, 21 July 1827; and *Carolina Gazette*, 26 January 1822 (quoted in Grayson, 496). See also "Capuchin Chapel," *Boston Weekly Messenger*, 27 November 1823.

50.   Peale to Jefferson, 3 July 1820, *The Selected Papers of Charles Willson Peale and his Family*, ed. Lillian B. Miller et al., 4 vols. (New Haven: Yale University Press [1983–1996]), 3: 831; Peale to Raphaelle Peale, 14 May 1820, ibid., 3: 821; Peale to Rembrandt Peale, 23 July 1820, ibid., 3: 840–41; Rembrandt Peale to Sully, 4 July 1820, ibid., 3: 834 (spelling and grammar following the original, as published). For a good discussion of class divisions around large-scale trompe l'oeil presentations, see Angela Miller, "The Panorama, the Cinema, and the Emergence of the Spectacular," *Wide Angle* 18 (April 1996): 41–44.

51.   Peale to Rubens Peale, 5 May 1822, *Selected Papers.*, 4: 116; Charles Willson Peale, diary, 8 June 1817, ibid., 3: 524; and Peale to Raphaelle Peale.

52.   Jonathan Crary, *Techniques of the Observer: On Vision and Modernity in the Nineteenth Century* (Cambridge, Mass.: MIT Press, 1990), 98. See also chaps. 1 and 4, passim. Crary makes the important point (124) that the "realism" seen by nineteenth-century viewers, enthusiastically described by texts such as the *Capuchin Chapel* reviews, is unavailable to modern viewers and is largely unrecoverable. Our culturally produced vision of the late twentieth century simply will not permit us to "see" these images as their original audiences perceived them.

53.   Ibid., 18; Catherine Bell, *Ritual Theory, Ritual Practice* (New York: Oxford University Press, 1992), 93, 107; and Chidester and Linenthal, *American Sacred Space*, 10, 17–18, 28. See also Duncan, 10–12.

54.   Clifford Geertz, "Religion as a Cultural System," in *The Interpretation of Cultures* (New York: Basic Books, 1973), 113. A thorough discussion of the "observability" of ritual performance is found throughout Bell, *Ritual Theory*, especially 27–29, 37–41. On "misreading," see Duncan, *Civilizing Rituals*, 13. One could argue that the perspective of the nonparticipant is encoded into Granet's *Capuchin Chapel*, for as a Frenchman, he was reviled by the Capuchin monks in Rome, whose order had essentially been disbanded and destroyed by Napoleon. The artist's memoirs (Munhall, *François-Marius Granet*, 38) make it clear that he felt very much the intruder in this space. Alone among Granet commentators, Jacques Thuillier has commented on his "strange faith," which kept him

on the edges of religious life without addressing the truths of Catholic belief ("Etrange foi, que celle qui s'arrête au cadre de la vie religieuse sans toucher aux vérités du *Credo*"). Jacques Thuillier, "Préface," in Néto-Daguerre and Coutagne, *Granet*, 9. See also Bruno Foucart, "Saint François d'Assise et l'art français du XIXe siècle," *Revue d'Histoire de l'Eglise de France* 70, 184 (1984): 160–62.

CHAPTER 6

1. Robert Gober's *Untitled* (1995–97) was featured in the "Robert Gober" exhibition held at the Geffen Contemporary at MOCA, 7 September–14 December 1997; for illustrations and further discussion of the installation, see the exhibition catalogue *Robert Gober* (Los Angeles: The Museum of Contemporary Art, 1997), with essays by MOCA curator Paul Schimmel and critic Hal Foster; for information on the making of the installation components, see *Robert Gober: The 1996 Larry Aldrich Foundation Award Exhibition* (Ridgefield, Conn.: The Aldrich Museum of Contemporary Art, 1998), with an essay by Aldrich Museum director Harry Philbrick and an interview, conducted by Lena Howansky, with Gober's assistants in October 1997.

2. Robert Wuthnow, *After Heaven: Spirituality in America since the 1950s* (Berkeley and Los Angeles: University of California Press, 1998), 1; Anne Lewis Black and Dennis McCafferty, "The Age of Contentment," *USA Weekend* (3–5 July 1998), 4–6; Leslie Petrovski, "Modern Pilgrims Search for Meaning in Ancient Labyrinth," *The Denver Post* (24 August 1997): 6-H. For the "What Would Jesus Do?" website, see http://www.walkwith jesusdaily.com; on contemporary spiritual trends see Don Lattin and Richard Cimino, *Shopping for Faith: American Religion in the New Millennium* (New York: Jossey-Bass, 1998).

3. Edward Weisberger, ed., *The Spiritual in Art: Abstract Painting, 1890–1985* (Los Angeles: Los Angeles County Museum of Art and Abbeville Press, 1986); *Winged Evocations: A Kinetic Sculptural Installation & A Meditation on Flight and Its Association with Divinity* (Oberlin, Ohio: Allen Memorial Art Museum, 1998). Other exhibitions include "Seven Visions: The Spirit of Religion in Contemporary Regional Art" (Elmira, N.Y.: Arnot Art Museum, 1991); "Ceremony of Spirit: Nature and Memory in Contemporary Latino Art" (The Mexican Museum: San Francisco, 1993–94); "Consecrations: The Spiritual in Art in the Time of AIDS" (St. Louis University, Museum of Contemporary Religious Art, 1994–95); "Negotiating Rapture" (Chicago Museum of Contemporary Art, 1996); "Art & Religion: The Many Faces of Faith" (Philadelphia: The Balch Institute for Ethnic Studies and Villanova University Art Gallery, 1997); for further information see *Seven Visions: The Spirit of Religion in Contemporary Regional Art* (Elmira, N.Y.: Arnot Art Museum, 1991); *Ceremony of Spirit: Nature and Memory in Contemporary Latino Art*, curated by Amalia Mesa-Bains (San Francisco: The Mexican Museum, 1993); Victoria Carlson, "Consecrations at an Exhibition: Religious and Spiritual Art in the Time of AIDS," *The Critic: A Catholic Review of Books and the Arts* 49, no. 4 (1995): 2–17; Richard Francis, ed., *Negotiating Rapture* (Chicago: Museum of Contemporary Art, 1996); *Art & Religion: The Many Faces of Faith* (Philadelphia: The Balch Institute for Ethnic Studies, 1997).

4. Roger Lipsey, *An Art of Our Own: The Spiritual in Twentieth Century Art* (Boston: Shambhala Publications, 1988); David Morgan, ed., *Icons of American Protestantism: The Art of*

Warner Sallman (New Haven: Yale University Press, 1996), and *Visual Piety: A History and Theory of Popular Religious Images* (Berkeley and Los Angeles: University of California Press, 1998).

5. Wade Clark Roof, *A Generation of Seekers: The Spiritual Journeys of the Baby Boom Generation* (New York: HarperCollins, 1993).

6. César Grana, "The Private Lives of Public Museums," *Trans-Action* 4, no. 5 (1967): 20–25, as noted in Carol Duncan, *Civilizing Rituals: Inside Public Art Museums* (New York: Routledge, 1995), 17 n. 31.

7. John Berger, *Ways of Seeing* (London: British Broadcasting Corporation, 1972), 21; Jenny Franchot, "Unseemly Commemoration: Religion, Fragments, and the Icon," *American Literary History* 9, no. 3 (fall 1997): 502–21. For one critique of Berger see Peter Fuller, *Seeing Berger: A Revaluation of Ways of Seeing* (London: Writers and Readers Publishing Cooperative, 1980).

8. Frank McEntire, *Dreams and Shields: Spiritual Dimensions in Contemporary Art* (Salt Lake City: Salt Lake Art Center, 1992), 11–46, with a foreword by Edward G. Leffingwell, 5–10; Joanne Cubbs, *Religious Visionaries* (Sheboygan, Wis.: John Michael Kohler Arts Center, 1991), 3; see also Joanne Cubbs, "Rebels, Mystics, and Outcasts: The Romantic Artist Outsider," in *The Artist Outsider: Creativity and the Bounds of Culture*, ed. Michael D. Hall and Eugene W. Metcalf Jr. (Washington, D.C.: Smithsonian Institution Press, 1994), 76–93.

9. Lucy Lippard, *Overlay: Contemporary Art and the Art of Prehistory* (New York: Pantheon Books, 1983), 49; Irit Rogoff, "In the Empire of the Object: The Geographies of Ana Mendieta," in *Outsider Art: Contesting Boundaries in Contemporary Culture*, ed. Vera L. Zolberg and Joni Maya Cherbo (Cambridge, Eng.: Cambridge University Press, 1997), 159–71.

10. Suzi Gablik, *Has Modernism Failed?* (New York: Thames and Hudson, 1984), 97; Gablik, *The Reenchantment of Art* (New York: Thames and Hudson, 1991); Rachel Sadinsky, catalogue essay, *Seven Visions*, n.p. On CIVA see the organization's quarterly newsletter, published in Minneapolis, and its website: http://www.civa.org; on MOCRA see Alison Schneider, "Religion and Modern Art Find Common Ground," *The Chronicle of Higher Education* (26 April 1996): B3–B5.

11. Gober quoted in Joan Simon, "Robert Gober and the Extra Ordinary," in *Robert Gober* (Paris: Galarie Nationale du Jeu de Paume, 1991), 78–84; Dave Hickey, *Robert Gober* (New York: Dia Center for the Arts, 1992), 37.

12. Gober quoted in Paul Schimmel, "Gober Is in the Details," in *Robert Gober* (Los Angeles: The Museum of Contemporary Art, 1997), 44.

13. Eleanor Heartney, "Postmodern Heretics," *Art in America* (Feb. 1997): 32–39; Smith quoted in M. A. Greenstein, "A Conversation with Kiki Smith," *Artweek* (7 Jan. 1993): 23. See also Hal Foster's remarks regarding abjection in *The Return of the Real: The Avant-Garde at the End of the Century* (Cambridge, Mass.: MIT Press, 1996), 152–68.

14. Heartney, "Postmodern Heretics," 33.

15. Gary Garrels, "New Sculpture," in *Robert Gober, Jeff Koons, Hans Steinbach: New Sculpture* (Chicago: The Renaissance Society at The University of Chicago, 1986), n.p.; Nancy Spector, "Robert Gober: Homeward Bound," *Parkett* 27 (March 1991): 82.

16. Gober quoted in Steven Henry Madoff, "After the 80's, a decade of Quiet," *New York*

Times (2 Nov. 1997): Arts and Entertainment 1, 45, and in Richard Flood and Lynne Cooke, *Robert Gober* (Liverpool: Tate Gallery, 1993), 13.

17. Spector, "Robert Gober," 82, and Sigmund Freud, "The Uncanny" (1919), in *On Creativity and the Unconscious: Papers on the Psychology of Art, Literature, Love, Religion* (1925, reprint, New York: Harper, 1958), selected with an introduction by Benjamin Nelson.

18. Spector, "Robert Gober," 80.

19. Libby Lumpkin, "Robert Gober, Museum of Contemporary Art, Los Angeles," *Artforum* 36 (Dec. 1997): 107–8; Gober quoted in Schimmel, "Gober Is in the Details," 44.

20. Mike Davis, *City of Quartz: Excavating the Future in Los Angeles* (New York: Verso, 1990), and *Ecology of Fear: Los Angeles and the Imagination of Disaster* (New York: American, 1998).

21. Schimmel, "Gober Is in the Details," 47; St. Teresa of Avila, *Interior Castle*, trans. E. Allison Peers (Garden City, N.J.: Image Books, 1961), 136.

22. Gober quoted in Suzanne Muchnic, "Stop, Look and Look Again," *Los Angeles Times* (31 August 1997): Calendar-6, 76–77.

23. Schimmel, "Gober Is in the Details," 54. Thanks to Ljubica Popovich of Vanderbilt University for helpful insights regarding the staircase.

24. Gober quoted in Karel Schampers, "Robert Gober," in *Robert Gober* (Rotterdam: Museum Boymans van-Beuningen, 1990), 33, and in Muchnic, "Stop, Look and Look Again," 76.

25. Lynne Cooke, "Los Angeles, Robert Gober," *Burlington* 140, no. 1140 (March 1998): 227.

26. Christopher Knight, "Articles of Faith for This World, Robert Gober's new installation at MOCA," *Los Angeles Times* (9 September 1997): F-1; Smith quoted in Greenstein, "A Conversation," 23–24; Steven L. Douglass, "Kiki Smith, PaceWildenstein," *Flash Art* (Nov./Dec. 1997): 112; Fawbush quoted in Michael Boodro, "Blood, Spit, and Beauty," *Artnews* (March 1994): 130.

27. "Counterpunch Letters" and "Saturday Letters," respectively, *Los Angeles Times* (29 Sep. 1997): F-3, and (13 Sep. 1997): F-6; Father Gregory Coiro, "Gober Exhibition Insults Virgin Mary," *Los Angeles Times* (22 Sep. 1997): F-3; Catholic League referenced in Linda Ekstrom, "Gober's Mary Fires Debate on Art, Religion," *National Catholic Reporter* (15 Dec. 1997): 18.

28. "Saturday Letters" and "Counterpunch Letters" respectively, *Los Angeles Times* (25 Oct. 1997): F-12, F-14, and (29 Sep. 1997): F-3.

29. Ekstrom, "Gober's Mary," 18.

30. See *Betye Saar* (Los Angeles: Museum of Contemporary Art, 1984), with an essay by Peter Clothier.

CHAPTER 7

1. Such a fundamental and integrative role for religion is envisioned by such classical thinkers as Durkheim and Weber but is also present in such works as Peter Berger and Thomas Luckman, *The Social Construction of Reality* (Garden City: Anchor Books, 1967).

2. R. Stephen Warner, "Work in Progress toward a New Paradigm for the Sociological Study of Religion in the United States," *American Journal of Sociology* 98, no. 5 (1993): 1044–93.

3. Wade Clark Roof, *A Generation of Seekers: The Spiritual Journeys of the Baby Boom Generation* (San Francisco: HarperCollins, 1993).

4. Anthony Giddens, *Modernity and Self-Identity: Self and Society in the Late-Modern Age* (Stanford: Stanford University Press, 1991).

5. Catherine Albanese, "Fisher Kings and Public Spaces: The Old New Age in the 1990s," *The Annals of the American Academy* 527 (May 1993).

6. Martin Marty, "Where the Energies Go," *The Annals of the American Academy* 527 (May 1993).

7. Peter Williams, *Popular Religion in America: Symbolic Change and the Modernization Process in Historical Perspective* (Urbana: University of Illinois Press, 1989).

8. David Morgan, *Visual Piety: A History and Theory of Popular Religious Images* (Berkeley and Los Angeles: University of California Press, 1998); Sally M. Promey, *Spiritual Spectacles: Vision and Image in Mid-Nineteenth Century Shakerism* (Bloomington: Indiana University Press, 1993).

9. R. Laurence Moore, *Selling God* (New York: Oxford, 1993).

10. David Paul Nord, *The Evangelical Origins of Mass Media in America, 1815–1835,* Journalism Monograph No. 88 (Columbia, S.C.: Association for Education in Journalism and Mass Communication, 1984).

11. Pierre Bourdieu, *Distinction: A Social Critique of Judgment of Taste,* trans. R. Nice (London: Routledge, 1984).

12. For an example of what may emerge, see the discussion of the visualization of angels in Lynn Schofield Clark, "Identity, Discourse, and Media Audiences: A Critical Ethnography of the Role of Visual Media in Religious Identity-Construction among U.S. Adolescents," Ph.D. diss., University of Colorado, 1998.

13. See, in particular, Morgan, *Visual Piety;* Promey, *Spiritual Spectacles;* John Davis, *The Landscape of Belief: Encountering the Holy Land in Nineteenth-Century American Art and Culture* (Princeton: Princeton University Press, 1996); see also the other chapters in this volume.

14. See, in particular, David Harvey, *The Condition of Postmodernity: An Enquiry into the Origins of Cultural Change* (Cambridge, Eng.: Blackwell, 1989).

CHAPTER 8

1. The term "Sioux" will be used throughout this chapter to designate the whole or any part of the loose alliance that was known by its members as the *Oceti Sakowin,* or Seven Council Fires. Four of these fires—the *Mdewakanton, Wahpekute, Wahpetuwan,* and *Sissituwan*—belonged to a division alternatively referred to as the Dakotas, Santees, or Eastern Sioux; two others—the *Ihanktuwan* (Yanktons) and the *Ihanktuwannai* (Yanktonais)—to the Nakotas or Middle Sioux; and one fire to the Lakotas, Teton, or Western Sioux. The Teton Sioux, in turn, comprised seven tribes: *Oglalas, Sicangus, Hunkpapas, Mnikowojus, Sihasapas, O'ohenumpas,* and *Itazipcolas.* The words Dakota, Nakota, and Lakota are dialectical variants of a term meaning "friend" or "ally." The word "Sioux" is based on the French transliteration and abbreviation of a term *Nadouweso,* an Ojibwa (Chippewa) word meaning "snake," "adder," or "enemy."

2. The Federal Indian Bureau's efforts to suppress the Lakota Sun Dance represented only one front in its prolonged struggle to abolish social and ceremonial dancing among all American Indian tribes. From 1871 to 1934, reservation agents employed a variety of strategies and sanctions to compel Indians to forsake their dances. This policy reached its apex during the administration of Indian Commissioner Charles Henry Burke (1921–29) who issued a series of circulars and "messages" to convince Indians to redirect to acquiring practical knowledge of American civilization and Christianity the time they "squandered" on dancing. For a summary of issues and controversies surrounding Indian dancing, see Francis Prucha, *The Great Father* (Lincoln: University of Nebraska Press, 1984), 800–805.

3. James R. Walker, *Lakota Belief and Ritual* (Lincoln: University of Nebraska Press, 1980), 70.

4. Ibid., 69–70.

5. James R. Walker, *The Sun Dance and Other Ceremonies of the Oglala Division of the Teton Dakota*, American Museum of Natural History Anthropological Papers, vol. 16, pt. 2 (1917), 160.

6. Ibid., 159–60.

7. Ibid., 152.

8. Walker, *Lakota Belief and Ritual*, 215.

9. Walker, *The Sun Dance*, 159.

10. Raymond J. DeMallie and Robert Lavenda, "Wakan: Plains Siouan Concepts of Power," in *The Anthropology of Power: Ethnographic Studies from Asia, Oceania, and the New World*, ed. Richard Adams and Raymond D. Fogelson (New York: Academic Press, 1977), 155–56.

11. Walker, *Lakota Belief and Ritual*, 127–28.

12. Ibid., 116.

13. DeMallie and Lavenda, *Wakan*, 157.

14. Walker, *Lakota Belief and Ritual*, 69.

15. Raymond J. DeMallie, "Lakota Belief and Ritual in the Nineteenth Century," in *Sioux Indian Religion*, ed. Raymond J. DeMallie and Douglas R. Parks (Norman: University of Oklahoma Press, 1987), 31.

16. Walker, *Lakota Belief and Ritual*, 70. Consider also the following extract from James Walker's interview with the Oglala holy man, Finger:

> [WALKER]: Is *Skan, Wanka Tanka?*
> [FINGER]: Yes . . .
> [WALKER]: Are *Wi* and *Skan* one and the same?
> [FINGER]: No . . .
> [WALKER]: Are they both *Wanka Tanka?*
> [FINGER]: Yes.
> [WALKER]: Are there any other *[W]akan* that are *Wanka Tanka?*
> [FINGER]: Yes. *Han Wi*, the Moon; *Tate*, the Wind; *Wakiyan*, the Winged; and *Wohpe*, the Beautiful Woman.
> [WALKER]: Are there any others that are *Wanka Tanka?*
> [FINGER]: No.
> [WALKER]: Then there are eight *Wakan Tanka*, are there?
> [FINGER]: No, there is but one.

[WALKER]: How can that be?

[FINGER]: That is right. I have named eight. There are four, *Wi, Skan, Iyan,* and *Maka.* These are the *Wakan Tanka.*

[WALKER]: You named four others, the Moon, the Wind, Winged, and the Beautiful Woman and said they were *Wanka Tanka,* did you not?

[FINGER]: Yes. But these four are the same as the *Wanka Tanka.* The Sun and the Moon are the same, the *Skan* and the Wind are the same, Earth and the Beautiful Woman are the same. These eight are only one. The shamans know how this is, but the people do not. It is *wakan* (a mystery). (Walker, *The Sun Dance,* 154–55).

17. Ibid., 159.

18. James R. Walker, *Lakota Myth,* ed. Elaine Jahner (Lincoln: University of Nebraska Press, 1983), 212.

19. Walker, *Lakota Belief and Ritual,* 108.

20. Ibid., 181.

21. Ibid., 182.

22. Walker, *The Sun Dance,* 60

23. Walker, *Lakota Belief and Ritual,* 181.

24. Walker, *The Sun Dance,* 61.

25. Ibid., 95–96.

26. Ibid., 96–100.

27. Ibid., 100–121.

28. Frances Densmore, *Teton Sioux Music,* Smithsonian Institution, Bureau of American Ethnology, Bulletin 61 (1918), 131.

29. Ibid. Ella Deloria's Hunkpapa informants assured her that Sun Dance piercing seldom caused infection or lasting injury. They stated, "In terrible ways they dance with their chests pierced. And so long as they don't tear themselves away they continue to dance. But nobody ever got infected from the wounds nor were they permanently injured by the cuts. Only once a man by the name of Lone Man who had his chest pierced in two places pulled out not only the pegs from their pinnings, but the whole flesh off his chest, leaving a hideous, red circular wound. When this happened they took some pine charcoal and pulverized it and dusted the wound with it and healed it." (Ella Deloria, "The Sun Dance of the Oglala Sioux," *Journal of American Folklore* 42 [1929]: 412).

30. Walker, *Lakota Belief and Ritual,* 180.

31. Walker, *The Sun Dance,* 105–8.

32. Short Bull stated that the four men chosen to deliver these blows were elders from the Silent Society (Walker, *Lakota Belief and Ritual,* 191).

33. Walker, *The Sun Dance,* 106.

34. Ibid., 107.

35. Walker, *Lakota Belief and Ritual,* 108. In a narrative detailing how the Lakotas first received and celebrated the Sun Dance, Oglala holy man Nicholas Black Elk wrote of the painting of the sacred pole that "Kablaya [the man to whom the spirits had communicated the ceremony] painted stripes of red on the west, north, east, and south sides of the tree, and then he touched a very little paint to the tip of the tree for the Great Spirit, and he also put some at the base of the tree for Mother Earth." (Joseph Epes Brown,

ed., *The Sacred Pipe: Black Elk's Account of the Seven Rites of the Oglala Sioux*, [Norman: University of Oklahoma Press, 1989], 78).

36. Deloria, "The Sun Dance," 398–99.

37. Walker, *Lakota Belief and Ritual*, 189.

38. Ibid.

39. Densmore, *Teton Sioux Music*, 118.

40. Walker, *Lakota Belief and Ritual*, 100.

41. James Dorsey, *A Study of Siouan Cults*, Smithsonian Institution, Bureau of American Ethnology, Annual Report 11 (1894), 454.

42. Deloria, *The Sun Dance*, 378.

43. Ibid., 402.

44. Walker, *Belief and Ritual*, 187.

45. Dorsey, *Siouan Cults*, 460.

46. Densmore, *Teton Sioux Music*, 125.

47. James R. Walker, *Lakota Society*, ed. Raymond J. DeMallie (Lincoln: University of Nebraska Press, 1982), 99.

48. The highly formalized drawings of the first Sun Dance seen on some Lakota winter counts (for example, that by the Hunkpapa Lakota High Dog) may, arguably, be cited as prereservation representations of the ceremony.

49. DeMallie, *Lakota Belief and Ritual*, 300.

50. John Ewers, *Plains Indian Painting: A Description of an Aboriginal American Art* (Stanford: Stanford University Press, 1939), 15–22.

51. John A. Day and Margaret Quintal, "Oscar Howe, 1915–1983: Father of the New Native American Art," *Southwest Art* (June 1984).

52. Ibid., 59.

53. Ibid.

54. Ibid.

55. Arthur Amiotte, "The Lakota Sun Dance, Historical and Contemporary Perspectives," in *Sioux Indian Religion*, ed. Raymond J. DeMallie and Douglas Parks (Norman: University of Oklahoma Press, 1987), 89.

56. Ibid.

CHAPTER 9

1. 12 April 1847 diary entry, *William Sidney Mount*, ed. Alfred Frankenstein (New York: Harry N. Abrams, 1975), 174.

2. Deborah J. Johnson, *William Sidney Mount: Painter of American Life* (New York: The American Federation of Arts, 1998), 18–22.

3. 19 August 1846 diary entry, *Mount*, ed. Frankenstein, 143.

4. 19 October 1847 diary entry, *Mount*, ed. Frankenstein, 180.

5. In his Spiritualist diaries of 1854–55, which describe various encounters with spirits and mediums, Mount briefly alludes to the "hermetic philosophy" of Henry Cornelius Agrippa of Nettesheim (1486–1535) and mentions several other alchemists and magicians, including Roger Bacon (1214–94), John Dee (1527–1608), Paracelsus (c. 1493–1541)

and Count Cagliostro (1743–95). See *Mount*, ed. Frankenstein, 291. On the importance of the hermetic tradition for the democratic poetry of Walt Whitman, who also hailed from Long Island, see Ernest Lee Tuveson, *The Avatars of Thrice Great Hermes: An Approach to Romanticism* (London: Associated University Presses, 1982), 202–51. Wouter J. Hanegraaf persuasively argues that Tuveson overstated the difference between hermeticism and neoplatonism in "Romanticism and the Esoteric Connection," *Gnosis and Hermeticism from Antiquity to Modern Times*, ed. Roeof van den Broek and Wouter J. Hanegraaf (Albany, N.Y.: State University of New York Press, 1998), 253–62.

6. Deborah J. Johnson, *William Sidney Mount*, 62–65. In 1818, George Washington Strong formed a partnership with the upstate New York Federalist and prominent Freemason John Wells. It became New York City's largest and most prestigious law firm, focusing on real estate and probate issues for a wealthy, upper-class clientele. See Frederic Cople Jaher, *The Urban Establishment: Upper Strata in Boston, New York, Charleston, Chicago, and Los Angeles* (Urbana: University of Illinois Press, 1982), 224–25. On Wells's membership in Freemasonry and his 1823 nomination to become grand master of New York's City Grand Lodge (an honor he declined because of business obligations), see the *Sesquicentennial Commemorative Volume of Holland Lodge, No. 8 of the Ancient and Honorable Fraternity of Free Accepted Masons* (New York: Holland Lodge No. 8, 1938), 29. Although Strong moved in Masonic circles, I have not found any evidence that he belonged to Freemasonry, which attracted a significant number of New York's political and social elite and was a conduit for hermetic thought. See Thomas Bender, *New York Intellect: A History of Intellectual Life in New York City, from 1750 to the Beginnings of Our Own Time* (New York: Alfred A. Knopf, 1987), 58–60.

7. Mount to Charles Lanman, 17 November 1847, *Mount*, ed. Frankenstein, 120, 122.

8. Ibid., 122.

9. Shining fish eyes emerging from blackness traditionally symbolized the processes of alchemical transmutation from lower to higher forms of matter. See William R. Newman, *Gehennical Fire: The Lives of George Starkey, an American Alchemist in the Scientific Revolution* (Cambridge, Mass.: Harvard University Press, 1994), 47.

10. Mount to Benjamin Franklin Thompson, 31 December 1848, *Mount*, ed. Frankenstein, 235.

11. David Bjelajac, *Washington Allston, Secret Societies and the Alchemy of Anglo-American Painting* (New York: Cambridge University Press, 1997), 35–37.

12. Ibid.

13. John Galt, *The Life and Studies of Benjamin West*, 2d ed. (London: T. Cadell and W. Davies, and T. and G. Underwood, 1817), 18.

14. Ibid., 132. As Galt notes, West was instructed in the mysteries of Egyptian hieroglyphics by the Anglican clergyman and provost of the College of Philadelphia (the University of Pennsylvania), the Reverend William Smith (1727–1803). Smith also promoted the secretive social fraternity of Freemasonry, which played an important role in popularizing the notion of an ancient Egyptian wisdom or hieroglyphic knowledge of God's creation. On Smith and Freemasonry, see Steven C. Bullock, *Revolutionary Brotherhood: Freemasonry and the Transformation of the American Social Order, 1730–1840* (Chapel Hill: University of North Carolina Press, 1996), 53, 103–4, 109, 132.

15. American followers of the Swedish hermetic prophet Emanuel Swedenborg (1688–1772) especially argued for the metaphysical content of Egyptian hieroglyphics. See John T. Irwin, *American Hieroglyphics: The Symbol of the Egyptian Hieroglyphics in the American Renaissance* (Baltimore, Md.: Johns Hopkins University Press, 1980), 6–9. Though not a member of the Swedenborgian New Jerusalem Church, Mount quoted passages from Swedenborg's visionary writings in his 1854 Spiritualist diary. See his diary entry for 18 April 1854, *Mount*, ed. Frankenstein, 292. The Swedenborgian doctrine of correspondences supported the hermetic belief that the hieroglyphic book of nature was an actual manifestation of the divine, corresponding to the invisible world of spirit. See Sally M. Promey, "The Ribband of Faith: George Inness, Color Theory and the Swedenborgian Church," *The American Art Journal* 26 (1996): 49–50. A number of Swedenborgians were Freemasons. See Samuel Woodworth's discussion of Egyptian hieroglyphics in relation to the Swedenborgian "science of correspondences" in "The Christian Mason," *The American Masonic Register and Ladies' and Gentlemen's Magazine* 1 (July 1821): 409–14. Woodworth later wrote *The Forest Rose; or, American Farmers* (1825) a pastoral, comedic play of Yankee manners that influenced Mount's genre paintings of Yankee farmers. Woodworth's play portrayed farms and villages as "havens of peace and prosperity" in contrast to the "wickedness and materialism" of city life. See Sarah Burns, *Pastoral Inventions: Rural Life in Nineteenth-Century American Art and Culture* (Philadelphia: Temple University Press, 1989), 134, 150–51.

16. Thomas Cole, "A Lecture on Art," in *Thomas Cole: The Collected Essays and Prose Sketches*, ed. Marshall Tymn, The John Colet Archive of American Literature, 7 (St. Paul, Minn.: The John Colet Press, 1980), 104–5.

17. Ibid., 103, 109.

18. Following in the footsteps of Benjamin West, the Boston painter Washington Allston (1779–1843) was particularly influential in elevating the craft of painting into a hermetic medium for spiritual knowledge. See Bjelajac, *Washington Allston*, 10–65. A letter from Allston to the American art chronicler William Dunlap (1766–1839) helped to establish Mount's reputation. See William Dunlap, *History of the Rise and Progress of the Arts of Design in the United States*, vol. 2 (1834, reprint, vol. 2, part II, New York: Dover Publications, 1969), 452.

19. Brian P. Copenhaven, introduction to *Hermetica: The Greek 'Corpus Hermeticum' and the Latin 'Asclepius,'* trans. Brian P. Copenhaven (Cambridge, Eng.: Cambridge University Press, 1992), xvi–li.

20. On the importance of alchemy for Newton and his contemporaries, see B. J. T. Dobbs, *The Janus Faces of Genius: The Role of Alchemy in Newton's Thought* (Cambridge, Eng.: Cambridge University Press, 1991). See also Lawrence M. Principe, *The Aspiring Adept: Robert Boyle and His Alchemical Quest* (Princeton: Princeton University Press, 1998).

21. John L. Brooke, *The Refiner's Fire: The Making of Mormon Cosmology, 1644–1844* (Cambridge, Eng.: Cambridge University Press, 1994), 10–11.

22. Karin Johannisson, "Magic, Science, and Institutionalization in the Seventeenth and Eighteenth Centuries," in *Hermeticism and the Renaissance*, eds. Ingrid Merkel and Allen G. Debus (Washington, D.C.: Folger Books; The Folger Shakespeare Library, 1988), 251–61.

23. Theodore Dwight Bozeman, *Protestants in an Age of Science: The Baconian Ideal and Antebellum American Religious Thought* (Chapel Hill: University of North Carolina Press, 1977), 49–51, 71–175.

24. Samuel Miller, *A Brief Retrospect of the Eighteenth Century*, vol. 1 (New York: T. and J. Swords, 1803), 414.

25. Ibid., 53.

26. Thomas Bender, *New York Intellect*, 60. On Freemasonry and American art, see Bjelajac, *Washington Allston*, 3–7, 73–79.

27. By 1825, there was at least one Masonic lodge in virtually every town in America. Steven C. Bullock, *Revolutionary Brotherhood*, 138.

28. Toivo H. Nekton, *Morton Lodge No. 63 of Free and Accepted Masons of the State of New York* (Hempstead, N.Y.; Morton Lodge No. 63, 1949), 7–10.

29. Edward P. Buffett, "William Sidney Mount: A Biography," *Port Jefferson Times*, 1 December 1923–12 June 1924, chapter 4.

30. Charles Bergengren, " 'Finished to the Utmost Nicety': Plain Portraits in America, 1760–1860," in *Folk Art and Art Worlds*, ed. John Michael Vlach and Simon J. Bronner (Logan: Utah State University Press, 1992), 107. John D. Hamilton lists a number of artists and engravers who decorated Masonic aprons, including Amos Doolittle (1754–1832), Ezra Ames (1768–1836), Nathaniel Jocelyn (1796–1881), John Sartain (1808–97), and James Barton Longacre (1794–1869). See Hamilton, *Material Culture of the American Freemasons* (Lexington, Mass.: Museum of our National Heritage, 1994), 288–91. The portrait painter James Herring (1794–1867), who founded the American Art Union, was for many years the grand secretary of the Grand Lodge of New York. See Ossian Lang, *History of Freemasonry in the State of New York* (New York: Grand Lodge of New York, 1922), 126–27, 213. The New York theatrical scene painter Hugh Reinagle (c. 1788–1834) was a Freemason and had connections with the Mount family. Reinagle painted the scenery for the New York production of *The Saw Mill, or, a Yankee Trick* (1824), a musical comedy written by Mount's favorite uncle, Micah Hawkins (1777–1825). Reinagle became the architect for New York's Gothic-revival Masonic Hall on Broadway. See Brother Hugh Reinagle's address as the lodge architect in "Grand Lodge of New York. Proceedings of the Grand Lodge, with Respect to the Masonick Hall," *American Masonic Record, and Albany Saturday Magazine* 1 (1 Dec. 1827): 345. On Hugh Reinagle and Micah Hawkins, see Vera Brodsky Lawrence, "Micah Hawkins, the Pied Piper of Catherine Slip," *New York Historical Society Quarterly* 62 (April 1978): 156–59. As Lawrence points out, the critics wrote more favorably of Reinagle's beautiful pastoral scenery than they did of Hawkins's songs and libretto. On the close relationship between Mount and his talented musical uncle, see Peter G. Buckley, " 'The Place to Make an Artist work': Micah Hawkins and William Sidney Mount in New York City," in *Catching the Tune: Music and William Sidney Mount*, ed. Janice Gray Armstrong (Stony Brook, N.Y.: The Museums at Stony Brook, 1984): 22–39.

31. Bjelajac, *Washington Allston*, 131, 198 n. 67.

32. Jeremy L. Cross, *The True Masonic Chart or Hieroglyphic Monitor Containing all the Emblems Explained*, 2d ed. (1820; reprint, Waco: Texas Lodge of Research, 1983), 42.

33. Ibid. "Castle Building," *Masonic Mirror and Mechanics' Intelligencer* 2 (29 April 1826):

140. Samuel Ward Jr. (1814–84), who drew up the terms of the commission for *The Voyage of Life*, was a Freemason. See the *Sesquicentennial Commemorative Volume of Holland Lodge* No. 8, 45. The landscape painter Albert Bierstadt (1830–1902) also became a member of this prestigious lodge. On Cole and Samuel Ward Jr., see Ellwood C. Parry III, *The Art of Thomas Cole* (Newark: University of Delaware Press, 1988), 226–28, 234–36, 251–52.

34. "History of Chemistry," *American Masonic Record, and Albany Saturday Magazine* 1 (25 August 1827): 234.

35. See diary entries for 13 October 1844 and November 1844 in *Mount*, ed. Frankenstein, 129–30.

36. R. D. Harley, *Artists' Pigments c. 1600–1835: A Study in English Documentary Sources*, 2d ed. (London: Butterworth Scientific, 1982), 152–54.

37. Douglas Brooks-Davies, *The Mercurian Monarch: Magical Politics from Spenser to Pope* (Manchester, Eng.: Manchester University Press, 1983), 5. Like Mount, John Quidor had been a sign painter and, perhaps, painted signs for the Freemasons or for the Masonic-style fraternity, the Odd Fellows. When, in May of 1818, Quidor became an apprentice to the New York portrait painter John W. Jarvis, he signed an agreement promising that he would not publicly reveal his master's craft "secrets." In return Jarvis promised "to teach or cause to be taught or instructed, the said apprentice in the trade or mystery of a Portrait Painter." Later in 1822–23, Quidor sued Jarvis for failing to teach him the mysteries or secrets of portraiture. During the trial, Mount's older brother Henry and Henry's partner in the sign-painting business, William Inslee both testified on behalf of Jarvis's defense. Ultimately, the New York court found that Jarvis had failed to live up to the contract in teaching Quidor the trade or "mystery" of portraiture. On the relationship between hermeticism and artists' and artisans' craft secrets, see William Eamon, *Science and the Secrets of Nature: Books of Secrets in Medieval and Early Modern Culture* (Princeton: Princeton University Press, 1994). On hermetic secrecy and the craft tradition in America, see W. J. Rorabaugh, *The Craft Apprentice from Franklin to the Machine Age in America* (New York: Oxford University Press, 1986), 33–36. While Rorabaugh argues that there was a decline in craft secrecy and mysteries with economic modernization and the increased publication of informative books, journals, and newspapers, Quidor's experience with Jarvis clearly suggests continuing resistance to the new culture of openness.

38. In describing his 1843 search for Long Island pigments with his brother Henry, Mount discovered "several *brimstone balls* of a sea green color . . . smelling strong of sulphur." The smell caused the two brothers to imagine with humor that "old cloven foot" and the ghost of Captain Kidd, the notorious seventeenth-century pirate, were standing behind them. See William Sidney Mount to Benjamin Franklin Thompson, 31 December 1848, *Mount*, ed. Frankenstein, 236. On the popular mania for money digging, see Alan Taylor, "The Early Republic's Supernatural Economy: Treasure Seeking in the American Northeast, 1780–1830," *American Quarterly* 38 (spring 1986): 6–33. On treasure seeking and Joseph Smith's hermetic "discovery" of the hieroglyphic *Book of Mormon* on gold plates, see John L. Brooke, *The Refiner's Fire*, 149–83.

39. "National Academy of Design: Second Notice," *The Knickerbocker* 27 (June 1846): 556.

40. George Richardson, *Iconology; or, a Collection of Emblematical Figures*, vol. 1 (1779; reprint, N.Y.: Garland Publishing, 1979), 148–49.

41. William Hogarth, *The Analysis of Beauty*, ed. Ronald Paulson (New Haven: Yale University Press, 1997), 33.

42. Ibid., 32.

43. Hogarth appropriates this phrase from Giovanni Paolo Lomazzo (1538–1600), a Milanese artist who wrote an influential art treatise, *Trattato dell'Arte della Pittura, Scultura ed Architettura* (1584). Ibid., 3 n. 5. On how Hogarth's Freemasonry may have influenced his *Analysis of Beauty*, see Ronald Paulson, *Hogarth*, vol. 3: *Art and Politics, 1750–1764* (New Brunswick, N.J.: Rutgers University Press, 1993), 127–31.

44. Ibid., 30.

45. Ibid., 12. On the appeal of Hogarth's *Analysis of Beauty* for American painters see Susan Rather, "A Painter's Progress: Matthew Pratt and *The American School*," *Metropolitan Museum Journal* 28 (1993): 176–77. On Mount's indebtedness to Hogarth, see Deborah Johnson, *William Sidney Mount*, 19.

46. On St. George and the Elizabethan revival of the Order of the Garter, see Frances A. Yates, *The Rosicrucian Enlightenment* (London: Routledge and Kegan Paul; Ark Paperbacks, 1986), 3–4.

47. Letter from four Yale classmates to George Washington Strong, 25 November 1806, in Allen Nevins, preface to *The Diary of George Templeton Strong: Young Man in New York, 1835–1849*, ed. Allan Nevins and Milton Halsey Thomas (New York: Octagon Books, 1974), xii.

48. Bjelajac, *Washington Allston*, 17, 46, 52, 99.

49. Mount makes an extensive list of pigments "fit to be employed as glazing and finishing colours . . . according to Field's work" in his diary entry for 22 June 1847. He also makes several other references to Field in later diary entries. See *Mount*, ed. Frankenstein, 178–79, 315, 342. Mount visited Washington Allston in 1839 for the older artist's Boston retrospective. Allston strongly recommended Field's books on color theory to his fellow painters. See Bjelajac, *Washington Allston*, 43. For Field's influence on Mount's close friend, Thomas Cole, see William Inness Homer, "Thomas Cole and Field's Chromotography," *Record of the Art Museum, Princeton University* 19 (1960): 26–30. See also John Gage, *George Field and His Circle: From Romanticism to the Pre-Raphaelite Brotherhood* (Cambridge, Eng.: Fitzwilliam Museum, Cambridge University, 1989) and David Brett, "The Aesthetical Science: George Field and the 'Science of Beauty,'" *Art History* 9 (September 1986): 336–50. For Field's influence on Samuel F. B. Morse, president of the National Academy of Design, see Samuel F. B. Morse, *Lectures on the Affinity of Painting with the Other Fine Arts*, ed. Nicolai Cikovsky Jr. (Columbia: University of Missouri Press, 1983), 18 n. 44, 88 n. 8, 89 n. 11.

50. George Field, *Chromatics, or an Essay on the Analogy and Harmony of Colours* (London: A. J. Valpy, 1817). Field published new editions of *Chromatics* in 1835 and 1845. See David Brett, "The Aesthetical Science," 337. For a fuller discussion of Field's emblem see Bjelajac, *Washington Allston*, 43–46. The uroboros is a common symbol in Masonic furniture and decorative arts. See John D. Hamilton, *Material Culture of the American Freemasons*, 55. It also appeared as a symbol of revolution and regeneration on Revolutionary

War currency and popular prints. See Lester C. Olson, *Emblems of American Community in the Revolutionary Era: A Study in Rhetorical Iconology* (Washington, D.C.: Smithsonian Institution Press, 1991), 24–74.

51. Llyndy Abraham, *Marvell and Alchemy* (Hants, Eng.: Scolar Press, 1990), 49–55, 232–33. The revered New York author Washington Irving, who steeped himself in alchemical lore, described gold "as an intimate combination of pure sulphur [fire] & mercurial earth." See Washington Irving, *Journals and Notebooks, 1807–1822*, ed. Walter A. Reichart and Lillian Schissel, vol. 2 (Boston: Twayne, 1981), 350.

52. Daniel V. Thompson Jr., *The Materials and Techniques of Medieval Painting* (New York: Dover, 1956), 103. Cennino D'Andrea Cennini, *The Craftsman's Handbook: The Italian Il Libro Dell' Arte,"* trans. Daniel V. Thompson Jr. (1933, reprint, New York: Dover, 1960), 24. Originally published c. 1390, Cennini's treatise, which credited alchemy for the production of vermilion, was first published in an English translation in London by Mary P. Merrifield (fl. 1840–70) in 1844. Merrifield made repeated editorial references to the work of George Field in her preface. See John Gage, *George Field and His Circle*, 74. On the intense interest in old-master painting techniques in England during the 1840s, see Hugh Trevor-Roper, "Mayerne and His Manuscript," *Art and Patronage in the Caroline Courts: Essays in Honour of Sir Oliver Millar*, ed. David Howarth (Cambridge, Eng.: Cambridge University Press, 1993), 264–93.

53. George Field, *Chromatics*, 43. The English Landscapist J. M. W. Turner sang the praises of vermilion, or the color red, in his alchemical poem "The Origin of Vermilion or the Loves of Painting and Music." See Andrew Wilton, *Painting and Poetry: Turner's 'Verse Book' and His Work of 1804–1812* (London: Tate Gallery, 1990), 33–35.

54. In Mount's painting, the boy's bright red hat band visually unites him with the black woman, who wears an even more prominent red scarf around her head and neck. Mount's patron, George Washington Strong, would have associated these red garments with Long Island's Revolutionary War history. According to Mount's close friend and teacher, Benjamin Franklin Thompson, who wrote an exhaustive *History of Long Island*, the British occupation army ordered Long Island's royalist citizens to signify their sympathetic political views by wearing red rags in their hats. Soon, however, being convinced that "there was magic in a red rag," all manner of "negroes, boys, old and young, wore red rags" unauthorized by British officials. Originating as royalist "badges of submission," the popular proliferation of red rags became emblematic of Long Island's resistance to British domination. See Benjamin F. Thompson, *The History of Long Island from Its Discovery and Settlement to the Present Time*, vol. 1 (New York: Gould, Banks, 1843), 193.

55. "National Academy of Design: Second Notice," *The Knickerbocker* 27 (June 1846): 556. James P. Mapes, a chemist and color theorist affiliated with the National Academy of Design, wrote that Mount's earlier painting of *Cider Making* was "so closely painted to nature that its location is readily discovered to be Suffolk County" on Long Island. See "National Academy of Design. Review of Exhibition," *American Repository of Arts, Sciences and Manufactures* 3 (June 1841): 358. This favorable review of Mount's ability to capture the objective reality of the Long Island environment was fully quoted in Benjamin F. Thompson, *The History of Long Island*, vol. 2 (1843), 529. Mapes was a Freema-

son and, as a chemist specializing in the development of agricultural fertilizers, he was deeply influenced by the hermetic, alchemical tradition. As the editor of *The American Repertory of Arts, Sciences and Manufacturers*, he informed artisans and mechanics of ancient craft traditions descended from ancient Egypt and their importance for contemporary science. See his review of a series of lectures by a Dr. Quin at the Mechanics' Institute in New York in "Lectures at the Mechanics' Institute," *The American Repertory of Arts, Sciences and Manufactures* (April 1840): 179. On Mapes's membership in Freemasonry, see William J. Duncan, *History of Independent Royal Arch Lodge No. 2 . . . of the State of New York* (New York: Independent Royal Arch Lodge No. 2, 1904). In a draft of an 1861 speech before the National Academy of Design, Mount identifies Mapes as a distinguished member of the National Academy and calls him a "chemist, agriculturalist and spiritualist." See *Mount*, ed. Frankenstein, 355. A patron of Thomas Cole, Mapes also wished to commission a painting from Mount. He also advised Mount on a "cure for worms." See Mount's diary entry for 3 April 1854 in *Mount*, ed. Frankenstein, 273. Mount would have been interested in Mapes's journal, since the chemist published a number of articles on pigments and colors. See especially Hyde Clarke, "On Color as Applied in Decoration," *The American Repertory of Arts, Sciences, and Manufactures* 4 (January 1842): 425–30. Excerpted from the *Civil Engineer and Architect's Journal*, the article discusses the French theorist Eugène Chevreul's (1786–1889) law of simultaneous contrast of colors.

56. W. Alfred Jones, "A Sketch of the Life and Character of William Sidney Mount," *The American Review* 8 (August 1851): 123. Jones appropriates the phrase "finger of God" from the German poet and critic Heinrich Heine (1797–1856).

57. Charles Lanman, *Haphazard Personalities: Chiefly of Noted Americans* (Boston: Lee and Shepard, 1886), 173. Lanman was a landscape painter and travel writer as well as ardent admirer of Mount's painting and fishing talents. He published *Letters from a Landscape Painter* (1844), which praised nature for instructing him in the "magic of mysteries." Quoted in Mary Watkins Hardaway, "Charles Lanman, June 14, 1819–March 4, 1895, with Particular Emphasis on His Contributions as an Artist," (master's thesis, George Washington University, 1968), 43.

58. Review of *The History of Long Island* by Benjamin F. Thompson, *The Knickerbocker* 27 (March 1846): 257.

59. Benjamin F. Thompson, *The History of Long Island*, 1: 63. In his 1841 painting *Cider Making*, Mount prominently displays a weathervane decorated with a fish, thereby signifying the crucial, fertilizing role of fish for Long Island agriculture. See Elizabeth Johns, *American Genre Painting: The Politics of Everyday Life* (New Haven: Yale University Press, 1991), 50.

60. Quoted in Reginald Horsman, *Race and Manifest Destiny: The Origins of American Racial Anglo-Saxonism* (Cambridge, Mass.: Harvard University Press, 1981), 220.

61. On the history of the township of Brookhaven, see Benjamin F. Thompson, *The History of Long Island*, 1: 408–23. Thompson lists Zachariah Hawkins (1639–99), Mount's great-great-great-grandfather as one of fifty-five original proprietors of Brookhaven. See also Deborah Johnson, *William Sidney Mount*, 91 n. 1.

62. Thompson, *History of Long Island*, 1: 409, 413–14.

63. *The Diary of George Templeton Strong: Young Man in New York, 1835–1849,* 43.

64. William R. Newman, *Gehennical Fire,* 39–44. On John Winthrop Jr., and the Winthrop genealogy, see Lawrence Shaw Mayo, *The Winthrop Family in America* (Boston: Massachusetts Historical Society, 1948).

65. Ronald Sterne Wilkinson, "The Alchemical Library of John Winthrop Jr. (1606–76) and His Descendants in Colonial America," *Ambix* 11 (Feb. 1963): 33–51. In 1846, William Templeton Johnson, a nephew of George Washington Strong, married Laura Winthrop, the daughter of Strong's former Yale classmate Francis Bayard Winthrop (1787–1841). See *The Diary of George Templeton Strong,* 278. In 1749, Thomas Strong, George Washington Strong's grandfather, purchased Long Island property from the Winthrop family. See Benjamin F. Thompson, *The History of Long Island,* 1: 414.

66. On 24 May 1836, George Washington Strong's son, George Templeton Strong, attended a lecture delivered by the Yale University scientist Benjamin Silliman, who attempted to prove the veracity of Holy Scripture based upon geology and a discussion of volcanoes and the earth's "internal heat." Strong closely supervised the education of his son, who, shortly later, in June of 1836, purchased a book by Henry Cornelius Agrippa (1486–1535), the German alchemist whose *Occulta philosophia* (1533) represents a major expression of hermetic philosophy in its attempt to synthesize science, religion, and magic. *The Diary of George Templeton Strong,* 21, 24–25.

67. Ibid., 276.

68. Ibid., 94. On Mount's attitude toward slavery and African Americans, see Elizabeth Johns, *American Genre Painting,* 33–38, 114–17. See also Albert Boime, *The Art of Exclusion: Representing Blacks in the Nineteenth Century* (London: Thames and Hudson, 1990), 5–6, 88–100.

69. Boime, *The Art of Exclusion,* 5.

CHAPTER 10

Additional support from the Center for the Humanities, Oregon State University, enabled me to develop this research. A fully referenced study will appear as *Transforming Images: Locating New Mexican Santos In-between Worlds* (University Press of Colorado), coauthored with Donna Pierce, with additional contributions. Thanks to Keith Bakker, Erika Doss, Elizabeth Dunn, Samuel Y. Edgerton Jr., Robin Farwell Gavin, Pamela Jones, Wendy Madar, David Morgan, Donna Pierce, Sally Promey, and David H. Snow for their advice and expertise on this essay.

1. Yvonne Lange, "Lithography, an Agent of Technological Change in Religious Folk Art: A Thesis," *Western Folklore* 33, no. 1 (Jan. 1974): 51–64, first presented this groundbreaking thesis.

2. The art historian was Aby Warburg, who spent time with Mennonite missionary H. R. Voth at Second Mesa, Hopi, Arizona, and much later (1923) presented an illustrated lecture, posthumously published (1938) as an essay about Hopi "serpent rituals" that is widely known today as an innovative study for its time; see Aby M. Warburg, *Images from the Region of the Pueblo Indians of North America,* trans. Michael P. Steinberg; introduction by Michael P. Steinberg (Ithaca: Cornell University Press, 1995.)

3. The term "popular culture" is not meant to suggest "low" as opposed to "high" culture. I follow Peter Burke, Hugh Cunningham, Roger Chartier, Robert Scribner, and others for whom the term "popular" designates the entire culture and is associated with artifacts available to working people; see discussion with references in Patricia Anderson, *The Printed Image and the Transformation of Popular Culture 1790–1860* (Oxford: Clarendon Press, 1991), 8; Tessa Watt, *Cheap Print and Popular Piety, 1550–1640* (Cambridge, Eng.: Cambridge University Press, 1991), 1–8.

4. What we refer to collectively as the Pueblo Indians can be differentiated into seven distinct linguistic groups belonging to four families: the Tanoan language family composed of Tiwa, Tewa, Piro, and Towa; Keresan; Zuni; and Hopi. Athapaskan and Plains Indians carried their linguistic histories and material cultures into the region shortly before Europeans arrived in 1539 or earlier. There is no consensus on this issue, but the dominant theory is that undifferentiated nomadic bands of Athapaskans entered the southern Plains east of the Pueblos around 1525; D. Wilcox and W. Masse, eds., *The Protohistoric Period in the North American Southwest, A.D. 1450–1700* (Tempe: University of Arizona Press, 1981), 213–320. Moreover, the colonists who began arriving in 1598 from Mexico City, Zacatecas, Nueva Galicia, the Iberian peninsula, Africa, and elsewhere, were already ethnically and culturally diverse. After Mexico won its independence from Spain in 1821, and New Mexico became a U.S. territory in 1848, other European and Anglo-American settlers entered in significant numbers. See George Hammond and Agapito Rey, *Don Juan de Oñate: Colonizer of New Mexico, 1595–1628*, 2 vols. (Albuquerque: University of New Mexico Press, 1953), 1: 7ff.; José Esquibel, *Remembrance/Recordación: The Spanish Colonists That Arrived in Santa Fe, 23 June 1693* (Denver: Genealogical Society of Spanish America, 1994).

5. David Morgan, *Protestants and Prints*, typescript 34. (I thank the author for making his study available to me in typescript). David Morgan, *Protestants and Pictures: Religion, Visual Culture, and the Age of American Mass Production* (New York: Oxford University Press, 1999).

6. For the concept of "market revolution," see Charles Sellers, *The Market Revolution: Jacksonian America, 1815–1846* (New York: Oxford University Press, 1991); and Paul E. Johnson, "The Market Revolution," in *Encyclopedia of American Social History*, ed. Mary Kupiec Cayton, Elliott J. Gorn, and Peter Williams, 3 vols. (New York: Scribner's, 1993), 1: 545–60, with further references.

7. See, for example, John Baptiste Salpointe, *Soldiers of the Cross: Notes on the Ecclesiastical History of New Mexico, Arizona, and Colorado* (Albuquerque: Calvin Horn, 1967), who recounts his initial efforts to reach Santa Fe from the East Coast and the travels of Jean Lamy, the first archbishop of New Mexico, stationed in Santa Fe in 1851.

8. Typically, according to David Morgan, the intricate system of relationships involved in production and sales in mass culture separates the consumer from the raw goods and the skill of the craftsman in local culture; *Protestants and Pictures*, 33. My summary of mass culture is indebted to Morgan's discussion, and I have also benefited from Leigh Eric Schmidt, *Consumer Rites: The Buying and Selling of American Holidays* (Princeton: Princeton University Press, 1995); Grant McCracken, *Culture and Consumption: New Approaches to the Symbolic Character of Consumer Goods and Activities* (Bloomington: Indi-

ana University Press, 1990); and Daniel Miller, *Material Culture and Mass Consumption* (Oxford: Blackwell, 1987).

9. Gabrielle Palmer, ed., "*El Camino Reale de tierra adentro*" (New Mexico Bureau of Land Management, Cultural Resources Series, forthcoming); Keith Bakker, "Aesthetic and Cultural Considerations for the Conservation of Hispanic New Mexican Religious Art" (master's thesis, Antioch College [Yellow Springs, Ohio], 1994), 24–38. A great deal of valuable information about these goods is contained in wills; significant examples can be found in Claire Farago and Donna Pierce, eds., "Transforming Images: New Mexican Santos between Worlds" (unpublished manuscript).

10. Lane Coulter and Maurice Dixon Jr., building on Lange's groundwork, stress the effects of improved transportation (*New Mexican Tinwork, 1840–1940* [Albuquerque: University of New Mexico Press, 1990], 1–4). Since the sixteenth century, French firms played a leading role in the distribution of inexpensive prints of single standing saints. After invention of the process in 1798, lithographs of religious subjects were marketed first by French firms, such as the Turgis family, LeMercier, and Boasse Lebel (Coulter and Dixon, *New Mexican Tinwork*, 13), who exported devotional prints including single-leaf broadsheets, holy cards, and prayer cards, to the United States since the 1820s. Yvonne Lange, "In Search of San Acacio: The Impact of Industrialization on Santos Worldwide," *El Palacio* 94, no. 1 (summer/fall 1988): 18–24, has also identified and dated prints published by the Swiss firm of Benziger, still operating in the Swiss pilgrimage town of Einsiedeln today, which sold its chromolithographs in Cincinnati beginning in 1838 and became the most important Catholic publishing house in the United States. By 1835, American firms adopted the lithographic process and imitated the style of European productions, notably Currier (joined by Ives in 1857) of New York and Kurz (who founded his firm in the 1860s and was joined by Allison) of Chicago. Coulter and Dixon reproduced prints by these firms and others. By the 1850s, European-born merchants sold European and American prints, primarily lithographs, in Santa Fe and Albuquerque. The firm of Spiegelberg Brothers, established in 1846, was one of the leading wholesale houses in the territory for the duration of the nineteenth century. The Huning Company of Albuquerque even established a branch at Zuni Pueblo. See Floyd S. Fierman, *Merchant-Bankers of Early Santa Fe, 1844–1893* (El Paso: Texas Western Press, 1964), 11–20. Subjects of religious prints are catalogued by Beatrice Farwell, *French Popular Lithographic Imagery, 1815–1870*, 12 vols. (Chicago: University of Chicago Press, 1981–), vol. 1; Harry T. Peters, *America on Stone: The Other Printmakers to the American People* (Garden City, N.Y.: Doubleday, 1931); *Currier and Ives, A Catalogue Raisonné*, vol. 1 (Detroit: Gale Research Company Press, 1984). European popular religious prints have been studied recently, notably by Catherine Rosenbaum-Dondaine, *L'Image de Pieté en France, 1814–1914* (Paris: Musée-Galerie de la Serita, 1984); Christa Pieske, *Bilder für Jedermann: Waldbilddrucke, 1840–1940* (Museum für Deutsche Volkskunste, Staatliche Museum Preussischer Kulturbesitz, 1988); and see further bibliography in Lange, as cited above.

11. Kelly Donahue-Wallace, "Hide Paintings, Print Sources, and the Expression of a New Mexican Colonial Identity," in "Transforming Images," ed. Farago and Pierce (I thank Donahue-Wallace for allowing me to cite her ms. in typescript), brings together several important references in published and forthcoming scholarship, culled from church in-

ventories and domestic collections: in 1715 and 1728, the hide painter and shoemaker Francisco Xavier Romero of Santa Cruz de la Cañada had forty and sixty-seven prints, respectively (as discovered by Thomas Steele); the 1762 will of a Santa Cruz woman included four prints; a neighbor of hers had ten prints, while a Taos man listed ten engravings of saints in his will; in 1776, Fray Athanasio Dominguez counted seventy-two prints in 312 churches, as well as many books with printed images.

12. Yvonne Lange, "In Search of San Acacio," 18–24, esp. 19.

13. Lange, "Lithography, an Agent of Technological Change" and "In Search of San Acacio"; Kelly Donahue-Wallace, "Print Sources of New Mexican Colonial Hide Paintings," *Anales del Institutio de Investigaciones Estéticas* 68 (1996): 43–69, and "Hide Paintings, Print Sources."

14. Notably, Mark S. Schantz, "Religious Tracts, Evangelical Reform, and the Market Revolution in Antebellum America," *Journal of the Early Republic* 17 (fall 1997): 425–66.

15. Yvonne Lange and Christa Pieske conducted a survey of prints in the collection of the Museum of International Folk Art, Santa Fe; report dated 28 February 1989, from the museum files.

16. The example reproduced here is particularly reminiscent of temporary shrines for feast days of patron saints at the Pueblo mission churches, as documented by twentieth-century Pueblo artists such as printmakers Lilia Torivio and Pablita Velarde in two screenprints, c. 1936, Museum of Indian Arts and Culture of the Museums of New Mexico, Santa Fe. Thanks to Joanne Rubino for calling these images to my attention.

17. Coulter and Dixon write that these goods could have been purchased through trade over the Santa Fe Trail or obtained during expeditions organized by local families for trading in St. Louis and further east (*New Mexican Tinwork*, ix).

18. As discussed by Morgan, *Protestants and Pictures*, chap. 1. Coulter and Dixon write that these prints, primarily lithographs, created a demand for frames made by tinsmiths, but the print trade itself has never been the subject of a separate study (*New Mexican Tinwork*, x, 3).

19. Colleen McDannell's, *Material Christianity: Religion and Popular Culture in America* (London: Yale University Press, 1995), 17–67, 132–97, which builds on her earlier specialized studies and has an extensive bibliography, takes theories of mass consumption into account; and Celeste Olalquiaga, *Megalopolis: Contemporary Cultural Sensibilities* (Minneapolis: University of Minnesota, 1992). In a very different context, valuable information is presented in recent literature on the African diaspora; see Robert Farris Thompson, *Face of the Gods: Art and Altars of Africa and the African Americas*, exh. cat. (New York: The Museum for African Art, 1993); Donald J. Cosentino, ed., *Sacred Arts of Haitian Voudou*, exh. cat., (Los Angeles: UCLA Fowler Museum of Cultural History, 1995). David Freedberg's *The Power of Images: Studies in the History and Theory of Response* (Chicago: The University of Chicago Press, 1989) is an invaluable synthetic study of the early modern period framed "from below" that touches upon material culture at many points.

20. W. W. H. Davis writes that the new priests (who, directed by Lamy, established eighteen parishes by 1859), distributed devotional lithographs themselves and discouraged the veneration of handpainted *retablos* produced locally (*El Gringo or, New Mexico and her People* [Santa Fe: Rydal Press, 1938], 49). From c. 1853/4–56, Davis was the U.S. attor-

ney general for New Mexico and editor of the *Santa Fe Weekly Gazette*. Cited by Coulter and Dixon, *New Mexican Tinwork*, 3; 166 n. 13.

21. The subject needs investigation. My thanks to Yvonne Lange, personal communication with the author, 9 November 1998, for the view that American firms imitated the latest European innovations, particularly French ones made accessible when these firms opened offices in New York. On French prints and holy cards, see Rosenbaum-Dondaine, *L'Image de Pieté*.

22. Rosenbaum-Dondaine discusses the use of these cards for First Communion, celebrated at age twelve, and reproduces three variants of the same iconography (*L'Image de Pieté*, 162–71 nn. 245, 246; 191).

23. Coulter and Dixon reproduce a number of new introductions, including: Virgin labeled "Corazon de miraculado de Maria/pedid por nosostros," chromolithograph, pl. 8; praying Virgin, French lithograph, 5.5; The Sacred Heart of Mary, lithograph, 5.6; Jesus Christ, French lithograph, 5.12; S. Vincentius A. Poulo, Benziger lithograph, 5.14; Holy Card with Christ and St. John the Baptist as children, Benziger lithograph, 5.15; St. Ann and the Virgin Mary, Benziger lithograph, 5.16; St. Rupert, German lithograph, 5.29; scene of Holy Communion, Currier and Ives lithograph, 5.30 and 5.102; Resurrected Christ, French oleograph, 5.38; Sacred Heart of Jesus, German lithograph, 5.42; souvenir from Our Lady of Lourdes, French lithograph, 5.44; and St. Louis contemplating a crucifix, Benziger oleograph, 5.87 (*New Mexican Tinwork*).

24. We are fortunate in this case to know the name of the tinsmith, José María Apodaca, and to have firsthand information from his grandson that he did not read English: see Coulter and Dixon, *New Mexican Tinwork*, 91–93.

25. A brief chronology of the major studies is: Mitchell A. Wilder with Edgar Breitenbach, *Saints: The Religious Folk Art of New Mexico* (Colorado Springs: The Taylor Museum of the Colorado Springs Fine Arts Center, 1943); Roland Dickey, *New Mexico Village Arts* (1949, reprint, Albuquerque: University of New Mexico, 1990); George Kubler, *Santos: An Exhibition of the Religious Folk Art of New Mexico* (Fort Worth: Amon Carter Museum, 1964); José E. Espinosa, *Saints in the Valley: Christian Sacred Images in the History, Life, and Folk Art of Spanish New Mexico* (rev. ed., Albuquerque: University of New Mexico Press, 1967); Robert L. Shalkop, *Wooden Saints: The Santos of New Mexico* (Colorado Springs: The Taylor Museum of the Colorado Springs Fine Arts Center, 1967); E. Boyd, *Popular Arts of Spanish New Mexico* (Santa Fe: Museum of New Mexico Press, 1974); William Wroth, *Christian Images in Hispanic New Mexico: Taylor Museum Collection of "Santos"* (Colorado Springs: The Taylor Museum of the Colorado Springs Fine Arts Center, 1982); William Wroth, *Images of Penance, Images of Mercy: Southwestern Santos in the Late Nineteenth Century* (Norman: University of Oklahoma Press, 1991); Larry Frank, *New Kingdom of Saints: Religious Art of New Mexico, 1780–1907* (Santa Fe: Red Crane Press, 1992); Robin Farwell Gavin, *Traditional Arts of New Mexico: The Hispanic Heritage Wing of the Museum of International Folk Art* (Santa Fe: Museum of New Mexico Press, 1994); and Donna Pierce, "Saints in New Mexico," in *Spanish New Mexico: The Spanish Colonial Arts Society Collection*, ed. Donna Pierce and Marta Weigle, 2 vols. (Santa Fe: Museum of New Mexico Press, 1996), 1: 29–60.

26. At the end of the sixteenth century, when Franciscans began evangelizing in this re-

gion, then the northernmost territories claimed for Spain, they failed to learn the native languages. Consequently, they did not prepare prayers and other ritual materials for this region, as missionaries produced elsewhere. Henry Kelly writes that the missionaries were ordered to instruct in the native dialects "in accordance with La Nueva Recopilación," but they ignored the royal law due to the bewildering number of dialects and their use of children as translators (children quickly mastered Spanish) (*Franciscan Missions of New Mexico, 1740–1760* [Albuquerque: University of New Mexico Press, 1940], 10).

The other reason New Mexico's religious art is largely undocumented before the twentieth century is that institutionalized forms of artistic instruction apparently did not develop in the region. In Mexico and Peru, craft guilds, art academies, and a brisk trade in imported academic paintings resulted in a legacy of colonial art including narrative subjects, iconic representations, richly articulated church interiors, portraits, and domestic furnishings. See Edward J. Sullivan, "European Painting and the Art of the New World Colonies," in *Converging Cultures: Art & Identity in Spanish America*, ed. Diane Fane, exh. cat. (New York: The Brooklyn Museum in Association with Harry N. Abrams, 1996), 28–41; Jeanette Peterson, *The Paradise Garden Murals of Malinalco: Utopia and Empire in Sixteenth-Century Mexico* (Austin: The University of Texas Press, 1993), 50–57; both with further bibliography. While there may have been workshops at the village level in New Mexico, little is known about private patronage or artistic instruction and the transmission of artistic skills.

27.   Peterson, *The Paradise Garden Murals of Malinalco*, 7.

28.   The contemporary term for devotional artworks produced in New Mexico is Spanish—colonialist—in derivation. "Santos" is said to have been introduced into Mexico at an early date by missionaries to designate holy beings of lesser stature than the *teotl*, or impersonation of god (Louise Burkhart, *The Slippery Earth: Nahua-Christian Moral Dialogue in Sixteenth-Century Mexico* [Tucson: University of Arizona Press, 1989], 39). In present-day New Mexico, such concerns are forgotten and "santos" simply denote historical and contemporary images of the Virgin, Christ, saints, and other holy figures, usually painted on wood panel (*retablos*) or carved and painted in the round (*bultos*). This terminology, used in the predominantly English-speaking commercial art world, exemplifies the modernist reduction of New Mexican culture to its Spanish cultural roots.

29.   There is considerable disagreement on how their identities have changed: cf. Ramón Gutiérrez, *When Jesus Came, the Corn Mothers Went Away: Marriage, Sexuality, and Power in New Mexico, 1500–1846* (Stanford: Stanford University Press, 1991), xxxvi; and the native American response: "Commentaries on *When Jesus Came, the Corn Mothers Went Away*," *American Indian Culture and Research Journal* 17, no. 3 (fall 1993).

30.   Cheryl Foote, "Spanish-Indian Trade along New Mexico's Northern Frontier in the Eighteenth Century," *Journal of the West* 24 (1985): 22–33; Oakah L. Jones Jr., *Los Paisanos: Spanish Settlers on the Northern Frontier of New Spain* (Norman: University of Oklahoma Press, 1979), 109–66; L. R. Bailey, *Indian Slave Trade in the Southwest: A Study of Slave-taking and the Traffic of Indian Captives* (Los Angeles: Westernlore Press, 1973), with references to the earlier literature.

31.   The best work to date focuses on the economy of exchange: Ross Frank, "From Settler

to Citizen: Economic Development and Cultural Change in Late Colonial New Mexico, 1750–1820" (Ph.D. diss., University of California, Berkeley, 1992), and "The Changing Pueblo Indian Pottery Tradition: The Underside of Economic Development in Late Colonial New Mexico, 1750–1820," *Journal of the Southwest* 33, no. 3 (autumn 1991): 282–321. Interactions among women encouraged these forms of cultural exchange, but the issues of ethnic identity are more complex than I can suggest here; see David H. Snow, "Spanish American Pottery Manufacture in New Mexico: A Critical Review," *Ethnohistory* 31, no. 2 (1984): 93–113.

32. See *"El Camino Reale de tierra adentro,"* ed. Gabrielle Palmer (New Mexico Bureau of Land Management, Cultural Resources Series, forthcoming); Keith Bakker, "Aesthetic and Cultural Considerations for the Conservation of Hispanic New Mexican Religious Art" (master's thesis, Antioch College [Yellow Springs, Ohio], 1994), 24–38.

33. Lange, "Technology, an Agent of Change," and "In Search of San Acacio"; Kelly Donahue-Wallace, "An Odyssey of Images: The Flemish, Spanish, and New Spanish Print Sources of New Mexican Colonial Hide Paintings" (master's thesis, University of New Mexico, 1994). "Prints Sources," and "Hide Paintings, Print Sources" are the most extensive studies to date; see also Pierce, "Saints in New Mexico"; Wroth, *Christian Images;* and Boyd, *Popular Arts,* all passim; Kubler, *Santos,* 6; and Wilder and Breitenbach, *Santos,* 47.

34. France Scholes, *Troublous Times in New Mexico, 1659–1670* (Albuquerque: University of New Mexico Press, 1942); Eleanor Adams, ed., *Bishop Tamaron's Visitation of New Mexico, 1760* (Albuquerque: Historical Society of New Mexico, 1954), n. 15.

35. See especially, Karen McCarthy Brown, *Mama Lola: A Voudou Priestess in Brooklyn* (Berkeley and Los Angeles: University of California Press, 1991); Robert A. Orsi, *The Madonna of 115th Street: Faith and Community in Italian Harlem, 1880–1950* (New Haven: Yale University Press, 1985), and *Thank You, St. Jude: Women's Devotion to the Patron Saint of Hopeless Causes* (New Haven: Yale University Press, 1996); and the extensive writings of William A. Christian Jr., in this context especially, *Visionaries: The Spanish Republic and the Reign of Christ* (Berkeley and Los Angeles: University of California Press, 1996); Thomas Tweed, *Our Lady of the Exile: Diasporic Religion at a Cuban Catholic Shrine in Miami* (Oxford: Oxford University Press, 1997).

36. Fray Dominguez ordered the destruction of images: see Eleanor Adams and Fray Angélico Chavez, *The Missions of New Mexico, 1776: A Description by Fray Atanascio Dominguez with Other Contemporary Documents* (Albuquerque: University of New Mexico Press, 1956); other primary sources are cited in José Espinosa, *Saints in the Valleys: Christian Sacred Images in the History, Life, and Folk Art of Spanish New Mexico* (Albuquerque: University of New Mexico Press, 1960).

37. For an introduction, see Victor I. Stoichita, *Visionary Experience in the Golden Age of Spanish Art* (London: Reaktion Books, 1995).

38. Mihalyi Csikzentmihalyi and Eugene Rochberg-Halton, *The Meaning of Things: Domestic Symbols and the Self* (New York: Cambridge University Press, 1981).

39. Documentation for Fresquís suggests his ability to navigate between cultural and economic settings: Pierce, "Saints in New Mexico": 37–39; Boyd, *Popular Arts,* 327–40; his ethnic identity is listed in the 1790 Spanish census as *mestizo:* Marianne L. Stoller, "The

Early Santeros of New Mexico: A Problem in Ethnic Identity and Artistic Tradition" (unpublished ms.), 48.

40. Another example of the same motif in the same medium is found in the Museum of International Folk Art, Santa Fe, accession no. A69.45–49.

41. Cited in Donahue-Wallace, "Hide Paintings, Print Sources"; an example published in Madrid and collected in Mexico, is reproduced in Donna Pierce, "Saints in the Hispanic World," in *Spanish New Mexico*, 1: 18, fig. 25: Francisco Muntañer, *Our Lady of Atocha*, 1786.

42. This approach is common in reception aesthetics; see Wolfgang Iser, *The Act of Reading: A Theory of Aesthetic Response* (Baltimore: Johns Hopkins University Press, 1978), esp. 33–34, and most recently, *The Fictive and the Imaginary: Charting Literary Anthropology* (Baltimore: Johns Hopkins University Press, 1993), esp. 9, 118.

43. This statement is not intended to suggest that a pan-Pueblo perspective, to the extent that one exists, was homogeneous. See n. 2, above.

44. Homi Bhabha, "Signs Taken for Wonders: Questions of Ambivalence and Authority under a Tree outside Delhi, May 1817," *Critical Inquiry* 12, no. 1 (autumn 1985): 156.

45. Néstor García Canclini, *Hybrid Cultures: Strategies for Entering and Leaving Modernity*, trans. C. Chiappari and S. López (Minneapolis: University of Minnesota Press, 1995).

46. Canclini, *Hybrid Cultures*, 204.

47. Complex acts of translation are involved in comparing natural plants to botanical illustrations, and the plants depicted in the *retablos* are often too stylized to permit any identification. Some tentative identifications based on the literature and consultations with ethnobotanists and *curanderas*, will appear in Farago and Pierce, eds., "Transforming Images."

48. J. J. Brody, *Anasazi and Pueblo Painting* (Albuquerque: University of New Mexico Press, 1991), 9.

49. See examples and bibliography in Polly Schaafsma, *Rock Art in New Mexico*, rev. ed. (Santa Fe: Museum of New Mexico Press, 1992). Thanks to Sara Rockwell for calling my attention to the imagery in figure 8.

50. Common forms of wall decoration at other mission churches at other pueblos, such as Laguna and Acoma, include friezes of rainbow arcs, cloud terraces, birds, stylized corn plants, sun, moon, and other motifs that are traditional to the vocabulary of Pueblo sacred space. J. J. Brody argues that native symbols, secular in character when viewed from a Catholic perspective, were also intentionally meaningful "visual prayers." (Brody, *Anasazi and Pueblo Painting*, 147, 174.) In Brody's view, native imagery transformed a Catholic church into a ritual space on the order of a kiva or society house. But a mission church is *not* a kiva, and Brody's interpretation of how Pueblo symbols performed in a Catholic colonial context is undertheorized.

51. Until indisputably prehispanic murals at Kuaua and other sites were excavated in the 1930s, leading anthropologists hypothesized that the Katsina cult developed only after the introduction of Christian images of saints. For the history of the scholarship and current state of the issues, see Curtis Schaafsma, "Pueblo Ceremonialism from the Perspective of Spanish Documents," in *Kachinas in the Pueblo World*, ed. P. Schaafsma (Albuquerque: University of New Mexico Press, 1994), 121–38.

52. Frederick J. Dockstader, *The Kachina and the White Man: The Influences of White Culture on the Hopi Kachina Religion*, rev. ed. (Albuquerque: University of New Mexico Press, 1985), 11 ff.

53. Charles W. Hackett, *Historical Documents Relating to New Mexico, Nueva Vizcaya, and Approaches Thereto, to 1773*, 3 vols. (Washington: The Carnegie Institution, 1923–37).

54. Little has been published on this topic; the most extensive references, in passing, are found in Sylvia Rodriguez, *The Matachines Dance: Ritual Symbolism and Interethnic Relations in the Upper Rio Grande Valley* (Albuquerque: University of New Mexico Press, 1996); Alfonso Ortiz, *The Tewa World: Space, Time, and Becoming in a Pueblo Society* (Chicago: University of Chicago Press, 1969); and Edward P. Dozier, *The Pueblo Indians of North America* (New York: Holt, Rinehart and Winston, 1970), citing specialized studies in the anthropological literature, by Dozier, Leslie White, Florence Ellis, and Elsie Clews Parsons.

55. According to Albert Schroeder, "Rio Grande Ethnohistory," in *New Perspectives on the Pueblos*, ed. Alfonso Ortiz (Albuquerque: University of New Mexico Press, 1972), 41–72; see also Ramón A. Gutiérrez, *When Jesus Came, the Corn Mothers Went Away: Marriage, Sexuality, and Power in New Mexico, 1500–1846* (Stanford: Stanford University Press, 1991), 166–75. Gutiérrez's figures have been questioned as being too low by David H. Snow, "So Many Mestizos, Mulatos, and Zambohigos: Colonial New Mexico People without History" (paper presented at the Western History Association, 1995). The most extensive, comparative study is by Alicia V. Tjarks, "Demographic, Ethnic, and Occupational Structure of New Mexico, 1790," *Americas* 35, no. 1 (July 1978): 45–88, citing 83 here, who reports the following percentages for Santa Fe in 1790: 54 percent Spanish; 16 percent Indian; and 28 percent mixed blood; with Albuquerque reporting 38 percent mestizo. Tjarks observes, 72–74, that at the end of the eighteenth century, "the process of ethnic hybridization was proceeding in high gear and the increase in exogamic or interracial marriages contributed to create a more homogeneous population." The terms of classification are also inconsistent; see Adrian Bustamante, "'The Matter Was Never Resolved': The Casta System in Colonial New Mexico, 1693–1823," *New Mexico Historical Review* 66, no. 2 (April 1991): 143–64.

56. See Frances Leon Swadesh, *Los Primeros Pobladores: Hispanic Americans on the Ute Frontier* (Notre Dame: University of Notre Dame Press, 1974), 35–48.

57. Penitential societies, the most widely practiced form of community-based devotion outside the Pueblos, multiplied rapidly in the 1820s and 1830s, indicating that a culturally as well as genetically fragmented population was creating new, cohesive forms of social organization at the community level. By the second half of the nineteenth century, however, the same New Mexican villages were losing their emerging autonomy to much wealthier Mexican and Anglo-American businessmen, investors, and speculators who acquired the villages' lands and precious water rights, and soon controlled their means of production; see Roxanne Ortiz, *Roots of Resistance: Land Tenure in New Mexico, 1680–1980*, Chicano Studies Center, Monograph no. 10 (Los Angeles: University of California Press, 1980), 82. During this period, santo production declined and the use of printed images, especially chromolithographs, increased dramatically.

58. Lange, "Lithography, an Agent of Technological Change," 55–56. Lange argues, in part, that sculptures continued to be locally produced for Penitente processions, which required figures with reticulated limbs.

59. Coulter and Dixon, *New Mexican Tinwork*, xvii, citing Davis, *El Gringo*, 49. The problems perceived were artistic and religious: the humble execution and graphic Spanish realism of New Mexican santos clashed with French sensibilities. Yvonne Lange, personal archives, has an unpublished receipt from Francis Saler, Bookseller, St. Louis, dated 30 December 1864, for "merchandise" purchased by Bishop Lamy—suggesting the process by which the new print technology entered New Mexico with ecclesiastical endorsement. (Thanks to Dr. Lange for sharing this information with me.) On Lamy's harsh treatment of lay confraternities, see Marta Weigle, *Brothers of Light, Brothers of Blood: The Penitentes of the Southwest* (Albuquerque: University of New Mexico Press, 1976), 57–60. On Lamy, see also the account by his successor Salpointe, *Soldiers of the Cross*. In New Spain, the Inquisition apparently did little to regulate commerce in printed images. The few records on the control of prints that exist demonstrate that Tridentine ideas about the proper appearance of images were considered applicable, but mostly ignored, especially when it came to images produced in the colonial world. Eldemira Ramirez Leyva, "Censura inquisitorial novohispana sobre imagenes y objetos," in *Arte y coerción* (Mexico City: UNAM/IIE, 1992), 149–62 (cited by Donahue-Wallace, "Print Sources, Hide Paintings"). Yet the fact that Catholic Reformation criteria for the appearance of images were known and occasionally acted upon is enough to suggest a chain of negotiations between representatives of the Church and the population concerning access to the supernatural through images.

60. The foundational argument for cultural sociology, mass culture studies in particular, is Max Weber's classic study of Protestant ethics, with its emphasis on disenchantment and the overall presence of rationalization. Max Weber, *The Protestant Ethic and the Spirit of Capitalism*, trans. Talcott Parsons (London: University Books, 1930). I follow Colin Campbell, *The Romantic Ethic and the Spirit of Modern Consumerism* (Oxford: Basil Blackwell, 1987), 9–14, 72, who is critical of theories that explain consumer desire either as an inherent character trait (an essentialist explanation) or as the product of external manipulation (a determinist explanation). Campbell proposes instead a cycle rooted in individual disillusionment, on the Weberian model, in which "the [consumers'] basic desire to experience in reality the pleasurable dramas they have already enjoyed in their imagination" lead to literal disillusionment with each purchase, followed by renewed desire (Campbell, 205). This reinterpretation is still based on the case of Protestantism (see my remarks below, n. 63).

61. Thomas J. Steele, S.J., *Santos and Saints: The Religious Folk Art of Hispanic New Mexico* (Santa Fe: Ancient City Press, rev. ed., 1982), 84–85.

62. Campbell, *The Romantic Ethic*, 36–57, reviews theories of modern consumerism in these terms.

63. The term "resonance" derives from Stephen Greenblatt, *Marvelous Possessions: The Wonder of the New World* (Chicago: University of Chicago Press, 1991), who distinguishes it from "wonder," which he defines as reaction devoid of cultural understanding.

CHAPTER 11

1. William Frederick Pinchbeck, *The Expositor; Or Many Mysteries Unravelled* (Boston: n.p., 1805), 28–38, 81–82, 90–91; James M. Barriskill, "The Newburyport Theatre in the 18th Century," *Essex Institute Historical Collections* 91 (Oct. 1955): 339–42; "Astonishing Invisible Lady. The Acoustic Temple, and Incomprehensible Crystal" (Wilmington, Del.: [1804]; Broadsides Collection, American Antiquarian Society, Worcester, Mass.); William Frederick Pinchbeck, *Witchcraft, Or the Art of Fortune-Telling Unveiled* (Boston: n.p., 1805), 46–49, 81.

2. "Astonishing Invisible Lady," broadside; Pinchbeck, *Expositor*, 25, 91; Pinchbeck, *Witchcraft*, 7–18.

3. Pinchbeck, *Witchcraft*, 46–49; "Astonishing Invisible Lady," broadside; "The Mystery of the Invisible Lady Unfold[e]d and Explained" (Salem, Mass.: 1805; Broadsides Collection, American Antiquarian Society, Worcester, Mass.). For two especially evocative treatments of rational recreations and illusionist demonstrations in early modern Europe, see Barbara Maria Stafford, *Artful Science: Enlightenment Entertainment and the Eclipse of Visual Education* (Cambridge, Mass.: MIT Press, 1994); Grete de Francesco, *The Power of the Charlatan*, trans. Miriam Beard (New Haven: Yale University Press, 1939), 229–49.

4. "Astonishing Invisible Lady," broadside. For the mixing of the verbal and the visual, see especially W. J. T. Mitchell, *Picture Theory: Essays on Verbal and Visual Representation* (Chicago: University of Chicago Press, 1994).

5. Jonathan Edwards, *A History of the Work of Redemption*, ed. John F. Wilson (New Haven: Yale University Press, 1989), 392–93.

6. *Lettres édifiantes et curieuses, écrites des missions étrangères*, 26 vols. (Paris: Mérigot, 1780–83), 11: 42–79. For the uses of this script in the suppression of Incan "oracles," see Constance Classen, *Worlds of Sense: Exploring the Senses in History and across Cultures* (London: Routledge, 1993), 113. For the missionary argument, see also [J. S. Forsyth], *Demonologia; Or, Natural Knowledge Revealed; Being an Exposé of Ancient and Modern Superstitions, Credulity, Fanaticism, and Imposture* (London: Bumpus, 1827), 160–61.

7. H. W. Parke, *Sibyls and Sibylline Prophecy in Classical Antiquity*, ed. B. C. McGing (London: Routledge, 1988), 169–70; H. W. Parke, *Greek Oracles* (London: Hutchinson University Library, 1967), 144–48; James H. Charlesworth, ed., *The Old Testament Pseudepigrapha*, 2 vols. (Garden City, N.Y.: Doubleday, 1983), 1: 317–26, 345, 426. For the ongoing vitality of Christian Sibyllinism, see Bernard McGinn, *Visions of the End: Apocalyptic Traditions in the Middle Ages* (New York: Columbia University Press, 1979), 18–21, 40, 43–50, 130–33. For eighteenth-century uses, see John Floyer, *The Sibylline Oracles Translated from the Best Greek Copies, and Compar'd with the Sacred Prophesies, especially with Daniel and the Revelations, and with so much History as Plainly Shews, that Many of the Sibyls Predictions Are Exactly Fulfill'd* (London: Bruges, 1713); William Whiston, *A Vindication of the Sibylline Oracles* (London: n.p., 1715).

8. Walter Scott, ed., *Hermetica: The Ancient Greek and Latin Writings which Contain Religious or Philosophic Teachings Ascribed to Hermes Trismegistus*, 4 vols. (Oxford: Clarendon Press, 1924), 1: 339–41.

9. Henry Cornelius Arippa, *Three Books of Occult Philosophy* (London: R. W., 1651), 77–78;

[Montfaucon de Villars], *The Count of Gabalis: Or, the Extravagant Mysteries of the Cabalists, Exposed* (London: B. M., 1680), 85. For occultists, the ancient oracles were taken with the utmost seriousness, for they themselves lived in a Neoplatonist world charged with divine presences, speaking angels, and celestial visions. On voices and oracles, see Agrippa, *Three Books*, 411–13, 499–519; de Villars, *Count of Gabalis*, 62–99. For a work that takes on the Western fascination with animated statues broadly, though only in very limited ways its Hermetic dimensions, see the wonderfully evocative work of Kenneth Gross, *The Dream of the Moving Statue* (Ithaca: Cornell University Press, 1992).

10. For the debate over the oracles in the early Enlightenment, see Marcel Bouchard, *L'Histoire des oracles de Fontenelle* (Paris: Sfelt, 1947), 75–104; Gianni Paganini, "Fontenelle et la critique des oracles entre libertinisme et clandestinité," in *Fontenelle*, ed. Alain Niderst and Jean Mesnard (Paris: Presses Universitaires de France, 1989), 333–49; Marian Skrzypek, "La Contribution de Fontenelle à la science des religions," in ibid., 657–66; J. Samuel Preus, *Explaining Religion: Criticism and Theory from Bodin to Freud* (New Haven: Yale University Press, 1987), 47–55; Frank E. Manuel, *The Eighteenth Century Confronts the Gods* (Cambridge, Mass.: Harvard University Press, 1959), 47–53, 65–70.

11. Whiston, *Vindication*, 81; David Blondel, *A Treatise of the Sibyls* (London: T. R., 1661), 9, 15, 49, 57–63, 70, 148. For a contemporary summary of the array of modern critics, see John Beaumont, *Gleanings of Antiquities* (London: J. Roberts, 1724), 55–68. See also Lynn Thorndike, *A History of Magic and Experimental Science*, 8 vols. (New York: Columbia University Press, 1968), 8: 476–79. For one belated attempt to recover the pious use of these texts, see Alfred Canon White and Mariana Monteiro, *"As David and the Sibyls Say": A Sketch of the Sibyls and the Sibylline Oracles* (Edinburgh: Sands, 1905).

12. George Hickes, "Letter to the Translator," in [Jean Baltus], *An Answer to Mr. de Fontenelle's History of Oracles* (London: W. B., 1709), unpaginated; "A Letter to the Author of this Translation," in [Jean Baltus], *A Continuation of the Answer to the History of Oracles* (London: W. B., 1710), iv-vi; Voltaire, *Philosophical Dictionary*, in *The Works of Voltaire*, 42 vols. (Akron, Ohio: Werner, 1904), 12: 94, 97–98; [Bernard de Fontenelle], *The History of Oracles, and the Cheats of the Pagan Priests* (London: n.p., 1688), unpaginated preface, 155; Antonius van Dale, *De oraculis veterum ethnicorum dissertationes duæ* (Amsterdam: 1683; Amsterdam: Boom, 1700). For a critical French edition of Fontenelle's text, including a concordance comparing the contents of van Dale, Baltus, and Fontenelle, see Bernard de Fontenelle, *Histoire des oracles*, ed. Louis Maigron (Paris: Cornély, 1908). On the relationship of van Dale's work to Fontenelle's, see Bouchard, *L'Histoire*, 92–104. Baltus offered the fullest Christian response to the new history, and Anglicans appropriated his works, with due notation of where his Catholicism led him astray, to defend a view of history that largely overarched the Protestant-Catholic divide. For the French versions, see [Jean Baltus], *Réponse à l'histoire des oracles, de Mr. de Fontenelle, de l'Academie Francoise*, 2d ed. (Strasbourg: Doulssecker, 1709); [Jean Baltus], *Suite de la réponse à l'histoire des oracles* (Strasbourg: Doulssecker, 1708). For examples of how this scholarship flowed into English and American deism, see John Toland, *Letters to Serena* (London: Lintot, 1704), unpaginated preface and letter 3; Conyers Middleton, *An Examination of the Lord Bishop of London's Discourses Concerning the Use and Intent of Prophecy* (London: Manby and Cox, 1750), title page, 107–11; Charles Blount, *The Oracles of Reason* (London: n.p.,

1693); [Walter Anderson], *The History of Croesus King of Lydia* (Edinburgh: Hamilton, Balfour, and Neill, 1755), 21; Thomas Paine, *Rights of Man* in *The Complete Writings of Thomas Paine*, ed. Philip S. Foner, 2 vols. (New York: Citadel, 1945), 1: 277; Elihu Palmer, *An Enquiry Relative to the Moral and Political Improvement of the Human Species* (New York: Crocker, 1797), 25–26; *Prospect, Or, View of the Moral World*, 22 September 1804, 330–33; "Craft," *Temple of Reason*, 20 February 1802, 31; "Oracles," *Temple of Reason*, 18 September 1802, 234–35; John Stewart, *The Moral or Intellectual Last Will and Testament of John Stewart, the Traveller, the Only Man of Nature that Ever Appeared in the World* (London: n.p., 1810), 372; John Stewart, *The Sophiometer; Or, Regulator of Mental Power* (London: Gosnell, [1812]), 6–9, 75–76, unpaginated appendix; John Stewart, *Opus Maximum; Or, the Great Essay to Reduce the Moral World from Contingency to System* (London: Ginger, 1813), frontispiece, 10, 18, 53, 120–21; Ethan Allen, *Reason, the Only Oracle of Man*, ed. John Pell (New York: Scholars' Facsimiles and Reprints, 1940).

13. The longer history of how natural magic shaped the rational recreations of the Enlightenment is beyond the scope of this essay. But for these specific examples, see Athanasius Kircher, *Phonurgia nova* (Campidonae: Rudolphum Dreherr, 1673), 113; John Baptista Porta, *Natural Magick* (London: Young and Speed, 1658), 385–86. For an excellent treatment of the roots of these acoustic technologies in natural magic, see Thomas L. Hankins and Robert J. Silverman, *Instruments and the Imagination* (Princeton: Princeton University Press, 1995), 178–220.

14. David Brewster, *Letters on Natural Magic*, 5th ed. (London: Murray, 1842), 157–78; "The Invisible Lady," *Nicholson's Journal of Natural Philosophy, Chemistry, and the Arts* 16 (1807): 69–71, 80. See also Eusebe Salverte, *The Occult Sciences: The Philosophy of Magic, Prodigies, and Apparent Miracles*, trans. Anthony Todd Thomson, 2 vols. (New York: Harper and Brothers, 1847); P. T. Barnum, *The Humbugs of the World* (New York: Carleton, 1866), 387–400.

15. For other possibilities beyond Clarke, see the varied allusions to "the researches of modern antiquaries and travellers" in the chapter on oracles in [Richard A. Davenport], *Sketches of Imposture, Deception, and Credulity* (Philadelphia: Zieber, 1845), 21, 23–24, 28, and also in D. P. Kidder, *Remarkable Delusions: Or, Illustrations of Popular Errors* (New York: Lane and Scott, 1852), 169–71. See also similar connections in Henry Cockton's novel of the same period, *Life and Adventures of Valentine Vox the Ventriloquist* (New York: Burt, n.d.), 145–56. In this case, thanks to collectors like Clarke, the antiquities have been brought to the skeptical viewer in the British Museum, who is sure that "there is nothing . . . that can have so great a tendency to prove the rapid progress of the human intellect as an oracle" (148).

16. Edward Daniel Clarke, *Travels in Various Countries of Europe Asia and Africa*, 6 vols. (London: Cadell and Davies, 1811–23), 2: 239–40; 3: 677–78; 4: 179–80. There were several American editions of these *Travels* as well.

17. Clarke, *Travels*, 3: 678–79.

18. For indications of the Romantic backlash against the school of van Dale and Fontenelle, see, for example, Thomas De Quincey, *Essays on Christianity, Paganism, and Superstition* (New York: Hurd and Houghton, 1878), 465–532 (quotation on 497); Théodore Bouys, *Nouvelles considérations puisées dans la clairvoyance instinctive de l'homme, sur les oracles,*

les sibylles et les prophètes, et particulièrement sur Nostradamus (Paris: Desennne, 1806), 2–3, 7–12; "Modern Spiritualism," *Christian Examiner and Religious Miscellany* 61 (Nov. 1856): 362–64. At the popular level, fortune-telling books continued to be legion. See, for example, *The Oracles of the Ancients Explained: Wherein a True Answer May Be Obtained to Any Question Whatever* (London: n.p., 1815).

19. John La Farge, *The Gospel Story in Art* (New York: Macmillan, 1913), 19–20, 50.

20. Elihu Vedder, *Doubt and Other Things* (Boston: Porter Sargent, 1922), 21. The key secondary work on Vedder, which includes a complete catalogue of his paintings, is Regina Soria, *Elihu Vedder: American Visionary Artist in Rome (1836–1923)* (Rutherford, N.J.: Fairleigh Dickinson University Press, 1970). See also Regina Soria, Joshua C. Taylor, Jane Dillenberger, and Richard Murray, *Perceptions and Evocations: The Art of Elihu Vedder* (Washington, D.C.: Smithsonian Institution Press, 1979); Nola H. Tutag, "A Reconstruction of the Career of Elihu Vedder Based upon the Unpublished Letters and Documents of the Artist, his Family, and Correspondents Held by the Archives of American Art," (Ed.D. diss., Wayne State University, 1969); Abraham A. Davidson, *The Eccentrics and Other American Visionary Painters* (New York: E. P. Dutton, 1978), 63–66, 77–83; Gail Gelburd, *Elihu Vedder: Mystic Figures of the Nineteenth Century* (Hempstead, N.Y.: Hofstra Museum, 1989). Vedder's papers, consisting mostly of correspondence, drafts of his literary manuscripts, family photographs, and miscellaneous clippings, are at the Archives of American Art, Smithsonian Institution, Washington, D.C. The few journals (for 1878, 1882, 1889–90) add little to the understanding of his religious life; they are mostly terse jottings about travels, visitors, the weather, and the like.

21. Elihu Vedder, *The Digressions of V.* (Boston: Houghton Mifflin, 1910), 42–44, 48, 64–65.

22. Ibid., 19–20.

23. Ibid., 40–41.

24. Ibid., 61, 75–76. For examples of the Buddhist appropriations, see Gelburd, *Vedder*, unpaginated; "Nirvana," in "Thoughts while Dressing and Undressing," Vedder Papers.

25. Vedder, *Doubt*, 140.

26. Vedder, *Digressions*, 451–54. On the New York Historical Society exhibition, see Joshua C. Taylor, "Perceptions and Digressions," in Soria, Taylor, Dillenberger, and Murray, *Perceptions*, 58. More generally, see Richard G. Carrott, *The Egyptian Revival: Its Sources, Monuments, and Meaning, 1808–1858* (Berkeley and Los Angeles: University of California Press, 1978); Timothy Mitchell, *Colonising Egypt* (Cambridge, Eng.: Cambridge University Press, 1988), esp. 1–33. For a tourist's fascination with the Sphinx and the desert (who employed Vedder's *Questioner* as a lens), see Amelia B. Edwards, *A Thousand Miles up the Nile* (London: G. Routledge and Sons, 1891), xvi–xvii, 489–92.

27. James Jackson Jarves, *The Art-Idea*, ed. Benjamin Rowland Jr. (Cambridge, Mass.: Belknap Press of Harvard University Press, 1960), 200.

28. Elihu Vedder, *Miscellaneous Moods in Verse* (Boston: Porter Sargent, 1914), unpaginated (poem #16); Vedder, *Digressions*, 452; Vedder, *Doubt*, 44; Brewster, *Letters*, 234–40. On the myths of animation surrounding Memnon, see also Gross, *Dream of the Moving Statue*, 163–66.

29. Vedder, *Digressions*, 89, 197. There is also a scarcely whispered prayer in *Miscellaneous Moods*, #63.

30.   Vedder, *Digressions*, 42, 136, 318–20, 451; Vedder, *Doubt*, 42, 51, 53; Vedder, *Miscellaneous Moods*, unpaginated (poems #16 and #30).

31.   On the Pabst episode, see Soria, *Elihu Vedder*, 246; Tutag, "Reconstruction," 244, 246–47, 249; Elihu Vedder to Caroline Vedder, 25 February 1896, 5 March 1896, 8 March 1896, 19 March 1896, 11 April 1896, Vedder Papers.

CHAPTER 12

1.   On Rosh Hashanah, see the *Encyclopedia Judaica* (Jerusalem: Keter Publishing House Jerusalem Ltd., 1972); and Philip Goodman, ed., *The Rosh Hashanah Anthology* (Philadelphia: Jewish Publication Society, 1970).

2.   This article is based on examination of the collections of Jewish New Year postcards in the American Jewish Historical Society, New York, New York, and Waltham, Massachusetts (hereafter referred to as the AJHS); The Library of the Jewish Theological Seminary of America, New York, New York (hereafter referred to as JTS); the private collections of Peter Schweitzer, New York City, and Alan Scop, Brooklyn, New York; and selections from the collection of the Judah L. Magnes Museum, Berkeley, California. Published collections of postcards that were extremely helpful include the exhibition catalog, *Past Perfect: The Jewish Experience in Early 20th Century Postcards* (New York: The Library of the Jewish Theological Seminary of America, 1998), with an introduction by Shalom Sabar; and Christraud M. Geary and Virginia-Lee Webb, eds., *Delivering Views: Distant Cultures in Early Postcards* (Washington: Smithsonian Institution Press, 1998). Also useful are Gabriel Goldstein, "Shana Tovah! Jewish New Year's Cards—A Short History," in *Ephemera News* (fall 1997): 7–9; Rachel Schnold, ed., *Shanah Tovah—Happy New Year: Early 20th-Century Jewish Greeting Postcards from the National Library, Warsaw* (Tel Aviv: Beth Hatefutsoth and Palphot, 1996), which features text in Hebrew and English as well as the work of Polish artist Hayyim Goldberg (1890–1943), one of the rare artists whose work on postcards can be documented; David Tartakover, *Shanah Tovah: 101 Kartisei Berakhah la-Shanah ha-Hadashah* (Jerusalem: Keter Publishing House, 1978), in Hebrew; and Jacob Zidkoni, "Kartsei Berakhah k-Rosh ha-Shanah," in *Mahanayim* 60 (1961): 170–77, in Hebrew. On Jewish postcards in general see Gérard Silvain, "The World of Jewish Postcards," *Encyclopedia Judaica Yearbook, 1988/89* (Jerusalem: Keter Publishing House, 1989), 196–200; and Willy Lindwer, ed., *Classic Jewish Postcards for All Occasions* (New York: Schocken, 1996). Grateful acknowledgments are due to Chava Shiel and Joellyn Wallen Zollman, who helped organize and catalog the American Jewish Historical Society postcard collection, and to Elka Deitsch, Chava Charm, and especially Sharon Liberman Mintz, who made the collections of The Library of the Jewish Theological Seminary available to me under many varieties of conditions. Translations from Yiddish in this essay were made by Paul Glasser of YIVO Institute for Jewish Research, unless otherwise indicated.

3.   On the Jewish custom of exchanging Jewish New Year greetings, see Goodman, ed., *The Rosh Hashanah Anthology*, 274–79; Shalom Sabar, introduction to *Past Perfect*, 11–12; and Shalom Sabar, "The Custom of Sending Jewish New Year Cards: Its History and Artistic Development," *Jerusalem Studies in Jewish Folklore* 19/20 (1997–98), in Hebrew.

4. See, for example, such lists in publications ranging from *American Hebrew* (English-language and Reform), *Der Forwarts* (Yiddish language with a radical labor focus); synagogue publications; and virtually every early-twentieth-century American Jewish newspaper published throughout the United States.

5. For the history of the picture postcard, see especially Frank Staff, *The Picture Postcard and its Origins* (New York: Frederick A. Praeger, 1966); and Howard Woody, "International Postcards: Their History, Production, and Distribution (Circa 1895–1915)," in *Delivering Views*, 13–45. Other useful books include Miriam Klamkin, *Picture Postcards* (New York: Dodd, Mead, 1974); and Dorothy B. Ryan, *Picture Postcards in the United States, 1893–1918* (New York: C. N. Potter, 1982).

6. Woody, "International Postcards," 29.

7. Ibid., 42. According to Woody, sales peaked in 1912 (42). These figures do not include postcards purchased but never mailed.

8. In England, the house of Raphael Tuck, a Jewish immigrant and entrepreneur whose stationer's business made him a millionaire, helped pioneer and market the Christmas and Christian New Year card, but his stock included *Rosh Hashanah* cards as well. According to Staff, *The Picture Postcard*, 58, "Germany was undoubtedly the centre of the picture postcard industry . . . especially Saxony and Bavaria. The business seems to have been largely controlled by Jewish interests, and they were undisputedly the exponents in the technique of colour printing of this sort." Schnold, *Shanah Tovah*, n.p., cites early-twentieth-century Warsaw as "the hub of the Hebrew printing and publishing industry in Eastern Europe." Picture postcards were part of the larger technological advances in photography and graphic production of the late nineteenth and early twentieth centuries. Related graphic forms included *cartes de visite*, cabinet cards, and advertising cards and brochures. Photography was employed by a variety of photographers, artists, anthropologists, folklorists, and adventurers, among others, who toured the world cataloging the places and people to be found. On the technology and production innovations that enabled the growth of the picture postcard industry, see Staff, *The Picture Postcard*; Woody, "International Postcards," esp. 17–21, 23–36; and Peter C. Marzio, *The Democratic Art: Pictures for a Nineteenth-Century America, Chromolithography, 1840–1900* (Boston: Godine, 1979).

9. I could not locate early business records of any of these American companies, and neither could other historians who have tried before. Bloch Publishing Company is still run by the Bloch family, but early company records do not survive. Conversation with Charles Bloch, New York City, 8 July 1999.

10. "New Year Greetings: The Development of a New Custom," *American Hebrew* (18 August 1905): 325, as quoted in Jenna Weissman Joselit, *The Wonders of America: Reinventing Jewish Culture, 1880–1950* (New York: Hill and Wang, 1994), 249.

11. Gabriel Costa, "Some Quaint New Year Cards," *The American Hebrew* (26 September 1913): 554.

12. Gabriel Costa revealed that "at this time of the year, [the] display [in the windows of the Ghetto stationers] appeals to me particularly, so anxious am I to discover anything approaching originality in the latest thing in New Year greeting cards. . . . Alas and alack!" he reported with disappointment in 1913. "'Tis little originality that meets my eye." Ibid., 553.

13. See, for example, the advertisement for "New Year Cards and Art Calendars" and "Camée Candies" in *The American Hebrew* (26 September 1913): 561.
14. Collection of Peter Schweitzer.
15. The same brochure also advertises "Printed, Embossed and Engraved . . . Greeting or Visiting Cards for New Year," that are designed to be mailed in envelopes.
16. There is a growing literature and number of exhibition catalogues on postcards of Jews in specific nations. See, for example, Costis Copsidas, *The Jews of Thessaloniki through the Postcards, 1886–1917* (Thessaloniki: n.p., 1992), in Greek, French, and English; Eugeniusz Duda and Marek Sonsenko, *Old Jewish Postcards* (Cracow, Poland: Historical Museum of Cracow, 1997); and Gérard Silvain, *Images et traditions juives: un millier de cartes postales (1897–1917) pour servir à l'histoire de la Diaspora* (Paris: Astrid, 1980.)
17. Beyond the postcard format there were embossed, cut-out, and pop-up cards and fold-over notecards for mailing in envelopes.
18. Sabar, introduction to *Past Perfect*, 11.
19. See, for example, AJHS card 3333.129; 3333.131; 3333.139; 3333.183; and 3333.332. Means of delivering New Year greetings as depicted on the New Year cards themselves are also illustrated in *Past Perfect*, figs. 25–32, 38, 43.
20. See, for example, AJHS 3333.017 and 3333.028.
21. For valentines made into New Year cards, see, for example, AJHS 3333.109 and 3333.133.
22. AJHS 3333.105. Translation: "What does the new year bring them?/ What do the times tell them? / They say that their luck / will soon change for the better." A related card is illustrated in *Past Perfect*, fig. 49.
23. Thoroughly contemporary images of the secular new year could also be appropriated. AJHS 3333.191a depicts a quartet of men and women dressed in early 1920s clothing raising champagne toasts to the new year. A Jewish Theological Seminary copy of the card is printed in *Past Perfect*, fig. 47.
24. Most staged studio cards were initially photographed, sometimes had details added, and then issued in various versions of color: sepia, black and white, or black, blue, and white. Many of these images were also used in multiple formats, including postcards, embossed pop-up cards, and advertisements. The Jewish life-cycle postcard (fig. 12.4) marks important moments at ages one, two, three, six, thirteen (bar-mitzvah), twenty (chupah/marriage), thirty, fifty, seventy, and ninety.
25. See AJHS cards 3333.108; 3333.107; and 3333.110. The JTS copy of AJHS card 3333.107 appears in *Past Perfect* as fig. 51.
26. The same is true for most pastiche and collage postcards. For Jewish New Year postcards of this panoramic genre, see AJHS 3333.054; 3333.070; 3333.090; 3333.101; 3333.176; 3333.192; and *Past Perfect* figs. 91–93. For panoramic scenes of Paris, France, and an important interpretation of those postcards, see Naomi Schor, "*Cartes Postales:* Representing Paris 1900," *Critical Inquiry* 18 (winter 1992): 188–244. Her self-described "light" version of the article can be found as Naomi Schor, "Collecting Paris," in *The Cultures of Collecting*, ed. John Elsner and Roger Cardinal (Cambridge, Mass.: Harvard University Press, 1994), 252–302.
27. On Jewish "emancipation," see Paula E. Hyman, *The Emancipation of the Jews of Alsace: Acculturation and Tradition in the Nineteenth Century* (New Haven: Yale University Press,

1991); Marion Kaplan, *The Making of the Jewish Middle Class: Women, Family, and Identity in Imperial Germany* (New York: Oxford University Press, 1991); and Jacob Katz, *Out of the Ghetto: The Social Background of Jewish Emancipation, 1770–1870* (Cambridge, Mass.: Harvard University Press, 1973). For introductions to the rise of nineteenth- and early-twentieth-century European antisemitism, see Leonard Dinnerstein, *Uneasy at Home: Antisemitism and the American Jewish Experience* (New York: Columbia University Press, 1987); and Sander Gilman, *The Jew's Body* (New York: Routledge, 1991), which links political and visual antisemitism. Richard Cohen also raises important issues regarding antisemitism and images of European Jews in *Jewish Icons: Art and Society in Modern Europe* (Berkeley and Los Angeles: University of California Press, 1998).

28. Gilman, *The Jew's Body*. See also Linda Nochlin, "Starting with the Self: Jewish Identity and Its Representation" in *The Jew in the Text: Modernity and the Construction of Identity*, ed. Linda Nochlin and Tamar Garb (London: Thames and Hudson LTD, 1995), 7–19; Alfred David, "An Iconography of Noses: Directions in the History of a Physical Stereotype" in *Mapping the Cosmos*, ed. Jane Chance and R. O. Wells Jr. (Houston: Rice University Press, 1985), 76–97; and Jay Geller, "(G)nos(e)ology: The Cultural Construction of the Other" in *People of the Body: Jews and Judaism from an Embodied Perspective*, ed. Howard Eilberg-Schwartz (Albany: State University of New York Press, 1992), 243–82. Richard Cohen addresses images of Jews from additional perspectives in his *Jewish Icons*.

29. For typical illustrations of such period antisemitic stereotypes, see, for example, the illustrations in Gilman, *The Jew's Body*. On syphilis and the Jews, see Sander Gilman, "Salome, Syphilis, Sarah Bernhardt, and the Modern Jewess," in Nochlin and Garb, *The Jew in the Text*, 97–120.

30. The exaggerations of eyes, ears, nose, and mouth, plus the ascribing of sexually transmitted diseases to Jews, further denigrates Jews as a racial type by linking them to danger and chaos. All body parts mentioned, plus sexual organs and the rectum (related to the reputed gastronomic and digestive disorders of Jews) provide a complete inventory of the entrances and egresses of the human body. Such places potentially violate the otherwise fixed boundaries of the body's self-contained system, and like all boundaries, are potentially dangerous and threatening. Furthermore, in the human body, fluids of all types, many of them putrid, enter and leave the body through these openings. I think it no accident that these are the sites of emphasis and distortion when creating the antisemitic, fictionalized body of a Jew.

31. Instructive articles here include Carol Ockman, "'Two Large Eyebrows a l'Orientale': The Barrone de Rothschild," in Carol Ockman, *Ingres's Eroticized Bodies: Retracing the Serpentine Line* (New Haven: Yale University Press, 1995), 67–83; and Kathleen Adler, "John Singer Sargent's Portraits of the Wertheimer Family" and Carol Ockman, "When Is a Jewish Star Just a Star? Interpreting Images of Sarah Bernhardt," both in Nochlin and Garb, *The Jew in the Text*, 83–96, 121–39.

32. See the illustrations in Patricia C. Albers, "Symbols, Souvenirs, and Sentiments: Postcard Imagery of Plains Indians, 1898–1918"; Virginia-Lee Webb, "Transformed Images: Photographers and Postcards in the Pacific Islands"; and especially Christraud M. Geary, "Different Visions? Postcards from Africa by European and African Photographers and Sponsors" where Geary argues strongly that "the sitter's intention" needs to be taken

into account in decoding the postcards. All articles cited are in Geary and Webb, *Delivering Views*, 65–85; 115–45; and 147–77. Images of Jews are not addressed in the Geary and Webb volume. For parallel images of Jewish subjects on postcards see *Past Perfect*, figs. 94–109.

33. The question of whether the postcard companies used Jewish and/or non-Jewish actors cannot at present be answered, and perhaps never will be, given the paucity of production records surviving from the postcard companies. It is clear from viewing the cards that the same actors and actresses are reused in a variety of scenes, sometimes posing as modern Jews, sometimes as traditional Jews, sometimes posing in nearly the same scene with only a costume or detail change. Regardless of whether these are "actual" or "staged" Jews in the cards, however, the producers are clearly portraying a visual image of the Jew in stark contrast to the antisemitic physical image current at the time. The fact that these cards are for a Jewish audience suggests that this is less an act of polemics to convince non-Jewish audiences than it is a reflection of how Jews saw themselves or at least how they wished to see themselves. Even if the constructed images are conscious antidotes to antisemitic stereotypes, they are constructed to reassure, not to argue, and to reinforce not so much what Jews look like per se but that they fit in visually to their new environments.

34. The interpretation of antisemitic images by Jews at the time of their publication, as well as by present historians, is complex. The Jewish Theological Seminary has several postcards with caricatures of Jews and Jewish behavior that were purchased and sent by Jews to Jews, and appropriated by them as jokes or transformed through the addition of written text, into jokes. Much more work needs to be done on Jewish response to, and use of, antisemitic imagery.

35. The AJHS, for example, has a series of cards sent from the Cohen family in Nashua, New Hampshire, to friends and relatives throughout the northeast over a series of years. See AJHS 3333.005 and 3333.008.

36. See, for example, AJHS 3333.285.

37. See, for example, AJHS 3333.283; 3333.284; 3333.347; 3333.348; and 3333.349, and *Past Perfect*, figs. 66–71.

38. The eagle would likely also resonate with the Jewish patrons of the card as references to Isaiah, for example, Isaiah 40:31.

39. See, for example, AJHS 3333.136; 3333.148; 3333.185; 3333.188; 3333.339; and 3333.341, and *Past Perfect*, figs. 24–30. The greeting for fig. 12.6 translates as "We announce: / A New Year is coming! / Awaken quickly to light and joy / Be more cheerful and joyful!" Happiness, love, and wealth were among the most common New Year requests. Jewish New Year postcards were marketed to immigrant populations for whom such blessings were sometimes in short supply.

40. A related card, with a newly arrived immigrant walking with a steamship and the Statue of Liberty in the background, is illustrated in *Past Perfect*, fig. 61. Fig 12.7 translates as: "Tashlikh. / And thou wilt cast all their sins into the depths of the sea." Among the fullest celebrations of the American opportunity is AJHS 3333.014 from 1909. The American flag flies boldly over a camp of military tents. Many Jews emigrated to America to es-

cape oppressive Eastern European Jewish conscription laws. In America, the Jewish New Year postcard proudly combines images of military service, the American flag, and Jewish New Year greetings.

41. Personal conversation with Alan Scop, Brooklyn, New York, 6 April 1998, and personal conversations with Alan Scop and Ira Reznik, The Jewish Museum, New York City, 7 June 1999.

42. Andrew R. Heinze, *Adapting to Abundance: Jewish Immigrants, Mass Consumption, and the Search for American Identity* (New York: Columbia University Press, 1990), and Joselit, *The Wonders of America*. See also the exhibition catalogs, Susan L. Braunstein and Jenna Weissman Joselit, *Getting Comfortable in New York: The Jewish American Home, 1880–1950* (New York: The Jewish Museum, 1990); and Barbara Shreier, *Becoming American Women: Clothing and the Jewish Immigrant Experience, 1880–1920* (Chicago: Chicago Historical Society, 1994). On consumer culture and early twentieth-century America in general, see Leigh Eric Schmidt, *Consumer Rites: The Buying and Selling of American Holidays* (Princeton: Princeton University Press, 1995); Simon J. Bronner, ed., *Consuming Visions: Accumulation and Display of Goods in America, 1880–1920* (New York: Norton, 1988); and Richard Wightman Fox and T. J. Jackson Lears, *The Culture of Consumption: Critical Essays in American History* (New York: Pantheon Books, 1983).

43. Cards that were actually sent from a small portion of the AJHS and all other Jewish New Year postcard collections that I examined. Of the AJHS collection, fewer than 7 percent were actually written and mailed.

44. The topic of Jewish women as consumers is addressed by Heinze, *Adapting to Abundance;* and Joselit, *The Wonders of America*. On changing roles of women in American Jewish history, see Hasia Diner, *A Time for Gathering: The Second Migration, 1820–1880* (Baltimore: Johns Hopkins University Press, 1992); Paula E. Hyman, *The Jewish Woman in America* (New York: New American Library, 1975); and Paula E. Hyman, *Gender and Assimilation in Modern Jewish History: The Roles of Representation of Women* (Seattle: University of Washington Press, 1995). Issues of women, religion, and consumerism are also productively addressed in Schmidt, *Consumer Rites* and Colleen McDannell, *Material Christianity: Religion and Popular Culture in America* (New Haven: Yale University Press, 1995).

45. See Cohen, *Jewish Icons*. Most treatment of the images of Jewish women in this period has come in the context of analyzing antisemitic imagery. No historian has yet assessed these staged, photographed, manipulated, and ubiquitous postcard depictions of Jewish women.

46. "New Year Greetings: The Development of a New Custom," *The American Hebrew* (18 August 1905): 325, as quoted in Joselit, *The Wonders of America, 249.*

47. See Diner, *A Time for Gathering;* Hyman, *Jewish Women* and Hyman, *Gender and Assimilation*. Similar changed opportunities were also opening up in Europe, but the powerful and sometimes devastating impacts of mass out-migration from Jewish Europe and of World War I and World War II interrupted what might have been a smoother evolution of Jewish women's roles in Europe. Historians are just beginning to examine the parallels and differences of Jewish women's experiences in early-twentieth-

century Europe and America. See Kaplan, *Making of the Jewish Middle Class,* for European parallels.

48. AJHS 3333.314. JTS copy also illustrated in *Past Perfect,* figs. 14, 21. Translation quoted above is by Shalom Sabar in *Past Perfect,* 13.

49. AJHS 3333.335. JTS copy also illustrated in *Past Perfect,* figs. 41, 36. Translation quoted above is by Shalom Sabar in *Past Perfect,* 37.

50. AJHS 3333.336. JTS copy also illustrated in *Past Perfect,* fig. 43. Translation quoted above is by Shalom Sabar in *Past Perfect,* 37.

51. Naomi Schor, *"Cartes Postales,"* 211. See also Colleen McDannell, *Material Christianity,* especially "Christian Kitsch and the Rhetoric of Bad Taste," 163–97; and McDannell, "Christian Retailing," 222–69. Leigh Schmidt perhaps sees more power residing with women in the gendered collecting of postcards and greeting cards and in the gendered management of holidays overall. See Schmidt, *Consumer Rites.* See also Susan Stewart, *On Longing: Narratives of the Miniature, the Gigantic, the Souvenir, the Collection* (Baltimore: Johns Hopkins University Press, 1984.)

CHAPTER 13

1. "Jesus Handed Me a Ticket," in *God Struck Me Dead: Religious Conversion Experiences and Autobiographies of Ex-Slaves,* ed. Clifton H. Johnson (Philadelphia: Pilgrim Press, 1969), 145, 147.

2. The literature on the cultural influence of the railroad is quite large. See particularly the classic work by Leo Marx, *The Machine in the Garden: Technology and the New Pastoral Idea in America* (New York: Oxford University Press, 1964). More recently, and for a guide to the historiography, see William Deverall, *Railroad Crossing: Californians and the Railroad, 1850–1910* (Berkeley and Los Angeles: University of California Press, 1993). For an informative discussion on the influence of the railroad on the perception of time, see Michael O'Malley, *Keeping Watch: A History of American Time* (New York: Viking Press, 1994), esp. chap. 2.

3. On trains and migration as symbols of freedom for African Americans after the Civil War, see James Grossman, *Land of Hope: Chicago, Black Southerners, and the Great Migration* (Chicago: The University of Chicago Press, 1989), 18–32, esp. 28; and William Cohen, *Freedom's Edge: Black Mobility and the Southern White Quest for Racial Control, 1861–1915* (Baton Rouge: Louisiana State University Press, 1991), 201–48.

4. See the testimony of Mose Banks in George Rawick, ed., *The American Slave: A Composite Autobiography, Arkansas Narratives,* vol. 1, part I, 101–3.

5. C. Vann Woodward, *Origins of the New South* (Baton Rouge: Louisiana State University Press, 1971), 146–47; James M. McPherson, *Ordeal by Fire: The Civil War and Reconstruction* (New York: McGraw-Hill, 1982), 599–600. On the New South business ideology, see Paul M. Gaston, *The South Creed: A Study in Mythmaking* (New York: Alfred A. Knopf, 1970); and Raymond B. Nixon, *Henry W. Grady: Spokesman of the New South* (New York: Alfred A. Knopf, 1943).

6. *The Dallas Express,* 13 January 1900. See also the banner for the *Arkansas Mansion,* 5 January 1884, which features a chugging train.

7. John L. Pratt, ed., *Currier & Ives: Images of America* (Maplewood, N.J.: Hammond, 1968), 143.

8. On the notion of manifest destiny, the best introductions are Malcolm J. Rohrbough, *The Trans-Appalachian Frontier: People, Societies, and Institutions, 1775–1850* (New York: Oxford University Press, 1978); and Ray Allen Billington, *The Far Western Frontier, 1830–1860* (New York: Harper, 1956).

9. Charles A. Lofgreen, *The Plessy Case: A Legal-Historical Interpretation* (New York: Oxford University Press, 1987), 1–6; Catherine A. Barnes, *Journey from Jim Crow: The Desegregation of Southern Transit* (New York: Columbia University Press, 1989), 6–7; and Otto Olsen, ed., *The Thin Disguise: Turning Point in Negro History—Plessy v. Ferguson: A Documentary Presentation (1864–1896)* (New York: Humanities Press, 1967).

10. For a perceptive review of the ways that, in matters of railroad segregation, the nineteenth-century legal system legitimated racial discrimination on the basis that integrated public space was a social pathology regardless of the class of the black passengers, see Elizabeth Dale, "'Social Equality Does Not Exist among Themselves, Nor among Us': *Baylies vs. Curry* and Civil Rights in Chicago, 1888," *American Historical Review* [*AHR*] 102 (April 1997): 311–40; and the commentary in the same issue by Kevin Gaines, "Rethinking Race and Class in African-American Struggles for Equality, 1885–1941," 378–88.

11. Editorial. "Separating the Races on the Cars." 13 March 1890, *Southwestern Christian Advocate* [*SWCA*].

12. It is important to note that, in the North during the antebellum and early national periods, the railroad trip as an allegory for a journey gained literary notice, most prominently in the 1834 short story, "The Celestial Rail-road," by Nathaniel Hawthorne. Hawthorne used the train trip to depict the decline of a society run by men and women seeking profit and pleasure at all costs. In the story, the narrator, recalling a dream, took a train destined for the Celestial City. But it never got there. Instead, the train hurtled its passengers—greedy capitalists, lovers of indulgence, foes of bookish learning, and enemies of devout religion—to hell. The story is reprinted in *Nathaniel Hawthorne: Tales and Sketches* (New York: Library Classics of the United States, 1972), 808–24.

13. Jesse Hutchinson Jr., "Get off the Track" (Boston: Thayer & Company, 1844). American Antiquarian Society, Worcester, Mass.

14. C. H. Andrews Jr., "Discussed. African Migration—Washington's Birthday Celebration." 24 February 1894, *Indianapolis Freeman* [*IF*]. See also the letter to the editor by E. W. Johnson, of Little Bay, Arkansas. 29 October 1891, *SWCA*.

15. William Holmes, *History, Anniversary Celebration and Financial Report of the Work of the Phillips, Lee, and Monroe County Missionary Baptist District Association from Its Organization, November 10th, 1879 to November 9th, 1889* (Helena, Ark.: Helena World Job Print, 1890), 70. Arkansas History Commission, Little Rock, Arkansas.

16. J. W. Hudson, "Baton Rouge District." 1 January 1891, *SWCA*.

17. J. W. Spearman, "A Word to the Ministers." 16 January 1904, *Christian Index* [*CI*].

18. Editorial [untitled] on Reverend Pierre Landry. 2 January 1890, *SWCA*.

19. "North Little Rock Conference." 13 August 1904, *CI*.

20. On metaphors as forces that can shape the telling of individual histories, see Mary Hesse, *Revolutions and Reconstruction in the Philosophy of Science* (Bloomington: Indiana Uni-

versity Press, 1980), 111–24; Donald Davidson, "What Metaphors Mean," in his *Inquiries into Truth and Interpretation* (Oxford: Oxford University Press, 1984); and Bonnie G. Smith, "Gender and the Practices of Scientific History: The Seminar and Archival Research in the Nineteenth Century," *AHR* 100 (October 1995): 1150–53.

21. B. P. Williamson, Letter to the Editor. 7 August 1904, *CI.*

22. Letter to the Editor. 24 December 1904, *CI.*

23. Rev. A. Nix and His Congregation, "Black Diamond Express to Hell." Vocalion 1098. 1927. Blues Archive. University of Mississippi, Oxford, Miss. For background information on Nix, and a partial transcription of the lyrics, see Paul Oliver, *Songsters and Saints: Vocal Traditions on Race Records* (Cambridge, Eng.: Cambridge University Press, 1984), 150–52.

24. "The Two Railroads to Eternity" (Cincinnati: "The Revivalist," c. 1900). I would like to thank Bradford Verter for giving a copy of this diagram to me.

25. Rev. J. M. Gates, "Death's Black Train Is Coming," in *Roots N' Blues: The Retrospective, 1925–1950* (New York: Columbia-Sony, 1992) C4K 47901I. Four Compact Disks. Blues Archive. University of Mississippi, Oxford, Miss. For background information on Gates, see Oliver, *Songsters and Saints,* 160.

26. Mary Church Terrell, *A Colored Woman in a White World* (Washington, D.C.: Ransdell, 1940), 298.

27. Testimony of Mrs. V. K. Glenn in Mrs. L. D. McAfee, *History of the Woman's Missionary Society in the Colored Methodist Episcopal Church Comprising Its Founders, Organizations, Pathfinders, Subsequent Developments and Present Status* (1934; reprint, Phoenix City, Alabama: Phoenix City Herald, 1945), 83–86.

28. Testimony of Peggy Lesure in McAfee, *History of the Woman's Missionary Society in the Colored Methodist Church,* 43–45.

29. Ibid., 46.

30. This paragraph is based on David Evans, *Big Road Blues: Tradition and Creativity in the Folk Blues* (Berkeley and Los Angeles: University of California Press, 1982), 44; Edward Ayers, *The Promise of the New South: Life after Reconstruction* (New York: Oxford University Press, 1992), 390.

31. W. C. Handy, *Father of the Blues: An Autobiography,* ed. Arna Bontemps (1941; reprint, New York: Collier, 1970), 91–92; and Evans, *Big Road Blues,* 107.

32. Paul Harvey, *Redeeming the South: Religious Cultures and Racial Identities among Southern Baptists* (Chapel Hill: University of North Carolina Press, 1997), 115–16, 180.

33. Evans, *Big Road Blues,* 107.

34. Tommy Johnson, "Slidin' Delta," *Complete Recorded Works in Chronological Order, 1926–1929* (Vienna, Austria: Document Records, 1990) DOCD 5001. One Compact Disk. Blues Archive. University of Mississippi, Oxford, Miss. In this song and those that follow, I follow the lead of scholars of the early blues and date the origins of them in the 1890s and 1900s, even though they were actually recorded years later.

35. Henry Thomas, "When the Train Comes Along," *Henry Thomas Sings the Texas Blues.* Origin Records. OJL V3. Blues Archive. University of Mississippi, Oxford, Miss.

36. Blind Lemon Jefferson, "All I Want Is That Pure Religion," *Complete Recorded Works of Blind Lemon Jefferson, 1925–1929* (Vienna, Austria: Document Records, 1990) DOCD 8OCD 520. 3 Compact Disks. Blues Archive. University of Mississippi, Oxford, Miss.

37. *[Indianapolis] Freeman*, 17 August 1888.

38. See Nell Irvin Painter, *Exodusters: Black Migration to Kansas after Reconstruction* (New York: W. W. Norton, 1976).

39. David M. Lubin, *Picturing a Nation: Art and Social Change in Nineteenth-Century America* (New Haven: Yale University Press, 1994), 56–66.

40. Song quoted from Emmett J. Scott, *Negro Migration during the War* (New York: Oxford University Press, 1920), 45–46.

41. Quote from essay by Sharon F. Potter in *Memory and Metaphor: The Art of Romare Bearden, 1940–1987* (New York: Oxford University Press, 1991), 39, 109 n. 25. On the broader theme of art and images of African American life, see Guy C. McElroy, *Facing History: The Black Image in American Art, 1710–1940* (San Francisco: Bedford Arts, 1940); and Ellwood Parry, *The Image of the Indian and the Black Man in American Art, 1590–1900* (New York: G. Braziller, 1974).

42. Potter, in *Memory and Metaphor*, 39.

43. See also Bearden's *The Prevalence of Ritual: Baptism* (1964). Here he framed the upper-left corner of a scene of a river baptism with a distant silhouette of a church and, closer, of a train. The visual effect is to integrate the train as an intimate part of the drama and portray it as a vehicle connecting the spiritually reborn individual to the larger community of the faithful. Bearden incorporates the train in other works, most notably *Southern Limited* (1976) and *Memories* (1979). On Bearden, see Romare Bearden and Derek Walcott, *The Caribbean Poetry of Derek Walcott and the Art of Romare Bearden* (New York: Farrar, Straus, and Giroux, 1983). On his use of the train, see the brief comment by Sharon F. Potter in *Memory and Metaphor: The Art of Romare Bearden, 1940–1987* (New York: Oxford University Press, 1991). For another example of the significance of the train to modern African American life, see the paintings by Jacob Lawrence, especially *The Migration of the Negro Series* (1940–41).

CHAPTER 14

1. "Test Your Bible Knowledge," *Publisher's Weekly* (9 Oct. 1995), 63. For a partial listing of these English translations, also see Margaret Hills, *The English Bible: A Bibliography of Editions of the Bible & the New Testament Published in America, 1777–1957* (New York: American Bible Society, 1962).

2. Cathy Lynn Grossman, "The Bible Business," *USA TODAY* (27 May 1998): D: 1. According to Barna Research commissioned by Tyndale House Publishers, the King James Version still commands 37 percent of the American Reading Market, while the New International Version comes in second at 7 percent. "Huge Share of Market, Low Share of Mind: The Struggle of the Bible to Penetrate American Life," *The Barna Report* 1, no. 3 (Sep. 1996): 3–5.

3. Certain versions such as the Revised Version (1881), the New American Bible (1941), and the Revised Standard Version (1951) have all gained considerable followings since their introductions.

4. Folder "Historical Essays TEV—Secondary Material," RG 53, Box 2, Historical Essays, Studies Nos. 10–15, American Bible Society Archives, New York, N.Y., 2.

5. Ibid., 2, 12.

6. Initially it could be purchased for the extremely low price of twenty-five cents, roughly a third of the price of other paperbacks of the time. "The Today's English Version: A Bible for Today's Church," Press release by John D. Erickson, RG 53, Box 2, Historical Essays, Studies Nos. 10–15, American Bible Society Archives, New York, N.Y., 4. The translation's "standard, everyday, natural form of English" also appealed to a wide range of readers who found that its new, accessible language invigorated their Bible reading. Folder "Historical Essays TEV—Secondary Material," RG 53, Box 2, Historical Essays, Studies Nos. 10–15, American Bible Society Archives, New York, N.Y., 1. Further, a wide range of denominations and church groups quickly adopted the version; even a slightly revised Roman Catholic version won ecclesiastical approval in 1969 and soon became immensely popular among Catholics. Ibid., 3.

7. Vallotton's artistic philosophy focused on using simple lines to give maximum expression. Peter Wosh, "Today's English Version and the Good News Bible: A Historical Sketch," ts. RG 53, Box 2, Historical Essays, Studies Nos. 10–15, 1987, American Bible Society Archives, New York, N.Y., 9.

8. Annie Vallotton to Mr. K. A. Olenik, American Bible Society, 19 July 1965, "Biographical Sketch of: ANNIE VALLOTTON," Annie Vallotton Biographical File, American Bible Society Archives, New York, N.Y., 1.

9. Ibid., 6.

10. Article in the *Bible Translator*, January 1968, Annie Vallotton Biographical File, American Bible Society Archives, New York, N.Y., 29.

11. American Bible editions illustrated either by the works of famous artists or in conventions that resonate with refined cultural values are found throughout the two hundred years following the appearance of Thomas's folio edition. Just a few examples of this trend include: *The Holy Bible* (Boston: R. H. Hinkley, 1904?); *The Holy Bible . . . The Only Family Bible Richly Illustrated with Beautiful Colored Plates of the Old Masters* (Chicago: John A. Hertel, 1924?); *The Holy Bible . . . with Illustrations by Celebrated Old Masters* (Chicago: Consolidated Book Publishers, 1952); and the *Washburn College Bible* (Topeka, Kans.: Washburn College, 1979).

12. The engravers included: Joseph H. Seymour of Philadelphia, Amos Doolittle of New Haven, Samuel Hill, and H. Norman. Charles Lemuel Nichols, *Bibliography of Worcester* (Worcester, Mass.: Printed privately, 1899), 37.

13. Biographical material on Isaiah Thomas (1749–1831) can be found in: Clifford K. Shipton, *Isaiah Thomas: Printer, Patriot and Philanthropist, 1749–1831* (Rochester, N.Y.: The Printing House of Leo Hart, 1948); Benjamin Franklin Thomas, *Memoir of Isaiah Thomas* (Boston: Printed privately, 1874); Isaiah Thomas, *Three Autobiographical Fragments* (Worcester, Mass.: American Antiquarian Society, 1812); and Isaiah Thomas, "The Diary of Isaiah Thomas, 1805–1828," in *Transactions and Collections of the American Antiquarian Society*, vols. 9–10 (Worcester, Mass.: American Antiquarian Society, 1909). For discussions of the influence of various strains of Enlightenment thought on notions of refinement and cultural formation, see Richard Bushman, *The Refinement of America: Persons, Houses, Cities* (New York: Alfred A. Knopf, 1992), 3–206; Richard D. Brown, *Knowledge Is Power: The Diffusion of Information in Early America*

(New York: Oxford University Press, 1989), 42–64. For the rococo's connection to ideas of high culture and gentility, see William Park, *The Idea of Rococo* (Newark, N.J.: University of Delaware Press, 1992), 42. See also: Morrion H. Heckscher and Leslie Greene Bowman, *American Rococo, 1750–1775: Elegance in Ornament* (New York: The Metropolitan Museum of Art, 1992), 4. Along with Park's, Heckscher's, and Bowman's works, good treatments of the rococo style in the eighteenth and nineteenth century include: Jean Starobinski et al., *Revolution in Fashion: European Clothing, 1715–1815* (New York: Abbeville Press, 1989); Eric M. Zafran, *The Rococo Age: French Masterpieces of the Eighteenth Century* (Atlanta: High Museum of Art, 1983); and Michael Levey, *Rococo to Revolution: Major Trends in Eighteenth-Century Painting* (New York: Thames and Hudson, 1966).

14.   For a good discussion of the role of feeling in the midst of eighteenth-century Enlightenment thought, see Simon Schama, *Citizens: A Chronicle of the French Revolution* (New York: Alfred A. Knopf, 1992), 145–62.

15.   For an informative treatment of breasts in seventeenth- and eighteenth-century art and literature, see Clive Hart and Kay Gilliland Stevenson, *Heaven and the Flesh: Imagery of Desire from the Renaissance to the Rococo* (New York: Cambridge University Press, 1995), 74–91; Marilyn Yalom, *A History of the Breast* (New York: Alfred A. Knopf, 1997), 105–23. See also: Zafran, *The Rococo Age*, 12.

16.   E. T. Andrews to Isaiah Thomas, Boston, 26 May 1791, Isaiah Thomas Papers, Box 1, Folder 9, American Antiquarian Society, Worcester, Mass.

17.   Natalie Z. Davis, "Printing and the People," in *Rethinking Popular Culture*, ed. Chandra Mukerji and Michael Schudson (Berkeley and Los Angeles: University of California Press), 83–84.

18.   The best recent scholarly discussions on the interplay between juxtaposed visual and verbal texts include: W. J. T. Mitchell, ed., *Iconology: Image, Text, Ideology* (Chicago: University of Chicago Press, 1987), and J. Hillis Miller, *Illustration* (Cambridge, Mass: Harvard University Press, 1992). For a path-breaking study on popular religious imagery found both inside and outside of written texts, see David Morgan, *Visual Piety: A History and Theory of Popular Religious Images* (Berkeley and Los Angeles: University of California Press, 1998).

19.   Hills, *The English Bible*, 15–77. The Catholic Carey actively marketed Bibles to Protestant readers.

20.   Emily Ellsworth Ford Skeel, *Mason Locke Weems: Letters,* 3 vols. (New York: Privately published by the author, 1929), 3: 359.

21.   Skeel, *Mason Locke Weems*, 2: 201.

22.   Shirley Teresa Wajda, "And a Little Child Shall Lead Them," Children's Cabinets of Curiosities, 1790–1860," *Reader* 38/39 (fall/spring 1997–98): 5–19. See also: Stephen Bann, "Shrines, Curiosities, and the Rhetoric of Display," in *Visual Display: Culture beyond Appearances*, ed. Lynne Cooke and Peter Wollen (Seattle: Bay Press Seattle, 1995); Barbara Maria Stafford, *Artful Science: Enlightenment Entertainment and the Eclipse of Visual Education* (Cambridge, Mass.: MIT Press, 1994), 217–79.

23.   David R. Brigham, *Public Culture in the Early Republic: Peale's Museum and Its Audience* (Washington, D.C.: Smithsonian Institution Press, 1995); Brandon Brame Fortune, "Charles Willson Peale's Portrait Gallery: Persuasion and the Plain Style," *Word and Im-*

age 6, no. 4 (Oct.–Dec. 1990): 308–24. Charles Coleman Sellers, *Mr. Peale's Museum: Charles Willson Peale and the First Popular Museum of Natural Science and Art* (New York: W. W. Norton, 1980); Bluford Adams, *E Pluribus Barnum: The Great Showman and the Making of U.S. Popular Culture* (Minneapolis: University of Minnesota Press, 1997); and Neil Harris, *Humbug: The Art of P. T. Barnum* (Chicago: University of Chicago Press, 1981).

24. Skeel, *Mason Locke Weems*, 3: 148.

25. James Early, *Romanticism and American Architecture* (New York: A. S. Barnes, 1965).

26. Colleen McDannell, *The Christian Home in Victorian America, 1840–1900* (Bloomington: Indiana University Press, 1986), 30.

27. Jay Fliegelman, *Prodigals & Pilgrims: The American Revolution against Patriarchal Authority, 1750–1800* (New York: Cambridge University Press, 1982); and Ellen G. D'Oench, *Prodigal Son Narratives, 1480–1980*, exh. cat. (New Haven: Yale University Art Gallery and Davison Art Center, Wesleyan University, 1995).

28. John Albert Wilson, *Signs & Wonders upon Pharaoh: A History of American Egyptology* (Chicago: University of Chicago Press, 1964), 1–43. See also: John T. Irwin, *American Hieroglyphics: The Symbol of the Egyptian Hieroglyphics in the American Renaissance* (Baltimore: Johns Hopkins University Press, 1980).

29. Yeshayahu Nir, *The Bible and the Image* (Philadelphia: University of Pennsylvania Press, 1985); Naomi Shepherd, *The Zealous Intruders: The Western Rediscovery of Palestine* (New York: Harper & Row, 1987), 1–106; John Davis, *The Landscape of Belief: Encountering the Holy Land in Nineteenth-Century American Art and Culture* (Princeton: Princeton University Press, 1996); and Lester I. Vogel, *To See a Promised Land: Americans and the Holy Land in the Nineteenth Century* (University Park: Pennsylvania State University Press, 1993), 1–93.

30. Instructive discussions of the developments in nineteenth-century American biblical criticism include: Robert M. Grant, *A Short History of the Interpretation of the Bible,* rev. ed. (New York: Macmillan, 1963), 139–64; Theodore Dwight Bozeman, *Protestants in an Age of Science: The Baconian Ideal and Antebellum American Religious Thought* (Chapel Hill: University of North Carolina Press, 1977); John H. Giltner, *Moses Stuart: The Father of Biblical Science in America* (Atlanta: Scholars Press, 1988), 45–88; Jerry Wayne Brown, *The Rise of Biblical Criticism in America, 1800–1870* (Middletown, Conn.: Wesleyan University Press, 1969); Charles Cashdollar, *The Transformation of Theology, 1830–1890* (Princeton: Princeton University Press, 1989); James Turner, *Without God, Without Creed: The Origins of Unbelief in America* (Baltimore: Johns Hopkins University Press, 1985), 143–50; David N. Livingstone, *Darwin's Forgotten Defenders: The Encounter between Evangelical Theology and Evolutionary Thought* (Grand Rapids, Mich.: W. B. Eerdmans, 1987).

31. Although it is impossible to prove, Naomi Shepherd has called Thomson's book the best selling volume between Stowe's *Uncle Tom's Cabin* and Wallace's *Ben-Hur.* Shepherd, *The Zealous Intruders*, 90. Whether this claim is accurate or not, the book's popularity is testified to by the fact that it went through eighteen printings and remained in print for thirty years.

32. William McClure Thomson, *The Land and the Book,* 2 vols. (New York: Harper and Brothers, 1880), 1: 1.

33. Brown, *The Rise of Biblical Criticism*, 111–24.

34. Edward Robinson, *Biblical Researches in Palestine and Later Biblical Researches: Palestine*, 3 vols. (Boston: Crocker and Brewster, 1856), 1: viii–xii, 251–57.

35. For an excellent introduction to the philological debates in theology in the early nineteenth century, see: Philip Gura, *The Wisdom of Words: Language, Theology, and Literature in the New England Renaissance* (Middletown, Conn.: Wesleyan University Press, 1981), 15–71.

36. Herbert Hovenkamp, *Science and Religion in America, 1800–1860* (Philadelphia: University of Pennsylvania Press, 1978), 147–64. See also: Robert T. Handy, *The Holy Land in American Protestant Life, 1800–1948: A Documentary History* (New York: Arno Press, 1981), 3–40; Joseph Wentwork Ingraham, *An Historical Map of Palestine, or the Holy Land* (Boston: Thomas B. Wait and Joseph W. Ingraham, 1828); and "Palestine, a Perpetual Witness for the Bible," *The New Englander* 17 (1859): 192–223.

37. Shepherd, *The Zealous Intruders*, 170–92.

38. One traveler wrote, "A perfect knowledge of the *Land* is needful to a perfect knowledge of the Holy *Scriptures*." Robert Morris, *Freemasonry in the Holy Land* (New York: Masonic Publishing, 1872), 14. The biblical scholar Horatio B. Hackett summed up the thoughts of many pilgrims to Palestine in writing that the "agreement between the scriptures and the geography of the holy land . . . furnishes a direct proof of the truthful character of the sacred word." Horatio B. Hackett, *Illustrations of Scripture: Suggested by a Tour of the Holy Land* (Boston: William Heath, 1857), 73.

39. "Constitution," Article 1, *Annual Reports of the American Bible Society* (New York: Daniel Fanshaw, 1838), 10.

40. *American Bible Society Annual Report* (New York: American Bible Society, 1954), 138: 31–32.

41. Michael R. Flood. "Production and Supply, 1931–1966," American Bible Society Historical Essay #18, Part VI-A, B, fall 1968, ts., American Bible Society Archives, New York, N.Y., 151.

42. Versions Committee Minutes, 15 May 1953, ts., American Bible Society Archives, New York, N.Y., 233. Second quotation found in William F. Asbury, AA Publication Milestone: "The Illustrated New Testament—a Five-Year Project—Has Now Been Completed," *Bible Society Record* 100, no. 5 (May 1955): 84.

43. William F. Asbury, AA Publication Milestone: "The Illustrated New Testament—a Five-Year Project—Has Now Been Completed," *Bible Society Record* 100, no. 5 (May 1955): 84.

44. Hills, *The English Bible*, 422.

45. It should be noted that an early use of photography to link the Holy Land to the biblical text occurred in the mid-1890s, when the Thompson Publishing Company created a *Self-Interpreting Bible*. It included "Over Four Hundred Photographs Showing the Places of Bible Events as They Appear Today." Hills, *The English Bible*, 320.

46. *The Bible for To-Day*, ed. John Stirling (New York: Oxford University Press, 1941), dust jacket.

47. Ibid.

48. Ibid., 990, 992.

49. Ibid., dust jacket.

50. *The Way: An Illustrated Edition of the Living Bible* (Wheaton, Ill.: Tyndale House Publishing, 1971).

51. Sales statistic taken from *The Way: An Illustrated Edition of The Living Bible* (Wheaton, Ill.: Tyndale House Publishing, seventeenth printing, July 1976), t.p.

52. *The Way*, 1971, 833.

53. Ibid., 832–33.

54. *The Story of the Hamitic Peoples*. Quotation from a single sheet advertisement entitled "The Hamitic Bible" placed within the American Bible Society's copy of this edition. American Bible Society Library, New York, N.Y.

55. For a brief, yet informative, treatment of the popularity of study and specialty Bibles in the United States, see: "A Bible for Everybody: The Niche Phenomenon," *Publishers Weekly* (9 Oct. 1995): 58ff.; Nick Harrison, "Sacred Texts: It's Still the Good Book," *Publishers Weekly* (13 Oct. 1997): 32–40; "Niche Bibles: Good News and Bad News," *The Christian* (June 1996): 6; Glenn Paauw, "What's So Special about Specialty Bibles?" *The Banner* (19 Feb. 1996): 12–15.

56. *The Story of the Hamitic Peoples of the Old and New Testaments together with Original Subject Illustrations* (Philadelphia: A. J. Holman, 1940), 2.

57. Ibid.

58. Perry Nodelman, *Words about Pictures* (Athens: University of Georgia Press, 1988), 243.

59. *Catalogue of Books Published by Harper & Brothers, 1845* (New York: Harper & Brothers, 1845), 13. See also: Edward O'Callagahn, *A List of Editions of the Holy Scriptures and Parts Thereof* (Albany, N.Y.: Munsell & Rowland, 1861), 288–89.

60. David Morgan, *Protestants & Pictures: Religion, Visual Culture and the Age of American Mass Production* (New York: Oxford University Press, 1999), 65–66.

61. Eugene Exman, *The House of Harper: One Hundred and Fifty Years of Publishing* (New York: Harper & Row, 1967), 24; Edward K. Spann, *The New Metropolis: New York City, 1840–1857* (New York: Columbia University Press, 1981), 409.

62. Exman, *The House of Harper*, 34–35. See also: *American Dictionary of Printing and Bookmaking* (New York: Howard Lockwood, 1894), 157–66; and Bamber Gascoigne, *How to Identify Prints* (London: Thames and Hudson, 1986), 33b, 72.

63. *Contract Book*, Harper and Brothers Collection (New York: Chadwyck-Healy) Reel A1, 330–31, originals located in the Harper and Brothers Collection, Columbia University Library, Special Collections, Morningside Heights, New York. See also: Paris Marion Simms, *The Bible in America: Versions That Have Played their Part in the Making of the Republic* (New York: Wilson-Erickson, 1936), 266; Joseph Henry Harper, *The House of Harper* (New York: Harper & Brothers, 1912), 80.

64. *The Illuminated Bible* (New York: Harper & Brothers, 1846), thirty-sixth installment of printed sheets, back cover. A copy of the loose sheets for this Bible edition are located at Columbia University Library, Special Collections, Morningside Heights, New York.

65. *The Bible Alive* (San Francisco: HarperCollins, 1993), dust jacket.

66. Just one example of the wide exposure this edition received upon its introduction is Sophronia Scott Gregory, "'Diss' Is the Word of the Lord," *Time* (27 May 1998), 61.

67. Miller, *Illustration*, 67–70.

68. Although they have paid no attention to the role of pictures in the process, numerous scholars have noted a move away from logic-based argumentation in American religious rhetoric and thought. Examples include: David Reynolds, "From Doctrine to Narrative," *American Quarterly* 32, no. 5 (winter 1980): 479–98; Ann Douglas, *The Feminization of American Culture* (New York: Anchor Books, 1977), 121–64; and Laurence R. Moore, *Selling God: American Religion in the Marketplace of Culture* (New York: Oxford University Press, 1996), 12–39. Similar issues concerning method of production and meaning surround the rising use of websites bent on giving readers easy access to God's word. As one sees in the interaction between the visual and verbal in the *Illuminated Bible* and *The Bible Alive*, the medium does influence the message.

SELECTED BIBLIOGRAPHY

Adams, Doug. *Transcendence with the Human Body in Art: Christo, De Staebler, Johns and Segal.* New York: Crossroad, 1991.

Adams, Doug, and Diane Apostolos-Cappadona, eds. *Art as Religious Studies.* New York: Crossroad, 1987.

Addleshaw, G. W. O., and F. Etchells. *The Architectural Setting of Anglican Worship.* London: Faber & Faber, 1948.

African American Experience in Worship and the Arts. New Haven: Yale University Institute of Sacred Music, Worship, and the Arts, 1992.

African American Religion: Research Problems and Resources for the 1990s. New York: Schomburg Center for Research in Black Culture, 1992.

Ahlborn, Richard E. *The Sculpted Saints of a Borderland Mission.* Los Bultos de San Xavier del Bac: Tucson Southwestern Mission Research Center, 1974.

Albanese, Catherine L. "Fisher Kings and Public Places: The Old New Age in the 1990s." *Annals of the American Academy of Political and Social Science* 527 (May 1993): 131–43.

———. *America: Religions and Religion.* Belmont, Cal.: Wadsworth, 1981.

———. *Sons of the Fathers: The Civil Religion of the American Revolution.* Philadelphia: Temple University Press, 1976.

Alloway, Lawrence. "Barnett Newman. The Stations of the Cross and the Subjects of the Artist." In *Abstract Expressionism: A Critical Record,* ed. David Shapiro and Cecile Shapiro. Cambridge, Eng.: Cambridge University Press, 1990.

———. "Color, Culture, the Stations: Notes on the Barnett Newman Memorial Exhibition." *Artforum* 10 (Dec. 1971): 31–39.

Apostolos-Cappadona, Diane. *The Spirit and the Vision: The Influence of Christian Romanticism on the Development of 19th-century American Art.* Atlanta: Scholars University Press, 1995.

———, ed. *Art, Creativity, and the Sacred: An Anthology in Religion and Art.* New York: Crossroad, 1984.

Art & Religion: The Many Faces of Faith. Exh. cat. Philadelphia: The Balch Institute for Ethnic Studies, 1997.

Baigell, Matthew. *Jewish-American Artists and the Holocaust.* New Brunswick, N.J.: Rutgers University Press, 1997.

Bann, Stephen. "Shrines, Curiosities, and the Rhetoric of Display." In *Visual Display: Culture beyond Appearances,* ed. Lynne Cooke and Peter Wollen. Seattle: Bay Press, 1995.

Barnes, Susan J. *The Rothko Chapel. An Act of Faith.* Houston: Rothko Chapel. Distributed by The University of Texas Press, Austin, 1989.

Beardsley, John. *Gardens of Revelation: Environments by Visionary Artists.* New York: Abbeville Press, 1995.

Benes, Peter. *The Masks of Orthodoxy: Folk Gravestone Carving in Plymouth County, Massachusetts, 1689–1805.* Amherst: University of Massachusetts Press, 1977.

———, ed. *New England Meeting House and Church: 1630–1850.* Annual Proceedings of the Dublin Seminar for New England Folklife. Boston: Boston University Press, 1979.

Benes, Peter, and Philip D. Zimmerman. *New England Meeting House and Church, 1630–1850.* Exh. cat. Currier Gallery of Art, Manchester, New Hampshire. Boston: Boston University for the Dublin Seminar for New England Folklife, 1979.

Benson, Cynda L. "Early American Folk Art from the Ephrata Scriptorium." In *Early American Illuminated Manuscripts from the Ephrata Cloister,* exh. cat. Northampton, Mass: Smith College Museum of Art, 1994.

Bjelajac, David. *Washington Allston, Secret Societies, and the Alchemy of Anglo-American Painting.* New York: Cambridge University Press, 1996.

———. *Millennial Desire and the Apocalyptic Vision of Washington Allston.* Washington, D.C.: Smithsonian Institution Press, 1988.

Black, Gregory D. *The Catholic Crusade against the Movies, 1940–1975.* Cambridge, Eng.: Cambridge University Press, 1998.

Blaettler, James, S.J., ed. *The One Chosen: Images of Christ in Recent New York Art.* Exh. cat. New York: Thomas J. Walsh Gallery, 1997.

Bonomi, Patricia U. *Education and Religion in Early America: Gleanings from The New England Primer.* 13th Annual Phi Alpha Theta Distinguished Lecture on History. Albany, N.Y.: Department of History, State University of New York, 1993.

Borhegyi, Stephen F. de. "The Miraculous Shrines of Our Lord of Esquipulas in Guatemala and Chimayó, New Mexico." *El Palacio* 60 (1953): 83–111.

Boyd, Elizabeth. *Popular Arts of Spanish New Mexico.* Santa Fe: Museum of New Mexico Press, 1974.

———. *The New Mexican Santero.* Santa Fe: Museum of New Mexico Press, 1969.

Brew, Kathy. *Concerning the Spiritual: The Eighties.* Exh. cat. Curated by David S. Rubin. San Francisco: San Francisco Art Institute, 1985.

Briggs, Charles. *The Wood Carvings of Cordova, New Mexico: Social Dimensions of an Artistic "Revival."* Knoxville: University of Tennessee Press, 1980.

Brilliant, Richard. *Facing the New World: Jewish Portraits in Colonial and Federal America*. Exh. cat. New York: The Jewish Museum, 1997.

Bronstein, Léo. *Kabbalah and Art*. 2d ed. New Brunswick, N.J.: Transaction Publishers, 1997.

Brooke, John L. *The Refiner's Fire: The Making of Mormon Cosmology, 1644–1844*. Cambridge, Eng.: Cambridge University Press, 1994.

Brown, Frank Burch. *Religious Aesthetics. A Theological Study of Making and Meaning*. Princeton: Princeton University Press, 1989.

Brown, Glen R. "Toward a Topography of the Spiritual in Contemporary Art." *New Art Examiner* 26, no. 6 (March 1999): 23–27.

Buggeln, Gretchen. "Protestant Material Culture and Community in Connecticut, 1785–1840." Ph.D. diss., Yale University, 1995.

Bullock, Steven C. *Revolutionary Brotherhood: Freemasonry and the Transformation of the American Social Order, 1730–1840*. Chapel Hill: University of North Carolina Press, 1996.

Burnham, Patricia Mullan. "The Religious Paintings of John Trumbull: An Anglo-American Experiment." Ph.D. diss., Boston University, 1984.

Bushman, Richard L. *The Refinement of America: Persons, Houses, Cities*. New York: Knopf, 1992.

Butler, Jon. *Awash in a Sea of Faith: Christianizing the American People*. Cambridge, Mass.: Harvard University Press, 1990.

Campo, Juan Eduardo. "American Pilgrimage Landscapes." *Annals of the American Academy of Political and Social Science* 558 (July 1998): 40–56.

Carmack, Noel. "Of Prophets and Pale Horses: Joseph Smith, Benjamin West, and the American Millenarian Tradition." *Dialogue: A Journal of Mormon Thought* 29 (fall 1996): 165–76.

Carmean, A. E., Jr. "The Church Project: Pollock's Passion Themes." *Art in America* 70, no. 6 (summer 1982): 110–20.

Carmer, Carl. "A Panorama of Mormon Life." *Art in America* 58 (May–June 1970): 52–65.

Carrott, Richard G. *The Egyptian Revival: Its Sources, Monuments, and Meaning, 1808–1858*. Berkeley and Los Angeles: University of California Press, 1978.

Chidester, David, and Edward T. Linenthal, eds. *American Sacred Space*. Bloomington: Indiana University Press, 1995.

Classen, Constance. *The Color of Angels: Cosmology, Gender, and the Aesthetic Imagination*. London: Routledge, 1998.

Colbert, Charles. *A Measure of Perfection: Phrenology and the Fine Arts in America*. Chapel Hill: University of North Carolina Press, 1997.

Contemporary Religious Imagery in American Art. Exh. cat. Sarasota: Ringling Museum of Art, 1974.

Cook, John W. "A Willem de Kooning Triptych." *Theological Education* 31, no. 1 (autumn 1994): 59–73.

———. "Sources for the Study of Christianity and the Arts." In *Art as Religious Studies*, ed. Doug Adams and Diane Apostolos-Cappadona. New York: Crossroad, 1987.

Cooper, Jacqueline. "Comprehending the Circle: Wicca as a Contemporary Religion," *New Art Examiner* 26, no. 6 (March 1999): 28–33.

Cosentino, Donald J., ed. *Sacred Arts of Haitian Voudou*. Exh. cat. Los Angeles: UCLA Fowler Museum of Cultural History, 1995.

Coulter, Lane, and Maurice Dixon Jr. *New Mexican Tinwork, 1840–1940*. Albuquerque: University of New Mexico Press, 1990.

Cram, Ralph Adams. *The Catholic Church and Art*. New York: Macmillan, 1930.

Craven, Wayne. *Colonial American Portraiture: The Economic, Religious, Social, Cultural, Philosophical, Scientific, and Aesthetic Foundations*. Cambridge, Eng.: Cambridge University Press, 1986.

Cubbs, Joanne. "Rebels, Mystics, and Outcasts: The Romantic Artist Outsider." In *The Artist Outsider: Creativity and the Bounds of Culture*, ed. Michael D. Hall and Eugene W. Metcalf Jr. Washington, D.C.: Smithsonian Institution Press, 1994.

———. *Religious Visionaries*. Exh. cat. Sheboygan, Wis.: John Michael Kohler Arts Center, 1991.

Curl, James Stevens. *The Art and Architecture of Free Masonry*. Woodstock, N.Y.: The Overlook Press, 1993.

Curran, Kathleen. "The Romanesque Revival, Mural Painting, and Protestant Patronage in America." *Art Bulletin* 81, no. 4 (Dec. 1999): 693–722.

Currier & Ives: Catalogue Raisonné. 2 vols. Detroit: Gale Research Company, 1984.

Curtis, James R. "Miami's Little Havana: Yard Shrines, Cult Religion and Landscape." In *Rituals and Ceremonies in Popular Culture*, ed. Ray B. Browne. Bowling Green: Bowling Green University Popular Press, 1980.

Davidson, Abraham A. *The Eccentrics and Other American Visionary Painters*. New York: E. P. Dutton, 1978.

Davies, Horton, and Hugh Davies. *Sacred Art in a Secular Century*. Collegeville, Minn.: Liturgical Press, 1978.

Davis, John. *The Landscape of Belief: Encountering the Holy Land in Nineteenth-Century American Art and Culture*. Princeton: Princeton University Press, 1996.

———. "Holy Land, Holy People? Photography, Semitic Wannabes, and Chautauqua's Palestine Park." *Prospects: An Annual of American Cultural Studies* 17 (1992): 241–71.

Davis, Norma S. *A Song of Joys: The Biography of Mahonri Mackintosh Young, Sculptor, Painter, Etcher*. Provo, Utah: Brigham Young University Press, 1999.

Day, John A., and Margaret Quintal. "Oscar Howe, 1915–1983: Father of the New Native American Art." *Southwest Art* (June 1984): 52–60.

De Concini, Barbara. "State of the Arts: The Crisis in Meaning in Religion and the Arts." *Christian Century* 108, no. 10 (20–27 March 1991): 323–26.

Desmangles, Leslie G. *The Faces of the Gods: Voudou and Roman Catholicism in Haiti*. Chapel Hill: University of North Carolina Press, 1999.

Dewhurst, C. Kurt, Betty MacDowell, and Marsha MacDowell. *Religious Folk Art in America: Reflections of Faith*. Exh. cat. New York: Museum of American Folk Art, 1983.

Dillenberger, Jane [Daggett]. *Image and Spirit in Sacred and Secular Art*. New York: Crossroad, 1990.

———. *The Religious Art of Andy Warhol*. New York: Continuum, 1998.

Dillenberger, Jane, and John Dillenberger. *Perceptions of the Spirit in Twentieth-Century Art*. Exh. cat. Indianapolis: Indianapolis Museum of Art, 1977.

Dillenberger, Jane, and Joshua C. Taylor, eds. *The Hand and the Spirit: Religious Art in America, 1700–1900*. Exh. cat. Berkeley: University Art Museum, 1972.

Dillenberger, John. *A Theology of Artistic Sensibilities: The Visual Arts and the Church*. New York: Crossroad, 1986.

———. *The Visual Arts and Christianity in America. The Colonial Period through the Nineteenth Century*. Chico, Cal.: Scholars Press, 1984.

———. "The Diversity of Disciplines as a Theological Question: The Visual Arts as Paradigm." *Journal of the American Academy of Religion* 48, no. 2 (June 1980): 233–43.

Dixon, John W. Jr. *Images of Truth: Religion and the Art of Seeing*. Atlanta: Scholars Press, 1996.

———. "What Makes Religious Art Religious?" *Cross Currents* 43, no. 1 (spring 1993): 5–25.

———. "The Bible in American Painting." In *The Bible in American Arts and Letters*, ed. Giles Gunn. Philadelphia: Fortress Press, 1982.

Dockstader, Frederick. *Oscar Howe: A Retrospective Exhibition*. Tulsa, Okla.: Thomas Gilcrease Museum Association, 1982.

Donnelly, Marian C. *The New England Meeting Houses of the Seventeenth Century*. Middletown, Conn.: Wesleyan University Press, 1968.

Doss, Erika. *Elvis Culture: Fans, Faith, and Image*. Lawrence: University Press of Kansas, 1999.

Dresser, Louisa. "The Chapel of the Virgin at Subiaco by Samuel F. B. Morse." *Worcester Art Museum Annual* 4 (1941): 65–71.

Duncan, Carol. *Civilizing Rituals: Inside Public Art Museums*. London: Routledge, 1995.

Egan, Martha. *Relicarios: Devotional Miniatures from the Americas*. Santa Fe: Museum of New Mexico Press, 1993.

Eldredge, Charles C. *American Imagination and Symbolist Painting*. Exh. cat. Grey Art Gallery and Study Center, New York University, 1979.

Espinosa, Jose Edmundo. *Saints in the Valleys: Christian Sacred Images in the History, Life, and Folk Art of Spanish New Mexico*. Albuquerque: University of New Mexico Press, 1967.

Ewers, John C. *Plains Indian Painting: A Description of an Aboriginal Art*. Stanford: Stanford University Press, 1939.

Fabric of Jewish Life: Textiles from the Jewish Museum Collection. Exh. cat. New York: The Jewish Museum, 1977.

Farago, Claire J. "Prints and the Pauper: Artifice, Religion, and Free Enterprise in Popular Sacred Art." In *El Favor de los Santos: The Retablo Collection of New Mexico State University*, exh. cat. Las Cruces: New Mexico State University, 1999.

Farago, Claire J., and Donna Pierce, eds. "Transforming Images: New Mexican Santos between Worlds." Unpublished manuscript.

Fennimore, Donald L. "Religion in America: Metal Objects in Service of the Ritual." *American Art Journal* 10 (Nov. 1978): 20–42.

Finney, Paul Corby, ed. *Seeing beyond the Word: The Visual Arts and Calvinist Tradition*. Grand Rapids: Eerdmans, 1999.

Finster, Howard [as told to Tom Patterson]. *Howard Finster: Stranger from Another World*. New York: Abbeville Press, 1989.

Fitzhugh, William W., and Valérie Chaussonnet, eds. *Anthropology of the North Pacific Rim*. Washington, D.C.: Smithsonian Institution Press, 1994.

Flint, Janet A. *The Way of Good and Evil: Popular Religious Lithographs of Nineteenth-Century America*. Washington, D.C.: National Collection of Fine Arts, Smithsonian Institution, 1972.

Flores-Pena, Ysamur, and Robert J. Evanchuk. *Santería Garments and Altars: Speaking without a Voice*. Jackson, Miss.: University of Mississippi Press, 1997.

Forms for Faith: Art and Architecture of Worship. A Collaborative Exhibition by the Judah L. Magnes Museum and the Interfaith Forum on Religion, Art, and Architecture. Exh. cat. Berkeley: Magnes Museum, 1986.

Franchot, Jenny. "Unseemly Commemoration: Religion, Fragments, and the Icon." *American Literary History* 9, no. 3 (fall 1997): 502–21.

———. *Roads to Rome: The Antebellum Protestant Encounter with Catholicism*. Berkeley and Los Angeles: University of California Press, 1994.

Francis, Richard, ed. *Negotiating Rapture*. Exh. cat. Chicago: Museum of Contemporary Art, 1996.

Frank, Frederick. *New Kingdom of the Saints: Religious Art of New Mexico, 1780–1907*. Santa Fe: Red Crane Books, 1992.

Frantz, Nadine Pence. "Material Culture, Understanding, and Meaning: Writing and Picturing." *Journal of the American Academy of Religion* 66, no. 4 (winter 1998): 791–815.

Freedberg, David. *The Power of Images: Studies in the History and Theory of Response*. Chicago: University of Chicago Press, 1989.

Frishman, Martin, and Hasan-Uddin Khan, eds. *The Mosque: History, Architectural Development, and Regional Diversity*. New York: Thames & Hudson, 1994.

Gambone, Robert L. *Art and Popular Religion in Evangelical America, 1915–1940*. Knoxville: University of Tennessee Press, 1989.

Garvan, Beatrice B., and Charles F. Hummel. *The Pennsylvania Germans: A Celebration of Their Arts, 1683–1850*. Exh. cat. Philadelphia: Philadelphia Museum of Art, 1982.

Gavin, Robin Farwell. *Traditional Arts of Spanish New Mexico: The Hispanic Heritage Wing at the Museum of International Folk Art*. Exh. cat. Santa Fe: Museum of New Mexico Press, 1994.

Gelburd, Gail. *Elihu Vedder: Mystic Figures of the Nineteenth Century*. Hempstead, N.Y.: Hofstra Museum, 1989.

Giffords, Gloria K. *The Art of Private Devotion: Retablo Painting of Mexico*. Exh. cat. The Meadows Museum, Southern Methodist University. Fort Worth: InterCultura, 1991.

Giles, Paul. *American Catholic Arts and Fictions: Culture, Ideology, Aesthetics*. Cambridge, Eng.: Cambridge University Press, 1992.

Gill, Sam. "Color in Navajo Ritual Symbolism: An Evaluation of Methods." *Journal of Anthropological Research* 31 (1975): 350–63.

Glaser, David J. "Transcendence in the Vision of Barnett Newman." *Journal of Aesthetics and Art Criticism* 40, no. 4 (summer 1982): 415–20.

Goethals, Gregor T. "Ritual and the Representation of Power in High and Popular Art." *Journal of Ritual Studies* 4 (summer 1990): 149–77.

———. *The Electronic Golden Calf: Images, Religion, and the Making of Meaning*. Cambridge, Mass: Cowley Publications, 1990.

———. *The TV Ritual: Worship at the Video Altar*. Boston: Beacon Press, 1981.

Goetz, Ronald. "Anselm Kiefer: Art as Atonement." *Christian Century* 105 (23–30 March 1988): 314–20.

Grayson, Ellen Hickey. "Art, Audiences, and the Aesthetics of Social Order in Antebellum America: Rembrandt Peale's *Court of Death*." Ph.D. diss., George Washington University, 1995.

Greeley, Andrew. "Catholics, Fine Arts and The Liturgical Imagination." *America* 174, no. 17 (18 May 1996): 9–12, 14.

Green, Harvey. "Rational Muscle Culture: Religion, Sport, and Photography in Turn-of-the-Century America." In *This Sporting Life, 1878–1991*, ed. Ellen Dugan. Atlanta: High Museum of Art; Seattle: University of Washington Press, 1992.

Greenhouse, Wendy. "Daniel Huntington and the Ideal of Christian Art." *Winterthur Portfolio* 31, nos. 2, 3 (summer/autumn 1996), 103–40.

———. "The American Portrayal of Tudor and Stuart History, 1835–1865." Ph.D. diss., Yale University, 1989.

Greenwald, Alice M. "The Masonic Mizrah and Lamp: Jewish Ritual Art as a Reflection of Cultural Assimilation." *Journal of Jewish Art* 10 (1984): 87–101.

Griffith, James. *Beliefs and Holy Places: A Spiritual Geography of the Pimeria Alta*. Tucson: University of Arizona Press, 1992.

Gunn, Giles, ed. *The Bible in American Arts and Letters*. Philadelphia: Fortress Press, 1982.

Guthrie, Stewart Elliot. *Faces in the Clouds: A New Theory of Religion*. New York: Oxford University Press, 1993.

Gutjahr, Paul. *An American Bible: A History of the Good Book in the United States, 1777–1880*. Stanford: Stanford University Press, 1999.

Gutmann, Joseph. "Jewish Participation in the Visual Arts of Eighteenth- and Nineteenth-Century America." *American Jewish Archives* 15 (April 1963): 21–57.

Haider, Gulzar. "Muslim Space and the Practice of Architecture: A Personal Odyssey." In *Making Muslim Space in North America and Europe*, ed. Barbara Daly Metcalf. Berkeley and Los Angeles: University of California Press, 1996.

Hall, Sarah. *The Colour of Light: Commissioning Stained Glass for a Church*. Chicago: LTP, 1999.

Halle, David, "The Truncated Madonna and Other Modern Catholic Iconography." *Inside Culture: Art and Class in the American Home*. Chicago: University of Chicago Press, 1993.

Hamilton, C. Mark. *Nineteenth-Century Mormon Architecture and City Planning*. New York: Oxford University Press, 1995.

———. "The Salt Lake Temple: A Symbolic Statement of Mormon Doctrine." In *The Mormon People: Their Character and Traditions*, ed. Thomas G. Alexander. Provo, Utah.: Brigham Young University Press, 1980.

Hamilton, John D. *Material Culture of the American Freemasons*. Lexington, Mass: Museum of Our National Heritage, 1994.

Harris, Neil. *The Artist in American Society: The Formative Years, 1790–1860*. Chicago: University of Chicago Press, 1966.

Hartigan, Lynda Roscoe. "Elijah Pierce and James Hampton: One Good Book Begets Another." *Folk Art* 19 (summer 1994): 52–57.

Haseltine, James L. "Mormons and the Visual Arts." *Dialogue: A Journal of Mormon Thought* 1 (summer 1966): 17–29.

Hayden, Dolores. *Seven American Utopias*. Cambridge, Mass.: MIT Press, 1976.

Hayes, Jeffrey R. *Signs of Inspiration: The Art of Prophet William J. Blackmon*. Exh. cat. Patrick and Beatrice Haggerty Museum of Art. Milwaukee: Marquette University, 1999.

Haynes, Deborah. *The Vocation of the Artist*. Cambridge, Eng.: Cambridge University Press, 1997.

Haywood, Robert E. "Heretical Alliance: Claes Oldenburg and the Judson Memorial Church in the 1960s." *Art History* 18, no. 2 (June 1995): 185–212.

Heartney, Eleanor. "Blood, Sex, and Blasphemy: The Catholic Imagination in Contemporary Art." *New Art Examiner* 26, no. 6 (March 1999): 34–39.

———. "Postmodern Heretics." *Art in America* 85, no. 2 (Feb. 1997): 32–39.

Henkes, Robert. *The Spiritual Art of Abraham Rattner: In Search of Oneness*. Lanham, Md.: University Press of America, 1998.

Heyer, George S. *Signs of Our Times: Theological Essays on Art in the Twentieth Century*. Grand Rapids: Eerdmans, 1980.

Hicks, Michael. "Notes on Brigham Young's Aesthetics." *Dialogue: A Journal of Mormon Thought* 16 (winter 1983): 124–30.

Holod, Renata, and Hasan-Uddin Khan. *The Contemporary Mosque: Architects, Patrons, and Designs since the 1950s*. New York: Rizzoli, 1997.

Holt, Elizabeth Gilmore. "Revivalist Themes in American Prints and Folksongs, 1830–1850." In *American Printmaking before 1876: Fact, Fiction and Fantasy*, papers presented at a symposium at the Library of Congress, 12–13 June 1972. Washington, D.C.: Library of Congress, 1975.

Hoover, Stewart M., and Lynn Schofield Clark, eds. *Practicing Religion in the Age of the Media: Explorations in Media, Religion and Culture*. New York: Columbia University Press, 2001.

Huntington, David C. *Art and the Excited Spirit: America in the Romantic Period*. Exh. cat. Ann Arbor: University of Michigan Museum of Art, 1972.

———. *The Landscapes of Frederic Edwin Church: Vision of an American Era*. New York: George Braziller, 1966.

Husch, Gail E. *Something Coming: Apocalyptic Expectation and Mid-Nineteenth-Century American Painting*. Hanover, N.H.: The University Press of New England, 2000.

———. "'Freedom's Holy Cause': History, Religion, and Genre Painting in America, 1840–1860." In *Picturing History: American Painting 1770–1930*, ed. William Ayres. New York: Rizzoli Publications, 1993.

Hutson, James H. *Religion and the Founding of the American Republic*. Exh. cat. Washington, D.C.: Library of Congress, 1998.

Influence of Spiritual Inspiration on American Art: Proceedings of the Seminar Organized by Galleria D'arte Religiosa Moderna Dei Musei Vaticani. Washington, D.C: Smithsonian Institution, 1977.

Irwin, John T. *American Hieroglyphics: The Symbol of the Egyptian Hieroglyphics in the American Renaissance*. Baltimore: Johns Hopkins University Press, 1980.

Isay, David, and Henry Wang. *Holding On: Dreamers, Visionaries, Eccentrics and Other American Heroes*. New York: W. W. Norton, 1996.

Ivey, Paul E. *Prayers in Stone: Christian Science Architecture in the United States, 1894–1930*. Champaign: University of Illinois Press, 1999.

———. "Building a New Religion." *Chicago History* 23, no. 1 (spring 1994): 16–31.

Jewish Art and Culture in Early America. Charleston, S.C.: Piccolo Spoleto, 1981.

John and Mable Ringling Museum of Art. *Contemporary Religious Imagery in American Art*. Exh. cat. Sarasota: Ringling Museum of Art, 1974.

Joselit, Jenna Weissman. *The Wonders of America: Reinventing Jewish Culture, 1880–1950*. New York: Hill and Wang, 1995.

Kalb, Laurie Beth. *Crafting Devotions: Tradition in Contemporary New Mexico Santos*. Albuquerque: University of New Mexico Press, 1994.

———. *Santos Statues and Sculpture: Contemporary Woodcarving from New Mexico*. Los Angeles: Craft and Folk Art Museum, 1988.

Kanof, Avram. *Jewish Ceremonial Art and Religious Observance*. New York: Abrams, 1969.

Kaplan, Stuart R. *The Encyclopedia of Tarot*. 2 vols. New York: U.S. Games Systems, 1978.

Karp, Abraham. *The Jews in America: A Treasury of Art and Literature*. New York: Hugh Lauter Levin, 1994.

Kayser, Stephen, and Guido Schoenberger. *Jewish Ceremonial Art*. 2d ed. Philadelphia: Jewish Publication Society of America, 1969.

Keifert, Patrick R. "Truth and Taste on Sunday Morning." *Dialog* 25, no. 3 (summer 1986): 193–200.

Kelly, Susan H., and Anne C. Williams. *A Grave Business: New England Gravestone Rubbings: A Selection*. New Haven: Art Resources of Connecticut, 1979.

Kibbey, Ann. *The Interpretation of Material Shapes in Puritanism: A Study of Rhetoric, Prejudice, and Violence*. Cambridge, Eng.: Cambridge University Press, 1986.

Kirk, John T. *The Shaker World: Art, Life, Belief*. New York: Abrams, 1997.

Kirschner, Ann. "From Hebron to Saron: The Religious Transformation of an Ephrata Convent." *Winterthur Portfolio* 32, no. 1: 39–63.

Kirshenblatt-Gimblett, Barbara. *Destination Culture: Tourism, Museums, and Heritage*. Berkeley and Los Angeles: University of California Press, 1998.

Kleeblatt, Norman, and Gerard Wertkin. *The Jewish Heritage in American Folk Art*. New York: Universe Books, 1984.

Kretzmann, Paul Edward. *Christian Art in the Place and in the Form of Lutheran Worship*. St. Louis: Concordia, 1921.

Kubler, George. *Santos: An Exhibition of the Religious Folk Art of New Mexico*. Exh. cat. Fort Worth: Amon Carter Museum, 1964.

Kugelmass, Jack. "Jewish Icons: Envisioning the Self in Images of the Other." In *Jews and Other Differences: The New Jewish Cultural Studies*, ed. Jonathan Boyarin and Daniel Boyarin. Minneapolis and London: University of Minnesota Press, 1997.

Landres, J. Shawn. "Public Art as Sacred Space: Asian American Community Murals in Los Angeles." *Religion and the Arts* 1, no. 3 (summer 1997): 6–26.

Lange, Yvonne. "Lithography, an Agent of Technological Change in Religious Folk Art: A Thesis." *Western Folklore* 33, no. 1 (Jan. 1974): 51–64.

Lears, T. J. Jackson. *No Place of Grace: Antimodernism and the Transformation of American Culture, 1880–1920*. Chicago: University of Chicago Press, 1981.

Linenthal, Edward Tabor. *Sacred Ground: Americans and Their Battlefields*. 2d ed. Urbana: University of Illinois Press, 1993.

Lipsey, Roger. *An Art of Our Own. The Spiritual in Twentieth-Century Art*. Boston: Shambhala, 1989.

Locating the Spirit: Religion and Spirituality in African-American Art. Exh. cat. Washington D.C.: Anacostia Museum, 1999.

Ludington, Townsend. *Seeking the Spiritual: The Paintings of Marsden Hartley*. Ithaca, N.Y.: Cornell University Press, 1998.

Ludwig, Allan I. *Graven Images: New England Stonecarving and Its Symbols, 1650–1815*. Middletown, Conn.: Wesleyan University Press, 1966.

Macdonald, Sharon, and Gordon Fyfe, eds. *Theorizing Museums: Representing Identity and Diversity in a Changing World*. Oxford: Blackwell/The Sociological Review, 1996.

Macnair, Peter, Robert Joseph, and Bruce Grenville. *Down from the Shimmering Sky: Masks of the Northwest Coast*. Vancouver, B.C.: Vancouver Art Gallery, 1998.

Martin, Joel W., and Conrad E. Ostwalt Jr., eds. *Screening the Sacred*. Boulder: Westview Press, 1995.

Marvin, Carolyn, and David Engle. *Blood Sacrifice and the Nation: Totem Rituals and the American Flag*. Cambridge, Eng.: Cambridge University Press, 1998.

Masonic Symbols in American Decorative Arts. Lexington, Mass.: Scottish Rite Masonic Museum of Our National Heritage, 1976.

Mather, Eleanore Price. *Edward Hicks: His Peaceable Kingdoms and Other Paintings*. Newark: University of Delaware Press, 1983.

Maurer, Evan M. *Visions of the People: A Pictorial History of Plains Indian Life*. Exh. cat. Minneapolis: Minneapolis Institute of Arts, 1992.

May, John, ed. *Image and Likeness: Religious Visions in American Film Classics*. New York: Paulist Press, 1986.

McCloud, Aminah Beverly. "'This is a Muslim Home': Signs of Difference in the African-American Row House." In *Making Muslim Space in North America and Europe*, ed. Barbara Daly Metcalf. Berkeley and Los Angeles: University of California Press, 1996.

McDannell, Colleen. *Material Christianity: Religion and Popular Culture in America*. New Haven: Yale University Press, 1995.

———. "Interpreting Things: Material Culture and American Religion." *Religion* 21 (1991): 371–87.

———. *The Christian Home in Victorian America, 1840–1900*. Bloomington: Indiana University Press, 1986.

Metcalf, Barbara Daly, ed. *Making Muslim Space in North America and Europe*. Berkeley and Los Angeles: University of California Press, 1996.

Miles, Margaret Ruth. *Seeing and Believing: Religion and Values in the Movies*. Boston: Beacon Press, 1996.

Miller, Angela. *The Empire of the Eye: Landscape Representation and American Cultural Politics, 1825–1875*. Ithaca: Cornell University Press, 1993.

Milroy, Elizabeth. "Consummatum est . . . : A Reassessment of Thomas Eakins's Crucifixion of 1880." *Art Bulletin* 71 (June 1989): 269–84.

Milspaw, Yvonne J. "Protestant Home Shrines: Icon and Image." *New York Folklore* 12, nos. 3, 4 (1986): 119–36.

Mitchell, W. J. T. *Picture Theory*. Chicago: University of Chicago Press, 1994.

———. *Iconology: Image, Text, Ideology*. Chicago: University of Chicago Press, 1986.

———. "What Do Pictures *Really* Want?" *OCTOBER* 77 (summer 1996): 71–82.

Moran, J. Anthony. *Pilgrim's Guide to America: U.S. Catholic Shrines and Centers of Devotion*. Huntington, Ind.: Our Sunday Visitor Publishing Division, 1992.

Morgan, David. "Religion and American LIFE: Imaging Religion in America's Premier Picture Magazine." In *Looking at LIFE*, ed. Erika Doss. Washington, D.C.: Smithsonian Institution Press, 2001.

———. "Spirit and Medium: The Video Art of Bill Viola." *Image* 26 (spring 2000): 29–39.

———. *Protestants and Pictures: Religion, Visual Culture, and the Age of American Mass Production*. New York: Oxford University Press, 1999.

———. *Visual Piety: A History and Theory of Popular Religious Images*. Berkeley and Los Angeles: University of California Press, 1998.

———. "Ambiguous Icons: The Art of Ed Paschke." *Image* 17 (fall 1997): 31–44.

———. "Secret Wisdom and Self-Effacement: The Spiritual in Art in the Modern Age." In *Negotiating Rapture*, exh. cat., ed. Richard Francis. Chicago: Museum of Contemporary Art, 1996.

———, ed. *Icons of American Protestantism: The Art of Warner Sallman*. New Haven: Yale University Press, 1996.

Morgan, David, and Sally M. Promey. *Exhibiting the Visual Culture of American Religions*. Exh. cat. Valparaiso, Ind.: Brauer Museum of Art, 2000.

Murtagh, William J. *Moravian Architecture and Town Planning: Bethlehem, Pennsylvania, and Other Eighteenth-Century American Settlements*. Philadelphia: University of Pennsylvania Press, 1997.

Nelson, Robert S., and Richard Schiff, eds. *Critical Terms for Art History*. Chicago: University of Chicago Press, 1996.

Neuerburg, Norman. "The Function of Prints in California Missions." *Southern California Quarterly* 55, no. 3 (fall 1985): 263–80.

Novak, Barbara. *Nature and Culture: American Landscape and Painting, 1825–1875*. Rev. ed. New York: Oxford University Press, 1995.

Numrich, Paul David. *Old Wisdom in the New World: Americanization in Two Immigrant Theravada Buddhist Temples*. Knoxville: University of Tennessee Press, 1996.

Olalquiaga, Celeste. "Holy Kitschen: Collecting Religious Junk from the Street." In *Megalopolis: Contemporary Cultural Sensibilities*. Minneapolis: University of Minneapolis Press, 1992.

Olmos, Margarite Fernandez, and Lizabeth Paravisini-Gebert, eds. *Sacred Possessions: Voudou, Santeria, Obeah, and the Caribbean*. New Brunswick, N.J.: Rutgers University Press, 1997.

Oman, Richard G. "Sources for Mormon Visual Arts." In *Mormon Americana: A Guide to Sources and Collections in the United States*, ed. David J. Whittaker. Provo, Utah.: BYU Studies, 1980.

Orsi, Robert A., ed. *Gods of the City: Religion and the American Urban Landscape*. Bloomington: Indiana University Press, 1999.

O'Shaughnessy, Michael. *A Kingdom of Saints: Early Bultos of New Mexico*. Santa Fe: Red Crane Books, 1993.

Paine, Crispin, ed. *Godly Things: Museums, Objects, and Religion*. London and New York: Leicester University Press, 2000.

Perlmutter, Dawn, and Debra Koppman, eds. *Reclaiming the Spiritual in Art: Contemporary Cross-Cultural Perspectives*. Albany: State University of New York Press, 1999.

Pistolesi, Donald, ed. *The Body on the Cross*, exh. cat., trans. Neil Kroetsch and Jeffrey Moore. Paris: Reunion des musées nationaux. Montreal: Montreal Museum of Fine Arts, 1992.

Powell, Kirsten Hoving. "Resurrecting Content in De Kooning's Easter Monday." *Smithsonian Studies in American Art* 4, nos. 3–4 (summer/fall 1990): 87–101.

Price, Joseph L. "Expressionism and Ultimate Reality: Paul Tillich's Theology of Art." *Soundings* 69 (winter 1986): 479–98.

Promey, Sally M. "Pictorial Ambivalence and American Protestantism." In *Crossroads: Art and Religion in American Life*, ed. Glenn Wallach and Alberta Arthurs. New York: The New Press, 2001.

———. *Painting Religion in Public: John Singer Sargent's "Triumph of Religion" at the Boston Public Library*. Princeton: Princeton University Press, 1999.

———. "Sargent's Truncated *Triumph*: Art and Religion at the Boston Public Library, 1890–1925." *Art Bulletin* 79, no. 2 (June 1997): 217–50.

———. "Interchangeable Art: Warner Sallman and the Critics of Mass Culture." In *Icons of American Protestantism: The Art of Warner Sallman*, ed. David Morgan. New Haven: Yale University Press, 1996.

———. "The Ribband of Faith: George Inness, Color Theory, and the Swedenborgian Church." *The American Art Journal* 26, nos. 1, 2 (1994): 44–65.

———. *Spiritual Spectacles: Vision and Image in Mid-Nineteenth-Century Shakerism*. Bloomington: Indiana University Press, 1993.

———. "Celestial Visions: Shaker Images and Art Historical Method." *American Art* 7, no. 2 (spring 1993): 78–99.

Pyne, Kathleen. *Art and the Higher Life: Painting and Evolutionary Thought in Late Nineteenth-Century America*. Austin: University of Texas Press, 1996.

———. "John Twatchman and the Therapeutic Landscape." In *John Twatchman: Connecticut Landscapes*, exh. cat. Washington: National Gallery of Art, 1989.

Raguin, Virginia. *Glory in Glass. Stained Glass in the United States: Origins, Variety, and Preservation*. Exh. cat. New York: American Bible Society, 1999.

———. *Santos: Devotional Images from the American Southwest*. Exh. cat. Worcester, Mass.: Iris and B. Gerald Cantor Art Gallery, 1992.

Rand, Harry. "The Potential of Scripture's Images: From Genesis to Abstract Expressionism." *Religion and the Arts* 1, no. 3 (summer 1997): 46–72.

Rashall, Jacob. *Jewish Artists in America*. New York: Vantage Press, 1967.

Regier, Kathleen J., ed. *The Spiritual Image in Modern Art*. Wheaton, Ill.: A Quest Book, The Theosophical Publishing House, 1987.

"Religion and the Visual Arts: A Case Study." *Religion and Intellectual Life*, 1, no. 1, with contributions by John W. Cook, Giles Gunn, John Dillenberger, and John W. Dixon Jr. (fall 1983): 3–103.

Religion, the Arts, Artifacts and Museums among the Indians of the Americas. Salt Lake City: American West Center, University of Utah, 1976.

Riess, Jana. "Stripling Warriors Choose the Right: The Cultural Engagements of Contemporary Mormon Kitsch." *Sunstone* (June 1999): 36–47.

Roberts, Allen D. "Religious Architecture of the LDS Church: Influences and Changes since 1847." *Utah Historical Quarterly* 43 (summer 1975): 301–27.

Rochelle, Mercedes. *Post-Biblical Saints Art Index: A Locator of Paintings, Sculptures, Mosaics, Icons, Frescoes, Manuscript Illuminations, Sketches, Woodcuts, and Engravings, Created from* the 4th Century to 1950, with a Directory of the Institutions Holding Them. Jefferson, N.C.: McFarland, 1994.

Rosenak, Chuck, and Jan Rosenak. *Museum of American Folk Art Encyclopedia of Twentieth-Century American Folk Art and Artists*. New York: Abbeville Press, 1990.

Sack, Daniel. *White Bread Protestants: Food and Religion in American Culture*. New York: St. Martin's Press, 2000.

Sacred Images in Secular Art. Exh. cat. New York: Whitney Museum of American Art, 1986.

Santos: An Exhibition of Holy Images Predominantly from New Mexico, Mexico, and South America. Exh. cat. Fullerton: California State University, 1974.

Sarna, Jonathan. "Seating and the American Synagogue." In *Belief and Behavior: Essays in the New Religious History*, ed. P. R. Vandermeer and R. P. Swierenga. New Brunswick, N.J.: Rutgers University Press, 1991.

Sarna, Jonathan, and Ellen Smith, eds. *The Jews of Boston*. Boston: Combined Jewish Philanthropies of Greater Boston, 1995.

Schjeldahl, Peter. "Rothko and Belief." *Art in America* 67 (April 1979): 79–85.

Schmidt, Leigh Eric. *Consumer Rites: The Buying and Selling of American Holidays*. Princeton: Princeton University Press, 1995.

Schubel, Vernon James. "Karbala as Sacred Space among North American Shi'a: 'Every Day Is Ashura, Everywhere Is Karbala.'" In *Making Muslim Space in North America and Europe*, ed. Barbara Daly Metcalf. Berkeley and Los Angeles: University of California Press, 1996.

Sciorra, Joseph. "Yard Shrines and Sidewalk Altars of New York's Italian Americans." In *Perspectives in Vernacular Architecture, III*, ed. Thomas Carter and Bernard L. Herman. Columbia: University of Missouri Press, 1989.

Seager, Richard Hughes. *Buddhism in America*. New York: Columbia University Press, 2000.

Sears, John. *Sacred Places: American Tourist Attractions in the Nineteenth Century*. New York: Oxford University Press, 1989.

Seerveld, Calvin. *A Christian Critique of Art and Literature*. Toronto: Association for Reformed Scientific Studies, 1968.

Shelley, Donald A. *The Fraktur-Writings or Illuminated Manuscripts of the Pennsylvania Germans*. Allentown, Penn.: Pennsylvania German Folklore Society, 1961.

Silber, Elisabeth G. *The Visual Arts Philosophy of Roman Catholicism as Manifested in the Works of Four Commissioned Artists Completed for the 1987 Sanctuary of St. Rita's Catholic Church*. Denton: University of North Texas Press, 1989.

Simpson, Moira B. *Making Representations: Museums in the Post-Colonial Era*. London and New York: Routledge, 1996.

Sinnott, Edmund M. *Meetinghouse & Church in Early New England*. New York: McGraw-Hill, 1963.

Skerry, Janine, and Jeanne V. Sloane. "Images of Politics and Religion on Silver Engraved by Joseph Leddel." *The Magazine Antiques* 141 (March 1992): 490–99.

Smith, Barbara Sweetland. *Heaven on Earth: Orthodox Treasures of Siberia and North America*. Anchorage: Anchorage Museum of History and Art, 1994.

Smith, Ellen. "Portraits of a Community: The Image and Experience of Early American Jews." In *Facing the New World: Jewish Portraits in Colonial and Federal America*, exh. cat., ed. Richard Brilliant. New York: The Jewish Museum, 1997.

———. *On Common Ground: The Boston Jewish Experience, 1620–1980.* Exh. cat. Waltham, Mass.: American Jewish Historical Society, 1980.

Smith, Jane I. *Islam in America.* New York: Columbia University Press, 1999.

The Spirit within: Northwest Coast Native Art from the John H. Hauberg Collection. New York: Rissoli; Seattle: Seattle Art Museum, 1995.

The Spiritual in Art: Abstract Painting, 1890–1985. Exh. cat. Los Angeles: Los Angeles County Museum of Art, 1986.

Staker, Mark L. "By Their Works Ye Shall Know Them: The World View Expressed in Mormon Folk Art." *BYU Studies* 35, no. 3 (1995–96): 75–94.

Stanton, Phoebe B. *The Gothic Revival and American Church Architecture: An Episode in Taste, 1840–1856.* Baltimore: Johns Hopkins University Press, 1968.

Stein, Roger B. "Thomas Smith's Self-Portrait: Image/Text as Artifact." *Art Journal* 44 (winter 1984): 316–27.

———. *John Ruskin and Aesthetic Thought in America, 1840–1900.* Cambridge, Mass.: Harvard University Press, 1967.

St. George, Robert Blair. *Conversing By Signs: The Poetics of Implication in Colonial New England Culture.* Chapel Hill: University of North Carolina Press, 1998.

Stocking, George W., Jr., ed. *Objects and Others: Essays on Museums and Material Culture. History of Anthropology.* Vol. 3. Madison: University of Wisconsin Press, 1985.

Stone, Lisa, and Jim Zanzi. *Sacred Spaces and Other Places: A Guide to Grottos and Sculptural Environments in the Upper Midwest.* Chicago: School of the Art Institute of Chicago Press, 1994.

Stott, Annette. "Transformative Triptychs in Multicultural America." *Art Journal* 57, no. 1 (spring 1998): 55–63.

Swanson, Wayne R. *The Christ Child Goes to Court.* Philadelphia: Temple University Press, 1990.

Sweeney, Kevin M. "Meetinghouses, Town Houses, and Churches: Changing Perceptions of Sacred and Secular Space in Southern New England, 1720–1850." *Winterthur Portfolio* 28, no. 1 (spring 1993): 59–93.

Sweetman, John E. *The Oriental Obsession: Islamic Inspiration in British and American Art and Architecture, 1500–1920.* New York: Cambridge University Press, 1988.

Szabo, Joyce M. *Howling Wolf and the History of Ledger Art.* Albuquerque: University of New Mexico Press, 1994.

Taylor, Joshua C. "The Religious Impulse in American Art." In *Papers in American Art,* ed. John C. Milley. Mapleshade, N.J.: Edinburgh Press, 1976.

Taylor, Mark C. *Disfiguring: Art, Architecture, Religion.* Chicago: University of Chicago, 1992.

———, ed. *Critical Terms for Religious Studies.* Chicago: University of Chicago Press, 1998.

Thompson, Robert Farris. *Face of the Gods: Art and Altars of Africa and the African Americas.* Exh. cat. New York: The Museum for African Art; Munich: Prestel, 1993.

Thompson, Vivian Alpert. *A Mission in Art: Recent Holocaust Works in America.* Macon, Ga.: Mercer University Press, 1988.

Treib, Marc. *Sanctuaries of Spanish New Mexico.* Berkeley and Los Angeles: University of California Press, 1993.

Truettner, William H., and Alan Wallach, eds. *Thomas Cole: Landscape into History.* Exh. cat.

New Haven: Yale University Press; Washington, D.C.: National Museum American Art, 1994.

Truettner, William H., and Roger B. Stein, eds. *Picturing Old New England: Image and Memory.* Exh. cat. Washington, D.C.: National Museum of American Art, 1999.

Tweed, Thomas A. *Our Lady of the Exile: Diasporic Religion at a Cuban Shrine in Miami.* New York: Oxford University Press, 1997.

Tweed, Thomas A., and Stephen Prothero, eds. *Asian Religions in America: A Documentary History.* New York: Oxford University Press, 1999.

Upton, Dell. *Holy Things and Profane: Anglican Parish Churches in Colonial Virginia.* 1986. Reprint. New Haven: Yale University Press, 1997.

Verplanck, Anne. "Facing Philadelphia: The Social Functions of Silhouettes, Miniatures, and Daguerreotypes, 1760–1860." Ph.D. diss., University of California, Berkeley, 1996.

Walker, James R. *Lakota Belief and Ritual.* Ed. Raymond J. DeMallie and Elaine A. Jahner. Lincoln: University of Nebraska Press, 1980.

Ward, Barbara McLean. "In a Feasting Posture: Communion Vessels and Community Values in Seventeenth- and Eighteenth-Century New England." *Winterthur Portfolio* 23, no. 1 (spring 1988): 1–24.

Weekley, Carolyn J. *The Kingdoms of Edward Hicks.* Exh. cat. Abby Aldrich Rockefeller Folk Art Center/Colonial Williamsburg Foundation. New York: Abrams, 1999.

Welch, John W., and Doris R. Dant, eds. *The Book of Mormon Paintings of Minerva Teichert.* Provo, Utah.: BYU Studies, 1997.

West, W. Richard, et al. *The Changing Presentation of the American Indian: Museums and Native Cultures.* Seattle: University of Washington Press, 1999.

White, James F. *Protestant Worship and Church Architecture: Theological and Historical Considerations.* New York: Oxford University Press, 1964.

Wilcox, D., and W. Masse, eds. *The Protohistoric Period in the North American Southwest, A.D. 1450–1700.* Tempe: University of Arizona Press, 1981.

Williams, Peter W. *Houses of God: Region, Religion, and Architecture in the United States.* Urbana: University of Illinois, 1997.

Willis-Braithwaite, Deborah. *VanDerZee, Photographer, 1886–1983.* New York: Abrams, 1993.

Winston, Diane. *Red-Hot and Righteous: The Urban Religion of the Salvation Army.* Cambridge, Mass.: Harvard University Press, 1999.

Wischnitzer, Rachel. *Synagogue Architecture in the United States: History and Interpretation.* Philadelphia: Jewish Publication Society, 1955.

Wolf, Edwin, II. "*The Prodigal Son* in England and America: A Century of Change." In *Eighteenth-Century Prints in Colonial America: To Educate and Decorate,* ed. Joan D. Dolmetsch. Williamsburg: The Colonial Williamsburg Foundation, 1979.

Wolterstorff, Nicholas. *Art in Action. Toward a Christian Aesthetic.* Grand Rapids: Eerdmans, 1980.

Wroth, William. *Images of Penance, Images of Mercy: Southwestern Santos in the Late Nineteenth Century.* Exh. cat. Norman: University of Oklahoma Press, 1991.

Wuthnow, Robert. *Practicing Spirituality: The Way of the Artist.* Berkeley and Los Angeles: University of California Press, 2000.

Yoder, Don. *Discovering American Folklife: Studies in Ethnic, Religious, and Regional Culture*. Ann Arbor: UMI Research Press, 1990.

Young, Chloe Hamilton. *Contemporary Religious Painting in America*. Exh. cat. Oberlin: Allen Memorial Art Museum, 1949.

Young, M. Jane. *Signs from the Ancestors: Zuni Cultural Symbolism and Perceptions of Rock Art*. Albuquerque: University of New Mexico Press, 1988.

Zalesch, Saul. "The Religious Art of Benziger Brothers." *American Art* 13, no. 2 (summer 1999): 58–79.

ARCHIVES AND COLLECTIONS

The study of religious visual culture relies heavily on access to images, objects, and archives. There are literally hundreds of collections around the country that offer important resources. The purpose of this short list of profiles is to provide information about the range of a few important collections and archives, with the hope that this will encourage researchers to seek out these and other institutions.

ADVENTIST HERITAGE CENTER
Andrews University
Berrien Springs, MI 49104-1400
phone: 616-471-3274
fax: 616-471-6166
e-mail: ahc@andrews.edu
www.andrews.edu/library/collections/departments/ahc

A major repository of Seventh-Day Adventist materials, the Adventist Heritage Center at Andrews University collects items in various media produced between 1830 and the present. The AHC holds more than 600 Seventh-Day Adventist periodicals, 30,000 photographs and 6,000 audio-visual materials. In addition to personal papers and other manuscripts, the AHC also maintains an extensive Bible collection. The George Suhrie Bible Collection consists of 132 Bibles and examples of scripture. The Adventist Evangelical Media Archives contains the historical records of major radio and television programs—including *Voice of Prophecy, Faith for*

Today, and *It Is Written*—as well as evangelical materials such as glass slides, cloth charts, and handbills.

AMERICAN ANTIQUARIAN SOCIETY

185 Salisbury Street
Worcester, MA 01609
phone: 508-755-5221
www.mwa.org

The American Antiquarian Society, founded in 1812, collects materials related to American history and culture dating from settlement until 1877. This research library maintains an important collection of objects related to American religious life, including a selection of illustrated Bibles, religious literature, and photographs. The substantial print collection features images of biblical scenes, the life of Jesus, and portraits of clergy as well as reproductions of church buildings. Sunday school rewards of merit, children's primers, sentiment cards, and greeting cards marking the celebration of Easter and Christmas are preserved at the AAS, as are literary annuals and tract society publications produced for religious organizations. The manuscript division also maintains a collection of sermons.

AMERICAN BIBLE SOCIETY

1865 Broadway
New York, NY 10023
phone: 212-408-1200
www.americanbible.org

Founded in 1816, the American Bible Society is a Christian organization which preserves, translates, and distributes the Christian scriptures. The ABS maintains a library as well as an exhibition space, and produces printed versions of the Bible as well as a variety of materials in video, CD-ROM, and Internet formats. The library boasts the largest collection of printed Christian scriptural materials in the Western world. Particularly notable are the first illustrated Bible printed in America, produced by Isaiah Thomas in 1791 in Worcester, Massachusetts, and the *Harper's Illuminated Bible* of 1846. The ABS archives also contain all of the original drawings for the popular *Good News for Modern Man* edition of the Bible. Additionally, the ABS preserves a substantial collection of nineteenth-century photographs documenting important events in American Protestantism.

AMERICAN JEWISH ARCHIVES

Jacob Rader Marcus Center
Hebrew Union College—Jewish Institute of Religion
3101 Clifton Avenue
Cincinnati, OH 45220
phone: 513-221-1875
fax: 513-221-7812
www.huc.edu/aja

This important archive holds over 650 major manuscript collections and close to 14,000 smaller collections of materials. In addition to manuscript holdings, AJA preserves substantial collections (5,000 linear feet) of ephemeral materials and artifacts, such as newspapers; pamphlets and brochures; broadsides; photographs; audio and video recordings of religious services, lectures, and oral histories; genealogies; papers; and microfilm.

AMERICAN JEWISH HISTORICAL SOCIETY

Massachusetts office	New York office
(New England collection)	(national collection)
2 Thornton Road	15 West 16th Street
Waltham, MA 02453	New York, NY 10011
phone: 781-891-8110	phone: 212-294-6160
fax: 781-899-9208	fax: 212-294-6161
www.ajhs.org	www.ajhs.org

Founded in 1892, the American Jewish Historical Society is the world's oldest archive, library, and museum dedicated to the cultural, political, and religious life of American Jewry. AJHS's collections total almost 40 million documents. Archival materials include extensive personal papers and institutional records, including the Emma Lazarus papers and documents from the American Jewish Congress. The A. S. W. Rosenbach collection of Judaica Americana features more than 350 books and pamphlets published before 1850. The AJHS also holds the first Hebrew books and Jewish prayer books published in America. The museum division of the AJHS maintains one of the largest national collections of Jewish visual culture, including portraits, miniatures, Yiddish theater, and film posters, sheet music, and Rosh Hashanah greeting cards.

This noncirculating, closed stack resource is open to researchers, with prior appointment strongly recommended.

ARCHIVES OF AMERICAN ART

Smithsonian Institution
Washington, DC 20560-0937
phone: 202-314-3900
www.archivesofamericanart.si.edu

The Archives of American Art has been part of the Smithsonian Institution since 1970. It is the largest collection of documents related to the visual arts of the United States from colonial times to the present. Holdings total approximately 13 million items, including letters, diaries, photographs, oral histories, gallery and museum records, exhibition and auction catalogues, and scrapbooks and sketchbooks. Documents dating to the first half of the twentieth century are most heavily represented and include the records of the 1913 Armory show as well as extensive materials relating to the federal art programs of the New Deal. Also notable is the Tomás Ybarra-Frausto Research Material on Chicano Art, which chronicles murals, posters, cholos, altars, santos, and santeros as related to Mexican and Chicano culture.

ASIAN ART MUSEUM OF SAN FRANCISCO
Golden Gate Park
San Francisco, CA 94118
phone: 415-379-8800
www.asianart.org

This collection consists of over 12,000 objects representing the arts of China, India, Japan, Iran, Korea, the Himalayas, and Southeast Asia. While this collection consists of predominantly Asian, rather than Asian-American, materials, it provides significant contextual and historical background for engagement of the latter. The Asian Art Museum Library, with over 30,000 titles and 225 periodical subscriptions, is an important center for the study of Asian art and culture. The library is open to visitors by prior appointment only (phone: 415-379-8826).

BEINECKE RARE BOOK AND MANUSCRIPT LIBRARY
P.O. Box 208240
New Haven, CT 06520-8240
phone: 203-432-2972
www.library.yale.edu

Part of the Yale University library system, the Beinecke collects early manuscripts and rare books on a variety of topics, including theology and Western Americana. The Western Americana collection comprises books, manuscripts, maps, art, prints, photographs, and ephemera related to western expansion in the United States through the First World War. Particularly significant are documents related to Native American history and early Mormonism. The Beinecke is also a valuable resource for government surveys related to expansion in the nineteenth century.

BOSTON ATHENAEUM LIBRARY
Ten and a Half Beacon Street
Boston, MA 02108
phone: 617-227-0270
fax: 617-227-5266

Established in 1807, the Athenaeum maintains a library of more than half a million volumes that focus on Boston and New England history as well as American literature and fine arts.

Given to the ministers of King's Chapel by William and Mary, the important King's Chapel Collection contains biblical commentaries, sermons, ecclesiastical works, editions of the Church Fathers from the seventeenth century, and features Walton's *Biblia Polyglotta*. The Athenaeum maintains a consistent record of the cultural life of Boston from the late eighteenth century as well as an admirable collection of early Boston newspapers. Other highlights include part of the personal library of Jean Lefebvre de Cheverus, the first Catholic bishop of Boston, and eighteenth- and nineteenth-century tracts documenting American political and religious history. The Henry Rowe Schoolcraft collection features more than 150 volumes, and contains early Native American primers, Bibles, spelling books, and dictionaries. The Athenaeum also collects broadsides, prints, and photographs.

BOSTON PUBLIC LIBRARY
700 Boylston Street
Copley Square
Boston, MA 12117
phone: 617-536-5400
www.bpl.org

The Boston Public Library archives many rich resources for students of visual culture and religion. Especially notable are its Fine Arts, Rare Books, and Prints and Drawings Departments and its Research Library Special Collections. The Fine Arts Department, for example, holds materials related to the city's visual, material, and architectural histories, including the papers of leading church architects, sculptors, and producers of stained glass as well as a substantial collection of early art reproduction catalogues. Of particular interest might be: the Boston/New England Art Archives; the Boston Picture File (photographs, postcards, and clippings related to Boston's built environment, including houses of worship and religious institutions); the Charles J. Connick and Associates (1913–86) Stained Glass Studio Archives; the Ralph Adams Cram Collection; the Cram, Goodhue, and Ferguson/Cram and Ferguson Architectural Firm Collections; the John Evans and Company Architectural Sculpture Firm Collections; the Bertram Grosvenor Goodhue (1869–1924) Collection; the Maginnis and Walsh Collections (representing the archives of these leading designers of American Roman Catholic buildings); the Museum of Fine Arts Picture Collection; the Peabody and Stearns Collection; and the William G. Preston (1842–1910) Collection. The Rare Books and Manuscripts Division holds, for example, the Josiah H. Benton Collection on the origin and growth of the *Book of Common Prayer* (including such rare items as the *Mohawk Prayer Book* of 1715); the Rev. Theodore Parker Collection (20,000 volumes including works on religion and philosophy, antislavery tracts, and Parker's complete writings); the Rev. Thomas Prince Collection (2,000 volumes including *The Bay Psalm Book*, Eliot's *Indian Bible*, and many Mather and Cotton tracts); and the Sabatier Collection of Franciscana (4,000 volumes including illustrated Franciscan periodicals).

THE CONGREGATIONAL LIBRARY
14 Beacon Street, #207
Boston, MA 02108
phone: 617-523-0470

This collection contains 225,000 books and pamphlets, with current American and British religious materials added every week. In addition to printed materials, the Congregational Library also maintains holdings of church music, religious art, and literature. Archival materials include documents pertaining to Congregational Councils and other church organizations, local history, early manuscripts, church architecture, hymns, sermons, Bibles, and theological works. Particularly noteworthy are the fifteenth-century Chained Bible and John Eliot's Indian Bible. This circulating library is open to the public.

DISCIPLES OF CHRIST HISTORICAL SOCIETY

1101 Nineteenth Avenue South

Nashville, TN 37212

phone: 615-327-1444

http://users.aol.com/dishistsoc/index.htm

The Disciples of Christ Historical Society was founded in 1941 for the purpose of collecting and preserving for study materials relating to the work of Thomas and Alexander Campbell, Barton Stone, and other religious pioneers. The Historical Society contains the largest collection of material of the Campbell-Stone Movement in the world and a significant collection in American Protestantism.

FREER GALLERY OF ART AND ARTHUR M. SACKLER GALLERY—
NATIONAL MUSEUM OF ASIAN ART FOR THE UNITED STATES

Arthur M. Sackler Gallery	Freer Gallery of Art
1050 Independence Avenue, SW	Jefferson Drive at 12th Street, SW
Washington, D.C. 20560	Washington, D.C. 20560
phone: 202-357-3200	phone: 202-357-4880
www.asia.si.edu	www.asia.si.edu

Within the Smithsonian Institution, the Freer and Sackler Galleries hold important collections of Asian visual and material culture. The Freer Gallery also houses an important collection of American art and related archival materials. Both institutions are significant venues for the study and presentation of Asian art (and, consequently, Asian religions) in the United States.

THE FRICK LIBRARY

10 East 71st Street (between Madison and Fifth Avenues)

New York, NY 10021-4967

phone: 212-288-8700

fax: 212-879-2091

e-mail: info@frick.org

www.frick.org

The library at the Frick Collection was founded in 1920 by Helen Clay Frick. It focuses primarily on collecting materials relating to European and American art, and possesses auction catalogues and an extensive photoarchive. The archival and special collections include gallery archives, photographs of artists and their studios, and the personal papers of important art critics and scholars.

THE GENERAL COMMISSION ON ARCHIVES AND HISTORY
FOR THE UNITED METHODIST CHURCH

36 Madison Avenue (on the campus of Drew University)

P.O. Box 127

Madison, NJ 07940

phone: 973-408-3189

www.gcah.org

Consisting of a museum and library, the Archives and History Center houses a large collection of books, documents, objects, records, photographs, and artifacts relating to United Methodist history, serving as the official archives for the denomination. The library contains one of the largest collections of Methodist materials in the world, including books, pamphlets, and manuscripts of John Wesley. The library also possesses important items on women and ethnic minorities.

THE HUNTINGTON LIBRARY
1151 Oxford Road
San Marino, CA 91108
phone: 626-405-2100
www.huntington.org

This research institution collects materials related to British and American art, history, and literature in a wide range of media. The library is part of a larger complex that includes botanical gardens and two art galleries. An excellent resource for research in American history, the library holds books, newspapers, pamphlets, and almanacs from the seventeenth through nineteenth centuries. It has particularly extensive collections of Civil War materials and houses numerous sets of personal papers. The manuscripts holdings are especially useful for the study of the American West and American religious movements, and include the Mormon collection of diaries and journals. The Huntington has more than 250,000 British and American prints, including biblical illustrations and representations of religious life, as well as 500,000 prints and negatives with a focus on the American West and a notable collection of ephemera. Other highlights include a copy of the Gutenberg Bible on vellum.

JESSE C. WILSON GALLERIES
Anderson University
Anderson, IN 46012
phone: 765-641-4325
fax: 317-641-4328

The Jesse C. Wilson Galleries hold the principal collection of works by Warner Sallman (1892–1968), one of the most popular religious commercial artists of the twentieth century. More than 150 paintings, drawings, and objects by Sallman are joined by archival materials that document Sallman's career and the enormous reception of his devotional imagery.

JEWISH THEOLOGICAL SEMINARY OF AMERICA
3080 Broadway
New York, NY 10027
phone: 212-678-8000
www.jtsa.edu/library

The Library of the Jewish Theological Seminary of America (JTSA) contains one of the world's largest and most comprehensive collections of Hebraica and Judaica, with holdings consisting of 350,000 volumes. The institution's General Collections include materials on Jewish liturgy and Jewish art, a large collection of periodicals, and an audio-visual collection. The Special Collections include a Jewish Art Collection, micrographs, ketubbot, genealogical charts, prints and original photographs, postcards, decorated megillot, broadsides, manuscripts, record books, a body of works related to Kabbalah and Jewish mysticism, and other rare items. The library is open to the public for on-site use with presentation of photo identification.

THE LIBRARY COMPANY OF PHILADELPHIA

1314 Locust Street
Philadelphia, PA 19107
phone: 215-546-3181
www. librarycompany.org

The Library Company of Philadelphia maintains one of the nation's largest collections of American books printed before 1860, providing thorough coverage of the colonial and antebellum periods. Holdings include a large quantity of illustrated Bibles, with an especially strong focus in those published before 1840. In addition to books, the collection features many religious magazines, gift books, annuals, and publications by American tract societies. The Library Company also provides an important resource for prints, graphics, and photographs. This division concentrates primarily on photographs and the graphic arts produced in Philadelphia from the colonial period until the 1940s.

LIBRARY OF CONGRESS

First & Independence Avenue, SE
Washington, DC 20540
phone: 202-707-5000
www.loc.gov

The vast collections of the Library of Congress are noncirculating, but open to the public. The *American Memory* project is an online resource that digitizes significant Americana from the library's collection as part of the National Digital Library Program. Materials are grouped thematically, and those that are being made available electronically include: *African-American Odyssey* (rare books, government documents, manuscripts, maps, musical scores, plays, films, and recordings), *African-American Perspectives* (pamphlets), *Architecture and Interior Design*, Civil War photographs, map collections, and early motion pictures. Other important collections make available American sheet music, regional histories, oral histories from the American South, photographs of the American West, presidential papers, broadsheets, prints, and ephemera. The permanent exhibition *American Treasures*, on display in the Jefferson building, places some of the library's most significant American material on public view; a web version of the Library of Congress exhibition *Religion and the Founding of the American Republic* is also featured.

MASSACHUSETTS HISTORICAL SOCIETY

1154 Boylston Street
Boston, MA 02215
phone: 617-536-1608
www.masshist.org

Founded in 1791, the Massachusetts Historical Society was the first institution to concentrate on collecting Americana. The manuscript collection at the MHS contains approximately 10 million holdings, including the personal papers of Paul Revere, Thomas Jefferson, and the Adams family, and is especially useful for New England history through the nineteenth century. Part of the manuscript collection also comprises materials relating to American religious history and Native American history, as well as holdings of rare books, maps, almanacs, and broadsides. The MHS also houses fine arts, photography, and decorative arts collections. The society's research institute, the Center for the Study of New England History, is currently preparing a Boston African American Database and maintains other directories of Boston inhabitants.

MUSEUM OF TELEVISION AND RADIO
25 West Fifty-second Street
New York, NY 10019
phone: 212-621-6600
465 North Beverly Drive
Beverly Hills, CA 90210
phone: 310-786-1000
www.mtr.org

Although this collection includes no expressly religious programming, scholars have the opportunity to research the use of religious themes in commercial programming on television and radio.

NATIONAL COUNCIL OF CHURCHES
475 Riverside Drive EcuFILM
New York, NY 10115-0050
phone: 212-870-2574
fax: 212-870-2030
810 Twelfth Avenue
South Nashville, TN 37203
phone: 1-800-251-4091
www.ncccusa.org

The National Council of Churches preserves a significant collection of 16mm films produced for network television during the 1960s, 70s, and 80s, comprising approximately 100 titles. Many of the films are documentaries examining the role of the church in the modern world, but the collection also features dramatic and humorous series. Much of the remainder of the film and video library is available through EcuFILM, which lends and sells videos through its facilities at United Methodist Communications.

NATIONAL FOUNDATION FOR JEWISH CULTURE
phone: 212-629-0500
fax: 212-629-0508
e-mail: nfjc@jewishculture.org
www.jewishculture.org

The National Foundation for Jewish Culture (NFJC), the central agency for Jewish culture in the United States, provides a range of cultural services, among these the organization oversees the Council of American Jewish Museums (CAJM). CAJM's directory of Jewish museums is an invaluable resource for the study of Jewish visual and material culture (including such items as paintings, graphics, sculpture, ceremonial and liturgical objects, textiles, photographs, prints, archaeological and ethnographic materials, manuscripts, posters, ephemera, and broadcast media materials). The NFJC and CAJM websites maintain contact and descriptive information for over sixty major collections nationwide, including such important cultural and collecting institutions as The Jewish Museum (New York); the Skirball Cultural Center (Los Angeles); the Skirball Museum (Cincinnati); the Spertus Museum of Judaica (Chicago); and the Yeshiva University Museum (New York).

NATIONAL GALLERY OF ART LIBRARY

National Gallery of Art
Washington, DC 20565
phone: 202-842-6511
www.nga.gov

The National Gallery of Art in Washington, D.C., possesses an important art library, containing more than 200,000 holdings. This institution specializes in European art from the medieval period to the present as well as American art and architecture from colonial times to the present. In addition to an extensive array of books and periodicals, the National Gallery library also collects exhibition and auction catalogues, and maintains a large number of vertical files. The National Gallery of Art library is available to qualified researchers through prior appointment. The reference staff is also available for phone and mail inquiries.

NEW YORK HISTORICAL SOCIETY

Seventy-seventh Street and Central Park West
New York, NY 10024
phone: 212-873-3400
www.nyhistory.org

Maintaining a library and a museum, the New York Historical Society has been preserving documents and objects related to American history since 1804. The NYHS has an impressive print and photographic collection that features portraits of religious leaders and representations of religious buildings, including churches, synagogues, and meetinghouses. Also notable are biblical illustrations, architectural drawings, blueprints, and watercolors as well as scenes of baptisms, revival meetings, and other spiritual activities. The Currier and Ives collection includes several sentimental and religious scenes. In addition, the NYHS library owns a considerable number of nineteenth-century religious periodicals, hieroglyphic Bibles intended for children, and Easter, Christmas, and Rosh Hashanah greeting cards. Early New York maps, locating houses of worship and burial grounds, can also be found at the NYHS library.

NEW YORK PUBLIC LIBRARY

Center for the Humanities
Fifth Avenue and Forty-second Street

New York, NY 10018-2788
phone: 212-930-0830
www.nypl.org

The NYPL is a network of 85 libraries that preserves more than 11.6 million items. The Center for the Humanities, housed in the main building, oversees a vast body of American historical material. The General Research Division maintains a substantial collection of religious Americana, including extensive Shaker materials, a substantial Mormon collection, theosophical documents, a Jewish Division, and an Oriental Division. The Mormon documents feature one of nine known copies of the early edition *Book of Mormon*, as well as pamphlets, newspapers, government documents, letters, and diaries.

NEWBERRY LIBRARY

60 West Walton Street
Chicago, IL 60610-3305
phone: 312-943-9090
www.newberry.org

This independent research library concentrates on the study of the humanities in America. Religious matter held in the special collections include Bibles, prayer books, Hebraica, hymnals, and psalm books as well as materials on Jansenism, Jesuits, Mormons, and Recusants. The Newberry Library's D'Arcy McNickle Center for American Indian History structures and enhances research efforts with respect to the library's two unparalleled collections of print and nonprint materials on the histories, cultures, and literatures of Native American peoples: the Edward E. Ayer Collection and the Everett D. Graff Collection. The Ayer collection consists of more than 130,000 volumes, 2,000 maps, 500 atlases, 6,000 photographs, and 3,500 drawings and paintings related to Native American history, Jesuit relations, and Westward expansion. The Graff Collection (comprising some 900 maps and 10,000 volumes as well as microfilmed government documents, scholarly journals, and related materials) complements the Ayer Collection and focuses on the exploration and settlement of the trans-Mississippi West in the nineteenth century, including documentation of Mormon migration and the Lewis and Clark expedition as well as other travel literature. In addition, the McNickle Center's curriculum library includes some 2,800 items—books, catalogues, guides, artworks, reports, audio tapes, video cassettes, slide-tape sets, and a tribal newspaper collection.

SAN ANTONIO MUSEUM OF ART

200 W. Jones Avenue
San Antonio, TX 78215
phone: 210-978-8100
www.c7a.com/studio/museum/sananton.htm

The San Antonio Museum of Art includes the Nelson A. Rockefeller Center for Latin American Art, the most comprehensive presentation of Latin American art in the United States. It contains four permanent galleries: Pre-Columbian, Spanish Colonial/Republican, Modern/Contemporary, and Folk. The Spanish Colonial collection contains religious paintings, statuary, silver, and an eighteenth-century baroque *retablo* or altar screen, about 25 feet tall.

In the center of this *retablo* is a large-scale depiction of Our Lady of Guadalupe. The folk gallery features a section on ceremonial art, which includes masks from ten countries, curing sticks from the Darien Forest of Panama, religious paintings, and votive art from throughout Latin America.

SCHOMBURG CENTER FOR RESEARCH IN BLACK CULTURE

515 Malcolm X Boulevard
New York, NY 10037-1801
phone: 212-491-2200
www.nypl.org/research/sc/sc

Part of the New York Public Library, the Schomburg Center is one of the nation's preeminent institutions for research on the culture of Africa and the African Diaspora. Collecting a wide array of media, the Schomburg is divided into five research divisions: Art and Artifacts Division; General Research and Reference Division; Manuscripts, Archives, and Rare Books Division; Moving Image and Recorded Sound Division; and Photographs and Prints Division. Holdings include art work from Africa and the African Diaspora, with a strong concentration in objects from the Harlem Renaissance and Works Progress Administration as well as more than 4,000 political and cultural posters. The center also maintains an important vertical file of ephemera in addition to the Ernest D. Kaiser Index to Black Resources. Manuscript and archival materials consist of personal papers and institutional records and are particularly useful for the study of the visual arts and African American religion. The sheet music collection also includes a number of spirituals. The Prints and Photographs Division features materials relating to fraternal and religious organizations.

SOUTHERN BAPTIST HISTORICAL LIBRARY AND ARCHIVES

901 Commerce Street
Nashville, TN 37203
phone: 615-244-0344
www.sbhla.org

The main repository for denominational records among Southern Baptists, this collection includes more than 12,000 photographs of Baptist leaders, pastors, missionaries, and church events. Collections also include prints, illustrated periodicals, 71,000 annuals of Baptist associations and conventions, 25,000 books, 16,000 reels of microfilm, audio-visual recordings and motion pictures, a collection of rare Bibles, and a collection of church music and hymnals.

SOUTHWEST MUSEUM

234 Museum Drive
Los Angeles, CA 09965
phone: 323-221-2163
www.southwestmuseum.org

Collections consist of art and material culture of prehistoric, historic, and contemporary Native Americans of North, Central, and South America; Spanish colonial and Mexican provincial artifacts and decorative arts; and manuscripts and photographs.

TAYLOR MUSEUM FOR SOUTHWESTERN STUDIES

Colorado Springs Fine Arts Center
30 West Dale Street
Colorado Springs, CO 80903
phone: 719-634-5581

Founded by Alice Bemis Taylor in 1935, the Taylor Museum is dedicated to the study of folk arts from the Southwest. The museum, as part of the Colorado Springs Fine Arts Center, acquires, exhibits, and publishes examples of Southwestern American folk art, including objects of religious significance. Particularly notable is the Taylor's extensive collection of *santos* from the nineteenth and twentieth centuries, which includes more than 750 objects executed in a variety of media. The Taylor Museum Archives also preserves historical photographs of the American Southwest, some of which document religious life.

UCLA FOWLER MUSEUM OF CULTURAL HISTORY

Box 951549
Los Angeles, CA 90005-1549
phone: 310-825-9672
www.fmch.ucla.edu

Based at the University of California-Los Angeles, the Fowler Museum is a collection of more than 790,000 works of art and material culture that represents contemporary, historic, and prehistoric cultures from Africa, Native and Latin America, Oceania, and Asia. Materials belonging to the Latin American category include Haitian works related to Vodou. Mexican holdings include pre-Columbian, colonial, contemporary folk, and ethnographic collections. Native American materials come from throughout North America. The museum's archaeological collections draw from more than 1,000 sites in California.

WINTERTHUR MUSEUM, GARDEN AND LIBRARY

Winterthur, DE 19735
phone: 1-800-448-3883
www.winterthur.org

The library and museum collections at Winterthur contain a rich variety of source materials that support the study of American history. The museum maintains numerous examples of Americana related to religious life, including Shaker objects, fireplace tiles, and cookie molds featuring biblical scenes. The library collects a range of materials, including religious literature and institutional records as well as architectural drawings of devotional buildings and holiday greeting cards. The Printed Book and Periodical Collection includes books of common prayer, hymnals, Bibles, martyrologies, materials related to church design, and decoration and embroidery. Also notable are Quaker publications, religious children's books, and psalm books, including that that belonged to John Hancock. In addition, the Downs Collection of Manuscripts and Printed Ephemera houses personal papers, institutional records, and ephemera related to American culture spanning three centuries. Important religious materials include church records, sermons, hymnals, photographs, and illustrations of churches, and sheet music. The Edward Deming Andrews Memorial Shaker Collection is the third largest library of Shaker materials in the United States, and includes approximately 1,400 photographs as well as watercolors, diaries, and journals.

CONTRIBUTORS

DAVID BJELAJAC, professor of art history and human sciences at The George Washington University, has written two books on Washington Allston, *Millennial Desire and the Apocalyptic Vision of Washington Allston* and *Washington Allston, Secret Societies, and the Alchemy of Anglo-American Painting*, and a thematic survey of American art titled *American Art: A Cultural History*.

GRETCHEN T. BUGGELN, assistant professor in the Winterthur Program of Early American Culture, assistant director of the Winterthur Office of Advanced Studies, and director of the Research Fellowship Program at the Winterthur Museum, Garden, and Library, is currently revising for publication her dissertation on religion and material culture in early republican Connecticut. She contributed a related essay to the recently published volume *Seeing beyond the Word: Visual Arts and the Calvinist Tradition*, edited by Paul Corby Finney.

JOHN DAVIS, Priscilla Paine Van der Poel Professor of Art History at Smith College, also teaches in the American Studies Program. He is author of *The Landscape of Belief: Encountering the Holy Land in Nineteenth-Century Art and Culture* and coauthor of *Smith College Museum of Art: European and American Paintings and Sculpture, 1760–1960*. His current research concerns art institutions in New York City in the late nineteenth and early twentieth centuries.

ERIKA DOSS, professor of art history at the University of Colorado, is also director of the American Studies Program. She is the author of several books and essays on twentieth-century American art, including *Benton, Pollock, and the Politics of Modernism: From Regionalism to*

Abstract Expressionism; Spirit Poles and Flying Pigs: Public Art and Cultural Democracy in American Communities; and *Elvis Culture: Fans, Faith, and Image.* She is currently completing a textbook on twentieth-century American art for the Oxford History of Art series.

CLAIRE FARAGO, associate professor of art history at the University of Colorado at Boulder, is the author of *Leonardo Da Vinci's "Paragone"* and contributing editor of *Reframing the Renaissance.* She is currently collaborating author for a volume titled *Transforming Images: New Mexican Santos between Worlds,* and she is writing an essay about the gendered ideology of Western aesthetic theory.

JOHN M. GIGGIE, assistant professor of history at the University of Texas at San Antonio, is currently completing *Exodus: African-American Religion and Modernity in the Mississippi Delta, 1875–1915* and *Frederick Law Olmsted's Civil War: Visions of Authority and Order in the North, 1848–1870.* He is also coediting two volumes: *The Limits and Liberties of Markets: Practices of Race, Religion, and Gender in United States History* and *The Sacred and the City: Religion and Urban Commercial Culture in the Americas, 1800–2000.*

PAUL GUTJAHR, assistant professor of English, American studies, and religious studies at Indiana University, is author of *An American Bible: A History of the Good Book in the United States, 1777-1880.* He has also coedited a collection of essays, *Illuminating Letters: Essays on Typography and Literary Interpretation,* and edited an anthology titled *American Popular Literature of the Nineteenth Century.*

STEWART M. HOOVER is a professor of media studies, religious studies, and American studies at the University of Colorado at Boulder. He is author of *Religion in the News: Faith and Journalism in American Public Discourse* and coeditor (with Knut Lundby) of *Rethinking Media, Religion, and Culture.* His other books include *Mass Media Religion* and *Religious Television: Controversies and Conclusions.*

HARVEY MARKOWITZ is field specialist on the curatorial staff of the Cultural Resources Center, National Museum of the American Indian, Smithsonian Institution. He is author of *American Indian Biographies;* editor of *Native Americans: An Annotated Bibliography;* and consulting editor to *Ready Reference: North American Indians.*

DAVID MORGAN holds the Duesenberg Chair in Christianity and the Arts in Christ College, the honors college, at Valparaiso University. He is the author of *Visual Piety: A History and Theory of Popular Religious Images* and *Protestants and Pictures: Religion, Visual Culture, and the Age of American Mass Production* and contributing editor of *Icons of American Protestantism: The Art of Warner Sallman.* He is currently working on the history of the religious tract in the United States.

SALLY M. PROMEY, professor of art history and archaeology at the University of Maryland, is author of *Spiritual Spectacles: Vision and Image in Mid-Nineteenth-Century Shakerism* and *Painting Religion in Public: John Singer Sargent's* Triumph of Religion *at the Boston Public Library.* She is currently writing a book on the history of the public display of religion titled *Religion in Plain View: The Public Aesthetics of American Belief.*

LEIGH E. SCHMIDT, professor of religion at Princeton University, is author of *Holy Fairs: Scottish Communions and American Revivals in the Early Modern Period; Consumer Rites: The Buying and Selling of American Holidays;* and *Hearing Things: Religion, Illusion, and the American Enlightenment.* He is currently working on interrelated projects on the making of American spirituality and the discovery of religion as an object of study.

ELLEN SMITH is curator of the American Jewish Historical Society and associate director of the Gralla Fellows Program for Religion Journalists at Brandeis University. Her recent books and exhibitions include *The Jews of Boston* (with Jonathan D. Sarna); *Facing the New World: Jewish Portraits in Colonial and Federal America;* and *Yiddish on Stage: The World of Yiddish Theater.* She is currently directing the creation of the new visitor center for Touro Synagogue, Newport, Rhode Island. She teaches material culture studies and American Jewish history as visiting instructor at Brandeis University and Northeastern University.

THOMAS A. TWEED, professor of religious studies and American studies and associate dean of arts and sciences at the University of North Carolina at Chapel Hill, is author of *The American Encounter with Buddhism, 1844–1912* and *Our Lady of the Exile: Diasporic Religion at a Cuban Catholic Shrine in Miami.* In addition, he is coeditor of *Asian Religions in America: A Documentary History* and editor of *Retelling U.S. Religious History.*

INDEX

Page numbers in *italics* denote illustrations.

Abbott, Jacob, 52

abolitionism: Baconian empiricism and, 189; and benevolent moment, inversion of, 58–59, *59*, *60*, 299n24; and the railroad, 252–53, *253*

academy: religion as marginalized by, 44; religious art as ignored by, xi–xiii

accessibility: and public display, 31–32, 45–47; as visibility, 31

Acoustic Temple, 211–14, *212*, 219

activism, biblical illustration and, 278

Adams, Joseph Alexander, 280–81, *282*

advertising: biblical illustration and, *279*, 280, 282; of Jewish New Year postcards, 233, 243; Vedder and, 227. *See also* commodification; consumerism; media

Advice to Freedmen (Brinckerhoff), 301n37

aesthetic construction, 199

aesthetics: invention of, 114; norms of, and loss of meaning, 201, 205; Protestant consumption of Catholic images and, 114–19, *116*, 317–18n27; spirituality and, 114

African Americans: biblical illustration addressed to, 278–80, *279*; and children of Israel, 261, *262*, 264; Freemasons and wisdom of, 183–84; and literacy, nineteenth-century, 51, 59–64, *63*, 300nn25,27, 300–301n35, 301nn37,42; migration of, 263–64, *263*; in military, 4, *5*; Mount and, 177, *178*, 184–85, 187, 189–90; newspapers of, 250–51, *250*, 252, 260, *260*, 263–64, *263*; and racism (*see* racism); railroad and (*see* railroad, African Americans and); and segregation, 4, 250, 251–52, 255, 261, 264, 357n10; violence against, 250, 260–61, 264. *See also* ethnicity

Africans, 183–84, 278–79, *279*

pluralism and, 38–39, 47; preservation of, 94–95; of railroad stations, 253, *263*, *264*; role of, 87–88; as spiritual, 97; of Washington, D.C. (*see* Washington, D.C., architecture of); and worship, 97–98, 100

Argos, 221–22

art: in Bibles (*see* Bible illustration); colonial (*see* colonial art); meaning of text affected by, 268–69, 270–71, 273, 280, 284–85, 365n68; as religion, 224–30. *See also* illustration

artists: and aestheticization of Catholic images, 114; Romanticism and, 222; tension with Catholicism and, 136–37, 140–41, 142, 144, 315n10

art world: spiritual revival in, 132, 134–36, 142–44; and the spiritual, suspicion of, xi–xiii, 132–36, 143–44

Assemblies of God, 75, 305n8

Athapaskan peoples, 192, 337n4

audience: of church buildings, 87–88; culture and, 204; hybridity and, 204; and media consumption, 155, 156–57, 158; of New Mexican art, 200, 202, 203, 204; and public display of religion, 29, 32–33, 40–42, 47. *See also* consumerism; viewer and viewing

auditory culture, 214, 219, 224

Augustine, 214, 216

authenticity, deconstruction of, 15

authority: of Catholic Church, anti-Catholicism and, 110; iconoclasm and, 14; prodigal son as cultural trope and, 273; tarot cards and, 13; of text (*see* text)

autonomy, religious, 152

avant-garde, spiritual in art and, 132–36, 142–44

Ave Maria (Mignot), 319n39

Awad, Nihad, 41

Bacon, Roger, 328–29n5

Bacon, Sir Francis, 181

Baconian empiricism, 181, 189–90, 229.

See also Enlightenment; Freemasonry; hermeticism

baggage, 141–42

Baird, Charles, 311n17, 312n21

Baltus, Jean, 215, *215*, 347–48n12

Baptism of Pocahontas at Jamestown, Virginia, 1613 (Chapman), 36, *37*, 289n8, *plate 4*

Baptista della Porta, John (Giovanni), 219

Baptist Church, 74, 305n8, 305–6n10

Barr, Alfred H., Jr., xii

Barzman, Karen-Edis, 293n30

Batterson, Mark, 75

Bearden, Romare, 264–66, *266*, 359n43, *plate 15*

Beardsley, John, 28

beauty, racism and standards of, 1–2

Belknap, Jeremy, 269–70, 271

Bell, Catherine, 127

Bellah, Robert, 304n6

Bells of St. Mary's, 156

benevolence, civil religion and, 54–57, *56*, *58*, 298n18

benevolent moment, 57–58, *58*, *59*, 62, *63*; inversion of, 58–59, *59*, 63–64, *64*

Benveniste, Emile, 119

Benziger Brothers, 193, *194*, *195*, 198, 338n10

Berger, John, 133

Berger, Peter, 45

Bernini, Gianlorenzo, 141

Bewick, Thomas, 298n18

Bhabha, Homi, 204

Bible, 181, 182, 216; apologetics and, 273–77, *274*, 282, 363n38. *See also* Bible illustration

The Bible Alive (HarperCollins), 282–84, *283*, *plate 16*

Bible for To-day (Stirling), 277–78, *278*

Bible illustration, 23, 267–69; advertising for, *279*, *280*, 282; apologetics and, 263n38, 273–74, *274*, 282; attracting the reader, 268, 271–73, *272*; economics and choice of, 273, 282; fine art and,

Carroll, James, 81–82

Carter, Jimmy, 74

Catholicism. *See* Roman Catholicism

Catholic Reformation, 201, 345n59

"The Celestial Rail-road" (Hawthorne), 357n12

Champollion, Jean-Francois, 180

Channing, William Ellery, 57

Chapel of the Virgin at Subiaco (Morse), 119–22, *121*, 318–19n38

Chapman, John G., 36, *37*, 289n8, *plate 4*

Cheverus, Jean Lefebvre de, 105–7, *106*, 117, 119, 128, 314nn3,4, 314–15n5

Chicago, Illinois, Chinatown of, 6, *7*

Chidester, David, 127

children: as blank slate, 296–97n5; and media, effect on, 146–47; and reading instruction, 51–52, 53, 296–97n5

The Child's Paper, 62, *63*

China: export ceramics of, *194–96*, *198*, *199–200*, 203; folk shrines of, 6, *7*

The Choir of the Capuchin Chapel (Granet), 123–27, *124*, 128, 321nn48,52, 321–22n54, *plate 9*

Chong, Albert, 132, 133–34, *133*

Chopra, Deepak, 154

Christ, Jesus, as activist, 278

Christian Examiner, 115

Christian Index, 254

Christianity: Enlightenment and (*see* Enlightenment); and oracles, 214–17, *215*; pluralism and, 295n54. *See also* *specific churches and people*

Christian Methodist Church, 255

Christians in the Visual Arts (CIVA), 136

Christian Watchman, 109

Christmas, 33, 38, 40, 227, 351n8. *See also* nativity scenes

Chromatics; Or An Essay on the Analogy and Harmony of Colors (Field), 187–88, *187*

Church of England, 114, 347–48n12

Church of God, 305n8

Church of Jesus Christ of Latter Day Saints temple, 38–39, *39*

Church of the Holy City (Washington, D.C.), 74, 305n8, 305–6n10

circle, as sacred, 161, 165

Citizens Committee for the Army and Navy, 4

Citizens Protesting Anti-Semitic Acts (Brenner), 33–35, *34*

City of Quartz (Davis), 141

civil religion, 18; benevolence as ideal in, 54–57, *56*, 58, 298n18; Catholicism in, 19, 64, 65–67; definitions of, 7, 72, 304n6; education of former slaves and breakdown of, 61; literacy and, 54; primers as espousing, 54–57; Protestantism in, 19, 20, 57, 64–67; sacralizing of public heroism, 7–10, *8*, *9*, 53–54, *55*, 61, 289n8. *See also* national identity; separation of church and state; United States of America

Clarke, Edward Daniel, 221–22

class: antisemitism and, 238, 239; benevolent acts and maintenance of, 54–56, *56*; consumerism and, 207, 208; land grants to *genízaros* and, 206–7, 344n57; and mass-produced santos, 207; scholarly resistance to religous art and, xii; segregation and, 252, 357n10; and trompe l'oeil, taste for, 126. *See also* poverty

clergy. *See* Roman Catholic clergy

Clinton, Bill, 74

Clinton, Hillary Rodham, 74

Cogdell, John S., 123

Cole, Thomas, 119–22, *120*, 180–81, *183*, *183*, 319n39, 334–35n55

collections: of curiosities, 271; of postcards, 230, 243, 246–47, 356n51

collective good: architecture and, 90; republican ideals and, 54

collectivity, and public display, 31

colonial art: and assimilation, native participation in, 200, 206; in Mexico and Peru, 340–41n26; models for, 201; survival of dispossessed and, 200 colonialism: hybridity and (*see* hybridity); and oracles, silencing of, 215–16; Southwestern Catholicism and, 192, 200, 206, 337n4, 340–41n26, 341n28. *See also* racism

color: meaning of, 163–64, 167, 169, 188; Mount and, 184, 188, 190, 333n49, 334n54; racism and, 2, 3, 37, 190; and Revolutionary War resistance, 334n54; theory of, hermeticism and, 179, 181, 187–88, *187*, 333n49, 334n52; Venetian, hoax concerning, 179, *180*, *181*

Comenius, Johann, 296n1

commemorative images, 10–12

Commercial Advertiser, 119

"Committing the Study of Religion in Public" (Marty), 290–91n1

commodification: of Bible (*see* Bible illustration); of spiritual longing, 229. *See also* advertising; consumerism

communication as visual operation, 2–6, 14; definition of, 3–4

communion as visual operation, 3, 6–10, 14. *See also* civil religion

community: and Jewish New Year postcards, 237, 244, 247–48; nonmember attachment to church buildings, 88, 95; service to (mission), 89, 91, 94–95, 99, 101, 312n21

competition among faiths: separation of church and state and, 72, 86; in Washington, D.C., 72, 73, 85, 309–10n33

computer effects, 282–84, *283*, *plate 16*

Congregationalists, 72

Connecticut, 189

consumer desire, 199, 207–8, 345nn60,61

consumerism, 293n29; agency and, 191–92, 199; class and, 207, 208; clergy and, 197, 339–40n20, 200, 207, 345n59; desire and, 199, 207–8, 345nn60,61; disenchantment and, 208, 345n60; disillusionment and, 345n60; display of religion and, 293n29,

295n55; identity and, 21–22, 243; and Jewish immigrant culture, 229, *230*, 242–43, 247, *plate 13*; lay Catholicism and, 208; and Mexican independence, 200; women and, 243. *See also* advertising; commodification

context: Sioux art and, 171

conversion: aesthetics of Church and, 115

Cook, John W., 96

Cooke, George, 123, 319–20n44

Cooledge, George, 57

Cooper, James Fenimore, 319–20n44

correspondences, doctrine of, 330

Costa, Gabriel, 232, 351n12

Cotter, John Rogerson, 316n14

Coulter, Lane, 338n10, 339nn17,18

counter-Enlightenment, 222–23, 227–28

Courbet, Gustave, 142

Covenant First Presbyterian Church, 75

craftsmanship: Gober and artisanal fabrication, 143; hermeticism and secrecy of, 179, 181, 332n37, 334–35n55; Mount and local pigments, 176, 178–79, 184, 188, 332n38

Crary, Thomas, 127, 321n52

creation myths, 181

criticism, spiritual in art and, 133, 143–44

"Crossing the Red Sea" (*Bible Alive*), 282–83, *283*, *plate 16*

crucifixes, and Protestant consumption of images, 117, 317–18n27

Csikszentmihalyi, Mihalyi, 201

Cubbs, Joanne, 134

cultural hierarchies, construction and enforcement of, xiii

cultural sociology, 345n60

culture: and audience, 204; auditory, 214, 219, 224; mass (*see* mass culture); mass media as defining, 146–47, 152, 158; and nature, conflicts with, 21, 188–89; pluralism as practice of, 48, 295n63; popular, defined, 337n3

curanderas, 204, 343n47

Currier and Ives, 193, 251, *251*, 338n10

Ekstrom, Linda, 144
electrotyping, 281
Eliade, Mircea, 319n41
Ellis, Reverend George E., 115
Elon, Dr. Edward, 75
Emancipation Proclamation, 61
empiricism, Baconian, 181, 189–90, 229.
    See also Enlightenment; Freemasonry;
    hermeticism
England, 351n8
Enlightenment: casualties of, 227–28;
    counter-Enlightenment, 222–23, 227–
    28; demythologizing of revelation and,
    22; and oracles, silencing of, 217–22,
    218, 220–22, 226, 227–28; postmodern
    abandonment of, 132; separation of
    church and state and, 31
envy. *See* Protestants, and consumption
    of Catholic images
Episcopal Cathedral Church of Saints
    Peter and Paul (National Cathedral),
    72–73, *73*, 76, 79, 81, 83, *84*, 85, 305n8
Episcopal Church: cultural power of, 72;
    high-church campaign of, 114–15,
    317n22; National Cathedral of, 72–73,
    73, 76, 79, 81, 83, *84*, 85, 305n8; other
    Washington, D.C., churches, 74,
    305n8, 305–6n10
ethnicity: biblical illustration and, 278–80,
    279; intolerance of, immigration and,
    109–10; national Catholic shrine and,
    76–77, 306–7n15; and Washington,
    D.C., area "Religion Row," 309–10n33.
    See also diversity; racism; *specific peoples*
Europe: antisemitism in, 231–32, 237–39;
    biblical criticism originating in, 275;
    and Jewish women, changes in roles
    of, 355–56n47; mass-marketed images
    produced in, 93, 338n10; norms of,
    and overlooked signifying elements,
    201; postcard production and, 231–32,
    351n8
European representational practices: and
    Pueblo peoples, 200, 202–3, 204, 206,
    340–41n26; Sioux artists and, 171–73,
    175
Everson v. Board of Education, 291n3
"The Excursion Craze" (*Freeman*), 260,
    260
exhibition, 36–37; performance distin-
    guished from, 38; production of
    observer and practices of, 127, 321n52;
    seasonal (*see* seasonal exhibition). *See
    also* display
exotic. *See* other
Eyck, Jan van, 140

Fallot, Roger, 42
familiar, postcards and the, 237
Farago, Claire, 4, 21–22, 191–208
Feather on Head, 162
Fetish #4 (Stout), 133–34
Ficino, Marsilio, 181
Field, George, 187–88, *187*, 333n49, 334n52
Filipino Americans, 306–7n15
Finger, 326–27n16
Finley, Karen, 137
First Amendment: establishment clause
    of (*see* separation of church and state);
    free exercise clause of, 27, 28, 291n3
First Baptist Church (Washington, D.C.),
    74, 305n8, 305–6n10
first communion cards, 197, *197*, 340n22
fish, as symbol, 178, 189, 329n9, 335n59
The Flagellants (Marr), xii
Flagg, George Whiting, 314n1
Florencia, Francisco de, 203
Fontenelle, Bernard le Bovier de, 218–19,
    220, 222
Forest Rose; or, American Farmers (Wood-
    worth), 330n15
formalism, 133, 142
fortune-tellers, 223–24
Founding Church of Scientology (Wash-
    ington, D.C.), 305n8
Foundry United Methodist Church
    (Washington, D.C.), 74, 85, 305n8,
    305–6n10

four, as sacred number, 161, 162–63, 164, 166

Fourteenth Amendment, 291n3

The Fourth Day of the Sun Dance (Short Bull), 170–71, *171*, *173*, *175*

Fourth Eclectic Reader (McGuffey), 57

fragmentation: mass-produced santos and, 208; penitential societies and, 344n57; and silence of God, 227–28

France: clergy of, and distribution of images, 197, *197*, 338n10, 340n21; mass-production of images by, 338n10

Franchot, Jenny, 108, 118, 315n8

Frankenstein (Shelley), 15

Fraser, Charles, 125

Freedmen's Aid Societies, 60–65

Freedmen's Bureau, 60–61, 300n27, 300–301n35

Freemasonry, 181–84; aprons of, *182*, *182*, 331n30; and black Africans, 182–84; and Egyptian wisdom, 329n14, 334–35n55; Mount and, 182–83; in New York, 182, 329n6, 331n30; and Swedenborgians, 330n15

Fresquís, Pedro Antonio, 202–3, *202*, 342–43n39

Freud, Sigmund, 138

frontality, 119, 125, 206

funding. *See* public funding

Gablik, Suzi, 136

Gallaudet, Thomas, 51–52

Galt, John, 179

Garrison, William Lloyd, 59, 252

Gates, Reverend J. M., 257–58

gay men, 136, 138, 139

gaze: of Protestantism, 108; Sun Dance and, 165

Geertz, Clifford, 128

gender: and anti-Catholicism, 318n28; postcards and, 230, 243, 246–47, 356n51; and railroad symbolization, 250, 258. *See also* men; women

Genesis, 181, 182

Genesis (Quick-to-See Smith), 134

genízaros, 206–7, 344n57

German immigrants, 315–16n12

Germany, postcards and, 231, 232, *235*, *236*, 351n8

"Get off the Track!" (Hutchinson), 252–53, *253*

Gibbons, James Cardinal, 68, 76

Giddens, Anthony, 152

Giggie, John, 22, 23, 249–68

Gillray, James, 179, *180*

Gilman, Sander, 238

Giurgola, Romaldo, 98

Glenn, Mrs. V. K., 259

Glennon, Cardinal, 307–8n18

globalization, and public display, 293n29

Gober, Robert, 129; alternative world/ spirituality of, 140–43, 144; and architecture, 138–40; autobiographical nature of work, 140, 142; and baggage, 141–42; and the body, 136, 137–38, 140, 141; and Catholicism, 136, 140–41, 142, 144; and context of spiritual in art, 130–36; critical and public response to, 143–44; and museums, change in, 144–45; and water as cleansing, 142. Works: *Prayers Are Answered*, 138–39; *The Silly Sink*, 137; *The Subconscious Sink*, 137; *Untitled* (1991), 138, *139*; *Untitled (House)*, 139; Virgin Mary installation (*Untitled*, 1995–97), 129–30, *130*, *131*, 136, 138, *139*–45, *140*, *143*

God: as everywhere, 176; hermeticism and, 181; voice of, as absent, 213–14, 225–28

Going My Way, 156

gold, 188, *189*, 334n51

Goodman, Walter, 156

Good News, The New Testament with Over 500 Illustrations and Maps, 276–77

Good News for Modern Man, 267–68, *268*, 360nn6,7

Goodrich, Samuel G., 56–57, 297n6

Good Seat, 161

Gore, Mrs. John, 314–15n5
Gothic style, 79, 81, 89–90, 91, 331n30;
    high-church campaign and taste for,
    115, 117
Goupil's Gallery, New York, 115, 118
Grace Methodist Church (Wilmington,
    Del.), 90
Grady, Monsignor Thomas J., 83,
    307–8n18
graffiti, 38–39
Granet, François-Marius, 123–27, 124, 128,
    321nn48,52, 321–22n54, *plate 9*
gravemarkers, 11
"The Great Southern Exodus" (*Freeman*),
    263–64, *263*
The Great West (Currier and Ives), 251, *251*
Greenhouse, Wendy, 317–18n27
Greenwood, Grace, 108, 316n16,
    319–20n44
Guthrie, Stewart, 13–14
Gutjahr, Paul, 23, 193, 267–85

Hackett, Horatio B., 363n38
Ham, 183–84, 279–80, *279*
Hamilton, George Heard, xii
Hamilton, John D., 331n30
handprints, 205
Hanegraaf, Wouter J., 328–29n5
Hanukkah, 33–34, 37, 38. *See also* menorah
Haring, Keith, 132, 134
Harper and Brothers, 23, 57, 280–82, *281*,
    284, 289n8
HarperCollins, 23, 282–84, *283*, *plate 16*
Harper's New Monthly Magazine, 110–14,
    110, 111, 113, 117
Harper's Weekly, 66
Hart, Rachel Holland, 178
Hartley, Marsden, 134
Has Modernism Failed? (Gablik), 136
Hatch, Nathan, 45
hate crimes. *See* violence
Hawkins, Jonas, 182
Hawkins, Micah, 331n30
Hawkins, Zachariah, 335n61

Hawthorne, Nathaniel, 357n12
Head of a Dead Man, Mexico (Witkin), 137
Head of Christ (Sallman), 38
healing: Pueblo culture and, 204, 343n47;
    shrines of, 71, 302–3n2; Virgin Mary
    and, 79–81, 302–3n2
hearing, disciplining of, 214, 219
Heartney, Eleanor, 137, 315n10
Hebrew Publishing Company, 230, 232,
    plate 13
Heine, Heinrich, 335n56
Heinze, Andrew, 242–43
Helms, Jesse, 28
Hermes Trismegistus, 181, 182, 216, 217
hermeticism, 21; color theory and, 179,
    181, 187–88, *187*, 333n49, 334n52; and
    correspondences, doctrine of, 330n15;
    Mount and, 12, 21, 177, 184–90,
    328–29n5; and oracles, 211–12, 216–
    17, 219; painting as medium of, 21,
    180–81, 188, 330n18, 334–35n55; racism
    and, 177, 189–90; signatures of, 21;
    symbolism of, 177, 184–90, 329n9;
    texts of, 181, 216, 328–29n5. *See also*
    alchemy; Freemasonry
Herring, James, 331n30
hexagram, 187, *187*, 188
Heywood, Ian, 295n61
Hickey, Dave, 136
hieroglyphics, 179–80, 184, *185*, 329n14,
    330n15
High and Low Mass (Hogan), 117
High Bear, 169
high culture, scholarly resistance to
    religous art and, xii
Hilder, Rowland, 277
Hill, Samuel, 360n12
Hindus, 45, 47
History of Quadrupeds (Bewick), 298n18
*History of the Oracles, and the Cheats of the
    Pagan Priests* (Fontenelle), 218–19, *220*
History of the Work of the Redemption
    (Edwards), 216
Hoffman, Randy, 38, 294n33

Hogan, William, 110, 117, 316n14

Holbrook, John, 274–75, *274*

Holman, A. J., 278–80, *279*

Holocaust, 231–32

Holy Land (Palestine), biblical apologetics and, 273–77, *274*, 282, 363n38

home, 138–39

homosexuality, 136, 138, 139. *See also* gay men

Hoover, Stewart M., 12, 19–20, 146–59

Houdon, Jean-Antoine, 9–10, *9*

Howe, Oscar, 171–73, *172, 173, 175, plate 10*

Hubard, William James, 317–18n27

Hudson, Elder J. W., 254

Huntington, Daniel, 117, 317–18n27

Hutchings, Joe, 255

Hutchinson, Jesse, Jr., 252–53, *253*

hybridity: audience and, 204; definition of, 204; and meaning, 198, 201–3, 204, 208; New Mexican santos and, 21–22, 201–3, 204–7, 208; resonance and, 208, 345n63

iconoclasm, xii, 14–15; as liberatory, 14; as performance, 37; power of images demonstrated by, 2, 14; and racism, responses to, 2, 3, *3*, 37; as violence in service of absolutism, 14–15

identity: capitalism and, 21–22; of Catholics, 7, 18–19, 78–79, 81, 84–85; communion as visual operation and, 6–7; consumerism and, 21–22, 243; and display of religion, 28, 29, 35, 37, 38, 40, 41, 47, 48; hybridity and, 204; loss of church building and, 87; and mass-produced santos, 21, 192, 193, 195, 208; material objects as securing continuity of, 201; media and, 147, 155, 158; and memory as visual operation, 3, 10–12, 14; national (*see* civil religion; national identity); nineteenth-century Southwest and, 21; and place, commitment to, 88, 101; and ritual, 128; seeker religiosity and, 152, 155. *See also* self

idolatry, charges of, 76, 112, 306–7n15

The Illuminated American Primer, 54, *55*

Illuminated Bible (Harper and Brothers), 280–82, *281*, 284, 289n8

illustration: of Bible (*see* Bible illustration); meaning of text affected by, 268–69, 270–71, 273, 280, 284–85, 363n45, 365n68

images. *See* power of images; presentation; representation

immigration, 22; anti-Catholicism and, 109; belonging and, 237, 239, 243; images and, 22; and Jewish New Year postcards, 229, 234, 237, 239–44, *240*, 247–48, 354nn33,39, 354–55n40, *plate 14*; and Judaism, 240–42, 244; and pluriformity, 45; population figures for, 45, 315–16n12; and technology, celebration of, 240, *241*, 247; women's changing roles and, 243, 244. *See also* migration of African Americans

Indianapolis Freeman, 260, *260*, 263–64, *263*

Indian art, Studio and, 172

Inman, Henry, 125

Inslee, William, 332n37

intent vs. static tradition, 174–75

Interior Castle (Teresa of Avila), 141

Interior of St. Peter's (Cook), 123

Internet: pluralism and, 46; privacy and, 32, 293n23; shrines and, 70; text erosion and, 365n68. *See also* technology

interpretation, biblical illustration and, 268–69, 270–71, 273, 280, 284–85, 363n45, 365n68. *See also* meaning

Irish immigrants, 109, 315–16n12

irony, lack of, 143

Irving, Washington, 334n51

Irwin, Robert, 134

Islam, 37, 40, 41, 42, 45, 47

Islamic Center of Washington, D.C., 309–10n33

McDannell, Colleen, 246

McGuffey, William, 56–57, 297n6

McKenna, Monsignor Bernard A., 77, 79, 80, 308n19

McLanathan, Richard, 314n2

McMillan, James, 304n6

meaning: aesthetic norms and loss of, 201, 205; of architectural spaces, 70–72; audience as determining, 40–42, 71–72; construction of, 199; display and, 29, 38–40, 42, 47; hybridity and construction of, 198, 201–3, 204, 208; mass media discourses and, 155, 156–57, 159; medium as influencing, 268–69, 270–71, 273, 280, 284–85, 363n45, 365n68; pluralism and, 47; postcards and construction of, 237, 245–46; religion as integration of, 147; visual culture and construction of, 17, 19–22; as visual operation, 3, 12–14, 15

media: advertising in (*see* advertising); changes in religion and, 147, 152–54; culture defined by, 146–47, 152, 158; effects of, 158; and exhibition vs. performance, distinctions of, 38; instrumentalist vs. meaning-making view of, 20; motivations for consumption of, 154–55, 156, 157; New Mexican santos and (*see* santos, mass-produced); news, 147; newspapers (*see* newspapers); nineteenth-century explosion of, 297–98n12; pluralism and, 46; and public vs. private, definitions of, 32, 293n23; and the spiritual, interest in, 131–32; and visual literacy, 158

media, and religious representation, 158–59; audience and, 155, 156–57, 158; discourses of, and meaning-making, 155, 156–57, 159; effects of, 158; marketplace and, 153–54; and seeker religiosity, 155, 156, 158–59; *Ten Commandments* film and visual language of, 158–59

megachurches, 131–32

memorials, 11–12; exhibition vs. performance and, 38; gravemarkers, 11; roadside crosses, 11, *11*, 12; of war, 12

memory: postcards and, 237; reuse of architectural elements and, 96, 100; as visual operation, 3, 10–12, 14

men: African American, and railroad symbolization, 258; antisemitism and, 238, 239. *See also* gender

Mendieta, Ana, 134, 136

menorah, 33, 34, 36, 37

mercury, 188

Merrifield, Mary P., 334n52

Mesa-Bains, Amalia, 132, 133–34

Methodist Church, 74, 85, 90, 305n8, 305–6n10

Methodist Episcopal Church, 61, 63

Methodist Freedman's Aid Society, 61, 63

Metropolitan African Methodist Episcopal Church, 74, 305n8

Mexico, 200, 340–41n26

Michelangelo, 216, 223

middle class. *See* class

Midnight Mass in the Church of St. Etienne du Mont (Daguerre), 122

Mignot, Louis Rémy, 319n39

migration of African Americans, 263–64, *263*

military: Jews and, 4, 5, 238, 354–55n40; war memorials, 12; worship by members of, 4, 4–5, 37

millennialism: and oracles, 216, 217; Protestant civil religion and, 64–65

Miller, Reverend Samuel Miller, 181

Minton, Sherman, 42

Mitchell, W. J. T., 16, 32

mobilization of religion, 43–44

MOCRA (Museum of Contemporary Religious Art), 136

modernism: paradigms of formalist and self-exploration in, 133, 142; reaction against religion compared to spiritual revival in art, 132–36, 142–44 modernity: hallmarks of, 22; and mobilization of religion, 43–44; and secularization, 42–44

The Monastery (Scott), 125

The Money Diggers (Quidor), 184, *185*

Montgomery County, Maryland, 47, 309–10n33

Moore, R. Laurence, 293n29

moral conduct, illustrated publications and, 53–55, *55, 56, 58–60, 63, 64*

Morey, Charles Rufus, xii

Morgan, David, 7, 18, 49–67, 192, 193, 337–38n8

Morrison, Toni, 1–2, 14–15

Morrow, James, 311n17

Morse, Samuel F. B., 109, 119–22, *121*, 125, 316n16, 318–19n38

Motherwell, Robert, 134

Mount, Henry Smith, 183, 332nn37,38

Mount, Shepard Alonzo, 178–79

Mount, William Sydney, 176; and African Americans, 177, 178, 184–85, 187, 189–90; Allston and, 330n18, 333n49; biblical paintings of, 176; *Cider Making*, 334–35n55, 335n59; and color, 184, 188, 190, 333n49, 334n54; *Eel Spearing at Setauket*, 176–78, *177*, 184–90, *plate 11*; fish and fishing and, 178, 189, 335n59; and Freemasons, 182–83; and hermeticism, 12, 21, 177, 184–90, 328–29n5; high- and low life portrayed by, 176, 188; and local pigments, 176, 178–79, 184, 188, 332n38; Mapes and, 334n54; and Micah Hawkins, 331n30; and Native Americans, 179; and nature, book of, 21, 176, 178, 179, 184, 190; and Spiritualism, 177, 328–29n5, 330n15; Woodworth and, 330n15

Muhammad's tomb, 70, 302–3n2

multilingualism: and mass-produced santos, 193, 195, 197–98, 340n24; postcard production and, 232

Murray, Nicholas, 110, 115

museums: change in, and the spiritual in

art, 144–45; and collection, culture of, 271

music: blues, 263–64; popular, 132

Muslims: and images of Muhammad, 40–41, *41*; as pilgrims, 302–3n2; and pluralism in United States, 45, 47; Washington, D.C., center for, 309–10n33

mysticism, 148

Nast, Thomas, 63–64, *64*, 66, *66*

National Apostolic Church, 305n8

National Baptist Memorial Church, 305n8

National Cathedral (Episcopal), 72–73, *73*, 76, 79, 81, 83, 84, *85*, 305n8

National Catholic Reporter, 144

National Church of God, 305n8

National City Christian Church, 75, 305n8, 306n12

National Community Church (Washington, D.C.), 75, 305n8

national identity: antisemitism and, 238; civil religion and, 7; pluralism and, 18. *See also* civil religion; identity; United States of America

National Memorial Church of God (Washington, D.C.), 305n8

National Presbyterian Church, 75, 76, 305n8

National Shrine of the Immaculate Conception, 68, *69, 71, 77, 82, 84, plate 6*; as "America's Church," 68, 72, 76–77, 81, 84, 306–7n15; awareness of existence of, 82–84, 86; design of, 76, 79, 81–82, *83*–84, 306–7n15, 307–8n18; as devotional shrine, 70; identity and, 7, 18–19, 79, 81; lay response to, 79–83, 307–8n19; as national center, 70, 71, 72, 76–79, 80–81, 84–86, 305n8; site of, reasons for, 79, 81, 307–8n18; size of, 68, 76, 302n1

National Spiritual Science Center, 75, 305n8

National Wesleyan Church, 305n8

and, 217–22, *220–21,* 226, 227–28;
indigenous, 215–16; and religious
vision, loss of, 213–14, *213,* 222–23,
224–28, *plate 12;* showmen and, 211–
14, *212,* 219
Orbis Pictus (Comenius), 296n1
*Origen de los dos célebres santuarios de la
Nueva Galicia* (Florencia), 302
ornament, Catholic theories of images
and, 201
Orthodox Church, 74, 305n8
O'Sullivan, John, 189
other: art and religiosity and, 132–34;
Catholicism as, 20; Jewish representation and, 230, 233, 239; Vedder and
appropriation of, 225. *See also* prejudice

paganism. *See* oracles, silencing of
Paine, Tom, 219
Painter's Studio (Courbet), 142
painting, as hermetic medium, 21, 180–81,
188, 330n18, 334–35n55
Palmer, Elihu, 219
Paracelsus, 328–29n5
parochial school funding, 64, 65–66
Pashke, Ed, 132
Peale, Charles Willson, 126
Peale, Rembrandt, 123, 126, 321n48
Penitente, New Mexico (Witkin), 137
penitential societies, 344n57, 345n58
Il Penseroso (Cole), 119–22, *120,* 319n39
performance, 37–38. *See also* display
persecution. *See* anti-Catholicism; antisemitism; racism
Peter Parley primers (Goodrich), 56–57,
297n6
Philosophical Dictionary (Voltaire), 219
photography: Bible illustration and, 276,
278, 282–84, *283,* 363n45, *plate 16;*
postcards and, 351n8
Pierpont, John, 297n6
pigments: of Egypt, 184; local, Mount and,
176, 178–79, 184, 188, 332n38. *See also*
color

Pinchbeck, William Frederick, 211–14, *212*
Piss Christ (Serrano), 134, 143
Pius IX, 19, 66
Pius X, 76
place, commitment to, 88, 101
Platonism: and beauty, 1; fear of images
and, 14–15; Jesus and Forms of, 2;
material culture of religion and, 16
pleasure, as motivation, 154
Plessy v. Ferguson, 251–52
pluralism: as cultural practice, 48, 295n63;
definition of, 291–92n7; immigration
and, 45; modernity and, 44; national
identity and, 18, 291–92n7; privatization and, 44; as public, 44–48; and
public display of religion, 28, 32–33,
38–39, 44–48, 291–92n7; truth claims
and, 45. *See also* diversity; republican
ideals
Poland, 234, 351n8
politics, and religious instruction in public
schools, 66
polytheism, Lakota spirituality vs., 163
Pope, John Russell, 75
popular culture, defined, 337n3
popular religion, repression of, 153
portraits, viewer engagement with, 119
postcards: Catholic national shrine and,
84, *84,* 309n29; gender and, 230, 243,
246–47, 356n51; international market
in, 229, 231, *232,* 233, 351n8; for Jewish
audience (*see* postcards, Jewish New
Year); non-Jewish representation of
Jews on, 238–39; production of, 231–
35, 351nn8,9, 352n24; related graphic
forms, 351n8, 352nn17,24; viewer
engagement and, 237, 239
postcards, Jewish New Year, 229, *230, 235,
236, 240, 241, 245–47, 247–48, plate 13,
plate 14;* belonging and, 237, 239, 243,
354n33; community and, 237, 244,
247–48; consumer culture and, 229,
230, 242–43, 247, *plate 13;* customs of
Rosh Hashanah and, 229, 230–31,

empiricism and, 181, 189–90; and biblical apologetics, 275–76, 363n38; biblical illustration and erosion of text, 268–69, 284, 365n68; Catholic images and (*see* Protestants, and consumption of Catholic images); and civil religion, 19, 20, 57, 64–67; iconoclasm and, xii; and military worship, 4; millennialism of, 64–65; and public schools, 57, 65–67

Protestants, and consumption of Catholic images, 12, 20, 107–8, 128, 315n8; aestheticization of images and, 114–19, *116*, 317–18n27; anti-Catholic context of, 107, 109–14, *110*, *111*, *113*, 117, 120, 124–26, 127–28, 315n8, 316nn14,16, 318n28, *plate 8, plate 9; Capuchin Chapel* as benchmark, 123–26; objections to, 118, 318n31; religious tourism and, 108–9, 114, 117, 122–23, 318n31, 319–20n44, 321n48; ritualization and, 127–28, 321–22n54; St. Peter's Basilica and, 122–23; Vedder and, 224–25; viewer engagement and, 119–23, 319n39

Protestants and Pictures (Morgan), 192, 337–38n8

Providence Patriot and Columbian Phenix, 125

Provis, Mary Ann, 179

public display of religion, 27–29, 48–49, 290–91n1; accessibility and, 31–32, 45–47; alternate responses to, 40; audience and, 29, 32–33, 40–42, *41*, 47, *plate 5; display* as term and, 28, 29, 33–40, 293n29; and meaning, 29, 38–40, 42, 47; mural projects, 4–5, *6*, 29, *30*, 32, 36, *37*, 289n8, *plate 2, plate 3, plate 4*; pluralism and, 28, 32–33, 38–39, 44–48, 291–92n7; *public* as term and, 28, 29–33, 293n25; *religion* as term and, 27–28, 29, 40–47; separation of church and state and, 27–28, 31, 42; visibility and, 31. *See also* civil religion

public domain: nineteenth-century visual culture and, 66–67; as term, 28, 29–33, 293n25

public funding: of art, xii; and public display of religion, 27, 28, 42; of public schools, 64, 65–66

public schools: funding of, 64, 65–66; movement for, 52, 57; violence in, responses to, 38

public schools, religious instruction in: Catholic and other religious objections to, 65–66, 67; civil religion and, 51, 65, 66–67; politicization of, 66; and primers, content of, 51–52, 54, 56–57; separation of church and state and, 28, 65–67

publishing: of Bibles (*see* Bible illustration); *Illuminated Bible*, effect of, 280; international market of images, 193, 338n10; market revolution in, 192; of postcards (*see* postcards); religiosity and, 147; technology of, 191, 192, 199, 251, 276, 280, 281, 282–84, *283*, 338n10, *plate 16. See also* books

Pueblo peoples, 192, 337n4; and Chinese export ceramics, 194–96, 198, 199–200, 203; Christianity of, 204–7, 208, 343nn50,51; colonization and, 192, 200, 206, 337n4, 340–41n26, 341n28; European representational practices and, 200, 202–3, 204, 206, 340–41n26; healing and, 204, 343n47; hybridity and, 21–22, 198, 201–3, 204–7, 208; indigenous artistic traditions of, 199–200, 201–3, 204–6, 207, 343n50; katsinas, 205–6, 343n51; kivas, 203, 343n50; language of, 206, 337n4, 340–41n26. *See also* New Mexico; santos, locally produced; santos, mass-produced

Pueblo Revolt, 200, 206

Puritans, 7; separation of church and state and, 31

Quaker Hill neighborhood (Wilmington, Del.), 88, 94–95
quester religiosity. *See* seeker religiosity
The Questioner of the Sphinx (1863, Vedder), *213*, 214, 225–26, 227, *plate 12*
The Questioner of the Sphinx (1875, Vedder), *213*, 225–26
Quidor, John, 184, *185*, 332n37
Quintal, Margaret, 172

race: biblical illustration and, 278–80, *279*; Jews as, 237–39, 353n30
racism: color theory and, 190; hermeticism and, 177, 189–90; iconoclastic rituals in response to, 2, 3, *3*, 37; manifest destiny and, 189; power of images and, 1–2; segregation, 4, 250, 251–52, 255, 261, 264, 357n10; violence of, 250, 260–61, 264. *See also* African Americans; anti-Catholicism; anti-semitism; colonialism
railroad: Long Island and, 188; manifest destiny and, 251, *251;* and the South, as economic force in, 250, 253; Southwest and, 191; and spiritual journey stories, 357n12; Whites and symbolization of, 251, *251*
railroad, African Americans and: abolitionists and, 252–53, *253;* and adversity, stories of overcoming, 255, 258–60; and blues music, 263–64; congregations of churches and, 253–54, 264; excursions, 260, *260;* gender and symbolization of, 250, 258; geographical deliverance and, 250, 261; progress and, 250–51, *250*, *251*, 263; as religious symbol, 23, 249–50, 264–66, *266*, 359n43, *plate 15;* segregation and, 250, 251–52, 255, 261, 264, 357n10; and spiritual journey stories, 254–58, *257*, 261, 357n12; violence and, 250, 260–61. *See also* African Americans
Raphael, Reverend P., 77–78, *78*
Rathbone, Perry T., xii

redemption, oracles as axis of, 214
Reed, Rebecca, 314n4
Reenchantment of Art (Gablik), 136
Reinagle, Hugh, 331n30
Reinhardt, Ad, 134
relevance in Bible illustration, 23, 277–82, *278*, *279*
religion: art as, 224–30; autonomy of, 152; changes in, 147, 152–54; civil (*see* civil religion); freedom of, 18; history of, art ignored in, xi–xiii; material culture of, 15–17; mobilization of, 43–44; popular, repression of, 153; practice of (*see* altars; ritual; sacred space; shrines; worship); privacy and (*see* privacy, religious); public display of (*see* public display of religion); railroad and (*see* railroad, African Americans and); return to, 130–32; seeker religiosity (*see* seeker religiosity); and self, creation of ideal, 152, 155; separation of state and (*see* separation of church and state); vs. spirituality, as term, 153; as term, 27–28, 29, 40–47, 153; trans-religiosity, 45. *See also* Christianity; Judaism; Protestantism; Roman Catholicism; spirituality; *other specific traditions*
Religious Tract Society, 57
representation: European (*see* European representational practices); and hybridity (*see* hybridity); of Jews, 229–30, 237, 238–39, 244–45, *245*, *246*, 353n30, 354nn33,34, 355n45; media and (*see* media, and religious representation); Sioux Sun Dance painting and, 21, 170–74, *171–74*, 175, 328n48, *plate 10;* of women, 238–39, 244–45, *245*, *246*, 269–70, *270*, 355n45. *See also* presentation
republican ideals, 53–54, 272–73. *See also* civil religion; democracy; pluralism
Republicans, and school funding, 66
resonance, 208, 223, 345n63
retablos, as term, 341n28

Strong, George Templeton, 189, 190, 336n66

Strong, George Washington, 177–78, 187, 189, 190, 329n6, 336nn65,66

Strong, Selah, 178

Stuart, Gilbert, 105–7, *106*, 119, 128, 314nn1,3, 314–15n5

Studio program, Indian art and, 172

Subconscious Sink (Gober), 137

subjectivity, and observer, construction of, 127, 321n52

suffering: Catholicism and, 137, 141. *See also* sacrifice

Sully, Thomas, 123–25, *124*, 126, *plate 9*

Sun Dance, 164–69, 174, 327n29; and colors, significance of, 163–64, 167, 169; dancers, painting of, 168–69; effigies and, 167–68, *168*; intent vs. static tradition and, 174–75; pole, painting of, 166–68, 327–28n35; presentation in, 21, 166, *168*, 175; representation of, in paintings, 21, 170–74, *171–74*, 175, 328n48, *plate 10*; sacrifice and, 165, 327n29; spirituality and, 21, 161–64, 326–27n16; suppression of, 160, 326n2

The Sun Dance (Amiotte), 174, *174*

The Sun Dance (Howe), 172–73, *172*

The Sun Dancers (Howe), 172–73, *173*, *plate 10*

superstition, vanquishing, 219–22

Supreme Court, U.S.: images in courtroom of, 40–42, *41*, *plate 5*; segregation and, 251–52, 357n10; separation of church and state and, 28, 291n3. *See also* United States of America

"Susanna Surprised by the Elders in the Garden" (Thomas), 269, *270*

Swanson, Wayne, 28

sweatbaths, 169

Swedenborg, Emanuel, 330n15

Swedenborgian Church, 74, 305n8, 305–6n10, 330n15

Sword, 162, 163–64

symbols, marketplace of, 153

syphilis, 238, 353n30

Taking the Veil (Weir), 115–19, *116*, 123, 128, 317–18n27, 318n31, *plate 8*

Tappan, Lewis, 61

tarot cards, 12–14, *13*, 289–90n13

Taves, Ann, 115

Taylor, Thomas, 222

technology: and African American upliftment, 250–51, *250*, 263; and biblical illustration, 276, 280–84, *281*, *283*, *plate 16*; celebration of, immigrants and, 240, *241*, 247; computer effects, 282–84, *283*, *plate 16*; cultural continuum and, 199; Internet (*see* Internet); media (*see* media); postcard production and, 231, 351n8; printing, 191, 192, 199, 251, 276, 280, *281*, 282–84, *283*, 338n10, *plate 16*; publishing and, 192; railroad (*see* railroad)

teens, 131, 277–78

television: clerical dress and, 149, 156; discourse in meaning-making and, 155, 156–57, 159; diversification of, and religious autonomy, 153–54; as dominant medium, 151–52; motivations for viewing of, 154–55, 156, 157; and spirituality, interest in, 131, 148, 153–54; traditional vs. seeker religiosity and, 147–49, 151, 155–56, 158, 159

temperance propaganda, 59

The Ten Commandments, 158

Teresa of Avila, 141

Terrell, Mary Church, 258–59

territorialism: display and, 48

text: illustration and medium affecting meaning of, 268–69, 270–71, 273, 280, 284–85, 363n45, 365n68; Protestantism and authority of, 49, 268–69, 284, 365n68; repression of popular religion and authority of, 153. *See also* language; literacy, nineteenth-century

DESIGN: Nicole Hayward
COMPOSITOR: Integrated Composition Systems
TEXT: 9.5/14 Scala
DISPLAY: Scala Sans
PRINTER AND BINDER: Thomson-Shore, Inc.